W9-BIY-966

Tenth Edition

PROCEDURES IN THE JUSTICE SYSTEM

Cliff Roberson, LLM, Ph.D.
Managing Editor,
Police Practices & Research: An International Journal

Harvey Wallace, J.D.

Gilbert B. Stuckey

Boston Columbus Indianapolis New York San Francisco Upper Saddle River
Amsterdam Cape Town Dubai London Madrid Milan Munich Paris Montreal Toronto
Delhi Mexico City Sao Paulo Sydney Hong Kong Seoul Singapore Taipei Tokyo

Vice President and Executive Publisher: Vernon Anthony
Senior Acquisitions Editor: Eric Krassow
Assistant Editor: Tiffany Bitzel
Editorial Assistant: Lynda Cramer
Media Project Manager: Karen Bretz
Director of Marketing: David Gesell
Marketing Manager: Cyndi Eller
Senior Marketing Coordinator: Alicia Wozniak
Production Manager: Holly Shufeldt
Creative Director: Jayne Conte
Cover Designer: Suzanne Duda
Cover Photo: Fotolia
Full-Service Project Management/Composition: Mohinder Singh/Aptara®, Inc.
Printer/Binder: Edwards Brothers Malloy
Cover Printer: Lehigh-Phoenix Color

Credits and acknowledgments borrowed from other sources and reproduced, with permission, in this textbook appear on appropriate page within text.

Library of Congress Cataloging-in-Publication Data

Roberson, Cliff,
   Procedures in the justice system / Cliff Roberson, Harvey Wallace,
Gilbert B. Stuckey.—10th ed.
      p. cm.
   Includes index.
   ISBN-13: 978-0-13-270584-4
   ISBN-10:   0-13-270584-2
1. Criminal procedure—United States.   2. Criminal justice,
Administration of—United States.   I. Wallace, Harvey.   II. Stuckey,
Gilbert B.   III. Title.
   KF9619.S8 2013
   345.73'05—dc23
                              2011035966

10 9 8 7 6 5 4 3
ISBN-13: 978-0-13-270584-4
ISBN-10: 0-13-270584-2

CONTENTS

PREFACE

In 1976, Gilbert Stuckey published the first edition of *Procedures in the Justice System.* In 1988, Gil asked Harvey Wallace and Cliff Roberson to assist him in revising the text. Gilbert died in 1989, From 1988 to 2007, Cliff Roberson and Harvey Wallace revised and updated the new editions. In 2007, Harvey passed away. This edition was revised and updated by Cliff Roberson. When the first edition was published, it contained 158 pages. The present edition contains almost three times that number.

The tenth edition of *Procedures in the Justice System* continues the tradition of providing the reader with a thorough understanding of our justice system from the time of arrest through the sentencing of the criminal offender. Legal rules of procedure are presented in language that is easy to understand. The high crime rate continues to be one of society's major problems, not only in the United States but also throughout the world. It is the primary responsibility of those directly connected with the justice system, such as members of law enforcement agencies, the courts, and correctional officers, to fight crime. Yet to effectively curb crime, society needs the assistance of every law-abiding person.

By studying history, we often see the mistakes of the past and thus can make efforts not to repeat those mistakes in the future. One past mistake was the failure to recognize that the members of the justice system are a team who must work together. Yet, to work as a team, it is necessary for each member to understand his or her own responsibility as well as that of each of the other members.

This book was written for those interested in our justice system, particularly police and correctional science students. It explains the duties and responsibilities of the law enforcement agencies, courts, and correctional departments in relation to law violators from the time of accusation until completion of the sentence. Criminal justice students should, however, study more than just judicial procedures. They should have some knowledge of why we have laws and why those laws are broken, should be cognizant of the constitutional rights of an accused, and should have a better understanding of the philosophy of correctional endeavors. Thus, material on these subjects is incorporated into the text. The information in this book will help the student, as well as others, attain a more thorough knowledge of our justice system and of the role that each member must play to achieve, through teamwork, law and order for all.

Special thanks to the following reviewers for their hard work and assistance on this edition: J.D. Elshoff, Texas State University—San Marcos; Kelli Florman, Rio Hondo College; David Forristal, Brown Mackie College—Salina, KS; Donna Nickolson, Manchester Community College; Victoria Time, Old Dominion University; and Larry Vick, Fayetteville Technical Community College.

The invaluable assistance of acquisitions editor Eric Krassow, Melanie Blake, copyeditor, Holly Shufeldt, production manager, Mohinder Singh, project manager at Aptara, and Jessica Sykes, production project manager, was necessary to accomplish this extensive revision to the text. Also a special thanks to the director of editorial development at Pearson, Vernon Anthony, for his support and faith in the project.

A warm and special thanks to the supplements author, J.D. Elshoff, Texas State University.

To assist the instructor in presenting the material in this edition, a Test Bank, *MyCrimeKit* companion website (www.mycrimekit.com), MyTest, and PowerPoint presentations are also available. Suggestions for improvement, corrections, and other comments are invited and may be forwarded to Cliff Roberson at cliff.roberson@washburn.edu.

New to the tenth edition

In addition to updating legal issues and cases, there have been numerous changes made to the tenth edition. These include:

- Capstone Cases have been replaced with Case Law. The new Case Law sections in each chapter provide summaries and excerpts of recent court decisions.
- New discussions on what constitutes justice, rule of law, concepts of law, classifications of law, and theories of law in Chapter 1 have been added.
- The glossary has been updated.
- New material on vehicle searches based on the latest U.S. Supreme Court decisions has been added.
- Discussion on the right of privacy of police officers' cell phones has been added.
- *Miranda* Rule discussions have been modified to reflect the latest court decisions.
- Material on the right of an undocumented alien to bail has been added.
- The discussion on motions at arraignment has been significantly expanded.
- A new table on the differences between grand juries and trial juries has been developed.
- Discussion on the reasons for which criminal cases are withdrawn from the court system prior to the cases' being adjudicated has been expanded.
- Discussions on the advantages and disadvantages of jury size have been added.
- Qualifications of defense counsel in capital cases have been included.
- A new section on the *Brady* v. *Maryland* Doctrine has been added.
- A new discussion on judicial notice has been added.
- New discussions on petitions for Writ of Certiorari have been added.

—**Cliff Roberson,** LLM, Ph.D.
Emeritus Professor of Criminal Justice
Washburn University;
Professor of Criminology (Retired),
California State University, Fresno;
Academic Chair, Graduate School of
Criminal Justice, Kaplan University;
Managing Editor, Police Practices &
Research: An International Journal.

The fourth through eighth editions have been dedicated to our colleague Gilbert Stuckey. This edition, like the ninth, is dedicated to my friend and colleague Paul Harvey Wallace. Harvey and I were fellow Marines, friends, and coauthors for sixteen years. We coauthored ten books together. I still miss him.

—CLIFF ROBERSON

CHAPTER 1

Historical Development of Law and the Justice System

The law embodies the story of a nation's development through many centuries, and it cannot be dealt with as if it contained only the axioms and corollaries of a book of mathematics.

—OLIVER WENDELL HOLMES, *THE COMMON LAW,* 1881

Chapter Outline

Key Terms

Abstract goals

Atonement

Code of Hammurabi

Court rules

Due process

Jurisdiction

Orientation goals	**Trial by ordeal**
Pragmatic goals	**Venue**
Standards	

Learning Objectives

After completing this chapter, you should be able to:

- Summarize the Constitutional basis for criminal procedure.
- Describe the impact of the Bill of Rights on criminal procedure.
- Summarize the history and legal foundations of criminal procedure.
- Explain the importance of precedent.
- Compare the theory of criminal procedure to the reality.
- Describe the public order (crime control) and individual rights (due process) perspectives of criminal justice and how criminal procedure balances the two.
- Outline the structure of the court system, including the responsibilities and jurisdictions of each level.
- Define terms related to the introduction of criminal procedure.

OVERVIEW

The study of our justice system should be viewed not as a set of rules for memorization, but as a cluster of ideas, principles, and values about which reasonable people can and do disagree. The system is not fixed in stone; it is changing and flexible. Understanding our concept of justice requires a thoughtful comprehension of the historical background, social values, moral standards, and political realities that give direction to our system. The major problem facing the state and federal court systems is their ever-increasing case loads.

Criminal courts are the heart of criminal justice system. They have three primary missions:

- to administer justice in a fair and impartial manner
- to protect the individual rights of persons accused of crimes
- to provide an authority for controlling crime

In the United States, there are two separate court systems in each state, the federal system and the state system. Generally, federal courts are involved only in matters concerning federal issues and state courts are involved in the other matters. The court systems of the federal and state governments in the United States operate on an adversarial system in that the prosecution or plaintiff is opposed by the defense with the judge and jury operating as the decision-makers.

Both the state and federal governments have enacted statutes to regulate the administration of the criminal justice system. The primary state regulatory statute is the state code of criminal procedure that regulates procedure in state courts. The primary federal statute that governs the trial of criminal cases in federal court is Title 18 of the U.S. Code. Except for constitutional issues, federal procedural rules apply only to federal criminal cases. State procedural rules apply only to state cases.

Courts are established either by the U.S. Constitution, state constitutions, or legislation. If the court is established under a constitution, it is considered as a constitutional court. Those established by a state or federal legislation are considered as legislative courts. According to Section 1, Article III, of the U.S. Constitution:

The Judicial Power of the United States shall be vested in one Supreme Court, and in such inferior Courts as Congress may from time to time ordain and establish. The Judges, both of the supreme and inferior Courts, shall hold their Offices during good Behavior, and shall, at Times, receive for their services, a compensation, which shall not be diminished during their continuance in office.

Judicial Guidance

JUDICIAL OPINIONS Judicial opinions construe the constitutionality, meaning, and effect of constitutional and statutory provisions. The court decisions included in each chapter of this text provide examples of the importance of judicial opinions in the justice system.

COURT RULES Court rules consist of the various standard procedures used by the courts that were developed as the result of a court's inherent supervisory power over the administration of the criminal justice system. Court rules regulate the guilt-determining process of the courts in the areas not regulated by other rules. Most students of the justice system fail to consider the importance of court rules in the trial of criminal cases.

Examples of court rules that have an impact on the courts follow.

Los Angeles County Municipal Court Rule 532.6:

Each judge is required to list [report] all causes [cases] under submission for more than 30 days, with an indication of the length of time each has been pending (30 through 60 days, 61 through 90 days; or over 90 days).

California Supreme Court Rule 22 (regarding oral arguments before the court):

Unless otherwise ordered: (1) counsel for each party shall be allowed 30 minutes for oral argument, except [that] in a case in which a sentence of death has been imposed each party shall be allowed 45 minutes. . . .

U.S. District Court (Eastern District California) Rule 5a:

(1) The trial of a defendant held in custody solely for purposes of trial on a federal charge shall commence within 90 days following the beginning of continuous custody.

Goals of the Justice System

Most experts on the justice system agree that the most basic goal of the system is to protect society from crime. Beyond that, there is little agreement. There are several competing philosophies concerning the purposes of the justice system, each with its own specific goals. To help us understand some of the more commonly accepted goals of the justice system, the goals are classified as **orientation goals**, **pragmatic goals**, **abstract goals**, or **standards**.

ORIENTATION GOALS Criminal justice professionals generally are oriented in one of two opposite directions—law and order or individual rights. The law and order orientation stresses the need to solve the crime problem. The individual rights orientation stresses the need to protect an individual's rights and considers this need greater than the need to punish offenders. Too great an emphasis on individual rights will restrict law enforcement and allow offenders to escape punishment. Arbitrary police practices that may occur under the law and order orientation may infringe on human and constitutional rights. As Chief Justice Earl Warren stated in *Miranda* v. *Arizona*:

The quality of a nation's civilization can be largely measured by the methods it uses in the enforcement of the criminal law. . . . All of these policies point to one overriding thought: the constitutional foundation underlying the privilege is the respect a government—state or federal—must accord the dignity and integrity of its citizens. To maintain a fair state–individual balance, the government must shoulder the entire load.

PRAGMATIC GOALS   The pragmatic goals of the justice system include:

Preventing Crime.   This goal includes providing potential criminals with conventional opportunities for success before they start a career of crime, building stronger social control units such as the family, providing guidance and counseling in our schools, and developing better environmental conditions in the neighborhoods that foster law-abiding behavior.

Diverting Offenders.   This refers to the efforts to remove offenders from the system and place them in nonpunitive treatment programs. The purpose of this effort is to correct offenders without placing the stigma of a criminal conviction on them.

Deterring Crime.   The justice system attempts to deter crime by making potential criminals believe that the punishments received for criminal behavior outweigh any potential benefit (i.e., crime does not pay).

Controlling Criminals.   The system attempts to control the behavior of known criminals by incarcerating the more serious offenders and placing the less serious ones in community correction programs.

Rehabilitating Offenders.   An objective of the system is to provide rehabilitation treatment to offenders in order to reduce the likelihood of future involvement in criminal behavior. The goal of rehabilitation was very popular in the 1960s. During the 1980s it was discounted because of the popular belief that existing rehabilitation programs were not effective. Today, rehabilitation is not a popular objective in most states.

ABSTRACT GOALS   Abstract goals are the underlying principles upon which our justice system is based. The most common abstract goals include:

Fairness.   The justice system should ensure that all persons involved in the criminal justice system are treated fairly and humanely. More specifically, socioeconomic status, ethnicity, and other factors should not determine the type of treatment or form of punishment one receives from various criminal justice agencies.

Efficiency.   The system should be organized and managed in a manner to ensure maximum utilization of personnel and resources.

Effectiveness.   The justice system should operate in an effective manner.

Justice.   Justice is considered as the ideal goal of all governments and the disposition of a criminal matter in such a manner that the best interest of society is served. It is not measured solely by its application to the accused. Justice is the broad concept of reward and punishment currently accepted as proper by a society. A state court judge in an early Texas case defined justice as follows:

> Justice is the dictate of right, according to the common consent of mankind generally, or of that portion of mankind who may be associated in one government, or who may be governed by the same principles and morals.

STANDARDS Organizations such as the American Bar Association and the American Correctional Association have developed detailed goals to improve the justice system. These goals are called standards. For the most part, standards are designed to protect individual rights and promote the efficiency of the justice process. (*Note:* Standards are goals, not binding rules.) Selected standards on criminal justice are as follows:

AMERICAN BAR ASSOCIATION STANDARDS RELATING TO PROSECUTION FUNCTION

1.4 Duty to Improve the Law

It is an important function of the prosecutor to seek to reform and improve the administration of criminal justice. When inadequacies or injustices in the substantive or procedural law come to his or her attention, he or she should stimulate efforts for remedial action.

2.7 Relations with the Police

a. The prosecutor should provide legal advice to the police concerning police functions and duties in criminal matters.
b. The prosecutor should cooperate with police in providing the services of his or her staff to aid in training police in the performance of their function in accordance with the law.

National Advisory Commission on Criminal Justice Standards and Goals

4.11 Priority Case Scheduling

Cases should be given priority for trial where one or more of the following factors are present:

a. The defendant is in pretrial custody;
b. The defendant constitutes a significant threat of violent injury to others;
c. The defendant is a recidivist;
d. The defendant is a professional criminal;
e. The defendant is a public official.

6.5 Further Review

After a reviewing court has affirmed a trial court conviction and sentence, or after the expiration of a fair opportunity for a defendant to obtain a review with the aid of counsel, the conviction and the sentence generally should be final and not subject to further review in any state or federal court. Further review should be available only in unusual circumstances.

JUSTICE SYSTEM STRUCTURE AND PROCESS

We refer to the justice system as a system as if it were a formal system. It would be more accurate to refer to it as a nonsystem. The term system refers only to the interrelationship among all those agencies concerned with the prevention of crime in society. The systems approach to criminal justice sees a change in one part of the system affecting change in all the others. It implies that a closely-knit, coordinated structure of organizations exists among the various components of the system.

The justice system, however, is not a close-knit, coordinated structure of organizations. It is actually three separate elements: police, courts, and correction institutions. Each operates almost independently of the others. In many cases, the goal orientations of the various elements within a local jurisdiction are in conflict with each other concerning the main functions of the criminal justice system. Thus, the system can best be described as fragmented or divided.

Accordingly, the criminal justice system is a group of agencies organized around various functions that each agency is assigned.

Evolution of Criminal Procedure

Our system of criminal justice is based on English common law. The colonists brought English traditions and concepts with them when they settled in our country. Except for a few modifications, English common law became the common law of the colonies. During and shortly after the American Revolution, there was hostility toward the English in the colonies. The hostility extended to the common law system of law as well. Most of the newly founded states enacted new codes and statutes defining criminal acts and establishing criminal procedures. The codes and statutes, however, were based on common law concepts. Included was the English concept of justice on which our system is based. To this foundation, a bit of Spanish and French influence was added as the system was developed and changed to meet the requirements of our growing nation.

Foundational Concepts in Criminal Procedure

As an introduction to the study of criminal procedure, the foundational concepts in criminal procedure below should be considered. These concepts will be explained in the text and are listed here to create an awareness of their existence.

- The guarantees of the Bill of Rights in the U.S. Constitution apply directly only to the federal government.
- The Due Process Clause of the Fourteenth Amendment by selective incorporation applies most of the rights contained in the Bill of Rights to the states.
- State constitutions may provide rights to citizens in addition to those provided for in the U.S. Constitution, but may not restrict the rights granted by the U.S. Constitution.
- The two basic questions regarding the burden of proof in criminal proceedings are: (1) Who has the burden of proving an issue? and (2) What is the magnitude of the burden? The magnitude may be (1) proof beyond a reasonable doubt, (2) clear and convincing evidence, or (3) preponderance of evidence. On issues relating to the guilt of a defendant, the burden is proof beyond a reasonable doubt and that burden rests on the prosecutor or state.
- Charges in a criminal trial must first be formalized either by an indictment returned by a grand jury or by information prepared by a prosecutor.
- Prior to trial, both the prosecution and the defense may submit pretrial motions, and both have discovery rights imposed on them.
- Our system of criminal procedure is based on the adversarial process.

Two famous quotes from U.S. Supreme Court Justice Oliver Wendell Holmes should be noted:

- "Whatever disagreement there may be as to the scope of the phrase 'due process of law,' there can be no doubt that it embraces the fundamental conception of a fair trial, with opportunity to be heard."[1]
- "The life of the law has not been logic, it has been experience."[2]

EARLY DEVELOPMENT OF LAWS

A law in its simplest form is merely a guideline for human behavior. The primary purpose of criminal law is to promote domestic peace by encouraging people to do what is right and discouraging them from doing what is wrong. Law is often described as a social tool to mold and regulate human conduct. Legally, a law is defined as an act of a legislative body written and recorded in some public repository, informing people of what is right and wrong. In the case of *Koenig* v. *Flynn,* it was stated as "that which must be obeyed and followed by citizens, subject to sanctions or legal consequences, is a law."[3]

The next question to be answered is: Are laws necessary today? It has been stated frequently that laws are made to be broken. Also, it has been alleged that if there were no laws, they would not be broken. In fairness to the declarant of this statement, it is only logical to assume that if there were nothing to break, nothing would be broken. So we return to the question: Are laws necessary? Before answering, it may be well to consider the origin of laws and why they came into being.

A human being comes into the world with certain basic needs that remain throughout his or her life. These are the needs for food, shelter, companionship, and sexual gratification. If untrained and uncontrolled, a person may attempt to satisfy these needs in a most animalistic manner. If one were completely isolated from all other human beings, the fashion in which one might try to satisfy personal needs would be relatively unimportant. However, the moment one comes in contact with another person, the needs of each individual must be considered, and each must respect the desires of the other. Each person must learn to realize that his or her liberties cease where other person's begin. Certain restraints upon activity must be imposed. Thus, there is a necessity for some guidelines about satisfying personal needs without infringing upon the rights of others.

People may agree upon a division of territory, and each will confine his or her activities to that territory. If this arrangement takes place, there is little reason for other guidelines, but if they agree to combine their efforts, further regulations must be made. It must be decided who will do what and how they will share. As more and more persons enter the picture, the necessity for more rules becomes apparent. Eventually, it will be necessary to choose a leader or chief to see that the rules are followed and to keep order within the tribe or society.

Undoubtedly, many of the early established guidelines came about through trial and error. When it was recognized that a tribal member committed an act that threatened the existence of the tribe, a restraint against that act was created, and a violation of that restraint was what we now know as a crime. It probably did not take long for members of a primitive tribe to learn that they could not kill each other and still have the tribe continue to exist. Therefore, rules against murder were established. To satisfy a person's need for food and shelter, that person devised certain tools that became his or her property. The taking of these tools by another, depriving the owner of their use, was a serious act, so a rule against theft was enacted. People took mates to satisfy their needs for companionship and sexual gratification. The mate was also personal property, and to violate that property right was an offense, so rules against adultery were formed.

As tribes or societies grew in number and became somewhat more sophisticated, so did their regulations. As time passed, people developed the belief in a deity. Regulations respecting this belief were also established, and the violation of these regulations was a serious offense against the society.

Code of Hammurabi

The **Code of Hammurabi** is considered one of the first known attempts to establish a written code of conduct. King Hammurabi ruled Babylon in approximately 2000 B.C. He was the sixth king of the First Dynasty of Babylonia for about fifty-five years. Babylon during that period of time was a commercial center for most of the known and civilized world. Since its fortune lay in trade and other business ventures, the Code of Hammurabi provided a basis for the order and certainty that were essential for commerce. The code established rules regarding theft, sexual relationships, and interpersonal violence. It was intended to replace blood feuds with a system sanctioned by the state. The Code is also one of the first known laws to discuss the rights of victims.

The Code of Hammurabi was divided into five sections:

A penal or code of laws;

A manual of instruction for judges, police officers, and witnesses;

A handbook of rights and duties of husbands, wives, and children;

A set of regulations establishing wages and prices;

A code of ethics for merchants, doctors, and officials.

The code established certain obligations and objectives for the citizens of Babylon to follow. These included the following elements:

AN ASSERTION OF THE POWER OF THE STATE This was the beginning of state-administered punishment. The blood feuds that had occurred previously between private citizens were barred under the code.

PROTECTION OF THE WEAKER FROM THE STRONGER Widows were to be protected from those who might exploit them, elder parents were protected from sons who would disown them, and lesser officials were protected from higher officials.

RESTORATION OF EQUITY BETWEEN THE OFFENDER AND THE VICTIM The victim was to be made as whole as possible and, in turn, he or she was required to forgive vengeance against the offender.

Of noteworthy importance in the code was its concern for the rights of victims. In reality, this code may have been the first victims' rights statute in history. Unfortunately, as will be seen, society began to neglect victims in its rush to punish the offenders, with the result that victims' rights would not resurface until the twentieth century.

Biblical historians tell us that when Moses led the Israelites out of Egypt, some thirteen hundred years before Christ, he quickly realized that these people must have some guidelines to follow if they were to continue to exist. Through an inspiration from God, ten basic rules known as the Ten Commandments were established. Included were not only those laws that earlier tribes found necessary for existence, that is, rules against murder, theft, and adultery, but also more sophisticated rules that pertained to admonitions against not respecting God. In addition were admonitions against certain thoughts that people may conceive that might lead them to greedy actions. Thus, a person should not covet his or her neighbor's property. When Moses gave these guidelines to the people of Israel, he commanded them to obey them, since they would ensure life and entrance into the possession of the land. He further indicated that these laws were not to be tampered with in the interest of human weakness. There was no mention that these laws were made to be broken. Nor has there been any suggestion by anyone in authority since that time that laws are made to be broken.

Because of the effect of ecclesiastical law on the nations of Europe, most of these commandments were incorporated into their laws and, in turn, were brought to this country by the colonists. Our early criminal laws included laws against murder, theft, adultery, working on Sunday ("blue laws"), profanity, and perjury, as well as rules describing family responsibilities. Although we have become a more permissive society and take some of the earlier guidelines less seriously, a few of the Ten Commandments are still found in the criminal laws of all the states of this nation, because they are necessary for the existence of any society. These are the laws against murder, theft, perjury, and adultery; other laws are added to these from time to time.

As societies become more complex, so do their laws. New restraints are placed upon people's activities. These laws are designed with the hope that people can and will live more peacefully and pleasantly with their fellow human beings. Again we see, from a sociological standpoint, that laws are necessary for humankind's existence. From a legal standpoint, laws are necessary to inform people of what is right and what is wrong. People must be made aware of the acts for which, if committed, they may be prosecuted. In our form of government, each criminal law must be spelled out in detail so that a person may know the exact act that, if committed, is a violation of the law. If a law is considered too vague, it will be declared null and void.

COMMON LAW

Much of the basic criminal law of this country originated from the common law of England. Originally, the common law of England was nothing more than a set of unwritten regulations and customs that acted as guidelines in settling disputes, determining the inheritance of property, and dealing with persons who committed misdeeds of a serious antisocial nature. As time passed, court decisions were made a part of the common law. Thereafter, the common law was further enlarged by legislative enactments and was brought to this country by the colonists to act as guidelines for conduct.

MODERN CRIMINAL LAW

Today, the criminal law of the various states is a written set of regulations that is largely the result of legislative action. These regulations are recorded in some official record within the states and are often referred to as the penal code. Criminal laws vary somewhat among the states. In some states, there is no reliance upon the common law to determine what is right and wrong. The statutes spell out specifically the act that is made a crime and the punishment that may be inflicted for the commission of such an act. For example, the law may state that manslaughter is the unlawful killing of a human being without malice. This definition will be followed by a statement that one convicted of manslaughter may be imprisoned for a period not to exceed four years. The statutes of other states provide that manslaughter is punishable by imprisonment not to exceed a prescribed number of years. But these latter statutes do not define what act constitutes manslaughter. The courts must then look to the common law to determine the interpretation of manslaughter.

WHAT CONSTITUTES JUSTICE?

The concept of "justice" is commonly used but seldom defined. It is a concept that relates to our ideas about morality or what is right and what is wrong. Most individuals associate the concept with our concepts of fairness, equality, and goodness. We expect justice in both our private lives and in our public ones. One text defines justice as "upholding what is just, especially fair treatment and due reward in accordance with honor, standards, or law."

[Jeffery A. Jenkins (2011) *The American Courts: A Procedural Approach*. Boston: Jones and Bartlett, p. 4.]

It is via our laws that we most often reflect our concept of justice. As noted in the below excerpt from the Preamble to the U.S. Constitution, we place a high premium on the concept of justice.

Preamble to the U.S. Constitution:

We the people of the United States, in Order to form a more perfect Union, establish justice, insure domestic tranquility, provide for the common defense, promote the general welfare, and secure the blessings of liberty to ourselves and our posterity, do ordain and establish this Constitution for the United States of America.

There are no bright line rules as to what constitutes "justice." It is a subjective concept and has different meanings in different situations. We rely on our court systems to make decisions that implement our concept of justice. Whether justice is served in a case depends upon the facts of the case, the law involved in the case, the behavior of the person being judged, as well as the behavior of the persons doing the judging. In summary, justice is a multifaceted concept.

RULE OF LAW

"What do we mean by the rule of law? We mean a judicial regime in which everyone is equal before the law, and everyone—and every institution—is subject to it."

[Source: Paul Johnson, *Laying Down the Law,* The Wall St. Journal, March 10, 1999, http://www.opinionjournal.com/extra/?id=65000285]

It means, in the first place, the absolute supremacy or predominance of regular law as opposed to the influence of arbitrary power, and excludes the use of arbitrariness, of prerogative, or even of wide discretionary authority on the part of the government. Englishmen are ruled by law, and by the law alone; a man may with us be punished for a breach of law, but he can be punished for nothing else.

[Source: A.V. Dicey, *The Law of the Constitution,* London: Macmillan (8th ed. 1915, p. 60)]

The "Rule of Law" refers to the concept that all individuals and institutions will abide by the laws and no one is above the law. In other words, we all have a duty to obey the law. This duty applies to everyone, including the president, or in Great Britain, even to the Queen. By choosing to become a part of a society, we agree to abide by the society's rules and laws. It addition, it refers to the concept that no one may be punished for conduct unless there is a law that forbids that conduct.

CONCEPT OF LAW

One method of understanding the concept of law is by examining the different theories of law that serve to explain the bases for law and how it operates. The various theories of law have their roots in philosophy or in sociological or political concerns. The goal of each theory is to explain the meaning and purpose of law.

Natural Law. The theoretical basis of law according to the natural law theory is that law has a moral basis. It is derived from "nature" or God, and human understanding of what morality requires gives the law meaning. Consider this concept: We should act in accordance with the law because morality demands it.

Positive Law. Law is manmade and does not depend on morality or a "higher order." Although moral principles may influence the creation of laws, the law operates in a vacuum devoid of morals or human conceptions of right or wrong. Laws are developed based on what the citizens believe to be in their own best interests and not based on morality.

Critical Legal Theory. Critical legal theory developed in the 1970s by individuals who were dissatisfied with the ability of the law to properly address social issues such as war, race, inequality, and distribution of social wealth. Critical legal theory, unlike both natural and positive law theories, is not a unified theory but a collection of theories related to each other by the view that law should be used as an agent of social change. It emphasizes that:

- Legal reasoning and political argument is the same;
- Law is not based on reason but on political dealing that allows for the dominance of one class of persons, groups, or institutions over others; and
- Legal decisions do not represent the final say on a matter.

Legal Realism. Legal realism is based on the actual practice of law and the outcomes achieved. It is a reaction to the natural and positive law theories. The legal realisms theorists view the role of judges as applying their notions of fairness to the legal cases based primarily on the facts of the case. Legal rules serve only as after-the-fact rationalization of what a judge has already decided on the basis of the judge's concept of fairness.

Economic Theory of Law. Legal decisions are based primarily on the application of economic principles to legal questions. Microeconomics affects our legal preferences and our preferences are driven by self-interest.

Theories of Law

Theory	Originated	Principle
Natural	1300s	God given
Positive	1800s	Reason
Critical Legal Reasoning	1970s	Political motivation
Legal Realism	1920s	Socialism
Economic	1980s	Money

CLASSIFICATION OF LAW

Collectively, the law is considered as a body of written rules issues by governmental authorities for the purpose of guiding and controlling individuals and institutions. The laws may be statutes, regulations, or codes enacted by a legislative body; ordnances passed by cities and counties; rules established by appellate courts; and executive orders issued by the president, a governor, or other executive body. The most common classification of law is based on its subject matter such as criminal law, insurance law, probate law, juvenile, and family law, and so on. Two additional common classifications of law are based on its applicability and its functions.

Applicability	Private	Concerns disputes between private parties (e.g., contract disputes)
	Public	Concerns government powers (e.g., criminal law)
Functions	Substantive	Establishes and defines rights, duties, and obligations (e.g., describes what conduct constitutes a crime)
	Procedural	Prescribes methods to enforce substantive law (e.g., the rules of evidence)
	Remedial	Determines the actual benefits or remedies that should be obtained by the successful party in a legal action (e.g., in a civil trial the winning party may receive damages in the form of a certain amount of money)

Consider the following scenario: Tom while driving under the influence of alcohol ignores a traffic control signal and causes an accident. Mike was injured in the accident.

- Mike sues Tom in civil court for damages that Mike suffered. This is a private action because it is between two private parties. It would also be a tort law issue (subject matter).
- The amount of money that Mike received as the result of the court's award of damages would be a function of remedial law.

- The state brings a criminal action against Tom for driving under the influence of alcohol, a violation of a state criminal law. The statute prohibiting driving under the influence would be a public law because it involves the power of a governmental body to prescribe obligations. It would also be a criminal law as to subject matter. In addition, it would be a substantive law because it defines the duty of a person not to drive while with a blood alcohol content above a certain pre-established point.
- The procedures required by the state in the prosecution of Tom for the crime would be considered as procedural law.

CLASSIFICATION OF CRIMES AND PUNISHMENT

In our present form of jurisprudence, not only do we tell people what a criminal act is, but we also tell them the punishment they may be subjected to if they commit the act. The following definition is generally found in the statutes of the states: A crime or public offense is an act committed or omitted in violation of a law forbidding or commanding it and to which is annexed, upon conviction, one or more of several punishments. The basic forms of punishment are death, imprisonment, fines, removal from office, or disqualification to hold and enjoy any office of honor, trust, or profit. We have classified criminal laws in accordance with their seriousness to society and have stated the punishment that could be inflicted upon conviction. Earlier in our history, we classified criminal laws as treason, felonies, and misdemeanors. Most states eliminated treason as a category of crime and listed it merely as another felony violation. Thus, two classifications remained: felonies and misdemeanors. However, in recent years, many states have added a third and a fourth classification, an infraction and a state jail felony. An infraction is a minor crime less serious than a misdemeanor. A state jail felony is a crime that has some aspects of a felony and some of a misdemeanor. In severity, it is classified as between a felony and misdemeanor.

With the felony being the most serious crime, the violator is subjected to the most severe punishment either by death, imprisonment in a state prison, or a sentence of more than one year. The misdemeanor, being a less serious threat to the existence of a society, carries a lesser punishment, the most severe of which is usually not more than a year in jail. The infraction is the least serious crime, carrying a fine or probation but, in most states, no imprisonment.

The procedure by which one accused of a crime is brought to trial and punished is known as a criminal action, and the one prosecuted is known as the defendant or accused. Criminal actions are commenced with the filing of a formal written document with the appropriate court. In some states, there is no requirement to file a formal written document in cases involving infractions.

The charging document is referred to as an accusatory pleading. In most felony prosecutions, the document will be an indictment or an information. In misdemeanor prosecutions, the accusatory pleading is generally a complaint, as explained in Chapter 4. When a criminal law is broken, it is done against society as a whole, so that the prosecutive action is brought in the name of the people; thus, the action is generally entitled "People versus [the defendant]," "State versus [the defendant]," or "Commonwealth versus [the defendant]," stating the defendant's name.

Frequently used classification of offenses are based on three broad categories:

- Based on the gravity of the offense and corresponding punishment—felonies, misdemeanors, and infractions/violations;
- Based on the degree of evilness—mala in se or mala prohibita offenses; and
- Based on the subject matter—offenses against the state, habitation, person, and so on.

JUSTICE SYSTEM

When examining the criminal justice system, we will discover many technical rules and procedures that must be followed. These rules and procedures are the result of a long evolutionary process. The process is interesting, particularly the development of the right of an accused to a trial by jury. Trial by jury, for example, is regarded by many as one of the greatest achievements of our justice system.

When considering trial by jury, we immediately visualize a comfortable courtroom with a judge sitting behind a desk on a raised platform and presiding over the trial proceedings in a dignified and formal manner. We see the jury sitting in the jury box listening to the testimony of witnesses who have some knowledge about the facts of the case and the prosecuting attorney presenting evidence in an effort to prove the defendant guilty beyond a reasonable doubt. We also tend to see the defense attorney as an Eleanor in *The Practice*. We may also picture the defendant conferring with the attorney throughout the trial. At the conclusion of the trial, we visualize the jury deliberating on the evidence that has been presented and returning a verdict of guilt or innocence. The actual practice may, however, be quite different.

Guilt or innocence has not always been decided by a jury trial. In fact, the jury system as we know it today is of comparatively recent origin, coming into existence at the start of the eighteenth century. The early history of efforts to determine guilt or innocence of an accused was primarily based on calls upon the supernatural or for signs from God.

As we trace the development of trial by jury, we focus primarily on England, from where most of our judicial system came. Many blank spots are encountered in tracing the history of a jury trial because of the lack of records. But it is known that the Christian church played an important role in the development of much of the law and procedure of early England. Most of the early records available for study of the beginnings of the judicial system were prepared by the clergy and are largely incomplete. These records were not compiled as a history of the time but were merely a documentation of certain customs and events of the era.

Invasion of England

History states that Julius Caesar invaded England in 55 B.C. and that Christianity was taught there as early as A.D. 64. At that time, Christianity was not accepted by the Romans, and any activity of the Christian church throughout the Roman Empire had to be underground. Yet despite the persecution of Christians, their church continued to grow. Religious societies and new congregations were formed. Rules, regulations, and laws were established to be followed by the Christians, but they were unlawful in the eyes of the Romans. However, these laws were soon to become the laws of the continent of Europe and of England. By the year A.D. 200, Roman jurisprudence had reached its peak, and from that time on, Roman law began to decline. Instead of looking forward, the Roman leaders were looking backward to what had been. The Roman persecution of Christians terminated in A.D. 303, and in A.D. 313, Christianity was established as a lawful religion. Almost immediately the bishops of the Christian church involved themselves in politics, and they soon became as powerful as the emperor. The Church law, also known as the canon or ecclesiastical law, began to dominate the lives of people throughout Europe.

There is little doubt that Julius Caesar imported much of the Roman law to England, but the Romans did not have an easy life there because other people invaded England. The Saxons conducted raids on the coastal plains as early as the third century and continued to do so thereafter. The Romans are said to have abandoned England sometime before A.D. 429, and the Anglo-Saxon invasions began on a large scale in A.D. 449. The Anglo-Saxons are believed to have established laws, since they were known to have existed on the continent of Europe at the time, but records of the Anglo-Saxon laws and procedures are mostly fragmentary. Those that are available shed little light upon the judicial procedures of that time. It is known that kings established themselves and ruled until they were overthrown or died. A king formulated his own laws, which were known as the king's laws, laws of the land, temporal laws, or secular laws. The Anglo-Saxons held reign in England until the Norman Conquest in A.D. 1066. Prior to this time, England had experienced considerable strife. Much of the administration of justice was left to the bishops of the church, to be processed through the ecclesiastical courts, and the canon law continued to play a dominant role. But as kings began to establish themselves more securely, they continued to formulate more and more laws affecting the people. These laws were enforced through the king's courts, known as secular or temporal courts. The king's court was presided over by the king's justices.

Although an effort was made to separate the jurisdiction of the secular courts and the ecclesiastical courts, rivalry still arose, particularly as it related to appeals. The ecclesiastical courts had jurisdiction over all matters pertaining to people's souls and church-related matters, including violations by the clergy. All laypeople were subject to both the ecclesiastical laws and the secular laws. The ecclesiastical laws regulated many affairs of the layperson's life, such as marriage, divorce, and the distribution of property after death. Through the ecclesiastical courts, laypeople could be tried and punished for various offenses, including such crimes as adultery, fornication, incest, bigamy, defamation, and blasphemy. Originally, the ecclesiastical courts were presided over by the bishops of the church, but as the caseload increased, charges were often heard by the bishops' assistants, known as archdeacons. Crimes of murder or theft and attacks on property or persons were violations of the secular laws, and the offender was tried and punished by the secular courts.

Magna Charta

When an offender was convicted, his or her property was usually forfeited. This forfeiture became a source of great revenue to the church or king, depending upon what law was broken. In order to increase their revenue, kings frequently made various acts a crime in order to confiscate the property of a landowner or merchant. How the people fared depended largely on the compassion of the king at the time. In tracing our judicial procedure, frequent mention is made of the Magna Charta (also spelled Magna Carta) and its influence on *people's* rights. This document is considered to be the forerunner of the present **due process** rights since the Magna Charta granted to the people of England certain political and civil rights. The Magna Charta, which is the result of a king's being unduly oppressive to the people of England, was signed during the reign of King John, who was known as the cruel ruler.

King John took over the reign of England in A.D. 1199, after the death of his brother King Richard, the "Lion Hearted." King John was described as being clever but greedy and tyrannical in ruling his people. Conditions under him became unbearable for both the nobleman and the commoner. In an effort to improve the situation, the noblemen gathered and prepared a document containing certain resolutions that they felt were in the best interest of the people. King John was maneuvered onto the Plains of Runnymede on June 15, 1215, where he was forced to sign the Magna Charta. Among other resolutions in the Magna Charta was the guarantee that, stated briefly, held that no free man shall be seized and imprisoned except by judgment of his peers or by the law of the land. Contrary to the beliefs of many, this guarantee did not give people the right to a trial by jury. Trial by jury, as we know it today, did not come into existence until the latter part of the seventeenth century. It merely meant that when a criminal accusation was made against a person, he or she was entitled to have the charge reviewed by a council consisting of members of the community. If the council concluded that the charge was well founded, they would command that the accused be held to answer for trial. Guilt or innocence was decided by the procedures of the time—**trial by ordeal** or trial by battle. This council, which became known as a grand jury, comprised between sixteen and twenty-four persons.

The right of an accused to appeal his or her case was practically unknown in early judicial procedure. But as time passed, a limited right of appeal was granted. Appeals in the ecclesiastical courts, in the twelfth century particularly, were taken to the bishop from the court presided over by an archdeacon, and from the bishop to the archbishop. The final appeal was to the pope in Rome. The final appeal from the king's court was to the king. Although the kings for the most part respected the jurisdiction of the ecclesiastical courts, this final appeal to the pope was upsetting to the kings. The inevitable result of this final appeal to the pope was to give recognition to the fact that the canon law was a worldwide system and was not limited to any national boundary. The kings were jealous of the pope's outside influence, over which the kings had little control, so that they often tried to restrict this influence. King William I declared that no one was to receive a letter from the pope unless it was first shown to him. Later, other kings declared that there should be no appeal to the pope without consent of the king. Yet with all the kings' jealousy of the pope, King John, in his desperation, sought the assistance of Pope Innocent III after he was forced to sign the Magna Charta on June 15, 1215. King John requested that the pope annul the Magna Charta, which he did on August 25, 1215. The pope further forbade the king to enforce the Magna Charta upon the grounds that this charter was extorted from King John by force and that the terms of the charter were "dishonorable, unjust, unlawful, and derogatory" to the king. But after the death of King John in October 1216, the Magna Charta was revised, and its provisions were again placed into operation. It was expected that kings thereafter would comply with these provisions.

Early Treatment of Offenders

With the church playing the paramount role in the administration of justice in the early history of England, it is only natural that the deity was called upon to assist when efforts were made to determine the guilt or innocence of one accused of a crime. From the time of the invasion of England by the Romans until the Norman Conquest, a person accused of breaking the law could be handled in one of four ways:

- The community could make war on the offender;
- the offender might be exposed to the vengeance of those he had offended;
- the offender might be permitted to make atonement for his crime; or
- the community might inflict upon the offender the penalty already established for the particular crime after his or her guilt had been determined.

Outlawry

Perhaps the earliest method of handling one who was accused of committing a crime was to wage war upon the accused. It was held that when one had gone to war with the community by committing a crime, the community was not only entitled to, but bound to, make war upon the offender. The accused was declared "outlawed," or without the protection of the law. Thus, the community was to pursue and slay the offender, burn the offender's house, ravage his or her land, and take his or her possessions. As time passed, this form of punishment was inflicted upon only the person of lowest status, the slave. The declaration was, in effect, the imposition of the death penalty, because without the protection of the community, the individual would soon be killed by others or by wild beasts.

Blood Feud

If the accused was not outlawed, the community might leave the accused unprotected against those he or she had offended, whereupon they might avenge themselves by taking whatever action they deemed appropriate in accordance with the crime committed, even to the slaying of the offender. Some of the offender's relatives might be slain also, since not all persons were of the same status in the early history of England. The lowest status was that of slave; next was the serf, who was bound to native soil instead of being the absolute property of a master like the slave; then status continued up to the highest, that of king. In between were a number of other classes of persons, such as the barons and knights, who were referred to as "thegns"; the freeman workers were known as "ceorls." It was alleged that six ceorls were the equivalent of one thegn. Thus, if a ceorl should slay a thegn, the slayer and five of his or her kinsfolk would also have to be slain. However, it might take time to locate the kinsfolk in order to slay them, and other members of the family might inherit the responsibility of avenging the crime; thus, the blood feud took place.

Atonement

There is no doubt that blood feuds were not the most popular method of settling a crime that had been committed, particularly when the blood feud reached a point where relatives of the offended or offender became involved in avenging the crime. It is only natural that the relatives would prefer to conduct some type of financial bargaining rather than engage in a lengthy hunt for the offender or the offender's relatives and then become involved in a bloody entanglement to avenge a crime. Frequently, a price of so many cows or horses or a sum of money was agreed upon, which the offender or the relatives could pay in order to bring about peace in the community. Thus, the system of atonement was established. Each particular crime developed a designated price that had to be paid when that crime was committed. Even murder could be atoned under certain circumstances, depending upon the status of the offender and the offended. **Atonement** was an accepted procedure in most instances, not only by the offended but also by the church and the king, since each would receive a portion of the atonement, depending upon the crime. For example, if a couple were caught committing adultery, the man paid the king in order to regain his peace in the community, whereas the woman paid the church for the sin she had committed. If the offender was without possessions, in order to make atonement, he or she might have to go into bondage or be subjected to a prescribed punishment. The system of atonement is the precursor to the present procedures of fining persons for having committed certain crimes.

Trial by Ordeal

Since not all persons were permitted to make atonement, other procedures had to be devised to bring those guilty of having committed a crime to justice. One of the most prevalent methods utilized in determining the guilt or innocence of an accused was the trial by ordeal. The accused was required to perform some physical feat. This procedure was a call to the deity for assistance in determining the guilt or innocence of the accused. The theory was that if the accused were innocent, God would enable him or her to perform the required ordeal. If guilty, the accused would fail in his or her performance. The accused would then be subjected to the prescribed punishment for the crime committed. When punishment was inflicted, it was usually severe. The punishment may have been death by hanging, beheading, stoning, burning, or drowning. If the punishment did not cause death, the guilty might have one or both ears cut off, have the nose or upper lip severed, have a hand or foot cut off, be castrated, or be flogged, tarred, and feathered. People who had falsely accused someone might lose their tongues. In addition, they might be banished from the land (a punishment that was later referred to as outlawry) or be sold into slavery.

The ordeal that the accused might be subjected to varied greatly in procedure, but whatever it may have been, it was preceded by an oath by the accused; this was an oath of innocence to God. If found guilty by failing in the ordeal, the accused would not only suffer the punishment inflicted upon him or her, but also would receive divine punishment according to the belief of the time. Most of the ordeals were supervised by priests.

The most prevalent ordeal used was that of the hot iron. The accused would appear before the altar, give the oath, and then have a hand sprinkled with holy water. A red-hot iron would be laid across the hand, and the accused would take nine paces and drop the iron. The accused would return to the altar, where a priest would bind the burned hand. Three days later, the accused would return to the priest and have the hand unbound. If the wound had healed, the accused was found innocent; if it had not healed, the accused was judged guilty and was then subjected to the prescribed punishment in accordance with the crime committed.

Another type of ordeal was that of the boiling pot of water from which the accused might be required to remove a large rock. The same binding procedure would be followed as in the ordeal of the hot iron. It would seem that under this system there would be few acquittals, but apparently many priests felt compassion for those accused and assisted God in determining guilt or innocence. Records reveal that in one period there were eighty-three acquittals out of eighty-four trials by ordeal. Upon viewing the wound, the priest declared that it had healed. This record of acquittals caused the king much displeasure because of the loss of revenue.

The accused might be subjected to other types of ordeals in addition to the hot iron and boiling pot of water. For example, the accused might be required to walk barefoot and blindfolded over nine red-hot ploughshares laid lengthwise at unequal distances, or the accused might have his or her thumbs tied to the toes and be thrown into a lake or pond. If the accused did not sink, he or she was declared innocent. Also used was the ordeal of the accursed morsel, whereby a piece of bread was prayed over. It was then given to the accused, who was to swallow it. If the person choked, he or she was found guilty. The decision of the cross involved laying two pieces of wood on an altar, one of which had been marked with a cross. After a prayer asking for a sign from God, a priest or young boy picked up one of the pieces of wood without looking at it. If it bore the mark of a cross, the accused was deemed to be innocent.

Trial by Battle

Another method of determining guilt or innocence was trial by battle. In this method, the accused and the accuser would go into actual combat with each other, usually using battle axes. Before the battle took place, both participants would swear to God that they were right. It is believed that the trial-by-battle procedure was brought to England by the Normans. It is known that trial by battle was used as a method of determining guilt on the continent before the Norman Conquest, and there is no record of its use in England before the Norman invasion. The church displayed less favor to trial by battle than to trial by ordeal because it involved a certain amount of pagan ceremony. However, trial by battle was tolerated because it also involved a call to God, and the one who came forth the victor did so not from brute force but through the assistance of God.

Trial by Compurgation

The church was always seeking ways to determine the guilt or innocence of an accused person without the tortures of the ordeal or the bloodshed of the battle, particularly when its own hierarchy was involved. It is believed that determining guilt by compurgation, through oath helpers or wager of the law, by which terms it was also known, originated within the church, but the method was not confined to church personnel. For a time, it was used for laypeople, since it related to violations of the secular and ecclesiastical laws. Trial by compurgation originated on the continent of Europe, but there are records indicating its existence in England before the Norman Conquest.

In the trial by compurgation, both the accused and the accuser would take an oath to God. The accused would swear to his or her innocence, and the accuser would swear that the accusation was true. Each would be assisted by oath helpers, or compurgators. The compurgators of the accused would swear to God that the oath given by the accused was a true oath. The accuser would be accompanied by oath helpers who would swear to his or her truthfulness.

Initially, the accused's oath helpers were often relatives, and if the accused failed in the oath-taking experience, the matter might turn into a blood feud; consequently, the relatives were usually very willing to assist, although their assistance frequently led to perjury. Because of the unreliability of the relatives as oath helpers, the accused soon had to select oath helpers from among persons in the community who were not relatives. If the accused had a bad reputation, he or she might experience difficulty in getting oath helpers. An oath helper might be compared with a character witness in our present judicial system. In some instances, the accused had to select oath helpers from a list supplied to him or her by the accuser or by one of the priests or justices involved. Many times the accused was unknown to these persons, so they were permitted to swear to the truthfulness of the accused's oath to the best of their knowledge and belief. The number of oath helpers that was called to assist varied considerably. Any number between four and sixty-six was called, but most frequently the number was twelve.

Although trial by compurgation was used for a time, it did not replace the trial by ordeal or the trial by battle. As time passed, the wording of the oath to be taken by the accused and the oath helpers became so complex that repeating it without error was almost impossible. If an error was made, the accused was automatically declared guilty, and the prescribed punishment was inflicted. Thus, with the technical language of the oath and the general unreliability of the oath helpers, trial by compurgation was somewhat of a farce. It therefore soon fell into decay and disuse, and other methods were adopted to determine guilt or innocence.

Establishment of Juries

As early as the ninth century, Frankish kings on the European continent would summon, through a public officer, the most trustworthy people of a community. These people were then placed under oath to answer truthfully all questions directed at them during sessions with the king. These sessions, which were called inquests, did not necessarily arise out of criminal activity or litigation, but were often merely fact-finding meetings in which the king could gather information about the community. During the inquest, the king might ask the following kinds of questions: What were the rights of the king in their particular community? Who were the landowners, and how much land did they own? What were the customs of their area? Who had a better title to a piece of property, John or James? The number of people summoned to serve on this body varied from three to seventy-two, but twelve was the number most frequently called.

In addition to seeking the answers to these kinds of questions, the king would ask this body whom they suspected of having committed murder, rape, or robbery. This body was the first crude form of an accusatory jury. But the Frankish kings did not always use the jury merely to accuse a person of a crime; in fact, they often called upon the jury to render a verdict of guilt or innocence. In order to collect their revenue for crimes committed, these kings frequently preferred the verdict of this body of people over that of a trial by ordeal, battle, or compurgation. During the early use of the jury by kings, it is not inconceivable that people may have found themselves accused and convicted without even knowing that an accusation had been directed at them.

To collect the wages of sin, the Frankish bishops were also known to have used the inquest to determine who had committed crimes against the church. Records reflect that certain Frankish bishops selected a number of trustworthy men from an assembled laity, or congregation, who were administered an oath to tell the truth and conceal nothing for love or hate, reward or kinship, and to report their suspicions about their neighbors who might have sinned against the church. These suspected sinners then would be put through the ordeal.

There is little record of the inquest being used in England until after the Norman Conquest. However, Ethelred the Unready, King of England, is alleged to have decreed early in the eleventh century that a moot was to be held in every "wapentake," and that the twelve eldest thegns were to go out with the "reeve" and swear on a relic that they would neither accuse an innocent person nor conceal a guilty person. In our terminology, a meeting was to be held in every county subdivision where the eldest trustworthy members of that community were to go out with a local representative of the king and swear on some religious object that they would neither accuse an innocent person nor conceal one guilty of a crime.

Accusatory Juries

Hardly had England been conquered in A.D. 1066 when William the Conqueror summoned bodies of people from all the communities to assist him in obtaining general as well as criminal information concerning their respective areas. In the mid-twelfth century, King Henry II made great use of the juries to determine what cases his justices should hear as they rode their circuits through the kingdom. He summoned twelve of the most trustworthy noblemen from a group one hundred noblemen (or county), and four men from each township, who were sworn to hear accusations and determine whether they were well founded. If so, the accused was given an opportunity to prove his or her innocence by one of the various trial procedures.

King Henry II also suggested that the bishops of the ecclesiastical courts should not rely merely upon an accuser's unsworn suggestion that someone had committed a crime before subjecting the accused to the ordeal, battle, or compurgation. Rather, the bishops should have the sheriff summon twelve of the most lawful men of the neighborhood to hear an accusation to determine its reliability before the accused was put on trial.

The accusatory jury had become such an important part of justice by the beginning of the thirteenth century that when King John ignored its use and acted upon his own knowledge of accusations, the right to an accusatory jury was made a part of the Magna Charta. Included in the provisions of the Magna Charta was this guarantee: "No freeman shall be taken, or imprisoned, or disseized, or outlawed, or exiled, in any way harmed—nor will we go upon or send upon him—save by the lawful judgement of his peers or by the law of the land." It was expected that King John and all following kings would comply with this guarantee—the forerunner of our grand jury system.

Development of Trial by Jury

As time passed, greater use of the jury was made. It was called upon not only to decide whether an accusation was well founded but also, as in the case of some of the Frankish kings' juries, to render a verdict of guilt or innocence. It was eventually believed that a jury should not be both an accusatory jury and a trial or verdict jury. Consequently, one jury would be summoned to hear the accusation (later referred to as the grand jury), and another jury was summoned to render a verdict of guilt or innocence (known as the petit jury). The petit, or trial, jury, which usually consisted of twelve persons, initially functioned entirely differently from the juries of today. These early trial juries assembled and stated what they knew about a particular crime, or they might be assembled and commanded to go forth into the countryside and ascertain facts about the alleged crime. Then the jurors would talk to neighbors, pick up hearsay information and rumors, and undoubtedly be contacted by the accused and the accuser. After gathering their evidence, they would reassemble and draw a conclusion as to guilt or innocence. If the accused was found guilty, the prescribed punishment for the crime was inflicted upon him or her. Soon it was not just the jurors who stated what they had learned about the crime, witnesses might appear before the jury and relate what they knew about the accusation. Since the knowledge of the witnesses was often no more than rumor or hearsay, the jury might give little weight to their testimony and decide contrary to the general consensus of the witnesses. This outcome was particularly likely if the witnesses believed the accused to be innocent. The reason that the jury might decide contrary to the belief of the witnesses was that the jury was fearful of rendering a false verdict, thus denying the king his revenue. The jurors knew that the king's justices often had advance information about a crime because of reports from the sheriffs and the coroners. If the jurors made a false verdict in the eyes of the justices, they would be required to make atonement and were even punished in some instances.

Because of the danger of conviction in a trial by jury, an accused would frequently revert to the trial by ordeal. However, after the ordeal was abolished around A.D. 1215 and trial by compurgation had met with disfavor, the only procedure remaining was trial by battle. But if the accuser was a woman or a noncombatant, trial by battle was impossible, so it was unknown what should be done with the accused who refused a trial by jury or who put himself or herself upon the country, as the jury trial was sometimes referred to. Occasionally, under the circumstances, the accused was hanged immediately or, in other instances, was imprisoned for a year and given only a sip of water daily and a small morsel of bread. Sometimes the accused was imprisoned and weights were placed on his or her chest in increasing amounts until the person submitted to a trial by jury. Often the accused preferred being crushed to death in an effort to save his or her possessions for his or her family, rather than having them confiscated by the king, should the jury pass a conviction.

As time passed and the king could no longer confiscate property as payment for crimes and jurors were no longer punished or required to make atonement for possibly erroneous verdicts, greater reliance was placed on the testimony of witnesses. Eventually, the development of trial by jury progressed to what we know today. However, it still had a way to go even when the colonists settled in this country. The Maryland Archives reveal that on September 22, 1656, a judge in Patuxent, Maryland, impaneled a jury of seven married women and four single women to determine the guilt of one Judith Catchpole, who was accused of murdering her child. She denied guilt and even denied having a child. The judge then commanded the jury to go forth and determine first whether Judith had a child and, if so, whether she had murdered it. At this time, the jury was to "go forth into the countryside and seek information" rather than depend upon the sworn testimony of witnesses. The all female jury inspected Catchpole's body and concluded that she had not recently given birth. It is also interesting that a jury of eleven instead of twelve was impaneled, because long before that time, the number of twelve jurors for a trial was well established in England. By the thirteenth century, the usual number for a petit jury in England was twelve. By the fourteenth century, a jury of twelve persons was firmly established, and thereafter the number of twelve persons composing a trial jury seems to have developed some superstitious reverence.

The reason why a jury of twelve evolved is lost in the annals of history, but it is believed to have been based on Christ having chosen twelve apostles. It has been suggested that twelve was a popular number at the time of Christ, as witnessed by the twelve tribes of Israel, the twelve tablets, Solomon's twelve judges, and the twelve signs of the zodiac. Thus, it is highly likely that the jury comprising twelve persons is based upon that fact, especially since the church played a dominant role in the development of the judicial systems in both Europe and England. One of the ancient kings of Europe, Morgan of Gla-Morgan, is believed to have adopted a form of trial by jury called the Apostolic Law, which declared that since Christ and his twelve apostles were finally to judge the world, so the king and twelve wise men should comprise the human tribunals. Furthermore, later the following oath is alleged to have been required of a trial jury of twelve: "Hear this, ye justices, that I will speak of that which ye shall ask of me on the part of the king, and I will do faithfully to the best of my endeavor. So help me God, and these holy Apostles."

When the colonists came to North America, they were well indoctrinated with the view that a trial jury should comprise twelve persons, although it is known that one or two of the colonies permitted a jury to comprise fewer than twelve. It is not entirely clear from historical data whether permitting fewer than twelve was a conscious effort to break from tradition, in defiance of the king and England, or whether it was because of the small number of people in the colonies involved, making it difficult to find twelve qualified jurors. This situation may have accounted for the fact that the judge in the Catchpole case impaneled only eleven women instead of twelve. It was also a break with tradition to impanel women instead of men, since women were not generally considered to be qualified as jurors.

Historical Development of the Bill of Rights

As we approach the study of the judicial procedure followed today, it is important to review some of the rights and guarantees granted to one accused of a crime. These rights and guarantees are to be found either in the Constitution of the United States or in the constitutions and statutes of the various states. Some of these rights are based upon the common law of England, but others were developed over time as a result of dealing with accused persons.

Returning now to the Magna Charta, we find that it created no panacea, but it did ensure the people certain liberties, which they had been denied previously, and made way for the establishment of due process of law. However, the people of England continued to be subjected to many oppressive practices, and many were persecuted because of their religious beliefs. To escape these practices, a number of people left for North America to establish colonies. The king considered these colonies to be his possessions; the colonists were still under the rule of the king, and all too often that rule laid heavily upon them. They were taxed excessively and were generally oppressed. When they objected, they were often taken to England for trial. As time passed, the colonists increased their opposition. This became a source of irritation to the king, who sent his armies to enforce his rule. Suspected objectors were frequently subjected to searches and seizures without cause and imprisoned without justification.

As a result of the king's extreme actions, the colonists banded together and adopted a resolution declaring their political independence from England. This document is the Declaration of Independence, which announced to the world that the colonists were serious in their aim to become an independent nation, and it asked for understanding and compassion from other nations. The Declaration of Independence set forth the reasons for their actions and grievances against the king. Among the charges were that the king

> has refused to assent to laws, the most wholesome and necessary for the public good; . . . has obstructed the administration of justice; . . . has kept among us, in times of peace, standing armies without the consent of our legislatures; . . . has deprived many of the benefits of trial by jury; . . . has transported us beyond seas to be tried for pretended offenses.

By reviewing the Declaration of Independence, we are able to appreciate the conditions of the time and the conflicts experienced by the people of America. The Declaration became the basis of the guarantees later to be embodied in our Constitution.

The king did not take this Declaration of Independence lightly. He sent additional armies to subdue the colonies, resulting in the Revolutionary War. When peace was restored in 1783, the colonies became a self-governing nation. A governmental structure had to be formed, and laws had to be made for governing the people. Although various efforts at governmental structures were attempted, each revealed weaknesses. In 1787, representatives of the colonies, now referred to as states, met in Philadelphia to attempt again to formulate an acceptable and a workable governmental structure. The result of this conference, known as the Constitutional

Convention, was the U.S. Constitution, which was finally adopted in 1789. It established three branches of government: executive, legislative, and judicial.

As the various state representatives reviewed this document, they felt that a vital weakness still remained in its structure: The people were not guaranteed protection against oppression should this central government become too strong and powerful. Therefore, it was agreed that certain additions should be made to the Constitution. Again representatives of the states met in Congress during 1789 and proposed twelve amendments to the Constitution. Ten of them were adopted in 1791 and are known as the Bill of Rights, which guarantees certain rights to the people. The two amendments that were not adopted did not pertain to guarantees but were related to the legislative structure of the government. Because of the importance of these amendments to the administration of justice, we review them next.

The Bill of Rights

Amendment I: Restriction on Powers of Congress. Congress shall make no law respecting an establishment of religion, or prohibiting the free exercise thereof, or abridging the freedom of speech, or of the press; or the right of the people peaceably to assemble, and to petition the government for a redress of grievances.

Amendment II: Right to Bear Arms. A well-regulated militia being necessary to the security of a free State, the right of the people to keep and bear arms shall not be infringed.

Amendment III: Billeting of Soldiers. No soldier shall, in time of peace, be quartered in any house without the consent of the owner; nor in time of war, but in a manner to be prescribed by law.

Amendment IV: Seizures, Searches and Warrants. The right of the people to be secure in their persons, houses, papers, and effects, against unreasonable searches and seizures shall not be violated, and no warrants shall issue but upon probable cause, supported by oath or affirmation, and particularly describing the place to be searched and the persons or things to be seized.

Amendment V: Criminal Proceedings, Condemnation of Property. No person shall be held to answer for a capital or otherwise infamous crime, unless on a presentment or indictment of a grand jury, except in cases arising in the land or naval forces, or in the militia, when in actual service in time of war or public danger; nor shall any person be subject for the same offense to be twice put in jeopardy of life or limb; nor shall be compelled in any criminal case, to be a witness against himself; nor be deprived of life, liberty, or property, without due process of law, nor shall private property be taken for public use without just compensation.

Amendment VI: Mode of Trial in Criminal Proceedings. In all criminal prosecutions the accused shall enjoy the right to a speedy and public trial, by an impartial jury of the State and district wherein the crime shall have been committed, which district shall have been previously ascertained by law; and to be informed of the nature and cause of the accusation; to be confronted with the witnesses against him; to have compulsory process for obtaining witnesses in his favor, and to have the assistance of counsel for his defense.

Amendment VII: Trial by Jury. In suits at common law, where the value in controversy shall exceed twenty dollars, the right of trial by jury shall be preserved; and no fact tried by jury, shall be otherwise reexamined in any court of the United States than according to the rules of common law.

Amendment VIII: Involuntary Servitude. Excessive bail shall not be required, nor excessive fines imposed, nor cruel and unusual punishment inflicted.

Amendment IX: Certain Rights Not Denied to the People. The enumeration in the Constitution of certain rights shall not be construed to deny or disparage others retained by the people.

Amendment X: State Rights. The powers not delegated to the United States by the Constitution, nor prohibited by it to the States, are reserved to the states, respectively, or to the people.

Due Process of Law

As we study these amendments, we must remind ourselves that when they were adopted, the oppressive conditions that brought them into being were still vivid in the memory of the people. Thus, these guarantees were to protect the people against any action that might be attempted by the federal government and as such were applicable only to federal officers. The states, as provided in the Ninth and Tenth Amendments, were free to establish their own guarantees relating to the actions permitted by state and local officials. We will find that the Fourth, Fifth, Sixth, and Eighth Amendments are most significant in the administration of justice.

As time passed, slavery and involuntary servitude, such as forcing men to build public roads or to serve in a state militia without pay, were permitted in some states. After the Civil War, the Thirteenth Amendment, abolishing slavery, was added to the U.S. Constitution. To prohibit other oppressive and arbitrary actions by the states, the Fourteenth Amendment was adopted in 1868. This amendment held that:

> All persons born or naturalized in the United States, and subject to the jurisdiction thereof, are citizens of the United States and of the State wherein they reside. No State shall make or enforce any law which shall abridge the privileges or immunities of citizens of the United States; nor shall any State deprive any person of life, liberty, or property, without due process of law; nor deny to any person within its jurisdiction the equal protection of the laws.

It should be emphasized that this amendment was directed to the states to prevent them from depriving any person of life, liberty, or property without due process of law. However, the amendment raised a question regarding the interpretation of the term due process of law as it related to the administration of justice. The courts later concluded that if an accused had his day in court with the right to appeal a conviction, the due process of law clause of the Fourteenth Amendment had been satisfied. We will find in our study of the judicial procedure throughout this text that the U.S. Supreme Court has since placed a different interpretation on the meaning of the due process of law clause of the Fourteenth Amendment. The Supreme Court has ruled that the following particular Bill of Rights guarantees are applicable to the states: the Fourth Amendment right to be free from unreasonable searches and seizures and to have any illegally seized evidence excluded from criminal trials[4]; the Fifth Amendment privilege against self-incrimination[5] and the guarantee against double jeopardy,[6] and the Sixth Amendment rights to counsel,[7] to a speedy trial,[8] to a public trial,[9] to confront opposing witnesses,[10] and to an impartial jury.[11] Decisions making these guarantees applicable to the states will be discussed as the judicial procedure is further explained. For practical purposes, these amendments are as applicable to state and local officers as they are to federal officers. Figure 1-1 indicates the relationship of the Bill of Rights and the Fourteenth Amendment to the Constitutional Rights of the Accused.

In addition to the guarantees provided by the Bill of Rights, each state has furnished to the people within that state additional guarantees and rights, which are contained in the statutes of the state constitution. To ensure that the guarantees of the Bill of Rights and the state statutes are properly afforded the people, court structures have been established.

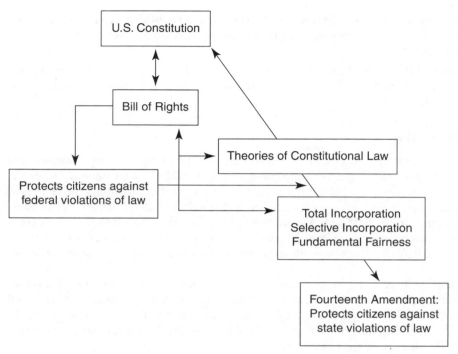

FIGURE 1-1 Relationship of the Bill of Rights and the Fourteenth Amendment to the Constitutional Rights of the Accused.

COURT STRUCTURES

The court system in the United States is based upon the principle of federalism.[12] The first Congress established a federal court system, and the individual states were permitted to continue their own judicial structure. There was general agreement among our nation's founding fathers that individual states needed to retain significant autonomy from federal control. Under this concept of federalism, the United States developed as a loose confederation of semi-independent states, with the federal court system acting in a very limited manner. In the early history of our nation, most cases were tried in state courts, and it was only later that the federal government and the federal judiciary began to exercise jurisdiction over crimes and civil matters. **Jurisdiction** in this context simply means the ability of the court to enforce laws and punish individuals who violate those laws.

As a result of this historical evolution, a dual system of state and federal courts exists today. Therefore, federal and state courts may have concurrent jurisdiction over specific crimes. For example, a person who robs a bank may be tried and convicted in state court for robbery and then tried and convicted in federal court for the federal offense of robbery of a federally chartered savings institution.

The second characteristic of the American court system is that it performs its duties with little or no supervision. A supreme court justice does not exercise supervision over lower court judges in the same way that a government supervisor or manager exercises control over his or her employees. The U.S. Supreme Court and the various state supreme courts exercise supervision only in the sense that they hear appellate cases from lower courts and establish certain procedures for these courts.

The third feature of our court system is the specialization that occurs primarily at the state and local levels. In many states, courts of limited jurisdiction hear misdemeanor cases.

Other state courts of general jurisdiction try felonies. Still other courts may be designated as juvenile courts and hear only matters involving juveniles. This process also occurs in certain civil courts that hear only family law matters, probate matters, or civil cases involving damages. At the federal level, there are courts, such as bankruptcy court, that hear only cases dealing with specific matters. Figure 1-2 depicts the structure of the federal court system.

A fourth characteristic of our court system is that generally the courts perform either trial or appellate functions. A trial court tries the case and issues a verdict and if appropriate a sentence. Evidence is presented at the trial court and the jury or judge when there is no jury makes the findings of fact, for example, did the defendant kill the victim. The evidence is presented by witnesses, documents, and so on to help the decision maker arrive at the verdict.

Generally an appellate court does not hear evidence or make findings of fact. The appellate court rules on the legal issues presented in the appeals of the parties from the judgment of the trial court. Witnesses do not appear in appellate court and the defendant does not have a right to be present at any hearing before an appellate court. The appellate court makes its decision on the record presented by the briefs of the parties, record of trial, and arguments of the parties.

The fifth characteristic of the American court system is the organization of state and federal courts into geographic areas. In many jurisdictions, these are called judicial districts and contain various levels of courts. For example, on the federal level, the Ninth Circuit Court of Appeals has district (trial) courts that hear matters within certain specific boundaries and an appellate court that hears all appeals from cases within that area. Several studies have been conducted regarding the difference in sentences for the same type of crime in geographic district courts. For instance, in Iowa the average sentence for motor vehicle theft was forty-seven months, whereas the average sentence for the same offense in New York was fourteen months.[13] This observation shouldn't be taken as a criticism; rather, it may reflect different social values and attitudes within specific geographic areas.

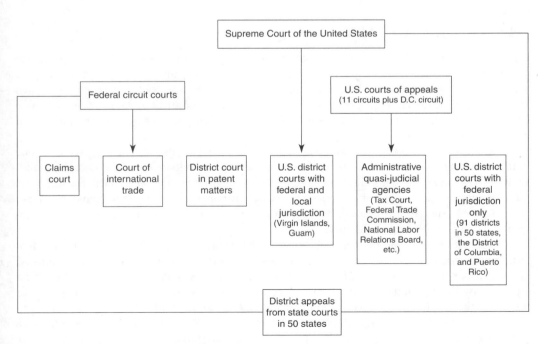

FIGURE 1-2 Structure of the Federal Court System.

After a person is arrested, unless the charge against him or her is dismissed, some prosecutive action must be taken, which will occur in the appropriate court. In order for students to have a clearer understanding of the judicial proceedings from the time of arrest through sentencing, a discussion of the court system follows. Although the court system may vary somewhat among the states, it is basically the same. The states are divided into territorial divisions known as counties, except in Louisiana, where they are called parishes, and in Alaska, which is divided into four judicial districts. Each county, parish, or district has its own trial court system. The chief trial court is known as the superior court, district court, or circuit court, depending upon the title that the court is given in a particular state. This court, in addition to trying civil matters, will hear trials involving felony cases and possibly some more serious, or high, misdemeanor charges. Generally, this court holds forth in the county seat. Although these courts are technically county courts, they are referred to in many books on judicial procedures as state courts, as distinguished from federal courts.

Law in Practice

Controversy over Sobriety Checkpoints

In 2011, four U.S. senators attempted to restrict the use of downloadable applications to cell phones that alert drivers to the locations of sobriety checkpoints. The Federal Centers for Disease Control and Prevention has concluded that sobriety checkpoints had reduced alcohol-related accidents.

The U.S. Supreme Court has ruled that these sobriety checkpoints are legal. This is one area where some state courts have disagreed with the U.S. Supreme Court and have concluded that the checkpoints were a violation of individual rights. This issue provides an example of how a state may offer more individual rights than provided by the U.S. Constitution. The reverse does not work in that a state may not restrict individual rights more than that permitted by the federal constitution.

As of June 2011, twelve state high courts or legislatures have ruled or concluded that sobriety checkpoints are unreasonable searches and seizures. In those 12 states; Alaska, Idaho, Iowa, Michigan, Minnesota, Montana, Oregon, Rhode Island, Texas, Washington, Wisconsin, and Wyoming; the police are restricted from using sobriety checkpoints.

STATE COURT SYSTEM

Historically, each of the thirteen states had its own unique court structure. This independence continued after the American Revolution and resulted in widespread differences among the various states; some of these differences still exist today. Because each state adopted its own system of courts, the consequence was a poorly planned and confusing judicial structure. As a result, there have been several reform movements whose purpose has been to streamline and modernize this system.

Many state courts can be divided into three levels: trial courts, appellate courts, and state supreme courts. It is in trial courts that criminal cases start, evidence is presented, the defendant is found guilty or not guilty, and a sentence is imposed if the defendant is found guilty. The trial court conducts the entire series of acts that culminate in either the defendant's release or sentencing. State trial courts can be further divided into courts of limited or special jurisdiction and courts of general jurisdiction.

The nature and type of case determines which court will have jurisdiction. Courts that hear and decide only certain limited legal issues are courts of limited jurisdiction. Typically, these courts hear certain types of minor civil or criminal cases. Approximately 13,000 local courts exist in the United States. They are county, magistrate, justice, or municipal courts. Judges in these courts may be either appointed or elected. In many jurisdictions, these are part-time positions, and the incumbent may have another job or position in addition to serving as a judge. Figure 1-3 depicts the hierarchy of the U.S. Court System.

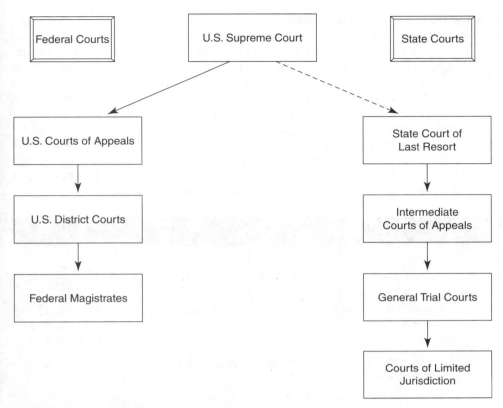

FIGURE 1-3 Hierarchy in the U.S. Court System.

Coming to the county seat from outlying areas of the county has often created hardship and expense for many of those involved in a trial. To accommodate these persons and to relieve part of the caseload of the superior court, some counties have been divided into judicial districts, each containing a lower court. This lower court is often referred to as an inferior court, as opposed to the superior court, and is known in many places as the justice court. The judge is frequently called the justice of the peace. This court has limited jurisdiction, hearing certain misdemeanor charges and civil matters involving small amounts of money. Usually the judge is elected by the people within the district, and generally in the past there was no requirement that he or she have legal training. The reason for no such requirement was that in many outlying judicial districts, there were no attorneys; however, the people of those districts were entitled to some judicial assistance. Today, since more attorneys are available, many states have phased out the judges of the inferior courts who are not attorneys. However, the elimination of the layperson judge has met with resistance. Some contend that the local inferior, or lower, court can provide a form of justice that is convenient for both the accused and the accuser and that the layperson justice of the peace is part of the American heritage. Others contend that to subject an accused to possible imprisonment after a conviction in a trial presided over by a layperson judge is to deny the accused the right to due process of law. This matter was brought before the U.S. Supreme Court in the case of *North* v. *Russell* after North was convicted of drunk driving and sentenced to thirty days in jail by a layperson sitting as a police court judge.[21] North contended that his conviction for drunk driving and sentencing to thirty days in jail was a violation of his right to due process of law as provided in the Fourteenth Amendment. The Court upheld the conviction upon the grounds that North could have taken his case to a higher court and had it completely tried again by a court presided over by an attorney judge. Therefore, North was not denied due process of law. The Court pointed out that there was an advantage to the accused in having the trial in a community near his residence rather than traveling to a distant court where a law-trained judge was provided. The decision did not rule out all laypersons judges as being a denial of due process of law, but it should be noted that the judicial structures of some states do not provide for a conviction in a lower court to be taken to a higher court and the case started anew. Where such a procedure is not available, courts could hold that an accused would be denied the right of due process of law in a proceeding before a layperson judge.

However, simply because they handle minor civil and criminal matters does not mean that these courts do not perform important duties. In many cases, the only contact the average citizen will have with the judicial system occurs at this level. Courts of limited jurisdiction hear and decide issues such as traffic tickets or set bail for criminal defendants.

Law in Practice

State Major Criminal Trial Courts

Circuit Court	Alabama, Arkansas, Florida, Hawaii, Illinois, Indiana, Kentucky, Maryland, Michigan, Mississippi, Missouri, Oregon, South Carolina, South Dakota, Tennessee, Virginia, West Virginia, and Wisconsin
Court of Common Pleas	Ohio and Pennsylvania
District Court	Colorado, Idaho, Kansas, Louisiana, Minnesota, Montana, Nebraska, Nevada, New Mexico, North Dakota, Oklahoma, Texas, Utah, and Wyoming
Superior Court	Alaska, Arizona, California, Connecticut, Delaware, District of Columbia, Georgia, Maine, Massachusetts, New Hampshire, New Jersey, North Carolina, Rhode Island, Vermont, Washington, and New York
Supreme Court	New York (New York also uses county courts and superior courts)

Source: David Rottman, Carol Flango, and R. Shedine Lockley, *State Court Organizations, 1993* (Washington, D.C.: U.S. Department of Justice, Bureau of Justice Statistics, Government Printing Office, 1995).

In addition, courts of limited jurisdiction may hear certain types of specialized matters such as probate of wills and estates, divorces, child custody matters, and juvenile hearings. These types of courts may be local courts or, depending on the state, courts of general jurisdiction that are designated by statute to hear and decide specific types of cases. For example, in California, a superior court is considered a court of general jurisdiction; however, certain superior courts are designated to hear only juvenile matters, thereby becoming courts of limited jurisdiction when sitting as juvenile courts.

Courts of general jurisdiction are granted authority to hear and decide all issues that are brought before them. These are the courts that normally hear all major civil or criminal cases. These courts are known by a variety of names, such as superior courts, circuit courts, district courts, or courts of common pleas. Since they are courts of general jurisdiction, they have authority to decide issues that occur anywhere within the state. Some larger jurisdictions such as Los Angeles or New York may have hundreds of courts of general jurisdiction within the city limits. Typically, these courts hear civil cases involving the same types of issues that courts of limited jurisdiction hear, although the amount of damages will be higher and may reach millions of dollars. These courts also hear the most serious forms of criminal matters, including death penalty cases. Figure 1-4 depicts the Commonwealth of Virginia's court system.

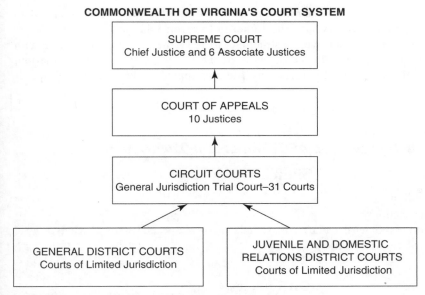

COMMONWEALTH OF VIRGINIA'S COURT SYSTEM

FIGURE 1-4 Commonwealth of Virginia's Court System.

Courts of general jurisdiction traditionally have the power to order individuals to do or refrain from doing certain acts. These courts may issue injunctions prohibiting certain acts or requiring individuals to perform certain functions or duties. This authority is derived from the equity power that resides in courts of general jurisdiction. Equity is the concept that justice is administered according to fairness, as contrasted to the strict rules of law. In early English common law, such separate courts of equity were known as courts of chancery. These early courts were not concerned with technical legal issues; rather, they focused on rendering decisions or orders that were fair or equitable. In modern times, these courts have been merged with courts of general jurisdiction, allowing them to rule on matters that require fairness as well as the strict application of the law. The power to issue temporary restraining orders in spousal abuse cases comes from this authority.

Appellate Courts

Appellate jurisdiction is reserved for courts that hear appeals from both limited and general jurisdiction courts. Except for appeals from minor courts that are heard "de novo" (as a new trial), these courts do not hold trials or hear evidence. Instead, they decide matters of law on the basis of the record of trial and appellate briefs, and they issue formal written decisions, or opinions. In a few states, the intermediate-level appellate courts have limited authority to make findings of fact. There are two classes of appellate courts: intermediate and final.

The intermediate appellate courts are known as courts of appeals. Approximately half of the states have designated intermediate appellate courts. These courts may be divided into judicial districts that hear all appeals within their district. They hear and decide all issues of law that are raised on appeal in both civil and criminal cases. Since these courts deal strictly with legal or equitable issues, there is no jury to decide factual disputes. These courts accept the facts as determined by the trial courts. Most criminal cases end at either the trial or intermediate appellate court level; less than 1 percent of the cases are appealed to the state highest appellate court. However, whereas all states have appellate courts for criminal appeals, there appears to be no constitutional duty for states to have appellate courts. Intermediate appellate courts have the authority to reverse the decision of the lower courts and to send the matter back with instructions to retry the case in accordance with their opinion. They also may uphold the decision of the lower court. In either situation, the party who loses the appeal at this level may file and appeal to the next higher appellate court.

A Comparison of Criminal and Tort Law

Similarities

- Goal of controlling
- Imposition of sanctions
- Some common areas of legal action—for example, personal assault, control of white-collar offenses such as environmental pollution

Differences

Criminal Law	Tort Law
Crime is a public offense.	A tort is a civil or private wrong.
The sanction associated with criminal law is incarceration or death.	The sanction associated with tort law is monetary damages.
The right of enforcement belongs to the state.	The individual brings the action.
The government ordinarily does not appeal.	Both parties can appeal.
Fines go to the state.	The individual receives damages as compensation for harm done.
The burden of proof is beyond a reasonable doubt.	The burden of proof is preponderance of evidence.
Remedies after verdict: punishment.	Remedies after verdict: money damages, injunctions, writs commanding certain action.

A Comparison of Criminal and Tort Laws.

Supreme Courts

Final appellate courts are the highest state appellate courts. They may be known as supreme courts or courts of last resort. There may be five, seven, or nine justices sitting on this court, depending on the state. This court has jurisdiction to hear and decide issues dealing with all matters decided by lower courts, including ruling on state constitutional or statutory issues. Its decision is binding on all other courts within the state. In two states, Oklahoma and Texas, the state supreme courts do not have jurisdiction over criminal matters. In these two states, the highest court of appeal for criminal matters is the Court of Criminal Appeals.

Once the highest state appellate court decides an issue, the conviction is considered final. The defendant may attack the judgment of a state court by filing a writ with a federal court. But before the federal court will accept a writ attacking a state court judgment, a federal issue must be involved. Normally, the federal issue is that the state court violated the federal constitutional rights of the defendant. This is regarded as a collateral attack.

Law in Practice

Cases Incorporating Provisions of the Bill of Rights into the Due Process Clause of the Fourteenth Amendment

The information below indicates how the U.S. Supreme Court has applied the Due Process Clause of the Fourteenth Amendment to incorporate certain rights contained in the U.S. Constitution's Bill of Rights into state proceedings.

First Amendment

Establishment of religion	*Everson* v. *Board of Education* (1947)
Free exercise of religion	*Cantwell* v. *Connecticut* (1940)
Freedom of speech	*Gitlow* v. *New York* (1925)
Freedom of the press	*Near* v. *Minnesota* (1931)
Freedom to peaceably assemble	*DeJong* v. *Oregon* (1937)

Fourth Amendment

Unreasonable search and seizure	*Wolf* v. *Colorado* (1949)
Exclusionary rule	*Mapp* v. *Ohio* (1961)

Fifth Amendment

Grand jury	*Hurtado* v. *California* (1884) [Held not applicable to the states.]
Double jeopardy	*Benton* v. *Maryland* (1969)
Self-incrimination	*Mallay* v. *Hogan* (1964)
Compensation for taking private property	*Chicago, Burlington and Quincy Railroad* v. *Chicago* (1897)

Sixth Amendment

Speedy trial	*Klopfer* v. *Worth Carolina* (1967)
Public trial	*In re Oliver* (1948)
Impartial jury	*Parker* v. *Gladden* (1966)
Jury trial	*Duncan* v. *Louisiana* (1968)
Confrontation of witnesses	*Pointer* v. *Texas* (1965)
Compulsory process	*Washington* v. *Texas* (1967)
Assistance of counsel	*Gideon* v. *Wainwright* [felony cases] (1963) *Argersinger* v. *Hanilin* [misdemeanors involving confinement] (1972)

Eighth Amendment

Excessive bail	*United States* v. *Salerno* (1987)
Cruel and unusual punishment	*Robinson* v. *California* (1962)

Law in Practice

The New York Unified Court System

The New York State court system is different from that of the other states. In New York, the Supreme Court is a trial court and the New York Court of Appeals is the court of last resort for the State of New York.

Mission

The mission of the New York Unified Court System is to promote the rule of law and to serve the public by providing just and timely resolution of all matters before the courts.

State Trial Courts in New York

The trial courts of superior jurisdiction are the supreme courts, the Court of Claims, the family courts, the surrogate's courts, and, outside New York City, the county courts. In New York City, the supreme court exercises both civil and criminal jurisdiction. Outside New York City, the supreme court exercises civil jurisdiction, while the county court generally handles criminal matters.

The trial courts of limited jurisdiction in New York City are the New York City Civil Court and the New York City Criminal Court. Outside New York City, the trial courts of limited jurisdiction are the city courts, which have criminal jurisdiction over misdemeanors and lesser offenses and civil jurisdiction over claims of up to $15,000. There are district courts in Nassau County and parts of Suffolk County. District courts have criminal jurisdiction over misdemeanors and lesser offenses and civil jurisdiction over claims of up to $15,000.

Upstate New York Trial Courts

The county court is established in each county outside of New York City. It is authorized to handle the prosecution of all crimes committed within the county. The county court also has limited jurisdiction in civil cases involving amounts of up to $25,000.

City courts outside of New York City exist in sixty-one cities, and have criminal jurisdiction over misdemeanors and lesser offenses and civil jurisdiction over claims of up to $15,000. Some city courts have separate parts to handle small claims or housing matters. City court judges act as arraigning magistrates and conduct preliminary hearings in felony cases.

Town and village courts have criminal jurisdiction over violations and misdemeanors and civil jurisdiction over claims of up to $3,000. As magistrates, town and village court justices hold arraignments and preliminary hearings for those charged with more serious crimes. Traffic infractions also are heard in these courts.

New York City Courts

The New York City Supreme Court is the trial court of unlimited original jurisdiction, but it generally only hears cases that are outside the jurisdiction of other trial courts of more limited jurisdiction. It exercises civil jurisdiction and jurisdiction over felony charges.

The Family Court hears matters involving children and families. Its jurisdiction includes custody and visitation, support, family offense (domestic violence), persons in need of supervision, delinquency, child protective proceedings (abuse and neglect), foster care approval and review, termination of parental rights, adoption, and guardianship.

The Surrogate's Court hears cases involving the affairs of decedents, including the probate of wills, the administration of estates, and adoptions.

The Civil Court of the City of New York has jurisdiction over civil cases involving amounts of up to $25,000 and other civil matters referred to it by the Supreme Court. It includes a small claims part for informal dispositions of matters not exceeding $5,000 and a housing part for landlord–tenant matters and housing code violations.

The Criminal Court of the City of New York has jurisdiction over misdemeanors and violations. Judges of the Criminal Court also act as arraigning magistrates and conduct preliminary hearings in felony cases.

State Appellate Courts

The appellate courts hear and determine appeals from the decisions of the trial courts. The appellate courts are the Court of Appeals (the highest court in the state), the appellate divisions of the Supreme Court, the appellate terms of the Supreme Court, and the county courts acting as appellate courts in the Third and Fourth Judicial Departments.

FEDERAL COURT SYSTEM

Although state courts had their origin in historical accident and custom, federal courts were created by the U.S. Constitution. Section 1 of Article III established the federal court system with the words providing for "one supreme Court, and . . . such inferior Courts as the Congress may from time to time ordain and establish." From this beginning, Congress has passed a series of acts that have resulted in today's federal court system. The Judiciary Act of 1789 created the U.S. Supreme Court and established district and circuit courts of appeals.

Federal district courts are the lowest level of the federal court system. These courts have original jurisdiction over cases involving a violation of federal statutes. Because these district courts handle thousands of criminal cases per year, questions have been raised regarding the quality of justice that can be delivered by overworked judges.

Federal circuit courts of appeals are the intermediate-appellate courts within the federal system. These courts are called circuit courts because the federal system is divided into eleven circuits. A twelfth circuit court of appeals serves the Washington, D.C., area. These courts hear all criminal appeals from the district courts. These appeals are usually heard by panels of three of the appellate court judges rather than by all the judges of each circuit.

The U.S. Supreme Court is the highest court in the land. It has the capacity for judicial review of all lower court decisions involving federal issues or federal questions. By exercising this power, the Supreme Court determines what laws and what lower court decisions conform to the mandates set forth in the U.S. Constitution, national treaties, and federal law. The concept of judicial review was first referred to by Alexander Hamilton in *The Federalist Papers,* where he referred to the Supreme Court as ensuring that the will of the people will be supreme over the will of the legislature.[22] This concept was firmly and finally established in our system when the Supreme Court asserted its power of judicial review in the case of *Marbury* v. *Madison.*[23] Figure 1-5 depicts the organization of federal courts handling criminal matters. The U.S. Supreme Court has original jurisdiction in the following cases:

- Cases between the United States and a state;
- cases between states;
- cases involving foreign ambassadors, ministers, and consuls; and
- cases between a state and a citizen of another state or country.

The Supreme Court hears appeals from lower courts, including the various state supreme courts (on issues involving federal questions). If four justices of the U.S. Supreme Court vote to hear a case, the Court will issue a writ of certiorari, which is an order to a lower court to send the records of the case to the Supreme Court for review. The Court meets on the first Monday of October and usually remains in session until June. The Court may review any case it deems worthy of review, but it actually hears very few of the cases filed with it. Of approximately 5,000 appeals each year, the Court hears about 100.

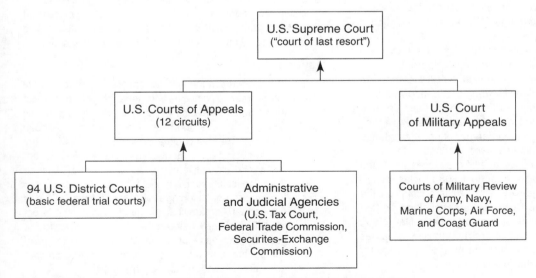

FIGURE 1-5 Organization of Federal Courts Handling Criminal Matters.

VENUE

Defined simply, **venue** is the geographic area in which a case may be heard. It is the place where a case is brought to trial and the area from which the jurors are selected. Usually, venue will lie within the county or judicial district in which a crime is committed. Venue may be waived by the defendant. There are times when a defendant may request that a trial be held in a county other than where the crime was committed.

Occasionally, situations arise when it is difficult to determine in which county a crime was committed in order to have venue established. Many states have set forth guidelines to overcome this dilemma. They include such provisions as the following:

- When an offense is committed in part in one county and in part in another, the trial may be held in either county, and
- when an offense is committed on the boundary of two or more counties, or within 500 yards (this distance may vary among states) of the boundary, the trial may be held in either jurisdiction.

Prior to the passage of such provisions, there was a joke among old-time sheriffs and prosecutors about wearing out bodies by dragging them across county lines to avoid the responsibility of investigations and prosecutions. It has also been held that when a crime is committed within the state in a boat, a motor vehicle, an aircraft, or a common carrier, the trial may be held in any county through which the trip passed or the one in which it was terminated.

Law in Practice

Motion for Change of Venue Denied

Defendant Joshua Komisarjevsky and others were charged with the killing of a family during a home invasion robbery. One defendant, Hayes, allegedly involved in the home invasion was previously convicted and sentenced to death. The defense moved for a change of venue contending that the defendant could not get a fair trial in New Haven, Connecticut, because the newspapers had described the crime as one of Connecticut's most notorious crimes.

Attached to the defense motion was a survey done after the Hayes trial that showed that 99 percent of the population of New Haven was familiar with the crime. The Hayes trial attracted nationwide media attention and lawyers say they are concerned whether an impartial jury can be impaneled in New Haven for Komisarjevsky's trial. At a hearing on the motion to change venue, the defense presented two expert witnesses who testified in the hearing they analyzed media coverage of the Hayes trial. One expert witness noted that she found 1,808 articles including the words "Komisarjevsky" and "William Petit" on the Internet. The other expert witness, a psychology professor at John Jay College of Criminal Justice in New York, said he analyzed the impact of pretrial publicity on juries in criminal and civil cases and found pretrial coverage for Komisarjevsky's case to be "overwhelming."

Decision

On March 1, 2011, Trial Judge Jon C. Blue denied the motion for a change of venue. But he suggested he might change his mind once jury selection begins, depending on how questioning of potential jurors goes. In his ruling, Blue said the New Haven judicial district is large and diverse, increasing the chance of getting a jury. He also pointed out that Hayes was acquitted on one arson charge, suggesting jurors can go by the evidence presented to them in court.

Issues

1. If and when can the defense appeal this ruling? [While the answer to this question depends on Connecticut law, in most states the defendant may not appeal this decision until after the case is over and he has been convicted. He then could appeal based on the fact that he did not get a fair trial because the jury was not impartial and did not render a decision based solely on the evidence presented at trial.]
2. If during the questioning (voir dire) of potential jurors (jury panel), a significant number of potential jurors indicate that they have formed an opinion as to the guilt or innocence of the defendant, at what point should the trial judge reconsider his decision and grant the motion for a change of venue?

Second Issue

Prior to the start of the trial, defense lawyers moved to ban reporters from tweeting details of the trial. Defense contends that the tweets are prejudicial to their client. Defense attorneys say the tweets violated laws prohibiting the broadcast of sexual-assault trials. Reporters were using cell phones and iPads to Tweet courtroom action as it occurs. The trial judge denied this motion. The defense then immediately appealed to the state supreme court to intervene.

1. As trial judge, would you have ruled differently? Why?
2. Would the requested ban on the reporters involved a freedom of the press issue under the First Amendment to the U.S. Constitution? Why?
3. Note that in most states the denial of the motion for a change of venue cannot be appealed until the conclusion of the trial, the refusal to ban reporters from Tweeting could immediately be appealed. Why the difference? [There is no simple answer to this question. It is a confusing area in court procedures in most states and an area in which attorneys often disagreed.]

Third Issue

During the earlier Hayes trial, the defense counsel for Komisarjevsky was cited for holding a news conference. The judge stated that the counsel violated the judge's order against making public comments on the case. Why would a judge order counsel not to make public comments on a pending criminal trial?

[*Source of facts:* http://www.upi.com/Top_News/US/2011/03/01/No-change-of-venue-in-Conn-home-invasion/UPI-22121299020252 and *State v. Hayes,* 2010 Conn. Super. LEXIS 3066 (Conn. Super. Ct. Nov. 26, 2010)]

JURISDICTION

Jurisdiction is the inherent power of a court to hear and decide a case, whereas venue designates a particular area in which a case may be heard and decided. Unfortunately, the statutes of some states use jurisdiction when in fact the statute refers to venue, thus creating confusion for the layperson. This dual use of the term jurisdiction stems from the fact that it is an all-encompassing word, embracing every kind of judicial action. Figure 1-6 depicts a jurisdictional map of the U.S. Courts of Appeal.

Federal versus Local Jurisdiction

Since we have learned that there are two court systems, that is, the state system and the federal system, it may be useful at this point to compare the jurisdiction of each. As we have previously stated, criminal laws enacted by the U.S. Congress are known as federal criminal laws and are enforced by federal officers. Criminal laws passed by the state legislatures are generally enforced by city police departments or sheriffs and their deputies, and are assisted by state officers where they have the authority to do so. Although most of the criminal laws within a state are state enacted, the violators are prosecuted in the county court or local system, since that is where the trial courts are located. Thus, our discussion of the jurisdiction of the two systems is directly related to the trial jurisdiction of the federal and county courts.

When a crime is committed, the violator may have broken either a federal law or a state law, depending upon the act. For example, a person may rob a liquor store, an act that would be a violation of a state statute, since all states have laws making robbery a crime. Or a person may violate the Sherman Antitrust Law, an act that would be a federal violation. The county court would have exclusive jurisdiction to try the case of robbery, whereas the federal government would have exclusive jurisdiction to try the antitrust violation. It is possible for a person to commit both a federal and a state violation with a series of acts arising out of a sequence of events. For example, a person may steal an automobile in one state and transport it to another state. Such an individual could be prosecuted in the local courts for the theft of the vehicle and prosecuted in the federal courts because it is a federal crime to transport a vehicle from one state to another knowing that it has been stolen. In this example, the offender has actually committed two violations as a result of two different acts—one being the theft and the other the transportation of the vehicle while knowing that it has been stolen. In these two examples, each court has its own trial jurisdiction exclusive of the other.

As stated, it is possible for an individual to violate both a federal and a state law by the same act. For example, an individual may kill a federal officer, thereby violating a federal statute, and the killing may also violate a state homicide statute. Under these circumstances, concurrent jurisdiction would exist. The question then would be whether the accused could be prosecuted in both the federal and the state courts. This question will be better discussed in Chapter 5, which deals with the plea of once in jeopardy. Where an act violates both federal and state statutes, the federal government can always take jurisdiction and prosecute the violation. In some states, like California, if the federal government prosecutes, the state prosecutor is barred by state statute from prosecuting for the same criminal act.

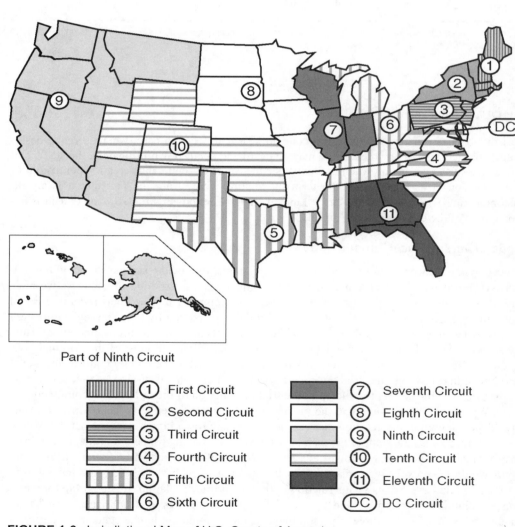

Part of Ninth Circuit

① First Circuit		⑦ Seventh Circuit		
② Second Circuit		⑧ Eighth Circuit		
③ Third Circuit		⑨ Ninth Circuit		
④ Fourth Circuit		⑩ Tenth Circuit		
⑤ Fifth Circuit		⑪ Eleventh Circuit		
⑥ Sixth Circuit		DC DC Circuit		

FIGURE 1-6 Jurisdictional Map of U.S. Courts of Appeal.

Although most crimes committed on government reservations are also local or state violations, the federal courts have exclusive jurisdiction to try those matters because they were committed on government reservations. It should be pointed out that government reservations are comparatively few in number. In order for a territorial area to be a government reservation, the land must have always been U.S. property, with the title still retained by the United States, or property acquired from a state for which all right and title was relinquished. Most military installations and national parks are government reservations; most post offices are not. Scattered throughout the United States are many national forests, but most of these are not government reservations, so that any crimes committed in these forests are within the jurisdiction of the local courts. However, any theft of the trees from these forests is a theft of government property, which would be a federal violation.

Law in Practice

Foundational Concepts in Criminal Procedure

As an introduction to the study of criminal procedure, the foundational concepts in criminal procedure below should be considered. These concepts will be explained in the text and are listed here to create an awareness of their existence.

- The guarantees of the Bill of Rights in the U.S. Constitution apply directly only to the federal government.
- The Due Process Clause of the Fourteenth Amendment, by selective incorporation, applies most of the rights contained in the Bill of Rights to the states.
- State constitutions may provide rights to citizens in addition to those provided for in the U.S. Constitution, but may not restrict the rights granted by the U.S. Constitution.
- The two questions regarding the burdens of proof in criminal proceeding are: (1) Who has the burden of proving an issue? and (2) What is the magnitude of the burden?
  - The magnitude may be proof beyond a reasonable doubt,
    - clear and convincing evidence, or
    - preponderance of the evidence.
- Formal charges in a criminal trial must first be formalized either by an indictment returned by a grand jury or by information prepared by a prosecutor.
- Prior to trial, both the prosecutor and the defense may submit pretrial motions, and both have discovery rights imposed on them.
- Our system of criminal procedure is based on the adversarial process.
- Two famous quotes from Oliver Wendell Holmes should be noted:
  - "Whatever disagreement there may be as to the scope of the phrase 'due process of law,' there can be no doubt that it embraces the fundamental conception of a fair trial, with opportunity to be heard."[24]
  - "The life of the law has not been logic, it has been experience."[25]

In review, jurisdiction—as it relates to the administration of justice—refers to the right and the power of a particular court to try a case. It includes jurisdiction over the person and the subject matter of the issue to be tried. For example, inferior courts have jurisdiction, or the right, to hear misdemeanor matters. The superior or district court has jurisdiction, or the right, to hear felony cases. Jurisdiction is basic to the trial of a case, and it cannot be waived. It is a right of the court established by law.

The Interrelationship of the Criminal Justice System and the Criminal Justice Process

The System: Agencies of Crime Control	The Process
1. **Police**	1. Contact
	2. Investigation
	3. Arrest
	4. Custody
2. **Prosecution and defense**	5. Complaint/charging
	6. Grand jury/preliminary hearing
	7. Arraignment
	8. Bail/detention
	9. Plea negotiations
3. **Court**	10. Adjudication
	11. Disposition
	12. Appeal/postconviction remedies
4. **Corrections**	13. Correction
	14. Release
	15. Postrelease

The Interrelationship of the Criminal Justice System and the Criminal Justice Process.

Law in Practice

The *Miranda* Citation

The full citation for *Miranda* is as follows: *Miranda* v. *Arizona*, 384 U.S. 436, 86 S.Ct. 1602, 16 L.Ed.2d 694 (1966). The lead name in the case usually refers to the party who lost in the lower court and is seeking to overturn that decision. That party is called the appellant. The second name refers to the other party (or parties) who won at the lower level (in this instance, the state of Arizona). The second party is called the appellee or the respondent. Miranda was seeking to overturn his conviction. The state of Arizona was named as the respondent because criminal prosecutions are brought in the name of the state.

After the names of the parties are three sets of references. All decisions of the U.S. Supreme Court are reported in the *Supreme Court Reports*, which is published by the U.S. Government Printing Office. It is the official reporting system and is abbreviated U.S. In addition, decisions of the Supreme Court are reported in two commercial reporting systems: the *Supreme Court Reporter*, which is abbreviated S.Ct, and *Lawyers Supreme Court Reports, Lawyers Edition*, which is abbreviated L.Ed.2d.

The numbers preceding the abbreviation for the volume refer to the volume number. Thus, *Miranda* can be found in volume number 384 of the *Supreme Court Reports*. The numbers after the abbreviation refer to the page number of the first page. Thus, the *Miranda* decision in volume 384 begins on page 436, in volume 86 of the *Supreme Court Reporter*, it is on page 1602, and so on.

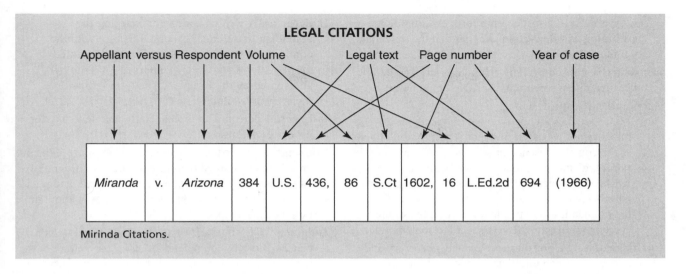

Mirinda Citations.

Law in Practice

Model Penal Code

The Model Penal Code (MPC) is not a statute, but a model code of laws recommend by Members of the American Law Institute (ALI). It has influence many changes in state statutes since it was completed in 1962. The MPC was developed in an attempt to standardize and organize the often-fragmentary criminal codes enacted by the states.

Members of the American Law Institute (ALI), a group made up of judges, lawyers, and legal scholars started working on the Model Penal Code in 1952. The group had abandoned two previous attempts to create a model criminal code. Their third attempt, which was successful, took ten years and a total of thirty-one drafts before the MPC was completed and published.

The MPC was organized into four parts: (1) general provisions containing definitional functions and presumptive rules; (2) definitions of specific offenses; (3) provisions governing treatment and correction; and (4) provisions governing the organization of corrections departments and divisions such as the divisions responsible for Parole or Proba-

tion. Many states have codified their criminal laws based on the MPC format.

Elements of the MPC have changed the way criminal law is administered in the United States. One example of this is on the issue of mens rea, meaning state of mind or guilty mind. Previous state criminal statutes took a scattershot approach to mens rea, requiring it for some crimes and not for others, and using multiple terms to measure culpability. The MPC stated simply that a person is not guilty of an offense unless he or she acted purposely, knowingly, recklessly, or negligently, as the law may require, with respect to each material element of the offense. The MPC then defined the terms in a criminal law context, and what types of conduct would satisfy these terms. The clarity and simplicity of this approach resulted in many states replacing their codes with MPC-influenced codes. Even some states that have not adopted the language have used the MPC's model of organization as a starting point. The MPC's influence is also felt in the courts, where judges often rely on the code when handling substantive criminal law decisions.

Judicial Definitions

This section contains some key definitions used in the judicial system.

Aggravation or circumstances in aggravation. Facts that tend to justify the imposition of the more severe punishment.

Civil contempt. Willful, continuing failure or refusal of any person to comply with a court's lawful

writ, subpoena, process, order, rule, or command that by its nature is still capable of being complied with.

Complaint. A written statement made upon oath before a judge, magistrate, or official authorized by law to issue warrants of arrest, setting forth essential facts constituting an offense and alleging that the defendant committed the offense.

Constructive contempt. Any criminal or civil contempt other than direct contempt. (*See* Direct contempt.)

Criminal contempt. Either:

- Misconduct of any person that obstructs the administration of justice and that is committed either in the court's presence or so near thereto as to interrupt, disturb, or hinder its proceedings, or
- willful disobedience or resistance of any person to a court's lawful writ, subpoena, process, order, rule, or command, where the dominant purpose of the contempt proceeding is to punish the contemptor.

Curtilage of a dwelling-house. A space, necessary and convenient and habitually used for family purposes and the carrying on of domestic employments. It includes the garden, if there is one, and it need not be separated from other lands by a fence.

Determination of guilt. A verdict of guilty by a jury, a finding of guilty by a court following a nonjury trial, or the acceptance by the court of a plea of guilty.

Direct contempt. Disorderly or insolent behavior or other misconduct committed in open court, in the presence of the judge, that disturbs the court's business, where all of the essential elements of the misconduct occur in the presence of the court and are actually observed by the court, and where immediate action is essential to prevent diminution of the court's dignity and authority before the public.

Duplicate. A counterpart produced by the same impression as the original, or from the same matrix, or by means of photography, including enlargements and miniatures, or by mechanical or electronic rerecording, or by chemical reproduction, or by other equivalent techniques which accurately reproduce the original.

Evidence relating to past sexual behavior. Such a term includes, but is not limited to, evidence of the complaining witness's marital history, mode of dress, and general reputation for promiscuity, nonchastity, or sexual mores contrary to the community standards and opinion of character for those traits.

Evidentiary hearing. A hearing held by the trial court to resolve contested factual issues.

Harmless error. Any error, defect, irregularity, or variance that does not affect substantial rights shall be disregarded.

Hearsay. A statement, other than one made by the declarant (person who makes the statement) while testifying at the trial or hearing, offered in evidence to prove the truth of the matter asserted.

Indictment. A written statement charging the defendant or defendants named therein with the commission of an indictable offense, presented to the court by a grand jury, endorsed "A True Bill," and signed by the foreman. The term indictment includes presentment.

Indigent. A person who is financially unable to pay for his or her defense.

Information. A written statement charging the defendant or defendants named therein with the commission of an indictable offense, made on oath, signed, and presented to the court by the district attorney without action by a grand jury.

Judgment. The adjudication of the court based upon a plea of guilty by the defendant, upon the verdict of the jury, or upon its own finding following a nonjury trial, that the defendant is guilty or not guilty.

Law enforcement officer and officer. Any person vested by law with a duty to maintain public order or to make arrests for offenses.

Magistrate. Includes magistrates, district judges, superior court judges, and any other judicial officer authorized by law to conduct a preliminary examination of a person accused of a crime or issue a warrant.

Mentally incompetent. Unable to stand trial or to be sentenced for an offense if the defendant lacks sufficient present ability to assist in his or her defense by consulting with counsel with a reasonable degree of rational understanding of the facts and the legal proceedings against the defendant.

Mitigation or circumstances in mitigation. Facts that tend to justify the imposition of a lesser punishment.

Order to show cause. An order in response to a habeas corpus petition directing the respondent (warden) to file a return. The order to show cause is issued if the petitioner (prisoner) has made a prima facie showing that he or she is entitled to relief; it does not grant the relief requested. An order to show cause may also be referred to as "granting the writ."

Original. In regard to a writing or recording, the writing or recording itself or any counterpart intended to produce the same effect by a person executing or issuing it. An original of a photograph includes the negative or any print from. If data are stored in a computer or a similar device, any printout or other output readable by sight, shown to reflect the data accurately, is an original.

Plain error. Plain errors or defects affecting substantial rights may be noticed, although they were not brought to the attention of the court.

Reasonable cause to believe. A basis for belief in the existence of facts that, in view of the circumstances under and purposes for which the standard is applied, is substantial, objective, and sufficient to satisfy applicable constitutional requirements.

Reasonable suspicion. A suspicion based on facts or circumstances that of themselves do not give rise to the probable cause requisite to justify a lawful arrest, but that give rise to more than a bare suspicion; that is, a suspicion that is reasonable as opposed to an imaginary or purely conjectural suspicion.

Release on own recognizance. Release of a defendant without bail upon his or her promise to appear at all appropriate times, sometimes referred to as personal recognizance.

Relevant evidence. Evidence having any tendency to make the existence of any fact that is of consequence to the determination of the action more probable or less probable than it would be without the evidence.

Return. The law enforcement officer executing an arrest warrant shall endorse thereon the manner and date of execution, shall subscribe his name, and shall return the arrest warrant to the clerk of the court specified in the arrest warrant.

Search. Any intrusion other than an arrest, by an officer under color of authority, upon an individual's person, property, or privacy, for the purpose of seizing individuals or things or obtaining information by inspection or surveillance, if such intrusion, in the absence of legal authority or sufficient consent, would be a civil wrong, criminal offense, or violation of the individual's rights under the Constitution of the United States or the state.

Search warrant. A written order, in the name of the state or municipality, signed by a judge or magistrate authorized by law to issue search warrants, directed to any law enforcement officer as defined by Rule 1.4(p), commanding him or her to search for personal property and, if found, to bring it before the issuing judge or magistrate.

Seizure. The taking of any person or thing or the obtaining of information by an officer pursuant to a search or under other color of authority.

Spousal privilege. A communication is confidential if it is made privately by any person to his or her spouse and is not intended for disclosure to any other person. An accused in a criminal proceeding has a privilege to prevent his spouse from testifying as to any confidential communication between the accused and the spouse. The privilege may be claimed by the accused or by the spouse on behalf of the accused. The authority of the spouse to do so is presumed. There is no privilege under this rule in a proceeding in which one spouse is charged with a crime against the other person or property of (1) the other, (2) a child of either, (3) a person residing in the household of either, or (4) a third person committed in the course of committing a crime against any of them.

Subpoenas. Orders issued by the clerk of the court in which a criminal proceeding is pending at any time for such witnesses as any party may require for attendance at trial and at hearings, for taking depositions, or for any other lawful purpose.

Summons. An order issued by a judicial officer or, pursuant to the authorization of a judicial officer, by the clerk of a court, requiring a person against whom a criminal charge has been filed to appear in a designated court at a specified date and time.

Verdict. In criminal proceedings, the decision of the jury in a jury trial or of a judge in a nonjury trial.

Victim. A person against whom a criminal offense has allegedly been committed, or the spouse, parent, lawful representative, or child of someone killed or incapacitated by the alleged criminal offense, except where the spouse, parent, lawful representative, or child is also the accused.

Voir dire. The preliminary examination of a potential juror to determine qualifications to serve as a juror; preliminary examination of a witness to determine his or her competency to speak the truth.

Waiver of error. No party may assign as error on appeal the court's giving or failing to give any instruction or portion thereof or to the submission or the failure to submit a form of verdict unless the party objects thereto before the jury retires to consider its verdict, stating distinctly the matter to which the party objects and the grounds of his or her objection.

Work product. Discovery cannot be required of legal research or of records, correspondence, reports, or memoranda to the extent that they contain the opinions, theories, or conclusions of the prosecutor, members of the prosecutor's legal or investigative staff or law enforcement officers, or of defense counsel or defense counsel's legal or investigative staff.

Writ. A formal written order issued by a court commanding an individual or party identified in the order to do, or abstain from doing, some specified act.

Summary

- The law is merely a guideline for human behavior.
- The study of our justice system should be viewed as a cluster of ideas, principles, and values about which reasonable persons can and do disagree.
- Judicial opinions construe the constitutionality, meaning, and effect of constitutional and statutory provisions.
- Most individuals agree that the most basic goal of the criminal justice system is to protect society from crime.
- Criminal justice professionals are generally oriented toward one of two opposite goals—law and order or individual rights.
- The pragmatic goals include the goal of preventing crime.
- Organizations have developed standards, which are detailed goals for improving the system.
- Although the criminal justice system is referred to as a system, it is more accurate to refer to it as a nonsystem.
- Two important questions regarding the burden of proof in criminal proceedings are: Who has the burden of proving an issue? and, What is the magnitude of the burden?
- The Code of Hammurabi is considered one of the first-known attempts to establish a written code of conduct.
- Most of our criminal law concepts and principles originated in the common law of England.
- Today, the criminal laws of the states are largely the result of legislative action.
- The Magna Charta is considered the forerunner of the present due process rights.
- The court system in the United States is based upon the principle of federalism.
- A dual system of state and federal courts exists today.
- Appellate jurisdiction is reserved for courts that hear appeals from both limited and general jurisdiction courts. In many states, the appeals from minor courts are heard de novo.
- The Judiciary Act of 1789 created the U.S. Supreme Court and established district and circuit courts of appeal.
- Venue is the geographic area in which a case may be heard.
- Jurisdiction is the power of a court to hear and determine an issue.

Review Questions

1. Why are laws necessary?
2. Define common law.
3. How do we classify laws?
4. What is civil law?
5. What is ecclesiastical law?
6. In what year was the Magna Charta signed?
7. What significant contribution did the Magna Charta make to the administration of justice?
8. How did the trial by ordeal and the trial by battle differ from each other?
9. Describe a trial by compurgation.
10. How did the English kings use early juries?
11. What was the accusatory jury?
12. The U.S. Bill of Rights is what part of what document?
13. What portions of the Bill of Rights are of particular significance to the administration of justice?
14. What amendment makes the Bill of Rights applicable to the states?
15. Define venue.
16. Define jurisdiction.
17. How do jurisdiction and venue differ from each other?

Local Procedure

Since judicial procedure differs slightly from state to state, the reader may wish to consult the local prosecuting attorney for the procedure within his or her state.

1. By what names are trial courts known in your state?

2. What are the trial jurisdictions of the trial courts in your state?

3. What are the qualifications of the judges presiding over the trial courts in your state?

Endnotes

1. *Frank* v. *Mangum,* 237 N.S. 309, 347 (1914).
2. The Common Law (1881) 1.
3. 258 NY 292 (1932).
4. *Mapp* v. *Ohio,* 367 U.S. 643 (1961).
5. *Malloy* v. *Hogan,* 378 U.S. 1 (1964).
6. *Benton* v. *Maryland,* 95 U.S. 784 (1969).
7. *Gideon* v. *Wainwright,* 372 U.S. 335 (1963).
8. *Kloper* v. *N.C.,* 386 U.S. 335 (196).
9. In re *Oliver,* 330 U.S. 257 (1942).
10. *Pointer* v. *Texas,* 380 U.S. 400 (1965).
11. *Duncan* v. *Louisiana,* 391 U.S. 145 (1968).
12. Portions of this section have been adapted from Harvey Wallace, "The Roles of Federal and State Law: The Judicial System and Victims of Crime" in *The National Victim Assistance Academy Text* (Washington, D.C.: OVC), 2001.
13. Robert D. Pursley, *Introduction to Criminal Justice,* 6th ed. (New York: Macmillan), 1994.
14. James Liebman, "The Overproduction of Death," *Columbia Law Review*, vol. 100, pp. 2030–2041, 2000.
15. *Miller-El* v. *Dretke,* 125 S. Ct. 2317 (2005) and *Miller-El* v. *Dretke,* 361 F.3d 849 (2004).
16. 99 U.S. 130 (1879).
17. Gilbert King, *The Execution of Willie Francis: Race, Murder and the Search for Justice in the American South.* (New York: Basic Civitas Books), 2008.
18. 136 U.S. 436, (1890).
19. 136 U.S.436 at 438 (1890).
20. 329 U.S. 459 (1947).
21. 437 U.S. 328 (1976).
22. *The Supreme Court of the United States* (Washington, D.C.: Government Printing Office), 2001.
23. 1 Cranh 137 (1803).
24. *Frank* v. *Mangum,* 237 N.S. 309, 347 (1914).
25. *The Common Law* (1881) 1.

CHAPTER 2

Search and Seizure

The right of the people to be secure in their persons, houses, papers, and effects, against unreasonable searches and seizures, shall not be violated, and no Warrants shall issue, but upon probable cause, supported by Oath or affirmation and particularly describing the place to be searched, and the persons or things to be seized.

—FOURTH AMENDMENT OF THE U.S. CONSTITUTION (1791)

Chapter Outline

History and Purpose of the Fourth Amendment

Exclusionary Rule

Fruits of the Poisonous Tree Doctrine

Protected Areas and Interests

Expectation of Privacy Zone

Exceptions to the Fourth Amendment

Inspections and Regulatory Searches

Independent State Grounds

Probable Cause

Search with a Warrant

Case Law

Summary

Key Terms

Abandonment

Exclusionary Rule

Expectation of privacy zone

Fruits of the Poisonous Tree Doctrine

Independent state grounds

Magistrate

Open fields

Plain View Doctrine

Probable cause

Search

Learning Objectives

After completing this chapter, you should be able to:

- Summarize the exclusionary rule and the issues associated with it.

- Summarize the Fruits of the Poisonous Tree Doctrine.

- Explain the requirements for obtaining a search warrant.

- Outline the history, purpose, and essential elements of the Fourth Amendment.

- Describe searches within the context of the Fourth Amendment.

- Summarize the Fourth Amendment's expectation of privacy.

- Explain the concept of probable cause and its implications.

- Summarize the plain view and related doctrines.

- Define terms related to the Fourth Amendment.

- Describe how search warrants are executed.

- Summarize the issues involved in warrantless searches.

- Summarize the special issues involved in automobile searches.

- Summarize the special issues involved in border and extraterritorial searches.

- Describe regulatory and administrative searches.

- Describe consent searches and the issues associated with them.

- Summarize the issues associated with seizures.

HISTORY AND PURPOSE OF THE FOURTH AMENDMENT

From a criminal procedure perspective, the Fourth and Fifth Amendments contain the most important language in existence within the U.S. legal structure. It must be stressed that not all searches are prohibited, only those that are unreasonable. The issues surrounding searches and seizures can become quite complex, and many times students or even professionals in the field lose sight of the rationale and reasons for the Fourth Amendment. Asking the following questions any time that a **search** or seizure situation arises will assist in analyzing this complex area of constitutional law:

1. **Does the Fourth Amendment apply?** If it does not apply, the question of reasonableness and warrants and probable cause are irrelevant. For example, as will be discussed later in this chapter, there are certain situations, such as evidence found in open fields, that can be seized because the Fourth Amendment does not apply to property found in open fields.

2. **If the Fourth Amendment does apply, has it been complied with?** If all the requirements have been satisfied, then any evidence will be admitted. If it has not been complied with, go to question 3.

3. **If the Fourth Amendment does apply and has not been complied with, what sanctions will the court impose on any evidence seized in violation of the amendment?** The court has a range of options available to it if it determines that the officers or agents have violated the Fourth Amendment.

These are simple questions and a seemingly simple approach to the concepts of search and seizure, but using this approach will enable students to focus on the correct issues within this area of criminal procedure.

When the U.S. Constitution was being drafted and considered by our forefathers, very little, if any, thought was given to including a declaration of rights for individual citizens. At that time, the original state constitutions contained language that purported to protect individuals from undue oppression by the government. However, the ratification process produced a movement to include amendments in the form of a Bill of Rights, which would address individual rights and restrict government action in the area of the criminal justice process. The drafters of the U.S. Constitution and the Bill of Rights were influenced by a number of factors, including our English heritage, the misuse of the criminal justice process within the colonies during English rule, and a belief in the limited role of government.[1] Thus, the Fourth Amendment was based upon a distrust of government and a desire to prevent arbitrary actions by that government or its agents in personal areas such as the unreasonable seizure of persons, property, or other items without proper justification.

1. The right of the people to be secure in their
   a. persons,
   b. houses,
   c. papers,
   d. and effects
   against unreasonable searches and seizures, shall not be violated, and
2. No warrants shall issue, but
   a. upon probable cause
   b. supported by oath or affirmation and
3. Particularly describing the
   a. place to be searched
   b. and the persons or things to be seized.

FIGURE 2-1   Fourth Amendment Diagrammed

Source: U.S. Constitution, Fourth Amendment (designations added)

However, before the rights that are guaranteed in the Bill of Rights could have an impact on individuals within the criminal justice system, two critical events would have to occur: First, since most criminal prosecutions take place at the local or state level, the U.S. Supreme Court would have to make the Bill of Rights apply to local criminal justice procedures; and second, the Court would have to interpret those rights and the way that they impact local government and individual citizens. As will be seen later in this chapter, both of those events would occur, with the result that individuals are protected from invasive governmental action.

The Fourth Amendment deals with the "seizures" of both persons and property. To properly understand its scope and ramifications within the criminal justice system, we should examine a concept known as the Exclusionary Rule. Figure 2-1 is a diagramed breakdown of the Fourth Amendment to the U.S. Constitution.

EXCLUSIONARY RULE

In 1914, the U.S. Supreme Court decided *Weeks* v. *United States* that established the **Exclusionary Rule** and its applicability to the federal government.[2] In *Weeks,* local and federal law enforcement officers seized evidence from the home of the defendant. The Court excluded the evidence seized by the federal officers, holding that to allow it would defy the prohibitions of the Constitution that were intended to protect the people against such unauthorized actions. While the federal prohibition remained in effect, local police were still able to conduct searches and seizures according to the rules established by the individual states, since the Fourth Amendment applied only to federal action for the next thirty-five years.

The Byron White Federal Court Building, Denver, Colorado. (*Source:* Cliff Roberson)

In 1949, the Court issued its ruling in *Wolf* v. *Colorado.*[3] This was the first time the Supreme Court considered whether the Fourth Amendment should be imposed upon state proceedings by using the Fourteenth Amendment due process clause. In *Wolf,* the Court addressed the question of whether a conviction by a state court for a state offense denies due process of law as required by the Fourteenth Amendment solely because evidence admitted at the trial was obtained in a manner that would have rendered it inadmissible in a federal court, since such evidence would have been obtained in violation of the Fourth Amendment. Although acknowledging that individuals should be secure from arbitrary intrusion by police and that such security is basic to a free society, the *Wolf* Court reviewed the states' acceptance of the *Weeks* doctrine and pointed out that at the time of the decision, thirty states rejected the concept. The justices therefore held that the Fourteenth Amendment does not forbid admission of evidence obtained in violation of the Fourth Amendment. It would take another twelve years before the Court would overrule *Wolf* when it decided its landmark case of *Mapp* v. *Ohio.*[4]

In *Mapp* v. *Ohio,* the Court expressly overruled *Wolf* by acknowledging that *Wolf* was founded on factual considerations that lacked validity in today's society. The Court found that in the intervening years (since its decision in *Wolf*), a number of states had accepted the validity of the Exclusionary Rule, and experience had demonstrated that other options and remedies to prevent illegal searches were worthless and futile.

In *Mapp,* three Cleveland police officers arrived at Mapp's home to search for a person who was wanted for questioning in connection with a recent bombing. Miss Mapp and her daughter lived on the second floor of the two-family dwelling. Upon arrival at the home, the officers knocked on the door and demanded entry, but Miss Mapp, after telephoning her attorney, refused to admit them without a search warrant. Three hours later, after additional officers were on the scene, the officers forced a door in the house. By that time, Miss Mapp's attorney had arrived, but the officers would not allow him to enter the house or consult with Miss Mapp. Meanwhile, as the officers entered the house, Miss Mapp demanded to see their search warrant. One of the officers held out a paper and claimed that it was the warrant. Miss Mapp grabbed the paper and placed it in her bosom. The officers struggled with her, regained possession of the "warrant," and placed her under arrest. The officers searched the house, dressers, and trunks, finding some obscene material in a trunk. Miss Mapp was charged with and convicted of possession of obscene material. At the trial no search warrant was produced, nor was the failure to produce one explained. Miss Mapp was convicted, and she appealed.

In overturning her conviction, the Supreme Court stated:

> Moreover, our holding . . . is not only the logical dictate of prior cases but it also makes very good sense. There is no war between the Constitution and common sense. Presently, a federal prosecutor may make no use of evidence illegally seized [because of *Weeks*], but a State's attorney across the street may. . . . Thus the State, by admitting evidence unlawfully seized, serves to encourage disobedience to the Federal Constitution which it is bound to uphold. . . .
>
> Our decision, founded on reason and truth, gives to the individual no more than that which the Constitution guarantees him, to the police officer no less than that to which honest law enforcement is entitled, and, to the courts, that judicial integrity so necessary in the true administration of justice. . . .

The deterrence effect on unreasonable searches and seizure is a major purpose of the Exclusionary Rule. However, the rule also serves at least two other purposes. The judicial integrity approach is to ensure that courts will not become accomplices in violating the rules they were sworn to uphold. Another purpose is to ensure that citizens understand that the government will not profit by unlawful activity, thereby minimizing the lack of trust in our government.

What happens if the officers conducting the search were acting in good faith? This is exactly the situation in *United States* v. *Leon.*[5] This case presented the question of whether the Exclusionary Rule should be modified to allow the use of evidence obtained by officers acting in reasonable reliance on a search warrant issued by a detached and neutral magistrate but ultimately found to be unsupported by probable cause. During trial, respondents filed motions to suppress evidence seized pursuant to a warrant and said that motions were granted in part based on the conclusion that the warrant was not supported by probable cause despite the fact that the police officer was acting in good-faith reliance on what he believed to be a valid warrant. The lower court affirmed and held that there was no good-faith exception to the Exclusionary Rule. The U.S. Supreme Court reversed this decision and held that the Exclusionary Rule should be modified so as not to bar the admission of evidence seized in reasonable, good-faith reliance on a search warrant that was subsequently held to be defective. The Court concluded that the marginal or nonexistent benefits produced by suppressing evidence obtained in objectively reasonable reliance on a subsequently invalidated search warrant could not justify the substantial costs of exclusion.

Law in Practice

What If the Wrong Warrant Is Used in a Search and Seizure Case?

Suppose a detective investigating a homicide case needed a search warrant, but because it was Sunday, he could find only one that was used for controlled substances. He took it to a magistrate and pointed out the problems. The magistrate told him to cross out the language regarding controlled substances and to use the warrant; however, the detective neglected to make some of the changes. After the warrant was served, the defendant challenged its validity.

Should the warrant be declared valid under the principles set forth in *Leon*? In *Massachusetts* v. *Sheppard,* the court upheld such a process and allowed the seized evidence to be used against the defendant.[6]

FRUITS OF THE POISONOUS TREE DOCTRINE

What happens if law enforcement violates the protections offered by the Fourth Amendment? The most straightforward explanation of the **Fruits of the Poisonous Tree Doctrine** is that courts will not allow the "fruit," or evidence obtained as a result of an illegal search, to be used against the accused. In explaining this doctrine, one court stated: "The essence of a provision forbidding the acquisition of evidence in a certain way is that not merely evidence so acquired shall not be used before the Court, but that it shall not be used at all."[7]

The Fruits of the Poisonous Tree Doctrine applies to searches, arrests, confessions, and other evidence-gathering activities of law enforcement. However, not all evidence is automatically barred simply because it may have initially been gathered in violation of the Constitution. In *Wong Sun* v. *United States,* the Supreme Court held that the issue was whether the originally obtained illegal evidence can be admitted because it could or was obtained by means sufficiently distinguishable to be purged of the primary taint of illegality.[8] *Wong Sun* also restated the rule that the Exclusionary Rule has no application when the government learned of the evidence from a source independent of any taint. Another theory used to cleanse or avoid the Fruits of the Poisonous Tree Doctrine is the so-called Inevitable Discovery Rule, which allows the admission of evidence if it would have been found and discovered legally at a later time.

The Supreme Court has been hesitant to apply the rule to violations of the *Miranda* warning requirements. In *United States* v. *Patane,*[9] the defendant had violated a restraining order and officers going to his home to investigate the matter were told that he, a convicted felon, illegally possessed a pistol. They arrested Patane but were interrupted when they attempted to advise him of his *Miranda* rights. An officer then asked about the gun and he revealed where it was. The Court noted that unlike unreasonable searches under the Fourth Amendment or actual violations of the Due Process Clause or the Self-Incrimination Clause, there was, with respect to mere failures to warn, nothing to deter since failure to give the *Miranda* warnings neither violated the *Miranda* rule or the Self-Incrimination Clause. There was therefore no reason to apply the Fruits of the Poisonous Tree Doctrine.

In *Hudson* v. *Michigan,* the Supreme Court declined to hold that all evidence is "fruit of the poisonous tree" simply because it would not have come to light but for the illegal actions of the police.[10] The Court in *Hudson* created another reason not to apply the Fruits of the Poisonous Tree Doctrine, which was that the application of the rule would cause substantial social costs. Justice Scalia, in the majority opinion, stated:

> Suppression of evidence has always been the United States Supreme Court's last resort, not the Supreme Court's first impulse. The exclusionary rule generates "substantial social costs," which sometimes include setting the guilty free and the dangerous at large. The Supreme Court has therefore been cautious against expanding it, and has repeatedly emphasized that the rule's "costly toll" upon truth-seeking and law enforcement objectives presents a high obstacle for those urging its application. The Supreme Court has rejected "indiscriminate application" of the rule and has held it to be applicable only where its remedial objectives are thought most efficaciously served—that is, where its deterrence benefits outweigh its "substantial social costs."

PROTECTED AREAS AND INTERESTS

Exactly what interest is protected by the Fourth Amendment? The language in the Amendment states that persons, houses, papers, and effects shall be protected or secure against unreasonable searches. Does that mean that a person can carry a bomb on an airplane without being searched? Can a person commit a crime inside his or her home and be secure against a search? The courts have established a "zone of constitutional protection" that surrounds a person and moves with that person wherever he or she travels.

Law in Practice

Sanchez-Llamas v. Oregon, 548 U.S. 331 (2006)

The defendant, a Mexican national, argued that his incriminating statements to police in an attempted murder case should have been suppressed, as he was not informed of his right under Vienna Convention art. 36 to have the Mexican Consulate notified of his detention.

How Would You Rule?

The Vienna Convention on Consular Relations does not prescribe specific remedies for violations of Vienna Convention art. 36. Rather, it expressly leaves the implementation of Vienna Convention art. 36 to domestic law: Rights under Vienna Convention art. 36 are to be exercised in conformity with the laws and regulations of the receiving state. The exclusionary rule as it is known is an entirely American legal creation. The exclusionary rule is unique to American jurisprudence. More than forty years after the drafting of the Vienna Convention on Consular Relations, the automatic exclusionary rule applied in American courts is still universally rejected by other countries. It is implausible that other signatories to the Vienna Convention thought it to require a remedy that nearly all refuse to recognize as a matter of domestic law. Under the United States' domestic law, the exclusionary rule is not a remedy that is applied lightly. The rule's "costly toll" upon truth-seeking and law enforcement objectives presents a high obstacle for those urging application of the rule. Because the rule's social costs are considerable, suppression is warranted only where the rule's remedial objectives are thought most efficaciously served. [The Supreme Court ruled that exclusion of the evidence was not appropriate.]

Law in Practice

Identity Theft: A Top Concern

Identity theft is the top concern for consumers although they are not taking immediate steps to prevent it, according to new data released by the National Crime Prevention Council (NCPC). According to an NCPC survey conducted by Harris Interactive, identity theft and credit card fraud top the list of crimes about which Americans are extremely concerned.[13]

The NCPC data also show identity theft is a concern across all income levels and regions of the country. Ninety-three percent of Americans believe that identity theft is a major or moderate crime problem today. Other major statistics include:

- Sixty-six percent of women are more likely to be concerned about identity theft, compared with 47 percent of men.

- Identity theft is of greater concern to adults with older children at home (45 percent) versus those with younger children at home (27 percent).
- Eighty percent of those who feel vulnerable being on the Internet were more likely to say identity theft is a major problem.
- Nearly 24 percent of adults said they knew someone close to them who has been a victim of identity theft.
- Fourteen percent reported being a victim of identity theft.
- Those Americans with higher incomes and education levels considered themselves more knowledgeable about how to prevent identity theft.

EXPECTATION OF PRIVACY ZONE

The older view was that a search required a physical intrusion into a "constitutionally protected area."[11] In the leading case of *Katz* v. *United States,* the Supreme Court expanded the scope of the Fourth Amendment by establishing an "**expectation of privacy zone**" that is protected by the Constitution.[12] In *Katz,* FBI agents had attached an electronic listening device to the outside of a public phone booth that the defendant used to make wagering calls. The Court held that the Fourth Amendment protects people, not places. Justice Harlan, in a concurring opinion, went on to state that the test for any expectation of privacy is based upon two requirements: (1) that a person exhibit an actual or subjective expectation of privacy and (2) that the expectation is one that society is prepared to recognize as reasonable. In this case, the defendant went to a public phone booth, closed the glass door, and made a call. It is clear that while people could see him in the booth, he had an actual expectation that the phone call itself would not be overheard. It is also clear that society would deem that making any calls from a public phone booth with the door closed is a situation in which there is a reasonable expectation of privacy.

Practicum

Using Justice Harlan's two-prong test for a citizen's expectation of privacy, answer the following questions regarding search and seizure:

> If a person leaves narcotics on his desk at work and that location is open to the public, is there any expectation of privacy?
>
> What if a criminal leaves plans for a burglary in a hotel room after she checks out of the hotel?
>
> If a person leaves a murder weapon in an open field, is there any expectation of privacy?

These and other questions will be discussed in the following section.

EXCEPTIONS TO THE FOURTH AMENDMENT

If the police activity is not a search, the Fourth Amendment does not apply. Therefore, the question becomes: How far does the protection of the Fourth Amendment extend? This section deals with areas and interests that are considered exceptions to the Fourth Amendment and therefore are considered outside the scope of protection of the Fourth Amendment.

Consent

If a party consents to a search, there are no Fourth Amendment protections. Whether the consent is valid is a question of fact to be determined from the totality of the circumstances.[14] The Supreme Court in *Schneckloth* v. *Bustamonte* held that although the subject's knowledge or a right to refuse is a factor to be taken into account, it is not a requirement to establishing a voluntary search.[15]

The Supreme Court held that individual consent could only be ascertained by analyzing all of the circumstances. The traditional definition of voluntariness, which the Court adhered to, did not require proof of knowledge of a right to refuse as the sine qua non of an effective consent to a search. In determining whether a defendant's will was overborne in a particular case, a court assesses the totality of all the surrounding circumstances—both the characteristics of the accused and the details of the interrogation. Some of the factors taken into account include the youth of the accused; his lack of education or his low intelligence; the lack of any advice to the accused of his constitutional rights; the length of detention; the repeated and prolonged nature of the questioning; and the use of physical punishment such as the deprivation of food or sleep.

Another issue that sometimes arises concerns consent obtained by deception. What if an undercover officer is invited into a home that is being used to distribute narcotics? When a criminal gives consent to another person to enter an area normally protected by the Fourth Amendment, knowing that as a result he will reveal to that person criminal activity, such consent is not invalid merely because the consent was given to an undercover police officer.[16] What happens when a third party gives consent? The Supreme Court has adopted a common authority test for consent by third parties. Common authority rests upon the mutual use of the property by persons generally having joint access or control for most purposes, so that it is reasonable to recognize that any of the coinhabitants has the right to permit the inspection in his own right and that the others have assumed the risk that one of their number might permit the common area to be searched.[17]

Who can give consent? It is generally agreed that one spouse can give consent to search the family residence. If a son or daughter is a minor, parents are presumed to be able to consent to a search of the child's room. What happens if a child consents to a search of the parents' home? If the child is older, courts generally uphold such consent on the theory that older children acquire authority and discretion to admit whom they want into the family house. Property relationships raise special issues regarding consent. An owner may not consent to a search of the renter when the owner has given the renter exclusive possession of the property.

In *Georgia* v. *Randolph*, the wife gave permission to search and her husband objected. The Supreme Court held that since a wife had no recognized authority in law or social practice to prevail over her husband's objections to consenting to the police searching their home, her consent, without more, gave police no better claim to reasonableness in entering than they would have had in the absence of any consent at all under the Fourth Amendment.[18] Exceptions to the Fourth Amendment are listed in Figure 2-2.

EXCEPTIONS TO THE FOURTH AMENDMENT

Open fields	*Oliver* v. *U.S.:* No expectation of privacy therefore no search.
Plain view	*Arizona* v. *Hicks:* No expectation of privacy of an item in plain view
Abandonment	*California* v. *Greenwood:* No expectation of privacy in abandoned property and no property interest protected.
Consent	*Schneckloth* v. *Bustamonte:* Consent constitutes a waiver of Fourth Amendment rights against unreasonable searches and seizures.
Airport searches	Waiver of rights in order to travel by air.
Border searches	A country has a right to protect its borders.
Parolees and Probationers	In most states individuals on parole or probation must consent to be searched as a condition of release from confinement.
School searches	If the search is conducted by school officials and not for law enforcement reasons or at the direction of law enforcement. Search must be reasonable.
Searches incident to an arrest	*Chimel* v. *California:* Must be a lawful arrest and scope of search is limited.

EXCEPTIONS TO THE EXCLUSIONARY RULE

Good faith exception	*Massachusetts* v. *Shepherd* and *U.S.* v. *Leon:* Police are acting in good faith and generally the error is made an official other than a police officer.
Inevitable discovery	*Nix* v. *Williams:* Police would have inevitably discovered the evidence independently of the unconstitutional action.
Purged taint or attenuation	*Wong Sun* v. *U.S.:* Where connection between taint and obtaining new evidence has become so attenuated as to dissipate the taint, e.g., a statement given two weeks after an illegal arrest and while the individual was on bail from the arrest.
Independent source	*Murray* v. *U.S.:* Evidence was obtained in a constitutional manner from an independent source that was unconnected to the illegal actions.

FIGURE 2-2

EXCEPTIONS TO THE WARRANT REQUIREMENT

Exigent circumstances	Must establish that it was impractical or impossible to get a warrant. Generally need probable cause.
Automobile searches	Because of the mobility of automobiles, an automobile may be searched if on a public road or public property without a warrant but probable cause generally needed
Stop and Frisk	*Terry* v. *Ohio:* Quick investigatory stop-need reasonable suspicion.

FIGURE 2-2   (*Continued*)

Plain View Doctrine

The Supreme Court has established an exception to the Fourth Amendment in the form of the **Plain View Doctrine**. This concept holds that the Plain View Doctrine authorizes seizure of illegal evidence visible to a police officer if the officer's access to the object has a Fourth Amendment justification. In *Horton* v. *California* the Court summed up this doctrine by stating, ". . . not only must the officer be lawfully located in a place from which the object can be plainly seen, but he or she must also have a lawful right to access to the object itself."[19] Compare and contrast the following situations: (1) The officer is standing on a public sidewalk and can see inside a home through an open window. He observes narcotics on a table. (2) The officer is responding to a loud party complaint, and after identifying herself to the owner, the officer is invited into the house. Once inside, she observes narcotics lying on the table in the room where she is standing. In the first situation, the officer is on a public sidewalk and therefore lawfully in a place from which he can observe the object, but to gain entrance to the house, he must obtain a search warrant.[20] In the second situation, the officer is lawfully located in a place from which the object can be seen, since she was given consent to enter the home; and once in the home, she has a lawful right to access to the object itself.

Law in Practice

Is There a "Plain Feel" Rule?

In *State* v. *Ortiz*[21] the Hawaii Supreme Court granted certiorari to determine whether a search warrant was required before a police officer opened a knapsack made of thin material through which the officer felt, after lawfully seizing the sack, what seemed to be the butt of a handgun. The trial court had suppressed the gun, ruling that the officer was not entitled to open the knapsack once it was removed from the immediate control of the defendant. The appellate court reversed, upholding the search under a plain feel rule. The Supreme Court affirmed the appellate court's result, but vacated its plain feel ruling and found that the warrantless search was a valid protective weapons search under *Terry*. The Court found that the officer's belief that the defendant was armed and that a search of the knapsack was necessary for his own protection was a reasonable belief when the defendant had made a quick grab for his allegedly empty knapsack; the officer was one-on-one with the defendant; it was late at night; the officer had no idea whether the defendant had a hidden confederate who might suddenly appear; and after feeling what seemed like a gun butt, the officer had a strong firsthand suspicion that the knapsack contained a gun.

How far does the expectation of privacy extend when dealing with the Plain View Doctrine? Does a defendant who is growing marijuana in a fenced backyard have a right of privacy from a plane flying over the property? In *California* v. *Ciraolo,* the Supreme Court held that the defendant did not have any reasonable expectation of privacy.[22] The officers were in a private plane flying at 1000 feet when they saw the marijuana. They obtained a search warrant, seized the property, and charged the defendant. The court upheld the procedure, explaining that there was no reasonable expectation of privacy from aircraft flying overhead. This concept has been expanded to include helicopters flying at 400 feet over a partially enclosed greenhouse. In that case, the court upheld the search, reasoning that helicopters can lawfully fly lower than planes and that again there was no reasonable expectation of privacy.[23]

Abandonment

If a person abandons property, is there any continuing expectation of privacy regarding that property? **Abandonment** requires intent by the party abandoning the property to give up all claim of ownership to the item or items.[24] In *California* v. *Greenwood,* the Supreme Court held that evidence of the defendant's narcotic use obtained from his garbage bags left on the sidewalk for pickup by the trash collector was properly admitted, since the defendant had evidenced an intent to abandon the property.[25] The Court held that the defendant had no subjective expectation of privacy for garbage bags left on the sidewalk that society deems reasonable. It went on to state that such bags were readily accessible to animals, children, snoops, and other members of the public. What if a person checks out of a hotel room and leaves incriminating evidence in the room's trash container? Does the person have any expectation of privacy? Would the manager or a maid have a right to observe the material in the container? Could the manager of the hotel authorize the police to enter the vacant hotel room and seize the evidence? When someone checks out of a hotel and leaves property behind, there is no reasonable expectation of privacy. Furthermore, once having checked out, the person has no authority to prevent any member of the public or an employee from entering that room to clean it for the next guest or to inspect it for damage. Since technically the manager now controls the room, that person can grant police access to the abandoned room and any evidence in the trash container.[26]

Open Fields

In an early case dealing with the Fourth Amendment and seizure of evidence from an open field, Justice Holmes pointed out in *Hester* v. *United States* that the special protection offered by the Fourth Amendment to citizens in their persons, places, papers, and effects does not extend to open fields. He went on to point out that the distinction between **open fields** and the home is as old as the common law.[27]

The concept of the sanctity of a person's home developed during early times. Curtilage includes the home and the land immediately surrounding it.

What effect did *Katz* have on *Hester? Hester* was decided in 1924, and *Katz* established the expectation of privacy in 1967. Did *Katz,* by implication, overrule *Hester? Oliver* v. *United States* addressed this issue.[28] The Court in *Oliver* held that open fields do not provide the setting for those intimate activities that the Fourth Amendment was designed to protect.

Businesses

Does a business owner have any protection or expectation of privacy within a commercial establishment open to the general public? The question revolves around whether or not the activity engaged in by the police is classified as a search. This in turn depends on the physical characteristics of the business. An officer may enter a commercial business during the time it is open to the public and may go anywhere within that business that members of the public go, and that access will not be considered a search. However, if the officer opens a door marked private and observes criminal activity, that activity falls under the *Katz* zone of privacy rule, and it would be deemed an illegal search.

Federal rules do not recognize an expectation of privacy in business, financial, telephone, and post office box records. Accordingly, no warrant is required to search these records. Most states, including New York, California, and Texas, require a warrant or subpoena to search the records unless (1) exigent circumstances exist, (2) consent is obtained, or (3) the search is part of a valid inventory.[29]

Vehicles

There is a lesser expectation of privacy when dealing with vehicles. If the officer is lawfully present at the vehicle (issuing a traffic ticket, for example) and the officer observes or smells what is inside the vehicle, or even examines the exterior of the vehicle, such activity is not considered a search within the meaning of the Fourth Amendment. However, if the officer intrudes into "protected" places, that activity may be classified as a search. Automobile Inventory Searches raise special issues.

Automobiles or motorcycles by their very nature are mobile and can be moved or relocated very easily. The Court addressed the issue of the scope of a search incident to a lawful arrest in *Arizona* v. *Gant*.[30] In *Gant*, the Court held that evidence seized pursuant to a search of a vehicle incident to an arrest must fall within one of those two narrow situations in order to avoid suppression where (1) the arrestee is unsecured and within reaching distance of the passenger compartment at the time of the search, or (2) it is reasonable to believe evidence relevant to the crime of arrest might be found in the vehicle.

In *Illinois* v. *Caballes*,[31] the U.S. Supreme Court held that police may use a drug-sniffing dog around the outside of a vehicle during a routine traffic stop even when police have no grounds to suspect illegal activity. This case stands for the proposition that a sniff is not a search. A state trooper stopped Caballes for speeding. A second trooper drove to the scene with his dog and walked the dog around the respondent's car while the first trooper wrote a warning ticket. When the dog was alerted at Caballes's trunk, the officers searched the trunk and found marijuana. The Court held that the Fourth Amendment did not require reasonable, articulable suspicion to justify using a drug-detection dog to sniff a vehicle during a legitimate traffic stop. The Court noted that the use of a well-trained narcotics-detection dog—one that did not expose noncontraband items that otherwise would have remained hidden from public view—during a lawful traffic stop generally did not implicate legitimate privacy interests. The dog sniff was performed on the exterior of the respondent's car while he was lawfully seized for a traffic violation. Any intrusion on the respondent's privacy expectations did not rise to the level of a constitutionally cognizable infringement.

The government's authority to conduct suspicionless inspections at the Mexico border included the authority to remove, disassemble, and reassemble a vehicle's fuel tank.[32] Where defendant exited his vehicle after seeing a police officer, but prior to being contacted by the officer, the officer was entitled to search the vehicle incident to defendant's arrest even though defendant was not an occupant of the vehicle at the time of the arrest.[33]

Law in Practice

Vehicle Searches—When and Where

- If search is based on warrant, the officers must search in accordance with the terms of the warrant.
- A valid consent to search waives Fourth Amendment requirements and the search may be as extensive as the consent.
- A vehicle search incident to an arrest must be completed at or near the time and place of arrest—not at a later time (*Arizona* v. *Gant* and *Dyke* v. *Taylor*).
- If you have probable cause to believe that there is sizable contraband, fruits of the crime, instrumentalities,

(continued)

or evidence inside the vehicle and the vehicle is parked in an area with public access; you may search any part of the vehicle that could contain the objects of the search. This includes locked containers in the vehicle. May search at anytime, as long as probable cause exists (*U.S.* v. *Ross* and *California* v. *Acevedo*).

- At a lawful traffic stop, if officer sees evidence of a danger or that the suspect may be armed, a pat down is permitted. This search would be limited to areas, compartments, and containers that may conceal a weapon (*Michigan* v. *Long*).
- If the vehicle is an instrumentality of the crime, e.g., vehicle used to transport narcotics or a child was molested in the vehicle, it may be seized and subjected to search and laboratory examination (*California* v. *Carney*). Note: Mere use of the vehicle for transportation to or from a crime scene does not make the vehicle an instrumentality of the crime.
- When any recent occupant of the vehicle is lawfully arrested, the passenger compartment and all compartments and containers may be searched (but not the trunk). This search may be conducted only while the arrestee is within reaching distance of the vehicle and is unsecured (*Arizona* v. *Gant*).
- If the vehicle is impounded, any personal property in the vehicle may be inventoried (*Colorado* v. *Bertine*).
- Note: there may be some variance based on local rules.

Tracking of Movements

Is it a search for law enforcement to monitor the movements of a suspect? Clearly, law enforcement officers may surveil or follow a suspect without his or her knowledge or consent on public roads and public property. The courts have stated that persons traveling in an automobile on public roads have no reasonable expectation of privacy in their movements from one place to another.[34] Additionally, the courts allow officers to attach electronic beepers to the exterior of cars and to follow the movement of those cars from a distance. In *United States* v. *Karo,* the Supreme Court held that the use of a beeper attached to the suspect's car was not a search within the scope of the Fourth Amendment because it did not infringe on any privacy interest and conveyed no protected information.[35] The court went on to state that no possessory interest had been interfered with in any meaningful way. The Court in *Karo* did hold, however, that the monitoring of a beeper in a private residence, a location not open to visual surveillance, violates the Fourth Amendment rights of those who have a justifiable interest in the privacy of the residence.

Random Drug Testing

In *Board of Education of Independent School Dist. No. 92 of Pottowotomie County* v. *Earls,* the Supreme Court upheld a school district's policy of requiring random drug testing as a condition for participating in interscholastic activities.[37] The Court held that the Fourth Amendment was not violated because the school's interest in protecting its students' health and safety and in deterring drug usage served an important governmental concern. The Court went on to state that there was a minimal invasion of privacy caused by the tests. The Court relied upon its earlier decision of *Vernonia School District* v. *Action* that allowed suspicionless drug testing of athletes.[38]

Student Searches by Educators

In *N.J.* v. *T. L. O.,*[39] a student's purse was searched after she was suspected of having cigarettes. The principal discovered that the student had the cigarettes in her possession, and discovered evidence of marijuana and a list of alleged users from the school. The State of New Jersey brought delinquency charges against the student. The student alleged that the search of her purse violated her Fourth Amendment rights. The U.S. Supreme Court held that the search did not violate the Fourth Amendment. The Court stated that a search by a school official was permissible in its scope when the measures adopted were reasonably related to the objectives of the search and were not intrusive in light of the age and sex of the student.

Law in Practice

United States v. *Simms*[36]

A police officer observed a traffic violation by Simms, the defendant, and was subsequently alerted that Simms was suspected of drug activity and was being monitored with a tracking device in his vehicle, although the device was only authorized for use in another state. After a warning was issued and Simm's documents were returned to him, the officer obtained Simms's consent to search the vehicle and discovered the drugs in a hidden compartment. The appellate court first held that the alert concerning Simms and his apparent nervousness warranted prolonging the traffic stop, and there was no indication that his consent to search was involuntary. Further, the use of the tracking device outside the scope of a state warrant did not raise constitutional issues and was irrelevant to his guilt.

The Court noted that school officials need not obtain a warrant before searching a student who is under their authority. The accommodation of the privacy interests of students with the substantial need of teachers and administrators for freedom to maintain order in the schools does not require strict adherence to the requirement that searches be based on probable cause to believe that the subject of the search has violated or is violating the law. The Court stated that under ordinary circumstances, a search of a student by a teacher or another school official will be justified at its inception when there are reasonable grounds for suspecting that the search will turn up evidence that the student has violated or is violating either the law or the rules of the school. Such a search will be permissible in its scope when the measures adopted are reasonably related to the objectives of the search and not excessively intrusive in light of the age and sex of the student and the nature of the infraction.

School locker searches made under the auspices of a previously promulgated school locker search policy have been upheld as constitutional [*Zamora* v. *Pomeroy*, 639 F.2d 662 (10th Cir. 1981)]. In the *Zamora* case, an appellate court held that school officials had authority to conduct a warrantless search of the student's high school locker after a drug detection dog's positive response provided reasonable cause.

Highway Checkpoints

The Fourth Amendment does not treat a motorist's car as his castle.

JUSTICE BREYER IN *ILLINOIS* V. *LIDSTER*

540 U.S. 419 (2004) *A highway checkpoint stop that was designed to obtain more information about a recent hit-and-run accident was constitutional because the relevant public concern was grave, the stop advanced the concern, and the stop interfered only minimally with liberty.[40] The Court held that the law ordinarily permits police to seek the voluntary cooperation of members of the public in the investigation of a crime. Law enforcement officers do not violate the Fourth Amendment by merely approaching an individual on the street or in another public place, by asking him if he is willing to answer some questions, or by putting questions to him if the person is willing to listen. That, in part, is because voluntary requests play a vital role in police investigatory work. The Court held that special law enforcement concerns will sometimes justify highway stops without individualized suspicion.*

Canine Sniffing

Defendant was stopped by a state officer for speeding. A second officer arrived on the scene with his dog and walked the dog around defendant's car while the first officer wrote a warning ticket. When the dog alerted at defendant's trunk, the officers searched the trunk and found marijuana. The U.S. Supreme Court held that the use of a well-trained narcotics-detection dog—one that did not expose noncontraband items that otherwise would have remained hidden from public view—during a lawful traffic stop, generally did not implicate legitimate privacy interests. The dog sniff was performed on the exterior of defendant's car while he was lawfully seized for a traffic violation. Any intrusion on defendant's privacy expectations did not rise to the level of a constitutionally cognizable infringement.[41]

Law in Practice

Mi Casa es su Casa

When does the search of a residence violate the rights of a guest?

To answer this question, you need to look at three U.S. Supreme Court decisions; *Rakas* v. *Illinois*, *Minnesota* v. *Olson*; and *Minnesota* v. *Carter*.

Rakas v. Illinois, 439 U. S. 128 (1978): A person can have a legally sufficient interest in a place other than his own home so that the Fourth Amendment protects him or her from unreasonable governmental intrusion into that place.

Minnesota v. Olson, 495 U.S. 91 (1990): An overnight guest has a reasonable expectation of privacy in the residence. Evidence obtained in a warrantless, non-consensual, non-exigent entry into the private home where he was an overnight guest could not be used against him in court.

Minnesota v. Carter, 525 U.S. 83 (1998): A temporary guest had no expectation of privacy in the search of a private residence. In this case Carter was merely present in the residence doing business (in drug dealing) with the consent of the householder.

What general rule would you devise regarding the rights of a houseguest to challenge evidence based on an unreasonable search of a private residence from the three cases?

Sobriety Checkpoints

The U.S. Supreme Court in *Michigan Department of State Police* v. *Sitz*[42] held that sobriety checkpoints were reasonable considering the increasing number of alcohol-related deaths and mutilations on the nation's roads. The court considered that the state program was consistent with the Fourth Amendment, and that the balance of the state's interest in preventing drunken driving and the degree of intrusion upon individual motorists who were briefly stopped weighed in favor of the state program.

The Court noted that no allegations were made of unreasonable treatment of any person after an actual detention at a particular checkpoint. The Court noted that only the initial stop of each motorist passing through a checkpoint and the associated preliminary questioning and observation by checkpoint officers were before the court and stated that the detention of particular motorists for more extensive field sobriety testing may require satisfaction of an individualized suspicion standard.

Law in Practice

State v. *Michael G*[43]

A swimming coach at a high school informed two assistant principals that an unidentified student had told him that another juvenile was selling marijuana. The assistant principals then searched the juvenile's locker and discovered two cigarettes that looked like marijuana joints. The cigarettes subsequently tested positive for marijuana. The court held that the assistant principals had reasonable grounds to suspect that the juvenile was violating the law or school rules. The information that provided the basis of the search was the specific statement of a student that the juvenile had tried to sell some marijuana to him. It was not a mere rumor or belief, but an eyewitness account of a breach of school rules and the law. Statements by eyewitness citizen-informants were subject to much less stringent credibility verification requirements. The fact that the principals did not know the identity of the complaining student did not affect the finding that this search was based upon reasonable grounds. The court further held that substantial evidence was present for the children's court to find that the juvenile was in possession of marijuana.

INSPECTIONS AND REGULATORY SEARCHES

These are administrative searches that fall outside the scope of the day-to-day activities normally associated with law enforcement activities. They are considered outside the scope of the protection of the Fourth Amendment and therefore are judged by a different standard. The courts have established a reasonable legislative or administrative standard for use in these situations. This standard is less than the probable cause requirement used in Fourth Amendment situations. It is a test that balances the need to search against the invasion that the search entails. This balancing test considers (1) whether the practice has a long history of judicial and public acceptance, (2) whether the practice is necessary to achieve acceptable results, and (3) whether the practice involves a relatively limited invasion of privacy.[44]

Welfare Inspections

The courts have considered that a visit by caseworkers to a welfare recipient's home does not constitute a search within the meaning of the Fourth Amendment. In *Wyman* v. *James,* the U.S. Supreme Court reasoned that a welfare recipient may be required to consent to such visits as a condition of continued receipt of benefits.[45]

Inspections at Fire Scenes

Can a fire inspector or an arson inspector remain in a building after a fire to conduct an investigation without obtaining a search warrant? Clearly, fire personnel can enter a building to put out a fire. This is a form of emergency that is outside the protection of the Fourth Amendment. The courts have stated that whereas inspectors or firefighters can remain in a building once the fire is extinguished, if they leave and desire to reenter, they must obtain a warrant.

Border Searches

The Supreme Court addressed the issue of competing rights and values in a border search in *United States* v. *Ramsey.*[46] The Court held that searches at the border are per se reasonable because of the right of a sovereign nation to protect itself by stopping and searching persons and property entering its soil. Therefore, searches of persons and property entering the country may be made without obtaining a warrant or establishing probable cause. This activity is a form of balancing the national interest in preventing illegal persons and goods from entering the United States against the limited intrusion that occurs when a person decides to cross the border. The authority to conduct suspicionless inspections at the border includes the authority to remove, disassemble, and reassemble a vehicle's fuel tank.[47]

Airport Searches

In the late 1960s, the United States began limited searches of persons traveling on airlines if they matched a predetermined profile. This process was abandoned in 1973, and then all persons traveling on airlines were required to pass through a magnetometer and have their carry-on luggage X-rayed and/or inspected. The courts have upheld such airport searches on the basis of balancing the need for the search with its limited scope. Additionally, the search is limited to a certain process, and passengers have advance notice of its existence. This notice allows them to avoid the search simply by choosing not to fly.

Searches of Prisoners

It has been said that prisoners do not lose all of their Fourth Amendment rights simply because they are incarcerated. However, the courts have ruled in favor of correctional institutions in a number of situations. For example, a prisoner's mail may be read; after a visit with friends or family, prisoners may be searched; and their religious practices may be curtailed. The courts balance the security of the institution against the rights of the inmate and in most situations find for the institution. It is said that courts are loath to second-guess prison administrators.

INDEPENDENT STATE GROUNDS

State constitutions may provide greater protection to an individual than that provided by the U.S. Constitution. This occurs when the state highest court decides an issue on **independent state grounds**. A classic example is the *Sitz* case discussed under "Sobriety Checkpoints." After the U.S. Supreme Court determined that the checkpoints did not violate the Fourth Amendment, the state appellate court held that they violated Article I, Section 11 of the Michigan Constitution. On appeal, the Michigan Supreme Court affirmed, holding that the checkpoints were unconstitutional under the Michigan Constitution because there was no support in Michigan's constitutional history for the proposition that police were permitted to engage in warrantless and suspicionless seizures of automobiles in order to enforce criminal laws. The state court's review of cases construing Article II, Section 10 of the Michigan Constitution (1908) showed no support for the proposition that police could engage in warrantless, suspicionless seizures of automobiles. The state court also held that the Michigan Constitution offered more protection than the U.S. Constitution.[48]

PROBABLE CAUSE

There are two parts to the Fourth Amendment. In the event that a warrant is not used, the first part of the amendment comes into play and requires that the people be secure "against unreasonable searches and seizures." However, when a warrant is used, the second part of the amendment requires that "no Warrants shall issue, but upon probable cause." Therefore, for a search warrant to be valid, the issuing authority must find that there are statements or other evidence that establishes probable cause.

The Supreme Court has a long history of expressing a strong preference for the use of search warrants. Warrants impose an orderly process with an independent review by the judiciary. This process has resulted in a slight shading or difference in evaluating searches with or without a warrant. The Court gives more deference to searches conducted with a warrant, holding that the reviewing court is not to conduct a de novo or an independent evaluation of the magistrate's probable cause determination; rather, the review is merely intended to decide whether the evidence taken as a whole forms a substantial basis for the magistrate's finding of probable cause.[49] **Probable cause** is an objective test that requires the facts to be such as would warrant a belief by a reasonable person that criminal conduct has occurred or is about to occur.

Information received from informants can complicate evaluations by the courts of whether or not probable cause exists. An informant is a person who learns of criminal conduct by being involved in the criminal culture. The term does not refer to a citizen who is a witness or victim. In *Aguilar* v. *Texas,* the Supreme Court set forth a two-prong test to determine whether probable cause existed when dealing with information from an informant.[50] This test requires (1) that the informant have a basis of knowledge for his or her allegations that someone is committing a criminal act and (2) that there must be facts to support the credibility of the informant or his or her information.

In *Illinois* v. *Gates,* the Supreme Court later adopted a "totality of the circumstances" analysis that traditionally has been used in probable cause determinations.[51] The *Gates* court continued to state that an informant's veracity, reliability, and basis of knowledge are critical in determining whether probable cause exists in any given situation.

The Court views witnesses or victims in a different light. Witnesses or victims are not passing on rumor; rather, they are reciting information that they observed regarding criminal activity. The knowledge or veracity of witnesses or victims is seldom questioned for purposes of probable cause. Courts look at a variety of factors in determining whether statements by victims/witnesses establish probable cause, including the particularity of the description of the perpetrator.

SEARCH WITH A WARRANT

As indicated earlier in this chapter, the courts prefer that a law enforcement officer obtain a search warrant. The warrant process involves (1) a neutral and detached magistrate, (2) an oath or affirmation, (3) establishment of probable cause, (4) particular description of the place to be searched, (5) particular description of the items to be seized, and (6) the time and manner of execution.

Importance of a Search Warrant

The U.S. Supreme Court has indicated a strong preference for obtaining a search warrant prior to conducting a search. The general rule is that the police must get a warrant unless they cannot. In the trial of a criminal case, searches conducted pursuant to a valid search warrant are presumed to be legal, and the party, normally the defendant, who attacks the validity of the search has the burden of proof to establish that the search was invalid. In the case of search without a warrant, the search is presumed to be invalid and the party, normally the prosecutor, who is attempting to enter into evidence the results of the search has the burden to establish that the search was legal.

A Neutral and Detached Magistrate

The court has stated that police and prosecutors cannot be expected to remain neutral when dealing with their own investigations. A neutral and detached **magistrate** provides a fresh, unbiased determination regarding the sufficiency of the evidence supporting the request for the warrant. The magistrate cannot receive any funds for issuing the warrant; otherwise, he or she has a financial interest in the case. Nor can the magistrate be involved in the execution of the warrant.

An Oath or Affirmation

Typically, warrants require a written record under an oath or affirmation. Courts are reluctant to allow other information to be brought in at a later date to rehabilitate an otherwise defective warrant. This rule should be distinguished from the oral or the telephonic issuance of warrants that is now common in many jurisdictions. Whether the information is presented in writing or over the telephone, it must be attested to by an oath or affirmation.

Establishment of Probable Cause

Once probable cause has been established in the warrant, it can be issued. What happens if the facts supporting the probable cause are false? In *Franks* v. *Delaware,* the Supreme Court allowed the defendant to present evidence to show that the information contained in the search warrant was false and therefore that no probable cause had been established.[52] The Court stated that banning such a process would destroy the probable cause requirement in a warrant because an officer could lie about the facts and there would be no way or method to counter such false allegations.

Particular Description of the Place to Be Searched

The warrant does not have to describe every detail of the place to be searched. In urban areas, for single-family residences, the street address is usually sufficient. However, warrants must be more specific when dealing with multiple-family apartments. For example, there may be an apartment No. 3 on each floor, and if the warrant simply states "425 S. Swift, Apt 3" without stating the floor, the warrant may well be defective, since it does not describe the particular place to be searched. As a practical matter, many jurisdictions require that officers describe the place to be searched to avoid mistakes. "The address of the premise to be searched is 323 N. Apple Street. It is a single-family residence, with an attached two-car garage. The premise has white exterior stucco walls and a brown shingle roof with two tall trees in the front yard. It is the third house on the western side of the street in a northern direction from the cross street of S. Apple."

Particular Description of the Items to Be Seized

The leading case in this area is *Marron* v. *United States.*[53] *Marron* required that any item seized be particularly described in the warrant. However, in *Coolidge* v. *New Hampshire,* this concept was broadened to allow officers to seize evidence that was not described in the warrant if (1) it was in plain view and (2) it was of an incriminating nature.[54] Although *Coolidge* does not allow officers to go on a fishing expedition searching for evidence, if they are conducting a search of a premise and during the search observe other items that are incriminating, they may lawfully seize those items. For example, officers may have a warrant that allows them to search for bank records that show the commission of a mail fraud, and if after opening a desk drawer they observe narcotics, they may seize the narcotics.

Law in Practice

Can the Police Chief Monitor Police Officers' Use of Official Devices?

As a police officer, you are issued a cell phone. Do you have a right to privacy on and in that cell phone?

City of Ontario v. *Quon*, S. Ct. 2619: (2010):

The City provided alphanumeric pagers to police officers on its SWAT team. After Sergeant Quon exceeded his allotted usage limit, the City acquired transcripts from the pager provider and discovered that Quon had used the pager for personal purposes and that some messages were sexually explicit. Quon and those with whom he had exchanged messages sued claiming an unlawful search in violation of the Fourth Amendment. The trial court found that officers had a reasonable expectation of privacy in the text messages, but that the search did not violate the Fourth amendment. The Ninth Circuit reversed, holding that the search was unreasonable as matter of law.

The US Supreme Court reversed, holding that the search of Quon's text messages was reasonable and did not violate the Fourth Amendment. The search was motivated by a legitimate work-related purpose, and it was not excessive in scope. (Note: The Court assumed—without deciding—that Quon had a reasonable expectation of privacy.) The Court noted or held:

- While individuals do not lose Fourth Amendment rights merely because they work for the government, some expectations of privacy held by government employees may be unreasonable due to the "operational realities of the workplace."
- The warrantless review of Quon's pager transcript was reasonable because it was motivated by a legitimate work-related purpose, and because it was not excessive in scope in that Chief Scharf had ordered the audit to determine whether the City's contractual character limit was sufficient to meet the City's needs.
- Individuals do not lose their Fourth Amendment rights merely because they work for the government instead of a private employer.
- The concept of legitimate expectation of privacy may evolve with changing technology.
- It is important that departments have clear, comprehensive policies that put employees on notice of the conditions of use of department-issued equipment.

Time and Manner of Execution

Some jurisdictions allow warrants to be executed only within a limited number of days after issuance. For example, a warrant might be issued October 15 and can be served any time within the next ten days. Approximately half of the states require that warrants be executed only during the daylight hours unless the officers can show some special need to serve the warrant at other times, such as during the evening hours.

An individual's detention in handcuffs during the search of a particular residence was permissible where a warrant existed to search that residence, the individual was an occupant of that residence at the time of the search, and the use of handcuffs minimized the inherent risk in searching a gang house for dangerous weapons.[55] Execution of search warrant for a house formerly occupied by suspects was not unreasonable, even though current residents were not the same race as suspects. Also ordering residents from their bed and requiring them to remain unclothed for brief period was justified to determine that residents were not armed and that suspects were not at house.[56]

Law in Practice

Are Anticipatory Warrants Legal?

An anticipatory warrant is a warrant based upon an affidavit showing probable cause that at some future times (but not presently) certain evidence of crime will be located at a specified place. Most anticipatory warrants subject their execution to some condition precedent other than the mere passage of time—a so-called triggering condition.

In *United States* v. *Grubbs*,[57] the defendant purchased a videotape containing child pornography from a web site operated by an undercover postal inspector. Postal inspection officers arranged a controlled delivery of a package containing the videotape to defendant's residence. The postal inspector then submitted a search warrant application to a magistrate with an affidavit describing the proposed operation in detail. The magistrate judge issued the warrant on the basis of an affidavit but directed the inspector that the warrant could not be executed until after the controlled delivery. The warrant did not, however, indicate this requirement. The Court held that anticipatory warrants were lawful and that the occurrence of the triggering condition plainly established probable cause for the search. The Court noted that the affidavit established probable cause to believe the triggering condition would be satisfied even though it was possible that the defendant could have refused delivery of the videotape, which was unlikely.

Law in Practice

Example of an Affidavit for an Arrest Warrant—*Davis* v. *State*[58]

[A jury convicted Appellant Davis of the manufacture of more than 400 grams of methamphetamine and assessed punishment at fifty years' confinement and a $100,000 fine. The trial court sentenced him accordingly. In one issue, Davis challenged the trial court's denial of his motion to suppress the fruits of the search warrant subject to which the contraband was seized. The appellate court held that the trial court abused its discretion in denying his motion to suppress and reversed the trial court's judgment. Because the affidavit was silent as to the officer's experience, his proximity to the residence at 701 Young Street other than the fact that he "drove past" the residence, the length of time he spent outside the residence, or anything else that would show the reliability of his suspicion, the affidavit was insufficient to establish probable cause needed to support the warrant.]

The affidavit in question, submitted to the magistrate by Officer John Spragins of the Wichita Falls, Texas, police department:

Case # TF-03-0081 Warrant (DA) # Affidavit for Search and Arrest Warrant the State of Texas County of Montague

The undersigned Affiant, being a Peace Officer under the laws of the State of Texas and being duly sworn, on oath makes the following statement and accusations:

(continued)

1. There is in MONTAGUE County, Texas, a suspected place and premises described and located as follows: A single family mobile home that is known as 701 Young Street, Nocona, Montague County, Texas. Said residence is grey in color with white trim. S[ai]d residence is located on the west side of the roadway and the front door faces east.

   Said suspected place and premises, in addition to the foregoing description, also includes all other buildings, structures, places, vehicles on said premises and within the curtilage, if said is a residence, that are found to be under the control of the suspected party named below and in, on, or around which said suspected party may reasonably reposit or secrete property that is the object of the search requested herein.

2. There is at said suspected place and premises property concealed and kept in violation of the laws of the State of Texas and described as follows: drugs kept, prepared, or manufactured in violation of the laws of this state, to-wit, Methamphetamine. Further, Affiant believes that suspected party has at said suspected place other paraphernalia, implements, and instruments used in the commission of the offense of Manufacture and Distribution of Methamphetamine.

3. Said suspected place and premises are in charge of and controlled by each of the following persons: Jeffery Scott Davis, white male, DOB 01-22-76[.]

4. It is the belief of Affiant, and he hereby charges and accuses, that: Jeffery Scott Davis is intentionally and knowingly in unlawful possession of a controlled substance listed in the Texas Health and Safety Code, to wit, Methamphetamine.

5. Affiant has probable cause for said belief by reason of the following facts: Your Affiant is a Texas commissioned Peace Officer and has been so commissioned for over 10 years. Your Affiant is employed by the Wichita Falls Police Department and assigned, as a Narcotics Investigator, to the North Texas Regional Drug Enforcement Task Force. During the time your Affiant has been assigned as a Narcotics Investigator, your Affiant has been responsible for several investigations of controlled substances violations including the Manufacture and Distribution of Methampheta-mine. In addition, your Affiant has attended training in narcotics investigations including search warrant preparation, evidence collection and investigations of individuals who derive substantial income from the illegal importation, manufacture, distribution, and sale of illegal controlled substances. Your Affiant has also attended basic and advanced training in clandestine laboratories and is certified by the Drug Enforcement Administration to enter and seize clandestine drug manufacturing laboratories.

   Your Affiant, along with Task Force investigators and DPS Investigators, ha[s] been conducting a joint investigation regarding Jeffery Scott Davis[‘s] involvement in the Manufacture and Distribution of Methamphetamine. During this investigation investigators have gathered information that Davis was manufacturing methamphetamine at 701 Young Street, Nocona, Texas. Investigators have received information from confidential informants that stated Davis was manufacturing the methamphetamine inside the residence as well as in a shed located in the backyard of said residence. Investigators have received information that Davis was purchasing items used in the manufacture of methamphetamine including starter fluid (ether) and coffee filters. Investigators have received information from Crime Stoppers that described a chemical odor emitting from the residence at 701 Young Street and that Davis was manufacturing methamphetamine at the residence.

   On 03-18-03, at approximately 0400 hrs, Officer Mitchell Westervelt was on patrol in Nocona and drove past residence. Westervelt stated that he could smell a strong chemical odor he has associated with the manufacture of methamphetamine emitting from the residence at 701 Young Street. Westervelt informed Chief Holcomb of the odor and Holcomb contacted your Affiant.

   Based on the information received from numerous sources and the odor emitting from the residence, your Affiant firmly believes that Jeffery Scott Davis is intentionally and knowingly in possession of a quantity of methamphetamine at the above listed location.

   Further, based on your Affiant's experience as an Investigator, it is known that drug dealers normally keep certain records indicating drug quantities handled, cost, prices, names and telephone number of buyers and suppliers as well as information regarding bank accounts. It can also be presumed that these and other records indicating premise occupancy/residence will be found on the said property. Your Affiant further alleges that weapons found on the said property are seizable as indicative of drug dealings since possession of a firearm tends to demonstrate a likelihood that the dealer took steps to prevent contraband, paraphernalia, and the proceeds (money) from being stolen, similarly as other tools of the trade (scales, plastic baggies, cutting equipment and narcotics equipment) which are also seizable would be kept. Further, your Affiant alleges the above constitute specific articulable facts from which a reasonable person could draw [a] rational inference that large sums of cash found at the premise (absent proof to the contrary) were derived from illegal narcotics sales and therefore subject to seizure.

Law in Practice

Notice of Service of a Search Warrant

Many states require that when a person's property has been searched, the officers must provide the person with a notice of service of a search warrant. The following is a copy of a notice given in a West Covina, California, case:

Search Warrant: Notice of Service to Whom It May Concern:

1. THESE PREMISES HAVE BEEN SEARCHED BY PEACE OFFICERS OF THE (name of searching agency) *West Covina Police* DEPARTMENT PURSUANT TO A SEARCH WARRANT ISSUED ON (date) *5-20-93*, BY THE HONORABLE (name of magistrate) *Dan Oki*,

JUDGE OF THE SUPERIOR/MUNICIPAL COURT, *Citrus* JUDICIAL DISTRICT.

2. THE SEARCH WAS CONDUCTED ON (date) *5-21-93*. A LIST OF THE PROPERTY SEIZED PURSUANT TO THE **SEARCH WARRANT IS ATTACHED.**

3. IF YOU WISH FURTHER INFORMATION, YOU MAY CONTACT:
   (name of investigator) **Det. Ferrari or Det. Melnyk** AT [telephone number].
   "LT. SCHIMANSKI [telephone number]."
   [Italicized characters represent those portions of the original document that were handwritten on the form.]

CASE LAW

Recent Cases

Excerpts from U.S. Supreme Court decision in *Kentucky* v. *Hollis King*
563 U. S. _____ (2011) No. 09–1272. Argued January 12, 2011—Decided May 16, 2011

Were the actions of the Lexington, Kentucky, police officers legal?

Police officers in Lexington, Kentucky, followed a suspected drug dealer to an apartment complex. They smelled marijuana outside an apartment door, knocked loudly, and announced their presence. As soon as the officers began knocking, they heard noises coming from the apartment; the officers believed that these noises were consistent with the destruction of evidence. The officers announced their intent to enter the apartment, kicked in the door, and found the respondent and others. They saw drugs in plain view during a protective sweep of the apartment and found additional evidence during a subsequent search. King entered a conditional plea of guilty and reserved his right to appeal the failure of the trial court to suppress the drugs.

The Supreme Court of Kentucky reversed the conviction. The Kentucky court assumed that exigent circumstances existed, but it nonetheless invalidated the search. The exigent circumstances rule did not apply, the court held, because the police should have foreseen that their conduct would prompt the occupants to attempt to destroy evidence.

The U.S. Supreme Court held:

The exigent circumstances rule applies when the police do not create the exigency by engaging or threatening to engage in conduct that violates the Fourth Amendment.

The Fourth Amendment expressly imposes two requirements: All searches and seizures must be reasonable; and a warrant may not be issued unless probable cause is properly established and the scope of the authorized search is set out with particularity. Although "searches and seizures inside a home without a warrant are pre-sumptively unreasonable," (*Brigham City* v. *Stuart*, 547 U. S. 398), this presumption may be overcome when "the exigencies of the situation make the needs of law enforcement so compelling that a warrantless search is objectively reasonable under the Fourth Amendment," (*Mincey* v. *Arizona*, 437 U. S. 385, 394). One such exigency is the need "to prevent the imminent destruction of evidence." (*Brigham City*, supra, at 403).

Under the "police-created exigency" doctrine, which lower courts have developed as an exception to the exigent circumstances rule, exigent circumstances do not justify a warrantless search when the exigency was "created" or "manufactured" by the conduct of the police. The lower courts have not agreed, however, on the test for determining when police impermissibly create an exigency.

The proper test follows from the principle that permits warrantless searches: warrantless searches are allowed when the circumstances make it reasonable, within the meaning of the Fourth Amendment, to dispense with the warrant requirement. Thus, a warrantless entry based on exigent circumstances is reasonable when the police did not create the exigency by engaging or threatening to engage in conduct violating the Fourth Amendment. A similar approach has been taken in other cases involving warrantless searches. For example, officers may seize evidence in plain view if they have not violated the Fourth Amendment in arriving at the spot from which the observation of the evidence is made; see *Horton* v. *California,* 496 U. S. 128, 136–140; and they may seek consent-based encounters if they are lawfully present in the place where the consensual encounter occurs; see *INS* v. *Delgado*, 466 U. S. 210, 217, n. 5. Pp. 8–10.

Some courts, including the Kentucky Supreme Court, have imposed additional requirements—asking whether officers deliberately created the exigent circumstances with the bad faith intent to avoid the warrant requirement; reasoning that police may not rely on an exigency if it was reasonably foreseeable that their investigative tactics . . . would create the exigent circumstances; faulting officers for knocking on a door when they had sufficient evidence to seek a warrant but did not do so; and finding that officers created or manufactured an exigency when their investigation was contrary to standard or good law enforcement practices. Such requirements are unsound and are thus rejected.

Respondent contends that an exigency is impermissibly created when officers engage in conduct that would cause a reasonable person to believe that entry was imminent and inevitable, but that approach is also flawed. The ability of officers to respond to an exigency cannot turn on such subtleties as the officers' tone of voice in announcing their presence and the forcefulness of their knocks. A forceful knock may be necessary to alert the occupants that someone is at the door, and unless officers identify themselves loudly enough, occupants may not know who is at their doorstep.

Respondent's test would make it extremely difficult for officers to know how loudly they may announce their presence or how forcefully they may knock without running afoul of the police-created exigency rule. And in most cases, it would be nearly impossible for a court to determine whether that threshold had been passed.

Assuming that an exigency existed here, there is no evidence that the officers either violated the Fourth Amendment or threatened to do so prior to the point when they entered the apartment.

Assuming an exigency did exist, the officers' conduct—banging on the door and announcing their presence—was entirely consistent with the Fourth Amendment. Respondent has pointed to no evidence supporting his argument that the officers made any sort of "demand" to enter the apartment, much less a demand that amounts to a threat to violate the Fourth Amendment. If there is contradictory evidence that has not been brought to this Court's attention, the state court may elect to address that matter on remand. Finally, the record makes clear that the officers' announcement that they were going to enter the apartment was made after the exigency arose. [The decision of the Kentucky Supreme Court was reversed on the federal issue as to whether or not the search violated the Fourth Amendment of the U.S. Constitution.]

United States v. *Williams,* 2010 U.S. App. LEXIS 22787 (7th Cir. 2010)

Issue: The Drug Enforcement Administration (DEA) has probable cause to stop and search a vehicle, but the DEA officers who actually stopped the vehicle do not have probable cause.

Was the search legal?

Court's decision: Where the Drug Enforcement Agency (DEA) has probable cause to stop and search a vehicle, under the collective knowledge doctrine, that probable cause is imputed to the officers who actually make the stop at the direction of the DEA.

Facts: The district court denied the motion to dismiss citing the collective knowledge doctrine as the stop and search was at the request of another Chicago police officer who was a member of a DEA task force. As part of an ongoing drug-trafficking investigation in Chicago run by the DEA, court authorized wiretaps were employed to intercept telephone calls made by and to individuals believed to be involved in the drug-trafficking organization targeted. As a result of the intercepted calls, DEA agents stopped individuals leaving a suspected stash house and were able to confirm location of drug transaction and identify some of the participants in the organization.

On the day the defendant was stopped, members of the DEA task force watched him and another person arrive at the stash house in a Chevy Suburban at approximately 11:30 a.m. The two men were observed walking into the backyard of the house and after about 15 minutes leave the house with a brown shoebox.

One of the Chicago police officers working with the DEA task force observed them leave the house and called Officer Simon with a description of the vehicle, license plate, and the route they took leaving the stash house.

Simon and his partner stopped the vehicle after observing that defendant was not wearing his seatbelt. Once stopped, the defendant and the driver were instructed to exit the car. A pat-down search revealed two bags of marijuana in the defendant's pocket. A search of the vehicle revealed a "brown shoebox in the back seat of the Suburban ... containing a brick of what was later confirmed to be a kilogram of cocaine."

Court's decision: The knowledge of a team of officers working together closely in monitoring a drug transaction as it unfolds may be mutually imputed even the absence of express testimony that the specific or detailed information creating the justification for the stop was conveyed. Therefore, knowledge of the information contained in the intercepted phone calls by the DEA was properly imputed to the members of the Chicago Police Department working with them.

Warrantless searches are considered per se unreasonable under the Fourth Amendment unless one of a few specifically established and well-delineated exceptions applies. One of the more notable exceptions to the warrant requirement is the 'automobile exception,' which allows law enforcement to conduct a warrantless search of a vehicle if there is probable cause to believe the vehicle contains contraband or evidence of a crime. 'When probable cause exists to search a vehicle, law enforcement agents are permitted to search all parts of the vehicle in which contraband or evidence could be concealed, including closed compartments, containers, packages, and trunks. The appellate court held that the DEA task force had probable cause to search the vehicle, and second, can the information can be imputed to the officers who conducted the stop and search under the collective knowledge doctrine.'

Probable cause to search will exist, when based on the known facts and circumstances, a reasonably prudent person would believe that contraband or evidence of a crime will be found in the place to be searched. The critical inquiry was whether there was a fair probability that contraband or evidence of a crime would be found in the Suburban; absolute certainty of such a discovery is not required. The determination whether suspicious circumstances rise to the level of probable cause is a common-sense judgment, and officers are entitled to draw reasonable inferences based on their training and experience in making that determination.

United States v. *Epps*, 2010 U.S. App. LEXIS 16309, 22 Fla. L. Weekly Fed. C 1311 (11th Cir. 2010).

Issue: During the robbery of a bank, the teller provided the robber with several stacks of money that contained "dye packs." The dye packs were designed to burst and produce a pink-colored stain when the money bundles were opened. Shortly after the robbery and in a mall near the robbery, an individual was stopped while carrying a white pillowcase with pink stains and the shapes of the objects in the pillowcase looked like bundle of money.

Were the actions of the police in inspecting the contents of the pillowcase legal?

Court's decision: There was no reasonable expectation of privacy where a container's contents can be inferred from its outwardly visible stains and shape.

Facts: A deputy heard the report of a carjacking en route to the bank robbery. A number of police cars were already present when he arrived at the bank and so he proceeded across the street in the direction of a shopping mall. He noticed a blue Cavalier parked by a pawnshop as he approached the mall. The car matched the description of the carjacked vehicle and was parked with the driver's door open. The deputy continued toward the mall, and saw a man running quickly through the mall parking lot with a white bag in his hand. The path that the runner was taking led away from the Cavalier toward the mall entrance. The deputy, with lights and siren already activated, announced his presence over the car's P.A. system and ordered the individual running to stop.

The fleeing individual looked back over his shoulder at the police car and pointed a gun in the deputy's direction, while continuing to run. A bystander in the mall parking lot also saw the gun being pointed at the officer. At this point, the runner was approximately ten feet in front of the police car.

The deputy tried to stop the man by hitting him with the front passenger corner of the police car. The man rolled off the hood and landed on the ground—the gun, a pocketknife, and the white bag went flying. The deputy covered the suspect with a gun until another officer arrived and handcuffed the man. The individual, defendant, was already under arrest when Investigator Dawson came to process the scene. She photographed the gun, knife, and white bag where they came to rest on the pavement after being dropped by the appellant.

The white bag was a pillowcase, with pink stains on it. The pillowcase was later moved to the back of a police vehicle, where the police opened it and found the following items: currency that was partially burned and marked with red dye; two dye packs; a dreadlock wig; a black bag; a shirt; and a can of pepper spray.

Decision: On appeal, appellant (defendant) asserted that the district court erred when it denied his motion to suppress evidence. He argued that the police lacked the authority to conduct a warrantless search of the pillowcase he was carrying. He further asserted that deputy had no lawful justification to stop him, and that everything obtained from his unlawful detention must therefore be suppressed as the fruit of the poisonous tree.

The appellate court noted that it was well settled that the Fourth Amendment to the United States Constitution prohibits unreasonable searches and seizures. However, Fourth Amendment protections are extended to only those individuals who have a legitimate expectation of privacy in the area invaded. The party alleging an unconstitutional search must establish both a subjective and an objective expectation of privacy. The subjective component requires that a person exhibit an actual expectation of privacy, while the objective component requires that the privacy expectation be one that society is prepared to recognize as reasonable.

The appellate court opined that appellant manifested his subjective expectation of privacy by placing personal items inside the pillowcase and holding it shut in one hand. The fact that the pillowcase could not be fastened was not dispositive.

It was the objective component that could not be substantiated, because society is not willing to accept that his subjective privacy expectation was objectively reasonable. Some containers (e.g., a kit of burglary tools or a gun case) by their very nature cannot support any reasonable expectation of privacy because their contents can be inferred from their outward appearance.

The Eleventh Circuit noted that it had upheld a warrantless search of closed, opaque packages that reeked of marijuana and the warrantless search of a paper sack lying in full view on the floor of a car, where the paper sack was labeled as being from a pharmacy suspected of involvement in illicit activities and the sack's contents could be inferred from the observing police officers' first-hand knowledge that it had been brought directly from the pharmacy under unusual circumstances

Based on circuit precedent, the Eleventh Circuit Court of Appeals held that the totality of the circumstances, the fact that the pillowcase contained dye packs and possibly other items associated with the bank robbery could be inferred from its outward appearance, supported the conclusion that the search was valid.

Because the pillowcase's contents could be inferred from its outwardly visible stains and the circumstances under which the police obtained it, the pillowcase was one of those containers that by its very nature cannot support any reasonable expectation of privacy. The pillowcase therefore fell outside the protective ambit of the Fourth Amendment, and the police did not violate defendant's constitutional rights when they opened the pillowcase without first obtaining a warrant.

The denial of defendant's motion to suppress was affirmed.

United States v. *Villasenor*, 2010 U.S. App. LEXIS 11833 (9th Cir. 2010)

Issue: One of the exceptions to the probable cause requirement of the Fourth Amendment is border searches. A person entering the United States may be searched without a warrant and without probable cause. The search may be conducted at the border or under the extended border doctrine within a reasonable distance of the border. If a person is searched as he crosses the border, can he legally be searched a second time within a reasonable distance of the border under the border exception?

Court's Decision: The fact a search takes place at the border does not prohibit the government from legally conducting a subsequent search of the same person or vehicle under the extended border search doctrine.

Facts: Immigration and Customs Enforcement (ICE) agents interviewed a drug smuggler arrested at the Calexico West Port of Entry in Southern California. The smuggler provided dates and details of the future activities planned by the larger drug organization for which he worked. Those details included that in the near future he was to meet up with a white Toyota Tacoma, which would serve as a load vehicle, and a white PT Cruiser, which would serve as a scout vehicle. The meeting was to occur on the California side of the border and then proceed to a separate drop-off location. The smuggler provided detailed descriptions of the cars involved, he also provided pictures from his cell phone from which the agents were able to obtain a license plate. The license plate number was then entered into the Treasury Enforcement Communications System ("TECS"), a computer-based information system designed to identify individuals crossing the border who are suspected of violating federal law.

The next morning, the defendant Villasenor, an 82-year-old man, drove a white PT Cruiser to the Calexico West Port of Entry. The plate triggered an automatic referral to a secondary inspection but the narcotics detecting dog (NDD) sniffed the car but did not alert for the presence of drugs. (The dog was later fired.)

A short time later, an agent driving southbound on Imperial Avenue looked for a parking spot at the Point of Entry. When he found none, he made a U-turn and headed north on Imperial. At the second red light, he realized that he was behind a white PT Cruiser. He decided to follow the car. Villasenor stopped at a gas station for ten minutes, used the rest room and left the gas station, never filling up. He was on the cell phone the entire time.

In two miles, he stopped at another gas station, still on the cell phone, walked around the car, did not fill up and left that gas station as well. Next he drove thirty minutes to the DMV, parked his car, entered the DMV, and returned two to three minutes later and again drove away.

While at the DMV, the agent asked the El Centro Police Department, the local police, to send a marked police car to conduct a traffic stop of Villasenor's car. An officer responded to the call, tailing Villasenor's car just as it was leaving the DMV. Before long, the officer noticed a ten-inch rosary hanging from Villasenor's rearview mirror. Relying on California Vehicle Code § 26708(a)(2), which prohibits driving any motor vehicle with any object placed in or upon the vehicle that obstructs or reduces the driver's clear view through the windshield, Villasenor was then stopped.

The officer used the stop as an opportunity to call another NDD officer to conduct a sniff of the car. In the meantime, Villasenor was being ticketed for failure to provide proof of insurance. Once he received the ticket, Villasenor asked if he could leave, but was told to wait.

Forty-five minutes later, Agent Biella arrived with an NDD. The officer was aware that Villasenor's car had gone through secondary inspection that morning. During the ensuing dog sniff, the NDD alerted to the rear rocker panel. The agents looked behind the panel and discovered fifteen packages of cocaine weighing a total of 37.36 pounds. Villasenor was arrested and indicted on charges of importing and possessing an illegal substance, violations of 21 U.S.C. §§ 952 and 960.

Court's Opinion: In reversing the district court's decision to suppress the evidence seized in this case, the appellate court determined that the search in this case was authorized under the extended border search doctrine. In explaining the reasons behind its ruling, the Ninth Circuit Court of Appeals began its decision with a cursory review of the Fourth Amendment protections.

The Fourth Amendment protects against unreasonable searches and seizures. Generally, searches made at the border, pursuant to the longstanding right of the sovereign to protect itself by stopping and examining persons and property crossing into this country, are reasonable simply by virtue of the fact that they occur at the border. As a result, most border searches need not be justified by a search warrant or by any level of individualized suspicion.

Border searches are unique, in that they do not always occur at the physical border. This is because the logistical reality that it is impossible to search every vehicle or carrier at the precise moment it crosses land or sea borders, id., border searches sometimes occur at the functional equivalent of a border. The court cited the Supreme Court case of *Almeida-Sanchez* v. *United States*, 413 U.S. 266 (1973), where the search of passengers and cargo that occurred when a non-stop flight from Mexico City landed in St. Louis, was an example of the functional equivalent of a border search.

The appellate court also explained that the distinct but closely related type of border search is the so-called extended border search. Extended border searches usually occur near the border but after the border has already been crossed. Because extended border searches intrude more on an individual's normal expectation of privacy, id., their reasonableness depends on two factors: (1) whether the totality of the surrounding circumstances, including the time and distance elapsed as well as the manner and extent of surveillance, convince the fact finder with reasonable certainty that any contraband in or on the vehicle at the time of search was aboard the vehicle at the time of entry into the United States; and (2) whether government agents conducting the search have reasonable suspicion that the search may uncover contraband or evidence of criminal activity. The driving force behind the extended search doctrine is the recognized government interest in stopping drug traffic.

The court also acknowledged that in the balance between legitimate privacy interests of individuals and the government's recognized right to control drug trafficking, there will be instances where repeated and continual searches near or at the border become unreasonable; however, this was not one of those instances.

Conclusion: Judgment of the district court suppressing the search was reversed.

United States v. *Vongxay*, 2010 U.S. App. LEXIS 2682 (9th Cir. 2010)

Issue: What constitutes a consent to search?

Decision: In terms of consent for a valid search, voluntariness is a question of fact to be determined from all the surrounding circumstances.

Facts: The charges in this case arose after defendant was arrested outside a nightclub known for its gang activity. He was with a group of Asian males dressed in dark blue athletic wear, characteristic of the gangs that frequented the area, when he was spotted by Officer Campos. The appellant and the group dispersed when they saw Campos in a marked police car drive past the club. Campos called for backup as he drove away from the club. By the time he drove around the corner and headed back to the club on foot, the group had reassembled outside the club. The first person Campos encountered was defendant. Campos spoke to the defendant and asked if he was leaving the area or going into the club. During the conversation, he noticed the defendant trying to hide something in his waistband.

Based upon his training and experience, Campos believed that the defendant was armed as asked if he had any weapons. Although the defendant answered no, Campos was not convinced and asked defendant if he could search him for weapons. Defendant said nothing but placed his hands on his head. Campos started touching around defendant's waistband and felt the outline of a large gun. As soon as Campos felt the gun, the defendant pulled away. A struggle ensued, and a loaded semiautomatic handgun fell from defendant's waistband.

Court's Decision

The defendant willingly lifted his arms, so as to enable a search, in response to Campos's request for permission to search him. Given the facts surrounding the search, the defendant's attempt to pull away after the gun was found is better understood as a flight response than as evidence that he had not consented in the first place. Implied consent to the search was established.

Officer Campos never asserted that he had probable cause to search defendant upon finding him standing in a group outside a club. However, he was entitled to ask defendant questions including whether defendant would consent to a search as long as that consent was not coerced. The burden of proof to establish free and voluntary consent lay squarely with the government. Voluntariness is a question of fact to be determined from all the surrounding circumstances.

The appellate court reviewed the facts and circumstances surrounding the encounter to determine the free and voluntary nature of the consent. Campos approached defendant on foot and alone and asked him why he was in front of the club and if he had a gun. Although the defendant answered "no," he nevertheless asked if he could search him. Defendant did not verbally respond but simply placed his hands on his head.

The voluntariness of consent is determined by the totality of the circumstances as evaluated in light of five factors:

1. whether the defendant was in custody;
2. whether the arresting officer had his guns drawn;
3. whether *Miranda* warnings were given;
4. whether the defendant was notified that he had a right not to consent; and
5. whether the defendant had been told that a search warrant could be obtained.

The government need not establish all five factors in order to establish that the consent was voluntary; 3, 1113 (9th Cir. 2000). In addition, the defendant was not informed that a search warrant could be obtained. Therefore, the only one of the five factors listed above not satisfied here is that appellant was not informed that he could "decline" the request to be searched. The Supreme Court has held that an officer need not inform an individual of his or her right to decline the request for a search, only that doing so satisfies one of the five factors in determining consent.

The appellate court affirmed the district court's holding that defendant's act of raising his hands to his head constituted implied consent to search.

United States v. *Ruckes*, 2009 U.S. App. LEXIS 24578 (9th Cir. 2009).

Issue: Under *Arizona* v. *Gant*, 129 S. Ct. 1710, 1719, 173 L. Ed. 2d 485 (2009), evidence seized pursuant to a search incident to an arrest must fall within one of those two narrow situations in order to avoid suppression where (1) the arrestee is unsecured and within reaching distance of the passenger compartment at the time of the search, or (2) it is reasonable to believe evidence relevant to the crime of arrest might be found in the vehicle. The appellant (defendant) argued that the search was not valid incident to his arrest because he was not arrested until the contraband was recovered from his car.

Facts: The charges in this case arose after appellant was stopped for speeding. According to Trooper

Wiley, appellant was traveling 15 miles per hour over the posted speed limit on Interstate Highway 5 near Seattle, Washington. Trooper Wiley asked appellant for his driver's license, registration, and proof of insurance but appellant could produce none of the documents requested. The officer noticed that there was loose change and an unlabeled prescription bottle in the open center console next to appellant. The officer then asked appellant to accompany him back to his police car. The appellant was patted down before entering the police car. He was then asked for his full name and date of birth. The resulting computer check revealed that appellant's driver's license had been suspended in order to enforce child support payments.

The trooper asked appellant whether a search of his vehicle would reveal any contraband or illegal materials. When asked why the trooper would search the car, the officer answered that his suspended license offense warranted his arrest as well as an inspection of the vehicle. Trooper Wiley further explained that because Ruckes had been ticketed for driving with a suspended license in the past, it was permissible to impound the car for thirty days. When Trooper Wiley asked appellant if there was anyone who could take control of the car, appellant told him that although the car belonged to his mother, he doubted she would be in a position to remove it from the side of the highway. The stop was both audio and video tape-recorded.

At the suppression hearing, Trooper Wiley testified that although he would not have allowed appellant to drive the car away because his license was suspended, "he might have considered permitting the owner— Ruckes's mother—to take possession of the vehicle, [but] she was unavailable to do so." The district court concluded that Trooper Wiley acted properly in impounding appellant's car.

An inventory search of the car revealed the large bottle of crack cocaine in the center console. The officer then returned to the police car and put appellant in handcuffs. A more thorough search revealed a loaded 9mm handgun under the driver's seat. Trooper Wiley called in the discovery of the weapon then administered *Miranda* warning to appellant.

Holding

The recent Supreme Court case of *Arizona* v. *Gant*, 129 S. Ct. 1710 (2009), which limits the search of the vehicle to situations where (1) the arrestee is unsecured and within reaching distance of the passenger compartment at the time of the search, or (2) it is reasonable to believe evidence relevant to the crime of arrest might be found in the vehicle. Because we find

that Trooper Wiley's search of Ruckes's vehicle does not fit within either of these two narrow situations to satisfy the search-incident-to-arrest exception to the warrant requirement, we hold that this search cannot be sustained on this theory under the Fourth Amendment. However, the drugs and loaded firearm would have been discovered during the course of an inventory search, so that the denial of the motion to suppress under the doctrine of inevitable discovery was proper.

Generally, a search is presumed to be unreasonable under the Fourth Amendment if it is not supported by probable cause and conducted pursuant to a valid search warrant. There are a few specific and narrow exceptions to this general rule. Cars have their own exceptions to the warrant requirement. However, officers must still possess probable cause to conduct a search.

The "search-incident-to-arrest" exception to the warrant requirement was first annunciated in *United States* v. *Robinson*, 414 U.S. 218 (1973). The Robinson Court explained that "in the case of a lawful custodial arrest a full search of the person is not only an exception to the warrant requirement of the Fourth Amendment, but is also a reasonable search under that Amendment." The search incident to lawful arrest doctrine permitted "officers to search an arrestee's person subsequent to the arrest of that individual." *New York* v. *Belton*, 453 U.S. 454 (1981), established the proper scope of this doctrine in the context of a search of the interior of a car incident to a lawful custodial arrest of its occupants. A permissible search incident to arrest may not extend past an area within the immediate control of the arrestee—on the search of an arrestee's automobile. When a policeman has made a lawful custodial arrest of the occupant of an automobile, he may, as a contemporaneous incident of that arrest, search the passenger compartment of that automobile.

Since this "workable rule" was still subject to much litigation, it was further clarified in *Arizona* v. *Gant*, 129 S. Ct. 1710 (2009). After Rodney Gant was arrested for driving in Arizona with a suspended license and placed in handcuffs in the back seat of the patrol car, officers conducted a search of his vehicle. Cocaine was found in the pocket of a jacket located in the backseat of the car. The Arizona Supreme Court held that "search-incident-to-arrest doctrine did not stretch so far as to permit the search of a vehicle when the occupant could not have accessed the vehicle to retrieve weapons or evidence."

The Gant Court annunciated a bright-line rule to govern situations where searches of automobiles are permitted: "Officers are only permitted to search the passenger compartment of an arrestee's automobile if the search is required for officer safety or is necessary to prevent destruction of evidence of the crime for which the recent occupant was arrested." The Court opined that neither the possibility of access nor the likelihood of discovering offense-related evidence authorized the search in *Gant* because Gant clearly was not within reaching distance of his car at the time of the search [, and an] evidentiary basis for the search was also lacking. The Supreme Court found that the search of Gant's car was an unreasonable warrantless search conducted in violation of the Fourth Amendment.

The Ninth Circuit Court of Appeals determined that 'Trooper Wiley's search here cannot be classified as a valid search incident to arrest in light of the intervening decision in Gant.' Although there was a loaded gun found during a search of the car, appellant was "secured in the back seat of the patrol car—clearly beyond lunging distance of the handgun—at the time Trooper Wiley conducted the automobile search." Additionally, there was no likelihood that Trooper Wiley might have discovered evidence of Ruckes's driving offense within the vehicle. Moreover, driving with a suspended license is not an offense which the police could reasonably expect to find evidence of in the passenger side of appellant's car. As neither of the narrow circumstance for which the *Gant* Court ruled provided justification for a search incident to an arrest existed in this case, the search is not valid under this theory in light of Gant.

However, the court did find that the inventory search of the car conducted when it was properly impounded did provide a legitimate and legal ground upon which to conduct the search. Since there was no one else that could remove the car from the side of the road, once appellant was found to have a suspended license, the decision to impound the car was legal and the resulting inventory search was legal as well. Since the contraband would have been discovered during that inventory search, the evidence was properly admitted pursuant to the inevitable discovery doctrine.

This exception to the exclusionary rule permits the government to rely on evidence that ultimately would have been discovered absent a constitutional violation. *Nix* v. *Williams*, 467 U.S. 431 (1984). The Supreme Court has held that the purpose of this rule is to avoid setting aside convictions that would have been obtained without police misconduct.

Here the appellate court found the government has shown that the firearm and illicit substances would have been uncovered by law enforcement officers through some permissible means. Therefore, the district court properly found the government had met its burden on this alternative ground.

The appellate court cautioned that although the inevitable discovery doctrine "saved" a search that would have been otherwise invalidated under *Gant*, this certainly will not always be the case. Therefore, while the government met its burden here, the district court must conduct a case-by-case inquiry to determine whether a lawful path to discovery—such as inevitability—exists in each case. To hold otherwise would create an impermissible loophole in the Court's bright-line *Gant* determination.

Because appellant's gun and crack cocaine would have inevitably been discovered notwithstanding Trooper Wiley's invalid search incident to arrest, the evidence was properly admitted pursuant to the inevitable discovery exception to the exclusionary rule. Judgment of the district court was affirmed.

Briefly Noted

United States v. *Orozco*, **2009 U.S. App. LEXIS 17991 (7th Cir. 2009)**. A law enforcement officer's experience, without more, can be sufficient under certain circumstances to support probable cause to support a search warrant application.

Arizona v. *Gant*, **129 S. Ct. 1710 (2009)**. Where officers searched defendant's car after arresting him, handcuffing him, and locking him in a patrol car, the search-incident-to-arrest exception did not justify the search under the Fourth Amendment, because he clearly was not within reaching distance of his car at the time of the search and an evidentiary basis for the search was lacking.

Kansas v. *Ventris*, **129 S. Ct. 1841 (2009)**. A jailhouse informant's testimony, concededly elicited in violation of the Sixth Amendment, was admissible to challenge defendant's inconsistent testimony at trial because the interests safeguarded by such exclusion were outweighed by the need to prevent perjury and to assure the integrity of the trial process.

Illinois v. *Caballes*, **125 S. Ct. 834 (2005)**. The Supreme Court held that when these four-legged law enforcers arrive at the scene of a traffic stop and circle and sniff a car, even in the absence of evidence suggesting that a narcotics search is warranted, that activity is not a search that implicates the Fourth Amendment.

Michigan v. *Fisher*, **130 S. Ct. 546 (2009)**. When officers, responding to a disturbance report, encountered a tumultuous situation and observed what looked like blood on a damaged car and defendant inside scream-ing and throwing things with a cut on his hand, the emergency aid exception to the Fourth Amendment's warrant requirement was reasonably invoked.

***Safford Unified Sch. Dist. #1* v. *Redding*, 129 S. Ct. 2633 (2009).** Extending search of student to the point of making student pull out her underwear was unrea-sonable and violated Fourth Amendment because there was no indication of danger to the students from the power of the drugs or their quantity, and there was no reason to suppose that student was carrying pills in her underwear. Principal was entitled to qualified immunity.

***City of Ontario* v. *Quon*, 130 S. Ct. 2619 (2010).** The U.S. Supreme Court noted that the employee probably had a reasonable expectation of privacy in the text messages sent on the pager provided to him by the city, the search was justified at its inception because there were reasonable grounds for suspect-ing that the search was necessary for a non-investigatory work-related purpose. The search was done in order to determine whether the character limit on the city's contract was sufficient to meet the city's needs. Also, the city and a police department had a legitimate interest in ensuring that employees were not being forced to pay out of their own pock-ets for work-related expenses, or on the other hand that the city was not paying for extensive personal communications. The search was permissible in its scope because reviewing the transcripts was reason-able because it was an efficient and expedient way to determine whether the employee's overages were the result of work-related messaging or personal use. The search was reasonable. The city did not violate respondents' Fourth Amendment rights.

***Montejo* v. *Louisiana*, 129 S. Ct. 2079 (U.S. 2009).** The Court held that defendant must request counsel, or otherwise assert his Sixth Amendment right when being questioned. It was unjustified to presume that a defendant's consent to police-initiated interrogation was involuntary or coerced simply because he had previously been appointed a lawyer.

***FCC* v. *AT&T* Inc., 2011 U.S. LEXIS 1899 (2011).** The protection afforded by 5 U.S.C.S. § 552(b)(7)(C), FOIA's Exemption 7(C), against disclosure of law enforcement information on the ground that it would constitute an unwarranted invasion of personal pri-vacy, did not extend to a corporation, as "personal" ordinarily referred to individuals.

***Berghuis* v. *Thompkins*, 130 S. Ct. 2250 (U.S. 2010).** Where petitioner inmate did not say that he wanted to remain silent or that he did not want to talk with the police, he did not invoke his rights. Had he made either of those simple, unambiguous state-ments, he would have invoked his right to cut off questioning. He did neither, so he did not invoke his right to remain silent. There was no basis to conclude that he did not understand his rights; and it followed that he chose not to invoke or rely on those rights when he did speak. His answer to a detective's ques-tion about whether the inmate prayed to God for for-giveness for shooting the victim was a course of conduct indicating waiver of the right to remain si-lent. If the inmate wanted to remain silent, he could have said nothing in response to the detective's ques-tions, or he could have unambiguously invoked his *Miranda* rights and ended the interrogation. The fact that the inmate made the statement about three hours after receiving a *Miranda* warning did not overcome the fact that he engaged in a course of conduct indi-cating waiver. There was no evidence that the state-ment was coerced. It was not reasonably likely that a jury instruction would have made any difference in light of all the other evidence of guilt.

Hiibel v. *Sixth Judicial District Court of Nevada* 542 U.S. 177 (2004)

When an officer approaches you and asked for identi-fication, are you required to provide identification?

A police officer responded to a call reporting that a man assaulted a woman. The officer found defendant standing outside a parked truck with a woman inside the truck. The officer asked for defendant's identification 11 times and was refused each time. The officer ar-rested defendant. Defendant was convicted for obstruct-ing the officer in carrying out his duties under Nev. Rev. Stat. 171.12, a "stop and identify" statute that re-quired defendant to disclose only his name. The U.S. Supreme Court determined that the *Terry* stop, the re-quest for identification, and the State's requirement of a response did not contravene the guarantees of the Fourth Amendment, because the request for identity had an immediate relation to the purpose, rationale, and practical demands of the *Terry* stop. Also, the request for identification was reasonably related in scope to the circumstances which justified the *Terry* stop. The Court also determined that defendant's conviction did not vio-late the Fifth Amendment's prohibition on compelled self-incrimination, because disclosure of his name pre-sented no reasonable danger of incrimination.

Summary

- Not all searches are prohibited; only those that are unreasonable.
- The Fourth Amendment deals with the seizures of both persons and property.
- The U.S. Supreme Court imposed the Exclusionary Rule on the states in the case of *Mapp* v. *Ohio*.
- The Fruits of the Poisonous Tree Doctrine prevents the use of evidence that is tainted by illegal activities of law enforcement.
- The Fourth Amendment protects only persons, houses, papers, and effects.
- A search is a governmental intrusion into an area where a person has a reasonable expectation of privacy.
- Exceptions to the Fourth Amendment include consent, the Plain View Doctrine, and open fields.
- A person has no reasonable expectation of privacy in property that the person has abandoned.
- There is a lesser expectation of privacy when dealing with vehicles.

- The federal government does not recognize an expectation of privacy in business, financial, telephone, and post office box records.
- There is a lesser standard of probable cause for inspections and regulatory searches.
- The Supreme Court has upheld the use of sobriety checkpoints.
- There are two parts to the Fourth Amendment; the Warrant Clause and the Probable Cause Clause.
- State constitutions and statutes may provide greater protections to an individual than are provided by federal law.
- Only a neutral and detached magistrate may issue a valid search warrant.
- The general rule is that to conduct a search, you must get a warrant unless you cannot.
- A general search warrant is illegal.
- The search warrant must specifically describe the place to be searched and the items to be seized.

Review Questions

1. Explain the purpose of the Fourth Amendment. Is it an absolute bar to all searches? Why? Why not?
2. What principle is the Exclusionary Rule based upon? Does it work? Can you list other ways that the objective of the Exclusionary Rule could be accomplished?
3. What is the zone of privacy? How does it work? Does it attach to places or persons?

4. List some of the exceptions to the Fourth Amendment. Which one is the most important in your opinion?
5. Describe the requirements for the issuance of a search warrant. Which one is the most important and which is the least important? Justify your answer.

Endnotes

1. Wayne LaFave et al., *Criminal Procedure,* 3rd ed. (St. Paul: West), 2000.
2. 232 U.S. 383 (1914).
3. 338 U.S. 25 (1949).
4. 367 U.S. 643 (1961).
5. 468 U.S. 897 (1984).
6. 468 U.S. 981 (1984).
7. *Silverhorne Lumber Co.* v. *United States*, 251 U.S. 385 (1920).
8. 371 U.S. 471 (1963).
9. 542 U.S. 630 (2004).
10. *Hudson* v. *Michigan*, 547 U.S. 586 (2006).
11. See *Silverman* v. *United States,* 365 U.S. 505 (1961).
12. 389 U.S. 347 (1967).

13. National Crime Prevention Council website, www. ncpc.org (accessed May 5, 2008).
14. *Schneckloth* v. *Bustamonte*, 412 U.S. 218 (1973).
15. Ibid.
16. See, for example, *On Lee* v. U.S., 343 U.S. 747 (1952) and *Hoffa* v. U.S., 385 U.S. 293 (1966).
17. *United States* v. *Matlock*, 415 U.S. 164 (1974).
18. 547 U.S. 103; (2006).
19. 496 U.S. 128 (1983).
20. There are some situations in which police officers may enter the house without a warrant, but these are exceptions to the general rule.
21. Supreme Court of Hawaii; 67 Haw. 181; 683 P.2d 822; 1984 Haw. LEXIS 107.

22. 476 U.S. 207 (1986).
23. *Florida* v. *Riley*, 488 U.S. 445 (1989).
24. *Abel* v. *United States,* 362 U.S. 217 (1960).
25. 486 U.S. 35 (1988).
26. *Abel* v. *United States,* 362 U.S. 217 (1960).
27. 265 U.S. 57 (1924).
28. 466 U.S. 170 (1984).
29. *People* v. *Chapman,* 36 Cal.3d 98 (1984).
30. 129 S.Ct. 1710, 1719, 173 L. Ed. 2d 485 (2009)
31. 125 S.Ct. 834 (2005).
32. *United States* v. *Flores-Montano*, 541 U.S. 149 (2004).
33. *Thornton* v. *United States*, 541 U.S. 615 (2004).
34. 460 U.S. 276 (1983).
35. 468 U.S. 705 (1984).
36. U.S. Court of Appeals, 11th Cir. 2004; 385 F.3d 1347; 2004 U.S. App. LEXIS 20293.
37. 122 S.Ct. 2559 (2002).
38. 515 U.S. 646 (1995).
39. 469 U.S. 325 (1985).
40. *Illinois* v. *Lidster*, 540 U.S. 419 (2004).
41. *Illinois* v. *Caballes*, 543 U.S. 405 (2005).
42. 496 U.S. 4 (1993).
43. 106 N.M. 644 (1987).
44. See *Camara* v. *Municipal Court,* 387 U.S. 523 (1967).
45. 400 U.S. 309 (1971).
46. 431 U.S. 606 (1977).
47. *United States* v. *Flores-Montano*, 541 U.S. 149 (2004).
48. *Sitz* v. *Department of State Police*, 443 Mich. 744 (1993).
49. *Massachusetts* v. *Upton*, 466 U.S. 727 (1984).
50. 378 U.S. 108 (1964).
51. 462 U.S. 213 (1983).
52. 438 U.S. 154 (1978).
53. 275 U.S. 192 (1927).
54. 403 U.S. 443 (1971).
55. *Muehler* v. *Mena*, 544 U.S. 93 (2005).
56. *L.A. County* v. *Rettele*, 127 S.Ct. 1989 (2007).
57. 547 U.S. 90 (2006).
58. 165 S.W.3d 393; 2005 Tex. App. LEXIS 2229 (2005).

CHAPTER 3

Arrest and Custody

> He always has an alibi, and one or two to spare: At whatever time the deed
> took place—Macavity wasn't there.
>
> —T. S. ELIOT, "MACAVITY: THE MYSTERY CAT" (1939)

Chapter Outline

Arrest of the Law Violator

Arrests and Warrants

Stop and Frisk and Other Detentions

Territorial Jurisdiction to Make
    an Arrest

Force in Effecting an Arrest

Miranda and Its Effect

Immunity from Arrest

Booking

Issuance of a Citation

Summons

Case Law

Summary

Key Terms

Arrest

Booking

Consular immunity

Diplomatic immunity

Legislative immunity

Miranda warning

Private person arrest

Reasonable suspicion

Resisting arrest

Stop and frisk

Summons

Temporary detention

Terry stop

Terry-type stop

Learning Objectives

After completing this chapter, you should be able to:

- Summarize the issues involving stop and frisk.
- Explain the requirements of a valid arrest.
- Summarize the issues involving force in making an arrest.

- Describe the situations in which warrantless arrests may be made.

- Describe the booking, citation, and summons processes.

- Describe the immunities from arrest.

- Illustrate the *Miranda* requirements.

- Discuss the issue of using force in making an arrest.

- Explain the concept of territorial jurisdiction to make an arrest.

- Explain the protections granted an out-of-state witness.

- Define terms related to stops and arrests.

ARREST OF THE LAW VIOLATOR

Under the Fourth Amendment, there are three distinct levels of interaction between the police and an individual[1]:

- Consensual encounters
- Detentions
- Arrests

Consensual encounters occur when the individual is not detained by the police and the police have not in any manner indicated that the individual is not free to terminate the encounter and leave. If the police temporarily restrict the freedom of the individual, the actions of the police may constitute a detention. To constitute a detention, the police must have communicated in some manner, oral or by actions, which would leave a reasonable person to believe that he or she is not free to leave. Generally, before the police may effect a lawful detention, the officers need to possess a reasonable suspicion that the person may be involved in criminal behavior. The two most common types of detention are the pedestrian stop (*Terry* v. *Ohio*) and the vehicle stop (*U.S.* v. *Hensley*).

An arrest generally involves a person being taken into custody. Typically the taking is by physical restraint (handcuffs or caging) or by informing the person that he or she is under arrest. To constitute a valid warrantless arrest, the police need probable cause (PC). Rutledge notes that it is common for officers to refer to their "PC for the stop" which is a misnomer.[2] For consensual encounters there is no need for any justification. For detention stops, the police need at least reasonable suspicions based on articulable facts; and for an arrest, the officers need PC.

When a person violates a criminal law, society's traditions generally demand that society should take some action against that person: An **arrest** should be made. Originally, the members or citizens of society were responsible for taking the violator into custody. In fact, it was such a responsibility for members of society to make the arrest that failure to do so was a violation. Even withholding information about a known crime from the authorities was a violation. In both instances, the violation was called a misprision of a felony. As law enforcement agencies were created, the citizen was relieved of much of the responsibility for making arrests. Yet the citizen, or private person, has not given up the right to make a **private person arrest**.

Private Person Arrest

A private person arrest is an arrest performed by a civilian who lacks official government authority to make an arrest (as opposed to an officer of the law).

The arrest by a private person is sometimes referred to as a citizen's arrest, but the private person does not have to be a citizen to make an arrest. The right to make an arrest by a private person can be traced back to early English common law. Historically, before the modern infrastructure of police departments, "citizen's arrests" were an important part of community law enforcement. Today, arrests by private persons are legal in every state, although state laws pertaining to the requirements for arrests are not uniform.

The private person may make arrests under certain conditions, which are restrictive in order to discourage the private person from making unnecessary arrests. Arrests should be made by the professional, that is, the law enforcement officer. Even though arrests by a private person are discouraged, thousands of private person arrests are made annually in this country. These arrests are made primarily by security guards employed by private companies to curb shoplifting and employee thefts. The records of one drug store chain indicate that the security guards of that chain average more than 12,000 private person arrests annually. It is important, therefore, that the private person know his or her rights and limitations in making a private person arrest. A private person arrest generally requires that the crime for which the arrest is made has been committed or attempted in the presence of the arresting person. The statutes of some states provide for the arrest of a felon even though the crime occurred in the absence of the private party. A felony must have been committed, and the private person must have had reasonable cause to believe that the person arrested committed the felony.

Although the powers of arrest and the procedure in making arrests may have been covered in other areas of study, a brief discussion of arrests is useful because of their importance in the prosecution of cases. If an arrest is not made lawfully, any information learned or physical evidence obtained will in most instances be inadmissible in court. In *Legrand* v. *Bedinger,* the court stated the following:

> The term "arrest" is derived from the French, arrester, to stop or stay, and signifies a restraint of a man's person; depriving him of his own will and liberty, and binding him to become obedient to the will of the law. It is called the beginning of imprisonment.[3]

Legally, an arrest has been defined as the taking of a person into custody in the manner authorized by law. The arrest is made by actual restraint of the person or by submission of the offender to the custody of an officer. The person arrested may be subjected to such restraint as is reasonable for the arrest and detention. There must be sufficient probable cause for the arrest to be made. Briefly, it has been held that probable, or reasonable, cause is shown if a person of ordinary prudence would be led to believe that a crime had been committed. Reasonable cause may exist even though there may be some room for doubt, but it must be more than a mere suspicion that a crime had been committed. It is difficult to set forth guidelines in determining probable cause. One might ask what facts would cause an ordinary, prudent person to believe that a crime had been committed. The test for probable cause must be determined by the circumstances of each individual case on the basis of the situation confronting the officer at the time that the arrest is made. The ordinary, prudent person test has been criticized as being unrealistic because the officer, through training and experience, could recognize certain facts that would cause him or her to believe that a crime had been committed. Such facts may not be of a suspicious nature to the ordinary, prudent person. Yet the courts have consistently adhered to this test. However, most courts will consider the facts as seen by the officer before dismissing a charge because of lack of probable cause.

Arrest by a Law Enforcement Officer

We should define the terms "law enforcement officer" or "peace officer" before continuing this discussion. A law enforcement officer or peace officer is a person employed by some branch of the government and is sworn to uphold the laws of the United States and the state, county, or city by which he or she is employed. The statutes of some states specifically spell out who are law enforcement or peace officers within that state; if not listed in the statutes, a person is not a law enforcement officer within that state. Law enforcement or peace officers may be placed in four basic categories: federal officers, employed by the U.S. government; state officers, employed by the state; sheriffs, employed by the county or parish; and city police officers, employed by their respective cities.

ARRESTS AND WARRANTS

As we indicated earlier, the Fourth Amendment protects against unreasonable searches and seizures. This language makes it clear that the amendment applies both to searches of persons and places and to arrests of persons. An arrest may be made in two ways: with or without a warrant. As indicated, in both situations the arresting officer must have probable cause to arrest. There are two elements to probable cause to arrest: (1) there is reason to believe that a crime has been committed and (2) the person to be arrested committed the offense.[4]

Arrest without a Warrant

An arrest without a warrant is the most common form of arrest. Historically, warrantless arrests have always been allowed under the common law. The courts have held that requiring a warrant for every arrest is impractical.[5] However, there is one situation in which an arrest warrant is required. The Supreme Court held that unless there are exigent or emergency circumstances or consent, the police may not enter a private home to make a warrantless arrest.[6]

The courts have held that entry into a home is an extreme intrusion and that entry to make an arrest is very similar to entry to search a home; therefore, the Fourth Amendment requires that a neutral magistrate make a determination that there is probable cause to make the arrest before such an intrusion is allowed. The exception to this warrant requirement is exigent or emergency circumstances. Courts have ruled that fresh or hot pursuit of a suspect as he or she runs into a home does not require a warrant.[7] Additionally, if the police believe that if they wait for the issuance of a warrant the suspect will destroy the evidence, they may enter and make an arrest without a warrant.[8]

ATWATER V. *CITY OF LAGO VISTA*, 532 U.S. 318 (2001)

Gail Atwater was driving her pickup truck in Lago Vista, Texas, with her three-year-old son and five-year-old daughter in the front seat. None of them was wearing a seatbelt. A Lago Vista police officer observed the seatbelt violations and pulled Gail Atwater over. According to Atwater's complaint, the officer approached the truck and "yelled" something to the effect of "we've met before" and "you're going to jail." He then called for backup and asked to see Atwater's driver's license and insurance documentation, which state law required her to carry. Atwater was charged with driving without her seatbelt fastened, failing to secure her children in seatbelts, driving without a license, and failing to provide proof of insurance. She ultimately pleaded no contest to the misdemeanor seatbelt offenses and paid a $50 fine; the other charges were dismissed.

Atwater asked to take her "frightened, upset, and crying" children to a friend's house nearby, but the officer told her, "you're not going anywhere." As it turned out, Atwater's friend learned what was going on and soon arrived to take charge of the children. The officer then handcuffed Atwater, placed her in his squad car, and drove her to the local police station, where booking officers had her remove her shoes, jewelry, and eyeglasses, and empty her pockets. Officers took Atwater's "mug shot" and placed her, alone, in a jail cell for *about one hour, after which she was taken before a magistrate and released on $310 bond. She sued the city and the officer for false arrest.*

In Texas, if a car is equipped with safety belts, a front-seat passenger must wear one, Tex. Tran. Code Ann. §545.413(a), and the driver must secure any small child riding in front, §545.413(b). Violation of either provision is a misdemeanor punishable by a fine not less than $25 or more than $50, §545.413(d). Texas law expressly authorizes any peace officer to arrest without warrant a person found committing a violation of these seatbelt laws, §543.001, although it permits police to issue citations in lieu of arrest.

Justice SOUTER delivered the opinion of the Court:

"The question is whether the Fourth Amendment forbids a warrantless arrest for a minor criminal offense, such as a misdemeanor seatbelt violation punishable only by a fine. We hold that it does not. The Fourth Amendment, as originally understood, did not forbid peace officers to arrest without a warrant for misdemeanors not amounting to or involving breach of the peace."

Arrest with a Warrant

Even though officers may arrest a suspect without a warrant, there is legal preference for arrests made with a warrant. This is the case because it places the determination of finding of the existence of probable cause in the hands of a neutral magistrate. The Supreme Court, though upholding warrantless arrests, has stated that the deliberate determination of magistrates is preferred over the hurried actions of police officers.[9]

An arrest warrant is a written order issued by the proper judicial officer upon showing of probable cause commanding the arrest of a particular person. Arrest warrants must conform to certain requirements. Although these vary from jurisdiction to jurisdiction, most warrants require the following information:

- The caption or title of the court from which the warrant is issued.
- The name of the person to be arrested. The warrant must describe with particularity the person to be seized. (Many warrants also require a detailed description of the person, including height, weight, and hair color.)
- A description of the offense. This normally is described in the language of the statute or law that the suspect violated.
- The date of issuance of the warrant.
- A command that officers take the suspect into custody and bring him or her before the proper judicial officer.
- The signature of the issuing official.

Many states require officers to have warrants of arrest for misdemeanors committed outside of their presence. This circumstance usually means that the officer must witness the criminal act. The officer doesn't have to see the offense; the courts have ruled that use of any of the officer's senses is sufficient. The officer may hear the offense (sounds of gunfire) or even smell the offense (marijuana burning). Recently, some states have enacted statutory exceptions to this requirement. Most notable is the duty of officers to arrest suspects in domestic violence cases, even if the officer did not see the suspect strike the victim.

Some jurisdictions allow for the use of telephonic arrest warrants. These warrants are most often used after normal working hours and when it is considered necessary to arrest the suspect immediately. In these jurisdictions, officers telephone a prosecuting attorney and explain why they need a warrant. The prosecutor then calls a judge at his or her home, who listens to the officer's testimony over the phone. The judge may authorize the issuance of a warrant and direct the officer to fill in the blanks on the warrant and print the judge's name. A copy of this warrant is then given to the judge when he or she comes to work.

STOP AND FRISK AND OTHER DETENTIONS

Until 1967, a search was an all-or-nothing concept. Either it was a search subject to the probable cause and warrant requirements or it was not a search. This situation often was referred to as the bright-line approach. In 1967 and 1968, the Supreme Court devised nontraditional definitions of probable cause on the basis of the concept of a floating reasonableness standard. The 1967 case of *Camara* v. *Municipal Court of the City and County of San Francisco*[10] involved administrative inspections. The 1968 case was *Terry* v. *Ohio.*[11] *Terry* developed the concept of searches of differential intrusiveness, and in those cases in which the intrusiveness is minimal, the standard of "**reasonable suspicion**" was deemed sufficient. The Supreme Court in *Terry* stated that "there is no ready test for determining the reasonableness other than by balancing the need to search against the invasion which the search entails. The procedures used by the police in these situations must be governed by the exigencies which justify its initiation."

The *Terry* case developed the concept of **stop and frisk**. A stop and frisk is less than an arrest. The rules applying to **temporary detention** also apply to stop-and-frisk situations. It was a standard police practice to stop suspicious persons in public places for the purposes of questioning them or conducting an investigation. Until the *Terry* case, there was a question as to whether this procedure constituted a violation of the Fourth Amendment, since the officers generally do not have probable cause to detain and question the individuals. As noted, the stop is not an arrest and the frisk is not a search but a pat-down for the officer's safety. Despite these facts, the stop-and-frisk doctrine is discussed in this chapter on arrest and custody as a matter of convenience.

In *Terry* v. *Ohio,* an officer observed Terry and two other men walking back and forth in front of a store. The officer decided that the men were casing the store for a possible robbery. When he approached them and asked for identification, he received only mumbled replies. He then grabbed Terry, turned him around, and patted him down. The officer found a pistol in Terry's pocket. Terry, an ex-convict, was arrested for carrying a concealed weapon. The Court upheld the search and found no Fourth Amendment violation.

The Court held that a police officer may temporarily detain a person for questioning if the officer has a reasonable suspicion that criminal activity may be involved. The officer may pat down the person for weapons only if the officer has the additional reasonable suspicion that the pat down is necessary for safety reasons. If, during the pat-down for weapons, the officer feels a weapon on the individual, the officer then has probable cause to conduct a complete search.

Law in Practice

Differences Between an Arrest and a *Terry*-Type Stop

	Formal Arrest	*Terry* Stop
Justification required	Probable cause to believe that the person to be arrested has committed or is committing a crime.	Reasonable suspicion supported by articulable facts that criminal activity is ongoing.
Warrant	Warrant is preferred but not required unless there is a requirement to enter a private home.	None needed.
Notice	Officer is required to notify the person to be arrested that he or she is under arrest.	No special notice required.
Time requirement	No time limits as long as the warrant has not been withdrawn.	Stop must be temporary and no longer than necessary to effectuate the purpose of the stop.
Extent of search allowed	Full body search and search of the area immediately surrounding the area where the person is arrested is allowed.	Officer may pat down the individual for a weapon only if the officer has reason to believe that the individual may be armed.

Temporary Detention

Mere temporary detention for questioning is not considered to be an arrest.[12] If, however, police restraint goes beyond that which is reasonably necessary for questioning, an arrest may result. For example, handcuffing an alleged drug dealer and moving to another area of the airport for questioning is considered to be an arrest.[13]

A temporary detention of a vehicle is less than a full arrest, and, accordingly, the level of probable cause necessary to support a temporary detention is less than that required for a full arrest. A detention starts the moment that the officer directs the vehicle to stop—for example, when an officer turns on the red lights. It is not a detention if the vehicle is already parked and the officer asks the driver for his or her license or other identification.[14]

Reasonable Suspicion

A detention requires at least reasonable suspicion. (*Note:* Reasonable suspicion is less than probable cause. The officer must have reasonable suspicion that criminal activity is occurring, is about to occur, or has recently occurred and that the vehicle or a person in the vehicle is connected with that criminal activity.) The reasonable suspicion must be based on specific facts that can be articulated to a court. If the suspicion relates to any person in the vehicle (including a passenger), the officer may stop the vehicle.

In *People* v. *Remiro,*[15] a state appellate court upheld the stopping of the vehicle on the basis of the officer's reasonable suspicion. In this case, the officer saw a van he did not recognize that was driving slowly in a residential neighborhood at 1:30 a.m. The officer followed the van and noticed that it was traveling in a circle. He stopped the van. His stop was upheld on the basis of the following articulable facts:

1. The van's speed and route were suggestive of a casing operation.
2. The officer was familiar with the neighborhood, its vehicles, and its driving patterns.
3. He did not recognize the vehicle.
4. He knew that many residential burglaries had occurred in the neighborhood.
5. He knew that vans were frequently used in such burglaries.

In *People* v. *Dominguez,*[16] a state court upheld a detention of the vehicle when the identities of the persons within the vehicle were unknown and a warrant existed for the registered owner. The court indicated that if none of the people could be the registered owner, that is, of a different race, then the legality of the detention would be questionable. While the *Remiro* and *Dominguez* cases are controlling only in California, their rationale appears to be accepted by most other states.

A stop based on a "wanted flyer" or a similar notice or bulletin issued by another jurisdiction and related to completed criminal activity is sufficient basis to detain a vehicle and its occupants if the other jurisdiction had a valid basis to issue the flyer, and so forth.[17]

Distinguishing an Arrest from a *Terry*-Type Detention

Often it is necessary to distinguish an arrest from a stop-and-frisk situation, especially if evidence is found during the detention. The leading Supreme Court decision on this question is *United States* v. *Sharp.*[18] In that case, the length of the detention was considered. The Court indicated that a *Terry*-**type stop** will ordinarily be for a fairly short duration and that the detention will be no longer than necessary to effectuate the purpose of the detention. Other factors considered include the following: Did the police pursue the investigation diligently? Was the method of investigation likely to confirm or dispel the officer's suspicions quickly?

A warrantless protective sweep of a residence by the police who are making a lawful arrest in the residence is considered to be legal if the police have a reasonable suspicion that the residence may contain an individual who poses a danger to the officers or to others.[19] The protective sweep should be a quick and limited search of the premises and narrowly confined to a cursory visual inspection of those places where an individual may be hiding.

When an individual is arrested, the officer may search the individual based solely on the fact of a legal arrest. In a *Terry* stop, the officer may only pat-down the individual for presence of weapons and only if the officer has reasonable suspicion that the individual may be a danger to the officer or others.

Law in Practice

Frisking for Weapons

While the U.S. Supreme Court approved the "stop and frisk" in the 1968 case of *Terry* v. *Ohio*, it should be pointed out that while it is common to pair the terms "stop and frisk" that they are two different concepts. Each has different standards. A "stop" is a temporary detention of a person, and a frisk is a limited search of the stopped person's outer clothes for a weapon. A stop is justifiable if there is a reasonable suspicion that the person is involved in criminal activity. A frisk is justifiable only if there is reason to believe that the person may be armed and is dangerous.

Arizona v. *Johnson,* 129 S.Ct. 781 (2009): Lemon Johnson was a passenger in a car stopped by Tucson police officers. The vehicle was stopped because of a vehicle registration violation. Johnson was wearing Crips colors including a blue bandana. He had a scanner in his pocket, which suggested that he was monitoring police traffic. This information suggested that the occupants of the car were engaged in some kind of illegal activity. Johnson disclosed to the officers that he had served time in prison for robbery and gave an address in a Crips area. One of the officers ordered Johnson to step out of the car. She then patted down his outer clothing and discovered a handgun. Since Johnson was a convicted felon, the possession of the handgun was a felony. The Arizona state appellate court held that the officer had no right to question and then frisk Johnson.

On appeal to the U.S. Supreme Court, the Court reversed the state court's ruling that the frisk violated the Fourth Amendment to the U.S. Constitution. [Note: Had the state court ruled that the frisk violated the state constitution, then the U.S. Supreme Court would not have had jurisdiction to overrule that determination.]

The Court noted that all passengers in a stopped vehicle are necessarily detained during a traffic stop. The Court stated that a lawful roadside stop begins when a vehicle is pulled over for investigation of a traffic violation. It ends when the police no longer have need to control the scene and allow the driver and passengers to leave.

An officer's inquiries into an unrelated matter did not make the stop illegal as long as those inquiries did not measurably extend the duration of the stop. The Supreme Court remanded the case to the state court for the state court to determine if the officer had reasonable suspicion to frisk Johnson.

Pennsylvania v. *Mimms,* 434 U.S. 106 (1977): In *Mimms,* the U.S. Supreme Court noted that statistics indicated that 30 percent of the officers shot in the line of duty were shot as they approached a vehicle. The Court held that when officers make a traffic stop, they may routinely order the driver out of the car without giving any reason.

Maryland v. *Wilson,* 519 U.S. 408 (1997): The Supreme Court extended the *Mimms* rule to passengers and held that all passengers in a lawfully stopped vehicle may be ordered out of the vehicle without giving any reason.

TERRITORIAL JURISDICTION TO MAKE AN ARREST

From a procedural standpoint, it is important to determine if an officer has the authority to make an arrest, particularly when he or she has no warrant. If the officer does not have the authority, the arrest will be declared unlawful. One factor that becomes significant in determining the officer's authority is whether the officer was in his or her territorial jurisdiction. In most states, the territorial jurisdiction of the city police is confined to the city limits. Any arrest without a warrant made beyond the city limits would have to be made as a private person and meet the restrictions of a private person arrest. Similarly, the territorial authority of the sheriff of a county or parish is limited to the county or parish line. Some states limit the jurisdiction of the sheriff within the county, allowing arrests only in unincorporated areas. These states remove the sheriff's authority to make arrests within an incorporated city. However, in most states the sheriff is considered to be the chief law enforcement officer of the county and has authority to make arrests anyplace within the county. The sheriff, when within city limits, would have concurrent authority with the city police.

It was held for a long time that if an outlaw was able to outdistance a sheriff to the county line, the sheriff had to discontinue the pursuit since he had no authority to make an arrest in the adjoining county. To prevent the escape of an outlaw under these circumstances, the hot pursuit rule was developed. This rule provided that if an officer was in hot or fresh pursuit of an offender, the officer could follow the offender into another jurisdiction to make an arrest. The problem presented by this rule was: What would be interpreted as fresh pursuit? In early times when the local officer made the pursuit on horseback, it was concluded that if the officer could keep the outlaw in sight or still see the dust kicked up by the outlaw's horse, the officer was in fresh pursuit. With the advent of the motor vehicle as a means of escape, as well as pursuit, the in sight theory became impractical. Therefore, it is generally held today that if a pursuit is uninterrupted and continuous, it is a fresh pursuit. But even with this concept of fresh pursuit, the local officer had no authority to cross a state line to make an arrest. Thus, if the fleeing offender was able to reach the state line before apprehension, he or she had sanctuary in the next state. With rapid transportation available to criminals, new rules and regulations concerning the extent of pursuit had to be formulated.

Uniform Act of Fresh Pursuit

Today, most states have adopted what is known as the Uniform Act of Fresh Pursuit. This act provides that a peace officer of one state may enter another state in fresh pursuit to arrest an offender who has committed a felony in the state from which he or she fled. In adopting the Uniform Act of Fresh Pursuit, a few states have made the act applicable not only to felonies but also to certain misdemeanors, usually those involving moral turpitude. Moral turpitude has been defined as conduct contrary to justice, honesty, modesty, or good morals. There is no specific distance set forth in the act that the officer may travel within the state in order to make the arrest. The act does provide that after the arrest is made, the officer must take the arrested person before a local magistrate, without unnecessary delay, for a hearing to determine the lawfulness of the arrest. If the magistrate concludes that the arrest was lawful, the magistrate will either commit the accused or release him or her on bail pending extradition proceedings.

Limited Arrest Powers

A few states do grant local officers the right to make an arrest without a warrant anywhere in the state. This right is based on the theory that, when sworn as a peace officer within a city or county, the officer swears to uphold the constitution and laws of the state as well as local ordinances, thereby giving the officer statewide arrest powers. But as stated, in most states the local officer has authority to make arrests without a warrant only within the territorial jurisdiction in which he or she is employed, except in fresh pursuit instances. Some people in the justice system believe that this limited arrest power by local officers hampers law enforcement. As a result, statutes have been passed in some states extending the arrest power of local officers.

Although extended authority differs among states, the power to make arrests without a warrant beyond the territorial area in which an officer is employed is usually confined to one of three situations. Authority has been granted in some states permitting an officer to make a lawful arrest beyond the officer's area if the officer has prior permission from the chief or sheriff of the area in which the arrest is to be made. This granted authority is based upon an old posse comitatus right of a sheriff. The posse comitatus right came into being early in the history of this country and particularly in the western part of the United States. The sheriff was often the only law enforcement officer within the county and therefore frequently needed assistance in locating and apprehending a criminal. To obtain this assistance, the sheriff was authorized by law to call on citizens of the county and deputize them to assist in the location and apprehension of a dangerous felon. These deputies were formed into a posse. Under posse comitatus, the officer making the arrest, in a sense, is a temporary officer of the jurisdiction in which the arrest is made. Further, the right to make an arrest beyond the officer's area of employment has been granted in instances when the offender is wanted for a crime committed in the officer's area of employment. In other instances, authority has been granted to an officer to make arrests beyond the officer's jurisdiction with extended private person arrest power. This extended right permits the officer to arrest a person who has committed a crime or where there is reasonable cause to believe that a crime was committed in the presence of the officer and that lives may be in danger, property may be immediately damaged, or the offender may escape.

State Police Agencies

All states except Hawaii have some type of state police or law enforcement system. The state police agencies have statewide territorial jurisdiction, but states vary considerably in the power of the state police to make arrests. In some states, the state police have the power to enforce all state laws and have concurrent power throughout the state with local law enforcement agencies. In other states, the state police have limited jurisdiction that confines them to enforcing criminal laws only on state property. In addition to the state police, a number of investigative agencies in most states have limited authority and arrest powers and are employed to perform specific duties. Examples of persons with limited investigative authority and arrest powers are game wardens and drug law administrators. In some states, the state police not only enforce state laws generally but also patrol the highways; other states have a separate agency for this purpose: a highway patrol. Although the territorial jurisdiction of state police is restricted to the state boundaries, the Uniform Act of Fresh Pursuit is applicable to these agencies as well as to local officers.

Federal Law Enforcement Agencies

Technically, the only peace officers of the U.S. government are the U.S. marshals within the Department of Justice. But as with the states, a number of federal investigative agencies have emergency arrest powers. All federal officers have territorial jurisdiction throughout the United States and its possessions. Also within the U.S. Department of Justice is the Federal Bureau of Investigation (FBI), which was established in 1908, and has investigative jurisdiction over all federal violations not specifically assigned to some other federal agency. The FBI began in 1908 as the Bureau of Investigation.[20] It was created in part because of other law enforcement agencies' inability to investigate and arrest corrupt politicians and business leaders. The Bureau began as a small organization; however, it grew and became a household name under the guidance of J. Edgar Hoover. The FBI investigates a wide range of violations. Examples of FBI investigations include bank robberies; kidnapping when the victim has been, or is presumed to have been, transported across a state line; theft from interstate shipment; internal security matters; and interstate organized crime activities.

Within the U.S. Treasury Department is the Secret Service, created in 1865 to investigate and curtail counterfeiting of U.S. currency. After the assassination of President William McKinley in 1901, the Secret Service was charged with the duty of protecting the president of the United States. This duty has been expanded to include not only the president but also his immediate family, certain other high governmental officials, and some foreign dignitaries. Other agencies within the U.S. Treasury Department are the Customs and Border Protection Service; the Alcohol, Tobacco, and Firearms Service; the Internal Revenue Service; and the U.S. Postal Service. Among the duties of the Customs and Border Protection Service are investigations of smuggling operations. The Alcohol, Tobacco, and Firearms Service investigates violations pertaining to the illegal manufacture of alcoholic beverages, illegal possession of certain firearms, and tobacco infractions. The Internal Revenue Service oversees the collection of federal income taxes and violations of federal income tax law. U.S. Postal Service inspectors investigate violations pertaining to the mail, such as use of the mails to defraud and mail theft. There are a number of other investigative agencies of the federal government, but the foregoing are the ones most frequently encountered in law enforcement.

After the terrorist attacks of September 11, 2001, and in response to a number of factors, President George W. Bush created the Office of Homeland Security. He appointed Tom Ridge as its first director. The office was later replaced by the U.S. Department of Homeland Security (DHS). Many of the federal law enforcement agencies were placed under the DHS, the mission of which is to do the following:

- Prevent terrorist attacks within the United States;
- reduce America's vulnerability to terrorism; and
- minimize the damage and recover from attacks that do occur.

The Department of Homeland Security has four divisions:

> ***Border and Transportation Security.*** The department is responsible for securing our nation's borders and transportation systems, managing who and what enters our homeland, and working to prevent the entry of terrorists and the instruments of terrorism while ensuring the speedy flow of legitimate traffic.

> ***Emergency Preparedness and Response.*** The department will ensure the preparedness of our nation's emergency response professionals, provide the federal government's response, and aid America's recovery from terrorist attacks and natural disasters.

> ***Chemical, Biological, Radiological, and Nuclear Countermeasures.*** The department leads the federal government's efforts in preparing for and responding to the full range of terrorist threats involving weapons of mass destruction.

> ***Information Analysis and Infrastructure Protection.*** The department merges under one roof the capability to identify and assess current and future threats to the homeland, map those threats against our current vulnerabilities, inform the president, issue timely warnings, and immediately take or effect appropriate preventive and protective action.

FORCE IN EFFECTING AN ARREST

The laws of the states are comparatively uniform as to the amount of force that may be used by a peace officer in making an arrest, but there seems to be some doubt as to the degree of force that may be used by a private person. The statutes of most states provide that any peace officer who has reasonable cause to believe that the person to be arrested has committed a public offense may use reasonable force to effect the arrest, to prevent escape, or to overcome resistance. It is also generally held that the officer may break open a door or window of a house in which the person to be arrested is, or is believed to be, located. Unless there is a danger to the life of the officer or others, the officer must first demand admittance and explain the purpose for which the admittance is desired.

Although the officer may use whatever force is reasonably necessary to overcome the resistance of the accused, the officer may not use force that is disproportionate to the resistance met. If undue force is used, the officer could be guilty of violating the civil rights of the accused and be prosecuted in a federal court under the Civil Rights Acts (see Title 18 U.S. Code, section 242, and Title 42 U.S. Code, section 1983). That is exactly what happened in *Tennessee* v. *Garner.*[21] In that case, Memphis police officers responded to a call of a burglary in progress. One of the officers went into the backyard of the house and saw Edward Garner flee from the house and attempt to climb a chain-link fence. The officer fired his weapon and killed the suspect. The perpetrator's father filed a federal civil rights lawsuit, and the U.S. Supreme Court held that the use of deadly force was a form of seizure protected by the Fourth Amendment and that it was unreasonable under these circumstances. The Court reasoned that the officer was not in fear for his safety and had no evidence that the suspect was armed or a danger to any other person. In its opinion in the *Garner* case, the Court created a new rule concerning the use of deadly force in an attempt to arrest an individual suspected of having committed a serious felony. The Court concluded that the use of deadly force while attempting to make an arrest or prevent an escape can be justified only as an absolute last resort if there are no other means of apprehending the felon and the failure to stop the felon creates a serious risk of bodily injury or death to others.

Whether excessive force was used in a particular instance is a matter of fact that would be determined by some board of inquiry, jury, or judge. The question to be determined is whether the force used was that which an ordinary, prudent person would have used under the circumstances. Any mistreatment of an accused person once he or she is under control could also be a violation of the accused's civil rights. In addition to having violated the federal laws on civil rights, the officer could possibly be charged with assault and battery under a state statute.

FOCUS

Excessive Force and Videotapes

In March 1991, several Los Angeles police officers were videotaped beating an African American male named Rodney King with their batons as he lay on the ground. The officers were charged with state crimes and tried in a superior court in Simi Valley, a suburb of Los Angeles. The state jury acquitted the officers, and they were then tried and found guilty of the federal crime of violating Mr. King's civil rights.

The videotape that was broadcast across the world shows the officers beating Mr. King for nineteen seconds. The tape does not show that the officers had chased Mr. King for eight miles, surrounded him, and used electronic darts carrying 50,000 volts that failed to subdue him. When he ran for the nearby park, the officers began to wildly beat Mr. King. That was the portion that was captured on videotape and shocked the world.

Approximately eleven years later, on July 6, 2002, Inglewood police officers were involved in an altercation with a young African American male that was also videotaped. The tape shows the officers pulling the handcuffed male to his feet and slamming his body onto the top of the police cruiser. Officer Jeremy More is then shown striking the male with his fist as he lay on the vehicle. The officer claims that the male was squeezing his testicles, so he had to apply force to make him let go.

When should an officer be able to use force to effect an arrest?

When does force become excessive?

What can be done to prevent officers from using excessive force?

An increasing number of law enforcement agencies are using dogs to locate and capture suspects. In order to avoid a possible excessive force accusation in the capture of a suspect, the dog handler should warn the suspect that a dog will be released unless the suspect surrenders peacefully. Also, the dog should be restrained when the suspect is under control.

But what about the private person? How much force may he or she use to effect an arrest? The statutes of many states are silent on this issue. Although it is generally conceded that a private person may also use that degree of force reasonably necessary to make the arrest and to overcome resistance, most states do not give a private person the right to break into a dwelling to make an arrest for a misdemeanor violation.

Calling for Assistance

In making an arrest, an officer or a private person may call upon as many people as are deemed necessary for assistance in making the arrest. In general, no prosecutive action can be taken against anyone for refusing to assist the private person in making an arrest. However, the statute of one state provides that any person making an arrest may orally summon as many people as he or she finds necessary, and that all those failing to obey such a **summons** for assistance will be guilty of a misdemeanor. This provision implies that anyone failing to assist a private person will be subject to prosecution. Most states make it a violation for certain persons to refuse to assist an officer in making an arrest when summoned to do so. As was the case with states that allow officers to arrest outside their jurisdiction, this provision is based upon the old posse comitatus policy that a sheriff had the authority to deputize members of a community and demand that they assist him in the location and apprehension of an outlaw. In modern practice, it is not necessary in an emergency situation to deputize a person before requesting assistance. Many times an officer is confronted with circumstances in which immediate help is needed in making an arrest. Under these circumstances, an officer may orally summon those present to assist him or her, and a failure to come to the officer's aid may subject those persons to prosecution.

Law in Practice

Arrest Warrant

Scott Peterson's wife, Laci, a twenty-seven-year-old woman who was eight months pregnant, disappeared on Christmas Eve 2002, prompting a nationwide search. When her body and the body of her unborn child were found four months later, her husband was charged with two counts of murder. Scott Peterson was convicted and formally sentenced to death for the murders of the mother-to-be and the fetus. Following is a copy of the arrest warrant issued in the case.

PEOPLE OF THE STATE OF CALIFORNIA)

)

Plaintiff,)

)

vs.   )

)

<u>Scott Lee PETERSON</u>   Defendant)

**PROBABLE CAUSE
WARRANT OF ARREST**

(P.C. §5814 and §1427

Peo. v. Ramey, 16 Cal. 3rd 263;

Peo. v. Sesslin, 68 Cal. 2nd 418)

COUNTY OF STANISLAUS:
THE PEOPLE OF THE STATE OF CALIFORNIA
To any Peace Office of said State:
    Complaint upon oath having been this day made before me by Detective Craig Grogan, I find that there is probable cause to believe that two counts of the crime of: 187 PC, homicide committed on or about Monday December 23, 2002 or Tuesday December 24, 2002, in the County of Stanislaus by Scott Lee Peterson, date of birth, 10/24/72.
    YOU ARE THEREFORE COMMANDED forthwith to arrest the above-named Defendant and bring him/her before any magistrate in Stanislaus County pursuant to Penal Code Section 187.

The within named defendant may be admitted to bail in the sum of: ____*no bail*____ Dollars.
WITNESS, my hand this____*17ᵗʰ*____ day of ____*April*____ 2003.

____*(signed by judge)*____
Judge of the Superior Court
County of Stanislaus, State of California

[*Note:* The italicized words and figures were handwritten.]

States differ considerably in who must assist an officer in making an arrest. The statutes of several states provide that an officer making a lawful arrest may command the aid of every male person over eighteen years of age to assist him or her, and any male failing to obey the command for assistance shall be guilty of a misdemeanor. This provision makes no mention of the male's being "able-bodied." This provision was excluded purposely. When an officer is presented with an emergency situation, he or she should not have to spend time determining who is physically capable of providing assistance. It also prohibits an individual from using the excuse that he is not physically able to assist. Not all requests for assistance entail a physical encounter with the accused. The assistance may be only a request that the individual radio for other police units to come to the aid of an officer, a task that could be performed by a person in a wheelchair.

The statutes of some states provide that every able-bodied person over the age of eighteen years who refuses to aid an officer in making an arrest after being commanded to do so is guilty of a misdemeanor. Such a provision makes both men and women subject to prosecution should they fail to assist in making an arrest after being summoned to do so by an officer. The problem created by the provision that the person be able-bodied is how to determine whether the person summoned was able-bodied. It has been held that the mere fact that there may be some danger involved in rendering assistance is not sufficient reason to refuse to assist. The statutes of a few states provide that every person who fails to obey a command by an officer to assist him or her in making an arrest shall be guilty of a misdemeanor. Such a provision is all-encompassing, since no mention is made of the person's being able-bodied, male or female, or within a specific age designation.

The statute of one state provides that the officer requesting assistance must be in uniform for prosecutive action to be applicable. This requirement is again designed to eliminate the possibility of an individual's using the excuse that he or she did not know that the person requesting assistance was an officer. However, this restriction is not without complications. In view of the wording of the statute, even if an individual knows that the person summoning assistance is an officer, unless the officer is in uniform when summoning aid, the individual cannot be prosecuted if he or she fails to assist the officer. This provision also raises the question: What is a uniform? Some law enforcement agencies have adopted the sport coat or blazer and sport pants style of uniform, which gives the appearance of civilian clothing. Would this be considered a uniform within the meaning of the statute?

When a person responds to an officer's call or demand for assistance, he or she has the same rights and privileges as the officer. Such a person is, in effect, a temporary law enforcement officer and has the right to use reasonable force to effect the arrest. If the person called upon to assist the officer acts in good faith, he or she is protected from civil liability.[22]

Resisting Arrest

Generally, it is a violation to willfully resist, delay, or obstruct a peace officer in the performance of his or her duty, including making an arrest. Yet, may an individual who is being arrested by a private person resist that arrest without being subjected to prosecution for the resistance? Most state statutes are silent on this point. Since there is no provision that an individual can be charged with an act of **resisting arrest** by a private person, presumably one is not subject to any additional charge except the one for which the arrest is being made, and the only peril is in meeting the resistance of the private person.

In this discussion, a question regarding the right of a person to resist an unlawful arrest must also arise. As previously stated, it is generally held that resisting an officer in the performance of his or her duty is a violation. But is an officer performing his or her duty by making an unlawful arrest? It was previously held at common law that a person could resist an unlawful arrest, and this view is followed in some of the states whether the arrest is being made by an officer or a private person. This situation results in many curbside court sessions and brawls between the accused and the arresting person, with each claiming to be right and with violent resistance taking place. Other states have provided that if a person is being arrested or has reasonable cause to believe that he or she is being arrested by an officer, the person is under the duty to refrain from using force or any weapon to resist such arrest. By court interpretation, it has been held that this provision refers to unlawful arrests as well as lawful ones. Note, however, that the provision pertains only to officers and is still silent about resisting arrest by a private person.

The justifications under the common law rule allowing for individuals to resist an unlawful arrest include:

- A state may not indiscriminately take away a person's liberty.
- Citizens are responsible for governing the governors (police).
- Innocent persons may resist by virtue of the injustice attempted to be placed on them.

Although a person may not resist an unlawful arrest in most states, he or she is not without recourse. One is entitled to seek immediate release from custody by a writ of habeas corpus proceeding and may sue those responsible for the illegal arrest for damages in civil court. Once the arrest of a suspect is completed, he or she should be searched for weapons and evidence. Depending upon the circumstances of the case, it may be advisable to search the immediate area where the arrest took place for any additional evidence, including instruments that may have been used in committing the crime. A search may also be made for any hidden weapons that the suspect might use to attempt an escape or to harm the arresting officer or others. These searches are considered reasonable as incidental to the arrest because if the search were not done at the time, evidence could be lost or destroyed.

MIRANDA AND ITS EFFECT

Before the U.S. Supreme Court decided *Miranda* v. *Arizona,* confessions and the accompanying interrogations were decided on a case-by-case method.[23] This approach reviewed the circumstances surrounding the interrogation to determine whether the suspect's will was broken by the police. The interrogation was considered improper if it violated the suspect's due process rights.

Interrogation has been broadened by the courts to include not only questioning of a suspect by a law enforcement officer but to also include the functional equivalent of questioning. For example, two police officers talking to each other in the presence of a suspect in a manner designed to encourage the suspect to make a statement is considered as interrogation by the officers.

Pre-*Miranda* Techniques

In *Brown* v. *Mississippi,* the defendant was taken to the crime scene, where he was questioned regarding his involvement in a murder.[24] After denying guilt, he was hung by a rope from a tree. He continued to claim innocence and was tied to the tree and whipped. Brown was released but subsequently seized again and whipped until he finally confessed. The court held that the confession was a product of coercion and brutality and therefore violated the defendant's Fourteenth Amendment due process rights.

In *Ashcraft* v. *Tennessee,* the defendant was taken to the police station and questioned continuously for two days regarding the murder of his wife.[25] The officers questioned Ashcraft in relays because they became exhausted during the interrogation; however, the defendant was denied rest and sleep during the entire time. The court held that the prolonged interrogation of Ashcraft was coercive, and therefore the confession was involuntary and inadmissible.

In *Spano* v. *New York,* the defendant was suspected of a murder.[26] Spano informed a friend who was a rookie police officer that he had in fact killed the victim. Spano was arrested, and the rookie officer was instructed to tell Spano that he (the officer) was in trouble and might lose his job unless Spano confessed. Spano finally confessed to the killing. The Supreme Court held that the use of deception as a means of psychological pressure to obtain a confession was a violation of the defendant's constitutional rights and that therefore the confession was involuntary and suppressed.

In *Escobedo* v. *Illinois,* the defendant was arrested for murder and interrogated for several hours at the police station.[27] During the interrogation, Escobedo repeatedly requested to see his attorney, who was also at the police station demanding to see his client. The police refused both requests and finally obtained the confession. The court held that Escobedo was denied his right to counsel and that therefore no statement obtained from him could be used at a criminal trial.

Law in Practice

Handwriting Exemplars

Timothy McVeigh was arrested for bombing the Oklahoma City federal building, which caused many deaths. A federal grand jury issued a subpoena ordering him to furnish exemplars of his handwriting. He refused, contending that the subpoena was a violation of his Fifth Amendment privilege against self-incrimination.[28] As a judge, how would you rule?

The *Escobedo* decision was confusing because it is not clear when the right to counsel attaches during the interrogation. Trial courts began interpreting the meaning of *Escobedo* differently. Thus, the stage was set for the U.S. Supreme Court to clear up the confusion that had resulted from its previous rulings.

Miranda Safeguards

In *Miranda* v. *Arizona,* the U.S. Supreme Court established certain safeguards for individuals who are being interrogated by police.[29] Most people know that the *Miranda* decision requires police officers to advise suspects of their constitutional rights prior to in-custody interrogation. In reality, *Miranda* established a four-prong test that must be satisfied before a suspect's statements can be admitted into evidence. The test requires affirmative answers to all four of the following questions:

1. Was the statement voluntary?
2. Was the *Miranda* warning given?
3. Was there a waiver by the suspect?
4. Was the waiver intelligent and voluntary?

Unless all these questions are answered in the affirmative, none of the suspect's statements can be admitted into evidence. In *Miranda,* the defendant was arrested at home in Phoenix, Arizona, in connection with the rape and kidnapping of a female and was taken to a police station for questioning. At the time, he was twenty-three years old, poor, and basically illiterate. After being questioned for two hours, he confessed to the crime. The Supreme Court issued its now famous *Miranda* **warning** requirement stating the following:

> We hold that when an individual is taken into custody or otherwise deprived of his freedom . . . the privilege against self-incrimination is jeopardized. . . . He must be warned prior to any questioning that he has a right to remain silent, that anything he says can be used against him in a court of law, that he has a right to an attorney, and that if he cannot afford an attorney one will be appointed for him prior to any questioning if he so desires.

The *Miranda* decision has drawn a bright line for admissibility of confessions and admissions obtained during investigations. It changed the way police interrogated suspects. The decision was sweeping in its scope, but it still left questions unanswered.

Law in Practice

Requirements of an Admissible Confession

- The confession must be given knowingly and not as the result of lies or deception.
- If in custody, the suspect must be informed of his or her rights.
- The confession must be voluntary.
- Confessions may not be obtained through threats, such as
  - threatening to turn an illegal foreign alien over to immigration authorities for deportation;
  - threatening to report a mother to child protective services for child abuse to have her children taken away from her;
  - threatening to report suspects to a welfare agency for the purpose of having their welfare benefits suspended.
- Confessions may not be obtained through use of pain or through constructive force.

In *Berkemer* v. *McCarty,* the Supreme Court held that the *Miranda* warning must be given during any custodial interrogation.[30] The Court held that a person subjected to a custodial interrogation must be given the warning regardless of the severity of the offense, but questioning a motorist at a routine traffic stop does not constitute custodial interrogation.

The *Miranda* decision has generated both support and criticism since its inception. Supporters argue that it protects the rights of those accused of crimes, whereas detractors claim that it allows the guilty to go free because the officer may not have followed all the rules. In recent years, the courts have begun to allow statements to be admitted into evidence despite the absence of the *Miranda* warning.

Eroding of *Miranda*

Miranda did not prevent statements obtained in violation of its rules from being used to impeach the credibility of a defendant who took the witness stand. In *Harris* v. *New York,* the U.S. Supreme Court held that it was proper to use such statements so long as the jury was instructed that the confession was not to be considered evidence of guilt but only to determine whether the defendant was telling the truth.[32] Voluntary statements made by the defendant without having received the *Miranda* warning are admissible even though the defendant is later advised of his or her rights and waives those rights. In *Oregon* v. *Elstad,* the defendant was picked up at his home as a suspect in a burglary and made incriminating statements without receiving his *Miranda* warning.[33] After being advised of his rights, he waived them and signed a confession. The Supreme Court held that the self-incrimination clause of the Fifth Amendment did not require suppression of the written confession because of the earlier unwarned admission.

In *Illinois* v. *Perkins,* the Supreme Court held that an undercover officer posing as an inmate need not give a jailed defendant the *Miranda* warning before asking questions that produce incriminating statements.[34] The Court held that no coercive atmosphere is present when an incarcerated person speaks freely to someone whom he believes is a fellow inmate. The Court added that the *Miranda* warning does not forbid strategic deception by taking advantage of a suspect's misplaced trust.

Recent U.S. Supreme Court decisions have made it clear that the Constitution does not forbid an officer from talking to a suspect just because the suspect has an attorney. Instead, the rules now focus on whether or not the suspect is willing to talk without his or her attorney present. In *Moran* v. *Burbine,* the police officer did not tell *Burbine* that a lawyer had phoned on his behalf. The officer gave Burbine the *Miranda* warning, conducted an interrogation, during which Burbine confessed to killing a woman with a metal pipe. The confession was held to be admissible. The Supreme Court noted that they had no doubt that Burbine validly waived his rights to remain silent and to the presence of counsel. And that events occurring outside the presence of the suspect and entirely unknown to him can have no bearing on the capacity to comprehend and knowingly relinquish a constitutional right.

In *Berghuis* v. *Thompkins,* the Supreme Court held that the waiver of counsel for *Miranda* rule purposes need not be expressed. That waiver may be implied by the suspect's receipt of the *Miranda* warning, followed by his or her acknowledgement of the right and then making a statement.

Law in Practice

Using Psychological Tactics in Interrogation

The defendant Hawkins was arrested for rape and murder. While being interrogated by Officer LeFavers, he asked the police officer if he would be sentenced to death for his crime. The police officer stated: "Sam, to be honest with you, I would think that the courts in your situation would be very lenient. I really do. I think that they will observe the fact that you need help—you're trying to seek that help already, psychological, psychiatric help, and I think they would recommend a psychiatrist." The defendant was black and had professed a dislike for "honkies." The police used a black officer to interrogate him, hoping to obtain a psychological advantage. Taken together, does the statement of the police officer and use of the black officer establish improper psychological techniques and thus result in a confession that is not the result of the free will and rational choice of the defendant?

The court held in the above factual situation that the confession was admissible. The court stated that the comments were not a promise of leniency and that predictions about future events are not the same as a promise of leniency. The court also stated that there is nothing inherently wrong with the police's efforts to create a favorable climate for confession and that the use of the black police officer, even though designed to gain a psychological advantage, was not improper.[31]

In *Arizona* v. *Fulminante,* the Supreme Court held that the harmless error rule is applicable to cases involving involuntary confessions.[35] The harmless error rule holds that an error made by the trial court in admitting illegally obtained evidence does not require a reversal of the conviction if the error was determined to be harmless. The burden of proving harmless error rests with the prosecution and must be proved beyond a reasonable doubt.

In *Davis* v. *United States,* the Supreme Court considered the degree of clarity that was necessary for a suspect to invoke his *Miranda* rights.[36] Agents of the Naval Investigative Service were questioning the defendant in connection with the death of a sailor. The defendant initially waived his rights, but approximately ninety minutes later he stated, "Maybe I should talk to a lawyer." The agents asked clarifying questions, and when the defendant stated that he did not want an attorney, the interrogation resumed and elicited incriminating statements. The Court held that an equivocal request for a lawyer is insufficient to invoke the right to counsel and that there is no need for clarifying questions before proceeding with the interrogation.

Two years after *Miranda* was decided, Congress passed Title 18 U.S. Code, Section 3501, which set forth only voluntariness as the touchstone of admissibility for statements. In 2000, the Supreme Court finally had a case before it that allowed it to examine this law. In *Dickerson* v. *United States,* the Court held that the *Miranda* decision was of constitutional origin and that therefore Congress may not overrule its scope or effect.[37]

After years of allowing suspects to avoid police interrogation by invoking their *Miranda* rights, the Supreme Court is beginning to take a more reasonable and practical approach to this controversial issue.[38] However, police officers must still carefully tailor their interrogations so that they obtain information from the suspects while protecting their constitutional rights.

Law in Practice

Significant Cases Involving Interrogation

Brown v. *Mississippi* (1936)	The use of physical force (hanging in this case) to obtain a confession violated the Due Process Clause of the Fourteenth Amendment.
Ashcraft v. *Tennessee* (1944)	Psychologically coerced confessions are not voluntary and therefore not admissible in court.
Miranda v. *Arizona* (1966)	An in-custody suspect must be advised of his or her rights prior to being interrogated.
Harris v. *New York* (1971)	A voluntary statement taken from an in-custody defendant (without being advised, as required by *Miranda*) could be used at trial to impeach his or her in court testimony.
New York v. *Quarles* (1984)	Public safety concerns justified the police officer's failure to provide a *Miranda* warning before asking about the location of a loaded weapon apparently abandoned immediately prior to arrest.
Duckworth v. *Eagan* (1989)	Advising a suspect that an attorney would be appointed only if he goes to court did not render the *Miranda* warning inadequate.
Illinois v. *Perkins* (1990)	When a police officer poses as a prison inmate and is placed in a cell with a defendant, there is no requirement that the officer advise the defendant of his or her *Miranda* rights prior to asking questions of the defendant.
Minnick v. *Mississippi* (1990)	Once a suspect invokes his or her right to counsel, the police may not resume interrogation unless the suspect has an attorney. (*Note:* This rule does not apply if the suspect initiates the latter questioning.)
Pennsylvania v. *Muniz* (1990)	Police officers are not required to give a *Miranda* warning prior to asking suspected drunken drivers routine questions and recording their answers.
Arizona v. *Fulminate* (1991)	The Court upheld a conviction even though the confession admitted may have been coerced. The Court noted that the evidence of guilt even without the confession was overwhelming.
Davis v. *United States* (1994)	Police were not required to stop questioning a suspect merely because the suspect made an ambiguous statement about wanting an attorney.
Dickerson v. *United States* (2000)	The Court noted that *Miranda* had become embedded in police practices and did not overrule *Miranda*.
United States v. *Patane* (2004)	The introduction at trial of the physical evidence of a gun that had been found due to statements given by an arrestee who had not been given his *Miranda* warnings did not violate the *Miranda* rule or the Self-Incrimination Clause. Public emergency exception.

Missouri v. *Seibert* (2004)	Question-first interrogation tactic where defendant was questioned, confessed, was Mirandized, and then requestioned, did not comply with *Miranda's*; both pre- and post-warning confessions were inadmissible.
Sanchez-Llamas v. *Oregon* (2006)	Defendant was not entitled to suppression of evidence as a remedy for violation of the consular notification provision of Vienna Convention.
Montejo v. Louisiana (2009)	Defendant may waive Sixth Amendment rights whether or not he is already represented by counsel.
Berghuis v. *Thompkins* (2010)	The suspect's waiver of his or her *Miranda* rights need not be expressed and may be implied.

Practicum

You are a detective in a local police department and are investigating a murder. An individual whom you have targeted as a "person of interest" in the murder case has been arrested for shoplifting. She has been given the *Miranda* warnings and informed that she was suspected of committing the crime of shoplifting. After questioning her on the shoplifting charge, you want now to question her regarding the murder case. Do you need to issue new *Miranda* warning before questioning her regarding the murder case? She is still in custody.

The answer to the above question may be determined by reading the following cases:

> *Colorado* v. *Spring* 479 U.S. 564 (1987),
> *Arizona* v. *Roberson* 486 U.S. 675 (1988),
> *Davis* v. *United States* 512 U.S. 452 (1994).

Law in Practice

City of Indianapolis v. *Edmond*, 531 U.S. 32 (2000)

The City of Indianapolis decided to establish vehicular checkpoints for narcotics. The police set up lighted signs that stated: "Narcotics Checkpoint 1 mile ahead. Narcotics K-9s in use. Be prepared to stop." At the checkpoint, a predetermined number of vehicles were stopped only long enough to run a dog around the cars and ask a couple of questions. The "hit" rate on stopped vehicles was a very high 9 percent.

Two motorists who had been stopped sued the city and the city police department claiming that their Fourth Amendment rights against unreasonable seizure had been violated.

In a 6-3 opinion written by Justice Sandra Day O'Connor, the Supreme Court held that because the checkpoint program's primary purpose was indistinguishable from the general interest in crime control, the checkpoints violated the Fourth Amendment. Justice O'Connor stated that the

Court cannot sanction stops justified only by the generalized and ever-present possibility that interrogation and inspection may reveal that any given motorist has committed some crime. Chief Justice William H. Rehnquist and Justices Antonin Scalia and Clarence Thomas dissented, arguing that the reasonableness of the city's roadblocks depended on whether they served a "significant state interest with minimal intrusion on motorists."

Note: In *Illinois* v. *Caballes,* the Supreme Court upheld the actions of a state trooper in walking a dog around a car that had been stopped for speeding. In *Caballes,* the Court held that the use of a well-trained narcotics detection dog during a lawful traffic stop does not implicate legitimate privacy interests.

How do you distinguish between the above two cases?

IMMUNITY FROM ARREST

Certain classes of persons are immune from arrest because of statutory regulations. These include representatives of foreign countries, legislators, and out-of-state witnesses.

Diplomatic Immunity

International law and various agreements between nations exchanging representatives are the bases for **diplomatic immunity**. For example, in the United States, as provided by international law, diplomatic officers, their staff, members of their families, and their servants are free from local jurisdiction, and as such they should not be arrested or detained for any offense except in cases of grave crime and pursuant to a decision by a competent judicial authority unless they are citizens of or permanent residents of the United States (Title 22 U.S. Code, Section 252). The diplomatic officers who enjoy this unlimited immunity are ambassadors, ministers, their assistants, and attachés. The purpose behind the doctrine of diplomatic immunity is to contribute to the development of friendly relations between nations and to ensure the efficient performance of the diplomatic missions.

Although these persons have complete immunity from arrest, detention, or prosecution, the immunity does not give them blanket authority to disregard the laws of the United States and of the individual states. As established by international law, it is the duty of all foreign representatives to respect the laws and regulations of the land. If a member of the diplomatic corps commits a crime, the offense should be brought to the attention of the U.S. Department of State, and if the crime is a serious one, the State Department may request that the member be recalled from the country.

Consular Immunity

Consuls and their deputies are also representatives of foreign nations but have only limited immunity. In all cases, however, they are to be treated with due respect. The consular officers are not liable for arrest or detention pending a trial except in cases of a serious felony having been committed. Since **consular immunity** is limited to acts in performance of their duties, the immunity does not include members of their families or servants, but they too should be treated with proper respect. A police officer may treat a consular officer who commits a traffic violation the same as he or she does anyone else. The police officer may simply warn the consular officer, or the police officer may issue a citation, since this is not considered in violation of the immunity of arrest and detention.

Most diplomatic corps are stationed either in Washington, D.C., or with the United Nations in New York City, but consular officers are assigned to stations in many large cities throughout the United States. Peace officers in the United States may encounter members of these groups anywhere, since many of them travel extensively. Each member of these groups should have official identification in his or her possession, whereby a peace officer may determine the official status of the member and the immunity to which he or she is entitled.

Legislative Immunity

Most states have some type of provision in their statutes granting immunity to legislative members, but this immunity is limited. Many of the states hold that **legislative immunity** relates only to arrest arising out of some civil matter and that there is no immunity from arrest on a criminal charge.

Out-of-State Witnesses

The Uniform Act to Secure the Attendance of Witnesses from Without the State in Criminal Cases has been adopted by most of the states. This act provides that if a person enters a state in obedience of a subpoena to testify in that state, he or she shall not be subject to arrest in connection with any crime committed in the state prior to his or her entrance into the state to testify. The person is also granted a reasonable time to leave the state after testifying without being subject to such an arrest but is not granted any immunity from arrest for a crime that he or she may commit while in the state to testify. A similar immunity is given to persons passing through a state to testify in another state in obedience of a subpoena. One might question this immunity from arrest given to a witness. The reason is that the testimony is more important to a particular case than is the prosecution of a witness for some past violation of the law. In addition, if the prosecution were significant, there is no reason that extradition proceedings could not be brought against the witness.

BOOKING

When people are arrested, the usual procedure is to take them to the police station for booking. **Booking** consists of recording the arrest in official law enforcement records, fingerprinting, and photographing the accused. If the charge is a bailable offense, the accused is entitled to post bail at this time. If bail is not posted, the accused will be searched and placed in jail until he or she does post bail or until final prosecution takes place. Even though the accused was searched in the field at the time of the arrest, a more thorough search may be made at the time of booking for weapons or evidence that may have been missed during the field search.

Right to Telephone Calls

Whether an arrest is made by a law enforcement officer or by a private person, the accused is entitled to certain rights. One of these rights is to be informed of the offense for which the accused is being arrested. Another right provided by the statutes of some states is the right to make telephone calls. This right has been incorporated into the laws to prohibit individuals from being held indefinitely without anyone knowing that they have been arrested—in other words, to prevent them from being held incommunicado.

In those states in which the arrested person is permitted to make telephone calls, there are considerable differences in the rights afforded the arrested person. These rights differ as to the number of calls that may be made; to whom, how soon after the arrest, and at whose expense they may be made; whether the calls can be monitored; and whether the arrested person must be advised of the right to make the calls. It is generally held that the arrested person is entitled to make the calls immediately after being booked or, except where physically impossible, within a prescribed time, such as three hours, after the arrest. It is also generally provided that the arrested person is entitled to make at least one or more completed calls to an attorney, bail bondsman, relative, or other person. The calls are to be made free of charge to a local area; otherwise, they are made at the expense of the arrested person. Some jurisdictions require that the arrested person be advised of the right to make the calls; others merely require that the right be posted in a conspicuous place in the area of detention. This right is a continuing one and is not waived if the arrested person does not request to make the calls immediately after being booked. Some states also require that if the arrested person is physically unable to make the calls, he or she is entitled to the assistance of an officer.

ISSUANCE OF A CITATION

At one time in our history, all criminal offenders were brought to court with force. Even in civil matters, an arrest was frequently used to bring the defendant to court. Today, the defendant in a civil matter is not forced to appear in court. If the defendant fails to appear as requested, the person bringing the suit, who is known as the plaintiff, is given the judgment by default. Even in criminal matters, particularly involving minor violations, efforts are made to persuade the accused to come to court with as little inconvenience to all as possible. But when a warrant of arrest is issued, the person named in the warrant must be taken into custody, booked, and transported for arraignment unless he or she posts bail before arraignment. This same procedure is followed in most arrests made without a warrant. Each of these steps is time-consuming, and if the person does not post bail, he or she must be confined to jail pending the judicial proceedings. This detention often causes overcrowding of the jail facilities and, in some instances, an injustice to the accused. To alleviate this situation, many states have adopted legislation whereby an officer may issue a citation for a misdemeanor or an infraction violation instead of taking the person into custody.

A citation (sometimes referred to as a summons) is a written notice issued to a violator to appear in court. The citation lists the violator's name, address, and the offense committed. It also sets forth the time, place, and date that the violator is to appear in court. If the arrested person signs the citation agreeing to appear in court as directed, he or she is entitled to be released without further action being taken at that time.

In most instances, a citation will be issued for an infraction and for a traffic violation. But it is generally within the discretion of the law enforcement officer whether a citation will be issued for a misdemeanor violation. Many law enforcement agencies have established guidelines on which misdemeanor violations a citation may be issued for in lieu of taking the offender into custody. One reason for the selective practice is that it may be felt that the violator would not appear in court and that booking and confinement until he or she posts bail is the preferable procedure. Some law enforcement agencies have established a policy of taking an offender into custody, booking him or her, and then releasing the offender on a citation. This procedure defeats part of the purpose of issuing the citation in that the offender is taken into custody, transported to the station, and booked. Those following this process feel that the identifying data obtained from the booking justify the time consumed, particularly if the violator does not appear as agreed and must be sought on a bench warrant. To discourage the book-and-then-release practice, some jurisdictions require that the arresting agency conduct a background investigation to determine whether the person should be released on a citation. The investigation should include the person's name, address, length of residence at that address, length of residence in the state, marital and family status, current employment, length of current employment, prior arrest record, and such other facts as would bear on the question of the release of the individual.

Even though the violator is released in the field by signing the citation, most jurisdictions permit the law enforcement agency involved to request that the violator be booked prior to commencement of final judicial proceedings in order to get identifying data for future reference.

Citation Court Procedure

In some jurisdictions, a copy of the citation is filed with the appropriate court. This citation will become the accusatory document, eliminating the necessity of the officer's filing a complaint. In other jurisdictions, a copy of the citation is furnished to the prosecuting attorney, and on the basis of this citation, a complaint will be filed with the court that is to hear the case. After the citation has been issued and before the arraignment, the violator may post bail for his or her appearance. If the violator fails to appear as agreed, the bail may be forfeited. The judge, at his or her discretion, either may order that no further proceedings shall take place on the matter or may issue a bench warrant for the arrest of the violator. The judge will then proceed on the original charge for which the citation was issued, and in most jurisdictions, the violator can be charged with a misdemeanor for failure to appear.

SUMMONS

Although a citation is sometimes referred to as a **summons**, technically a summons differs from a citation. The true summons is issued by a judge in lieu of a warrant of arrest. The summons commands the accused to appear in court at a specified time and eliminates the need for arresting the accused and bringing him or her before the court. The summons may be issued by a judge when he or she feels that the accused will appear as commanded without the need to make an arrest. The summons, like the warrant of arrest, is based upon a complaint filed with the court. After the summons is issued, it may be personally delivered or mailed to the accused. If the person named in the summons fails to appear as commanded, a warrant of arrest will be issued. A summons differs from a citation in that a summons is issued by a judge and either mailed to or served upon the accused personally, commanding his or her appearance; a citation is generally issued by an officer in the field.

CASE LAW

Recent Cases

United States v. *Lall*, 2010 U.S. App. LEXIS 10938 (11th Cir. 2010)

Issue: Is a confession that was improperly coerced by state law enforcement officers admissible in a federal prosecution?

Holding: An involuntary confession is inadmissible in a federal prosecution if it was improperly coerced by state law enforcement officers.

Facts: The appellant (defendant) challenged his convictions after jury trial of conspiracy to commit credit card fraud in violation of 18 U.S.C. § 1029(a)(2),(4), and (b)(2), possession of device-making equipment with intent to defraud in violation of 18 U.S.C. § 1029(a)(4), and aggravated identity theft in violation of 18 U.S.C. §§ 1028A(a)(1) and (2). His appellate arguments targeted the denial of his motion to suppress evidence obtained after police responded to an armed burglary at his parents' home where he lived with his family.

In November 2007, North Miami Police Detectives Michael Gaudio ("Gaudio") and Fred Desir ("Desir") responded to a 911 call after an armed robbery at the home where the appellant, then twenty years old, lived with his parents Erroll and Hannah and his brother and sister, Joel and Anissa. The appellant's mother, Hannah, and his two siblings were at home when two armed masked men entered the home demanding money. The robbers made comments to the appellant's family about appellant's money and equipment and searched the room he shared with his brother, Joel. The two men threatened the family and eventually left with a laptop and the appellant's father's car.

The two detectives responded to the call to investigate the crime. During the course of that investigation, Joel told the officers that appellant was into credit card fraud and making "IDs and stuff" with the Internet. The two detectives determined that the bedroom shared by Joel and Lance was the focus of this home invasion, whatever these criminals were looking for, they were looking for in his room. When appellant arrived home, the officers read him his *Miranda* rights before he stepped inside the house. Gaudio testified that he told Lance, my main concern was the home invasion, about who had done this to his family, you know, this was a pretty serious crime, and that Gaudio needed to find out more information.

Gaudio then took appellant into his bedroom to try to collect any evidence that might help and to develop any leads to who might have committed the home invasion robbery. The appellant recounted that he, then twenty years old, was questioned in his bedroom with four officers and the bedroom door closed. Gaudio testified that he along with one or two other officers were present behind closed doors while speaking with appellant. Gaudio admitted that Lall's father and other family members were purposefully excluded from the room and not permitted to enter, despite objections from the family. Significantly, prior to entering the bedroom, Detective Gaudio told Lall and his family that any information Lall shared with the police would not be used to prosecute him.

During this encounter behind closed doors, appellant showed the officers the equipment he used to commit identity theft and how each device worked. Based on these admissions, Gaudio seized, inter alia, two skimmers, which Lall used to capture account information from swiped credit cards and driver's licenses, and one encoder, which he used to transplant that information onto new cards or licenses for fraudulent purposes.

Although Gaudio did not arrest appellant, he did notify the secret service of the evidence seized less than a day after assuring appellant the police would not use the information to prosecute him.

Several days later, Gaudio called Lall and told him to come to the police station with his father. According to Lall, Gaudio told Lall's father that they would not need to be accompanied by a lawyer, and Gaudio testified at the suppression hearing that he again told Lall he wasn't going to be charging him with any of this. While at the station, Lall was again given *Miranda* warnings, and proceeded to further "expound" on his initial statement. Lall was not aware at this time that Gaudio had already notified the Secret Service of the evidence originally taken. Ultimately,

Lall was arrested by Secret Service and charged with the offenses of which he was convicted.

Prior to trial, Lall moved to suppress the statements made to Gaudio during the initial interrogation and the physical evidence seized from his bedroom. Lall argued that the statements, which provided the probable cause for the seizure of the physical evidence, were improperly obtained. After a suppression hearing, the district judge denied the motion to suppress. Specifically, he held that Lall was not in custody—a holding which obviated any *Miranda* violation—and that there was sufficient probable cause to seize evidence found in Lall's bedroom.

Court's Opinion: The principal issue presented by this appeal is the voluntariness of Lall's statements to Detective Gaudio. Lall's challenge to the admissibility of those statements encompasses two separate yet interrelated arguments: first, that Gaudio's promises of non-prosecution prevented Lall from making a voluntary, knowing, and intelligent waiver of his *Miranda* rights; and second, that these promises rendered any subsequent confession by Lall involuntary and thus inadmissible. The U.S. Attorney argues that Lall freely and voluntarily confessed to committing identity and credit card fraud and explained to Detective Gaudio how his equipment facilitated the commission of those crimes. Moreover, he argues that Lall was not in custody at the time of the questioning, notwithstanding the fact that he was given the *Miranda* warnings. Consequently, he argues, it is immaterial whether Lall knowingly and voluntarily waived his *Miranda* rights. The same argument is repeated with respect to Lall's challenge to the admissibility of the second statement he made a few days later after he was summoned to the police station for additional interrogation.

We begin with Lall's first confession made to Detective Gaudio on the night of the robbery. Before a suspect's uncounseled incriminating statements made during custodial interrogation may be admitted, the prosecution must show that the suspect made a voluntary, knowing and intelligent waiver of his privilege against self-incrimination and his right to counsel. In *Miranda* v. *Arizona*, 384 U.S. 436, (1966), the Supreme Court explained that a warning that statements could be used against the suspect would make him aware of the consequences of foregoing the right to remain silent. It is only through an awareness of these consequences that there can be any assurance of real understanding and intelligent exercise of that privilege. Two factors are relevant to whether a waiver of the privilege was voluntary, knowing, and intelligent:

First, the relinquishment of the right must have been voluntary in the sense that it was the product of free and deliberate choice rather than intimidation, coercion, or deception. Second, the waiver must have been made with a full awareness of both the nature of the right being abandoned and the consequences of the decision to abandon it. Only if the totality of the circumstances surrounding the interrogation reveal both an uncoerced choice and the requisite level of comprehension may a court properly conclude that the *Miranda* rights have been waived.

Lall contends that the promises of non-prosecution made by Gaudio undermined the *Miranda* warnings he had initially been given. Detective Gaudio gave Lall the *Miranda* warnings on the front lawn of the house. Nevertheless, Gaudio testified that before he entered the bedroom, he told Lall that he was not going to pursue any charges against him. This representation contradicted the *Miranda* warnings previously given. Our holding there compels the conclusion that, as a result of Gaudio's statements, Lall did not truly understand the nature of his right against self-incrimination or the consequences that would result from waiving it.

Even if Lall was not in custody in the technical sense and thus *Miranda* warnings were not required, we would still be required to address the voluntariness of his confession. While the failure to comply with *Miranda* creates a presumption that a confession was not voluntary, an examination of the totality of the circumstances is necessary to determine whether the confession was actually voluntarily given.

While we look to the totality of the circumstances to determine the voluntariness of Lall's confession, a significant aspect of that inquiry here involves the effect of deception in obtaining a confession. We begin by observing that the deception at issue here did not involve a misrepresentation of fact. Such misrepresentations are not enough to render a suspect's ensuing confession involuntary, nor does it undermine the waiver of the defendant's *Miranda* rights. Police misrepresentations of law, on the other hand, are much more likely to render a suspect's confession involuntary.

Given the uniquely influential nature of a promise from a law enforcement official not to use a suspect's inculpatory statement, such a promise may be the most significant factor in assessing the voluntariness of an accused's confession in light of the totality of the circumstances.

If the officers, fully intending to use anything Rutledge said against him, had said to him, 'Tell us all you know about the drug trade, and we promise you that nothing you tell us will be used against you, then he would have a strong argument that any ensuing confession had been extracted by fraud and was involuntary. As already discussed, Gaudio explicitly assured Lall that anything he said would not be used to prosecute him. Moreover, there is ample record evidence to support a finding that Gaudio's promise was deceptive. Lall testified that Gaudio told him he would not be charged for any statements or evidence collected on the night of the robbery, and this was corroborated by Gaudio's testimony at the suppression hearing. It is inconceivable that Lall, an uncounseled twenty-year-old, understood at the time that a promise by Gaudio that he was not going to pursue any charges did not preclude the use of the confession in a federal prosecution. Indeed, it is utterly unreasonable to expect any uncounseled layperson, especially someone in Lall's position, to so parse Gaudio's words. On the contrary, the only plausible interpretation of Gaudio's representations, semantic technicalities aside, was that the information Lall provided would not be used against him by Gaudio or anyone else. Under these circumstances, Gaudio's statements were sufficient to render Lall's confession involuntary and to undermine completely the prophylactic effect of the *Miranda* warnings Gaudio previously administered.

The judgment of conviction is reversed and the case is remanded to the district court for further proceedings consistent with this opinion.

Melendez-Diaz v. *Massachusetts* 129 S. Ct. 2527, 2530 (2009)

Issue: Did defendant have a right to confront the lab analysts?

Facts: The defendant was charged with distributing and trafficking cocaine. At trial, the prosecution introduced several bags that purportedly contained cocaine into evidence. Prosecution also submitted three certificates of analysis showing the results of the forensic analysis performed on the seized substances. The certificates reported the weight of the seized bags and stated that the bags had been examined and the substance was found to contain to be cocaine. The certificates were sworn to before a notary public by analysts at the State Laboratory Institute of the Massachusetts Department of Public Health, as required under Massachusetts law.

Defendant objected to the admission of the certificates, asserting that the Confrontation Clause required the analysts to testify in person. The objection was overruled, and the certificates were admitted pursuant to state law as "prima facie evidence of the composition, quality, and the net weight of the narcotic analyzed." Specifically, the question presented was

whether those affidavits are testimonial, rendering the affiants witnesses subject to the defendant's right of confrontation under the Sixth Amendment.

In a 5-4 decision, the Court held the documents at issue were within the core class of testimonial statements. The description of that category mentions affidavits twice. The documents at issue here, while denominated by Massachusetts law "certificates," are quite plainly affidavits: declarations of facts written down and sworn to by the declarant before an officer authorized to administer oaths. They are incontrovertibly a solemn declaration or affirmation made for the purpose of establishing or proving some fact. The fact in question is that the substance found in the possession of Melendez-Diaz was cocaine. The precise testimony that the analysts would be expected to provide if called at trial. The "certificates" are functionally identical to live, in-court testimony, doing precisely what a witness does on direct examination. Forensic evidence is not uniquely immune from the risk of manipulation. Confrontation is designed to weed out not only the fraudulent analyst, but the incompetent one as well. Serious deficiencies have been found in the forensic evidence used in criminal trials. Like expert witnesses generally, an analyst's lack of proper training or deficiency in judgment may be disclosed in cross-examination.

Briefly Noted

Michigan v. *Bryant*, **131 S. Ct. 1143 (2010).** Because the primary purpose of an interaction between a mortally wounded shooting victim and the police was to enable the police to meet an ongoing emergency, the victim's identification and description of the shooter and the location of the shooting were not testimonial statements and the statements could be used in a criminal prosecution. Their admission at trial did not violate the Confrontation Clause.

Florida v. *Powell*, **130 S. Ct. 1195 (2010).** The U.S. Supreme Court has jurisdiction to review a state-court decision that advisement of rights of the defendant in a guilty plea was inadequate since decision did not distinguish between state and federal law, and advisement was proper since advice that defendant had right to counsel before questioning, which could be invoked at any time, conveyed right to counsel during questioning.

Maryland v. *Shatzer*, **130 S. Ct. 1213 (2010).** In 2003, a police detective tried to question the inmate, who was incarcerated at a state prison pursuant to a prior conviction, about allegations that he had sexually abused his son. The inmate invoked his *Miranda* right to have counsel present during interrogation, so the interview was terminated. The inmate was released back into the general prison population, and the investigation was closed. Another detective reopened the investigation in 2006 and attempted to interrogate the inmate.

In *Edwards* v. *Arizona*, the U.S. Supreme Court determined that the traditional standard for waiver was not sufficient to protect a suspect's right to have counsel present at a subsequent interrogation if he had previously requested counsel; additional safeguards were necessary. The Court therefore superimposed a second layer of prophylaxis. When an accused has invoked his right to have counsel present during custodial interrogation, a valid waiver of that right cannot be established by showing only that he responded to further police-initiated custodial interrogation even if he has been advised of his rights.

He is not subject to further interrogation by the authorities until counsel has been made available to him, unless the accused himself initiates further communication, exchanges, or conversations with the police. Under this rule, a voluntary *Miranda* waiver is sufficient at the time of an initial attempted interrogation to protect a suspect's right to have counsel present, but it is not sufficient at the time of subsequent attempts if the suspect initially requested the presence of counsel. The Edwards presumption of involuntariness ensures that police will not take advantage of the mounting coercive pressures of prolonged police custody by repeatedly attempting to question a suspect who previously requested counsel until the suspect is badgered into submission.

Shatzer waived his *Miranda* rights and made inculpatory statements. The Court held that the break-in-custody provided plenty of time for a suspect to get reacclimated to his normal life, to consult with friends and counsel, and to shake off any residual coercive effects of his prior custody. The inherently compelling pressures of custodial interrogation ended when the inmate returned to his normal prison life, so his release back into the general prison population after the 2003 interview constituted a break in custody. The defendant's inculpatory statements were admissible despite an earlier inadmissible statement. A judgment overturning a conviction based upon the admission of defendant's own inculpatory statements was reversed.

***Montejo* v. *Louisiana*, 129 S. Ct. 2079 (U.S. 2009)**. The Court held that defendant must request counsel, or otherwise assert his Sixth Amendment right when being questioned. It was unjustified to presume that a defendant's consent to police-initiated interrogation was involuntary or coerced simply because he had previously been appointed a lawyer.

***Berghuis* v. *Thompkins*, 130 S. Ct. 2250 (2010)**. The suspect's waiver of his or her *Miranda* rights need not be expressed, but may be implied from by the suspect's receipt of the *Miranda* warning, followed by an acknowledgement of his or her understanding of it, and then making a statement or answering a question.

Summary

- Police encounters are of three types: consensual, detention, and arrest.
- The arrest by a private person is sometimes referred to as a citizen's arrest.
- Thousands of arrests are made by private persons in this country.
- An arrest is the taking of a person in custody in a manner authorized by law.
- Probable cause to arrest exists when there is evidence that a crime has probably been committed and that the person to be arrested committed it.
- An arrest with a warrant is presumed to be legal.
- There is a legal preference for arrests made with a warrant.
- The *Terry* v. *Ohio* case developed the concept of stop and frisk.
- A mere temporary detention is not considered an arrest.
- A detention requires at least reasonable suspicion.
- A nonfederal law enforcement officer's jurisdiction to make an arrest is determined by state law.
- The Uniform Act of Fresh Pursuit has been adopted by most states. It permits a continuous pursuit of a fleeing person across jurisdictional lines.
- Generally, federal law enforcement officers have jurisdiction to arrest anywhere within the United States.
- An officer may use reasonable force to effect an arrest.
- Under most circumstances, it is illegal to willfully resist, delay, or obstruct a peace officer in the performance of his or her duty, including making an arrest.
- The *Miranda* rule requires that before a suspect is interrogated while in custody, the suspect must be advised of his or her *Miranda* rights.
- Certain individuals are immune from arrest because of statutory regulations.

Review Questions

1. Define an arrest.
2. Define probable cause for an arrest.
3. Who are peace officers?
4. What is meant by fresh pursuit?
5. What charges may be brought against an officer who uses excessive force in making an arrest?
6. What is meant by diplomatic immunity?
7. Which officials fall within the diplomatic immunity provisions?
8. For what reason is an arrested person entitled to make telephone calls?
9. What is a citation?
10. How does the procedure followed in issuing a citation differ from that used in executing a warrant of arrest?

Local Procedure

1. Do peace officers have statewide arrest powers?
2. Who, if anyone, must come to the aid of an officer in making an arrest when called upon to do so or else be subject to prosecution?
3. Does an arrested person have the right to make telephone calls, and, if so, to whom and how many calls may he or she make? Must the person under arrest be advised of this right to make the calls?
4. Has your state adopted the Uniform Act of Fresh Pursuit? If so, does the act apply to felony violations only, or has it been made applicable to misdemeanors? If applicable to misdemeanors, what types?

Endnotes

1. DeVallis Rutledge, "Unmixing Mixed-up Concepts," *Police Magazine*, January 2008, Vol. 32, No. 1 pp. 66–68.
2. Ibid, at p. 66.
3. 20 Ky. 539.
4. *Wong Sun* v. *U.S.,* 371 U.S. 471 (1963).
5. *U.S.* v. *Watson*, 423 U.S. 411 (1976).
6. *Payton* v. *New York,* 445 U.S. 573 (1980).
7. *U.S.* v. *Santana*, 427 U.S. 38 (1976).
8. *U.S.* v. *Davis*, 461 F.2d 1026 (3d Cir. 1972).
9. *Aguilar* v. *Texas,* 378 U.S. 108 (1964).
10. 387 U.S. 523.
11. 392 U.S. 1.
12. 50 Cal. Rev. 99.
13. *People* v. *Campbell,* 118 C.A. 3rd 588, 1981.
14. *People* v. *Gonzales,* 164 C.A. 3rd 1194, 1981.
15. 89 C.A. 3rd 809 (1979).
16. 118 C.A. 3rd 1315 (1985).
17. *U.S.* v. *Hemsley,* 105 S. Ct. 675, 1985.
18. 470 U.S. 675 (1990).
19. *Maryland* v. *Buie,* 494 U.S. 325, 1985.
20. See Wallace, Roberson, and Steckler, *Fundamentals of Police Administration* (Upper Saddle River, N.J.: Prentice Hall), 1995.
21. 471 U.S. 1 (1985).
22. See *Peterson* v. *Robison,* 277 P.2d 19, 24 (Cal. 1954).
23. This section has been adapted from Harvey Wallace, Cliff Roberson, and Craig Steckler, *Written Interpersonal Communication Methods for Law Enforcement* (Upper Saddle River, N.J.: Prentice Hall), 1997.
24. 297 U.S. 278 (1936).
25. 322 U.S. 143 (1944).
26. 360 U.S. 315 (1959).
27. 378 U.S. 748 (1964).
28. *United States* v. *McVeigh*, 896 F. Supp. 1549 (W.D. Okla, 1995).
29. 384 U.S. 436 (1966).
30. 468 U.S. 420 (1984).
31. *Hawkins* v. *Lynaugh*, 844 F.2d. 1132 (5th Cir. 1988).
32. 401 U.S. 222 (1971).
33. 470 U.S. 298 (1985).
34. 495 U.S. 292 (1990).
35. 111 S. Ct. 1246 (1991).
36. 114 S. Ct. 2350 (1994).
37. 539 U.S. 428 (2000).
38. Kimberly A. Crawford, "Invoking the Miranda Right to Counsel," *FBI Law Enforcement Bulletin*, 3, pp. 27–31 (March 1995).

CHAPTER 4

Initial Appearance

To implement the Fourth Amendment's protection against unfounded invasions of liberty and privacy, the Court has required that the existence of probable cause be decided by a neutral and detached magistrate whenever possible.

—JUSTICE POWELL IN *GERSTEIN* V. *PUGH* 420 U.S. 103 (1975)

It's better to enter the mouth of a tiger than a court of law.

—OLD CHINESE PROVERB

Chapter Outline

Purpose of the Initial Appearance
Complaint
Bail

Case Law
Summary

Key Terms

Arraignment
Bail
Complaint
Demur

Exoneration of bail
Initial appearance
Material witness

Learning Objectives

After completing this chapter, you should be able to:

- Explain the purpose and process of the initial appearance.
- Explain the purpose and process of the probable cause hearing.

- Summarize bail and other types of pretrial release.
- Explain the purpose and process of the preliminary hearing.

- Understand the legal requirements of a complaint.
- Discuss the restrictions on bail.

- Explain what happens when the de fendant violates the conditions of his or her bail.

PURPOSE OF THE INITIAL APPEARANCE

Although there is no mention of the **initial appearance** in our Bill of Rights, it is a basic right of an arrested person to be taken before a magistrate without unnecessary delay. This right is included in the federal rules of procedure and in the laws of the states. The initial appearance consists of the accused's appearing before a magistrate to be advised of certain rights to which he or she is entitled. A magistrate may be defined as anyone having the authority to issue an arrest warrant or a search warrant. From a practical standpoint, a magistrate generally is a judge of one of the inferior courts who spends much of his or her time conducting initial appearance hearings. The initial, or first, appearance is sometimes referred to as an arraignment. The term **arraignment** is used in many areas, and even the U.S. Supreme Court in the landmark cases of *McNabb* v. *United States*[1] and *Mallory* v. *United States*[2] referred to the initial appearance as an arraignment. In some states, the accused is permitted to enter a plea at the initial appearance, which adds to the tendency to call the initial appearance an arraignment.

At the initial appearance, the accused will be officially informed of the charge against him or her. Although the person is entitled to be informed of the charge at the time of the arrest, the charge is often changed between the time of the arrest and the initial appearance. For example, a person may be arrested on a charge of aggravated assault, but between the time of the arrest on that charge and the initial appearance, the victim dies. The charge is usually changed from aggravated assault to homicide. Further, at the initial appearance, if the offense is one for which bail may be posted, a bail amount is set and the accused will be informed of the right to make bail if he or she is not already out on bail. If the accused is not represented by an attorney, the rights to the assistance of counsel and to remain silent will be explained. Each of these rights is discussed in detail.

Differences Between Civil and Criminal Trials

Type of Case	Criminal Case	Civil Case
How case is started	Filing an indictment or other charging instrument with the court	Filing of a petition or complaint by plaintiff
Party responsible to bring the case forward	Prosecutor or district attorney in name of United States, a state or commonwealth	Plaintiff (party who filed the petition)
Burden of proof	On matters of guilty or not guilty—proof beyond a reasonable doubt. On other issues it varies.	On almost all issues—preponderance of evidence
Jury verdicts	In most states—unanimous	Many states—less than unanimous
Exclusionary rule	Applies regarding most issues	Generally not applicable
Remedies	Penal sanctions	Money damages or injunctions
Defendant's testimony	Right to remain silent	May be forced to testify
Right to attorney (retained)	Constitutional right	May be restricted, e.g., small claims courts
Right to appointed counsel	Rights for indigent defendants in certain cases	No right
Right to confront witnesses	Sixth Amendment	May be limited

Law in Practice

Federal Rules of Criminal Procedure: Rule 5. Initial Appearance

(a) In General

(1) Appearance Upon an Arrest

(A) A person making an arrest within the United States must take the defendant without unnecessary delay before a magistrate judge, or before a state or local judicial officer as Rule 5(c) provides, unless a statute provides otherwise.

(B) A person making an arrest outside the United States must take the defendant without unnecessary delay before a magistrate judge, unless a statute provides otherwise.

(2) Exceptions

(A) An officer making an arrest under a warrant issued upon a complaint charging solely a violation of 18 U.S.C. § 1073 need not comply with this rule if:

(i) the person arrested is transferred without unnecessary delay to the custody of appropriate state or local authorities in the district of arrest; and

(ii) an attorney for the government moves promptly, in the district where the warrant was issued, to dismiss the complaint.

(B) If a defendant is arrested for violating probation or supervised release, Rule 32.1 applies.

(C) If a defendant is arrested for failing to appear in another district, Rule 40 applies.

(3) Appearance Upon a Summons

When a defendant appears in response to a summons under Rule 4, a magistrate judge must proceed under Rule 5(d) or (e), as applicable.

(b) Arrest Without a Warrant

If a defendant is arrested without a warrant, a complaint meeting Rule 4(a)'s requirement of probable cause must be promptly filed in the district where the offense was allegedly committed.

(c) Place of Initial Appearance; Transfer to Another District

(1) Arrest in the District Where the Offense Was Allegedly Committed

If the defendant is arrested in the district where the offense was allegedly committed:

(A) the initial appearance must be in that district; and

(B) if a magistrate judge is not reasonably available, the initial appearance may be before a state or local judicial officer.

(2) Arrest in a District Other Than Where the Offense Was Allegedly Committed

If the defendant was arrested in a district other than where the offense was allegedly committed, the initial appearance must be:

(A) in the district of arrest; or

(B) in an adjacent district if:

(i) the appearance can occur more promptly there; or

(ii) the offense was allegedly committed there and the initial appearance will occur on the day of arrest.

(3) Procedures in a District Other Than Where the Offense Was Allegedly Committed

If the initial appearance occurs in a district other than where the offense was allegedly committed, the following procedures apply:

(A) the magistrate judge must inform the defendant about the provisions of Rule 20;

(B) if the defendant was arrested without a warrant, the district court where the offense was allegedly committed must first issue a warrant before the magistrate judge transfers the defendant to that district;

(C) the magistrate judge must conduct a preliminary hearing if required by Rule 5.1;

(D) the magistrate judge must transfer the defendant to the district where the offense was allegedly committed if:

(i) the government produces the warrant, a certified copy of the warrant, or a reliable electronic form of either; and

(ii) the judge finds that the defendant is the same person named in the indictment, information, or warrant; and

(E) when a defendant is transferred and discharged, the clerk must promptly transmit the papers and any bail to the clerk in the district where the offense was allegedly committed.

(d) Procedure in a Felony Case

(1) Advice

If the defendant is charged with a felony, the judge must inform the defendant of the following:

(A) the complaint against the defendant, and any affidavit filed with it;

(B) the defendant's right to retain counsel or to request that counsel be appointed if the defendant cannot obtain counsel;

(C) the circumstances, if any, under which the defendant may secure pretrial release;

(D) any right to a preliminary hearing; and

(E) the defendant's right not to make a statement, and that any statement made may be used against the defendant.

(2) Consulting with Counsel

The judge must allow the defendant reasonable opportunity to consult with counsel.

(3) Detention or Release

The judge must detain or release the defendant as provided by statute or these rules.

(4) Plea

A defendant may be asked to plead only under Rule 10.

(e) Procedure in a Misdemeanor Case

If the defendant is charged with a misdemeanor only, the judge must inform the defendant in accordance with Rule 58(b)(2).

(f) Video Teleconferencing

Video teleconferencing may be used to conduct an appearance under this rule if the defendant consents.

Steps in the Pretrial Process

1. **Arrest:** suspect taken into custody
2. **Booking:** administrative record of arrest
3. **Initial appearance:** notice of charge, advice of rights, setting of bail
4. **Preliminary hearing:** test of evidence against defendant
5. **Grand jury/information:** review of evidence by grand jury; charge filed by prosecution
6. **Arraignment:** appearance for plea; defendant elects trial by jury or judge
7. **Pretrial motions:** motion to dismiss charges and motions regarding the admissibility of evidence
8. **Guilty plea/trial:** plea accepted or trial scheduled

Time of the Initial Appearance

One of the more troublesome problems involved in an initial appearance concerns when it must be held once the arrest is made. For many years, neither the courts nor law enforcement agencies were particularly concerned about the timing of the initial appearance. As a result, many arrested persons were held incommunicado in jail for days and sometimes weeks before being taken before a magistrate. To overcome the injustice of this procedure, it is now provided that an arrested person must be taken before a magistrate without unnecessary delay. However, this provision is not without its complications. What will the courts accept, if anything, as necessary or reasonable delay in taking the defendant before a magistrate, and what penalties will be attached if there is an unnecessary delay deemed in the initial appearance? To assist officers in determining time limits, most states have enacted provisions setting forth the time within which the initial appearance must take place. The time limit varies considerably among the states, but the following is typical of the wording of such statutes:

> The arrested person must be taken before a magistrate without unnecessary delay, and in any event no longer than two days, Sundays and holidays excluded. If the

two-day period expires when the Court is not in session, the time for the initial appearance will be extended until the next regular court session.

This provision implies that the two-day period is actually based on a forty-eight-hour limit. It is pointed out that the forty-eight-hour restriction does not provide blanket authority to hold all arrested persons for that time without taking them before a magistrate. A delay in the initial appearance for a much shorter time could be interpreted as an unnecessary delay. Some states have a seventy-two-hour limit, and a few states merely provide that an arrested person must be taken before a magistrate without unnecessary delay. If an arrested person is not taken before a magistrate within the prescribed time, he or she must be released. Whether the person could be arrested again after the release is doubtful; much would depend on the facts of the particular case and the reason for the delay in the initial appearance. In some instances, the release of the accused will result in a dismissal of the charge and will bar further prosecutive action, particularly in misdemeanor cases.

The time within which an initial appearance must occur and the penalties that may be attached for the delay were given particular emphasis by the landmark decision handed down by the U.S. Supreme Court in 1943 in the case of *McNabb* v. *United States*. The facts of that case reveal that some of the defendants were held for six days after the arrest before being arraigned, during which time confessions were obtained from them. These confessions were introduced against the defendants in their trial for the murder of a federal officer. The conviction was appealed to the U.S. Supreme Court upon the grounds that the confessions had been involuntarily given. The Court concluded that there was an unnecessary delay in the arraignment, during which time these confessions were obtained. To discourage unnecessary delay in arraignments, the Court held that any confession obtained during an unnecessary delay would be inadmissible as evidence in a court proceeding. This was an entirely new approach to the admissibility of confession. Prior to the *McNabb* decision, the test of admissibility was voluntariness in giving the confession. So the Court, in that case, attached a very significant penalty to a delay in arraigning an arrested person.

Although this decision pertained only to federal officers, several states have adopted the rule set forth in the *McNabb* decision by maintaining that confessions obtained by local officers during a delay in arraignment are inadmissible as evidence. It becomes important to determine what, if anything, might be considered a necessary delay in arraigning an arrested person. Following the *McNabb* case, the U.S. Supreme Court handed down other decisions relative to the time factor in arraignments. It was indicated in one case that the Court took into consideration that an arrested person should be booked before being arraigned. In another case, it was held that some investigative activity to verify information furnished by the defendant before being arraigned would be tolerated (see *Mallory* v. *United States*).

The U.S. Supreme Court cases mentioned are of little assistance in furnishing guidelines on how long an accused may be held within the prescribed time limit before the initial appearance and still have the delay considered necessary. The courts have held that if the delay is solely for the purpose of interrogating the accused, such delay is not considered necessary. Yet it is recognized that some questioning after an arrest may be in order, followed by a reasonable investigation to verify or refute information given by the arrested person. Such questioning could assist in the early release of an innocent person or could act as a justification for the arrest. For example, in one case, the delay in initial appearance for almost the entire prescribed time was upheld. In that case, the owner of an old model car took the car to a garage to be repaired. The mechanic told the owner that the car would be ready in three days. When the owner did not return for the car for more than a week, the mechanic checked the car in an effort to locate some identification in order to notify the owner that the car was ready. The mechanic found no identification, but he did find $1,500 in the glove compartment. He became suspicious and notified the local authorities. The officers were also unable to determine the owner and asked to be called if he returned for the car. Upon returning for the car a few days later, the owner was questioned by the officers but gave evasive answers. He was arrested for reasonable cause to believe that a crime had been committed since it was thought that an ordinarily prudent person would hold such a belief under the circumstances. But what crime should he have been booked for? Had he committed robbery, burglary, grand theft, or some other crime? He was arrested for grand theft, but there were no facts to verify such a crime in the area. He was further questioned by the officers but refused to reveal his identity or place of residence. The investigation revealed no damaging evidence. As the forty-eight-hour limit approached, the authorities realized that the accused would have to be released, yet they believed that he had been involved in some type of crime because an innocent person would have assisted in getting his own release much earlier. Just before the time limit was reached, the officers received a call from a woman reporting her husband as missing. The description of the missing husband fit that of the man in custody. It was learned that the accused had cashed a number of forged checks and that the money in the glove compartment was from his check-cashing activity. He had forgotten that it was in the glove compartment when he took the car to the garage. It is interesting that he stated that he was cashing the forged checks to get enough money to buy a small ranch where he could raise his children in a wholesome atmosphere.

Generally, a delay in an initial appearance or arraignment is not sufficient grounds for a reversal of a conviction on appeal unless it can be shown that the delay deprived the defendant of a fair trial. A few states have adopted the *McNabb* rule of excluding a confession obtained during a delay in arraignment. But there are other penalties besides the procedural one pertaining to the admissibility of a confession that may be attached to a delayed arraignment. Many states hold that a public officer who willfully delays bringing a defendant before a magistrate for the arraignment is guilty of a misdemeanor. It has also been held that once the time limit has been reached wherein an arrested person must be taken before a magistrate, any detention beyond that period is illegal, and that the officer responsible for such detention is subject to a civil suit for damages on a false imprisonment allegation.

Accepting the Accused for the Initial Appearance

Whether the accused was arrested by a private person or by an officer, he or she must be taken before a magistrate. The laws of many states provide that a private person who arrests another must take that person before a magistrate without unnecessary delay or deliver the arrested person to a peace officer who will in turn see that the accused is taken before a magistrate. The usual procedure is that the private person will deliver the arrested person to a peace officer rather than take the person before a magistrate personally. This situation creates the problem of how far the officer should go in determining the legality of the arrest before accepting the accused. There seems to be no uniformity in the answer to this problem. The courts of some states have held that if a competent private person informs the officer of the charge for which the arrest was made and demands that the officer take the accused, the officer has no right to refuse. This approach is reinforced by the further provision in some states that an officer who willfully refuses to accept one who has been charged with a crime is also subject to prosecution. Under the circumstances, an officer is not civilly liable for false arrest by accepting one arrested by a private person. The officer in reality is only a transportation officer and not an arresting one.[3] Other states permit the officer to make a determination concerning the legality of the arrest by the private citizen before accepting the accused. Such a ruling places a tremendous burden upon the officer. The officer is partially acting as a court in making a determination as to the legality of the arrest. If the officer incorrectly concludes that the arrest was legal, he or she could possibly be held civilly liable for accepting the accused.

COMPLAINT

Prior to the initial appearance, a legal document must be filed with the court setting forth the charge against the accused, who will be referred to as the defendant hereinafter in relation to the judicial procedure. In most instances, this legal document will be a **complaint**. The complaint is comparatively simple. It sets forth the name of the defendant, the date and place that the offense took place, and the nature of the offense. The complaint must contain enough facts to enable the judge to determine whether a crime has been committed and whether there is reasonable cause to believe that the defendant committed it. If the defendant is not in custody, a warrant of arrest will be issued on the basis of this complaint. The complaint is sometimes referred to as an accusatory pleading. As we discuss the judicial procedure further, it will be determined that other accusatory pleadings follow the complaint in felony cases, but in misdemeanor matters, it is usually the only accusatory pleading filed with the court.

Demurrer to Complaint

In most states, a person named as the accused in an accusatory pleading (indictment, information, or complaint) may demur to the pleadings. A **demur** is the formal mode of disputing the sufficiency in law of the pleadings. The grounds upon which a demur may be based include:

- The grand jury that issued the indictment had no legal authority to inquire into the offense charged or, in the case of information or a complaint, that the court had no jurisdiction for the offense charged.
- The accusatory pleadings do not conform to required provisions of the state's penal code.
- More than one offense is charged (in those states that require a separate pleading for each charge).
- The facts stated in the pleading do not constitute a public offense (crime).
- The pleading contains matter that, if true, would constitute a legal justification or excuse for the offense charged or another legal bar to prosecution.

A demur must be in writing, signed either by the defendant or by his or her counsel, and filed with the court. It must distinctly specify the grounds of objection to the pleading. When a demur is filed with the court, generally the court will hold a hearing and then make an order overruling (denying) or sustaining (approving) it. Generally if the demur is overruled, a court must then allow the defendant to plead. If the demur is sustained, a court must, if the defect can be corrected, allow the indictment to be resubmitted to the grand jury or in the case of other pleadings to the prosecutor to amend the pleadings. If the demur is sustained and the pleading is not correctable, the court must dismiss the charge.

BAIL

The Right to Post Bail

The right of an arrested person to post bail to obtain release from custody is an inherent right. As stated in the case of *Stack* v. *Boyle*[4]:

> This traditional right to freedom [by posting bail] before conviction permits the unhampered preparation of a defense, and serves to prevent the infliction of punishment prior to conviction. . . . Unless this right to bail before trial is preserved, the presumption of innocence, secured only after centuries of struggle, would lose its meaning.

Law in Practice

Does an Undocumented Alien Have a Constitutional Right to Bail?

If you were the trial judge in a bail hearing where the defendant is an undocumented alien and is charged with burglary. What would you consider in making the bail decision?

Consider the following:

In 1896, the U.S. Supreme Court ruled in *Wong Wing* v. *United States*, 163 U.S. 228 (1896) that:

> The Fourteenth Amendment to the Constitution is not confined to the protection of citizens. It says: 'Nor shall any state deprive any person of life, liberty or property without due process of law; nor deny to any person within its jurisdiction the equal protection of the law.' These provisions are universal in their application to all persons within the territorial jurisdiction, without regard to any differences of race,

of color, or nationality; and the equal protection of the laws is a pledge of the protection of equal laws.

All persons in the United States, therefore, have constitutional rights. Among these are the right to equal protection of the law and the right to due process.

Stack v. *Boyle*, 342 U.S. 1, 4–6 (1951): Bail is "excessive" in violation of the Eighth Amendment when it is set at a figure higher than an amount reasonably calculated to ensure the asserted governmental interest.

United States v. *Ong*, 2010 U.S. Dist. LEXIS 136170 (N.D. Ga., 2010): Where the risk of flight is unusually high as in this case where the defendant is an undocumented alien, there is no constitutional right to bail.

Law in Practice

Setting Bail Amount

The amount of bail necessary to secure the defendant's presence at trial varies according to the circumstances of each case. Generally, the following factors are considered by judges in setting bail amounts:

1. Seriousness of the offense charged—some crimes, such as capital murder, may be assumed to be non-bailable offenses
2. Weight of the evidence against the defendant
3. Defendant's ties to the community, family, and employment

4. Defendant's prior criminal record
5. Any history of failure to appear

The right to be released before trial is conditioned upon the accused's giving adequate assurance to the court that he or she will return to stand trial. The assurance is often in the form of bail. Since the function of bail is the limited purpose of ensuring attendance at trial, the amount of bail varies with each defendant. Bail set at a figure higher than an amount reasonably calculated to fulfill this purpose is considered to be excessive under the Eighth Amendment.[5]

But the right to post bail is not a guarantee included in our Bill of Rights. The Eighth Amendment to the Constitution merely provides that "excessive bail shall not be required," implying that not all offenses are bailable. By constitutional provision or by statute, the right to post bail by someone arrested under certain conditions is granted by all states. If the defendant has not been released on bail by the time of the initial appearance, the right to post bail will be explained to him or her at that time.

Historical Development of Bail

The origin of the term **bail** has been obscured by time. Some believe that the term is from the Old French word *baillier,* meaning to deliver. Others hold that it originated from the common law procedure of bailments. A bailment is the deposit of something of value with another for a particular purpose. In the case of bail, the deposit was for the release of one in custody. The right to post bail is found in the early history of England. By the time of the Norman Conquest in A.D. 1066, the posting of a form of security to obtain the release of an accused was a common practice on the continent of Europe, and it became part of the common law of England. It was developed as a humanitarian procedure. Previously, people accused of crimes were thrown into the dungeons of local noblemen to make sure that they would be available for trial when the judge made his circuit. This custom was important to the king. If the charge was serious and the accused was convicted, his or her property was confiscated, thus providing a lucrative source of revenue for the king. Often by the time of the trial, the accused would have died from malnutrition and neglect. To prevent this from happening, relatives or friends of the accused sought his or her release to their custody upon a promise that they would produce the accused for the trial. To make certain that the relatives or friends would fulfill their promise, they were required to post some security in the form of chattels or objects of value. If the accused was not produced for trial, these chattels would be confiscated by the king. In addition, the persons posting the security had to suffer the punishment that the accused would have been subjected to had he or she been convicted. As time passed, the practice of punishing those who had posted security was discontinued, and they lost only the security.

Purpose of Bail

Today, we continue to place persons who are arrested in jail. We do so not as a form of punishment, because one cannot be punished or imprisoned until found guilty of a crime. We confine arrested persons to make sure that they will be available for trial. If we can obtain that surety by permitting accused persons to post bail, they are entitled to be released from custody until found guilty of the accusation. Thus, the only purpose of bail is to secure the release from custody of one who has been arrested upon his or her promise to appear at the various court proceedings related to the offense. These may include the arraignment, the preliminary hearing, the trial, and other such proceedings that the court may direct.

At common law, it was felt that there was no way to ensure the trial presence of one who was charged with a capital offense, so bail was denied to that type of offender. A capital offense is one for which the death penalty may be inflicted. The statutes of many states have included similar provisions, holding that one charged with a capital offense may be denied bail if the proof of guilt is great. Even in those states in which capital punishment has not been made a penalty, bail may be denied to one arrested for murder if the proof of guilt is evident.

Denial of Bail for Protective Reasons

In the past, a few jurisdictions held that bail may be denied to an arrested person if his or her release on bail would cause a danger to the public. This policy is based upon an interpretation of the Eighth Amendment to the Constitution by the U.S. Supreme Court in the case of *Carlson* v. *Lando*.[6] In review, the Eighth Amendment guarantees that "excessive bail shall not be required." In the *Carlson* case, the Court rested its interpretation of the Eighth Amendment on the common law, stating the following:

> The bail clause was lifted with slight changes from the English Bill of Rights Act. In England that clause has never been thought to accord a right to bail in all cases, but merely to provide that bail shall not be excessive in those cases where it is proper to grant bail. When this clause was carried over into our Bill of Rights, nothing was said that indicated any different concept. The Eighth Amendment has not prevented Congress from defining the classes of cases in which bail shall be allowed in this country. Thus in criminal cases bail is not compulsory where the punishment may be death. Indeed, the very language of the Amendment fails to say [that] all arrests must be bailable.

Thus, it was concluded that the Eighth Amendment does not grant the right to bail. The Eighth Amendment can be construed to mean only that bail shall not be excessive in those cases in which it is proper and that the denial of bail in certain cases is permissible. In recognition of the Court's interpretation of the Eighth Amendment and in response to the alarming problem of crimes committed by persons released on bail, Congress enacted an elaborate plan of preventive detention by enactment of the Bail Reform Act of 1984 (Title 18 U.S. Code, section 3242). This act provides that a federal officer may detain, pending trial, an arrestee who may be a danger to another person or a community. But before such an arrestee can be detained, a hearing must be held to determine "by clear and convincing evidence" that no condition exists that will assure the safety of a person or community if the arrestee were released on bail.

The constitutionality of this act was questioned by the defendant in the case of *United States* v. *Salerno.*[7] The defendant Salerno alleged that the act violated his right to the Due Process of Law clause embodied in the Fifth Amendment of the Constitution, which provides that "No person shall . . . be deprived of life, liberty or property without Due Process of Law. . . ." The U.S. Supreme Court did not agree with this contention, and stated that the act limits its application to those arrested on the most serious offenses and that the arrestee is entitled to a prompt hearing. During this hearing, the arrestee has the right to be represented by an attorney, to cross-examine witnesses, and to testify in his or her own behalf. In the opinion of the Court, this procedure fulfills the Due Process Clause of the Constitution.

The defendant also alleged that the act violated his right against excessive bail provided in the Eighth Amendment of the Constitution. To this allegation, the Court reiterated that the Eighth Amendment does not guarantee bail in all instances. When community safety is at stake, the government may deny bail and detain individuals believed to be dangerous to society.

Since the U.S. Supreme Court has upheld the "protective detention" of certain individuals arrested by federal officers, many states have enacted similar statutes permitting the detention pending trial of individuals arrested by state officers, who are believed to be dangerous. However, to abide by the Due Process Clause, those acts are required to provide for a prompt detention hearing similar to the Bail Reform Act of 1984.

Form of Bail

To post bail is to deposit an acceptable object of value with the appropriate court to ensure the appearance of the accused in court. Generally, the acceptable object of value is cash, U.S. or state bonds, or an equity in real property. If real property is pledged as security, most states require that the value of the property be twice that of the amount of bail. This requirement is made because of the possible fluctuation of real estate values and the difficulty of converting the real property into cash.

Since most arrested persons do not have these forms of security, they must rely upon someone to post bail for them. This person, known as a surety, may be a friend or relative, but in many cases, the person depositing the security will be one in the business of posting bail—a bail bondsperson. For a fee, the bail bondsperson will post the required security, which is usually a surety bond issued by some reliable company. Should the accused fail to appear as promised, the surety bond guarantees the bail payment in cash to the appropriate court. The fee that the bail bondsperson charges for this service is about 10 percent of the amount of the bail. A bail bondsperson who has some doubt about whether the accused will appear if released on bail may request relatives of the accused to deposit collateral funds to reimburse him or her if the accused does not appear. If the risk of the accused's not appearing is too great and no one will come to the aid of the accused by depositing collateral funds, the bail bondsperson may refuse to post the bail, and the accused will be detained until the judicial proceedings are completed. But once bail has been deposited, the accused is entitled to immediate release from custody. The law is silent in most jurisdictions on the amount of time that a defendant may be free on bail, but it is generally assumed that he or she is entitled to be free throughout all the proceedings up to the time of conviction. However, at his or her discretion, a judge may commit a defendant during the trial. Also, the defendant is not guaranteed the right to be free during an appeal time. Upon conviction, the defendant is no longer presumed to be innocent but rather to be guilty. But again, a judge, at his or her discretion, may permit a defendant to post bail during the appeal proceedings.

In some states, a bail bond is issued by a professional bond agency, which will issue the bond for a limited period and require renewal of bail. The usual period for which a professional bail bonds person or agency will issue a bond is one year, after which the bond must be renewed. This time limitation may be a problem in a lengthy trial.

Amount of Bail

The bail required to be posted is that amount that will ensure the court appearance of the accused. Anything above that amount could be considered excessive. This amount is not easy to determine. The amount that would guarantee the appearance of one person may be entirely different for another. Also, the amount that would ensure the appearance on one charge may differ from the amount for another charge. In determining the amount of bail, a judge may consider the seriousness of the crime; the criminal record of the defendant; his or her employment record; family ties; whether the defendant was a fugitive at the time of arrest; whether he or she is wanted in any other jurisdiction; how great the evidence of guilt may be; the financial burden that he or she may suffer by not appearing; and whether the defendant has more to gain than to lose by not appearing.

The amount of bail set by a judge will not necessarily remain the same throughout the proceedings. Circumstances may arise that justify an increase or decrease in the amount. If the defendant has been released on bail and the amount is increased, he or she must post the amount of the increase or be placed in custody again.

In some cases, especially those involving drug offenses or fraud, the trial court will require that the defendant establish that the money to secure the bail is from a legitimate source and is not fruits of the crime.

Bail Schedules

Since the amount of bail required largely depends on judicial discretion, it varies extensively. To establish uniformity in the amounts required, many states have adopted a procedure whereby judges of a county agree upon the amount of bail that is considered to be equitable on each misdemeanor violation. These amounts are listed in a schedule and act as guidelines for judges of the county. The amounts may still vary among counties. It has been recommended that a similar schedule be prepared for felony charges. But as we have pointed out, it is difficult to determine the amount that will ensure the appearance of a defendant in court, particularly in felony matters, so that such a schedule could be most unrealistic. A few states, however, have adopted a schedule for felony charges.

Forfeiture of Bail

Once the defendant is released on bail and if, without sufficient cause, he or she fails to appear when lawfully required to do so, the bail will be forfeited. Forfeiting bail means that the security posted by the defendant, or someone in his or her behalf, is confiscated by the court and deposited in an official fund. The confiscation is justified on the grounds that the security will be used to pay additional court costs and costs involved in locating the defendant. In felony cases particularly, if the defendant does not appear as agreed, the court will issue a bench warrant for the immediate arrest of the accused. When arrested, the defendant will be tried on the original charge and, in some jurisdictions, can also be charged with violation of "failing to appear" or, as it is more commonly known, bail-jumping. If a defendant does not appear on some minor misdemeanor charges or on most traffic violations, a judge may forfeit the bail, considering it the equivalent of the fine, dismiss the charge, and order that no further action be taken on the matter.

Surrender of Defendant by Surety

The surety who posted bail for a defendant may surrender him or her to the court having jurisdiction over the case any time before bail is forfeited. Upon surrendering the defendant, the surety is relieved of all responsibility and is entitled to have the security returned to him or her. For the purpose of surrendering the defendant, the surety may arrest the defendant. This arrest is an extension to the power of arrest by a private person. It is based upon the old theory that one posting bail has indirect custody of a defendant, and the surety may be relieved of that obligation by seizing the defendant and surrendering him or her to the court.

Exoneration of Bail

If the defendant appears in court at all times required, the bail has served its purpose, and the surety is entitled to have it returned. This return is known as the **exoneration of bail**.

Release on Own Recognizance

In the past, judges developed a practice of releasing defendants charged with minor offenses without posting bail—merely upon their promise to appear. This procedure be came known as releasing one on his or her own recognizance, or OR release. The statutes of most states have extended this practice to any bailable offense, including felony charges. The laws provide that a judge may release a defendant on his or her own recognizance if it appears that the defendant will comply with the agreement to appear as directed. However, these laws do not give the defendant the right to be released merely on his or her own recognizance. Even though a defendant is released on his or her own recognizance, a judge may later require the defendant to post bail or even to be committed to actual custody.

Pretrial Release Mechanisms

Stage	Mechanism	Description
Police	Field citation release	An arresting officer releases the arrestee on a written promise to appear in court, at or near the actual time and location of the arrest. This procedure is commonly used for misdemeanor charges and is similar to issuing a traffic ticket.
Police	Station house citation release	The determination of an arrestee's eligibility and suitability for release and the actual release of the arrestee are deferred until after he or she has been removed from the scene of an arrest and brought to the station house or police headquarters.
Police/pretrial	Jail citation release	The determination of an arrestee's eligibility and suitability for citation release and the actual release of the arrestee are deferred until after he or she has been delivered by the arresting department to a jail or other pretrial detention facility for screening, booking, and/or admission.
Pretrial/court	Direct release authority by pretrial program	To streamline release processes and reduce the length of stay in detention, courts may authorize pretrial programs to release defendants without direct judicial involvement. Where court rules delegate such authority, the practice is generally limited to misdemeanor charges, but felony release authority has been granted in some jurisdictions.
Police/court	Bail schedule	An arrestee can post bail at the station house or jail according to amounts specified in a bail schedule. The schedule is a list of all bailable charges and a corresponding dollar amount for each. Schedules may vary widely from jurisdiction to jurisdiction.

Prior to being released on his or her own recognizance, the defendant must agree in writing to appear at all times and places as ordered by the court, and if he or she does not appear and is apprehended in another state, the defendant waives extradition proceedings. In most states, it is provided that if the defendant who is released on his or her own recognizance fails to appear as agreed, he or she can be charged with the failure to appear. If the original charge was a felony, the defendant can be charged with a felony for failure to appear. If the original charge was a misdemeanor, the defendant can be charged with a misdemeanor for failure to appear. It has been recommended that greater use be made of OR releases, particularly in minor offenses, to obtain the release of those who are unable to post bail for financial reasons.

Bail for a Material Witness

The laws of most states permit a judge to demand that a **material witness** to a felony violation deposit security for his or her appearance at the trial if the judge believes that the witness will otherwise not appear. If the witness is unable to post the security (bail) for his or her appearance, the witness may be held in custody. The detention of a witness who is unable to post bail is unusual in our form of judicial procedure, since it permits the incarceration of one not charged with a crime. For this reason, it is not used extensively. To further overcome the inconvenience of a material witness's being detained, many jurisdictions provide that if a material witness cannot deposit security to ensure his or her appearance at the trial, his or her testimony may be incorporated into a deposition. A deposition is a written statement of a witness taken under oath before a magistrate, with both the prosecution and the defense having the right to be present.

CASE LAW

Recent Cases

Corley v. *United States*, 129 S. Ct. 1558 (U.S. 2009)

The defendant was presented to a magistrate 29.5 hours after his arrest for armed bank robbery and related charges. The defendant contended that his confession made during the delay should not have been admitted into evidence.

> [Presentment in the federal system is similar to the initial appearance in state courts. It is the point at which the judge is required to take several key steps to foreclose government overreaching: (1) informing the defendant of the charges against him, his right to remain silent, his right to counsel, the availability of bail, and any right to a preliminary hearing; (2) giving the defendant a chance to consult with counsel; and (3) deciding between detention or release. Fed. R. Crim. P. 5(d).]

The Supreme Court noted that the rule known simply as McNabb-Mallory generally renders inadmissible confessions made during periods of detention that violate the prompt presentment requirement of Fed. R. Crim. P. 5(a). The Court pointed out that 18 U.S.C.S. § 3501 modified McNabb-Mallory without supplanting it. Under the rule as revised by § 3501(c), a district court with a suppression claim must find whether the defendant confessed within six hours of arrest (unless a longer delay was reasonable considering the means of transportation and the distance to be traveled to the nearest available magistrate). If the confession came within that period, it is admissible, subject to the other Federal Rules of Evidence, so long as it was made voluntarily and the weight to be given to it is left to the jury. If the confession occurred before presentment and beyond six hours, however, the court must decide whether delaying that long was unreasonable or unnecessary under the McNabb-Mallory cases, and if it was, the confession is to be suppressed.

In this case, the Third Circuit did not apply this rule and in consequence never conclusively determined whether Corley's oral confession should be treated as having been made within six hours of arrest, nor did the Circuit consider the justifiability of any delay beyond six hours if the oral confession should be treated as given outside the six-hour window; and it did not make this enquiry with respect to Corley's written confession. We therefore vacate the judgment of the Court of Appeals and remand the case for consideration of those issues.

Presley v. Georgia, 130 S. Ct. 721 (U.S. 2010)

The defendant was convicted of a cocaine trafficking offense but asserted that his right to a public trial under the Sixth Amendment was violated when the trial court excluded the public from the voir dire of prospective jurors.

Before selecting a jury, the trial court noticed a lone courtroom observer. The trial judge explained that prospective jurors were about to enter and would be sitting in the seats normally used by the public. The trial judge then instructed the man that he was not allowed in the courtroom and had to leave that floor of the courthouse entirely.

The Court noted that the Sixth Amendment directs, in part, that in all criminal prosecutions the accused shall enjoy the right to a speedy and public trial. This right extends to the states. The Sixth Amendment right, as the language makes explicit, is the right of the accused.

The Court also noted that while an accused has a right to insist that the voir dire of jurors be public, there are exceptions to this general rule. The right to an open trial may give way in certain cases to other rights or interests, such as the accused's right to a fair trial or the government's interest in inhibiting disclosure of sensitive information. Such circumstances are rare, however, and the balance of interests must be struck with special care. The party seeking to close a hearing must advance an overriding interest that is likely to be prejudiced, the closure must be no broader than necessary to protect that interest, the trial court must consider reasonable alternatives to closing the proceeding, and it must make findings adequate to support the closure.

DA's Office v. Osborne, 129 S. Ct. 2308 (U.S. 2009)

A state prisoner filed an action under 42 U.S.C.S. § 1983, claiming that he had a constitutional right to have access to evidence that was introduced at his trial so he could have DNA testing conducted at his expense. The U.S. District Court ordered the state district attorney's office to give the inmate access, and the U.S. Court of Appeals for the Ninth Circuit affirmed. The state district attorney sought further review.

The inmate and another person were convicted of kidnapping, assault, and sexual assault after they forced a prostitute to perform fellatio and sexual intercourse and choked her, beat her, and shot her when she tried to flee. The inmate filed an action in federal district court, seeking an order requiring an Alaska district attorney's office to give him access to evidence that was introduced at his trial so he could have DNA tests conducted at his expense.

The U.S. Supreme Court held that the court of appeals erred when it found that the inmate had a right under the Due Process Clause of the Fourteenth Amendment to have access to the evidence he sought. The issue of access to DNA evidence following conviction is best left to Congress and state legislatures, and there was nothing inadequate about the procedures Alaska provided to inmates.

Briefly Noted

Caperton v. *A. T. Massey Coal Co.*, 129 S. Ct. 2252 (U.S. 2009). In a civil case, the U.S. Supreme Court explored whether a justice who received extraordinary campaign contributions from the board chairman and principal officer of appellant corporation violated the Due Process Clause of the Fourteenth Amendment when he denied a recusal motion. The Court held that the Due Process Clause incorporates the common-law rule that a judge must recuse himself when he has a direct, personal, substantial, pecuniary interest in a case. This rule reflects the maxim that no man is allowed to be a judge in his own cause; because his interest would certainly bias his judgment, and, not improbably, corrupt his integrity.

Summary

- The initial appearance of a defendant is sometimes referred to as an arraignment.
- At the initial appearance, the defendant will be informed of the charges against him or her and advised of his or her rights.
- An accused should be taken before a magistrate without unnecessary delay.
- Prior to the initial appearance, a legal document must be filed with the court setting forth the charge or charges against the accused.

- A demurrer to a complaint is a formal mode of disputing the sufficiency in law of the pleadings.
- Originally, the purpose of bail was to ensure the presence of the accused at trial. Presently, bail can be denied for protective reasons.
- There are several types of bail. The most common is money bail.

- Excessive bail is a violation of the U.S. Constitution.
- Bail may be forfeited if the defendant does not appear as promised.
- If the defendant makes his or her required court appearances, bail may be exonerated.

Review Questions

1. What is the purpose of the initial appearance?
2. Why is the initial appearance important?
3. How soon after an arrest must the accused be furnished with an initial appearance?
4. What is the purpose of bail?

5. In what form may bail be posted?
6. How much bail should a defendant be required to post?
7. What does forfeiture of bail signify?
8. What is the significance of the phrase "released on one's own recognizance"?

Local Procedure

1. Within what period of time must the initial appearance take place?
2. May an accused enter a plea at the initial appearance?
3. May a defendant be denied bail for protective detention?

4. Can a defendant be prosecuted for failure to appear after posting bail?

Endnotes

1. 318 U.S. 332 (1943).
2. 354 U.S. 449 (1957).
3. *Kinney* v. *County of Contra Costa*, 87 Cal Rptr 638 (1970).
4. 342 U.S. 1 (1951).

5. *Stack v. Boyle*, 342 U.S. 1 (1951).
6. 342 U.S. 524 (1952).
7. 95 L. Ed 2d 697 (1987).

CHAPTER 5

The Charging Function

No person shall be held to answer for a Capital, or otherwise infamous crime, unless on a presentment or indictment of a Grand Jury. . . .

—U.S. CONSTITUTION, AMENDMENT V, 1791

Prosecutors have so much sway over grand juries they could get them to "indict a ham sandwich."

—SOL WACHTLER, FORMER CHIEF JUDGE OF NEW YORK'S COURT OF APPEALS, 1985

They don't even have enough to indict a ham sandwich, much less Barry Bonds. [Bonds was being investigated by a grand jury as to whether he lied under oath.]

—STATEMENT BY MICHAEL RAINS, ATTORNEY FOR BASEBALL PLAYER BARRY BONDS AT A NEWS CONFERENCE ON JULY 20, 2006.

Chapter Outline

Preliminary Hearing

Arraignment

Grand Jury

Grants of Immunity for Witnesses

Case Law

Summary

Key Terms

Former acquittal

Grand jury

Indictment

Nolo contendere

Preliminary hearing

Right of discovery

Learning Objectives

After completing this chapter, you should be able to:

▪ Explain the purpose and process of the preliminary hearing.

▪ Explain the purpose, functions, and powers of a grand jury.

- Summarize the arraignment process.
- Explain the functions and purposes of a preliminary hearing.
- Discuss the duties of a grand jury.
- List and describe the types of witness immunity.

- Describe the history of the grand jury.
- Explain the differences between a grand jury and a preliminary hearing in charging an accused.
- Outline the elements of a valid guilty plea.
- Define terms related to the pretrial process.

PRELIMINARY HEARING

Many states use a preliminary hearing in lieu of a grand jury. It also is referred to as a preliminary examination. At the **preliminary hearing**, a magistrate decides whether there is adequate cause to require an accused to stand trial for the offense or offenses charged. The preliminary hearing is conducted before a magistrate. A magistrate has been described as any officer of the court who has the power to issue a warrant of arrest. Generally, a preliminary hearing is held before a judge of an inferior court—for example, a municipal court.

Before a preliminary hearing may be held, the defendant must have a complaint filed against him or her charging the defendant with a felony. In some jurisdictions, the complaint is known as an information. If the defendant enters a plea of not guilty, the judge will set the case over for a preliminary hearing. At the preliminary hearing, the prosecuting attorney presents evidence against the accused. This evidence may consist of witnesses and such physical evidence as the prosecutor deems appropriate. In most states, the evidence may be in the form of sworn statements of witnesses, and formal rules of evidence are relaxed during preliminary hearings. Most jurisdictions allow inadmissible hearsay evidence in the form of statements taken by a police officer to be considered in determining if there is sufficient evidence to hold the defendant over for trial. After the prosecution has presented its case, the defense may present a case. A defendant may waive a preliminary hearing in most jurisdictions. In most states, if there is a grand jury indictment, no preliminary hearing is required.

Bound Over for Trial

If the magistrate concludes that the evidence presented establishes probable cause that the defendant committed the crime(s) charged, the magistrate will bind or hold the defendant over for trial. If the magistrate concludes that the evidence supports only a misdemeanor charge, the magistrate will reduce the charges to the lesser offense. In some states, the magistrate has the authority to then handle the misdemeanor. In some states, if the defendant pleads guilty, the magistrate has the authority to accept the guilty plea in a felony case and then forwards the case to the felony trial court for sentencing. If the magistrate determines that probable cause does not exist to hold the defendant over for trial, the magistrate will dismiss the charges. When the magistrate dismisses the charges, jeopardy has not attached and the prosecutor may refile the charges and submit the case in another court. Most of the time, a prosecutor will not refile unless there is additional evidence of the defendant's guilt. Trial judges, in general, do not like to overrule another trial judge unless there are additional or new factors to consider.

The magistrates dismiss the charges in about 15 percent of the cases and reduce the charges to misdemeanors in about 10 percent of the cases. The remaining 75 percent of the defendants are bound over for trial.

Waiver of Preliminary Hearing

Although the preliminary hearing is a safeguard established for the benefit of the defendant, he or she may waive it if he or she so desires. However, in most jurisdictions, the waiver must be agreed to by the prosecuting attorney and the judge. There are advantages and disadvantages to both the defendant and the prosecution in the waiver of the preliminary hearing. If the defendant is unable to make bail, a waiver of the hearing results in an earlier trial date being set. On the other hand, by demanding a preliminary hearing, a defendant might bring about a dismissal of the charge and his or her release from custody. The judge might conclude as a result of the hearing that there is insufficient cause to hold the defendant for trial. Another advantage to the defendant in having a preliminary hearing is that he or she may discover evidence held by the prosecution as it is unfolded during the hearing. This outcome is particularly likely in those jurisdictions where the right of the defendant to examine the evidence held by the prosecution before the trial is not recognized. This right is known as the **right of discovery** or the right of inspection. It is granted to defendants in order that they may better prepare their defense.

A waiver of the hearing also limits the charges against the defendant to those existing in the complaint at the time of the waiver. Accordingly, the prosecution may not amend later without starting the process again or obtaining a new waiver from defendant.

As it relates to the prosecution, there may be advantages in holding a preliminary hearing because it gives the prosecuting attorney an opportunity to obtain the testimony of the witnesses on an official record or transcript at a time when the facts are fresh in their memories and they are less likely to falsify. This record can be used during the trial should a witness become unavailable. In those states in which the right of discovery is not recognized, the prosecuting attorney may agree with the waiver so that he or she will not have to reveal evidence to the defense. The waiver will also eliminate a dilemma for the prosecuting attorney. In a preliminary hearing, the prosecuting attorney must present enough evidence to convince the judge that the accused should be held for trial, but the prosecuting attorney does not want to reveal any more evidence than is necessary in order to prevent the defense from endeavoring to obtain perjured testimony to meet the prosecution's case.

Although the grand jury system was established to safeguard the accused, this system has been under attack by defendants. Some professionals contend that a preliminary hearing better fulfills the Due Process Clause of the Fourteenth Amendment. The reasoning behind this position is that the grand jury meets in secret and the defendant is not permitted to be present, nor can the defendant demand to present evidence in his or her own behalf. Generally, the courts have held that either the grand jury hearing or the preliminary hearing system may be adopted by the states, as they see fit, and both satisfy the due process of law requirement.

Law in Practice

E-Discovery

E-discovery is the discovery of any type or format of electronic information within the context of the litigation discovery process. The term is used to encompass every action involved in the discovery of electronic information, including collection, forensics, review, production, native file production, and native file review.

Forms of electronic data include email, application files, instant messages, text messages, phone messages, and video recordings.

In *United States* v. *Ferguson*,[1] a drug-trafficking prosecution, defendant Ferguson moved to suppress Yahoo! and MSN Hotmail email evidence obtained by the government, which was seized pursuant to the magistrate judge's order under the Stored Communications Act (SCA). The SCA regulates when an electronic communication service provider, like Yahoo or MSN Hotmail, may disclose the contents of or other information about a customer's emails and other electronic communications to private parties. Congress passed the SCA to prohibit a provider of an electronic communication service "from knowingly divulging the contents of any communication while in electronic storage by that service to any person other than the addressee or intended recipient except as provided by a court order." The defendant challenged the SCA's constitutionality, and in turn, the government argued that the constitutionality of the SCA had no bearing on whether the evidence warranted suppression. Denying the defendant's motion to suppress, the court found that the SCA does not provide a suppression remedy and concluded that the government's reliance on the SCA was objectively reasonable.

ARRAIGNMENT

An arraignment is the formal reading of charges against a person. Usually, the arraignment is a brief hearing although it may be combined with a hearing on bail if the crime is a serious felony.

When an indictment is returned or an information is filed with the trial court, the accused will be arraigned upon that accusatory pleading. Arraignment in many jurisdictions is the initial and first appearance before a judge where the state reads the official charges, called an information or indictment, against the defendant.

At the arraignment, the accused will be permitted to enter a plea to the charge set forth in that accusatory pleading. If a plea of not guilty or not guilty by reason of insanity is entered, a trial must take place. If the accused was not arrested before the indictment was returned, this arraignment may be the initial appearance for the accused. At the arraignment, the accused will again be advised of his or her constitutional rights. Even though the accused may have been taken before a judge after a complaint was filed, the accused is still entitled to be arraigned after the filing of the indictment or information. In a sense, the indictment or information is a separate formal charge. The arraignment under these circumstances is not to be confused with the initial appearance even though, in some areas, the initial appearance is referred to as an arraignment.

During the arraignment, the defendant is given an opportunity to enter a plea to the charge alleged in the complaint. The defendant may either enter the plea at that time or request time to consider the plea to be entered. Depending upon the jurisdiction, the defendant may enter any one or more of the following pleas: (1) guilty, (2) not guilty, (3) nolo contendere, (4) not guilty by reason of insanity, (5) former jeopardy, or (6) former judgment of acquittal or conviction. Generally, the law provides that if a defendant does not plead not guilty by reason of insanity, he or she shall be conclusively presumed to have been sane at the time the crime was committed.

Depending on the jurisdiction, many pretrial issues are often settled at arraignment.

Motions at Arraignment

While procedures vary in states and federal trials, there are some motions that must be made at arraignment or they are considered as waived. A motion to quash (dismiss) the indictment generally must be made prior to entering a plea. For example, if the defendant moves the court to quash the indictment against him or her and argues that the indictment fails to supply required information, and the indictment is also vague and ambiguous and does not apprise the defendant of the charge against him or her with sufficient specificity to permit adequate preparation of a defense. Figure 5-1 is an example of a motion that may be filed. Other motions or issues that could be considered in many jurisdictions include:

- Hearing to determine if a murder trial will be tried as a capital case.
- Motion regarding the defendant's competency to stand trial.
- Motion for the appointment of an interpreter.
- Notice of intent to use insanity defense.
- Request to withdraw as defense counsel.
- Request for the judge to recluse herself based on a conflict of interest.
- Motion to disqualify the prosecutor.

Guilty Plea

At one time in our history, defendants were not permitted to enter guilty pleas since it was thought that the only way justice could be accomplished was by a trial. A plea of guilty is an admission of every element of the offense charged, and no proof of the crime needs to be presented.[2] A plea of guilty is more than a confession that admits that the accused did various acts; it is itself a conviction; nothing remains but to give judgment and determine punishment. Thus, the plea of guilty cannot be accepted lightly by a judge.

IN THE STATE COURT FOR BULLOCH COUNTY
STATE OF GEORGIA

THE STATE OF GEORGIA

     VS.   **Criminal Action Number: 1B05CR1274-A**

ROBIN WYNN

     Defendant

MOTION TO QUASH INDICTMENT

     COMES NOW the Defendant in the above-styled case who moves the Court to quash the indictment against her on the following grounds:

1.

Defendant demurs to and moves to quash any and all such parts of the indictment that are based upon Chapter 13 of Title 16 of The Georgia Code in that said code section is unconstitutional in that those parts of the offending section and those other parts of the Code which attempt to enforce and/or reinforce it are nothing less than attempts by the socialist party that dominates this State to use the laws to "perfect the socialist man" in contravention of the following Paragraphs of the Georgia Constitution's Bill of Rights, to wit:

  1 [life, liberty, and property-due process],
  2 [protection of person the paramount duty of government which shall be impartial-equal protection],
  3 [each person has the natural and inalienable right to worship God, each according to the dictates of his own conscience and no human authority should in any case control or interfere with such rights],
  4 [freedom of religion],
 13 [searches and seizures],
 25 [social status of a citizen never to be subject of legislation] and
 28 [the enermeration of rights shall not be construed to deny to the people any inherent rights which they may have hetherto enjoyed]

2.

Defendant further shows that through its application of the aforesaid offending Code provisions the General Assembly of Georgia has unleashed upon the populace a swarm of officers like unto a plague to harrass and bother the people in a seemingly endless pursuit of the aforesaid unconstitutional and immorally democratic goals. Defendant respectfully reminds the Court that this is supposed to be a Republic—not a Republic—with minority rights protected from infringement by the majority.

     Wherefore having so moved, Defendant prays that the indictments against her be quashed and that the State be barred from entering into evidence against her any reference to her alleged refusal to submit to a test of urine or blood.

                                       William Bush
                                       Georgia Bar No. 3420675

FIGURE 5-1 A Typical Motion to Quash (Dismiss) an Indictment.

Generally, in felony cases, a plea of guilty must be made by the defendant in open court either orally or in writing. The purpose behind the requirement that the defendant personally enter the plea is to ensure that it is his or her own plea. Most states provide that a judge may not accept a plea of guilty, particularly in felony cases, unless the defendant is informed of his or her right to the assistance of counsel. If the defendant understands this right to counsel and waives the right, the judge may then accept the plea of guilty. However, some states will not permit a judge to accept a guilty plea to a capital offense charge, or one in which the punishment is life imprisonment without the possibility of parole, unless the defendant is represented by counsel. A few states will not permit a defendant to enter a guilty plea to a capital offense even with the assistance of counsel. In lesser offenses (misdemeanors and infractions), most states allow counsel to enter guilty pleas on behalf of their clients in open court and on the record.

In accordance with the U.S. Supreme Court's *Boykin* v. *Alabama* decision, before a judge may accept a guilty plea to any charge, misdemeanor or felony, the judge must inform the defendant of the significance of the guilty plea. The defendant must be informed that by pleading guilty, he or she waives all right against self-incrimination, the right to a jury trial, and all right to be confronted by his or her accusers. Even though the defendant is represented by counsel at the time of the guilty plea, the records of the case in felony cases must reflect that the judge advised the defendant of the guarantees that would be waived by the plea of guilty.

The defendant must be advised of all the major consequences of his or her plea of guilty including, if applicable, the period of confinement, the period of probation, and any registration requirements. In most cases, before the trial judge takes the defendant's plea of guilty in open court, defense counsel or the prosecutor will provide written waiver forms advising the defendant of the rights that he or she is waiving by pleading guilty and the range of punishment that may be adjudged in the case. The waiver forms are then witnessed by the defense counsel and submitted to the trial judge as exhibits to be attached to the trial record.

Law in Practice

Should a Trial Judge Accept a Defendant's Plea of Guilt When the Defendant Refuses to Admit that He or She Committed the Crime?

In *North Carolina* v. *Alford* 400 U.S. 25 (1970), Alford was charged with capital murder. He pleaded guilty, although disclaiming guilt, because of the strong evidence against him. The prosecutor agreed to reduce the charges from capital murder to second-degree murder if he pleaded guilty. The punishment for second-degree murder was imprisonment from two to thirty years. The punishment for capital murder could have been the death penalty.

Alford's gun fired the fatal bullet. Alford and the victim had gotten into a fight earlier that evening. The next morning when Alford was arrested, he stated that because of his intoxication he did not remember what happened the night the victim was killed.

The Supreme Court noted in its opinion that while most pleas of guilt consist of both a waiver of trial and an express admission of guilt, the latter element is not a constitutional requisite to the imposition of criminal penalty. The Court indicated that as long as the plea of guilt was made voluntarily, knowingly, and understandingly it was constitutional. The Court also noted in a footnote that a trial judge is not required to accept a valid plea of guilt.

The laws of some states provide that before the judge may accept a guilty plea, an inquiry must be made to make certain that the accused has actually committed a crime serious enough to justify the guilty plea. The extent of the inquiry will depend largely upon the facts of each case. The judge may confine the inquiry to the facts in the transcript of the preliminary hearing or of the grand jury, or the judge may use whatever procedure is best under the circumstances, including interrogating the attorneys involved in the case. The accused does not have to admit guilt expressly at the time of the guilty plea. In some states, a guilty plea may be accepted even though accompanied by a claim of innocence.[3] A judge does not have to accept a guilty plea, particularly if the judge feels that the defendant does not understand the significance of the plea or if there is some question about the plea being voluntarily given. Most jurisdictions hold that defendants who are not citizens of the United States must be advised that if they plead guilty, they may be subject to deportation.

After a plea of guilty is accepted, the next step is to sentence the defendant. If the charge is a misdemeanor, the judge of the inferior court has the authority to mete out the sentence, but if the charge is a felony, the case must be transferred to the superior court for sentencing. A judge of an inferior court has the authority to accept a guilty plea to a felony charge in most jurisdictions, and the plea will have the same effect as if it had been entered in the superior court. A few jurisdictions do not permit a defendant to enter a plea to a felony charge in the inferior court, and the case must be transferred to the superior court for both the acceptance of the plea and the sentencing.

Withdrawal of Guilty Plea

In most jurisdictions, a defendant, upon showing a good cause, may withdraw a guilty plea and enter a not guilty plea or one of the other pleas at any time before the pronouncement of sentence. A few jurisdictions hold that if the defendant was not represented by counsel at the time the guilty plea was entered, the judge must permit the defendant to withdraw the guilty plea upon showing good cause. For this reason, most judges are reluctant to accept a plea of guilty if the defendant was not represented by counsel, particularly in felony cases. The request of a defendant to withdraw a guilty plea is not taken lightly. If the withdrawal is permitted, then the defendant is entitled to a trial on one of the other pleas that may have been entered. This action could inconvenience witnesses, crowd court calendars, and cause additional expense. But if the defendant can show sufficiently good cause, the withdrawal should be permitted by the trial judge; otherwise, the denial of the withdrawal may be overturned by an appellate court. The problem created by this procedure is determining what would be considered good cause.

It has been held that if the defendant did not understand the meaning or significance of the guilty plea, this allegation is sufficient showing of good cause. In *Henderson* v. *Morgan*,[4] the U.S. Supreme Court permitted the withdrawal of a guilty plea nine years after it was originally entered upon the grounds that the plea had been involuntarily given. In that case, the trial court accepted a guilty plea to a charge of second-degree murder. The defendant later attempted to withdraw the guilty plea on the grounds that he did not know that "intent" was a necessary element of second-degree murder and, further, that he had not been sufficiently informed of the sentence he would receive if he pleaded guilty. The appellate courts of New York upheld the judge's denial of the withdrawal, and the case was appealed to the U.S. Supreme Court upon the grounds that the defendant had been denied due process of law. The Supreme Court held that since the defendant had not been advised by either the judge or the attorneys involved that intent was a necessary element of the crime of second-degree murder, his plea of guilty was "as a matter of law involuntary and must be set aside." It was stated that a plea could not have been voluntarily given unless the defendant had "received real notice of the true nature of the charge against him, the first and most universally recognized requirement of due process." But it was felt that the defendant had been sufficiently informed of the sentence that he might receive if the guilty plea was received. In most jurisdictions, there is no requirement that a defendant be advised of the exact sentence that the court may impose if the guilty plea is accepted, but he or she must be informed of the potential maximum sentence and any mandatory minimum sentence that must be imposed. The acceptance of a guilty plea upon the basis of the sentence that may be imposed is discussed in Chapter 9 under the heading "Plea Negotiation."

An additional reason some states require a judge to make an inquiry concerning the facts surrounding a guilty plea is to prevent a defendant from later challenging the plea as being a free and voluntary act, as was successfully done by Morgan some nine years after his guilty plea in the *Henderson* v. *Morgan* case. The dissenting justices in that case felt that the withdrawal of the guilty plea should have been denied. It was their opinion that the trial judge had held a factual inquiry and that the inquiry revealed that the defendant had sufficient knowledge of the elements of the crime. Thus, these justices believed that the guilty plea had been voluntarily given. The facts in *Parker* v. *North Carolina*[5] present an interesting attempt to withdraw a guilty plea. The defendant argued that his guilty plea was the product of a coerced confession. The court stated that even on the assumption that the confession had been coerced, the court could not believe that the alleged police conduct during the interrogation period was of such a nature or had such an enduring effect as to make involuntary a plea of guilty entered over a month later. According to the appellate court, the trial judge was within his rights to refuse the request for withdrawal of the guilty plea.

Not Guilty Plea

When a plea of not guilty is entered by the defendant, the case will start proceeding toward a trial. If the plea is to a misdemeanor charge, the case may be set immediately for trial, which, in most instances, will take place in the minor court. If the not guilty plea is to a felony charge, further proceedings must take place either by a grand jury hearing or by a preliminary hearing before the case can be set for trial in the superior or district court. This procedure protects the accused from being held for trial without sufficient cause. The grand jury and preliminary hearings will be discussed later. Most jurisdictions permit a defendant to withdraw a not guilty plea and to enter a plea of guilty at any time during the trial. This possibility eliminates much trial time, particularly if the change of plea takes place early in the trial proceedings.

Occasionally, a defendant will refuse to enter any plea and stand mute before the court. History reveals that when this behavior occurred in early common law, the defendant was returned to the prison from which he or she had been brought and made to lie naked on his on her back on the floor. Great weights of iron were placed on the defendant, who was fed only three "morsels of the worst bread" the first day and three sips of stagnant water the next, with this diet alternating daily until the prisoner died or entered a plea. In later years, a more humane procedure was followed. When the defendant stood mute before the court, the silence was treated as a guilty plea. Today, if the defendant refuses to plead, a plea of not guilty is entered for him or her, followed by a trial. By entering a plea of guilty, the defendant admits that he or she is the person named in the indictment or information.

Nolo Contendere Plea

A plea of **nolo contendere**, meaning "I will not contest it," or "no contest," is essentially equivalent to a plea of guilty. In some states, the nolo contendere plea is known as "non volt contendere" and is sometimes abbreviated as "non volt." As with the plea of guilty, the judge must inform the defendant of those rights that he or she is entitled to and of those that he or she waives by such a plea. In some jurisdictions, the nolo contendere plea may not be used against the defendant in a civil matter because the defendant has not admitted guilt. As pointed out, a plea of guilty is a formal type of confession of the act charged. Not all states permit a nolo contendere plea to be entered by a defendant. In those states in which the plea has been adopted, there is a variance in who must agree to accept the plea. In some states, only the judge must agree to accept the plea; in others, the prosecuting attorney also must agree before the nolo contendere plea may be accepted.

This plea has been adopted to satisfy the thinking of two types of defendants charged with a violation. Some defendants will admit to committing a particular act but will refuse to admit that the act was a crime, so they enter the "no contest" plea of nolo contendere. For example, a person may be charged with speeding on a freeway. She may admit to excessive speed but allege that, since no one was injured or endangered, no crime was committed. Thus, she merely enters the plea of nolo contendere.

Other defendants have committed acts that may subject them to civil suits for damages or restitution as well as to criminal prosecution. They feel that the evidence against them is so great that it would be useless to contest the criminal charges, but they do not want to permit the guilty plea to be introduced against them in a civil trial. Under these circumstances, they may wish to enter the nolo contendere plea. As an example, this plea is frequently entered by a defendant who has been arrested for driving under the influence of alcohol after being involved in a serious accident in which persons were injured or killed. The defendant may know that the evidence against him is strong enough that a trial would result in a conviction. To save the expense of a trial and to prevent the conviction from being used against him in a civil suit, the defendant will attempt to enter a plea of nolo contendere. In this instance, the judge may refuse to allow the defendant to enter the nolo contendere plea, since it could be an injustice to the victims of the accident. A defendant may not plead nolo contendere as a matter of right but must have the consent of the judge, its acceptance being entirely a matter of grace.

Not Guilty by Reason of Insanity Plea

By entering a plea of not guilty by reason of insanity, the defendant is admitting the commission of the act for which he or she is charged, but the defendant alleges that he or she cannot be held responsible for the crime because he or she was not sane at the time the act was committed. The whole issue of the ensuing trial is whether the defendant was sane or insane at the time the crime was committed.

Most states provide that if the defendant enters this plea, he or she has the burden of proving that he or she was insane at the time the offense was committed, and the prosecution may endeavor to meet that allegation by introducing evidence to prove that the defendant was sane at the time of the offense. A few states hold that the burden of proving beyond a reasonable doubt that the defendant was sane at the time he or she committed the act still rests with the prosecution. The defendant has only to meet the prosecution's case by creating a doubt of his or her sanity. If the defendant is found to have been sane at the time he or she committed the crime, the only procedure to follow is sentencing the defendant because he or she has already admitted that he or she has committed the acts at issue by the plea of not guilty by reason of insanity. If the defendant is found to have been insane at the time the offense was committed, then technically he or she is entitled to be set free because his or her present sanity is not in question. However, most jurisdictions provide that the judge hearing the case may demand that the defendant be confined for a period, usually not less than ninety days, for observation to determine that the defendant is not a danger to society. If, after the confinement period, it is determined that the defendant is not a danger, he or she must be released from custody.

A few states permit a defendant to enter dual pleas. He or she may enter a plea of not guilty and at the same time enter a plea of not guilty by reason of insanity. This procedure has been criticized, since the pleas are actually inconsistent. Upon entering the plea of not guilty, the defendant is denying his or her guilt. In the second plea, the defendant is confessing guilt but alleging that he or she cannot be held responsible for the offense because of his or her insanity at the time. Where this procedure is permitted, the trial on the not guilty plea takes place first. If the defendant is found not guilty, he or she is entitled to be released without further action being taken. If the defendant is found to be guilty, the trial on the plea of not guilty by reason of insanity must follow. If the defendant is found to be sane at the time of committing the act, the sentencing procedure will take place. But if the defendant is found to have been insane at the time he or she committed the offense, the same procedure for release or observation will be set in motion as was previously described.

Not all states permit a plea of not guilty by reason of insanity to be entered, but insanity may be raised as a defense to the crime charged. Appendix B consists of an actual psychological report entered in trial at a case involving the issue of not guilty by reason of insanity.

Double Jeopardy or Plea of Once in Jeopardy

Excerpt from Fifth Amendment, U.S. Constitution: ". . . nor shall any person be subject for the same offense to be twice put in jeopardy of life or limb."

The guarantee against being placed twice in jeopardy, also referred to as the right against double jeopardy, is of ancient origin, having been found in procedures of early Greek and Roman jurisprudence. It was established in the common law of England and brought to this country by the colonists. The guarantee is embodied in the Fifth Amendment to the U.S. Constitution and the laws of all the states. Basically, the guarantee provides that no person shall be placed in jeopardy of his or her life or liberty more than once for the same offense. It prohibits undue harassment and oppression by those in authority. If it were not for this guarantee against double jeopardy, an accused could be tried and retried until found guilty. Likewise, he or she might be retried if it was felt that the sentence resulting from the first trial was not severe enough.

If an accused is charged with a crime and believes that he or she has been previously placed in jeopardy by court action on that same charge, the accused may enter the plea of once in jeopardy. But many ramifications are involved in this plea, such as what comprises jeopardy and under what conditions an accused may be placed twice in jeopardy. Many persons are under the impression that an accused cannot be tried twice for the same offense. This is not always the case. There are situations in which a defendant may be tried two or more times for the same offense. Generally, if a defendant is acquitted of a crime, he or she cannot be tried again for that particular offense. But if a defendant is convicted, he or she may appeal the conviction to an appellate court. If the conviction is reversed upon appeal, the case may be retried. Upon appealing the conviction, the defendant is in a sense waiving his or her guarantee against double jeopardy. In the same manner, if the defendant requests a new trial after being convicted, he or she is waiving the double jeopardy guarantee. Furthermore, it has been held that if the jury cannot arrive at a verdict, the case may be retried by a different jury without the second trial's being a violation of the double jeopardy right.

The determination of when an accused has been placed in jeopardy involves complications. The Fifth Amendment guarantee against double jeopardy is of little assistance, since it merely provides that an accused shall not "be subject for the same offense to be twice put in jeopardy of life or limb." As the courts began to grant the guarantee against double jeopardy, it became necessary to determine when jeopardy attaches. In making this determination, the courts looked to the common law of England. The common law rule at the time that the Fifth Amendment was adopted was comparatively simple, merely providing that a defendant had been placed in jeopardy only when there had been a conviction or an acquittal after a complete trial. The early English history of jurisprudence reveals that, once commenced, most trials were completed. It is stated that the traditional practice was to keep the jury together, unfed and without drink, until they delivered a unanimous verdict. As late as 1866, an English court stated that the rule seemed to command the confinement of the jury until death if it did not agree on a verdict. At the time of the enactment of the Fifth Amendment, most criminal prosecutions in this country proceeded until a verdict was reached. At that time, neither the defendant nor the prosecution had any right to appeal an adverse verdict. The verdict in such a case was unquestionably final and barred further prosecution for the same offense.

But as time passed, this strict rule was relaxed through U.S. Supreme Court decisions. One of the first relaxations was the right granted to one convicted of a crime to be able to appeal the conviction if some error was committed during the trial. If the conviction was reversed upon appeal because of some error during the trial, the prosecution could retry the case. As stated, the appeal by the defendant amounted to a waiver of the right against double jeopardy. However, the U.S. Supreme Court in *Burks* v. *United States*[6] held that once a jury's verdict of acquittal is returned, that acquittal is a bar against further prosecutive action against the accused for the offense charged. The Court stated that the acquittal is an absolute bar "no matter how erroneous its [the jury's] decision" may be. In the past, some states held that if the jury returned an erroneous verdict of acquittal, the defendant could be retried because jeopardy did not set in until a just verdict had been rendered. The *Burks* decision has eliminated such a contention.

Since it was believed that jeopardy did not set in until the verdict stage was reached, many trials were commenced but did not reach the verdict state. A judge often would stop a trial if he or she believed that the defendant was guilty and that the jury selected would not return a guilty verdict. The judge would dismiss that particular jury and have the trial started over with a new jury. This procedure could be repeated until the judge and prosecution felt that the jury selected would return a guilty verdict. Since this procedure resulted in injustices, to prevent such injustices, rules were established that held that if a jury was dismissed without sufficient cause after the trial began, the defendant would have been placed in jeopardy and could not be retried.

The reason behind this rule was expressed by the U.S. Supreme Court in the *Burks* v. *United States* decision. The Court stated as follows:

> The Double Jeopardy Clause forbids a second trial for the purpose of affording the prosecution another opportunity to supply evidence which it failed to muster in the first proceeding. This is central to the objective of the prohibition against successive trials. The Clause does not allow the state to make repeated attempts to convict an individual for an alleged offense since the constitutional prohibition against double jeopardy was designed to protect an individual from being subjected to the hazards of trial and possible conviction more than once for an alleged offense.

The Court further stated in the case of *Crist* v. *Bretz*[7]:

> The basic reason for holding that a defendant is put in jeopardy even though the criminal proceeding against him terminated before verdict was perhaps best stated in *Green* v. *United States,* 355 US 184: "the underlying idea, one that is deeply ingrained in at least the Anglo-American system of jurisprudence, is that the State with all its resources and power should not be allowed to make repeated attempts to convict an individual for an alleged offense, thereby subjecting him to embarrassment, expense and ordeal and compelling him to live in a continuing state of anxiety and insecurity, as well as enhancing the possibility that even though innocent he may be found guilty."

The ruling that held that a defendant had been placed in jeopardy once the jury trial began created the problem of determining at what point the jury trial commenced. The legislatures and courts of the various states tried to establish guidelines to solve this problem, but there was no uniformity among the states. Some states held that a jury trial began once the jury was selected and sworn to do its duty in arriving at a verdict. Other states held that a jury trial did not commence until after the jury was selected and the first witness was sworn. The U.S.

Supreme Court settled the problem in *Crist* v. *Bretz* by holding that a jury trial commences once the jury is selected and sworn. The Court stated as follows:

> . . . the federal rule that jeopardy attaches when the jury is empaneled and sworn is an integral part of the constitutional guarantee against double jeopardy. . . . The reason for holding that jeopardy attaches when the jury is empaneled and sworn lies in the need to protect the interest of an accused in retaining a chosen jury. That right was described in *Wade* v. *Hunter* as a defendant's valued right to have his trial completed by a particular tribunal. It is an interest with roots deep in the historic development of trial by jury in the Anglo-American system of criminal justice. Throughout that history there ran a strong tradition that once banded together a jury should not be discharged until it had completed its solemn task of announcing a verdict.

The rule provides that the defendant will have been placed in jeopardy if, once the trial begins, the jury is dismissed without sufficient cause before the verdict stage is reached.

There is no clear criterion concerning what is considered sufficient cause for a trial not to continue to the verdict stage. A sufficient cause may result from a mistrial having been declared by a judge. Often during a trial, a situation such as misconduct by a juror or some improper remark by a witness while testifying may cause a judge to believe that the defendant could not receive a fair trial if the trial was allowed to proceed. Even when a mistrial is declared primarily for the benefit of the defendant, the defendant usually must agree to the mistrial's being declared; otherwise, an appellate court may conclude that jeopardy had set in and the defendant could not be retried.

The U.S. Supreme Court in *Crist* v. *Bretz* indicated that a court trial (i.e., a trial by the judge without a jury) begins when the first witness is sworn. Unless the trial is continued to the verdict stage, the defendant will be placed in jeopardy. Remember that the defendant may be retried if the trial is discontinued for good cause.

Plea of Former Judgment of Conviction or Acquittal

The plea of former conviction or **former acquittal** is not included in the statutes of all states. However, it has been held by some states that a defendant is not properly protected by the plea of double jeopardy in some instances. When a defendant commits an act and breaks both state and federal criminal laws, the defendant could be prosecuted by either the state or the federal government. The question arises: May the defendant be prosecuted by both without a violation of the double jeopardy guarantee? This question was answered by the U.S. Supreme Court in the case of *United States* v. *Lanza*[8] and reiterated in *Abbate* v. *United States,*[9] in which cases the Court concluded that a defendant could be tried by *both* federal and state governments. The Court based its decisions upon the fact that a citizen of this nation owes a duty to both the federal and state governments. When an act is committed that violates the laws of both sovereignties, both may prosecute. About half of the states have statutory provisions that hold that if a defendant is prosecuted by the state government, prosecution by the local court in that state for the same act is prohibited. The plea of former judgment of conviction or acquittal would be the proper plea under the circumstances.

The protection against double jeopardy extends to the conduct of an accused, not just to the charged crimes. Once jeopardy has attached, the prosecutor may not file new and different charges against the defendant based on the same conduct.

The plea of former judgment would also be proper if a defendant were acquitted of one charge and retried on a lesser charge arising out of the same act. However, most states hold that the plea of once in jeopardy covers this situation and have not included the former judgment of conviction or acquittal plea in their statutes.

United States v. *Lara*, 541 U.S. 193 (2004)

The defendant, an Indian, was convicted of violence to a policeman, a federal officer, in the court of a tribe to which defendant did not belong, and asserted that his subsequent federal prosecution for assaulting the officer was precluded by the double jeopardy prohibition. The government contended that 25 U.S.C.S. § 1301(2), which allowed a tribal court to prosecute an Indian of any tribe, merely lifted the political restriction on a tribe's inherent sovereign authority to prosecute violations of tribal law. The government thus argued that double jeopardy did not apply since the tribal prosecution and the federal prosecution involved separate offenses against separate sovereigns.

Can Defendant Be Prosecuted Twice, Once in Tribal Court and Once in Federal Court, for the Same Act?

JUSTICE BREYER: Defendant's federal prosecution was not barred by double jeopardy. Congress had broad power to legislate with regard to tribes, including the power to relax as well as restrict tribal sovereign authority to control events that occur upon the tribe's own land which existed prior to federal authority over the tribe. The Double Jeopardy Clause reflects the common-law conception of crime as an offense against the sovereignty of the government; when a defendant in a single act violates the peace and dignity of two sovereigns by breaking the laws of each, he has committed two distinct offenses.

GRAND JURY

A **grand jury** is a group of persons representing a cross section of a community, usually a county, whose primary purpose is to hear certain types of criminal accusations in order to determine whether there are sufficient facts to hold the accused for trial. As was stated in the U.S. Supreme Court case of *Wood* v. *Georgia*[10]:

> Historically, this body [the grand jury] has been regarded as a primary security to the innocent against hasty, malicious and oppressive persecution; it serves the invaluable function in our society of standing between the accuser and the accused, whether the latter be an individual, minority group, or other, to determine whether a charge is founded upon reason or was dictated by an intimidating power or by malice and personal ill will.

The grand jury procedure came into being early in the common law of England. The Magna Charta provided that no freeman was to be seized and imprisoned except by the judgment of his or her peers. This provision established the procedure that before a person could be held for trial on a serious charge, the accusation had to be presented to a council comprising the accused's peers to determine whether the charge was well founded. The council later became known as a grand jury, as opposed to the petit or trial jury. The grand jury consisted of no fewer than sixteen persons and no more than twenty-three. There is really no logical reason for these numbers having been selected, except that it was thought that since a person was accused of a serious crime, a reasonable number of his or her peers should hear the accusation and determine whether the accused should be held for trial. Also, to prevent the body from becoming too large and unwieldy, a maximum of twenty-three was selected.

The grand jury was created as a safeguard for the accused. It prevented the accused from being held on a serious charge without sufficient cause or justification. The idea of the grand jury was brought to this country from England, and it was embodied in the Fifth Amendment of the U.S. Constitution. This amendment provides that "no person shall be held to answer for a capital or otherwise infamous crime, unless on presentment or indictment of a grand jury." A capital offense is one punishable by death; an infamous crime has been defined as one punishable by hard labor or imprisonment for more than one year. For all practical purposes, an infamous crime is any felony. This amendment was applicable only to federal charges, and the states were free to establish their own safeguards. Approximately one-half of the states hold that all felonies, and in some instances serious misdemeanors, must be presented to a grand jury. The remaining states provide that the accusation may be presented to a judge or magistrate in the form of a preliminary hearing in lieu of grand jury action.

Selection and Qualification of Grand Jurors

The selection of grand jurors varies greatly from state to state. In some states, they are selected at random, often using the list of voters for the territorial jurisdiction. The clerk of the court will cut the names from the list and place them in a box from which the required number of names will be drawn. In other states, the trial judge, or judges, of the county will furnish to the clerk of the court the names of prospective jurors. These names will be placed in a box from which the required number will be drawn. In some areas, the grand jury comprises persons who volunteer their services because it is considered to be an honor to serve on a grand jury.

Law in Practice

Differences in Procedure in the Charging Process When Using a Grand Jury or Preliminary Hearing

Grand Jury Proceedings	Preliminary Hearing
Primary duty is to determine if there is probable cause to believe that the defendant committed the crimes or crimes charged.	Same.
If probable cause is found, an indictment is returned against the defendant.	If probable cause is found, the defendant is bound over for trial. (*Note:* In a few states, the defendant may be referred to a grand jury.)
Grand jury sessions are closed hearings.	Held in open court.
Proceedings are secret.	Proceedings are open to the public.
Proceedings are informal.	Formal judicial proceedings occur.
Nonadversarial proceedings—grand jury normally hears only evidence presented by the prosecutor.	Adversarial proceedings—both prosecution and defense may present evidence.
A judge does not preside over the sessions.	A judge presides over the hearings.
Defendant has no right to be present or to present evidence.	Defendant has a right to be present and to present evidence.
Grand jury has power to conduct its own investigations.	No investigative authority is granted.
Grand jury can subpoena witnesses and documents.	No subpoena power at preliminary examination.
Grand jury has power to grant immunity.	No immunity power at hearing.

Following the common-law tradition, grand juries in this country vary from sixteen to twenty-three persons, but most grand juries consist of nineteen persons. They are usually selected at the beginning of the calendar or fiscal year and generally serve for one year. The qualifications necessary to serve on the grand jury are very similar to those of a petit jury. The individual must be eighteen years of age or over, a citizen of the United States, a resident of the jurisdiction for at least one year, and have sufficient knowledge of the English language to properly communicate. After the grand jurors have been selected, they are given an oath in which they promise to do their duty and to keep their proceedings secret and confidential. The oath is generally administered by a superior court judge. At this time, the grand jury is considered to be impaneled. After the grand jury is impaneled, the judge either will appoint a member of the grand jury to act as foreperson or may instruct the grand jury to select one of their members to act as foreperson. When the appointment of a foreperson is completed, the grand jury is authorized to hear criminal charges to determine whether an accused should be held for trial.

Indictment

Prior to the grand jury hearings, the prosecuting attorney will prepare a formal document setting forth the charge against the accused. This document is known as an **indictment**. It is also referred to as a bill of indictment in some jurisdictions. At one time in our history, the indictment was a very technically worded document, and any failure to word it properly would give a judge the right to dismiss the charge. In fact, the wording became ridiculously technical. For example, if the charge was for murder and if the indictment did not particularly designate the deceased as a human being, the indictment was considered faulty. Or if the initials A.D. did not accompany the date, it was held that the indictment did not reflect that the charge had not been outlawed by the passage of time. Today, the indictment is a comparatively simply worded instrument. It is very similar in form to the complaint. The indictment sets forth the name of the accused, the crime that is alleged to have been committed, the date and place of the alleged crime, and a few pertinent facts about the crime. Figure 5-2 is a copy of the indictment of Michael Jackson that was issued in 2004.

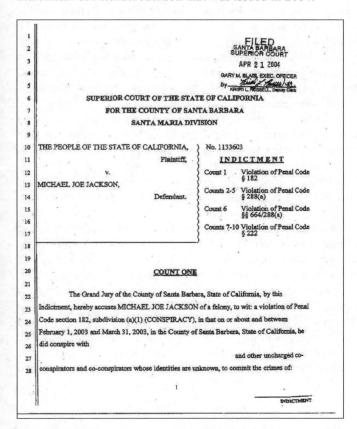

FIGURE 5-2 Copy of Michael Jackson Grand Jury Indictment.

The indictment serves several purposes. First, it informs the grand jury of the charge about which they will receive evidence during the hearing. Second, if the required number of grand jurors votes in favor of holding the accused for trial, they will so designate that fact by having the foreperson sign the indictment, or as it is known, "endorse the indictment." In some states, the grand jury in upholding the indictment finds it a "true bill of indictment." The indictment is then filed with the court in which the trial will take place. Third, if the accused is not in custody when the indictment is endorsed and filed with the court, the indictment will enable the judge to issue a warrant of arrest. The indictment is also an accusatory pleading and is the document that sets the trial in motion in the superior court. Finally, the indictment informs the defendant of the charge against which he or she must defend himself or herself. If the accused is charged with more than one crime, these additional crimes may be included in the same indictment, and they are referred to as counts.

Grand Jury Hearings

The frequency with which the grand jury meets depends upon the number of criminal charges that must be heard. In highly populated areas, the grand jury may meet daily, Monday through Friday. In other areas, it may meet only when there is an occasion to do so, which could be only once a month or less frequently. Although the grand jury may call a hearing on its own, the members usually meet at the request of the prosecuting attorney. The grand jury meets in closed hearings, and the procedure is secret. In determining whether an accused should be held for trial, jury members will question witnesses and receive the evidence that is deemed pertinent by the prosecuting attorney. Before testifying, each witness takes an oath to tell the truth and not to reveal the proceedings that take place during his or her presence before the grand jury. During the examination of the witnesses, the prosecuting attorney is usually present and does the questioning of witnesses and presents the other evidence to the jury. While members of the grand jury may question witnesses or present evidence, they rarely do. A court reporter who records the testimony of the witnesses is also usually present.

After hearing all the witnesses and receiving the evidence of the case, the grand jurors will deliberate on the facts of the matter among themselves. After deliberating on the facts, they will vote to determine whether in their minds there are sufficient facts to believe that a crime has been committed and whether the accused committed it. They do not have to believe beyond a reasonable doubt as to guilt; they require only sufficient probable cause to believe that the accused is guilty of the act. Only the grand jurors may be present during the deliberation and voting. Jurisdictions vary somewhat on the number who must vote to hold the accused for trial, or "vote for the indictment." If the grand jury comprises nineteen members, some states require only twelve to vote in favor of the indictment, whereas other states require fourteen. If the grand jury comprises twenty-three persons, some states require fourteen to vote in favor of the indictment, and others require sixteen. If the required number votes in favor of holding the accused for trial, the foreperson of the grand jury will endorse the indictment indicating that the grand jury believes in the truthfulness of the charge. Thus, we get the true bill as a name for an indictment that is returned by the grand jury holding an accused for trial. In some states, if a grand jury investigates a criminal charge that was not referred to them by the prosecuting attorney, the accusatory pleading is known as a presentment rather than an indictment.

Grand Jury Indictment

[The following grand jury indictment was taken from a case in Texas. The defendant was indicted for capital murder. He was charged with committing murder in a state prison while serving a sentence for another murder. Note that he is charged in two separate counts with the same murder. After the evidence is admitted, the State will generally move to dismiss one count, depending on how the evidence is developed at trial. Also note that at the end of the indictment, the crime is alleged as "against the peace and dignity of the state." Most states require that all crimes be against the peace and dignity of the state. This case ended with a plea bargain for a guilty plea to Count 1 and an agreed sentence of thirty-five years to be served at the end of his present prison term of thirty years.]

The State of Texas v. *Eric Roberto Acosta*
Charge: Capital Murder, Penal Code 19.03(a)(6)(A)

In the Name and by Authority of the State of Texas:

The Grand Jury, for the County of Bee, State of Texas, duly selected, impaneled, sworn, charged, and organized as such at the July Term A.D., 1999, of the 156th Judicial District Court for said County, upon their oaths present in and to said court at said term that:

Eric Roberto Acosta

Count 1

Hereinafter styled Defendant, on or about the 13th day of July A.D., 1996, and before the presentment of this indictment, in the County and State aforesaid, Eric Roberto Acosta while in a penal institution to-wit: The Garza East Unit of the Texas Department of Criminal Justice, Institutional Division and serving a sentence for the offense of Murder; did then and there intentionally and knowingly cause the death of another, Daniel Vela, by kicking the said Daniel Vela on or about the head and facial area with Eric Roberto Acosta's shoe clad feet.

Count 2

And hereinafter styled Defendant, on or about the 13th day of July, A.D., 1996, and before the presentment of this indictment, in the County and State aforesaid, Eric Roberto Acosta while in a penal institution to-wit: The Garza East Unit of the Texas Department of Criminal Justice, Institutional Division and serving a sentence for the offense of Murder, did then and there, intending to cause serious bodily injury to an individual, Daniel Vela, commit an act clearly dangerous to human life, to-wit: by kicking the said Daniel Vela on or about the head and facial area with Eric Roberto Acosta's shoe clad feet thereby causing the death of said Daniel Vela, against the peace and dignity of the state.

[Signed by Presiding Grand Juror chairperson]

If the required number does not vote in favor of holding the accused for trial, the foreperson will so designate on the indictment. At one time in our history, the foreperson would write the word "ignoramus" on the indictment, indicating that the grand jury ignored the indictment. Today, the foreperson will usually write on the indictment that the grand jury does not believe in the charge, or in other words, that there is no bill of indictment forthcoming, or a no bill.

The defendant is not entitled to be present during a grand jury hearing, and there is some doubt whether the defendant may demand to present evidence in his or her own behalf. If the grand jurors feel that other witnesses besides those presented by the prosecution would be helpful in determining the truth of the indictment, the grand jurors have the authority to call additional witnesses, including the accused. The accused does not have to answer any questions that might subject him or her to punishment.

If a grand jury fails to hold the accused for trial, the question arises whether the facts may be presented to a new grand jury. The answer varies from state to state. Most states permit the indictment to be submitted to a different grand jury. Some states have statutory regulations prohibiting this practice. Other states are silent on the matter, thereby indicating that there is no bar to presenting the case again, since a grand jury hearing is not an action in which jeopardy will attach.

Secret Indictment

If the defendant is not in custody at the time the indictment is returned, a warrant of arrest will be issued on the basis of this indictment. Under these circumstances, no public record is made of the indictment and warrant in order that the defendant will not be alerted to the fact that he or she is wanted, thereby making his or her location and apprehension more difficult. The indictment in this case is referred to as a secret indictment or sealed indictment.

Open Hearings

Frequently, a grand jury is called on to investigate and hold hearings concerning alleged acts of misconduct by public officials. In these situations, most jurisdictions permit the hearing to be open to the public when it is believed to be in the best interest of justice. To hold an open hearing usually requires that a request be made to the presiding judge by the prosecuting attorney and by the foreperson of the grand jury.

Law in Practice

Differences between a Grand Jury and a Petit Jury (Trial Jury)

	Grand Jury	Petit Jury
Function	Investigative body	Fact finders—judicial function
Selection of potential jurors	Selected by supervising judge and his or her assistants	Must be random selection
Final selection of members	Determined by supervising judge	By trial judge after voir dire and ruling on counsel challenges
Number of jurors	Generally varies from 16 to 23	Generally 12 but can be a few as six
Duration of service	For predetermined periods of time, e.g., six months in many states	For specific trial only
Right of defendant or accused to be present	In most states no right to be present	Sixth Amendment right to be present
Presentation of evidence	Normally by prosecutor although can be presented by jurors	By both prosecution and defense
Proceedings	Secret	Open to public except for deliberations
Findings	True bill or no bill on indictment presented by prosecutor	Guilty or not guilty on each charge

[Note: there are differences between states' and/or federal practices.]

Dismissal of Indictment

Prosecution does not necessarily follow even though an indictment has been returned by a grand jury. The indictment may be dismissed. In many jurisdictions, the prosecuting attorney is permitted to dismiss the indictment. This procedure is referred to as a "nolle prosequi action," a formal entry on the record of the case stating that no further prosecutive action will be taken in the matter. Other jurisdictions hold that only the presiding judge may dismiss the indictment. The presiding judge may dismiss the indictment on his or her own if he or she does not believe that the facts will support a conviction, or the judge may dismiss the indictment upon the recommendation of the prosecuting attorney. It may seem to be somewhat paradoxical for the prosecuting attorney to seek an indictment and then dismiss it. But the prosecuting attorney may take this action because a material witness has become unavailable or if facts have been developed that, in the best interest of justice, indicate that the case should not go to trial.

Additional Functions of the Grand Jury

In many states, the sole function of the grand jury is to hold hearings on criminal charges to determine whether a crime has been committed and whether the accused should be held for trial. But in a few states, the grand jury performs other functions, such as investigating public expenditures. It may also inspect jails, prisons, and mental institutions within its territorial jurisdiction to determine whether these facilities are complying with safety and health regulations.

Criticism of the Grand Jury System

Many legal scholars have severely criticized the grand jury system. It has been alleged that the grand jury is not a safeguard of the accused but is merely a rubber stamp of the prosecuting attorney. Another allegation is that the grand jury is not representative of the peers of the accused, as was indicated to be necessary by the Magna Charta. The term peers seems to weave its way into the legal language of criminal procedure, but it is seldom found in the qualifications necessary for being a member of either a petit or a grand jury. The dictionary definition of peers reflects that they are one's equals or associates. Under this definition, a grand jury of one's peers could result in the impaneling of an odd group of persons, particularly if the accused had spent much of his or her life in prison. Generally, it is held that if the grand jury is a representative group of citizens from throughout the county, or a cross section of the county, it is the equivalent of one's peers, and such a group will fulfill the due process of law provision. However, greater emphasis is being placed on what determines a representative group when a member of a minority society is the accused. The cross section of the county provision has also been challenged by younger defendants, particularly since the age qualification for service on juries has been changed from twenty-one to eighteen.

Although the argument that the grand jury does not represent a cross section of society is valid, it is most difficult to obtain a truly representative group. Most grand jurors receive little or no compensation for their services. In those areas in which the grand jury holds frequent hearings, most persons cannot afford to serve on a grand jury. This circumstance results in many grand jurors who are retired or wealthy individuals who can afford to give their services. It has also been alleged that the grand jury is a cumbersome system because it cannot do anything that a magistrate could not do more efficiently at less cost. Those advocating the retention of the grand jury system in lieu of a preliminary hearing by a magistrate often quote Justice Harlan's dissenting opinion in the case of *Hurtado* v. *California*.[11] Justice Harlan stated the following:

> . . . nothing stands between the citizen and prosecution for his life, except the judgment of a justice of the peace [in a preliminary hearing]. Anglo-Saxon liberty would, perhaps, have perished long before the adoption of our Constitution, had it been in the power of government to put the subject on trial for his life whenever a justice of the peace, holding his office at the will of the crown, should certify that he had committed a capital crime. That such officers are, in some of the States, elected by the people, does not add to the protection of the citizen; for, one of the peculiar benefits of the grand jury system, as it exists in this country and England [the grand jury system has since been abolished in England] is that it is composed, as a general rule, of a body of private persons, who do not hold office at the will of the government, or at the will of voters. In many if not in all of the States civil

officers are disqualified to sit on grand juries. In the secrecy of the investigations by grand juries, the weak and helpless—proscribed perhaps, because of their race, or pursued by an unreasoning public clamor—have found, and will continue to find, security against official oppression, the cruelty of mobs, the machination of falsehood, and the malevolence of private persons who would use the machinery of the law to bring ruin upon their personal enemies.

What Are the Most Common Reasons for Rejection or Dismissal of a Criminal Case?

Many criminal cases are rejected or dismissed because of:

1. **Evidence problems**—a failure to find sufficient physical evidence linking the defendant to the offense, insufficient evidence that a crime was committed, or the existence of a defense apparent from the available evidence.
2. **Witness problems**—for example, when a witness fails to appear, gives unclear or inconsistent statements, is reluctant to testify, or is unsure of the identity of the offender, or when a prior relationship exists between the victim/witness and the offender.
3. **The interests of justice**—deciding not to prosecute certain types of offenses, particularly those that violate the letter but not the spirit of the law (e.g., offenses involving insignificant amounts of property damage).
4. **Due process problems**—violations of the constitutional requirements for seizing evidence and for questioning the accused.
5. **A plea on another case**—for example, when the accused is charged in several cases and the prosecutor agrees to drop one or more of the cases in exchange for a plea of guilty on another case.
6. **Pretrial diversion**—agreeing to drop charges when the accused successfully meets the conditions for diversion, such as completion of a treatment program.
7. **Referral for other prosecution**—when there are other offenses, perhaps of a more serious nature, in a different jurisdiction, or deferring to a federal prosecution.

Thus, we find the grand jury system continuing to function in many states; however, as time passes, it is highly possible that more states will adopt the preliminary hearing procedure.

CASE LAW

Recent Cases

Padilla v. *Kentucky*, 130 S. Ct. 1473 (U.S. 2010)

Note: While deportation is a particularly severe "penalty," it is not, in a strict sense, a criminal sanction. Removal proceedings are civil in nature; deportation is nevertheless intimately related to the criminal process. If a defendant pleads guilty based on erroneous advice by his counsel regarding whether he will be deported does this erroneous advice amount to ineffective assistance of counsel?

Defendant Padilla, who pleaded guilty to drug charges, sought post-conviction relief based on ineffective assistance of counsel. The Supreme Court of

Kentucky denied relief. The United States Supreme Court granted certiorari.

The defendant was a lawful permanent resident who pleaded guilty to transporting marijuana. His crime was a removable offense (deportable) under 8 U.S.C.S. § 1227(a)(2)(B)(i). He claimed that his counsel incorrectly told him prior to entry of his plea that he did not have to worry about immigration status because he had been in the United States for so long. The state court held that the Sixth Amendment did not protect defendant from erroneous advice about deportation because it was merely a collateral consequence of his conviction.

The Supreme Court held that the distinction between collateral and direct consequences was ill suited to the deportation context, so advice regarding deportation was not categorically removed from the ambit of the Sixth Amendment. Counsel's alleged failure to correctly advise defendant of the deportation consequences of his guilty plea amounted to constitutionally deficient assistance under prevailing professional norms, as the consequences could easily have been determined from reading the removal statute. Whether the defendant was entitled to relief depended on whether he could demonstrate prejudice, a matter for the state courts to consider in the first instance.

The Court also noted that if a noncitizen has committed a removable offense after the 1996 amendments to the Immigration and Nationality Act, his removal is practically inevitable but for the possible exercise of limited remnants of equitable discretion vested in the attorney general to cancel removal for noncitizens convicted of particular classes of offenses.

The Court reversed the state court's judgment, and the case was remanded for further proceedings.

Renico v. *Lett*, 130 S. Ct. 1855 (U.S. 2010)

During the prisoner Lett's first murder trial, after receiving notes from the jury, the trial court asked the foreperson whether the jury would reach a unanimous verdict. The foreperson answered in the negative. The trial court then declared a mistrial, and Lett was convicted in a retrial.

The trial transcript indicates that the following exchange took place between the judge and jurors:

> THE COURT: I received your note asking me what if you can't agree? And I have to conclude from that that that is your situation at this time. So, I'd like to ask the foreperson to identify themselves, please?
>
> THE FOREPERSON: [Identified herself.]
>
> THE COURT: Okay, thank you. All right. I need to ask you if the jury is deadlocked; in other words, is there a disagreement as to the verdict?
>
> THE FOREPERSON: Yes, there is.
>
> THE COURT: All right. Do you believe that it is hopelessly deadlocked?
>
> THE FOREPERSON: The majority of us don't believe that —
>
> THE COURT: (Interposing) Don't say what you're going to say, okay?

> THE FOREPERSON: Oh, I'm sorry.
>
> THE COURT: I don't want to know what your verdict might be, or how the split is, or any of that. Thank you. Okay? Are you going to reach a unanimous verdict, or not?
>
> THE FOREPERSON: (No response.)
>
> THE COURT: Yes or no?
>
> THE FOREPERSON: No, Judge.

The trial judge then declared a mistrial, dismissed the jury, and scheduled a new trial for later that year. Neither the prosecutor nor Lett's attorney made any objection.

The Michigan Supreme Court found no violation of the Double Jeopardy Clause because the mistrial declaration was not an abuse of discretion. In finding that the prisoner was not entitled to habeas relief, the U.S. Supreme Court held that the state supreme court's decision was not an unreasonable application of clearly established federal law. The state court identified the "manifest necessity" standard for declaring a mistrial and noted the broad deference due to trial courts in deciding whether that standard had been met. It was reasonable for the state court to have found that the trial court exercised sound discretion given the length of deliberations, the notes from the jury, and the foreperson's statement.

The Supreme Court noted that when a judge discharges a jury on the grounds that the jury cannot reach a verdict, the Double Jeopardy Clause does not bar a new trial for the defendant before a new jury. Trial judges may declare a mistrial whenever, in their opinion, taking all the circumstances into consideration, there is a manifest necessity for doing so. The decision to declare a mistrial is left to the sound discretion of the judge, but the power ought to be used with the greatest caution, under urgent circumstances, and for very plain and obvious causes.

The U.S. Supreme Court concluded that Lett was not entitled to a writ of habeas corpus. The Court noted that the trial judge could have been more thorough before declaring a mistrial. As the Court of Appeals pointed out she could have asked the foreperson additional follow-up questions, granted additional time for further deliberations, or consulted with the prosecutor and defense counsel before acting. Any of these steps would have been appropriate under the circumstances. None, however, were required.

Briefly Noted

***United States* v. *Goddard*, 2011 U.S. App. LEXIS 4956 (6th Cir. Ky. 2011).** In a U.S. Court of

Appeals case, the defendant requested to withdraw his plea of guilty to attempting to possess with intent to distribute 500 grams or more of cocaine and criminal forfeiture on the basis that he would not have pled guilty if he had known that he would not have had an opportunity to try to obtain a motion to decrease his sentence for cooperation with the government. The district court denied the motion. On appeal, the court held that several factors supported the district court's denial, including that defendant was well educated, he did not claim to be innocent, and he had prior experience with the criminal justice system, having had two prior drug felony trafficking convictions along with at least two felony drug convictions. The court rejected defendant's claim that he was denied counsel during the hearing on his motion to withdraw the guilty plea because defendant unquestionably had representation at the hearing, and the district court effectively addressed defendant's motion for substitute counsel before it proceeded to the next stage of the proceedings, namely defendant's the sentencing hearing. The U.S.

Court of Appeals denied his appeal and upheld the actions of the district court.

***United States* v. *Briggs*, 623 F.3d 724 (9th Cir. Wash. 2010).** The defendant sought to withdraw his guilty plea contending that he had not understood the consequences of his plea agreement. A review of the record, however, uncovered no evidence that defendant was incapable of understanding his guilty plea. Although he had an IQ of 70, a psychological evaluation found that he had the capacity to make a knowing decision about his plea. In fact, the defendant discussed in detail with the psychologist his own calculation of the sentence he faced, the good-behavior time he expected to accrue, and the ultimate period of incarceration that would result. Contrary to defendant's assertions, his understanding of the consequences of his guilty plea appeared to have been quite sophisticated. Because defendant admitted to the charged drug quantities, his bare assertion that he was the victim of sentencing entrapment was rejected. The defendant's appeal was denied.

Summary

- During arraignment, the defendant is given the opportunity to enter a plea to the charge alleged in the complaint.
- At one time, defendants could not enter a guilty plea based on the belief that the only way justice could be accomplished was by a trial.
- Many states use a preliminary hearing in lieu of a grand jury.
- The purpose of a preliminary hearing is to determine if there is sufficient evidence to hold the accused for trial.
- Inadmissible evidence may be used in the preliminary hearing in most states.
- If the magistrate determines that there is sufficient evidence, the accused is bound over for trial.
- The grand jury system was established to safeguard the accused, but the system has been under attack by some attorneys and charged with being a tool for the prosecutor.
- When an indictment is returned or an information is filed with the trial court, the accused will be arraigned upon the accusatory pleadings.

- In most jurisdictions, the defendant may withdraw a guilty plea upon a showing of good cause.
- Before a guilty plea is accepted by the court, the judge must advise the accused of his or her rights as required by the *Boykin* v. *Alabama* decision.
- A defendant does not have a constitutional right to have his or her guilty plea accepted by the court.
- A plea of nolo contendere means that the defendant does not contest the charge. Some courts do not accept nolo contendere pleas.
- Whether a defendant may enter a plea of not guilty by reason of insanity depends on the law of the state involved.
- The defendant is required to assert a plea of double jeopardy or it will be waived.
- A grand jury's primary purpose is to hear criminal accusations in order to determine whether there are sufficient facts to hold the accused for trial.
- A grand jury may also investigate public agencies and public officers.
- Grand jury hearings are not open to the public.

Review Questions

1. What is a guilty plea?
2. Before a guilty plea may be accepted, of what must the defendant be advised?
3. What is the next procedural step after the acceptance of a guilty plea?
4. What is the significance of a nolo contendere plea?
5. Define double jeopardy.
6. What is a grand jury?
7. List the qualifications for being a grand juror.
8. What is an indictment?
9. Who may be present during a grand jury's deliberation on an indictment?
10. What is a no bill?
11. What is a secret indictment?
12. Explain a nolle prosequi action.
13. What criticisms have been made of the grand jury system?
14. What is the purpose of the preliminary hearing?
15. What is an information?

Local Procedure

1. What pleas may a defendant enter in your jurisdiction?
2. May a defendant enter a plea of guilty to a capital punishment charge? If so, under what circumstances?
3. How many members compose a grand jury in your state?
4. May a defendant be brought to trial on a felony charge by an information, or must he or she be indicted?
5. How are grand jurors selected?
6. May the prosecuting attorney enter a nolle prosequi?
7. In your state, is the accused entitled to a preliminary hearing even though indicted?

Endnotes

1. 508 F.Supp.2d 7 (D.D.C. Sept. 10, 2007).
2. *Boykin* v. *Alabama,* 395 U.S. 238 (1969).
3. *North Carolina* v. *Alford,* 400 U.S. 25 (1970).
4. 426 U.S. 637 (1976).
5. 397 U.S. 790 (1970).
6. 437 U.S. 1 (1978).
7. 437 U.S. 28 (1978).
8. 260 U.S. 377 (1922).
9. 359 U.S. 187 (1959).
10. 370 U.S. 375 (1962).
11. 110 U.S. 516 (1884).

CHAPTER 6

Place and Time of Trial

In all criminal prosecutions, the accused shall enjoy the right to a speedy and public trial, by an impartial jury of the State and district wherein the crime shall have been committed. . . .

—U.S. CONSTITUTION, AMENDMENT VI, 1791

Chapter Outline

Pretrial Action

Competency to Stand Trial

Place of the Trial

Time of the Trial

Case Law

Summary

Key Terms

Change of venue

Competency to stand trial

Constitutional right to a speedy trial

Continuance

Insanity

Statute of limitations

Statutory right to a speedy trial

Learning Objectives

After completing this chapter, you should be able to:

- Summarize how the place and time of a trial are determined.
- Discuss the constitutional requirements concerning the place of trial.
- Explain when a defendant may want a change of venue.
- Distinguish between insanity and competency issues.

- List the issues involved in determining if the defendant's constitutional right to a speedy trial has been violated.
- Explain the differences between the constitutional and statutory right to a speedy trial.
- Describe the differences between speedy trial and statute of limitations.

- Explain the issues that a trial judge must consider in determining whether to grant a motion for a continuance.

- Discuss the steps that a state must take when the defendant is confined in another state.

PRETRIAL ACTION

Before the trial phase of the administration of justice begins, many decisions must be made. It must be determined when and where the trial will take place, whether the trial will be by the judge alone or by a jury, whether the defendant will represent himself or herself or be assisted by counsel, what witnesses will be called, what physical evidence will be presented, and whether a pretrial hearing will be held. In view of the importance of each of these processes, we will discuss each in some detail. These decisions and the trial procedures are largely the same whether the charge involved is a felony or a misdemeanor. Appendix A contains an outline of the stages of a criminal trial.

COMPETENCY TO STAND TRIAL

The defense of **insanity** refers to the defendant's mental state at the time that the alleged crime was committed. **Competency to stand trial** refers to the defendant's mental state at the time of the trial. The due process clauses of the Fifth and Fourteenth Amendments of the U.S. Constitution prohibit the trial of an individual who is incompetent. A defendant is considered incompetent if he or she lacks the capacity to understand the nature and object of the proceedings against him or her, or lacks the ability to consult with the defense counsel or to assist the defense counsel in preparing a defense.

If no issue is raised as to the competency of the defendant to stand trial, then it is assumed that he or she is competent. If the defendant's competency is at issue, the burden of presenting the evidence as to his or her competency is on the defense. The U.S. Supreme Court in *Cooper* v. *Oklahoma*,[1] held that it was permissible for a state to place the burden on the defendant to establish his or her lack of competency, but that Oklahoma's requirement that the defense establish the incompetency by clear and convincing evidence was too much of a burden on the defense. Most states require that the defendant establish incompetency by the preponderance of the evidence, a lower level of proof.

If the defendant is determined to be incompetent, the state may detain him or her for a reasonable period of time necessary to determine whether there is a substantial probability that he or she will attain competency in the near future.[2] Unlike the insanity defense, if the defendant regains his or her competency, he or she may then be prosecuted.

Law in Practice

Mentally Incompetent Defendants Increase in Number

A 2008 review of the twelve largest states indicated that the number of accused felons that were declared by the trial courts to be mentally incompetent to stand trial had substantially increased from 2002 to 2007. In Florida the number of defendants in 2002 that were found incompetent was 1061 and in 2007 it was 2123. In Ohio in 2007, 32 percent of the 1,050 state mental hospital patients have been charged with crimes but declared unfit to stand trial. In 2007, California had 5,000 beds in its state mental hospitals. Approximately 4,500 of the California mental patients in those hospitals had been found incompetent to stand trial.

It is estimated that it costs approximately $250 million a year to treat individuals in state mental hospitals who are considered as mentally incompetent to stand trial.[3]

Law in Practice

Should a Defendant Be Forced to Take Medication in Order to Be Competent to Stand Trial?

A federal criminal defendant with a long history of mental illness was initially found competent to stand trial for alleged fraud and was released on bail. However, his bail was subsequently revoked because his condition had worsened. Later, the defendant asked for a reconsideration of his competence. After being examined at a medical center for federal prisoners, the defendant was found incompetent to stand trial and was hospitalized at the center for a determination as to whether he would attain the capacity to allow his trial to proceed.

While at the center, the defendant refused to take antipsychotic medication, but a psychiatrist at the center held a hearing and authorized involuntary administration of the drugs in question. A federal Bureau of Prisons official upheld

this decision. A United States magistrate judge issued an order authorizing forced administration of the drugs, on the grounds that (1) the defendant was a danger to himself and others, (2) medication was the only way to render him less dangerous, (3) any serious side effects could be ameliorated, (4) the benefits to the defendant outweighed the risks, and (5) the drugs were substantially likely to return the defendant to competence. The defendant appealed the magistrate's decision claiming that he could not be forced take the medicine because it was not medically necessary to sustain life.

As the appellate justice in this case, how would you rule?

How did the court rule? See *Sell* v. *United States*, 539 U.S. 166 (2003).[4]

PLACE OF THE TRIAL

Venue

The Sixth Amendment to the U.S. Constitution guarantees to an accused the right to a speedy and public trial, by an impartial jury of the State and district wherein the crime shall have been committed. This guarantee was placed in the Sixth Amendment as a result of the colonists' having been dragged from their homes to some secret place, often to England, and tried away from their peers. This guarantee applies to the states through the Due Process Clause of the Fourteenth Amendment. Thus, the place of the trial, or venue, lies within the judicial district in which the crime occurred. The term venue is derived from the French word *visne,* meaning neighborhood. If the charge is a felony, the judicial district is the county; if it is a misdemeanor, the judicial district is the specific area of the county so designated and established by law. The burden is on the prosecution to present evidence during the trial to prove that the crime was committed within the judicial district in which the trial is being held. Proving venue may be accomplished merely by an investigating officer's testifying on the specific location within the county where the crime was committed. If venue is not established by the prosecution, a conviction may be reversed on appeal because it is the right of the defendant to have the jury chosen from the judicial district in which the crime was committed.

MOTION TO CHANGE VENUE Although the defendant is entitled to have the trial in the district where the crime occurred, that right may be waived and a request made that the trial be held in some other district. This outcome is particularly true in felony cases. The defendant often believes that a fair and impartial trial cannot be had in the county in which the crime was committed. This viewpoint is usually based on a belief that adverse publicity, the nature of the crime, or community hostility makes it impossible for the defendant to obtain an impartial jury. Under these circumstances, the defendant will file with the trial court a written request, known as a motion to change venue. The trial judge will hold a hearing on this request, at which time the defendant will present evidence in an effort to convince the judge that a **change of venue** should be granted. It may be alleged that, because the defendant is an outsider and the victim of the crime was popular, there is adverse feeling toward the accused. Or it may be alleged that because of the widespread publicity given to the crime, most persons in the county already believe in the defendant's guilt. In most instances, the prosecuting attorney will oppose the change of venue because of the inconvenience to witnesses and staff and because of the cost involved. However, the cost is not to be considered by the judge in granting or denying a change of venue because the accused is entitled to a fair and impartial trial, regardless of cost. The prosecuting attorney will oppose the change of venue on grounds other than cost in most instances. Also, the prosecuting attorney may contend that even though many persons have formed opinions unfavorable to the defendant as a result of what was published, it does not follow that persons without such views could not be found within the county to act as jurors or that those who have adverse opinions could not set those opinions aside and try the case in a fair and impartial manner on the basis of the evidence. Or the prosecuting attorney may contend that because of the widespread publicity given to the crime, it would be equally difficult to obtain an impartial jury in another county. Another contention may be that the emotional involvement with the crime has subsided sufficiently by trial time so that an impartial jury could be selected.

If, from the evidence presented during the hearing, the judge feels that a change of venue should be granted, the trial will be held in a county in which it is believed that a fair trial can be had. In most instances, the trial will be moved to an adjoining county. The cost of the trial will be borne by the county where the crime occurred. If the rule were otherwise, a county could impose on an adjoining county a terrific cost burden for trials of crimes not taking place within that adjoining county. If the judge does not grant a change of venue and the defendant is convicted, the refusal to grant a change of venue may be grounds for appeal. If the appellate court concludes that a change of venue should have been granted, the conviction will be reversed.

TIME OF REQUEST FOR CHANGE OF VENUE Generally, a request for change of venue must take place before the date set for the commencement of the trial. A change may be made after the commencement date if the jury panel is exhausted without a jury's being selected or if there is danger of violence taking place within the district.

TIME OF THE TRIAL

The Sixth Amendment provision that the "accused shall enjoy the right to a speedy trial" is embodied in the laws of all the states. The **constitutional right to a speedy trial** is a fundamental right of an accused; otherwise, many injustices may be suffered. The people, or society, also have an interest in the guarantee that an accused will be brought to trial without unnecessary delay. This is the only way that society can be properly protected from the offender. These guarantees provide few guidelines on exactly when a trial must be held in order to comply with the speedy trial regulation, so the decision on when to hold a trial becomes a troublesome and difficult one to make. The right to a speedy trial does not permit the defendant to demand that a trial be held the same day as the arrest because the prosecution has the right to prepare its case against the defendant. But the prosecution may not take an indefinite time in its preparation. In setting the trial date, many factors must be considered, such as what is a reasonable length of time to permit each side to prepare its case and whether the accused is in jail or has posted bail. Further, the rules of procedure of most states require that criminal trials be set for those in jail ahead of those who have posted bail when other factors are equal. Even if a trial date is set, the trial may not necessarily begin on that date, since continuances may be granted that will cause delays.

The constitutional right to a speedy trial is set forth in the Sixth Amendment to the U.S. Constitution. The federal government and most states also have statutory rights to a speedy trial. In the case of federal trials, it is the Speedy Trial Act of 1974 that provides the statutory right.

Differences Between Constitutional Right to a Speedy Trial and the Statutory Right

Right to Speedy Trial	Constitutional	Statutory
Test to determine if right violated	Four factors: Length of delay; justification for delay; whether defendant asserted right; and prejudice cause by delay	Violation of time periods
Remedy for violation	Dismissal of charge or charges and defendant may not be retried on offense	Depends on statute— usually dismissal and in some cases defendant may be retried.

The people or the state also has a right to a speedy trial. In most cases, it is the prosecution that is trying to bring a case to trial because it has the burden of establishing guilt, and delay generally weakens the case.

Continuances

Although the right to a speedy trial is primarily for the benefit of the accused, this right, like others rights, may be waived by the defendant, and often is. Defendants make frequent requests for **continuances** in bringing the case to trial. Often months pass between the time that an arrest is made and when the defendant is brought to trial, particularly in felony cases. Regardless of the hardships that may be suffered in not having a speedy trial, the defendant often will delay the trial date as long as possible. Delay often works to the advantage of the accused because, with the passage of time, witnesses for the prosecution are more likely to become unavailable and their memories are more likely to dull. In addition, physical evidence becomes difficult to identify and is likely to become lost or contaminated.

Although the defendant may suffer from continuances, others also suffer, particularly witnesses who must return to court many times only to find that the case has been continued. These witnesses usually receive no notice that a continuance will be granted. A continuance often is not granted until the case is called for trial, so notice is not possible. As a result, many witnesses must take time off from work, thus losing pay and experiencing the expense and inconvenience of traveling to and from court many times. It is understandable that people become reluctant to admit witnessing a crime. Delays also cause overcrowding of the court calendar, and other trials must be delayed, particularly civil trials.

Although the statutes of most states provide that a continuance may be granted only upon sufficient grounds and with sufficient notice, in most instances no specific grounds or time for the notice is stated. The most frequent ground alleged for a continuance is adequate time to prepare the case. Other grounds include obtaining witnesses or physical evidence, securing adequate and effective counsel for the defense, and ensuring the sound physical condition of the defendant. Delay may not be caused by inactivity of the defense in not preparing the case for trial. There is no set procedure to be followed in making a request for a continuance. It may be made orally in open court or by written request in advance of the trial date. Whether a continuance will be granted is at the discretion of the trial judge.

The U.S. Supreme Court, in the case of *Barker* v. *Wingo*,[5] discussed many of the ramifications of a speedy trial and the effect of delays on both the accused and the people. The Court also discussed some of the factors to be considered in determining whether the guarantee to a speedy trial had been violated. In view of the enlightening language of this decision, it is set forth in some detail for review by the reader. The facts of this case indicate that July 20, 1958, in Christian County, Kentucky, an elderly couple was beaten to death by intruders wielding an iron tire tool. Two suspects, Silas Manning and Willie Barker, the petitioner, were arrested shortly thereafter. The grand jury indicted them September 15. Counsel was appointed September 17, and Barker's trial was set for October 21. The Commonwealth had a stronger case against Manning, and it believed that Barker could not be convicted unless Manning testified against him. Manning was naturally unwilling to incriminate himself. Accordingly, on October 23, the day Silas Manning was brought to trial, the Commonwealth sought and obtained the first of what was to be a series of sixteen continuances of Barker's trial. Barker made no objection. By first convicting Manning, the Commonwealth would remove the possible problem of self-incrimination and would be able to assure his testimony against Barker.

The Commonwealth encountered more than a few difficulties in its prosecution of Manning. The first trial ended in a hung jury. The second trial resulted in a conviction, but the Kentucky Court of Appeals reversed because of the admission of evidence obtained by an illegal search. At his third trial, Manning was again convicted, and the Court of Appeals again reversed because the trial court had not granted a change of venue. The fourth trial resulted in a hung jury. Finally, after five trials, Manning was convicted, in March 1962, of murdering one victim, and after a sixth trial in December 1962, he was convicted of murdering the other.

The Christian County Circuit Court holds three terms each year—in February, June, and September. Barker's initial trial was to take place in the September term of 1958. The first continuance postponed it until the February 1959 term. The second continuance was granted for one month only. Every term thereafter, for as long as the Manning prosecutions were in process, the Commonwealth routinely moved to continue Barker's case to the next term. When the case was continued from the June 1959 term until the following September, Barker, having spent ten months in jail, obtained his release by posting a $5,000 bond. He thereafter remained free in the community until his trial. Barker made no objection, through his counsel, to the first eleven continuances.

When on February 12, 1962, the Commonwealth moved for the twelfth time to continue the case until the following term, Barker's counsel filed a motion to dismiss the indictment. The motion to dismiss was denied two weeks later, and the state's motion for a continuance was granted. The state was granted further continuances in June 1962 and September 1962, to which Barker did not object. In February 1963, the first term of court following Manning's final conviction, the Commonwealth moved to set Barker's trial for March 19. But on the day scheduled for trial, the Commonwealth again moved for a continuance until the June term. It gave as its reason the illness of the ex-sheriff who was the chief investigating officer in the case. To this continuance, Barker objected unsuccessfully.

The witness was still unable to testify in June, and the trial, which had been set for June 19, was continued again until the September term, again over Barker's objection. This time the court announced that the case would be dismissed for lack of prosecution if it were not tried during the next term. The final trial date was set for October 9, 1963. On that date, Barker again moved to dismiss the indictment, and this time specified that his right to a speedy trial had been violated. The motion was denied; the trial commenced with Manning as the chief prosecution witness; Barker was convicted and given a life sentence.

Barker appealed his conviction through the Kentucky Court of Appeals and the U.S. District Court of Appeals. Both affirmed the conviction. The case was then appealed to the U.S. Supreme Court on the grounds that the Due Process Clause of the Fourteenth Amendment of the Constitution had been violated because the defendant had been denied a speedy trial as provided by the Sixth Amendment now made applicable to the states through U.S. Supreme Court decisions.

In studying the case, the U.S. Supreme Court stated the following:

The right to a speedy trial is generically different from any of the other rights enshrined in the Constitution for the protection of the accused. In addition to the general concern that all accused persons be treated according to decent and fair procedures, there is a societal interest in providing a speedy trial which exists separate from and at times in opposition to the interests of the accused. The inability of courts to provide a prompt trial has contributed to a large backlog of cases in urban courts which, among other things, enables defendants to negotiate more effectively for pleas of guilty to lesser offenses and otherwise manipulate the system. In addition, persons released on bond for lengthy periods awaiting trial have an opportunity to commit other crimes. It must be of little comfort to the residents of Christian County, Kentucky, to know that Barker was at large on bail for over four years while accused of a vicious and brutal murder of which he was ultimately convicted. Moreover, the longer an accused is free awaiting trial, the more tempting becomes his opportunity to jump bail and escape. Finally, delay between arrest and punishment may have a detrimental effect on rehabilitation.

If an accused cannot make bail, he is generally confined, as was Barker for 10 months, in a local jail. This contributes to the overcrowding and generally deplorable state of those institutions. Lengthy exposure to these conditions has a destructive effect on human character and makes the rehabilitation of the individual offender much more difficult. At times the result may even be violent rioting. Finally, lengthy pretrial detention is costly. The cost of maintaining a prisoner in jail varies from $3 to $9 per day, and this amounts to millions across the Nation. In addition, society loses wages which might have been earned, and it must often support families of incarcerated breadwinners.

A second difference between the right to speedy trial and the accused's other constitutional rights is that deprivation of the right may work to the accused's advantage. Delay is not an uncommon defense tactic. As the time between the commission of the crime and trial lengthens, witnesses may become unavailable or their memories may fade. If the witnesses support the prosecution, its case will be weakened, sometimes seriously so. And it is the prosecution that carries the burden of proof. Thus, unlike the right to counsel or the right to be free from compelled self-incrimination, deprivation of the right to speedy trial does not per se prejudice the accused's ability to defend himself.

Finally, and perhaps most importantly, the right to speedy trial is a more vague concept than other procedural rights. It is, for example, impossible to determine with precision when the right has been denied. We cannot definitely say how long is too long in a system where justice is supposed to be swift but deliberate. As a consequence, there is no fixed point in the criminal process when the State can put the defendant to the choice of either exercising or waiving the right to a speedy trial. If, for example, the State moves for a 60-day continuance, granting that continuance is not a violation of the right to speedy trial unless the circumstances of the case are such that further delay would endanger the values the right protects. It is impossible to do more than generalize about when those circumstances exist.

The nature of the speedy-trial right does make it impossible to pinpoint a precise time in the process when the right must be asserted or waived, but that fact does not argue for placing the burden of protecting the right solely on defendants.

A defendant has no duty to bring himself to trial; the State has that duty as well as the duty of ensuring that the trial is consistent with due process. Moreover, for the reasons earlier expressed, society has particular interest in bringing swift prosecutions, and society's representatives are the ones who should protect that interest.

The Court stated, however, that the defendant had some responsibility to assert his right to a speedy trial. The approach that the Court accepted was a balancing test in which the conduct of both the prosecution and the defendant was to be weighed. The Court continued by stating as follows:

A balancing test necessarily compels courts to approach speedy-trial cases on an ad hoc basis. We can do little more than identify some of the factors which courts should assess in determining whether a particular defendant has been deprived of his right. Though some might express them in different ways, we identify four such factors: length of delay, the reason for the delay, the defendant's assertion of his right, and prejudice to the defendant.

We have discussed previously the societal disadvantages of lengthy pretrial incarceration, but obviously the disadvantages for the accused who cannot obtain his release are even more serious. The time spent in jail awaiting trial has a detrimental impact on the individual. It often means loss of a job; it disrupts family life; and it enforces idleness. Most jails offer little or no recreational or rehabilitative programs. The time spent in jail is simply dead time. Moreover, if a defendant is locked up, he is hindered in his ability to gather evidence, contact witnesses, and otherwise prepare his defense. Imposing those consequences on anyone who has not yet been convicted is serious. It is especially unfortunate to impose them on those persons who are ultimately found to be innocent. Finally, even if an accused is not incarcerated prior to trial, he is still disadvantaged by restraints on his liberty and by living under a cloud of anxiety, suspicion, and often hostility. . . .

The difficulty of the task of balancing these factors is illustrated by this case, which we consider to be close. It is clear that the length of delay between arrest and trial—well over five years—was extraordinary. Only seven months of that period can be attributed to a strong excuse, the illness of the ex-sheriff who was in charge of the investigation. Perhaps some delay would have been permissible under ordinary circumstances, so that Manning could be utilized as a witness in Barker's trial, but more than four years was too long a period, particularly since a good part of the period was attributable to the Commonwealth's failure or inability to try Manning under circumstances that comported with due process.

Two counter-balancing factors, however, outweigh these deficiencies. The first is that prejudice was minimal. Of course, Barker was prejudiced to some extent by living for over four years under a cloud of suspicion and anxiety. Moreover, although he was released on bond for most of the period, he did spend 10 months in jail before the trial. But there is no claim that any of Barker's witnesses died or otherwise became unavailable owing to the delay. The trial transcript indicates only two very minor lapses of memory on the part of prosecution witnesses which were in no way significant to the outcome.

More important than the absence of serious prejudice, is the fact that Barker did not want a speedy trial. . . . The probable reason for Barker's attitude was that he was gambling on Manning's acquittal. The evidence was not terribly strong against Manning, as the reversals and hung juries suggest, and Barker undoubtedly thought that if Manning were acquitted, he would never be tried.

We hold, therefore, that Barker was not deprived of his due process right to a speedy trial.

Out-of-State Incarceration

In the past, an acceptable ground for delay in bringing a case to trial was the incarceration of the defendant in another state. Under these circumstances, it was assumed that the prosecution had no obligation to bring a defendant to trial if he or she was unavailable because of imprisonment beyond the jurisdiction of the court in which he or she was charged with a crime. This viewpoint was changed by the U.S. Supreme Court in the case of *Smith* v. *Hooey*.[6] The Court held that a defendant was entitled to a speedy trial even while serving time in another state, particularly if the defendant demanded to be brought to trial. The facts of the *Smith* case indicate that in 1960 the defendant was indicted in Harris County, Texas, upon a charge of theft. The defendant was then, and still was when the decision was handed down in 1969, a prisoner in the federal penitentiary at Leavenworth, Kansas. Shortly after the Texas charge was filed, the defendant mailed a letter to the Texas trial court requesting a speedy trial. The reply stated that a trial would commence within two weeks of any date on which the defendant could be present. For the next six years, the defendant made periodic efforts to be brought to trial. Texas authorities made no effort to obtain the defendant's appearance in the Harris County trial court. The defendant appealed the case to the U.S. Supreme Court on due process of law grounds in that a speedy trial had been denied.

Law in Practice

In a Federal Criminal Case, Does the Speedy Trial Act Permit Prospective Waivers of the Right to a Speedy Trial?

Zedner v. *United States*, 547 U.S. 489 (1960)

Defendant Jacob Zedner was convicted of attempting to defraud a financial institution in violation of 18 U.S.C.S. § 1344. The U.S. Supreme Court granted certiorari with respect to the issue of whether Zedner had made an effective waiver of his rights under the Speedy Trial Act of 1974, 18 U.S.C.S. §§ 3161- 3174.

Zedner was indicted in April 1996 for allegedly attempting to open accounts at financial institutions using counterfeit United States bonds. In November 1996, defendant requested an adjournment and signed a waiver of his rights under the Speedy Trial Act "for all time." The district court granted Zedner's counsel another continuance in January 1997, continuing the case for 91 days. Because of subsequent proceedings, his trial was delayed until 2003.

ALITO, J., delivered the opinion of the Court:

The Supreme Court held that prospective application of the Act could not be waived. The Court noted that 18 U.S.C.S. § 3162(a)(2), which provided for waiver of a completed violation of the Act due to failure to timely move for dismissal, did not permit prospective waivers. The Court also noted that the Speedy Trial Act of 1974 generally requires a trial to begin within 70 days of the filing of an information or indictment or the defendant's initial appearance, 18 U.S.C.S. § 3161(c)(1), but the Act recognizes that criminal cases vary widely and that there are valid reasons for greater delay in particular cases. To provide the necessary flexibility, the Act includes a long and detailed list of periods of delay that are excluded in computing the time within which trial must start. For example, the Act excludes delay resulting from other proceedings concerning the defendant, delay resulting from the absence or unavailability of the defendant or an essential witness, delay resulting from the fact that the defendant is mentally incompetent or physically unable to stand trial, and a reasonable period of delay when the defendant is joined for trial with a codefendant as to whom the time for trial has not run and no motion for severance has been granted. To promote compliance with its requirements, the Speedy Trial Act of 1974 contains enforcement and sanctions provisions. If a trial does not begin on time, the defendant may move, before the start of trial or the entry of a guilty plea, to dismiss the charges, and if a meritorious and timely motion to dismiss is filed, the district court must dismiss the charges, though it may choose whether to dismiss with or without prejudice. In making that choice, the court must take into account, among other things, the seriousness of the offense; the facts and circumstances of the case which led to the dismissal; and the impact of a reprosecution on the administration of the Act and on the administration of justice.

According to the Court, much of the Speedy Trial Act of 1974's flexibility is furnished by 18 U.S.C.S. § 3161(h)(8), which governs ends-of-justice continuances. This provision permitted a district court to grant a continuance and to exclude the resulting delay if the court, after considering certain factors, makes on-the-record findings that the ends of justice served by granting the continuance outweigh the public's and defendant's interests in a speedy trial. This provision gave the district court discretion—within limits and subject to specific procedures—to accommodate limited delays for case-specific needs. However since the District Court failed to make an on-the-record finding that the ends of justice would be served by the delay, the case must be reversed.

Law in Practice

People v. *Johnson* (1980; 26 Cal. 3rd. 557)

[Defendant Johnson was confined awaiting trial. At a hearing to set a court date for the trial, the defense counsel, a public defender, made a motion to continue the trial. The record of the trial reflects the following exchanges:]

[The Court] All right, Mr. Johnson, I must inquire for my record: Do you waive your right to a speedy trial?

[Public Defender Cohen] I am presently engaged in *People* versus *Marshall* in trial in this department. I also have the case of *People* versus *Phillip*, which is number five on this calendar, and which is an older case than Johnson. I also have the Hughes matter set for the 28th which is a custody kidnapping-robbery case and also older than Mr. Johnson's case and some unfortunate bailout over a year old out of Department[s] 122 and 123. Therefore the realistic earliest date I could be available for Mr. Johnson is May 6th. Mr. Johnson has informed me, being in custody, he will not waive any time.

[The Court] All right. . . . Mr. Johnson, do you waive your right to trial within the statutory period and personally consent to this matter set for trial on the date requested by your counsel, May 6th?

[Defendant Johnson] No.

[The Court] Very well. There being good cause shown, the matter is continued to May 6th.

On May 6, the court again called the matter for trial:

[The Court] Number 6 on the calendar, Raymond Johnson. . . . The matter is on the court's calendar for trial.

[Defense Counsel] For the following reason, I cannot announce ready this morning. The Perez matter which is on its 10th day is assigned for trial to Department 128. The court has thereafter ordered me to try the Stevens matter which is presently set for the 11th. I am hopeful I will be finished with the Perez matter then. With the trailing time necessary to handle Stevens, then the next matter I have is Mr. Anderson, which the court has also ordered me to try after Perez and then Stevens. That is set for the 27th. Therefore, we will probably be trailing on the Stevens matter, I would figure 10 days which would be to the 7th, approximately, of June, and that case will probably take four days to try which is to the 13th. I will be concluding that matter, and I have talked with [the deputy district attorney] and Mrs. Ornelas, your clerk, about putting the matter over to June 14 when it looks like I will be done with Perez, Stevens and Phillips. . . .

[The Court] Mr. Johnson regarding your right to trial within the statutory period, do you personally consent to this matter being set for trial on the date requested by counsel, June 14 which it appears to the court is the earliest opportunity counsel has to try your matter?

[Defendant] No, I don't.

[The Court] There being good cause shown, the matter is continued to that day, June 14.

Was the defendant's **statutory right to a speedy trial** violated? Remember, it was his counsel who delayed the trial, not the prosecutor.

The California Supreme Court affirmed his conviction, concluding that the conflicts in the defendant's attorney's schedule did not constitute good cause for the delay of the trial because the defendant, who was incarcerated pending trial, expressly objected to the continuances. However, the court found that the defendant was not entitled to relief because he had not been prejudiced by the delay. The court indicated that since the state controlled the number of public defenders available to the court, the delay was chargeable to the state and not the defendant.

In agreeing with the contention of the defendant the Court stated:

At first blush it might appear that a man already in prison under a lawful sentence is hardly in a position to suffer from "undue and oppressive incarceration prior to trial." But the fact is that delay in bringing such a person to trial on a pending charge may ultimately result in as much oppression as is suffered by one who is jailed without bail upon an untried charge. First, the possibility that the defendant already in prison might receive a sentence at least partially concurrent with the one he is serving may be forever lost if trial of the pending charge is postponed. Secondly, under procedures now widely practiced, the duration of his present imprisonment may be increased, and the conditions under which he must serve his sentence greatly worsened, by the pendency of another criminal charge outstanding against him.

And while it might be argued that a person already in prison would be less likely than others to be affected by "anxiety and concern accompanying public accusation," there is reason to believe that an outstanding untried charge (of which even a convict may, of course, be innocent) can have fully as depressive an effect upon a prisoner as upon a person who is at large. In the opinion of the former Director of the Federal Bureau of Prisons: "It is in their effect upon the prisoner and our attempts to rehabilitate him that detainees are most corrosive. The strain of having to serve a sentence with the uncertain prospect of being taken into the custody of another state at the conclusion interferes with the prisoner's ability to take maximum advantage of his institutional opportunities. His anxiety and depression may leave him with little inclination towards self-improvement."

Finally, it is self-evident that the possibilities that long delay will impair the ability of an accused to defend himself are markedly increased when the accused is incarcerated in another jurisdiction. Confined in a prison, perhaps far from the place where the offense covered by the outstanding charge allegedly took place, his ability to confer with potential defense witnesses, or even to keep track of their whereabouts, is obviously impaired. And, while evidence and witnesses disappear, memories fade, and events lose their perspective, a man isolated in prison is powerless to exert his own investigative efforts to mitigate these erosive effects of the passage of time.

The *Smith* case did not resolve the question of the action that must be taken, if any, when a defendant does not demand to be brought to trial, and the *Barker* decision was of little assistance. The Court in the *Barker* case stated that the prosecution is responsible for bringing the defendant to trial. However, the Court did not absolve the defendant of all responsibility in bringing about the trial. At first glance, it would appear that if the prosecution learns that a defendant is incarcerated in another state, some action should be taken by the prosecution to return the defendant for a speedy trial before the expiration date of the sentence in the other state. Otherwise, it could be held that the defendant was denied the right to due process of law. On the other hand, if a defendant knows that he or she is wanted in another place for a crime committed, the failure to demand to be brought to trial could be interpreted as a waiver of the right to a speedy trial.

Statutory Regulations

To assist those involved in the administration of justice, most states have enacted statutes setting forth guidelines on when a trial should take place, but even these guidelines have much flexibility. For example, many states have passed statutes similar to the following:

California Penal Code 1050(a)

The welfare of the people requires that all proceedings in criminal cases shall be set for trial and heard and determined at the earliest possible time, and it shall be the duty of all courts and judicial officers and of all prosecuting attorneys to expedite such proceedings to the greatest degree that is consistent with the ends of justice. In accordance with this policy, criminal cases shall be given precedence over, and set for trial and heard prior to any civil matters. Also no continuance of a criminal trial shall be granted except upon sufficient cause shown in open court, and upon reasonable notice to the opposition. It is held also that cases of those accused of a crime who are in custody are to take precedence over those who have been released on bail.

In addition, most states have provisions stating that unless an accused is brought to trial within a set number of days after the filing of the appropriate accusatory pleading, the charge shall be dismissed, and, if in custody, the defendant shall be released or bail shall be exonerated. The period of time is usually thirty days if the charge is a misdemeanor or within a period of sixty to 120 days, depending upon the jurisdiction, if the charge is a felony. This period may be waived by the defendant. In most instances, if a misdemeanor charge is dismissed, further prosecution will be barred on that particular offense, but states vary in the effect of a dismissal of a felony charge. Some states hold that further prosecution is barred. Other states hold that the defendant must be released after the dismissal but may be rearrested upon the filing of a new accusatory document, and the time clock begins to run again. How many times such a procedure could take place before it would be considered a violation of the speedy trial guarantee is uncertain. If it can be proved that the refiling was for harassment purposes, even one refiling would undoubtedly be considered a denial of due process.

It has also been held that unless reasonable efforts are made to execute a warrant of arrest after it has been issued, the accused may have been denied the right to a speedy trial. In one case, for example, a felony warrant of arrest was issued for an accused, but no efforts were made to execute it even though the accused had resided at the address listed on the warrant for nearly six months after the warrant was issued. The accused left the area for a few months but returned and again lived at the address listed on the warrant for several months before being arrested on a minor charge. After the conviction on the felony charge, the appellate court held that because of the delay in executing the warrant of arrest, the accused had been denied a speedy trial. However, if a reasonable effort is made to execute a warrant of arrest and the accused cannot be located, the delay in the execution of the warrant will not be interpreted as a denial of a speedy trial. It has been held that if there is a good reason for not serving the warrant of arrest immediately after it is issued, the defendant's right to a speedy trial is not denied. In one case, there was a delay of five months between the time that the warrant of arrest was issued and the time of service. The court held that since the delay was for the purpose of identifying other members of a narcotic ring and this undertaking would have been hampered by an immediate arrest, the delay was justified. Similarly, it has been held that if there is a good cause for a delay in having a warrant of arrest issued after a crime is committed, the defendant has not been denied the right to a speedy trial.

Statute of Limitations

To further assure that one accused of committing a crime is afforded a speedy trial, a **statute of limitations** is incorporated into the laws of all the states. This has been termed a humanitarian statute, since it provides that some prosecutive action must be commenced against an accused within a reasonable time after the crime is committed. The statute prevents the state or society from holding the threat of prosecutive action for an indefinite period over the head of an offender. The statute has also been described as an act of grace, since there is a surrendering by the sovereignty of its right to prosecute.

The statute forces society to take some action from two perspectives. It gives law enforcement the responsibility of taking immediate and continuous action upon a reported crime in order to identify the perpetrator so that he or she may be afforded a speedy trial. The statute also gives the prosecutive officials the responsibility of commencing prosecution within a specified time after the identity of an offender is established. There are occasions when a crime is committed and the law enforcement agency involved is unsuccessful in identifying the perpetrators of that crime until after the time stated in the statute of limitations has lapsed. Under those circumstances, the perpetrators may not be brought to trial even if later identified. In most states, the statute of limitations is considered to be a jurisdictional matter and may not be waived. If the perpetrators of a crime are identified before the statutory period runs out and their whereabouts are unknown, some prosecutive action, such as filing a complaint or indictment, must still be commenced before the statutory time expires or future prosecutive action will be barred.

There was no statute of limitations, as we know it today, at common law in England. If a crime was committed at common law, it was a crime against the king, and it was presumed that prosecution might occur at any time. This was particularly true in murder cases. This background may be the reason that even today, in the United States, the statute of limitations never lapses on a murder charge. With most other crimes, there is a specified time within which prosecutive action must commence. The time varies among states. On a felony charge, the statute of limitations varies from three to six years, depending upon the state. On a misdemeanor charge, the period is between six months and one year. A few states list other felonies besides murder, such as the embezzlement of public funds or falsification of public records, for which there are not statutory periods. If, during the investigation of a case, it is determined that the perpetrator of the crime has left the state in which the crime was committed, the statute of limitations is suspended, or tolled, while the perpetrator is out of state.

For some crimes that are difficult to detect, the statute of limitations does not begin to run until it is discovered the crime has occurred. For example, in many jurisdictions, the statute of limitations for embezzlement does not begin to run until the act of embezzlement is discovered or should have been discovered. In a number of jurisdictions, the statute of limitations for crimes against minors does not start to run until the minor has reached the age of majority. For example, a stepfather has sex with his twelve-year-old stepdaughter; the statute does not start to run until the victim reaches eighteen years of age.

CASE LAW

Recent Cases

Indiana v. *Edwards*, 554 U.S. 164 (U.S. 2008)

Can a defendant have the mental capacity to stand trial yet lack the mental capacity act as his or her own counsel?

Edwards tried to steal a pair of shoes from a department store, drew a gun, fired at a store security officer, and wounded a bystander. The State of Indiana charged Edwards with attempted murder, battery with a deadly weapon, criminal recklessness, and theft. He initially was found incompetent to stand trial and was committed to a state hospital.

Subsequently, Edwards was found competent to stand trial and requested to represent himself at trial. The trial court found that respondent was competent to stand trial, but that he was not competent to defend himself.

The appellate court ordered a new trial. The Indiana Supreme Court affirmed. The State sought review before the U.S. Supreme Court. Edwards was represented by appointed counsel at his retrial.

The U.S. Supreme Court held that under the Sixth and Fourteenth Amendments that a new trial was not warranted based on the denial of his self-representation request because the United States Constitution did not forbid the State from insisting that Edwards proceed to trial with counsel, thereby denying him the right to represent himself. The Court stated that the United States Constitution permitted the State to limit respondent's self-representation right by insisting upon representation by counsel at trial on the ground that he lacked the mental capacity to conduct his trial defense unless represented.

The Court noted that the competency standard is defined as including both (1) whether the defendant has a rational as well as factual understanding of the proceedings against him and (2) whether the defendant has sufficient present ability to consult with his lawyer with a reasonable degree of rational understanding. It has long been accepted that a person whose mental condition is such that he lacks the capacity to understand the nature and object of the proceedings against him, to consult with counsel, and to assist in preparing his defense may not be subjected to a trial.

The Sixth and Fourteenth Amendments include a constitutional right to proceed without counsel when a criminal defendant voluntarily and intelligently elects to do so. That right has been implied from: (1) a "nearly universal conviction," made manifest in state law, that forcing a lawyer upon an unwilling defendant is contrary to his basic right to defend himself if he truly wants to do so; (2) Sixth Amendment language granting rights to the "accused"; (3) Sixth Amendment structure indicating that the rights it sets forth, related to the "fair administration of American justice," are "personal" to the accused; (4) the absence of historical examples of forced representation; and (5) respect for the individual. A knowing and intelligent waiver of counsel must be honored out of that respect for the individual, which is the lifeblood of the law.

The Court concluded that one might not be insane in the sense of being incapable of standing trial yet lack the capacity to stand trial without benefit of counsel.

The United States Constitution permits judges to take realistic account of the particular defendant's mental capacities by asking whether a defendant who seeks to conduct his own defense at trial is mentally competent to do so. That is to say, the United States Constitution permits States to insist upon representation by counsel for those competent enough to stand trial but who still suffer from severe mental illness to the point where they are not competent to conduct trial proceedings by themselves.

Skilling v. United States, 130 S. Ct. 2896, 2899-2900 (U.S. 2010)

Founded in 1985, Enron Corporation grew from its headquarters in Houston, Texas, into the seventh highest-revenue-grossing company in America. Petitioner Jeffrey Skilling, a longtime Enron officer, was Enron's chief executive officer from February until August 2001, when he resigned. Less than four months later, Enron crashed into bankruptcy, and its stock plummeted in value. After an investigation uncovered an elaborate conspiracy to prop up Enron's stock prices by overstating the company's financial well-being, the government prosecuted dozens of Enron employees who participated in the scheme.

In time, the government worked its way up the chain of command, indicting Skilling and two other top Enron executives. These three defendants, the indictment charged, engaged in a scheme to deceive investors about Enron's true financial performance by manipulating its publicly reported financial results and making false and misleading statements. Count 1 of the indictment charged Skilling with, inter alia, conspiracy to commit "honest-services" wire fraud, 18 U.S.C. §§ 371, 1343, 1346, by depriving Enron and its shareholders of the intangible right of his honest services. Skilling was also charged with over 25 substantive counts of securities fraud, wire fraud, making false representations to Enron's auditors, and insider trading.

In November 2004, Skilling moved for a change of venue, contending that hostility toward him in Houston, coupled with extensive pretrial publicity, had poisoned potential jurors. He submitted hundreds of news reports detailing Enron's downfall, as well as affidavits from experts he engaged portraying community attitudes in Houston in comparison to other potential venues. The district court denied the motion, concluding that pretrial publicity did not warrant a presumption that Skilling would be unable to obtain a fair trial in Houston. Despite incidents of intemperate commentary, the court observed, media coverage, on the whole, had been objective and unemotional, and the facts of the case were neither heinous nor sensational. Moreover, the court asserted, effective voir dire would detect juror bias.

In November 2005, the district court mailed the questionnaire to 400 prospective jurors and received responses from nearly all the addressees. The court granted hardship exemptions to approximately 90 individuals and the parties, with the court's approval, further winnowed the pool by excusing another 119 for cause, hardship, or physical disability. The parties agreed to exclude, in particular, "each and every" prospective juror who said that a preexisting opinion about Enron or the defendants would prevent her from impartially considering the evidence at trial.

On December 28, 2005, three weeks before the date scheduled for the commencement of trial, one defendant (Causey) pleaded guilty. Skilling's attorneys immediately requested a continuance, and the district court agreed to delay the proceedings until the end of January 2006. In the interim, Skilling renewed his change-of-venue motion, arguing that the juror questionnaires revealed pervasive bias and that news accounts of Causey's guilty plea further tainted the jury pool. If Houston remained the trial venue, Skilling urged that "jurors need to be questioned individually by both the Court and counsel" concerning their opinions of Enron and "publicity issues."

The district court again declined to move the trial. Skilling, the court concluded, still had not "established that pretrial publicity and/or community prejudice raised a presumption of inherent jury prejudice." The questionnaires and voir dire, the court observed, provided safeguards adequate to ensure an impartial jury.

Denying Skilling's request for attorney-led voir dire, the court said that in seventeen years on the bench:

> "I've found . . . I get more forthcoming responses from potential jurors than the lawyers on either side. I don't know whether people are suspicious of lawyers— but I think if I ask a person a question, I will get a candid response much easier than if a lawyer asks the question."

But the court promised to give counsel an opportunity to ask follow-up questions, ibid., and it agreed that venire members should be examined individually about pretrial publicity. The court also allotted the defendants jointly fourteen peremptory challenges, two more than the standard number prescribed by Federal Rule of Criminal Procedure.

Voir dire began January 30, 2006. The district court first emphasized to the venire the importance of impartiality and explained the presumption of innocence and the government's burden of proof. The trial, the court next instructed, was not a forum "to seek vengeance against Enron's former officers," or to "provide remedies for" its victims. "The bottom line," the court stressed, "is that we want . . . jurors who . . . will faithfully, conscientiously and impartially serve if selected." In response to the court's query whether any prospective juror questioned her ability to adhere to these instructions, two individuals indicated that they could not be fair; they were therefore excused for cause.

After questioning the venire as a group, the District Court brought prospective jurors one by one to the bench for individual examination. Although the questions varied, the process generally tracked the following format: The court asked about exposure to Enron-related news and the content of any stories that stood out in the prospective juror's mind. Next, the court homed in on questionnaire answers that raised a red flag signaling possible bias. The court then permitted each side to pose follow-up questions. Finally,

after the venire member stepped away, the court entertained and ruled on challenges for cause. In all, the court granted one of the government's for-cause challenges and denied four; it granted three of the defendants' challenges and denied six. The parties agreed to excuse three additional jurors for cause and one for hardship.

Defendant was convicted in federal district court of charges that included conspiracy to commit "honest services" wire fraud under 18 U.S.C.S. §§ 371, 1343, and 1346. The United States Court of Appeals for the Fifth Circuit affirmed. The Supreme Court held that the failure to move the trial from Houston was not error, but remanded the case for further proceedings regarding the charge of wire fraud.

The U.S. Supreme Court noted that the Sixth Amendment secures to criminal defendants the right to trial by an impartial jury. By constitutional design, that trial occurs "in the State where the . . . Crimes . . . have been committed." Art. III, § 2, cl. 3. See also the Sixth Amendment (right to trial by "jury of the State and district wherein the crime shall have been committed"). The Constitution's place-of-trial prescriptions, however, do not impede transfer of the proceeding to a different district at the defendant's request if extraordinary local prejudice will prevent a fair trial—a "basic requirement of due process."

The Court concluded that although Causey's "well-publicized decision to plead guilty" shortly before trial created a danger of juror prejudice, the district court took appropriate steps to reduce that risk. The court delayed the proceedings by two weeks, lessening the immediacy of that development. And during voir dire, the court asked about prospective jurors' exposure to recent publicity, including news regarding Causey. Only two venire members recalled the plea; neither mentioned Causey by name, and neither ultimately served on Skilling's jury. Although publicity about a codefendant's guilty plea calls for inquiry to guard against actual prejudice, it does not ordinarily— and, we are satisfied, it did not here—warrant an automatic presumption of prejudice.

Persuaded that no presumption arose, the Court concluded that the district court, in declining to order a venue change, did not exceed constitutional limitations.

Briefly Noted

United States v. *Moore,* **2011 U.S. App. LEXIS 6905 (8th Cir. Neb. Apr. 6, 2011).** Defendant Moore was convicted in the United States District Court of conspiracy to distribute cocaine base and a detectable amount of cocaine. The defendant appealed. Moore was indicted on a charge of conspiracy to distribute crack cocaine and cocaine between on or about June 1, 2005, and March 31, 2007. A witness testified that he purchased crack cocaine from defendant in 2008. The government acknowledged that there was a variance between the indictment date and the proof at trial. The court of appeals held that the variance did not affect defendant's Sixth Amendment right to adequate notice because the time frame of the conspiracy was not an element of the crime, and the acts to which the witness testified were committed within the limitations period and prior to the return date of the indictment. The U.S. Court of Appeals affirmed the district court's judgment.

***United States v. Szilvagyi*, 2011 U.S. App. LEXIS 6516 (6th Cir. Mich. 2011).** Defendant Szilvagyi was convicted in the United States District Court of unlawful procurement of naturalization. Defendant appealed the district court's denial of her motion to dismiss the indictment.She had applied for naturalization in 1996 and took the citizenship oath in 1997. She was indicted for naturalization fraud in 2007 for making false statements regarding whether she had ever knowingly committed a crime for which she had not been arrested. The indictment was filed under seal based on the government's stated fears that defendant would obstruct justice; the indictment was unsealed more than 10 years after defendant was sworn in as a citizen. Defendant argued that the indictment violated the 10-year statute of limitations. The court of appeals held that the indictment was indictment fell within the limitations period. The statute of limitations did not begin to run until defendant took the oath of citizenship, which was when the crime was complete. The sealed indictment was filed within the limitations period. The indictment was not improperly sealed, as the government expressed a legitimate concern that knowledge of the naturalization fraud charge could have caused defendant to attempt to obstruct justice in a different case. The defendant did not establish that

preindictment delay violated her Fifth Amendment due process rights, as substantial prejudice was not shown.

The U.S. Court of Appeals affirmed the judgment.

***United States v. James*, 2011 U.S. App. LEXIS 6857 (10th Cir. Okla. Apr. 4, 2011).** Defendant James appealed from the U.S. District Court for the Eastern District of Oklahoma decision, where he was convicted on one count of being a felon in possession of firearms, pursuant to 18 U.S.C.S. §§ 922(g)(1), 924(a)(2), and 924(e). He contended that the indictment against him should have been dismissed under the Speedy Trial Act, 18 U.S.C.S. §§ 3161-74, because the delay caused by his codefendant's psychological evaluation rendered his trial untimely.

The U.S. Court of Appeals held that defendant's sole challenge on appeal was to the exclusion from his speedy-trial calculation of the delay resulting from his codefendant's mental evaluation. He argued that the unexpected length of the delay, viewed as a whole, amounted to an unreasonable amount of time. The court examined the three reasonableness factors under 18 U.S.C.S. § 3161(h)(6): (1) whether the defendant was free on bond, (2) whether the defendant zealously pursued a speedy trial, and (3) whether the circumstances furthered the purpose behind the exclusion to accommodate the efficient use of prosecutorial and judicial resources in trying multiple defendants in a single trial.

The first factor favored defendant's position. But even if he had sought release and still been detained, the weight of the first factor was offset by the other two. As for the second factor, defendant did not zealously pursue a speedy trial. Most important was the third factor: a single trial was preferred in circumstances when the exact same evidence and witnesses would be used in the prosecution of both defendants. The burden on defendant of being incarcerated for a few extra months did not overcome that preference. The Court of Appeals affirmed the district court's denial of defendant's motion to dismiss.

Summary

- The Sixth Amendment guarantees an accused the right to a "speedy and public trial by an impartial jury of the state and judicial district wherein the crime shall have been committed."
- Venue refers to the geographical location of the trial. Venue may be waived by a defendant.

- The defense of insanity refers to the accused's mental state at the time of the criminal act.
- The issue of competency refers to the mental status of the defendant at the time of trial.
- Most states require the defendant to establish incompetency by a preponderance of evidence.

- A defendant is considered incompetent if he or she lacks the capacity to understand the charges and the object of the proceedings against him or her.
- A motion to change venue may be made by the defendant if he or she contends that a fair trial in the district where the crime occurred is not possible.
- The prosecution may not force a change of venue because of the constitutional right of a defendant to be tried in the judicial district in which the crime occurred.
- The right to a speedy trial is a fundamental right of an accused.

- The question of whether the right to a speedy trial has been violated depends on a balancing of the issues. The nature of the right makes it impossible to pinpoint a precise time when the right must be asserted or is waived.
- The statutory right to a speedy trial is based on definite guidelines and specific time periods.
- The statute of limitations refers to the period between the time when the crime was committed and prosecution is started. Some crimes, like murder, have no statute of limitations.

Review Questions

1. Where must a criminal trial take place?
2. What is meant by a change of venue?
3. What is meant by a speedy trial?
4. List four factors that the U.S. Supreme Court set forth in the *Barker* v. *Wingo* decision that should be taken into account in determining whether a defendant has been denied a speedy trial.

5. List three societal disadvantages of lengthy pretrial incarceration.
6. Why should granting continuances be discouraged?
7. What effect, if any, does out-of-state incarceration have on a speedy trial?
8. What is the statute of limitations?

Local Procedure

1. In your home state, what is the statute of limitations for the following:
   a. Misdemeanors?
   b. Felonies?

2. In your home state, if a felony is dismissed for the failure to bring the defendant to trial within statutory limitations, may the charge be refiled?

Endnotes

1. 517 U.S. 348 (1996).
2. *Jackson* v. *Indiana,* 406 U.S. 715 (1972).
3. Kevin Johnson and Andrew Seaman (2008, May 29), "Mentally Incompetent defendants on the rise," *USA Today,* p. A12.
4. In *United States* v. *Lindauer,* 448 F. Supp. 2d 558 (2006), an appellate court applied a four-part test to determine whether the government's motion should be granted. The test required the government to prove that important

government interests were at stake, that administration of the drugs was substantially likely to render defendant competent to stand trial, that involuntary administration of the drugs was necessary to advance the government's interests because less drastic measures would not suffice, and that administration of such drugs was in defendant's best interest in light of her overall medical condition.

5. 407 U.S. 514 (1972).
6. 393 U.S. 374 (1969).

CHAPTER 7

Trial

The majestic equality of the law forbids the rich as well as the poor to sleep under bridges, to beg in the streets, and to steal bread.

—ANATOLE FRANCE, 1914

Chapter Outline

Bench Trial versus Jury Trial

Public Trial

Case Law

Summary

Key Terms

Alternate jurors

Bench trial

Court trial

Gag orders

Impartial trial by jury

Locked-down jury

Petty offenses

Public trial

Right of the press and the public to
   access to criminal trials

Right to a trial by jury

Learning Objectives

After completing this chapter, you should be able to:

- Summarize defendants' rights.
- Differentiate between a bench and jury trial.
- Outline the jury selection process.
- Outline the trial process from opening statements through closing statements.

- Summarize instructions to and deliberations of a jury.
- Define terms related to the trial process.
- Discuss the right of the public and press to attend a criminal trial.
- Identify what constitutes a public trial.

- Explain the defendant's right to a jury trial.
- Discuss the procedure for waiving a jury trial.
- List what constitutes a petty offense.
- Discuss the rules regarding the size of a jury.

BENCH TRIAL VERSUS JURY TRIAL

By the beginning of the eighteenth century, the accused was being confronted by the witnesses against him or her, and hearsay evidence was eliminated. Witnesses were placed under oath to relate facts of their own knowledge. Juries rendered their verdicts based upon the testimony of witnesses given in open court, not upon what the jurors had learned about an accusation outside of court. Rules of evidence were being formulated. The trial by jury as it is known today was rapidly becoming part of the judicial system in Great Britain and was adopted by the colonists. The colonists had deep reverence for trial by jury, and they strongly resented interference by the king of Great Britain in his efforts to subdue them. This resentment was manifested by the colonists in the Declaration of Independence. Among other provisions, they included in the Declaration the following: "The history of the present King of Great Britain is a history of repeated injuries. To prove this, let facts be submitted to a candid world. . . . For his [the King] depriving us in many cases, of benefits of trial by jury."

Accused's Right to Jury Trial

After the colonists gained their independence from Great Britain, a new government was established. To prevent possible future interference with the **right to a trial by jury** in this newly formed government, the Sixth Amendment to the U.S. Constitution contained the provision that all persons accused of a crime had the right to be tried by an impartial jury. The Sixth Amendment right to trial by jury is made binding on the states through the Due Process Clause of the Fourteenth Amendment, as is the right to a speedy trial. These rights are also contained in all state constitutions or statutes. Although the Sixth Amendment did not mention the number of persons required to constitute a jury, it was generally accepted that the common law rule of twelve persons would prevail. So strongly was it felt that a jury must consist of twelve persons in a criminal case that a trial by jury consisting of fewer than twelve would be a denial of due process of law. The idea of an accused's being permitted to waive a jury trial and have the case heard by a judge alone was practically unthought-of. It was not until 1930 in the case of *Patton* v. *United States*[1] that the U.S. Supreme Court held that a verdict rendered by a jury comprising fewer than twelve members was not a violation of an accused's constitutional right to a trial by jury. In the *Patton* case, the trial started with a jury comprising twelve persons, but during the trial one of the jurors became incapacitated. The defendant agreed to continue the trial with only eleven jurors. He was convicted, and the case was taken to the U.S. Supreme Court to determine whether a defendant has the right to waive a jury trial. The defendant did not waive the entire jury in the *Patton* case, but even waiving one juror and continuing with only eleven was so foreign to the common law procedure that the U.S. Supreme Court felt that the matter was worth their consideration. The Court in the *Patton* case stated that, after an examination of Article III, section 2, and the Sixth Amendment of the U.S. Constitution, they had come to the conclusion that a jury trial was a right that the accused might "forego at his election" and that this right was a privilege and not an "imperative right." As such, the defendant could waive a jury comprising fewer than twelve persons. This decision gave an implied permission to waive the jury entirely and have the case heard by a judge sitting alone.

Even though the Court in the *Patton* case sanctioned the right of an accused to waive his or her right to a jury, it did emphasize the necessity of preserving the jury trial system. The Court stated as follows:

> Not only must the right of the accused to a trial by a constitutional jury be jealously preserved, but the maintenance of the jury as a fact-finding body in criminal cases is of such importance and has such a place in our traditions that, before any waiver can become effective, the consent of government counsel and the sanction of the court must be had, in addition to the express and intelligent consent of the defendant.

The U.S. Supreme Court further emphasized the importance of the right of an accused to a trial by jury in the case of *Duncan* v. *Louisiana.*[2] The Court in that decision stated the following:

> Providing an accused with the right to be tried by a jury of his peers gave him an inestimable safeguard against the corrupt or overzealous prosecutor and against the compliant, biased, or eccentric judge. If the defendant preferred the common sense judgment of a jury to the more tutored but perhaps less sympathetic reaction of the single judge, he was to have it. Beyond this, the jury trial provisions in the Federal and State Constitutions reflect a fundamental decision about the exercise of official power—a reluctance to entrust plenary powers over the life and liberty of the citizens to one judge or to a group of judges. Fear of unchecked power, so typical of our State and Federal Governments in other respects, found expression in the criminal law in this insistence upon community participation in the determination of guilt or innocence. The deep commitment of the Nation to the right of jury trial in serious criminal cases as a defense against arbitrary law enforcement qualities for protection under the Due Process Clause of the Fourteenth Amendment, and must therefore be respected by the States.

Trial by Judge Alone

Further advantages of a jury trial over a trial by a judge sitting alone, also referred to as a court trial, include the belief that a jury of twelve persons, representing a cross section of society, may be better able to evaluate the demeanor of witnesses than a judge sitting alone; that the group judgment of a jury is better than that of a single person, the judge; that there is a value in community participation in the administration of justice; and that the jury injects the common law test into the legal system instead of the legalistic viewpoint.

With all these listed advantages to a trial by jury, why would a defendant wish to waive a jury and be tried by a judge sitting alone? Situations arise in which it may be advantageous to the accused to waive his or her right to a jury trial in favor of a court trial. The crime of which the defendant is accused may be a heinous one. The emotional involvement of the people within the community may make the selection of an impartial jury very difficult. The defendant's general appearance may be such that a jury may become prejudiced. There may be a serious past criminal record subjecting the defendant to possible impeachment should the witness stand be taken as a defense, and the probability of the jury's convicting the defendant on his or her past record rather than on the evidence contended in the present charge is great. Or the defendant may be a part of an organized criminal syndicate or of a minority group that local feeling is against, and the jury may convict the accused by association rather than on the facts of the case. A judge is considered less inclined to be affected by any of these situations than would a jury.

PROCEDURE IN THE WAIVER OF A JURY   Prior to the *Patton* decision, only a few states had considered allowing a defendant to waive a trial by jury. However, after the *Patton* decision, a large majority of the states began permitting the defendant to waive the right to a trial by jury. States differ considerably regarding the conditions and the procedure to be followed in permitting a waiver of a jury trial. A few states still do not permit the defendant to waive a jury trial. Others permit the waiver in misdemeanor cases but not on felony charges. Still others permit the jury to be waived in all cases except those with a maximum penalty of death. One state permits the defendant to waive the jury in capital cases and be tried by a panel of three judges. A few states permit the jury to be waived in any type of charge, including capital cases.

States also differ concerning who must give consent and how the consent is given. Some states provide that the waiver is solely the right of the defendant, whereas others hold that the waiver must be consented to by the prosecution as well as the defendant. A few states require that the defendant, the prosecution, and the judge all must agree to the waiver of the jury, and a few others provide that the defendant and the judge must agree to the waiver, but the consent of the prosecution is not required. This latter position has been criticized, since it is believed that the prosecution should be permitted to disagree with the waiver. The reasoning is that a judge may be known to be sympathetic to the defendant or may be under political pressure, making him or her feel forced to render a verdict in favor of the defendant. In most instances, the prosecution will agree with the waiver of the jury, since the waiver expedites the trial by eliminating the time-consuming selection of the jury. Time is also saved by not having to stop during a jury trial to explain the law of the case to the jury.

The manner in which the waiver of the jury takes place also varies among states. In some states, the defendant must waive the jury in open court by an express statement to that effect. Other states require the defendant to consent to the waiver in writing before the date of the trial. Some states hold that unless the defendant demands a jury trial at the time that he or she enters the plea of not guilty, a jury trial is automatically waived. If the waiver of a jury takes place, it is usually before the jury is selected, but a few states permit the defendant to waive the jury anytime before the verdict is rendered.

A question that sometimes arises is: After consent to a waiver of the jury, may the defendant later demand to be tried by a jury? Generally, unless there is sufficient evidence of a miscarriage of justice, the defendant may not demand a jury trial, particularly if the trial has begun. The reason is that a jury would have to be selected and the trial would have to start over. Once the trial has begun, the waiver of a jury creates no particular difficulty, since the judge will have heard all the evidence during the trial's progress and will be in a position to render the verdict. Whether the defendant is permitted to withdraw the waiver of the jury is within the discretion of the trial judge. In making the decision, the judge may consider such matters as the timeliness of the motion to withdraw the waiver, the reason for the requested withdrawal, and the possibility of undue delay of the trial or inconvenience to witnesses that would result from granting the withdrawal of the waiver.

MAY THE DEFENDANT DEMAND A BENCH TRIAL? As previously pointed out, there are times when a defendant may wish to be tried by a judge sitting alone. Under these circumstances, may the defendant waive the jury and demand a **bench trial**, also known as a **court trial**? This question was answered by the U.S. Supreme Court in the case of *Singer* v. *United States*.[3] In that decision, the Court held that although a defendant could waive the right to a jury trial, there is no correlative right to a bench trial. The Court recognized the fact that a prosecutor also has the right to demand a jury trial. The Court in the *Singer* decision stated:

> The ability to waive a constitutional right does not ordinarily carry with it the right to insist upon the opposite of that right. For example, although a defendant can, under some circumstances, waive his constitutional right to a public trial, he has no absolute right to compel a private trial. Although he can waive his right to be tried in the State and district where the crime was committed, he cannot in all cases compel transfer of the case to another district, and although he can waive his right to be confronted by the witnesses against him, it has never been seriously suggested that he can thereby compel the Government to try the case by stipulation. . . .

Trial by jury has been established by the Constitution as the "normal and . . . preferable mode of disposing of issues of fact in a criminal case."

In light of the Constitution's emphasis on jury trial, we find it difficult to understand how the petitioner can submit the bald proposition that to compel a defendant in a criminal case to undergo a jury trial against his or her will is contrary to his or her right to a fair trial or to due process. A defendant's only constitutional right concerning the method of trial is to an **impartial trial by jury**. We find no constitutional impediment in conditioning a waiver of this right on the consent of the prosecuting attorney and the trial judge when, if either refuses to consent, the result is simply that the defendant is subject to an impartial trial by jury—the very thing that the Constitution guarantees him or her.

The Court concluded that forcing a jury trial was not a violation of any constitutional right of an accused even though the defendant might feel that it was advantageous to have a court trial. In this regard, many states permit the judge to refuse to consent to a court trial in lieu of a trial by jury. Those states adopting this policy feel that protection against community criticism should be provided when the judge might have to render an unpopular verdict.

Denial of a Jury Trial: Petty Offenses

Although the right to a trial by jury is an established guarantee to one accused of a crime, it is not an absolute right in all instances. As early as 1937, the U.S. Supreme Court in the case of *District of Columbia* v. *Clawans*[4] sanctioned a nonjury trial to one accused of a **petty offense**. This same sanction has been reiterated from time to time by the Court.[5]

In the *Duncan* v. *Louisiana* decision, the Court stated the following:

> So-called petty offenses were tried without juries both in England and in the Colonies and have always been held to be exempt from the otherwise comprehensive language of the Sixth Amendment's jury trial provisions. There is no substantial evidence that the Framers intended to depart from this established common-law practice, and the possible consequences to defendants from convictions for petty offenses have been thought insufficient to outweigh the benefits to efficient law enforcement and simplified judicial administration resulting from the availability of speedy and inexpensive non-jury adjudications. These same considerations compel the same result under the Fourteenth Amendment. Of course the boundaries of the petty offense category have always been ill defined, if not ambulatory.

DETERMINING PETTY OFFENSES In determining whether an offense is a "petty" one, the courts have had to turn to some criteria upon which to work. Although the statutes of some states have designated certain offenses as petty ones, this designation is not conclusive, and the courts may render different interpretations of petty offenses.

As stated by the U.S. Supreme Court in the *Frank* decision, to determine whether a particular offense could be classified as petty, the Court sought objective indications of the seriousness with which society regarded the offense. The Court stated that the most relevant indication of the seriousness of an offense was the severity of the penalty that could be imposed for the commission of the offense. The severity of the penalty authorized by law, and not the penalty actually imposed by the judge, was to be the criterion.

In the *Frank* case, the Supreme Court implied that they were relying upon the criterion set forth in the *Cheff* decision for a definition of petty offense. The *Cheff* decision adopted the definition of a petty offense found in 18 U.S. Code, section 1, where it is described as any misdemeanor the penalty for which does not exceed imprisonment for a period of six months or a fine of $500.

It would appear from these U.S. Supreme Court decisions that the states could pass statutes denying an accused the right to a trial by a jury for the commission of an offense for which the penalty would not exceed six months' imprisonment or a fine of not more than $500, and the accused would not be denied due process of law. A few states grant a defendant the right to a jury trial in all misdemeanor charges irrespective of the penalty but deny him or her the right to a jury trial on infractions—violations for which no imprisonment may be imposed.

Juries Comprising Fewer Than Twelve Persons

In line with the common-law tradition, the laws of the United States, as well as of most of the states, require that a criminal trial jury consist of twelve persons. There are a few states where the law provides that in misdemeanor violations, the jury may comprise any number fewer than twelve, agreed upon in open court by the defendant and the prosecution. How many fewer than twelve is not indicated, but the U.S. Supreme Court has not approved the use of a jury with fewer than six members. As in the *Patton* case, in some states it is held that a felony trial must commence with twelve persons in the jury, but if one should become incapacitated and unable to act as a juror, the trial may continue with fewer than twelve if agreed to by the defendant, his or her attorney, and the prosecution. If it is not agreed to, the judge must declare a mistrial, and the case will have to be heard again with a new jury.

Due to the difficulty in obtaining and managing twelve jurors and alternate jurors, some states have broken with the traditional number of twelve in a jury, even in felony cases, and have passed laws providing that a jury may comprise fewer than twelve both in misdemeanor and in felony cases. The problem that arises is whether trial by a jury comprising fewer than twelve when not consented to, particularly by the defendant, is a denial of the right to trial by jury. This question was answered in the case of *Williams* v. *Florida*,[6] in which the U.S. Supreme Court held that a jury comprising fewer than twelve persons, in accordance with the laws of the state involved, did not violate the Due Process Clause of the Fourteenth Amendment. The facts in the *Williams* case indicate that Williams was charged with robbery in the state of Florida. Williams, referred to as the petitioner by the Court, filed a pretrial motion to impanel a twelve-person jury instead of the six-person jury provided by Florida law in all but capital cases. The motion was denied, and Williams was convicted and sentenced to life imprisonment. He appealed his case to the U.S. Supreme Court upon the grounds that his right to a jury trial, as provided in the Sixth Amendment to the U.S. Constitution, made applicable to the states by the Fourteenth Amendment, had been violated by requiring him to submit to a trial by a jury comprising only six persons. The Court stated as follows:

> The question in this case is whether the constitutional guarantee of a trial by "jury" necessarily requires trial by exactly 12 persons, rather than some lesser number, in this case six. We hold that the 12-man panel is not a necessary ingredient of "trial by jury," and that respondent's [state's] refusal to impanel more than six members provided for by Florida law did not violate petitioner's Sixth Amendment rights as applied to the States through the Fourteenth.
>
> We had occasion in *Duncan* v. *Louisiana* to review briefly the oft-told history of the development of trial by jury in criminal cases. That history revealed a long tradition attaching great importance to the concept of relying on a body of one's peers to determine guilt or innocence as a safeguard against arbitrary law enforcement. That same history, however, affords little insight into the considerations which gradually led the size of that body to be generally fixed at 12. Some have suggested that the number 12 was fixed upon simply because that was the number of the presentment jury from the hundred, from which the petty jury developed. Other, less circular, but more fanciful reasons for the number 12 have been given, "but they were all brought forward after the number was fixed," and rest on little more than mystical or superstitious insights into the significance of "12." Lord Coke's explanation that the "number twelve is much respected in holy

writ, as 12 apostles, 12 stones, 12 tribes, etc." is typical. In short, while sometime in the 14th century the size of the jury at common law came to be fixed generally at 12, that particular feature of the jury system appears to have been an historical accident, unrelated to the great purposes which gave rise to the jury in the first place. The question before us is whether this accidental feature of the jury has been immutably codified into our Constitution. . . .

It might be suggested that the 12-man jury gives a defendant a greater advantage since he has more "chances" of finding a juror who will insist on acquittal and thus prevent conviction. But the advantage might just as easily belong to the State, which also needs only one juror out of twelve insisting on guilt to prevent acquittal. What few experiments have occurred—usually in the civil area—indicate that there is no discernible difference between the results reached by the two different sized juries. In short, neither currently available evidence nor theory suggests that the 12-man jury is necessarily more advantageous to the defendant than a jury composed of fewer members.

Similarly, while in theory the number of viewpoints represented on a randomly selected jury ought to increase as the size of the jury increases, in practice the difference between the 12-man and the 6-man jury in terms of the cross section of the community represented seems likely to be negligible. Even the 12-man jury cannot ensure representation of every distinct voice in the community, particularly given the use of the peremptory challenge. As long as arbitrary exclusions of a particular class from the jury rolls are forbidden, the concern that the cross section will be significantly diminished if the jury is decreased in size from 12 to 6 seems an unrealistic one.

We conclude, in short, as we began: the fact that the jury at common law was composed of precisely 12 is an historical accident, unnecessary to effect the purposes of the jury system and wholly without significance "except to mystics."

Since the *Williams* decision has been handed down by the U.S. Supreme Court, it is highly possible that more and more states will enact laws permitting juries to comprise fewer than twelve members in all but capital cases. However, the U.S. Supreme Court, in *Ballew* v. *Georgia,*[7] held that a jury may not comprise fewer than six persons. Ballew was convicted of a misdemeanor charge by a jury of five persons, as provided for by a Georgia statute. The conviction was upheld by the Georgia appellate courts. Ballew appealed his case to the U.S. Supreme Court on the grounds that his constitutional guarantee of a trial by jury had been denied, thereby denying him due process of law. The U.S. Supreme Court stated that a jury of six persons had been upheld in the *Williams* case and that the "line between five and six member juries is not difficult to justify, but a line has to be drawn somewhere if the substance of the jury trial is to be preserved." The Court further stated that assembled research data

raise substantial doubt about the reliability and appropriate representation of panels smaller than six. Because of the fundamental importance of the jury trial to the American system of criminal justice, any further reduction that promotes inaccurate and possibly biased decision making, that causes untoward differences in verdicts, and that prevents juries from truly representing their communities, attains constitutional significance . . . and such reduction from six-member to five-member juries is not to be permitted.

Regardless of the size of the jury, many courts select **alternate jurors**. An alternate juror sits with the jury and is prepared to serve as a jury member if one of the regular jurors is excused or disqualified during the trial. Because only jury members may be present in the room when a jury is deliberating, alternate jurors are generally excused by the trial judge shortly before the jury is **locked-down** for deliberations.

Law in Practice

How Important is Jury Size?

Advantages of Jury Size

The main advantages of reducing the size of juries are as follows:

- Smaller juries would cost less to maintain than larger juries.
- The amount of time spent on the voir dire process would decrease because fewer jurors would be needed.
- Deliberation time would decrease, and as a result, the jury system would become more efficient because more cases could be heard.

Disadvantages of Smaller Juries

Even though it is constitutionally acceptable to reduce the jury's size to any number above six, opponents argue that this would result in the following adverse consequences:

- Juries with fewer than twelve persons are less representative, and thus, fewer voices in the community are represented.
- The quality of jury deliberations would be adversely affected by reducing the jury's size.
- Jury verdicts will be more erratic.
- Lessens the chances of minority representation on the juries.

Federal Study

In 1994, a committee on Rules of Practice and Procedure of the Judicial Conference of the United States issued a report that recommended that federal district courts use six-person juries in federal civil cases, but not in federal criminal cases. The committee's findings included the following conclusions:

- Twelve-person juries are more stable and deliberative.
- Larger juries were more representative of the interests of minorities than six-person juries.
- Savings gained by using smaller juries were small when compared to the overall judiciary budget.

The saving in using smaller juries would not compensate for the decrease in stability and the affects on jury community representation.[8]

Jury Size in Selected Jurisdictions [Not an inclusive list]

Arizona: Permits the use of eight-person juries except in capital cases or where the possible sentence is thirty or more years.

Connecticut and Florida: Permit the use of six-person juries except in capital cases.

Indiana: Six-person juries in municipal and county courts.

Kentucky: Six person juries at the district level.

Massachusetts: Six-person juries in Boston municipal court and district level courts.

Utah: Eight-person juries in all felony cases.

Law in Practice

Does Defendant Have the Right to a Unanimous Verdict before He or She Is Convicted of a Crime?

Unanimous verdicts were required at English common law as early as the mid to late fourteenth century. In 1972 in *Apodaca* v. *Oregon* [406 U.S. 404 (1972)], the U.S. Supreme Court concluded that the Sixth Amendment to the U.S. Constitution, which guarantees the right to a jury trial, did not require that the jury's verdict be unanimous. The *Apodaca* case stands for the rule that nonunanimous verdicts are permissible in state, noncapital cases. In cases where the jury size is less than twelve, only unanimous verdicts are permitted. Unanimous verdicts are required in federal cases.

Only three states allow the use of nonunanimous verdicts in criminal cases:

- Louisiana allows 10-12 decisions in noncapital cases.
- Oklahoma permits nonunanimous verdicts in misdemeanor cases.
- Oregon provides for a 5-6 rule in all except murder cases.

PUBLIC TRIAL

Not only does the Sixth Amendment to the U.S Constitution, as well as the laws of all the states, provide that an accused person is entitled to a trial by jury, but it also further provides that he or she is guaranteed a public trial. The purpose of this guarantee is to ensure that the accused is dealt with fairly and not unjustly convicted. As was stated by the U.S. Supreme Court in the case of *Estes* v. *Texas*[9]:

> History has proven that secret tribunals were effective instruments of oppression. As our Brother Black so well said in *In re Oliver,* 333 US 257 (1948): the traditional Anglo-American distrust for secret trials has been variously ascribed to the notorious use of this practice by the Spanish Inquisition, to the excesses of the English Court of Star Chamber, and to the French monarchy's abuse of the lettre de cachet. Whatever other benefits the guarantee to an accused that his trial be conducted in public may confer upon our society, the guarantee has always been recognized as a safeguard against any attempt to employ our courts as instruments of persecution.
>
> Clearly the openness of the proceedings (the trial) provides other benefits as well (as a safeguard against oppression): it arguably improves the quality of testimony, it may induce unknown witnesses to come forward with relevant testimony, it may move all the trial participants to perform their duties conscientiously, and it gives the public the opportunity to observe the courts in the performance of their duties and to determine whether they are performing adequately.

What Makes a Trial "Public"?

Although an accused's guarantee to a **public trial** appears on the surface to be a clear and explicit right, it is not without complications. Just what constitutes a public trial is not defined either by the Sixth Amendment or by any of the laws of the states. The problems that arise are the following: What is a public trial? Who constitutes the public? How many persons must be in attendance to make a trial a public one? And since the right to a public trial is basically a right of the accused, may the right be waived, resulting in a private trial? Over time, partial answers to these questions have come from court decisions, but the answers to some questions have not been unanimous.

Law in Practice

Was Defendant Denied the Right to a Public Trial? *Rodriguez* v. *Miller*, 499 F.3d 136, 2007 U.S. App. LEXIS 20606 (2d Cir. N.Y. 2007)

Jose Rodriguez was tried in Kings County, New York for selling cocaine to an undercover officer in the Bushwick section of Brooklyn. The State moved to close the courtroom during the officer's testimony to protect his identity. The state court held a hearing at which the officer testified that he: (1) had received numerous threats in the course of work in Bushwick; (2) planned to return to Bushwick to conduct additional investigations "in the near future"; (3) had never in his life testified in open court; and (4) feared Rodriguez's relatives would recognize him and spread the word that he was a police officer. He also admitted that he did not know any of Rodriguez's relatives and had not been threatened by them.

The state court found that this testimony was sufficient to close the courtroom. Rodriguez, himself, conceded that some closure was necessary, but argued that the court could not exclude his family on these facts alone. The court eventually ruled that it would permit Rodriguez's mother and brother to attend the proceedings, but only if they sat behind a screen to obscure the officer's appearance. Fearing prejudice to his defense, Rodriguez objected to the screen and instructed his family not to attend his trial.

(continued)

Rodriguez was convicted. The New York State Appellate Division affirmed his conviction despite his claim that the courtroom closure violated his right to a public trial. The New York Court of Appeals denied an appeal. Court's decision: As the parties agree, the sole issue confronting this Court on remand is whether the New York State Courts' decision to exclude Rodriguez's family from his trial involved an "unreasonable application of . . . clearly established Federal law." We conclude that it did not. It is clear that the State has an "overriding interest" in protecting the identity of its undercover officers. The officer here had been threatened before and intended to return to Bushwick in the near future. The closure was to last only for the duration of his testimony. The court made sufficient findings to support the closure based on his testimony at the hearing. The use of a screen to shield Rodriguez's family was a reasonable alternative to closure. Rodriguez conceded at the hearing that some form of closure was necessary, but argued that the court could not exclude his family based on the limited testimony in the record. Thus, Rodriguez's petition must be denied.

It is clear that a public trial is one that is not secret. The commonsense interpretation of a public trial is one that the general public is free to attend. The doors of the courtroom are expected to be kept open. However, if no member of the public is in attendance, there is no requirement that a trial be stopped in order to satisfy the guarantee of a public trial. Under ordinary circumstances, the public includes persons of all classes, races, ages, and both sexes.

In some cases, even though the trial is open to the public, certain items of evidence are not open for public view. For example, pictures of children involved in a sexual pornography case, if entered into evidence, would not be open for public view.

There are times when it may not be necessary to permit every person to attend trial proceedings in order for a trial to be a public trial. It has been held that to satisfy the constitutional guarantee to a public trial, it is not necessary to provide a stadium large enough to accommodate all who might want to attend a particular trial. Yet a courtroom should be large enough to permit a reasonable number of the public to observe the trial proceedings. It also has been held that a judge may limit the number of persons attending a trial to the seating capacity of the courtroom facilities without violating the right of a public trial. A judge may eject any spectator or member of the public who becomes unruly and disrupts the trial proceedings. The judge may even clear the courtroom of all spectators if they become disruptive. However, that action does not permit locking the courtroom doors and prohibiting other members of the public who conduct themselves properly from attending the trial.

Public Right to Attend

The courts were far from unanimous in answering the question of public exclusion from the courtroom. The issue is whether or not the public may be excluded in any situation without violating the guarantee to a public trial. The question usually surfaced when a trial involved salacious testimony. Two cases that addressed the exclusion of the public from trial were *Richmond Newspapers Inc.* v. *Virginia*[10] and *Globe Newspapers Co.* v. *Superior Court for the County of Norfolk.*[11]

CLOSING THE ENTIRE TRIAL The Court in the *Richmond Newspapers, Inc.* case recognized that the **right of the press and the public to access to criminal trials** was based on the First Amendment of the U.S. Constitution and not on the Sixth Amendment right of a defendant to a public trial. The defendant was charged with murder and had been brought to trial on three prior occasions, each time ending in a mistrial. At the time of the fourth trial, the defense attorney requested that the trial be closed to the public because of prior interference by spectators. The prosecution voiced no objection to a closed trial, and the judge granted the defense request to close the courtroom to the press and the public. This right was granted to judges by the Virginia statutes. Richmond Newspapers, Inc., filed an objection to being barred from the courtroom, and a hearing was held on the objection. The Virginia Appellate Court upheld the judge's ruling to close the courtroom. The case was appealed to the U.S. Supreme Court on the grounds that the First Amendment right to

Law in Practice

Key Decisions on Jury Trials

Griffin v. *California* (1965)	Prosecutor cannot comment on defendant's failure to testify during trial. It violates the defendant's privilege against self-incrimination.
Sheppard v. *Maxwell* (1966)	Defendant's right to a fair trial was denied because of prejudicial press coverage.
Duncan v. *Louisiana* (1968)	The Due Process Clause of the Fourteenth Amendment incorporates the Sixth Amendment's right to a jury trial in state criminal courts.
Baldwin v. *New York* (1970)	There is no right to a jury trial in state courts for petty offenses.
Williams v. *Florida* (1970)	State juries are not constitutionally required to consist of twelve members.
Johnson v. *Louisiana* (1972)	Federal criminal jury verdicts must be unanimous.
Apodaca v. *Oregon* (1972)	There is no federal requirement that state jury verdicts must be unanimous.
Taylor v. *Louisiana* (1975)	Women cannot be excluded from juries.
Ballew v. *Georgia* (1978)	State juries must have at least six members.
Burch v. *Louisiana* (1979)	Six-member jury verdicts must be unanimous.
Chandler v. *Florida* (1981)	The right to a fair trial is not violated by electronic media and still photographic coverage of the trial.
Batson v. *Kentucky* (1986)	Peremptory challenges may not be used by the prosecutor solely to exclude a racial group from the jury.
Georgia v. *McCullum* (1992)	The defense may not use peremptory challenges to exclude jurors based on race.
Daulbert v. *Merrell Dow* (1993)	Scientific evidence must be both relevant and reliable.
J.E.B. v. *Alabama* (1994)	Peremptory challenges may not be used to exclude jurors based on their gender.
United States v. *Scheffer* (1998)	Lie detector test results are not admissible because of doubts about their accuracy.
Apprendi v. *New Jersey* (2000)	Any fact that increases the penalty for a crime beyond the prescribed statutory maximum must be submitted to a jury.
Cunningham v. *California* (2007)	Defendant's crime of conviction was punishable by a lower term sentence of six years, a middle term sentence of twelve years, or an upper term sentence of sixteen years. Under California Penal Code § 1170(b), the trial court was required to impose the middle term unless there were mitigating or aggravating circumstances. Defendant had a right to a jury finding as to whether aggravating circumstances were present.

freedom of the press had been violated by barring the press from the trial. Since the defendant had requested that the trial be closed, the U.S. Supreme Court could not consider the case on the Sixth Amendment right to a public trial. Consideration of the case was then based on First Amendment rights. The Court pointed out that the First Amendment does not mention the right of public access to a criminal trial explicitly, but held that the First Amendment is broad enough in scope to encompass certain rights not specifically mentioned, including the right of access to criminal trials. The Court stated the following:

> Underlying the First Amendment right of access to criminal trials [by the public] is the common understanding that a major purpose of that Amendment was to protect the free discussion of governmental affairs. By offering such protection, the First Amendment serves to ensure that the individual citizen can effectively participate in and contribute to our republican system of self-government. . . . Thus to the

extent that the First Amendment embraces a right of access to criminal trials, it is to ensure that this constitutionally protected discussion of governmental affairs is an informed one.

CLOSING A PORTION OF A TRIAL *The Richmond Newspapers, Inc.* decision pertained to the closing of the entire trial to the press and public, which the Court held was in violation of the First Amendment. That decision still left the question of whether the press and public can be excluded from a portion of the trial when it may be in the interest of fairness to make such an exclusion. The U.S. Supreme Court discussed this issue in the *Globe Newspapers Co.* case. In *Globe,* the Court stated the following:

> Although the right of access to criminal trials is of constitutional stature, it is not absolute. But circumstances under which the press and public can be barred from a criminal trial are limited; the State's justification in denying access must be a weighty one. Where, as in the present case, the State attempts to deny the right of access in order to inhibit the disclosure of sensitive information, it must be shown that the denial is necessitated by a compelling governmental interest, and is narrowly tailored to serve that interest.

In the *Globe Newspapers Co.* case, the defendant was charged with the rape of three teenage girls. The law of the state of Massachusetts required that under all circumstances, the press and public must be excluded during the testimony of a minor victim in a sex offense trial. In *Globe,* the Supreme Court focused on the reasons behind the mandatory exclusion. By passing this law, the state of Massachusetts tried to protect minor victims of sex crimes from further trauma and embarrassment and to encourage such victims to come forward and testify in a truthful and credible manner. The Court stated that it agreed with the state of Massachusetts's interest in safeguarding the physical and psychological well-being of a minor, but that this interest did not justify a mandatory exclusion rule for all cases. The Court felt that the trial judge could determine case by case whether a closure is necessary to protect the welfare of a minor victim. Among the factors to be weighed by the judge are the minor victim's age, psychological maturity and understanding, the nature of the crime, the desires of the victim, and the interests of the victim's parents and other relatives.

The Court further stated in the *Globe Newspapers Co.* case that the identities of the victims were already a matter of public record and that there was no showing that they would not testify in the presence of the public and press. Additionally, there was no showing that a closure of a trial during the testimony of a minor victim would result in others' coming forth and reporting such crimes. For these reasons, the Court held that the mandatory exclusion of the press and public in all such matters violated the First Amendment to the U.S. Constitution. The *Globe* decision would appear to allow a trial judge to exclude the press and public during the giving of testimony by a witness when it would be in the best interest of fairness to make that exclusion. The burden of showing that such an exclusion was in the best interest of all would be on the trial judge.

In a state court case, the trial judge's exclusion of the press and public during the testimony of the prosecution's principal witness, a sixteen-year-old pregnant girl, was upheld by the state appellate court. The exclusion order was based partly on concern for the welfare of the young expectant mother and her unborn child and partly on her own subjective fear of reprisal if she testified in public. In another state case, the exclusion of the press and public by the trial judge was upheld by the state appellate court during the testimony of an undercover police officer whose safety might have been endangered if his identity had been publicly exposed.

PUBLIC EXCLUSION FROM PRETRIAL HEARINGS The *Richmond Newspaper, Inc.* and *Globe Newspapers Co.* cases are not to be confused with the case of *Gannett Co.* v.

DePasquale.[12] In *Gannett,* the U.S. Supreme Court held that the press and public may be excluded from pretrial hearings, such as a pretrial hearing on the suppression of evidence or a preliminary hearing. *Gannett* upheld the exclusion of the press and public from pretrial hearings on the grounds that adverse prepublicity given to such hearings could pose a risk to the defendant and prevent a fair trial. The Court pointed out that there is a difference between the trial itself and pretrial hearings. The Court in the *Gannett* case stated the following:

> Publicity concerning pretrial suppression hearings such as the one involved in the present case poses special risks of unfairness. The whole purpose of such hearings is to screen out unreliable or illegally obtained evidence and ensure that this evidence does not become known to the jury. Publicity concerning the proceedings at a pretrial hearing, however, could influence the public opinion against a defendant and inform potential jurors of inculpatory information wholly inadmissible at the actual trial. This Court has long recognized that adverse publicity can endanger the ability of a defendant to receive a fair trial.

The *Gannett* decision does not demand that all pretrial hearings be closed to the press and public, but should be done only on a request made to the trial judge or on the judge's own discretion. As a general rule, a court will not allow a closed hearing without a strong showing of prejudice to the requesting party.

Fair Trial versus Freedom of the Press

From the foregoing discussion, it may be concluded that the public is entitled to know that justice is taking place during a criminal trial. Therefore, the public, with some reservations, is permitted to attend trial proceedings. Since not all members of the public who may have an interest in a particular trial may be able to attend, the news media have assumed the responsibility of informing the public about what takes place during certain trials. The problem that arises is just how far the news media may go in obtaining information and reporting it to the public. The courts and the news media are often in conflict over the answer to this question. The news media rely upon the First Amendment to the U.S. Constitution for support of the uninhibited right to exercise their power in getting the news. This amendment provides, among other things, that "Congress shall make no law . . . abridging the freedom of speech, or of the press. . . ."

Law in Practice

Was Defendant Denied a Fair Trial? *Carey* v. *Musladin*, 549 U.S. 70 (2006)

Mathew Musladin shot and killed Tom Studer outside the home of Musladin's estranged wife, Pamela. At trial, Musladin admitted that he killed Studer but argued that he did so in self-defense. A California jury rejected Musladin's self-defense argument and convicted him of first-degree murder and three related offenses. At times during the accused's murder trial in a California trial court, some of the alleged murder victim's family members, sitting in the front row of the spectators' gallery of the courtroom, wore buttons displaying the alleged victim's image. After the accused was convicted, he claimed that the wearing of the buttons had deprived him of his fair-trial rights under the Federal Constitution's Sixth and Fourteenth Amendments.

JUSTICE THOMAS Delivered the Opinion of the Court

In Estelle v. Williams and Flynn, this Court addressed the effect of courtroom practices on defendants' fair-trial rights. In Williams, the Court considered "whether an accused who is compelled to wear identifiable prison clothing at his trial by a jury is denied due process or equal protection of the laws." The Court stated that "the State cannot, consistently with the Fourteenth Amendment, compel an accused to stand trial before a jury while dressed in identifiable prison clothes," but held that the defendant in that case had waived any objection to being tried in prison clothes by failing to object at trial.

(continued)

In Flynn, the Court addressed whether seating "four uniformed state troopers" in the row of spectators' seats immediately behind the defendant at trial denied the defendant his right to a fair trial. The Court held that the presence of the troopers was not so inherently prejudicial that it denied the defendant a fair trial. In reaching that holding, the Court stated that "the question must be whether an unacceptable risk is presented of impermissible factors coming into play."

Both Williams and Flynn dealt with government-sponsored practices: In Williams, the State compelled the defendant to stand trial in prison clothes, and in Flynn, the State seated the troopers immediately behind the defendant. Moreover, in both cases, this Court noted that some practices are so inherently prejudicial that they must be justified by an "essential state" policy or interest.

In contrast to state-sponsored courtroom practices, the effect on a defendant's fair-trial rights of the spectator conduct to which Musladin objects is an open question in our jurisprudence. This Court has never addressed a claim that such private-actor courtroom conduct was so inherently prejudicial that it deprived a defendant of a fair trial. And although the Court articulated the test for inherent prejudice that applies to state conduct in Williams and Flynn, we have never applied that test to spectators' conduct. Indeed, part of the legal test of Williams and Flynn—asking whether the practices furthered an essential state interest—suggests that those cases apply only to state-sponsored practices.

Reflecting the lack of guidance from this Court, lower courts have diverged widely in their treatment of defendants' spectator-conduct claims. Some courts have applied Williams and Flynn to spectators' conduct. Other courts have declined to extend Williams and Flynn to spectators' conduct. And still other courts have ruled on spectator-conduct claims without relying on, discussing, or distinguishing Williams or Flynn.

Given the lack of holdings from this Court regarding the potentially prejudicial effect of spectators' courtroom conduct of the kind involved here, it cannot be said that the state court "unreasonably" applied clearly established Federal law. No holding of this Court required the California Court of Appeal to apply the test of Williams and Flynn to the spectators' conduct here. Therefore, the state court's decision was not contrary to or an unreasonable application of clearly established federal law.

When the courts attempt to curtail the media in obtaining news, the media allege violation of their rights under the First Amendment. The courts, on the other hand, hold that an accused is entitled to a fair trial by an impartial jury, and when that right is interfered with by the news media, they have exceeded their prerogative. Because of the right of the public to be informed of what takes place during criminal trials, the courts generally have permitted reporters to be present during criminal trials; and in many instances, special areas in courtrooms are set aside for reporters in order that they may have a vantage point to assist them in obtaining the news. With the advent of the camera, radio, and television, conflicts have arisen over whether these types of equipment should be permitted in the courtroom. The courts concede that when the gathering of news during trial proceedings becomes too disruptive or otherwise denies the defendant a fair trial by an impartial jury, some control must be exercised.

This viewpoint was emphasized by the U.S. Supreme Court in the *Estes* case. Estes was convicted in the state court in Texas on an extensive swindling charge. His case was taken to the U.S. Supreme Court on the grounds that, because of massive pretrial and trial publicity, he had been denied the right of due process of law as provided by the Fourteenth Amendment to the U.S. Constitution. The Supreme Court concluded that the defendant had been denied a fair trial because of the live radio and television coverage, so the conviction was reversed. The Court set forth some pertinent arguments against permitting live news coverage of criminal trials; these arguments are still being presented by those opposing live coverage.

At the time the *Estes* case was heard by the U.S. Supreme Court, the attorneys representing the state of Texas contended that the television portions of the trial did not constitute a denial of due process, since there was no showing of prejudice of *Estes* resulting from the television coverage. The state also argued that the public has a right to know what goes on in the courts, and that televising criminal trials would be enlightening to the public and promote greater respect for the courts. To this argument, the Court stated the following:

It is true that the public has a right to be informed as to what occurs in its courts, but reporters of all media, including television, are always present if they wish to be and are plainly free to report whatever occurs in open court through their respective media. . . .

As has been said, the chief function of our judicial machinery is to ascertain the truth. The use of television, however, cannot be said to contribute materially to this objective. Rather its use amounts to the injection of an irrelevant factor into court proceedings. In addition experience teaches that there are numerous situations in which it might cause actual unfairness, some so subtle as to defy detection by the accused or control by the judge. We enumerate some in summary:

1. The potential impact of television on the jurors is perhaps of the greatest significance. They are the nerve center of the fact-finding process. . . . From the moment the trial judge announces that a case will be televised it becomes [a] *cause celebre.* The whole community, including prospective jurors, becomes interested in all the morbid details surrounding it. The approaching trial immediately assumes an important status in the public press and the accused is highly publicized, along with the offense with which he is charged. Every juror carries with him into the jury box these solemn facts and thus increase[s] the chance of prejudice that is present in every criminal case. And we must remember that realistically it is only the notorious trial which will be broadcast, because of the necessity for paid sponsorship. The conscious or unconscious effect on the juror's judgment cannot be evaluated, but experience indicates that it is not only possible but highly probable that it will have a direct bearing on his vote as to guilt or innocence. Where pretrial publicity of all kinds has created intense public feeling which is aggravated by the telecasting or picturing of the trial, the televised jurors can not help but feel the pressures of knowing that friends and neighbors have their eyes upon them. If the community is hostile to an accused, a televised juror, realizing that he must return to neighbors who saw the trial themselves, may well be led "not to hold the balance nice, clear, and true between the State and the accused. . . ."

2. The quality of the testimony in criminal trials will often be impaired. The impact upon a witness of the knowledge that he is being viewed by a vast audience is simply incalculable. Some may be demoralized and frightened, some cocky and given to overstatement; memories may falter, as with anyone speaking publicly, and accuracy of statement may be severely undermined. Embarrassment may impede the search for the truth, as may a natural tendency toward overdramatization. Furthermore, inquisitive strangers and "cranks" might approach witnesses on the street with jibes, advice or demands for explanation of testimony. There is little wonder that the defendant cannot "prove" the existence of such factors. Yet we all know from experience that they exist.

3. A major aspect of the problem is the additional responsibilities the presence of television places on the trial judge. His job is to make certain that the accused receives a fair trial. This most difficult task requires his undivided attention. Still, when television comes into the courtroom he must also supervise it. . . . In addition, laying physical interruptions aside, there is the ever-present distraction that the mere awareness of television's presence prompts. Judges are human beings also and are subject to the same psychological reactions as laymen. Telecasting is particularly bad where the judge is elected, as is the case in all save a half dozen of our States. The distractions inherent in broadcasting divert his attention from the task at hand—the fair trial of the accused.

But this is not all. There is the initial decision that must be made as to whether the use of television will be permitted. This is perhaps an even more crucial consideration. Our judges are high-minded men and women. But it is difficult to remain oblivious to the pressures that the news media can bring to bear on them both directly and through the shaping of public opinion. Moreover, where one judge in a district or even in a State permits telecasting, the requirement that the others do the same is almost mandatory. Especially is this true where the judge is selected at the ballot box.

Finally, we cannot ignore the impact of courtroom television on the defendant. Its presence is a form of mental—if not physical—harassment. . . . A defendant on trial for a specific crime is entitled to his day in court, not in a stadium, or a city or nationwide arena. The heightened public clamor resulting from radio and television coverage will inevitably result in prejudice.

After the *Estes* decision, courts for a time generally prohibited live coverage of criminal trials. But the news media eventually renewed their pressure to permit live coverage of trials. Many judges and attorneys have resisted this pressure principally on the grounds presented in the *Estes* decision. Regardless of these strong arguments against live coverage, more and more courts are permitting live coverage of trials. In 1996, the nation watched the televised trial of O.J. Simpson. As in the results of the coverage of that trial, many in the justice system are seriously concerned about the effects of this type of coverage, not only from the standpoint of the defendant but also concerning the safety of witnesses. Great strides have been made to protect the victims in rape cases from embarrassment during trials in order to encourage victims to come forth and report such offenses. It is believed that with live coverage of trials, many victims of all types of crime will refuse to report offenses rather than face embarrassment and possible harm from testifying before television cameras.

Gag Orders

Courts throughout the nation are aware that the news media are entitled to report events occurring during a trial as well as crimes taking place, and no effort is made to suppress this type of reporting. However, the courts have periodically issued orders limiting the information that may be given to the press. Referred to as "**gag orders**," they are issued to prevent extensive pretrial or trial publicity that could deny a defendant a fair trial because of the resulting difficulty in selecting and maintaining an impartial jury. But the news media have strongly protested the issuance of gag orders on the grounds that such orders violate the First Amendment. Thus, balancing the right of a defendant to a fair trial with the right of freedom of the press has continually plagued the courts. In *Sheppard* v. *Maxwell*,[13] the U.S. Supreme Court criticized the trial judge for the failure to restrain pretrial publicity. The facts of that case reveal that Dr. Sheppard was accused of killing his wife. Prior to the trial, there were numerous newspaper stories concerning the questioning of the accused as well as articles about his personal life and love affairs. The jury list was published, and many of the prospective jurors received telephone calls concerning the case. Inaccurate news releases were given to the press by the police. The judge, who was coming up for election, permitted extensive live news coverage of the trial. Sheppard was convicted and eventually appealed the case to the U.S. Supreme Court on the grounds that due process of law had been denied during the trial. The Court reversed the conviction because it felt that pretrial publicity and extensive live coverage of the trial had kept the defendant from receiving a fair trial. The Court stated

[that the trial judge] should have made some effort to control the release of leads, information, and gossip to the press by police officers, witnesses, and the counsel for both sides. . . . The courts must take steps by law and regulation that will protect their processes from prejudicial outside interference. Neither prosecutors, counsel for defense, the accused, witnesses, court staff nor enforcement officers coming under the jurisdiction of the court should be permitted to frustrate its function.

Although the Court in the *Sheppard* case stated that trial judges "have the duty of so insulating the trial from publicity as to insure its fairness," the Court did not set down any fixed rules to guide the trial judges and others on what could and could not be printed. But acting upon the suggestion of the *Sheppard* case, trial judges have occasionally issued gag orders. In *Nebraska Press Association* v. *Stewart,*[14] the U.S. Supreme Court discouraged, but did not rule out, the use of gag orders. The Court stated, "This Court has frequently denied that the First Amendment rights are absolute and has consistently rejected the proposition that a prior restraint can never be employed." The Court indicated that such prior restraint should be used only when absolutely necessary to assure a fair trial. As stated by one of the justices, before a prior restraint is to be used there must be "a showing that (i) there is a clear threat to the fairness of trial, (ii) such a threat is posed by the actual publicity to be restrained, and (iii) no less restrictive alternatives are available."

The U.S. Supreme Court in this case felt that the trial judge had overstepped his rights in issuing the gag order. He prohibited the publication of information brought out in an open preliminary hearing that the public was free to attend. The Court did not rule out the possible use of a gag order to prevent pretrial publicity concerning information not otherwise known that would prevent a fair trial from being obtained when other, less restrictive measures were unavailable. But the Court did not indicate what less restrictive measures might be substituted for the gag order.

Law in Practice

The Prosecutor and the Press

The prosecutorial role in a case, as stated by the Supreme Court, is to be an advocate of a sovereign "whose obligation to govern impartially is as compelling as its obligation to govern at all; and whose interest, therefore, in a criminal prosecution is not that it shall win a case, but that justice shall be done."[15] The prosecutor has unique burdens placed upon him or her due to the nature of the position. One of the chief differences between a prosecutor and any other attorney is that a prosecutor represents the entire community, including the victim, police, governmental agencies or officials, and even the prosecutor's adversary, the defendant. Because of this, the prosecutor has certain ethical responsibilities when releasing information to the press. The prosecutor should consider whether the release of information to the press will change or affect.[16]

- Endangerment of the lives, physical safety or the reputation of others;
- protection of confidential informants;
- potential prejudice to pending investigations;
- potential prejudice to pending cases;
- preservation of the trust of law enforcement agencies and law enforcement strategies; and
- any other factors which will affect the fair administration of justice.

One less restrictive measure suggested for use instead of issuing a gag order was the granting of a change in venue. But many crimes committed receive such extensive publicity that a change in venue would accomplish little. Under these circumstances, judges may still issue gag orders to prevent undue pretrial publicity and will undoubtedly receive the sanction of the U.S. Supreme Court.

Even before the *Sheppard* decision, law enforcement officers and prosecuting attorneys restricted the release of certain information to the news media. This restrictive action, taken even without a gag order, was the result of criticism directed at law enforcement officers in *Rideau* v. *Louisiana.*[17] The U.S. Supreme Court in that case was critical of the law enforcement agencies involved in permitting the televising of a confession while it was being given by the defendant. The facts of the case reveal the following: Some two months before the petitioner's (Rideau's) trial began and some two weeks before he was arraigned on charges of robbery, kidnapping, and murder, a local TV station broadcast three different times in the space of two days a twenty-minute film of the petitioner, flanked by the sheriff and two state troopers, admitting in detail the commission of the various offenses in response to leading questions by the sheriff.

Rideau was convicted of the charges against him, and his case was taken to the U.S. Supreme Court on the grounds that he had been denied due process of law when a change of venue request was denied by the trial judge. The Supreme Court reversed the conviction, stating the following:

> . . . we hold that it was a denial of due process of law to refuse the request for a change of venue, after the people of the Parish had been exposed repeatedly and in depth to the spectacle of Rideau personally confessing in detail to the crimes with which he was later to be charged. For anyone who has ever watched television the conclusion cannot be avoided that this spectacle, to the tens of thousands of people who saw and heard it, in a very real sense was Rideau's trial—at which he pleaded guilty to murder. Any subsequent court proceedings in a community so pervasively exposed to such a spectacle could be but a hollow formality.

After the *Rideau* decision, many law enforcement officers and prosecuting attorneys decided that it was generally best not to reveal to the press whether an accused person has confessed or to comment on the results of any tests that may have been given. Some officers will not reveal any criminal record of an accused. However, not all are in agreement with this viewpoint, since some contend that if an accused has been previously convicted, the court record of the conviction is a public record, and the news media should be able to obtain this information. But self-imposed restrictions by officers and prosecutors may help ensure a fair trial. Judges often impose further restrictions during a trial to prevent jurors from being influenced by comments made in the news media.

CASE LAW

Recent Cases

Presley v. *Georgia*, 130 S. Ct. 721 (U.S. 2010)

The defendant was convicted of a cocaine trafficking offense but asserted that his right to a public trial under the Sixth Amendment was violated when the trial court excluded the public from the voir dire of prospective jurors. The defendant petitioned for a writ of certiorari to appeal the judgment of the Supreme Court of Georgia, which had affirmed his conviction.

The defendant contended that he was denied his right to a public trial because the trial court directed a relative of the defendant, the sole observer, to leave the courtroom so that prospective jurors could be seated without their inadvertent comments being overheard. The Court held that the defendant's right to a public trial extended to voir dire and the trial court improperly failed to consider reasonable alternatives to closing the voir dire to the public in addressing the trial court's concerns. The public also has a right to be present during voir dire and the defendant, for whose benefit the right to a public trial was granted, could not be barred from asserting the same right. Further, even if the trial court's concerns warranted the closure of voir dire to the public, the trial court was required to consider alternatives to closure regardless of the defendant's failure to offer any alternative.

Excerpts from the Court's decision

- The Sixth Amendment directs, in part, that in all criminal prosecutions the accused shall enjoy the right to a speedy and **public trial**. This right extends to the States. The Sixth Amendment right, as the language makes explicit, is the right of the accused.

- The **public trial** right extends beyond an accused and can be invoked under the First Amendment.
- While an accused has a right to insist that the voir dire of jurors be public, there are exceptions to this general rule. The right to an open trial may give way in certain cases to other rights or interests, such as the accused's right to a fair trial or the government's interest in inhibiting disclosure of sensitive information. Such circumstances are rare, however, and the balance of interests must be struck with special care. The party seeking to close a hearing must advance an overriding interest that is likely to be prejudiced, the closure must be no broader than necessary to protect that interest, the trial court must consider reasonable alternatives to closing the proceeding, and it must make findings adequate to support the closure.
- Trial courts are obligated to take every reasonable measure to accommodate public attendance at criminal trials.

Caperton v. *A. T. Massey Coal Co.*, 129 S. Ct. 2252 (U.S. 2009)

[This is a civil case, but the concepts should apply to criminal cases. The facts in this case were somewhat similar to the scenario outlined in John Grisham's best-seller The *Pelican Brief.* Except in the real case there were no murders and no illegal actions. One party contributed heavily to a state judicial campaign to elect a judge that would be favorable to their cause. While this action was not illegal, the actions reflected on the integrity of the process.]

Certiorari was granted to review a Supreme Court of Appeals of West Virginia decision that reversed a trial court judgment in favor of a coal company and subsidiaries, against a corporation, on the question of whether the Fourteenth Amendment was violated when one of the majority justices refused to recuse himself due to receiving large campaign contributions from, and through the efforts of, the corporation's principal.

Facts: After a West Virginia jury found respondents, a coal company and its affiliates (hereinafter Massey), liable for fraudulent misrepresentation, concealment, and tortious interference with existing contractual relations and awarded petitioners (hereinafter Caperton) $50 million in damages, West Virginia held its 2004 judicial elections. Knowing the State Supreme

Court of Appeals would consider the appeal, Don Blankenship, Massey's chairman and principal officer, supported Brent Benjamin rather than the incumbent justice seeking reelection. His $3 million in contributions exceeded the total amount spent by all other Benjamin supporters and by Benjamin's own committee. Benjamin won by fewer than 50,000 votes. Before Massey filed its appeal, Caperton moved to disqualify now-Justice Benjamin under the Due Process Clause and the State's Code of Judicial Conduct, based on the conflict caused by Blankenship's campaign involvement. Justice Benjamin denied the motion, indicating that he found nothing showing bias for or against any litigant. The court then reversed the $50 million verdict. During the rehearing process, Justice Benjamin refused twice more to recuse himself, and the court once again reversed the jury verdict. Four months later, Justice Benjamin filed a concurring opinion, defending the court's opinion and his recusal decision.

The Court reversed the decision and remanded the case.

Excerpts from the Court's decision

- The Due Process Clause incorporated the common-law rule requiring recusal [withdrawal] when a judge has "a direct, personal, substantial, pecuniary interest" in a case.
- Objective standards may require recusal whether or not actual bias on the part of a judge exists or can be proved. Due process may sometimes bar trial by judges who have no actual bias and who would do their very best to weigh the scales of justice equally between contending parties. The failure to consider objective standards requiring recusal is not consistent with the imperatives of due process.
- States may choose to adopt recusal standards more rigorous than due process requires. The Due Process Clause demarks only the outer boundaries of judicial disqualifications. Congress and the States, of course, remain free to impose more rigorous standards for judicial disqualification. Because the codes of judicial conduct provide more protection than due process requires, most disputes over disqualification will be resolved without resort to the United States Constitution. Application of the constitutional standard will thus be confined to rare instances.

Summary

- A bench or court trial is a trial by judge alone.
- The Sixth Amendment right to a jury trial applies to all federal criminal proceedings.
- States may deny an accused a jury trial in cases involving petty offenses.
- Petty offenses are defined by the Supreme Court as offenses for which the maximum period of confinement is six months and a fine of not more than $500.
- The defendant may not demand a bench or court trial.
- In noncapital cases, a defendant may be tried by a jury of fewer than twelve persons, depending on state laws.
- If there are fewer than twelve jurors, in most states the verdict must be unanimous.
- A public trial is a trial in which the public has a right to attend.
- The public has a limited right to attend criminal trials.
- The First Amendment gives the press a limited right to attend a criminal trial.
- A trial judge may issue a gag order that directs the parties to the trial not to talk to the press or otherwise release information that would jeopardize a fair trial.

Review Questions

1. What amendment of the U.S. Constitution embodies the right to trial by jury?
2. List three advantages to an accused of a trial by jury over a court trial.
3. Why would an accused waive a trial by jury?
4. What reasons has the U.S. Supreme Court set forth in prohibiting the accused from demanding and receiving a court trial?
5. Some jurisdictions hold that an accused may be denied a jury trial on petty offenses. What criteria has the U.S. Supreme Court set forth in determining what qualifies as a petty offense?
6. What U.S. Supreme Court decision upheld that a trial by a jury comprising fewer than twelve persons was not a denial of the Due Process Clause of the Fourteenth Amendment?
7. What is considered a public trial?
8. Why is the accused guaranteed a public trial?
9. Must a demand by an accused for a private trial be granted?
10. Why did the Richmond case base the public right to access to criminal trials on the First Amendment of the U.S. Constitution instead of the Sixth Amendment?
11. In what way may a fair trial and the freedom of the press be in conflict?
12. What is meant by a gag order, and why may one be placed in effect?

Local Procedure

1. May a defendant waive a jury trial in your state? If so, are there any restrictions on the type of offense for which the jury trial may be waived?
2. If a jury trial may be waived, who must give consent to the waiver?
3. Can a jury comprise fewer than twelve persons in your state?
4. May a petty offense charge be tried without a jury in your state?

Endnotes

1. 281 U.S. 276 (1930).
2. 391 U.S. 145 (1968).
3. 380 U.S. 24 (1965).
4. 300 U.S. 617 (1937).
5. See *Duncan* v. *Louisiana*, 391 U.S. 145 (1968); *Cheff* v. *Schnackenberg*, 384 U.S. 373 (1966); and *Frank* v. *United States*, 395 U.S. 147 (1969).
6. 399 U.S. 78 (1970).

7. 55 L.Ed. 2d. 234 (1978).
8. "Background Materials on Jury Size," Committee on Rules of Practice and Procedure of the Judicial Conference of the United States (December 13, 1994).
9. 381 U.S. 532 (1965).
10. 448 U.S. 555 (1980).
11. 457 U.S. 596 (1982).
12. 443 U.S. 368 (1979).
13. 443 U.S. 368 (1979).
14. 427 U.S. 539 (1976).
15. *Berger* v. *United States,* 295 U.S. 78, 88 (1935).
16. Rachel Luna, "The Ethics of Kiss-and-Tell Prosecution: Prosecutors and Post-Trial Publications Fall," 26 Am. J. Crim. L
17. 373 U.S. 723 (1963).

CHAPTER 8

Assistance of Counsel

Once I decide to take a case, I have only one agenda: I want to win. I will try, by every fair and legal means, to get my client off—without regards to the consequences.

—ALAN DERSHOWITZ, *THE BEST DEFENSE*, 1983

The Sixth Amendment right to counsel of choice commands not that a trial be fair but that a particular guarantee of fairness be provided—to wit, that the accused be defended by the counsel he believes to be best. The U.S. Constitution guarantees a fair trial through the Due Process Clauses, but it defines the basic elements of a fair trial largely through the several provisions of the Sixth Amendment, including the Counsel Clause. In sum, where the right at stake is the right to counsel of choice, not the right to a fair trial, and that right is violated because a deprivation of counsel was erroneous, no additional showing of prejudice is required to make the violation complete.

—JUSTICE ANTONIN SCALIA IN *UNITED STATES* V. *GONZALEZ-LOPEZ*, 548 U.S. 140 (2006)

Chapter Outline

Presence of the Defendant at a Trial

Right to Counsel

Case Law

Summary

Key Terms

Appointed counsel

Bench warrant

Conviction in absentia

Effective counsel

Farce or sham test

Indigent defendant

Public defender

Retained counsel

Right of confrontation

Self-representation

Standby counsel

Learning Objectives

After completing this chapter, you should be able to:

- Outline the development of the right to counsel.

- Explain the test for effective assistance of counsel.

- Summarize the right to self-representation and the issues involved with it.

- Explain the right to effective counsel and the causes and problems of ineffective counsel.

- Summarize the issues involved with indigent counsel.

- Define terms associated with the right to counsel.

- Discuss when the state has an obligation to provide defendant with a counsel.

- List the duties of a defense counsel.

- Distinguish between appointed counsel and retained counsel.

- Discuss the functions of a standby counsel.

PRESENCE OF THE DEFENDANT AT A TRIAL

In some countries, an accused person may be tried and convicted of a crime without being present and without knowing that a trial has taken place. This procedure is referred to as **conviction in absentia**. To prevent such action from taking place in the United States, the Sixth Amendment of the U.S. Constitution, as well as the laws of all the states, includes a provision entitling an accused to be confronted with the witnesses for the prosecution. This provision has a dual purpose. It guarantees that witnesses against a defendant must appear in person in court to present their facts, and it provides a defendant with the right to be present during every phase of trial proceedings.

For many years, the interpretation of the right of an accused to be present during a trial was so rigid that, if a defendant was not present, the trial had to be halted until he or she was in attendance. Knowing the court's rigid interpretation of this right, defendants occasionally took advantage of it by being so disruptive that the trial could not continue with their presence or by failing to appear in court while out on bail, thus preventing the trial from taking place. Many states included provisions in their statutes stating that in felony cases, the defendant had to be present during all phases of the trial. But as time passed, some courts relaxed the rule requiring the defendant's presence when he or she voluntarily was absent.

When representing a defendant who has been in confinement for an extended period of time, a defense counsel may submit a motion that the defendant not be tried in jail or prison clothing or restraints (handcuffs, chains, etc.). The U.S. Supreme Court in *Estelle* v. *Williams,* 425 U.S. 501 (1976), stated that with few exceptions, an accused should not be compelled to go to trial in prison or jail clothing and/or with restraints because of the possible impairment of his or her presumption of innocence, which is basic to the adversary system.

Disruption of the Trial

A separate issue is raised when the defendant is present and demands to remain present but becomes so disruptive that the trial cannot take place. This question was answered in the case of *Illinois* v. *Allen,*[1] in which the U.S. Supreme Court held that a defendant had waived his right to be present at his trial by his own disruptive action.

Law in Practice

Motion Not to Be Tried in Jail Clothes or Restraints

To the Honorable judge of Said Court:

NOW COMES the Defendant in the above-entitled and numbered cause by and through his attorney of record and files this Motion not to be tried before the Jury in jail clothes and restraints and in support thereof would show the following:

I.

On Defendant's being placed in confinement, his regular civilian type clothing was taken from him and he has been compelled to be dressed in identifiable prison clothing. When Defendant is brought from the Prison to Court, he will be handcuffed and shackled or be required to wear other such restraints.

II.

Compelling the Defendant to be tried before a jury in such distinctive, identifiable attire and restraints will affect the jury's judgment and violates the Defendant's constitutional right of presumption of innocence.

WHEREFORE, PREMISES CONSIDERED, Defendant prays that the Court order the Sheriff or Warden not to bring the Defendant to the courtroom for the purpose of trial or into the presence of any member of the jury panel attired in a prison uniform or in restraints of any kind.

Respectfully submitted,
Public Defenders Office

_____
Attorney for Defendant

The facts of the *Allen* case state that Allen was convicted of armed robbery by an Illinois jury and was sentenced to serve ten to thirty years in the Illinois State Penitentiary. During the trial, Allen insisted upon acting as his own attorney, and when the judge appointed an attorney for him, Allen began to argue with the judge in an abusive and disrespectful manner. The judge ordered Allen to remain silent and to let his attorney speak for him. Despite this admonition, the defendant continued to talk and argue with the judge, proclaiming that the appointed attorney was not going to act for him. Allen also informed the judge that "when I go out for lunchtime, you're going to be a corpse here." At the same time, Allen tore up his attorney's file and threw the pieces on the floor. The judge informed Allen that he would be removed from the courtroom if another disruption occurred. This warning had no effect upon Allen, and the judge had him removed from the courtroom. The jury was selected in his absence. Later in the day, Allen was permitted to return to the courtroom but became disruptive again, forcing the judge to remove him a second time. Allen remained out of the courtroom during most of the prosecution's presentation of the case but, on promising that he would conduct himself properly, was permitted to return and remain in the courtroom during the presentation by his attorney.

The *Allen* conviction was upheld by the Illinois appellate courts but was reversed by the U.S. District Court of Appeals. This court held that Allen's removal from the courtroom was a denial of his guarantee of confrontation as provided by the Sixth Amendment to the U.S. Constitution. The court stated that Allen could have been bound and gagged to prevent him from being disruptive and that the judge erred in removing Allen from the courtroom.

The case was then taken to the U.S. Supreme Court to determine whether Allen was denied due process of law because his Sixth Amendment guarantee of confrontation had been violated. The Supreme Court upheld the conviction and stated that the Sixth Amendment guarantee of confrontation could be "lost by consent or at times even by misconduct." The Court further stated the following:

Although mindful that courts must indulge every reasonable presumption against the loss of constitutional rights . . . we explicitly hold today that a defendant can lose his right to be present at trial if, after he had been warned by the judge that he will be removed if he continues his disruptive behavior, he nevertheless insists on conducting himself in a manner so disorderly, disruptive, and disrespectful of the court that his trial cannot be carried on with him in the courtroom. Once lost, the right to be present can, of course, be reclaimed as soon as the defendant is willing to conduct himself consistently with the decorum and respect inherent in the concept of courts and judicial proceedings.

It is essential to the proper administration of criminal justice that dignity, order, and decorum be the hallmarks of all court proceedings in our country. The flagrant disregard in the courtroom of elementary standards of proper conduct should not and cannot be tolerated. We believe trial judges confronted with disruptive, contumacious, stubbornly defiant defendants must be given sufficient discretion to meet the circumstances of each case. No one formula for maintaining the appropriate courtroom atmosphere will be best in all situations. We think there are at least three constitutionally permissible ways for a trial judge to handle an obstreperous defendant like Allen: (1) bind and gag him, thereby keeping him present; (2) cite him for contempt; (3) take him out of the courtroom until he promises to conduct himself properly.

Trying a defendant for a crime while he sits bound and gagged before the judge and jury would to an extent comply with that part of the Sixth Amendment's purposes that accords the defendant an opportunity to confront the witnesses at the trial. But even to contemplate such a technique, much less see it, arouses a feeling that no person should be tried while shackled and gagged except as a last resort. Not only is it possible that the sight of shackles and gags might have a significant effect on the jury's feelings about the defendant, but the use of this technique is itself something of an affront to the very dignity and decorum of judicial proceedings that the judge is seeking to uphold. . . . However, in some situations which we need not attempt to foresee, binding and gagging might possibly be the fairest and most reasonable way to handle a defendant who acts as Allen did here.

In citing the unruly defendant for contempt of court, the Court in the *Allen* case stated:

It is true that citing or threatening to cite a contumacious defendant for criminal contempt might in itself be sufficient to make a defendant stop interrupting a trial. If so, the problem would be solved easily, and the defendant could remain in the courtroom. Of course, if the defendant is determined to prevent any trial, then a court in attempting to try the defendant for contempt is still confronted with the identical dilemma that the Illinois court faced in this case. Any criminal contempt has obvious limitations as a sanction when the defendant is charged with a crime so serious that a very severe sentence such as death or life imprisonment is likely to be imposed. In such a case the defendant might not be affected by a mere contempt sentence when he ultimately faces a far more serious sanction. Nevertheless, the contempt remedy should be borne in mind by a judge in the circumstances of this case.

Another aspect of the contempt remedy is the judge's power, when exercised consistently with state and federal law, to imprison an unruly defendant such as Allen for civil contempt and discontinue the trial until such time as the defendant promises to behave himself. This procedure is consistent with the defendant's right to be present at trial, and yet it avoids the serious shortcomings of the use of shackles and gags. It must be recognized, however, that a defendant might conceivably, as a matter of calculated strategy, elect to spend a prolonged period in confinement for contempt in the hope that adverse witnesses might be unavailable after a lapse of time. A court must guard against allowing a defendant to profit from his own wrong in this way.

The trial court in this case decided under the circumstances to remove the defendant from the courtroom and to continue his trial in his absence until and unless he promised to conduct himself in a manner befitting an American courtroom. As we said earlier, we find nothing unconstitutional about this procedure. Allen's behavior was clearly of such an extreme and aggravated nature as to justify either his removal from the courtroom or his total physical restraint. Prior to his removal he was repeatedly warned by the trial judge that he would be removed from the courtroom if he persisted in his unruly conduct, and, as Judge Hastings observed in his dissenting opinion, the record demonstrates that Allen would not have been at all dissuaded by the trial judge's use of his criminal contempt powers. Allen was constantly informed that he could return to the trial when he would agree to conduct himself in an orderly manner. Under these circumstances we hold that Allen lost his right guaranteed by the Sixth and Fourteenth Amendments to be present throughout his trial.

It is not pleasant to hold that the respondent Allen was properly banished from the court for a part of his own trial. But our courts, palladiums of liberty as they are, cannot be treated disrespectfully with impunity. Nor can the accused be permitted by his disruptive conduct indefinitely to avoid being tried on the charges brought against him. It would degrade our country and our judicial system to permit our courts to be bullied, insulted, and humiliated and their orderly progress thwarted and obstructed by defendants brought before them charged with crimes.

Law in Practice

Deck v. *Missouri*, 544 U.S. 622 (2005)

Defendant was convicted of capital murder and sentenced to death. At a sentencing proceeding, he was shackled with leg irons, handcuffs, and a belly chain. The trial court overruled counsel's objections to the shackles, and defendant was sentenced to death.

Was Defendant Denied the Right to a Fair Trial by Having to Wear the Shackles in Court?

JUSTICE BREYER delivered the opinion of the Court.

The Court held that courts could not routinely place defendants in shackles or other physical restraints visible to the jury during the penalty phase of a capital proceeding. However, the constitutional requirement was not absolute. It permitted a judge, in the exercise of his or her discretion, to take account of special circumstances, including security concerns that may call for shackling. In so doing, it accommodated the important need to protect the courtroom and its occupants. But any such determination had to be case specific; that is to say, it should reflect particular concerns, say special security needs or escape risks, related to the defendant on trial. [Conviction was reversed.]

Voluntary Absence from Trial

The *Allen* decision definitely established that a trial could take place in the absence of a defendant when he or she was so disruptive that his or her removal from the courtroom became necessary. This decision also provided that a defendant who voluntarily absented himself or herself waived all right to be present. Even before the *Allen* decision, the courts were beginning to accept that if a defendant was voluntarily absent from his or her trial, the trial could proceed in his or her absence. This viewpoint was expressed in the case of *Cureton* v. *United States*.[2] The Court concluded that "if a defendant at liberty remains away during his trial the court may proceed provided it is clearly established that his absence is voluntary. He must be aware of the processes taking place, of his right and of his obligation to be present, and he must have no sound reason for remaining away." This viewpoint is sometimes referred to as the *Cureton* test. In other words, the defendant must have "knowingly and voluntarily absented himself."

As a result of the *Allen* decision and the viewpoint expressed in the *Cureton* case, many states have passed provisions similar to that of the *Federal Rules of Criminal Procedure,* which provides that "in prosecutions for offenses, not punishable by death, the defendant's voluntary absence after the trial has been commenced in his presence shall not prevent continuing the trial to and including the return of the verdict." The federal rule, as well as the provisions of many states, holds that the trial may continue in the absence of the defendant if the trial was commenced in his or her presence. Under these circumstances, the trial cannot commence unless the defendant is present. After the trial date is set, a defendant out on bail could keep the trial from taking place merely by not showing up for the trial. Of course, the judge could issue a **bench warrant** for the defendant's arrest, but it could take time to locate the defendant, thus delaying the trial. To overcome this problem, several states have provisions stating that a trial may commence when the defendant, knowing that the case is set for trial, voluntarily fails to appear on that date.

In those states requiring a trial to begin in the defendant's presence, for it to continue if the accused is voluntarily absent, the court must establish that the trial actually began while the defendant was present. Remember that a jury trial begins once the jury is sworn, and a court trial begins when the first witness is sworn. In one case, the defendant was present during the selection of eleven jurors before court was adjourned for the day. The following day the defendant failed to appear for the trial. The judge concluded that the defendant had voluntarily absented himself. Over the objections of the defense attorney, the judge permitted a twelfth juror to be selected, and the trial continued to the verdict stage in the absence of the defendant. The defendant was convicted, and he appealed his conviction on the grounds that he had been denied due process. The conviction was reversed since the law of the particular state provided that a trial could continue only if it commenced in the presence of the defendant. Since the jury had not been selected and sworn in the presence of the defendant, the trial had not begun.

Even in those states that hold that a trial may continue only if it began in the presence of the defendant, this rule usually refers to felony charges. In a misdemeanor case, most states provide that if a defendant voluntarily fails to appear at the time the case is set for trial or is voluntarily absent during the course of the trial, the judge may proceed when the defendant has full knowledge that the trial was to be held. In most jurisdictions, whether the charge is a felony or misdemeanor, it is not necessary to advise the defendant that this action will take place in the event of voluntary absence.

The problem created by these rules is establishing that the defendant knowingly and voluntarily absented himself or herself from the trial. Establishing this could take time, and the judge would have to delay the progress of the trial until this could be determined. The delay might be only a few hours, but it could take several days. If the court cannot determine satisfactorily whether the defendant was absent knowingly and voluntarily, the judge must declare a mistrial or delay the present trial until the defendant can be located and arrested on a bench warrant. If it cannot be determined that the defendant was absent without cause and if a conviction results, a new trial must be granted unless a satisfactory reason for absence is given. Thus, the courts are cautious in continuing a trial in the absence of a defendant.

The Sixth Amendment provision that "an accused shall enjoy the right . . . to be confronted with the witnesses against him" has been interpreted to mean not only the right to be present during the trial against him or her but also the right of a face-to-face confrontation with the witnesses as held by the U.S. Supreme Court in the case of *Coy* v. *Iowa.*[3] The facts of the case indicate that the accused was charged with the sexual assault of two thirteen-year-old girls. In accordance with an Iowa state statute, a screen was placed between the accused and the girls during their testimony. The purpose of the statute was to protect young victims of sexual assault from the "fear and trauma of testifying in front of the accused" by placing a screen between the victim and the accused. The screen in this case was placed in such a way that the girls could be observed by the judge and the jury during their testimony. They could also be dimly seen by the accused, but the girls could not see the accused.

The accused was convicted of the assault, and he appealed his conviction to the U.S. Supreme Court on the grounds that his Sixth Amendment **right of confrontation** had been violated, since he had not been allowed the right to a face-to-face confrontation with the witnesses against him. The Court agreed with this contention, stating:

> There is something deep in human nature that regards face-to-face confrontation between accused and accuser as essential to a fair trial in a criminal prosecution. . . . It is more difficult to tell a lie about a person to his face than behind his back. . . . The screen issue [in this case] was specifically designed to enable the witnesses to avoid viewing the appellant [the accused] as they gave their testimony. . . . It is difficult to imagine a more obvious or damaging violation of the defendant's right to a face-to-face encounter.

Thus, the conviction was reversed.

RIGHT TO COUNSEL

Under the common law of England, a person on trial for a felony was not entitled to the assistance of counsel. If the charge was a misdemeanor, however, the defendant had the right of counsel. Various reasons have been given for this paradoxical situation. In felony cases, it was thought that the judge would be sympathetic to the defendant because if the defendant were convicted, he would be subjected to severe punishment and might have his property confiscated by the king. In misdemeanor cases, the judge would have less interest in protecting the accused. Another theory is that because the property of a felon could be confiscated, the king knew that the chances for the defendant's conviction would be greater if the assistance of counsel was not allowed. Thus, the king did not permit the assistance of counsel in a felony trial.

Law in Practice

Indigent Defense Statistics

States and localities use several methods for delivering indigent defense services: public defender programs, assigned counsel, and contract attorney systems.

Twenty-eight percent of state court prosecutors reported that their jurisdictions used public defender programs exclusively to provide indigent counsel.

About three-fourths of the inmates in state prisons and about half of those in federal prisons received publicly provided legal counsel for the offense for which they were serving time. About 80 percent of defendants charged with felonies in the nation's seventy-five largest counties relied on a public defender or on assigned counsel for legal representation.

Federal Defender Services

The federal justice system provides indigent defense to eligible defendants through the Federal Defender Services, community defender organizations, and private attorneys as established by the Criminal Justice Act of 1964, as amended.

Conviction Rates

Conviction rates for indigent defendants and those with their own lawyers were about the same in Federal and States courts. About 90 percent of the Federal defendants and 75 percent of the defendants in the most populous counties were found guilty regardless of the type of their attorneys.

Effectiveness of Appointed Counsel

Of those found guilty, however, those represented by publicly financed attorneys were incarcerated at a higher rate than those defendants who paid for their own legal representation 88 percent compared to 77 percent in federal courts and 71 percent compared to 54 percent in the most populous counties.

Sentence Length

On average, sentence lengths for defendants sent to jail or prison were shorter for those with publicly financed attorneys than those who hired counsel. In Federal district court those with publicly financed attorneys were given just under five years on average and those with private attorneys just over five years. In large state courts those with publicly financed attorneys were sentenced to an average of two and a half years and those with private attorneys to three years.

Racial Disparity and the Use of Publicly Financed Counsel

While 69 percent of white state prison inmates reported they had lawyers appointed by the court, 77 percent of blacks and 73 percent of Hispanics had publicly financed attorneys. In federal prison, black inmates were more likely than whites and Hispanics to have public counsel: 65 percent for blacks, 57 percent for whites, and 56 percent for Hispanics.

[Source: Bureau of Justice web site http://www.ojp.usdoj.gov/bjs/id.htm#counties, accessed on June 5, 2008.]

The denial of the assistance of counsel in felony cases was rejected by the colonists, and in most of the colonies the right of counsel became a part of their due process of law. The right to counsel had become such an accepted practice that when the Bill of Rights was formulated, the following provision was included in the Sixth Amendment of the U.S. Constitution: "In all criminal prosecutions, the accused shall . . . have the assistance of counsel for his defense." This guarantee pertained only to federal prosecutions, but the states included similar provisions in their constitutions or statutes upon admittance to the Union. These provisions are usually worded similarly to that of the following: "In criminal prosecutions the accused shall have the right to appear and defend, and in person and with counsel."

For many generations, this right to the assistance of counsel was interpreted as meaning that if an accused appeared in court with an attorney, the accused could not be denied the assistance of the attorney. If, however, defendants were unable to afford an attorney to assist in their defense, it was their misfortune. Little thought was given to providing counsel for the accused. Nor was assistance of counsel considered essential for the accused prior to the time of the trial. But as time passed, new interpretations were placed upon the Sixth Amendment guarantee of counsel, particularly by the U.S. Supreme Court.

Providing the Accused with Counsel

One of the earliest decisions in which the U.S. Supreme Court held that in certain instances an accused must be provided with an attorney, if he or she cannot afford one, was the case of *Powell* v. *Alabama*.[4] The facts of this case indicate that ignorant and friendless black youths, strangers in the community without means to obtain counsel, were hurried to trial in an Alabama state court for a capital offense without appointment of counsel. The youths were convicted, and their case was taken to the U.S. Supreme Court on the grounds that the defendants had been denied due process of law. The Court agreed that the defendants had been denied due process of law in that they had not been provided with counsel to assist them in their defense. The Court stated:

> All that is necessary now to decide, as we do decide, is that in a capital case, where the defendant is unable to employ counsel, and is incapable adequately of making his own defense because of ignorance, feeblemindedness, illiteracy, or the like, it is the duty of the court, whether requested or not, to assign counsel for him as a necessary requisite of due process of law. . . .

In the *Powell* case, the charge was a capital offense, and the Court held that in capital offenses, the judge must appoint an attorney when the accused is unable to obtain counsel. This decision remained in effect until the case of *Gideon* v. *Wainwright*,[5] when the U.S. Supreme Court held that counsel must be provided for any defendant brought to trial irrespective of the charge. The facts of the *Gideon* case indicate that Gideon (the petitioner) was charged in a Florida state court with breaking into and entering a poolroom with intent to commit a misdemeanor. This offense is a felony under Florida law. Appearing in court without funds and without a lawyer, the petitioner asked the court to appoint counsel, but the judge informed him that under the laws of the state of Florida, the only time that the court could appoint counsel to represent a defendant is when that person is charged with a capital offense. Gideon attempted to conduct his own defense by making an opening statement, cross-examining prosecution witnesses, and presenting witnesses in his own behalf. Gideon was convicted and sentenced to five years in the state prison. The case was taken to the U.S. Supreme Court on the grounds that he had been denied due process of law in that his Sixth Amendment guarantee to the assistance of counsel had been denied. The Court agreed with this contention and reversed the conviction. The Court, in its decision, stated that

> reason and reflection require us to recognize that in our adversary system of criminal justice, any person hauled into court, who is too poor to hire a lawyer, cannot be assured a fair trial unless counsel is provided for him. This seems to us to be an obvious truth. Governments, both state and federal, quite properly spend vast sums of money to establish machinery to try defendants accused of crime. Lawyers to prosecute are everywhere deemed essential to protect the public's interest in an orderly society. Similarly, there are few defendants charged with crime, few indeed, who fail to hire the best lawyers they can get to prepare and present their defenses. That government hires lawyers to prosecute and defendants who have the money hire lawyers to defend are the strongest indications of the widespread belief that lawyers in criminal courts are necessities, not luxuries. The right of one charged with crime to counsel may not be deemed fundamental and essential to fair trials in some countries, but it is in ours. From the very beginning, our state and national constitutions and laws have laid great emphasis on procedural and substantive safeguards designed to assure fair trials before impartial tribunals in which every defendant stands equal before the law. This noble ideal cannot be realized if the poor man charged with crime has to face his accusers without a lawyer to assist him. A defendant's need for a lawyer is nowhere better stated that in the moving words of Mr. Justice Sutherland in *Powell* v. *Alabama*: "The right to be heard would be, in many cases, of little avail if it did not comprehend the right to be heard by counsel. Even the intelligent and educated layman has small and sometimes no skill in the science of law. If charged with crime, he is incapable, generally, of determining for himself whether the indictment is good or bad. He is unfamiliar with the rules of evidence. Left without the aid of counsel he may be put on trial without a proper charge, and convicted upon incompetent evidence, or evidence irrelevant to the issue or otherwise inadmissible. He lacks both the skill and knowledge adequately to prepare his defense, even though he has a perfect one. He requires the guiding hand of counsel at every step in the proceedings against him. Without it, though he be not guilty, he faces the danger of conviction because he does not know how to establish his innocence."

Law in Practice

How Would You Rule?

In *Wright* v. *Van Patten*, 128 S. Ct. 743 (2008), Van Patten was charged with first-degree intentional homicide and pleaded no contest to a reduced charge of first-degree reckless homicide. His counsel was not physically present at the plea hearing, but was linked to the courtroom by speaker phone. After the state trial court imposed the maximum term of twenty-five years in prison, Van Patten retained different counsel and moved in the Wisconsin Court of Appeals to withdraw his no-contest plea. The thrust of the motion was

that Van Patten's Sixth Amendment right to counsel had been violated by his trial counsel's physical absence from the plea hearing. The Wisconsin Court of Appeals noted that, under state law, a postconviction motion to withdraw a no-contest plea will be granted only if a defendant establishes "manifest injustice" by clear and convincing evidence. While the court acknowledged that the violation of the defendant's Sixth Amendment right to counsel may constitute a manifest injustice, it found that the absence of Van Patten's lawyer from the plea hearing did not violate his right to counsel. Van Patten appealed to the U.S. Supreme Court.

JUSTICE STEVENS: No decision of this Court, however, squarely addresses the issue in this case. Our precedents do not clearly hold that counsel's participation by speaker phone should be treated as a complete denial of counsel, on par with total absence. Even if we agree with Van Patten that a lawyer physically present will tend to perform better than one on the phone, it does not necessarily follow that mere telephone contact amounted to total absence or "prevented counsel from assisting the accused." The question is not whether counsel in those circumstances will perform less well than he otherwise would, but whether the circumstances are likely to result in such poor performance that an inquiry into its effects would not be worth the time. Sixth Amendment ensures effective (not mistake-free) representation. Our cases provide no categorical answer to this question, and for that matter the several proceedings in this case hardly point toward one. Because our cases give no clear answer to the question presented, let alone one in Van Patten's favor, it cannot be said that the state court unreasonably applied clearly established Federal law. Therefore, relief is unauthorized. [The Court held that there was no constitutional reason to order a new trial.]

Right to Counsel in Petty Cases

Although the Court in the *Gideon* case held that any person haled into court who is too poor to hire a lawyer cannot be assured a fair trial unless counsel is provided for him or her, the charge in this case was a felony. Thus, there remained the question of whether counsel must be appointed for one brought to trial on a petty charge. This doubt was resolved in the case of *Argersinger* v. *Hamlin,*[6] in which the U.S. Supreme Court held that no person may be imprisoned for any offense, petty or otherwise, unless he or she is represented by counsel. The facts of the case show that Argersinger was charged in Florida with carrying a concealed weapon, an offense punishable by imprisonment for up to six months. Argersinger was tried before a judge and was not represented by counsel, since he could not afford one, and the state contended that since the charge was a petty one, counsel did not have to be appointed for the defendant. Argersinger was convicted and sentenced to jail for ninety days. The conviction was upheld by the Florida Supreme Court, and the case was taken to the U.S. Supreme Court on the grounds that the defendant had been denied the right to counsel. The Court stated the following:

> . . . The Sixth Amendment, which in enumerated situations has been made applicable to the States by reason of the Fourteenth Amendment . . . provides specified standards for all criminal prosecutions.
>
> One is the requirement of a public trial . . . the right to a public trial was applicable to a state proceeding even though only a 60-day sentence was involved.
>
> Another guarantee is the right to be informed of the nature and cause of the accusation. Still another, the right of confrontation. And another, compulsory process for obtaining witnesses in one's favor. We have never limited these rights to felonies nor to lesser but serious offenses. . . .
>
> While there is historical support for limiting the deep commitment to trial by jury to serious criminal cases, there is no such support for a similar limitation on the right to assistance of counsel. . . .
>
> The assistance of counsel is often a requisite to the very existence of a fair trial. . . .
>
> The requirement of counsel may well be necessary for a fair trial even in a petty offense prosecution. We are by no means convinced that legal and constitutional questions involved in a case that actually leads to imprisonment even for a brief period are any less complex than when a person can be sent off for six months or more.
>
> The trial of vagrancy cases is illustrative. While only brief sentences of imprisonment may be imposed, the cases often bristle with thorny constitutional questions.

Beyond the problem of trials and appeals is that of the guilty plea, a problem which looms large in misdemeanor as well as in felony cases. Counsel is needed so that the accused may know precisely what he is doing, so that he is fully aware of the prospect of going to jail or prison, and so that he is treated fairly by the prosecution.

We hold, therefore, that absent a knowing and intelligent waiver, no person may be imprisoned for any offense, whether classified as petty, misdemeanor, or felony, unless he was represented by counsel at his trial.

Law in Practice

Qualifications of Defense Counsel in Capital Cases

Most states have additional requirements that the chief or lead defense counsel must meet before defending an accused in a capital case (possible death penalty case). Florida's rules are typical of those states.

Excerpts from Florida Criminal and Traffic Court Rules of Procedure § 3.112

Statement of Purpose: The purpose of these rules is to set minimum standards for attorneys in capital cases to help ensure that competent representation will be provided to capital defendants in all cases. Minimum standards that have been promulgated concerning representation for defendants in criminal cases generally and the level of adherence to such standards required for noncapital cases should not be adopted as sufficient for death penalty cases. Counsel in death penalty cases should be required to perform at the level of an attorney reasonably skilled in the specialized practice of capital representation, zealously committed to the capital case, who has had adequate time and resources for preparation. These minimum standards for capital cases are not intended to preclude any circuit from adopting or maintaining standards having greater requirements.

Lead Counsel: Lead trial counsel assignments should be given to attorneys who:

1. are members of the bar admitted to practice in the jurisdiction or admitted to practice pro hac vice; and

2. are experienced and active trial practitioners with at least five years of litigation experience in the field of criminal law; and

3. have prior experience as lead counsel in no fewer than nine state or federal jury trials of serious and complex cases which were tried to completion, as well as prior experience as lead defense counsel or co-counsel in at least two state or federal cases tried to completion in which the death penalty was sought. In addition, of the nine jury trials which were tried to completion, the attorney should have been lead counsel in at least three cases in which the charge was murder; or alternatively, of the nine jury trials, at least one was a murder trial and an additional five were felony jury trials; and

4. are familiar with the practice and procedure of the criminal courts of the jurisdiction; and

5. are familiar with and experienced in the utilization of expert witnesses and evidence, including but not limited to psychiatric and forensic evidence; and

6. have demonstrated the necessary proficiency and commitment which exemplify the quality of representation appropriate to capital cases, including but not limited to the investigation and presentation of evidence in mitigation of the death penalty; and

7. have attended within the last two years a continuing legal education program of at least twelve hours' duration devoted specifically to the defense of capital cases.

Major U.S. Supreme Court Cases Granting the Right to Counsel

Case	Stage and Ruling
Moore v. *Michigan,* 355 U.S. 155 (1957)	The defendant has the right to counsel when submitting a guilty plea to the court.
Brady v. *United States,* 397 U.S. 742 (1970)	Counsel is required during the plea bargaining process.
Powell v. *Alabama,* 287 U.S. 45 (1932)	Defendants have the right to counsel at their trial in a state capital case.

Hamilton v. *Alabama,* 368 U.S. 52 (1961)	The arraignment is a critical stage in the criminal process, so denial of the right to counsel is a violation of due process of law.
Coleman v. *Alabama,* 399 U.S. 1 (1970)	The preliminary hearing is a critical stage in a criminal prosecution requiring the state to provide the indigent defendant with counsel.
United States v. *Wade,* 388 U.S. 218 (1967)	A defendant in a pretrial, postindictment lineup for identification purposes has the right to assistance of counsel.
Gideon v. *Wainwright,* 372 U.S. 335 (1963)	An indigent defendant charged in a state court with a noncapital felony has the right to the assistance of free counsel at trial under the Due Process Clause of the Fourteenth Amendment.
Argersinger v. *Hamlin,* 407 U.S. 25 (1972)	A defendant has the right to counsel at trial whenever he or she may be imprisoned, even for one day, for any offense, whether classified as a misdemeanor or a felony.
Faretta v. *California,* 422 U.S. 806 (1975)	The defendant has a constitutional right to defend herself or himself if her or his waiver of the right to counsel is knowing and intelligent.
Escobedo v. *Illinois,* 378 U.S. 478 (1964)	The defendant has the right to counsel during the course of any police interrogation.
Miranda v. *Arizona,* 384 U.S. 436 (1966)	Procedural safeguards, including the right to counsel, must be followed at custodial interrogation to secure the privilege against self-incrimination.
Massiah v. *United States,* 377 U.S. 201 (1964)	The defendant has the right to counsel during postindictment interrogation.
In re Gault, 387 U.S. 1 (1967)	Procedural due process, including the right to counsel, applies to juvenile delinquency adjudication that may lead to a child's commitment to a state institution.
Townsend v. *Burke,* 334 U.S. 736 (1948)	A convicted offender has a right to counsel at the time of sentencing.
Douglas v. *California,* 372 U.S. 353 (1963)	An indigent defendant granted a first appeal from a criminal conviction has the right to be represented by counsel on appeal.
Mempa v. *Rhay,* 389 U.S. 128 (1967)	A convicted offender has the right to assistance of counsel at probation revocation hearings where the sentence has been deferred.
Morrissey v. *Brewer,* 408 U.S. 471 (1972)	The defendant has the right to counsel in the court's discretion at parole revocation hearings.
Gagnon v. *Scarpelli,* 411 U.S. 778 (1973)	The defendant has a right to counsel in the court's discretion at probation revocation hearings.
Indiana v. *Edwards* 128 S. Ct. 2379 (2008)	Because the right of self-representation is not absolute, states can adopt a higher standard of competence for self-representation than for standing trial.

Waiver of Counsel

Although the Sixth Amendment guarantees the right to counsel, may this constitutional guarantee, like most others, be waived, or is it mandatory that the defendant be represented by counsel? This question was answered in *Adams* v. *United States,*[7] in which the U.S. Supreme Court held that a capable defendant could waive the right to the assistance of counsel. But it must be determined first that the accused is capable of defense without counsel's assistance.

The right of a defendant to represent himself or herself was carried one step further by the U.S. Supreme Court in *Faretta* v. *California,*[8] where the Court held that when a defendant "knowingly and intelligently" waives the right to the assistance of counsel, the defendant has the constitutional right to **self-representation**. The facts reveal that Faretta was charged with grand theft. At the arraignment, the judge appointed a public defender to represent him, but before the trial, Faretta requested that he be permitted to represent himself. In an effort to determine whether Faretta was capable of representing himself, the judge questioned Faretta and learned that he had represented himself in a prior criminal prosecution, that he had a high school education, and that he did not want to be represented by the public defender. After further questioning at a later time, the judge concluded that Faretta had not intelligently waived his right to the assistance of counsel. The judge also ruled that Faretta did not have a constitutional right to self-representation. Faretta was represented by a public defender, and he was convicted and sentenced to prison. He appealed his case to the U.S. Supreme Court, which agreed to hear it to settle the question of whether an accused has a Sixth Amendment right to decline counsel. The Court ruled that there is such a constitutional right. The Court pointed out that in early common law, those accused of serious crimes had to represent themselves and that only later was an accused given the choice of receiving the assistance of counsel. This was the practice at the time that the colonists came to America and at the time that the Sixth Amendment was written. The Court stated that it recognized the advantages of an accused's having the assistance of counsel, but was unable to find an instance where a colonial court required an accused to accept an unwanted attorney as his or her representative. The Court felt that when the framers of the Sixth Amendment included the right of an accused to have the assistance of counsel, they were not denying the accused the right of self-representation. The Court stated the following:

> . . . in most criminal prosecutions defendants could better defend with counsel's guidance than by their own unskilled efforts. But where the defendant will not voluntarily accept representation by counsel, the potential advantage of a lawyer's training and experience can be realized, if at all, only imperfectly. To force a lawyer on a defendant can only lead him to believe that the law contrives against him. Moreover, it is not inconceivable that in some rare instances, the defendant might in fact present his case more effectively by conducting his own defense. Personal liberties are not rooted in the law of averages. The right to defend is personal. The defendant, and not his lawyer or the State, will bear the personal consequences of a conviction. It is the defendant, therefore, who must be free personally to decide whether in his particular case counsel is to his advantage. And although he may conduct his own defense ultimately to his own detriment, his choice must be honored out of that respect for the individual which is the lifeblood of the law. When an accused manages his own defense, he relinquishes, as a purely factual matter, many of the traditional benefits associated with the right to counsel. For this reason, in order to represent himself, the accused must "knowingly and intelligently" forego those relinquished benefits. Although a defendant need not himself have the skill and experience of a lawyer in order competently and intelligently to choose self-representation, he should be made aware of the dangers and disadvantages of self-representation, so that the record will establish that "he knows what he is doing and his choice is made with eyes open." Here, weeks before trial, Faretta clearly and unequivocally declared to the trial judge that he wanted to represent himself and did not want counsel. The record affirmatively shows that Faretta was literate, competent, and understanding, and that he was voluntarily exercising his informed free will.

KNOWING AND INTELLIGENT WAIVER The Court in the *Faretta* case stated that "in order to represent himself the accused must knowingly and intelligently" waive the right to the assistance of counsel. This statement placed a serious burden on trial judges in determining whether a defendant is capable of knowingly and intelligently waiving the right to the assistance of counsel. The problem created by this decision is that if a trial judge concludes that the defendant is capable of self-representation and the defendant is convicted, the defendant may appeal, and the appellate court may hold that the defendant was not capable of making an intelligent waiver of the right to counsel. On the other hand, as in *Faretta*'s case, if the judge concludes that the defendant was incapable of intelligently waiving the right to the assistance of counsel and is convicted, the appellate court may decide that the defendant had been denied the right of self-representation. The dissenting justices in the *Faretta* case pointed out that the majority of justices had created a problem that undoubtedly would cause confusion for trial courts, since no guidelines were set forth for the trial courts to follow in their efforts to determine when an accused was capable of self-representation.

Since the U.S. Supreme Court has held that an accused has the constitutional right of self-representation when the right to the assistance of counsel is knowingly and intelligently waived, a trial court must make a careful evaluation of the accused's ability to make the waiver. When an accused requests permission for self-representation, it is usually necessary for the trial judge to hold a hearing to determine the capability of the accused to make the waiver. This hearing has been referred to as a *Faretta* hearing. The time required to conduct this hearing varies with the circumstances of each case. It may become obvious to the judge after a short questioning of the accused that he or she has a limited educational background or knowledge of court procedure. The judge will conclude quickly that such an accused is not capable of making a knowing and intelligent waiver and will require representation by counsel. Other defendants who have some education and some knowledge of court procedures may insist on self-representation, and the hearing can be lengthy. The appellate courts have held that a "perfunctory hearing is improper. The record must show that the defendant made a knowing and intelligent election" to waive assistance of counsel. Further, "the actual conducting of a *Faretta* hearing may be difficult, time-consuming and trying of the patience of the trial judge, particularly if the defendant is eccentric, or prone to causing exasperation in others, or engages in the playing of games, or harassing the establishment. However the judge should not be misled by a confusion of the issue to be determined, that is, whether the defendant is capable of making the waiver."

Judges are inclined to conclude that a defendant is not capable of intelligently waiving the right to the assistance of counsel because of the many problems encountered by an untrained defendant attempting self-representation. The untrained defendant causes the trial to last longer, tries to introduce inadmissible evidence, makes improper objections to questions, and often argues with the judge over rulings. Deciding whether assistance should be provided by the trial judge for the self-represented defendant becomes a further issue. Many judges believe that with all the other duties to be performed during the trial, it is dangerous to try to assist the defendant because of the possibility of mistaken or misunderstood assistance. Yet, some appellate courts have stated that one of the major functions of the trial judge is to make certain that the "innocence or guilt of those accused of a crime is based upon the merits of the trial and not upon their inability to understand legal procedure." Therefore, the trial judge should render that assistance necessary for a fair trial.

The dissenting justices in the *Faretta* case recognized that these problems would be encountered by trial judges and believed that the majority justices had read into the Sixth Amendment something not intended by its framers.

STANDBY COUNSEL The majority justices in the *Faretta* case did indicate that a trial judge, even over the objections of the defendant, could appoint a **standby counsel** to aid the defendant, if and when the defendant requests help, and to be available to represent the defendant in the event that termination of the defendant's self-representation should become necessary. The appointment of a standby attorney is not a practical solution, however, since trial judges may appoint standby attorneys in most instances, tying up the services of an attorney and increasing court costs.

In *McKaskle* v. *Wiggins,*[9] the U.S. Supreme Court reaffirmed the *Faretta* ruling that a trial judge may appoint a standby attorney over the objections of the defendant. The Court stated as follows:

> A defendant's Sixth Amendment rights are not violated when a trial judge appoints standby counsel even over the defendant's objection—to relieve the judge of the need to explain and enforce basic rules of courtroom protocol or to assist the defendant in overcoming routine obstacles that stand in the way of the defendant's achievement of his own clearly indicated goals.

The Court further stated the following:

> A defendant does not have a constitutional right to receive personal instruction from the trial judge on courtroom procedure. Nor does the Constitution require judges to take over chores for a pro se defendant [one representing himself] that would normally be attended to by trained counsel as a matter of course. The right of self-representation is not a license to abuse the dignity of the courtroom. Neither is it a license not to comply with relevant rules of procedure and substantive law.

Although the *McKaskle* decision reaffirmed a trial judge's right to appoint standby counsel over the defendant's objections, the decision did not solve all the problems connected with the appointment of a standby attorney. The trial judge is still faced with deciding how far a standby attorney may proceed over the defendant's objections without the assistance being a violation of the defendant's right to self-representation. The Court in the *McKaskle* case gave few guidelines in this respect, but stated that a defendant's rights to self-representation

> are not infringed upon when standby counsel assists the defendant in overcoming routine procedural or evidentiary obstacles to the completion of some specific task, such as the introducing [of] evidence or objecting to testimony, that the defendant has clearly shown he wishes to complete. Nor are they infringed when counsel merely helps to ensure the defendant's compliance with basic rules of courtroom protocol and procedure. In neither case is there any significant interference with the defendant's actual control over the presentation of his defense.

Why an Accused Chooses Self-Representation

With the advantages to an accused in having the assistance of counsel and with the disadvantages of self-representation, one might ask why a defendant would insist upon self-representation rather than having the assistance of counsel. The saying is that an attorney who chooses self-representation has a fool for a client. Yet many defendants either do not trust attorneys or question their capabilities. One defendant, for example, conceded that an attorney had "more on the ball" than he himself did, but he also stated that there are certain questions "the attorney might not ask certain witnesses that are very potent, important, in regard to the case itself." Some defendants feel that attorneys do not have their client's best interests at stake or that attorneys are in collusion with the prosecuting attorney, with the result that the defendants will be railroaded into prison. Other defendants receive a certain gratification from representing themselves. Some are aware that by representing themselves they are entitled to confer with codefendants and witnesses in private, enabling them to conspire against the prosecution.

A defendant who represents himself or herself is referred to as "appearing in propria persona" ("in one's own proper person"), or in person. This circumstance is sometimes referred to by the courts as "pro per."

Law in Practice

United States v. *Pena*, 2008 U.S. App. LEXIS 11368 (10th Cir., 2008)

In the midst of defendant's complaints about his attorney during jury selection, defendant asked the trial judge whether he could represent himself, and the judge failed to answer his question.

Was Defendant Denied the Right to Represent Himself?

Decision of the Court: The court noted that other courts of appeals had held that similar questions and remarks about self-representation did not constitute clear and unequivocal requests for self-representation. The court concluded that defendant failed to establish that he clearly and unequivocally asserted his intention to represent himself. When the judge did not answer his question about self-representation, defendant did not pursue the issue in any way. Affirming the conviction, the court held that the district court did not violate defendant's Sixth Amendment right to self-representation.

A defendant has a Sixth Amendment right to waive his right to counsel and to represent himself. The Sixth Amendment right of self-representation differs from other constitutional rights because it cannot be exercised without the concomitant waiver of another fundamental right that is also guaranteed under the Sixth Amendment: the right to counsel. Thus, in order to invoke the right to self-representation, a defendant must (1) clearly and unequivocally assert his intention to represent himself; (2) make this assertion in a timely fashion; and (3) knowingly and intelligently relinquish the benefits of representation by counsel. Additionally, a defendant must be willing and able to abide by rules of procedure and courtroom protocol.

Law in Practice

Kane v. *Garcia Espitia*, 546 U.S. 9 (2006)

Defendant claimed he had received no law library access while in jail before trial—despite his repeated requests and court orders to the contrary—and only about four hours of access during trial, just before closing arguments. The United States Court of Appeals for the Ninth Circuit held that the lack of any pretrial access to law books violated the petitioner's constitutional right to represent himself.

Was the Defendant's Constitutional Right to Represent Himself Violated?

Per Curiam [A per curiam decision is a decision delivered via an opinion issued in the name of the Court rather than specific justices.]:

Faretta v. California does not clearly establish the law library access right for prisoners. In fact, *Faretta* says nothing about any specific legal aid that the State owes a pro se criminal defendant. The United States Court of Appeals for the Ninth Circuit erred in holding, based on *Faretta*, that a violation of a law library access right is a basis for federal habeas relief.

When the Right to Counsel Begins

For many years, the Sixth Amendment guarantee to the assistance of counsel was interpreted as meaning assistance at the time of trial. The *Gideon* decision did not materially change that interpretation, since that decision referred to the fact that "any person hauled into court, who is too poor to hire a lawyer, cannot be assured a fair trial unless counsel is provided for him." It was generally accepted that counsel need not be provided for the indigent defendant until the time of trial. However, later U.S. Supreme Court decisions established a new interpretation of when the right to counsel began and when counsel had to be provided for the indigent defendant.

In the case of *Escobedo* v. *Illinois,*[10] the U.S. Supreme Court held that the right to the assistance of counsel begins long before the time of the trial and may occur even before an arrest is made. The Court stated that when the investigation of a crime "shifts from . . . investigatory to accusatory," the accused is entitled to the assistance of counsel and such assistance could be very hollow if denied until the time of trial.

The facts of the *Escobedo* case indicate that Escobedo was arrested on a charge of murder. He was taken to a Chicago police station for interrogation. En route, Escobedo asked to consult with his attorney. Shortly after Escobedo arrived at the police station, his attorney arrived and requested permission to talk to Escobedo. Both were advised by the police that they could confer after the interrogation was completed. During the interrogation, Escobedo made certain admissions that implicated him in the murder charge. These admissions were used against him during the trial. Escobedo was convicted of murder, and his conviction was upheld by the Illinois Supreme Court. The case was taken to the U.S. Supreme Court upon the grounds that Escobedo was denied the assistance of counsel in violation of the Sixth Amendment guarantee. The attorneys for the State of Illinois argued that the right to counsel was not operative until the indictment stage of proceedings. To this argument, the Court stated that

> in *Gideon* v. *Wainwright* we held that every person accused of a crime, whether state or federal, is entitled to a lawyer at trial. The rule sought by the State here, however, would make the trial no more than an appeal from the interrogation; and the "right to use counsel at the formal trial [would be] a very hollow thing if, for all practical purposes, the conviction is already assured by pretrial examination." *In re Groban,* 352 U.S. 330 (1957) (Black, J., dissenting): One can imagine a cynical prosecutor saying: "Let them have the most illustrious counsel, now. They can't escape the noose. There is nothing that counsel can do for them at a trial."
>
> It is argued that if the right to counsel is afforded prior to indictment, the number of confessions obtained by the police will diminish significantly, because most confessions are obtained during the period between arrest and indictment, and "any lawyer worth his salt will tell the suspect in no uncertain terms to make no statement to police under any circumstances." This argument, of course, cuts two ways. The fact that many confessions are obtained during this period points up its critical nature as a "stage when legal aid and advice" are surely needed. The right to counsel would indeed be hollow if it began at a period when few confessions were obtained. There is necessarily a direct relationship between the police in their quest for a confession and the criticalness of that stage to the accused in his need for legal advice. Our Constitution, unlike some others, strikes the balance in favor of the right of the accused to be advised by his lawyer of his privilege against self-incrimination.
>
> We hold, therefore, that where, as here, the investigation is no longer a general inquiry into an unsolved crime but has begun to focus on a particular suspect, the suspect has been taken into police custody, the police carry out a process of interrogations that lends itself to eliciting incriminating statements, the suspect has requested and been denied an opportunity to consult with his lawyer, and the police have not effectively warned him of his absolute constitutional right to remain silent, the accused has been denied "the assistance of Counsel" in violation of the Sixth Amendment to the Constitution as "made obligatory upon the States by the Fourteenth Amendment," *Gideon* v. *Wainwright,* and that no statement elicited by the police be used against him at a criminal trial. . . .
>
> Nothing we have said today affects the powers of the police to investigate "an unsolved crime" by gathering information from witnesses and by other "proper investigative efforts." We hold only that when the process shifts from investigatory

to accusatory—when its purpose is to elicit a confession—our adversary system begins to operate, and, under the circumstances here, to consult with his lawyer.

The *Escobedo* decision provided that once suspicion is focused upon a particular suspect, he or she is entitled to consult with an attorney, but nothing was said about having to furnish the accused with an attorney. In the *Miranda* case, as previously stated, the Court held that before an accused can be interrogated, he or she must be advised of the right to the assistance of counsel. The accused must be advised of the right to remain silent and of the right to the assistance of counsel during the interrogation; and if the accused cannot afford an attorney, then one will be provided free.

Although both the *Escobedo* and *Miranda* decisions are more closely related to the field of evidence and the admissibility of confessions than to procedure, these decisions emphasized the importance of the assistance of counsel and set forth guidelines on when that right to assistance begins.

Effective Counsel

A defendant is entitled not only to the assistance of counsel but also to effective counsel. An **effective counsel** is one who has knowledge of the defendant's rights and who is capable of presenting the defenses to which the accused is entitled. Establishing the effectiveness of counsel is not easy. A counsel may be knowledgeable in one field but unfamiliar with crucial problems in another. If counsel does not effectively represent a defendant, whether through lack of knowledge or interest or because of mere carelessness, a conviction could be overruled upon appeal because of the denial of assistance of counsel. When attorneys are found to be ineffective, they are frequently sanctioned by the state bar association. This is a powerful incentive to diligently represent a client.

FARCE OR SHAM TEST In determining whether a conviction should be reversed because of ineffective counsel, many state appellate courts have stated that it must appear that counsel's lack of diligence or competence reduced the trial to a farce or sham. Today's courts have rejected the traditional **farce or sham test** and have adopted a less stringent criterion for determining the competency of counsel. Counsel is considered ineffective if in representing the defendant, the counsel fails to meet the standard of competence expected of criminal case attorneys. Counsel is held to be ineffective when not exercising the customary skills and diligence that a reasonably competent attorney would have used under similar circumstances. Effective counsel has the duty to investigate carefully all defenses of fact and law of a case. If counsel's failure to do so results in the failure to present a crucial defense during the trial, the defendant has been denied proper assistance of counsel. Further, mere allegations by the defendant indicating a lack of preparation by or general incompetence of counsel are not enough to show ineffectiveness. The defendant must show acts or omissions resulting in a failure to present a crucial defense. Counsel does not have to interview or call every witness with knowledge of the case, since many witnesses may be of little assistance to the defense.

CRUCIAL ERROR BY COUNSEL The effectiveness of counsel is usually considered when the court appoints an attorney to represent the defendant who cannot afford to choose an attorney. There are times when a defendant will complain about the effectiveness of chosen counsel (**retained counsel**). If an attorney selected by the accused is so ineffective that the defendant was denied a fair trial, the conviction will be reversed on appeal. For a time, courts were inclined to require a lesser degree of competence from an attorney of the defendant's own choosing. Today, it is accepted that whether an attorney is appointed for the defendant or is one of the defendant's own choosing, competence will be measured by the same degree. As stated by the U.S. Supreme Court in *Strickland* v. *Washington,*[11] "An accused is entitled to be assisted by an attorney, whether retained or appointed, who plays the role necessary to ensure that the trial is fair." A defendant may not expect an error-free attorney, but if an error is crucial to the defense, effective counsel has been denied. Determining whether an error was crucial has been a major problem for appellate courts. Defendants who have been convicted have successfully appealed on the allegation that effective counsel had been denied. Since no guidelines were set forth to measure the effectiveness of counsel, many convictions have been reversed. In *Strickland,* the Court endeavored to correct this situation by providing some criteria to measure effectiveness. The Court stated that "when a convicted defendant complains of the ineffectiveness of counsel's assistance, the defendant must show that counsel's representation fell below an objective standard of reasonableness. More specific guidelines are not appropriate."

BURDEN OF PROOF The *Strickland* decision points out that the burden of proving ineffective assistance of counsel is on the defendant. When a convicted defendant claims that counsel's assistance was so defective as to require a reversal of a conviction or a death sentence, the defendant must prove two things. First, the defendant must show that counsel's performance was deficient. The defendant is thus required to show that the errors made were so serious that counsel did not function as a reasonably competent attorney. Second, the defendant must show that the deficient performance prejudiced the defense. Counsel's errors must be so serious as to deprive the defendant of a fair trial.

A defendant may allege ineffectiveness of counsel when there may have been acts or omissions such as the failure of counsel to enter a proper plea when applicable (such as a plea of not guilty by reason of insanity); the failure to raise the defense of diminished capacity; the failure to cross-examine prosecution witnesses; or the failure to object to the introduction of evidence improperly obtained. In one case, an appellate court overruled a conviction when the defense attorney's request for a continuance was denied, and the attorney thereafter refused to assist in the selection of the jury. The appellate court held that the defense counsel had reduced the trial to a sham.

Law in Practice

Schriro v. *Landrigan*, 127 S. Ct. 1933 (2007)

An Arizona jury found defendant Landrigan guilty of theft, second-degree burglary, and felony murder for having caused the victim's death in the course of a burglary. Defendant refused to allow his counsel to present the testimony of his ex-wife and birth mother as mitigating evidence at his sentencing hearing for a felony-murder conviction. He also interrupted as counsel tried to proffer other evidence, and he told the Arizona trial judge he did not wish to present any mitigating evidence and to "bring on" the death penalty. The court sentenced him to death, and the sentence was affirmed. Later, defendant filed a writ in federal court claiming ineffective assistant of counsel because his counsel did not present any evidence in mitigation. The federal district court denied his writ without holding a hearing. Defendant now appeals the refusal of the federal district court to hold a hearing on his writ.

How Would You Rule?

JUSTICE THOMAS delivered the court's opinion.

Defendant could not show prejudice from any failure of counsel to investigate additional mitigating evidence, since the record indicated that defendant would have interrupted and refused to allow his counsel to present any such evidence. Further, the record also showed that defendant understood the consequences of refusing to allow evidence in mitigation, and the facts which defendant sought to prove in an evidentiary hearing constituted weak evidence in mitigation and would not have changed the result. His counsel's performance did not fall below the standard required by *Strickland* v. *Washington,* 466 U.S. 668.

Public Defender and Appointed Counsel

As has been stated, an accused is entitled to the assistance of counsel when that assistance is requested. If the accused is not in a position to employ private counsel, the court must appoint effective counsel. It is not always easy for a judge to obtain effective counsel to represent one accused of a crime. If effective counsel cannot be readily obtained, all prosecutive action must be suspended. To overcome this problem, many counties have established the **public defender**, whose function is representing those defendants who cannot afford an attorney of their own. These defendants are referred to as indigent persons or **indigent defendants**. The public defender, like the prosecuting attorney, is paid out of public funds. Many do not understand the use of public funds to employ a prosecuting attorney to prosecute offenders and, at the same time, to pay a public defender to defend the accused. But until the indigent defendant is furnished with the assistance of counsel, no prosecutive action can be taken. This delay can be expensive in time and money. If there is no public defender in a particular jurisdiction, the court must draw local attorneys from private practice. This necessity creates a problem, since most of these attorneys practice civil law and have little knowledge of the intricacies of a criminal trial; furthermore, in case of a conviction, the question of whether there was effective assistance of counsel could arise.

Before an accused may have the assistance of the public defender or an appointed private attorney, it must be established that the defendant is an indigent person, and this is sometimes difficult. Approximately 85 percent of all those arrested on felony charges are without question unable to afford an attorney. Determining which of the others can afford an attorney is difficult. Some courts have held that if the defendant can post bail, he or she is not indigent. Others have ruled that counsel is to be provided for any defendant who is unable to obtain counsel without serious financial hardship. The mere fact that friends or relatives have posted bail is not sufficient ground for denying the defendant free counsel. Another test is whether or not a private attorney would be interested in representing the defendant in his or her present economic circumstances. Undoubtedly, there have been defendants who have taken advantage of these tests to obtain free counsel, but with the large number of defendants who claim indigency, a thorough inquiry into each case is impossible. Judges who doubt the indigency status of a defendant have required the defendant to file a financial statement under oath. If it is determined later that the defendant was not indigent, prosecution for perjury as well as civil charges may be filed for the cost of the **appointed counsel**.

Law in Practice

Halbert v. *Michigan,* 545 U.S. 605 (2005)

The defendant pleaded guilty at his trial. He then appealed his conviction. Michigan had a statute that provided that an indigent defendant had a right to appellate counsel for his or her first appeal except in cases involving a guilty plea. The appointment of appellate counsel for a defendant who had pleaded guilty was at the discretion of the trial judge.

Does That Statute Violate a Defendant's Right to Counsel on Appeal When the Defendant Pleaded Guilty at Trial?

JUSTICE GINSBURG delivered the opinion of the Court.

The Federal Constitution imposes on the states no obligation to provide appellate review of criminal convictions. Having provided such an avenue, however, a state may not bolt the door to equal justice to indigent defendants. When a state conditions an appeal from a conviction on the provision of a trial transcript, the state must furnish free transcripts to indigent defendants who seek to appeal. In first appeals as of right, states must appoint counsel to represent indigent defendants. However, a state need not appoint counsel to aid a poor person in discretionary appeals to the state's highest court, or in petitioning for review in the United States Supreme Court. For the reasons stated, we vacate the judgment of the Michigan Court of Appeals and remand the case for further proceedings not inconsistent with this opinion. [The Court found that the statute did not conform to the requirements of the Sixth Amendment.]

CASE LAW

Recent Cases

Premo v. *Moore*, 131 S. Ct. 733 (U.S. 2011)

State inmate filed a petition in district court under 28 U.S.C.S. § 2254 for a writ of habeas corpus based on ineffective assistance of counsel under the Sixth Amendment. The district court denied the petition. The United States Court of Appeals for the Ninth Circuit reversed. The Supreme Court granted certiorari.

The inmate pleaded no contest to felony murder in exchange for the minimum sentence allowed for the offense. The inmate had confessed to two witnesses and later to police. The inmate argued that his counsel should have moved to suppress the confession to the police before advising him regarding the plea. The attorney concluded that such a motion would have been fruitless in light of the earlier confession.

The Supreme Court held that the inmate was not entitled to habeas relief under § 2254(d) because the state court decision was not an unreasonable application of clearly established federal law. Under the circumstances, which included the potential for a capital charge, it was not unreasonable to conclude that counsel's decision to opt for a quick plea bargain did not amount to deficient performance. With regard to prejudice, the state court reasonably could have found that the inmate would have accepted the plea agreement even if the confession to police had been ruled inadmissible, given the strength of the other evidence.

The Court noted that to establish ineffective assistance of counsel a defendant must show both deficient performance by counsel and prejudice. To establish deficient performance, a person challenging a conviction must show that counsel's representation fell below an objective standard of reasonableness. A court considering a claim of ineffective assistance must apply a strong presumption that counsel's representation was within the wide range of reasonable professional assistance. The challenger's burden is to show that counsel made errors so serious that counsel was not functioning as the "counsel" guaranteed the defendant by the Sixth Amendment. With respect to prejudice, a challenger must demonstrate a reasonable probability that, but for counsel's unprofessional errors, the result of the proceeding would have been different.

Halbert v. *Michigan* 545 U.S. 605, 2005 U.S. LEXIS 5012, 2005)

[In *Douglas* v. *California*, 372 U.S. 353 (1963), the U.S. Supreme Court held that, in criminal proceedings, a state must provide counsel for an indigent defendant in a first appeal as of right. Two considerations were key: (1) an appeal "of right" yields an adjudication on the "merits," and (2) first-tier review differs from subsequent appellate stages "at which the claims have once been presented by a lawyer and passed upon by an appellate court." Later, in *Ross* v. *Moffitt*, 417 U.S. 600 (1974), the Court held that a state need not appoint counsel to aid a poor person seeking to pursue a second-tier discretionary appeal to the state's highest court or thereafter. The Douglas rationale does not extend to second-tier discretionary review, the Court explained, because, at that stage, error correction is not the reviewing court's prime function. Principal criteria for state high court review, Ross noted, include whether the issues presented are of significant public interest, whether the cause involves legal principles of major significance to the state's jurisprudence, and whether the decision below is in probable conflict with the high court's precedent. Further, a defendant who has received counsel's aid in a first-tier appeal as of right would be armed with a transcript or another record of trial proceedings, a brief in the appeals court setting forth his or her claims, and, often, that court's opinion disposing of the case.

Michigan has a two-tier appellate system. Its Supreme Court hears appeals by leave only. The intermediate Court of Appeals adjudicates appeals as of right from criminal convictions, except that a defendant convicted on a guilty or nolo contendere plea who seeks intermediate appellate court review must apply for leave to appeal. Under Michigan law, most indigent defendants convicted on a plea must proceed pro se in seeking leave to appeal to the intermediate court. In *People* v. *Bulger*, 462 Mich. 495 (2000), the Michigan Supreme Court held that the Fourteenth Amendment's Equal Protection and Due Process Clauses do not secure a right to appointed counsel for plea-convicted defendants seeking review in the intermediate appellate court for these reasons: Such review is discretionary; plea proceedings are shorter, simpler, and more routine than trials; and a defendant entering a plea accedes to the state's fundamental interest in finality.]

JUDGES: GINSBURG, J., delivered the opinion of the Court, in which STEVENS, O'CONNOR, KENNEDY, SOUTER, and BREYER, JJ., joined. THOMAS, J., filed a dissenting opinion, in which SCALIA, J., joined, and in which REHNQUIST, C.J., joined.

Petitioner Halbert pleaded nolo contendere to two counts of criminal sexual conduct. During Halbert's plea colloquy, the trial court advised him of instances in which it "must" or "may" appoint appellate counsel, but failed to tell him that it could not appoint counsel in any other circumstances, including Halbert's own case. The day after his sentence was imposed, Halbert moved to withdraw his plea. Denying the motion, the trial court stated that Halbert's proper remedy was to appeal to the State Court of Appeals. Twice thereafter, Halbert asked the trial court to appoint counsel to help him prepare an application for leave to appeal to the intermediate court, stating that his sentence had been mis-scored, that he needed counsel to preserve the issue before undertaking an appeal, that he had learning disabilities and was mentally impaired, and that he had been obliged to rely on fellow inmates in preparing his pro se filings. The court denied Halbert's motion, citing Bulger. Halbert then filed a pro se application for leave to appeal, asserting sentencing error and ineffective assistance of counsel and seeking, inter alia, remand for appointment of appellate counsel. The Court of Appeals denied leave "for lack of merit in the grounds presented." The Michigan Supreme Court declined review.

Two aspects of the Michigan Court of Appeals' process following plea-based convictions compel the conclusion that Douglas, not Ross, controls here. First, in ruling on an application for leave to appeal, that court looks to the merits of the appellant's claims. Second, indigent defendants pursuing first-tier review in the Court of Appeals are generally ill equipped to represent themselves. A defendant who pleads guilty or nolo contendere in a Michigan court, although he relinquishes access to an appeal as of right, is entitled to apply for leave to appeal, and that entitlement is officially conveyed to him. Of critical importance, the intermediate appellate court, unlike the Michigan Supreme Court, sits as an error-correction instance. A court rule provides that the intermediate court may respond to a leave application in a number of ways: It may grant or deny the application, enter a final decision, grant other relief, request additional material from the record, or require a certified concise statement of proceedings and facts from the lower court. The court's response to the leave application by any of these alternatives—including denial of leave—necessarily entails some evaluation of the merits of the applicant's claims.

Whether formally categorized as the decision of an appeal or the disposal of a leave application, the intermediate appellate court's ruling on a plea-convicted defendant's claims provides the first, and likely the only, direct review the defendant's conviction and sentence will receive. Parties like Halbert, however, are disarmed in their endeavor to gain first-tier review. Ross emphasized that a defendant seeking State Supreme Court review following a first-tier appeal as of right earlier had the assistance of appellate counsel, who will have reviewed the trial court record, researched the legal issues, and prepared a brief reflecting that review and research. Such a defendant may also be armed with an opinion of the intermediate appellate court addressing the issues counsel raised. Without such guides keyed to a court of review, a pro se applicant's entitlement to seek leave to appeal to Michigan's intermediate court may be more formal than real. *Swenson* v. *Bosler*, 386 U.S. 258 (per curiam). Persons in Halbert's situation, many of whom have little education, learning disabilities, and mental impairments, are particularly handicapped as self-representatives. See *Kowalski* v. *Tesmer*, 543 U.S. 125, (2004). Vacated and remanded.

THOMAS J., dissenting.

Further, appeals by defendants convicted on their pleas may be "no less complex than other appeals." Michigan's complex procedures for seeking leave to appeal after sentencing on a plea, moreover, may intimidate the uncounseled. The State does have a legitimate interest in reducing its judiciary's workload, but providing indigents with appellate counsel will yield applications easier to comprehend. Michigan's Court of Appeals would still have recourse to summary denials of leave applications in cases not warranting further review. And when a defendant's case presents no genuinely arguable issue, appointed counsel may so inform the court.

The Court disagrees with Michigan's contention that, even if Halbert had a constitutionally guaranteed right to appointed counsel for first-level appellate review, he waived that right by entering a nolo contendere plea. At the time he entered his plea, Halbert had no recognized right to appointed appellate counsel he could elect to forgo. Moreover, the trial court did not tell Halbert, simply and directly, that in his case, there would be no access to appointed counsel.

Summary

- The defendant has a right to be present at his or her trial.
- The defendant may waive the right by his or her conduct.
- The defendant has a right not to be tried before a jury while wearing jail clothes.
- An unruly defendant may be gagged.
- After the trial has started, the accused may waive his or her right to be present by a voluntary absence from the proceedings.
- Under early English law, a person being tried for a felony had no right to counsel.
- The defendant has a right to counsel in all criminal proceedings, but whether the state is required to appoint a counsel for an indigent defendant depends on the nature of the charges and the possible punishment.

- An indigent defendant has the right to appointed counsel in any felony trial or in any trial where he or she faces confinement.
- While an accused has a right to counsel in petty cases, he or she does not have a right to appointed counsel even if indigent.
- An accused has the right to waive counsel and represent himself or herself. The waiver must be knowing and intelligent.
- The judge may appoint a standby counsel to assist the defendant when the defendant is self-represented.
- The right to counsel begins at all important stages of the criminal.
- The defendant is entitled to the effective assistance of counsel.

Review Questions

1. What is the significance of the constitutional guarantee that an accused must be confronted with the witnesses against him or her?
2. May a trial ever be conducted in the absence of the defendant? If so, under what circumstances?
3. What procedure, suggested by the U.S. Supreme Court, might be used against an unruly defendant during trial proceedings, and in what decision was the procedure suggested?
4. In what amendment to the U.S. Constitution is the right to the assistance of counsel embodied?
5. What was the significance of the *Gideon* v. *Wainwright* decision in reference to the assistance of counsel?
6. In the *Argersinger* v. *Hamlin* decision, what arguments were presented by the Court in granting the accused the assistance of counsel in the trial of a petty charge?
7. Under what circumstances, if any, may an accused waive the assistance of counsel and represent himself or herself during a trial?
8. When does the accused's right to counsel begin?
9. What is the significance of the term "effective assistance of counsel"?
10. What is the function of a public defender?

Endnotes

1. 397 U.S. 337 (1970).
2. 130 U.S. App. DC 22 (1968).
3. 101 L.Ed. 2d 857 (1988).
4. 287 U.S. 45 (1932).
5. 372 U.S. 335 (1963).
6. 407 U.S. 25 (1972).
7. 317 U.S. 269 (1942).
8. 422 U.S. 806 (1975).
9. 79 L.Ed. 2d 122 (1984).
10. 378 U.S. 478 (1964).
11. 466 U.S. 668 (1984).

CHAPTER 9

Pretrial Motions, Hearings, and Plea Negotiations

If criminals wanted to grind justice to a halt, they could do it by banding together and all pleading not guilty. It's only because we have plea-bargaining that our criminal justice system is still in motion.

—DOROTHY WRIGHT WILSON, FORMER DEAN,
SOUTHERN CALIFORNIA LAW CENTER, 1974

Chapter Outline

Key Terms

Motion to suppress evidence

Negotiated plea

Notice-of-alibi defense

Pretrial discovery

Severance

Learning Objectives

After completing this chapter, you should be able to:

- Discuss the defendant's right to pretrial discovery.
- Explain the various motions that may be made by counsel.
- Identify and explain the importance of evidentiary motions.
- Discuss the reasons for pretrial conferences.
- Explain the rationale behind the requirement to provide notice of an alibi defense.
- Discuss the prosecutor's right to pretrial discovery.
- List and explain the issues involved in plea bargaining.

INTRODUCTION

Prior to a trial, the prosecution and defense each may request that the trial judge take some action on a particular matter. These requests are usually referred to as motions. The motion may be made orally to the judge, but in most instances, it will be in written form and filed with the appropriate court. Accompanying the motion will be an affidavit setting forth the reasons the judge should take the action requested. A copy of the motion will be furnished to the opposing side, and generally, the judge will hold a hearing on the motion during which each side may present arguments for and against it; however, not all motions are opposed. It is not mandatory that the defendant be present at these hearings in every instance, but many judges demand that the defendant be present at all proceedings. More motions are filed by the defense than by the prosecution, since more matters affect the rights of a defendant than of the prosecution. A few more prevalent motions will be discussed, but they are in no way inclusive of all motions that may be filed either before or during a trial. The sequence of the motions discussed here is not necessarily in the same order that will be taken at trial. One of the earliest motions that may be filed is for pretrial discovery.

PRETRIAL RIGHT OF DISCOVERY

The right of discovery, or inspection, is more closely related to the subject of evidence than to the procedures in the justice system. However, one of the responsibilities of the attorneys for both the prosecution and the defense is to exercise the right of discovery. The right of **pretrial discovery** in criminal matters is of comparatively recent origin. It was unknown at common law and still is not recognized in criminal matters in some states. As stated in Chapter 5, the right of discovery is the pretrial right of the adversary to inspect, review, and copy certain materials held by the opposition that are anticipated to be introduced as evidence during the trial.

Defendant's Right of Discovery

The right of pretrial discovery was created primarily for the benefit of the defendant. The theory was that the right would assist the defendant in case preparation and aid in getting a fair trial. The right would also enable the defense attorney to better cross-examine the witnesses for the prosecution and assist in impeaching witnesses who have questionable credibility. The purpose of a trial is to determine the truth of what happened in a particular case. The parties involved in a trial are not to play games or create surprises. As expressed in *People* v. *Riser*[1]:

Absent some governmental requirement that information be kept confidential for
the purposes of effective law enforcement, the state has no interest in denying
[to] the accused . . . all evidence that can throw light on issues in the case, and
in particular it has no interest in convicting on the testimony of witnesses who
have not been as rigorously cross-examined and as thoroughly impeached as the
evidence permits.

The right of pretrial discovery may come into being either by legislative action or by
appellate court decisions and may be exercised in two ways. The defense may make an oral
request to the prosecuting attorney or to the law enforcement agency involved for permission
to examine the material held in the case. The alternative method consists of a written request
by the defendant's attorney in the form of a motion to produce the evidence held by the prosecution. This motion is presented to the appropriate trial judge, who will issue an order to produce
the material for examination by the defense.

What the Defendant May Inspect

Even in those states in which the right of discovery is recognized, the material and the information that the defendant may examine vary. Some states and the federal government are
quite liberal in the matters that may be examined. Rule 16 of the Federal Rules of Criminal
Procedure is typical of the broader right of discovery by a defendant. This rule provides the
following:

. . . Upon request of the defendant the government shall permit the defendant to inspect and copy or photograph books, papers, documents, photographs, tangible objects, buildings or places, or copies or portions thereof, which are in the possession, custody or control of the government, and which are material to the preparation of his defense or are intended for use by the government as evidence in chief
at the trial, or were obtained from or belong to the defendant.

The defendant is entitled to the names and addresses of witnesses whom the government
intends to call in case preparation, as well as any record of prior felony convictions of such
witnesses. The defendant is also permitted to inspect and copy any statements made to officers
of the government as well as his or her prior criminal record.

Appendix B contains a copy of a motion for the production and inspection of evidence.

Denial of the Right of Discovery

A few states have not granted the right of pretrial discovery to a defendant in criminal matters. Those states allege that this right is a one-way street created for the defendant. It is also
alleged that the defendant already has the balance of advantages in his or her favor in a
criminal trial because the prosecution must prove the defendant guilty beyond a reasonable
doubt, and in most jurisdictions the verdict must be unanimous. The right of discovery would
be an additional advantage. Further, permitting the defendant the right of pretrial discovery
would enable him or her to secure perjured testimony and to fabricate evidence to meet the
prosecution's case. The chance of witnesses for the prosecution being intimidated is increased if the defendant learns prior to the trial the names and addresses of witnesses and the
nature of their testimony.

In states where the right of pretrial discovery is not recognized, the defendant must rely
on the preliminary hearing, when applicable, for any assistance received in case preparation.
In these instances, the defendant will probably demand a preliminary hearing even though the
defendant knows that he or she will be held for trial.

Decisions Affirming the Defendant's Constitutional Rights at Trial

Decision	Constitutional Right
Coy v. *Iowa*	Confrontation of witnesses
Duncan v. *Louisiana*	Jury trial
Gideon v. *Wainwright*	Right to counsel
Faretta v. *California*	Self-representation
Klopfer v. *North Carolina*	Speedy trial
Nebraska Press Association v. *Stuart*	Fair trial/free press
Richmond Newspapers, Inc. v. *Commonwealth of Virginia*	Public trial

Those arguing against permitting a defendant the right of discovery often quote a statement made by Judge Learned Hand in the case of *United States* v. *Garison,*[2] in which he stated the following:

> Under our criminal procedure the accused has every advantage. While the prosecution is held rigidly to the charge, he [the defendant] need not disclose the barest outline of his defense. He is immune from question or comment on his silence; he cannot be convicted when there is the least fair doubt in the minds of any one of the twelve. Why in addition he should in advance have the whole evidence against him to pick over at his leisure, and make his defense, fairly or foully, I have never been able to see. . . . Our dangers do not lie in the too little tenderness to the accused. Our procedure has been always haunted by the ghost of the innocent man convicted. It is an unreal dream. What we need to fear is the archaic formalism and the watery sentiment that obstructs, delays, and defeats the prosecution of crime.

Prosecution's Right of Pretrial Discovery

Even those states recognizing the right to pretrial discovery have granted little pretrial right of discovery to the prosecution. This trend supports the contention that the right of pretrial discovery is a one-way street. The most convincing argument against allowing pretrial discovery by the prosecution is that the right would compel the defendant to be a witness against himself or herself. Many legal scholars are at a loss to understand how furnishing the names and addresses of witnesses or the defense to be used—such as an alibi or insanity defense—would be self-incrimination, but there are state courts that have prohibited the prosecution from exercising the right of pretrial discovery upon the self-incrimination claim.

In addition to the self-incrimination allegation, the supreme court of one state has held that the prosecution must prove the defendant guilty beyond a reasonable doubt and that any discovery by the prosecution that would lessen that burden is not permissible. It is almost impossible to imagine any discovery that would not in some respect lessen the burden of the prosecution. This holding by that court has been highly criticized in legal circles as being too restrictive and without merit.

Rule 16 of the Federal Rules of Criminal Procedure grants to the government (the prosecution) almost the identical rights of pretrial discovery that are granted to the defendant. More states in the future may follow the precedent set by the federal government in granting the right of pretrial discovery to the prosecution. Several states and the federal government have adopted the requirement that a defendant advise the prosecution in advance of the trial that an alibi defense is to be used. In an alibi defense, the claim is that the accused was in another location at the time the crime was allegedly committed. This type of defense is most difficult to refute, since it usually comes late during the trial, catching the prosecution by surprise.

The requirement that this information be furnished to the prosecution upon demand has received the sanction of the U.S. Supreme Court in the case of *Williams* v. *Florida.*[3] The facts of the *Williams* case indicate that, prior to his trial for robbery, Williams filed a motion with the trial court to be excused from the requirements of the Florida Rules of Criminal Procedure. This rule requires a defendant, on written demand of the prosecuting attorney, to give notice in advance of the trial if the defendant intends to claim an alibi and to furnish the prosecuting attorney with information on the place where he or she claims to have been and with the names and addresses of the alibi witnesses. Williams, referred to as the petitioner, claimed that this rule compelled him to bear witness against himself in violation of the Fifth and Fourteenth Amendment rights. The motion was denied, and Williams was convicted and sentenced to life imprisonment. He took his case to the U.S. Supreme Court on the grounds that his constitutional rights had been violated. The Supreme Court upheld the conviction, the requirement for **notice-of-alibi defense**, and stated the following:

> Florida law provides for liberal discovery by the defendant against the State, and the notice-of-alibi rule is itself carefully hedged with reciprocal duties requiring state disclosure to the defendant. Given the ease with which an alibi can be fabricated, the State's interest in protecting itself against an eleventh hour defense is both obvious and legitimate. Reflecting this interest, notice-of-alibi provisions, dating at least from 1927, are now in existence in a substantial number of States. The adversary system of trial is hardly an end to itself; it is not yet a poker game in which players enjoy an absolute right always to conceal their cards until played. We find ample room in that system, at least as far as "due process" is concerned, for the instant Florida rule, which is designed to enhance the search for truth in the criminal trial by insuring both the defendant and the State ample opportunity to investigate certain facts crucial to the determination of guilt or innocence.
>
> Petitioner's major contention is that he was "compelled to be a witness against himself" contrary to the commands of the Fifth and Fourteenth Amendments because the notice-of-alibi rule required him to give the State the name and address of Mrs. Scotty in advance of trial and thus to furnish the State with information useful in convicting him. No pretrial statement of petitioner was introduced at trial; but armed with Mrs. Scotty's name and address and the knowledge that she was to be petitioner's alibi witness, the State was able to take her deposition in advance of trial and to find rebuttal testimony. Also, requiring him to reveal the elements of his defense is claimed to have interfered with his right to wait until after the State had presented its case to decide how to defend against it. We conclude, however, as has apparently every other court which has considered the issue, that the privilege against self-incrimination is not violated by a requirement that the defendant give notice of an alibi defense and disclose his alibi witnesses.
>
> The defendant in a criminal trial is frequently forced to testify himself and to call other witnesses in an effort to reduce the risk of conviction. When he presents his witnesses, he must reveal their identity and submit them to cross-examination which in itself may prove incriminating or which may furnish the State with leads to incriminating rebuttal evidence. That the defendant faces such a dilemma demanding a choice between complete silence and presenting a defense has never been thought an invasion of the privilege against compelled self-incrimination. The pressures generated by the State's evidence may be severe but they do not vitiate the defendant's choice to present an alibi defense and witnesses to prove it, even though the attempted defense ends in catastrophe for the defendant. However "testimonial" and "incriminating" the alibi defense proves to be, it cannot be considered "compelled" within the meaning of the Fifth and Fourteenth Amendments.

Despite the *Williams* decision, a number of states have not passed legislation requiring a defendant to notify the prosecution that he or she plans an alibi defense. Some state courts still contend that if furnishing the names and addresses of witnesses will incriminate the defendant, it is not necessary to provide them to the prosecution. Thus, the right of pretrial discovery by the prosecution is seriously curtailed.

Brady v. *Maryland* Doctrine

Excerpts from *United States* v. *Jensen*, 2011 U.S. Dist. LEXIS 36912, 28-32 (D. Alaska Apr. 5, 2011) discussing the *Brady* v. *Maryland*, 373 U.S. 83 (1963) regarding the right to discovery.

Federal Rule of Evidence 16 permits discovery that is "relevant to the development of a possible defense." *United States* v. *Clegg*, 740 F.2d 16, 18 (9th Cir. 1984). The defendant must make a prime facie showing of materiality to obtain discovery under Rule 16. Neither a general description of the information sought nor conclusory allegations of materiality suffice.

A defendant's mere speculation about materials in the government files does not require the district court under Brady to make materials available for the defendant's inspection. *United States* v. *Michaels*, 796 F.2d 1112, 1116 (9th Cir. 1986). Brady supra does not establish a "duty to provide defense counsel with unlimited discovery of everything known by the prosecutor." *United States* v. *Agurs*, 427 U.S. 97, 106, 96 S. Ct. 2392, 49 L. Ed. 2d 342 (1975).

Brady does not compel the government "to furnish the defendant with information which he already has or has, with any reasonable diligence, he can obtain himself." *United States* v. *Pelullo*, 399 F.3d 197, 213 (3rd Cir. 2005) citing *United States* v. *Campagnuolo*, 592 F.2d 852, 861 (5th Cir. 1979). In addition to the government providing an extensive number of documents, the government claims it lacks specific knowledge about the existence of favorable material evidence beyond what it has and is producing to the defendants.

The defendants' request for all government reports is overly broad. Not all government agent reports are discoverable under Federal Criminal Rule 16. An agent's evaluation of a case is his work product and not discoverable unless it specifically falls under Rule 16, the Jencks Act, or Brady/Giglio material. This includes special agent reports and 9131 reports. The defendants' mere speculation that such documents may contain references to civil liabilities is insufficient to compel their discovery. Mere speculation by the defendants does not entitle them to have documents produced on the chance that they might contain helpful information. *United States* v. *Reed*, 726 F.2d 570, 577 (9th Cir. 1984); *United States* v. *Davis*, 752 F.2d 963, 976 (5th Cir. 1985). The prosecution is not required to deliver its entire file to the defense counsel. *United States* v. *Bagley*, 473 U.S. 667, 675, 105 S. Ct. 3375, 87 L. Ed. 2d 481 (1985). Brady does not create any pretrial discovery privileges not contained in the Federal Rules of Criminal Procedure. Flores, 540 F.2d at 438.

Brady requires the disclosure of exculpatory evidence which the government is aware of and which is within its custody or control. *United States* v. *Flores*, 540 F.2d 432, 438 (9th Cir. 1976). In *United States* v. *Gordon*, 844 F.2d 1397 (9th Cir. 1988) the court cited *United States* v. *Bagley*, 473 U.S. 667, 682-685, 105 S. Ct. 3375, 87 L. Ed. 2d 481 (1985) and stated: Under Brady, the suppression by the prosecution of evidence favorable to an accused upon request violates due process where the evidence is material either to guilt or innocence. Favorable evidence includes impeachment evidence. See *Giglio* v. *United States*, 405 U.S. 150, 154, 92 S. Ct. 763, 31 L. Ed. 2d 104 (1972). Assuming the evidence is favorable (either exculpatory or as impeachment), failure to disclose only requires reversal if the evidence is material: "the evidence is material only if there is a reasonable probability that, had the evidence been disclosed to the defense, the result of the proceeding would have been different. A 'reasonable probability' is a probability sufficient to undermine confidence in the outcome." See also *United States* v. *Andersson*, 813 F.2d 1450, 1458-59 (9th Cir. 1987).

The Brady doctrine is not absolute. As stated in *United States* v. *Pollack*, 534 F.2d 964, 975, 175 U.S. App. D.C. 227 (D.C. Cir. 1976), "broad as this mandate may be, it does not require that all information concerning the government witnesses be made available to the defense." In addition with respect to alleged Brady material contained in Jencks Act statements, "disclosure is generally timely if the government complies with the Jencks Act." *United States* v. *Anderson*, 574 F.2d 1347, 1352 (5th Cir. 1978); *United States* v. *Martino*, 648 F.2d 367, 384 (5th Cir. 1981).

Under Brady, the prosecutor is charged with knowledge of the significance of the evidence in his file regardless of whether he overlooks it. *United States* v. *Agurs*, 427 U.S. 97, 96 S. Ct. 2392, 49 L. Ed. 2d 342 (1976). Whether the requested evidence is exculpatory to the issue of guilt or punishment is left in the first instance to the prosecutor. The materiality of such evidence should be judged by reference to the evidence considered collectively not piecemeal. According to the government's response, various documents and information have already been furnished to defendant.

The defendant's Due Process right to exculpatory information is independent of and supersedes the scope of discovery allowed under Rule 16. We are not considering the scope of discovery authorized by the Federal Rules of Criminal Procedure. We are dealing with the defendant's right to a fair trial mandated by the Due Process Clause. *United States* v. *DeMarco*, 407 F.Supp. 107, 111 n.2 (C.D. Cal. 1975) (fact that government memoranda are not discoverable under Rule 16 cannot qualify the government's duty under Brady. Evidence is material where it has some significant potential for actually influencing the outcome of the case. Evidence is "material" within the meaning of Brady when there is a reasonable probability that had the evidence been disclosed, the result of the proceeding would have been different. *Cone* v. *Bell*, 129 S.Ct. 1769, 173 L. Ed. 2d 701 (2009).

Motion for Reciprocal Discovery by Prosecutor

Federal Criminal Rule 16(b)(1)(A) and many state rules provide that if the defendant requests disclosure under Rule 16(a)(1)(E) or appropriate state rule and the government complies, then the defendant must permit the government, upon request, to inspect and copy a photographs, books, papers, documents, data, tangible objects, buildings or places or other copies or portions of any of these items. The request for reciprocal discovery is granted as to the items within the defendant's possession, custody, or control and the defendant intends to use the item in the defendant's case-in-chief at trial. Reciprocal discovery is triggered after partial production by the government.

MOTION TO SUPPRESS EVIDENCE

At common law, it was held that any evidence that would assist in determining the truth of what happened in a particular case was admissible during a trial. The same policy was followed in this country for a number of years in spite of the constitutional guarantee contained in the Fourth Amendment of the U.S. Constitution against unreasonable searches and seizures. In the early 1920s, a few states, either by legislation or court decisions, began to hold that unlawfully obtained evidence was not admissible during a trial in attempting to prove a defendant guilty. The inadmissibility of unlawfully obtained evidence is known as the Exclusionary Rule. In 1961, the landmark case of *Mapp* v. *Ohio*[4] placed the Exclusionary Rule in effect for all the states. Since that decision, much use has been made of the **motion to suppress evidence**.

(Title of Court)

Notice of Motion and Motion to Suppress Evidence

In the Matter of Property Cr. No. _____

Seized from (names of persons from whom the property was seized)

To (Names of all police officers known to have participated in the seizure of the property)

PLEASE TAKE NOTICE that on _____, 20 _____ at _____.m., or as soon thereafter as the matter can be heard, at the courtroom of the Criminal District Court, Parish of Orleans at _____, City of New Orleans, State of Louisiana; Defendant Jon Notguilty will move the Court for an order directing various levying officers, including the above-named, to return to the movants forthwith certain personal property, _____ a schedule of which is attached to this motion, and which on _____ 19_____, at the premises known as _____, was unlawfully seized and taken from the movants by those levying officers, and directing that the property seized be suppressed as evidence against _____ in any criminal proceeding.

This motion is made on the grounds that:

1. _____.

2. _____.

This motion is based on this notice, the pleadings, records, and files in this proceeding, the attached memorandum of points and authorities and the attached supporting declaration of _____.

Dated: _____

_____ (signed)

Attorney for Defendant

Either as a result of pretrial discovery or through the preliminary hearing, the defense may learn that the prosecution plans to introduce evidence during the trial that, in the opinion of the defense, was unlawfully acquired. This evidence may be material that the defense alleges was obtained through an unlawful search or seizure, or it may be a confession that the defense states was improperly obtained. When this occurs, the defense counsel will usually file a motion to suppress evidence with the appropriate trial court. A hearing will be held on this motion, and the prosecution will present facts and testimony in an effort to prove that the material or confession was lawfully obtained. The defense may present evidence in an effort to prove that the evidence should be suppressed or not be introduced because of illegality.

Hearing to Suppress

The hearing to suppress evidence must be held prior to the trial time in some jurisdictions; the hearing is held before a judge alone and not before a jury. If the judge concludes that the evidence was illegally obtained, he or she will suppress it or hold that it is not admissible during the trial. If the judge believes that the material was lawfully obtained, it may be introduced against the defendant during the trial, and the jury will give the evidence the weight to which they feel it is entitled.

The hearing on the motion must be made prior to the trial in some jurisdictions because it is felt that the trial judge should not be required to stop in midtrial to determine whether evidence presented by the prosecution was lawfully obtained. If the evidence is ruled inadmissible, the prosecuting attorney may decide to dismiss the charge if a conviction would not be possible without the suppressed evidence. Thus, the time and expense of a trial would be saved.

Some jurisdictions permit the defense to object to the introduction of the evidence again at the trial, and the judge may consider at that time whether the evidence is admissible. A few jurisdictions require that the motion to suppress be made prior to trial, holding that unless the motion is made prior to the trial, the defendant waives the constitutional right to object to the method of obtaining evidence. In these instances, courts have held that there is no waiver if the defendant could not have reasonably made the motion prior to the trial. A reasonable cause may be that the defendant was unaware of the allegedly illegal search or seizure or did not have reasonable time to make the motion before the trial. Other states hold that a pretrial motion to suppress evidence is premature and that the objection should take place during the trial. Pretrial motions and hearings to suppress evidence unnecessarily delay setting the case for trial, and, since an objection to the introduction of the evidence may be made again in most jurisdictions during the trial, it is a duplication of effort.

In jurisdictions where the pretrial motion to suppress is not mandatory, many defense attorneys will not file a pretrial motion. They will wait and object to the introduction of the evidence at the preliminary hearings. It is the prosecution's responsibility to present testimony in an effort to prove that the evidence was lawfully obtained. Through cross-examination by the defense and the testimony of witnesses, efforts will be made to prove that the offered evidence was unlawfully obtained. If the judge holds that the evidence was illegally obtained, the defendant will be released unless other evidence causes the judge to reasonably believe that the defendant should be held for trial. If the evidence is lawfully obtained and the defendant is held for trial, a second objection to the introduction of the evidence may be made during the trial.

Grounds for Evidence Suppression

Obtaining confessions and unreasonable searches and seizures are two areas that include numerous grounds for challenging the introduction of evidence. A confession obtained through the psychological pressure of threats or promises would be suppressed. Search warrants may be improperly issued, or permission for consent searches involuntarily may be given. An officer exceeding the permissible area on a search incident to arrest provides grounds for a motion to suppress. A sample document for a typical motion to suppress evidence appears in the accompanying illustration.

Law in Practice

Samson v. *California*, 547 U.S. 843 (2006)

Donald Curtis Samson was on state parole in California, following a conviction for being a felon in possession of a firearm. On September 6, 2002, Officer Rohleder of the San Bruno Police Department observed him walking down a street with a woman and a child. Based on a prior contact with Samson, Officer Rohleder was aware that he was on parole and believed that he was facing an at large warrant. Accordingly, Officer Rohleder stopped Samson and asked him whether he had an outstanding parole warrant. He responded that there was no outstanding warrant and that he "was in good standing with his parole agent." Officer Rohleder confirmed, by radio dispatch, that Samson was on parole and that he did not have an outstanding warrant. Based solely on Samson's status as a parolee, Officer Rohleder searched him. During the search, Officer Rohleder

found a cigarette box in his left breast pocket. Inside the box he found a plastic baggie containing methamphetamine.

How Should the Trial Judge Rule on a Motion to Suppress Based on an Alleged Illegal Search by Officer Rohleder?

JUSTICE THOMAS delivered the Court's Opinion.

California law provides that every prisoner eligible for release on state parole shall agree in writing to be subject to search or seizure by a parole officer or other peace officer at any time of the day or night, with or without a search warrant, and with or without cause. Parolees are on the continuum of state-imposed punishments. On this continuum, parolees have fewer expectations of privacy than

(continued)

probationers, because parole is more akin to imprisonment than probation is to imprisonment. Parole is an established variation on imprisonment of convicted criminals. . . . The essence of parole is release from prison, before the completion of sentence, on the condition that the prisoner abides by certain rules during the balance of the sentence. In most cases, a state is willing to extend parole only because it is able to condition it upon compliance with certain requirements. The Fourth Amendment does not render states powerless to address recidivism concerns effectively. California's ability to conduct suspicionless searches of parolees serves its interest in reducing recidivism in a manner that aids, rather than hinders, the reintegration of parolees into productive society.

A California inmate may serve his parole period either in physical custody, or elect to complete his sentence out of physical custody and subject to certain conditions. Under the latter option, an inmate-turned-parolee remains in the legal custody of the California Department of Corrections through the remainder of his term and must comply with all of the terms and conditions of parole, including mandatory drug tests, restrictions on association with felons or gang members, and mandatory meetings with parole officers. [The Court held that the search was legal.]

MOTION TO DISMISS CHARGES

After a complaint, an information, or an indictment has been filed against a defendant, facts are sometimes revealed that, in the interest of justice, demand that the charge be dismissed. In some jurisdictions, this action may be taken by the prosecuting attorney and is known as "entering a nolle prosequi." Other jurisdictions do not grant the prosecuting attorney nolle prosequi authority. In these jurisdictions, a charge may be dismissed only by a judge, by judicial motion, or upon recommendation of the prosecuting attorney.

There are many reasons a prosecuting attorney may recommend that a charge be dismissed after it is filed. The original allegation may be unfounded; the evidence to be introduced may have been unlawfully obtained, making a conviction impossible; or a material witness may no longer be available to testify. Dismissals have also been granted to a defendant to allow testimony against codefendants. The defense may file a motion to dismiss on the grounds that the indictment or information was seriously defective or that a case was not brought to trial within the prescribed time.

A dismissal by a judge on judicial or defense motion is not always a bar to further prosecutive action on the matter, particularly if the charge is a felony. The prosecuting attorney may refile the charge. How many times this action may take place is not firmly established, but the right to a speedy trial prevents too many dismissals and refilings from taking place.

MOTION FOR CONTINUANCE

Criminal cases are to be heard as soon as reasonably possible, and they are to be given precedence over civil matters. Most state codes provide that no continuance of a criminal trial shall be granted except where the ends of justice require a continuance. The codes also provide that the continuance shall not be for a period longer than justice requires. Despite these provisions, perhaps no motion is made with greater frequency than the motion for a continuance, particularly by the defense. What is within the ends of justice and how long justice requires the continuance to be are primarily within the discretion of the trial judge.

Grounds for a Continuance

There are no specified grounds on which the continuance may be based. Justice requires that a continuance be granted to obtain a material witness. But before a continuance to obtain such a witness will be granted, the side making the request must present further evidence on why the witness is material, what effort has been made to locate the witness, and why the testimony of this witness is not available through any other witness. Continuances have been granted to defendants so that they may obtain effective counsel, and they often take advantage of this opportunity. Defendants have employed counsel and then, at trial time, they have discharged counsel and requested a continuance to obtain new counsel. There are cases in which this request was made as many as ten to thirteen times. Occasionally, the defendant will have employed new counsel just prior to the trial date, and the defense counsel will make a motion for continuance on the grounds that additional time is needed to prepare the defense. Continuances have been granted when a defendant is not physically able to attend the trial or when the defense attorney is ill or engaged in another trial. The length of time a trial may be delayed for these reasons is undetermined. If the defendant is not feigning illness, the court has no alternative but to grant a continuance until the defendant recovers. But how long may defense counsel delay a trial? It has been held that unless a defense counsel is available for trial within a reasonable time, the defendant must obtain substitute counsel.

A continuance will not usually be granted for longer than thirty to sixty days. At the end of that period, a new request may be made, and frequently it is granted. As a result, many criminal trials are not heard for more than a year after the crime has been committed.

When a motion for a continuance is to be made, reasonable notice must be given to the trial judge and the opposing side. Reasonable notice is difficult to determine. Unfortunately, the notice may be given on the trial date. If a continuance is granted at that time, it is a hardship on everyone involved in the trial proceeding. It may be particularly inconvenient for witnesses who have taken time off from work and have traveled great distances to appear in court. The witnesses will have to reappear on the new date set for the trial. The defense makes these frequent requests for continuances because they usually work to the advantage of the defendant. The possibilities of prosecution witnesses' becoming unavailable and memories dulling increase with the passage of time.

MOTION FOR SEVERANCE OF OFFENSES

Criminals often commit a series of crimes in a relatively short period. For example, a burglar may commit a number of burglaries within a few days or weeks. If the burglar is caught and charged, it is logical to try the offender on all the charges at one time. Consolidating several charges into one trial saves time and expense by eliminating a separate trial for each crime. Most state laws permit a series of crimes committed in one jurisdiction to be combined into one accusatory pleading. Each of the crimes charged in the accusatory pleading is referred to as a count. Crimes must be of the same general nature to be consolidated. If the crimes are all similar, such as all burglaries or all robberies, there is no doubt about consolidating them into one accusatory pleading. It has also been held that if the crimes are of a different nature but are part of the same transaction, scheme, or plan, they may be consolidated. For example, if an offender commits a burglary and then commits arson to hide the burglary, these two offenses could be consolidated, since they are parts of the same transaction or plan. However, a crime of robbery and a crime of burglary could not be consolidated without being parts of the same transaction.

A defendant having a series of crimes consolidated into one trial has the advantage of avoiding a defense in separate trials. Yet there are times when a defendant will make a motion for a **severance** of offenses. This motion is based upon the premise that being tried on several counts during the same trial is prejudicial to the defendant. As stated in the case of *Cross* v. *United States*[5]:

> Prejudice may develop when an accused wishes to testify on one but not the other of two joined offenses which are clearly distinct in time, place and evidence. His decision whether to testify will reflect a balancing of several factors with respect to each count: the evidence against him, the availability of defense evidence other than his testimony, the plausibility and substantiality of his testimony, the possible effects of demeanor, impeachment, and cross-examination. But if the two charges are

joined for trial, it is not possible for him to weigh these factors separately as to each count. If he testifies on one count, he runs the risk that any adverse effects will influence the jury's consideration of the other count. Thus he runs the risk on both counts, although he may benefit on only one. Moreover, a defendant's silence on one count would be damaging in the face of his express denial of the other. Thus he may be coerced into testifying on the count upon which he wished to remain silent.

Also, in *Drew* v. *United States,*[6] the Court stated the following:

The justification for a liberal rule on joinder of offenses appears to be the economy of a single trial. The argument against joinder is that the defendant may be prejudiced for one or more of the following reasons: (1) he may become embarrassed or confounded in presenting separate defenses; (2) the jury, may use the evidence of one of the crimes charged to infer a criminal disposition on the part of the defendant from which is found his guilt of the other crime or crimes charged; or (3) the jury may cumulate the evidence of the various crimes charged and find guilt when, if considered separately, it would not so find. A less tangible, but perhaps equally persuasive, element of prejudice may reside in a latent feeling of hostility engendered by the charging of several crimes as distinct from only one. Thus, in any given case the court must weigh prejudice to the defendant caused by the joinder against the obviously important consideration of economy and expedition in judicial administration.

MOTION FOR SEVERANCE

The laws of most states hold that when two or more defendants are jointly charged with the same offense, they must be tried jointly unless the judge feels that in the best interest of justice separate trials should be granted. Jointly trying codefendants promotes economy and efficiency and avoids multiplicity of trials. But defendants often file a motion for severance to avoid the possibility of prejudice. The prejudice may stem from the fact that evidence against one defendant is not applicable to others, and a jury may have difficulty in separating the evidence. One defendant may have a particularly bad reputation, and a codefendant could be convicted by association. A defendant may have given a confession implicating other codefendants, and this confession is to be introduced during the trial. Under such circumstances, unless the identifying data concerning codefendants cannot be adequately deleted from the confession, they are not admissible. Otherwise, separate trials must be granted. The jury would then be expected to perform the overwhelming task of considering a confession in determining the guilt or innocence of the confessor and then ignoring the confession in determining the guilt or innocence of codefendants.[7]

Since the concern with joint trials stems principally from the fact that the jury might be prejudiced against the defendant, should a severance be granted if a jury is waived in favor of a court trial? Jurisdictions are divided on the answer to this question. Some hold that a judge is competent to separate evidence between codefendants, whether it be a confession, a testimonial, or physical evidence. Therefore, a severance of codefendants may be denied. Other jurisdictions hold that upon an allegation of prejudice, a defendant has an absolute right to a severance whether the trial is a court trial or a jury trial.

MOTION TO DETERMINE COMPETENCY

If the present mental state of the defendant is in question at any time prior to or during a trial, the defense counsel should make a motion for a hearing on competency. Insanity refers to the accused's mental state at the time of the act. Competency refers to the accused's mental state at trial time. A hearing may be ordered on the competency question if the actions of the defendant would cause doubt in the judge's mind. Competency of the defendant must be determined because a person cannot be tried, sentenced, or punished while insane. The procedure of determining competency is referred to as both a hearing and a trial. Usually the hearing is conducted before a judge sitting alone, unless the defense demands that a jury trial be held. In some states, like Texas, the accused has a right to a jury trial on the issue of competency.

The competency hearing should not be confused with a trial on a plea of not guilty by reason of insanity, as discussed later in the text. The hearing to determine the competency of the defendant has nothing to do with guilt or innocence; it ascertains the defendant's *present* mental capabilities. The test of competency determines the defendant's present ability to understand the nature and purpose of the proceedings, and it measures the capacity to assist in the defense in a rational manner. If the defendant is unable to understand the charge and possible defenses and is also unable properly to confer with counsel in regard to the conduct of the trial, the trial should not take place. The test to determine competency is not the same as that used in a trial on a plea of not guilty by reason of insanity.

Once the competency of the defendant is questioned, all prosecutive proceedings must be halted until the issue of competency can be determined. The next step is the competency hearing or trial. Prior to the hearing, the defendant will normally be examined by psychologists or psychiatrists appointed by the court and by those selected by the defense, if desired. During the hearing, these specialists and any other witnesses able to shed light on the defendant's competency may be called to testify. If the prosecution thinks that the defendant is presently able to defend himself or herself, evidence may be offered in an effort to prove that the defendant is competent. If determined incompetent, the defendant may be confined to a mental hospital until recovery. There is no formal procedure to determine that the defendant has recovered his or her competency other than certification to that effect by the hospital superintendent. After the defendant has recovered, he or she will be brought back for trial unless the recovery period is extensive and the charge has been dismissed in the interest of justice.

If the competency hearing determines that the defendant is presently sane, the prosecutive proceedings will commence again from the point where they stopped. This is the case unless the trial on guilt or innocence was in progress and the trial judge dismissed the jury and declared a mistrial. Under those circumstances, the trial would be resumed from the beginning with a new jury. Various other motions will be discussed as the trial proceedings unfold.

PRETRIAL CONFERENCE

Pretrial conferences in civil matters have been effectively used for years. These conferences are informal meetings, usually in the judge's chambers, between both attorneys and the judge. The strong and weak points of the case are discussed in an effort to arrive at a settlement without going to trial. With court calendars becoming more and more crowded, greater use is being made of the pretrial conference in criminal matters. As the trial date approaches, the trial judge will often call for a pretrial conference. During this conference, the judge will determine whether both sides will be ready for trial on the date set or if a continuance will be requested. The judge will also try to ascertain the approximate number of days each side anticipates taking to present its case. By gathering this information, the judge will be better able to set other cases for trial and decide whether alternate jurors should be selected.

The attorneys may try to arrive at some sequence in calling witnesses, particularly professional persons or expert witnesses. The attorneys will attempt to agree, or to stipulate, to certain testimony. There are advantages to each side in stipulating to certain facts that a witness may present if called to testify. The stipulation may concern some uncontroversial matter when the presentation of proof during the trial would be of little consequence—thus saving trial time. The stipulation of some fact that the prosecution can prove convincingly may be to the advantage of the defense because it prevents a witness from going into great detail to the detriment of the defendant. Those facts having a stipulation are brought to the attention of the jury at the appropriate time, and the jury considers those facts as though they had been presented in testimony during the trial. The presentation of facts by stipulation does not violate the defendant's right of confrontation, since the defendant has waived his or her right of confrontation of that particular witness, or witnesses, by agreeing to the facts.

PLEA NEGOTIATION

Plea negotiating, or plea bargaining, as it is more commonly known, is nothing more than agreement between the prosecuting attorney and the defense to reduce a charge to a lesser crime, to drop certain charges, or to receive a lessened sentence in return for a guilty or nolo contendere plea. Plea negotiating usually takes place shortly after the initial appearance or the arraignment of a defendant. In most jurisdictions, the negotiating can continue up to the time that the verdict is rendered. Plea negotiating is often discussed during the pretrial conference. Although it has been held that the judge should not be a part of the negotiation, he or she should be made aware of it, and in many instances must, by law, accept the conditions of the plea bargaining before the guilty or nolo contendere plea is acceptable.

Plea bargaining has been both praised and criticized. Some allege that plea bargaining is important in the administration of criminal law, is advantageous to the state by saving time and money, and increases efficiency and flexibility in the criminal process. The advantage to the defendant is reduced punishment. Plea bargaining has been criticized, particularly by some law enforcement officers, because it allows a criminal to take advantage of the justice system by not being convicted and sentenced for the crime actually committed. The result is a much lighter penalty.

Benefits of Plea Bargaining

Although the practice of accepting negotiated pleas has been criticized, many prosecuting attorneys state that the acceptance of a negotiated plea often is for more justifiable reasons than lightening caseloads and clearing crowded court calendars. Sometimes an offender is initially charged on a *more serious* crime than is warranted by the evidence. Or an offender may be charged with a more serious crime so that a higher bail will be set. Reducing the number of charges in exchange for a negotiated plea may be justified on the grounds that many judges tend to give concurrent sentences. There would be little advantage in going to trial on a larger number of charges over accepting a plea on a reduced number. As to accepting a negotiated plea on the promise of a lighter sentence, prosecutors point out that they have little or no control over the sentence that may be given one convicted of a crime. Even if the accused were convicted as a result of a trial, the sentence could be the same as that agreed to in the negotiated plea.

In the past, plea bargaining was not discussed openly since it was considered to be unethical, if not illegal. Judges seldom were aware of any agreements made by plea bargaining because, to be valid, a guilty or nolo contendere plea had to be freely and voluntarily given. If the plea was induced upon a promise of leniency, there was a question of its being freely and voluntarily given. The secrecy of plea bargaining was eliminated by legislative action and court decisions, and today plea bargaining is openly engaged in as part of the justice system.

Supreme Court and Plea Bargaining

Much of the change in viewpoint was brought about by the case of *Brady* v. *United States,*[8] in which the U.S. Supreme Court gave sanction to plea bargaining. The facts of the case show that Brady was charged with a kidnapping violation and faced a maximum penalty of death if the verdict of the jury should so recommend. Brady entered a plea of guilty to the charge and was sentenced to thirty years' imprisonment. The case was taken to the U.S. Supreme Court upon the grounds that the plea was not freely and voluntarily given because of representations of a reduction of sentence and clemency. Brady alleged that this inducement was compelling him to be a witness against himself in violation of the Fifth Amendment to the U.S. Constitution. The Supreme Court concluded that the guilty plea "was voluntarily and knowingly made" even though it may have been induced by representations with respect to reduction of sentence and clemency, and, as such, Brady's guarantee against self-incrimination had not been violated.

The Court in this decision stated the following:

> . . . That a guilty plea is a grave and so solemn act to be accepted only with care and discernment has long been recognized. Central to the plea and the foundation for entering judgment against the defendant is the defendant's admission in open court that he committed the acts charged in the indictment. He thus stands as a witness against himself and he is shielded by the Fifth Amendment from being compelled to do so, hence the minimum requirement that his plea be the voluntary expression of his own choice.

The voluntariness of Brady's plea can be determined only by considering all of the relevant circumstances surrounding it. One of these circumstances was the possibility of a heavier sentence following a guilty verdict after a trial. It may be that Brady, faced with a strong case against him and recognizing that his chances for acquittal were slight, preferred to plead guilty and thus limit the penalty to life imprisonment rather than to elect a jury trial, which could result in a death penalty.

The state to some degree encourages pleas of guilty at every important step in the criminal process. For some people, their breach of a state's law is alone sufficient reason for surrendering themselves and accepting punishment. For others, apprehension and charge, both threatening acts by the government, jar them into admitting their guilt. In still other cases, the postindictment accumulation of evidence may convince the defendant and his counsel that a trial is not worth the agony and expense to the defendant and his or her family. All these pleas of guilty are valid in spite of the state's responsibility for some of the factors motivating the pleas; the pleas are no more improperly compelled than is the decision by a defendant at the close of the state's evidence at trial that he or she must take the stand or face certain conviction.

Of course, the agents of the state may not produce a plea by actual or threatened physical harm or by mental coercion overbearing the will of the defendant. But nothing of the sort is claimed in this case; nor is there evidence that Brady was so gripped by fear of the death penalty or hope of leniency that he did not or could not, with the help of counsel, rationally weigh the advantages of going to trial against the advantages of pleading guilty.

The issue we deal with is inherent in the criminal law and its administration, because guilty pleas are not constitutionally forbidden, because the criminal law characteristically extends to the judge or jury a range of choices in setting the sentence in individual cases, and because both the state and the defendant often find it advantageous to preclude the possibility of the maximum penalty authorized by law. For a defendant who sees little possibility of acquittal, the advantages of pleading guilty and limiting the probable penalty are obvious—his or her exposure is reduced, the correctional processes can begin immediately, and the practical burdens of a trial are eliminated. For the state, there are advantages: the more promptly imposed punishment after an admission of guilt may more effectively attain the objectives of punishment; and with the avoidance of trial, scarce judicial and prosecutorial resources are conserved for those cases in which there is a substantial issue of the defendant's guilt or in which there is substantial doubt that the state can sustain its burden of proof. It is this mutuality of advantage that perhaps explains the fact that at present, well over three-fourths of the criminal convictions in this country rest on pleas of guilty, a great many of them no doubt motivated at least in part by the hope or assurance of a lesser penalty than might be imposed if there were a guilty verdict after a trial to judge or jury.

Of course, that the prevalence of guilty pleas is explainable does not necessarily validate those pleas or the system that produces them. But we cannot hold that it is unconstitutional for the state to extend a benefit to a defendant who in turn extends a substantial benefit to the state and who demonstrates by his or her plea that the defendant is ready and willing to admit his or her crime and to enter the correctional system in a frame of mind that affords hope for success in rehabilitation over a shorter period of time than might otherwise be necessary.

The Court further stated that even if a guilty plea were entered through some inducement of leniency, that plea could not be withdrawn at a later date if the plea had been freely and voluntarily given. The standard of voluntariness of a guilty plea was set forth in the *Brady* decision, which is as follows:

> A plea of guilty entered by one fully aware of the direct consequences, including the actual value of any commitments made to him by the court, prosecutor, or his own counsel, must stand unless induced by threats or promises to discontinue improper harassment, misrepresentation including unfulfilled or unfulfillable promises, or perhaps by promises that are by their nature improper as having no proper relationship to the prosecutor's business (e.g., bribes).

Generally, before a negotiated plea is accepted, the judge and the prosecuting attorney must agree on the terms involved. Some judges have held that they may accept a negotiated plea without the concurrence of the prosecution and may even accept such a plea over the objections of the prosecutor. This contention is based on the fact that a judge may accept an *unnegotiated plea* without the consent or concurrence of the prosecutor; therefore, it is believed that the judge may accept a **negotiated plea** without the consent of the prosecutor.

Pleas to Be Related to the Offense Charged

It has been held that a negotiated plea should be related to the crime charged in the accusatory pleading, but the plea does not have to be confined to the one in the accusatory pleading. The negotiated plea may be to a lesser offense than the one in the accusatory pleading. For example, a defendant may be charged in the pleading with the crime of murder but may be permitted to plead guilty to voluntary manslaughter. The plea to the offense of voluntary manslaughter would be a plea to a related crime of murder. It is also held that if the negotiated plea is to a crime committed in the course of conduct that leads to the charge in the accusatory pleading, this plea would be to a related crime. For example, during the course of a robbery, the defendant may take the victim from his or her home to his or her place of business to open a safe. The defendant may be charged in the accusatory pleading with kidnapping, but may be permitted to plead guilty to robbery. This would be a related crime, since the robbery offense was in the course of conduct that led to the kidnapping charge. It is important that the negotiated plea be to a related crime so that the plea will more nearly reflect the true history of the crime for which the defendant was arrested. Often if the accused is awaiting trial on two or more separate unrelated indictments, the plea bargain will include an agreement to dismiss the other indictments.

Statutory Prohibitions Against Plea Bargaining

Some states, like California, prohibit plea bargaining on serious felonies except under limited circumstances. For example, California Penal Code Section 1192.7(a) prohibits plea bargaining in any case in which it is alleged that a firearm was used by the defendant or in any offense of driving while under the influence of alcohol or controlled substances, unless there is insufficient evidence to prove the people's case, it is necessary to obtain the testimony of a material witness, or a reduction or dismissal would not result in a substantial change in the sentence.

Withdrawal of the Negotiated Plea

A guilty plea may be withdrawn if the bargain is not complied with by either the judge or the prosecuting attorney. The statutes of those states where negotiated pleas have been enacted usually provide that a negotiated plea of guilty or nolo contendere must be approved by both the judge and the prosecuting attorney. If the approval is not forthcoming, the defendant is permitted to withdraw the plea of guilty or nolo contendere and to enter another plea. Once the approval is given, the bargain must be complied with, or the defendant may also withdraw the guilty or nolo contendere plea. This is true even though the defendant may not have been entirely honest in dealing with the court. In *People* v. *Johnson,*[9] for a negotiated plea of guilty, the judge promised the defendant that the matter would be handled as a misdemeanor rather than as a felony and that the defendant would be given probation. After discovering that the defendant had concealed his true identity and past criminal record, the judge sentenced the defendant to the state prison.

Notable U.S. Supreme Court Cases on the Regulation of Plea Bargaining

Case	Decision
Boykin v. *Alabama* (1969)	The defendant must make an affirmative statement that the plea is voluntary before the judge can accept it.
Brady v. *United States* (1970)	Avoiding the possibility of the death penalty is not grounds to invalidate a guilty plea.
North Carolina v. *Alford* (1970)	Accepting a guilty plea from a defendant who maintains his or her innocence is valid.
Santobello v. *New York* (1971)	The promise of a prosecutor that rests on a guilty plea must be kept in a plea bargaining agreement.
Bordenkircher v. *Hayes* (1978)	A defendant's constitutional rights are not violated when a prosecutor threatens to reindict the accused on more serious charges if he or she is not willing to plead guilty to the original offense.
Hill v. *Lockhart* (1985)	To prove the ineffectiveness of defense counsel, the defendant needs to show a reasonable probability that, except for counsel's errors, the defendant would not have pleaded guilty.
Ricketts v. *Adamson* (1987)	The defendant is required to keep his or her side of the bargain to receive the promised offer of leniency, because plea bargaining rests on an agreement between the parties.
United States v. *Mezzanatto* (1995)	A defendant who wants to plea bargain in federal court can be required to agree that, if he or she testifies at trial, his or her statements during the plea bargain negotiations can be used against him or her.

Source: Adapted from Norvill Morris, "Insanity Defense," Crime File, National Institute of Justice, U.S. Department of Justice (Washington, DC, undated).

Upon appeal, the judgment was reversed, and the trial court was directed to permit the defendant to withdraw the guilty plea and enter a new plea. The appellate court relied upon the state statute providing that "where such plea [negotiated plea] is accepted by the prosecuting attorney in open court and is approved by the court, the defendant . . . cannot be sentenced on such plea to a punishment more severe than that specified in the plea." The statute further provided that if the court approves the plea, the defendant, before accepting it, must be informed that the court might withdraw the approval in light of other consideration of the matter. In such a case, the defendant shall have the right to withdraw the plea if so desired.

In the *Johnson* case, the judge failed to inform the defendant of his right to withdraw the plea. During the argument before the state supreme court in this case, Johnson's attorney requested that, since the trial judge erred, the Supreme Court should give Johnson the alternative of either enforcing the original bargain or withdrawing his plea. The Court held that since there was a serious misrepresentation by Johnson, it was reluctant to create a right, for a defendant, to a specific performance of an original plea bargain rather than permit a withdrawal of the plea of guilty.

Law in Practice

Psychological Report on the Issue of Insanity

Set forth here is an actual copy of a psychological report entered into evidence by a defense counsel in an attempt to establish that the defendant lacked competency to stand trial. (Note: Jury found a lack of competency in this case. The "TDC" referred to in the report is the Texas Department of Corrections.)

July 18, 2001

Competency to Stand Trial

NAME: Richard Cole Masters

DOB: 12/10/58

DATE OF EVALUATION: 06/29/2001

CAUSE NO.: 12,943

Presenting Problem

Richard was referred for competency and sanity evaluations in connection with an alleged aggravated assault on another inmate which occurred on 3/31/01, and which ultimately led to the death of the victim. The assault occurred in a day room at Skyview and was witnessed by numerous staff and inmates. Richard has a very extensive history of mental health and disciplinary problems while in TDC, including serious assaultiveness. He has been evaluated extensively and given many courses of psychiatric treatment, including treatment with antipsychotic, anti-seizure, and antidepressant medications. His TDC record documents extensive refusal of treatment. Aside from obvious antisocial personality symptoms, Richard's most common diagnosis has been paranoid schizophrenia; and his TDC medical record is replete with references to psychotic functioning. His TDC record includes frequent observations of his having played with feces, but there have also been incidents in which he uses feces or urine as an aggressive instrument—as when

on 10/5/00 he set up a cup of urine to fall on a guard's head when the guard came to give medication.

Evaluation Methods

Richard's TDC medical record was reviewed prior to the evaluation and he was given a mental status exam on 6/26/01. It was intended to do cognitive and personality testing but the interview was ended prematurely by the inmate. The Internal Affairs Division offense report with multiple witness statements was reviewed.

Prior to any interviewing, Richard's *Miranda* rights were reviewed as well as my connection to Inmate Legal Services and the disposition of a report of the evaluation. Richard did agree to proceed with the evaluation but focused his attention very aggressively and in a suspicious manner on the examiner's role; and Richard could never be worked out of this stance so that the cognitive and personality testing could proceed.

The total time spent face to face with the inmate was thirty-five minutes.

Findings

Richard is viewed as clearly not competent to stand trial on the charges against him. His mental status is so extremely poor that he cannot relate to someone who is even on his side of things. He is consistently aggressive and intrusive to the point where this completely disrupts even a superficial relationship. His behavior is viewed as quite unmanageable. His view of his involvement in the charged offense is highly distorted and shows little relationship to the witness[es'] statements, in so far as Richard was even able to comment on that event. He stated, "I believe someone is making a big issue out of nothing." He stated he has not been appointed a lawyer, and when the incident was raised with him for discussion he said, "They have not a witness."

Richard was incapable of understanding the role of the examiner in this evaluation and it is likely he will be confused and highly suspicious about a relationship with his defense attorney. He seemed unconcerned with the seriousness of the charges against him. He is so hypervigilant [that] it is unlikely [that] he would disclose all relevant material to his attorney. He is viewed as not capable of testifying effectively for his defense in his own behalf. His actions were clearly and consistently self-protective and self-justifying but were completely self-defeating in nature because of his extreme aggressiveness and distortion. These distortions are not viewed as psychotic but as merely very self-serving. Richard's presentation at this evaluation is consistent with his presentation when visited by his attorney who noted the following: that Richard had to be manipulated with food even to agree to see the attorney, that Richard said the attorney had no right to talk to him, and that Richard refused to talk with him. After review of his TDC record it is likely he will become competent for a reasonable period of time only if he is consistently on psychotropic medication.

(signed)

CASE LAW

Recent Cases

Brady v. *Maryland* 373 U.S. 83 (1963)

Brady and a companion were convicted of first-degree murder and were sentenced to death by a Maryland trial court. The U.S. Supreme Court granted certiorari to consider whether Brady was denied a federal right when the appeals court restricted its grant of a new murder trial to the question of punishment, leaving the determination of guilt undisturbed.

The Supreme Court held that suppression of evidence favorable to an accused upon request violated the Due Process Clause of the Fourteenth Amendment, where the evidence was material to guilt or punishment, regardless of the state's good or bad faith. The suppression of evidence violated Brady's due process rights and required a retrial on the sentence.

DA's Office v. *Osborne,* 129 S. Ct. 2308 (U.S. 2009)

William Osborne and another person were convicted of kidnapping, assault, and sexual assault after they forced a prostitute to perform sexual intercourse and choked her, beat her, and shot her when she tried to flee.

Osborne sought postconviction relief in an Alaska court, claiming that he received ineffective assistance of counsel because his counsel did not seek restriction-fragment-length-polymorphism DNA testing on sperm found in a condom at the scene of the crime; however, the state court denied relief. After the state court denied relief, Osborne filed an action in federal district court, seeking an order requiring an Alaska district attorney's office to give him access to evidence that was introduced at his trial so he could have DNA tests conducted at his expense.

The U.S. Supreme Court held that the court of appeals erred when it found that the inmate had a right under the Due Process Clause of the Fourteenth Amendment to have access to the evidence he sought. The issue of access to DNA evidence postconviction was best left to Congress and state legislatures, and there was nothing inadequate about the procedures Alaska provided to inmates.

The Court noted that DNA testing alone does not always resolve a case. Where there is enough other incriminating evidence and an explanation for the DNA result, science alone cannot prove a prisoner innocent. The availability of technologies not available at trial cannot mean that every criminal conviction, or even every criminal conviction involving biological evidence, is suddenly in doubt. The dilemma is how to harness DNA's power to prove innocence without unnecessarily overthrowing the established system of criminal justice. That task belongs primarily to the legislature.

The Court also noted that criminal defendant proved guilty after a fair trial does not have the same liberty interests as a free man. At trial, the defendant is presumed innocent and may demand that the government prove its case beyond reasonable doubt. But once a defendant has been afforded a fair trial and convicted of the offense for which he was charged, the presumption of innocence disappears. Given a valid conviction, the criminal defendant has been constitutionally deprived of his liberty. The State accordingly has more flexibility in deciding what procedures are needed in the context of postconviction relief. When a State chooses to offer help to those seeking relief from convictions, due process does not dictate the exact form such assistance must assume.

Briefly Noted

Padilla **v.** *Kentucky,* **130 S. Ct. 1473 (U.S. 2010).** The defendant Jose Padilla was a lawful permanent resident of the United States who pleaded guilty to transporting marijuana. His crime was a removable offense (subject to deportation) under 8 U.S.C.S. § 1227 (a)(2)(B)(i). He claimed that his counsel incorrectly told him prior to entry of his plea that he did not have to worry about immigration status because he had been in the United States for so long.

The state court held that the Sixth Amendment did not protect defendant from erroneous advice about deportation because it was merely a collateral consequence of his conviction.

The Supreme Court held that the distinction between collateral and direct consequences was ill suited to the deportation context, so advice regarding deportation was not categorically removed from the ambit of the Sixth Amendment. Counsel's alleged failure to correctly advise defendant of the deportation consequences of his guilty plea amounted to constitutionally deficient assistance under prevailing professional norms, as the consequences could easily have been determined from reading the removal statute.

United States **v.** *Coon,* **2010 U.S. Dist. LEXIS 118436 (W.D.N.Y. Nov. 8, 2010).** Although there is no general constitutional right to pretrial discovery in a federal criminal case, a defendant does have a pretrial discovery right with respect to certain matters. For example, under the Fifth Amendment's Due Process Clause, a defendant is entitled to specific exculpatory evidence which is material either to guilt or punishment. In addition, the government has certain disclosure obligations under Rule 16 of the Federal Rules of Criminal Procedure and the Jencks Act, 18 U.S.C. § 3500.

Summary

- Both the prosecutor and the defense have a right to pretrial discovery.
- The right of discovery was originally created primarily for the benefit of the defendant.
- There are limitations on what the defendant or defense may inspect.
- The defense has no right to look at the prosecutor's work product.
- The defense has no right to examine the prosecutor's trial folder.
- In a few states where the defendant's pretrial right of discovery is not recognized, the defendant must rely on the preliminary hearing for any assistance received in trial preparation.
- In federal trials, the prosecutor has an almost identical right to pretrial discovery.
- A motion to suppress evidence is used to determine the admissibility of evidence prior to trial.

- Whether to grant a motion for a continuance rests with the trial judge.
- There are no specified grounds on which a continuance may be based. Justice may require that a continuance be granted to obtain a material witness.
- A motion for the severance of offenses or defendants must be made before the start of the trial.
- If the mental state of the defendant is in question, during the pretrial the defense may request a competency hearing.
- A plea bargain is an agreement between the prosecutor and the defense.
- The Supreme Court has sanctioned plea bargaining.
- In some states, like California, there are statutory restrictions on plea bargaining.
- A guilty plea based on a plea bargain may be withdrawn if the bargain is not complied with.

Review Questions

1. What is the right of discovery?
2. What is the theory behind the right of discovery as it relates to the defendant?
3. In general, what may the defendant expect by exercising his or her right of discovery?
4. What reasons have been presented by some states in denying the defendant the right of discovery?

5. What is the chief argument against permitting the prosecution the right of discovery?
6. In relation to the right of discovery by the prosecution, what was the significance of the *Williams* v. *Florida* decision?
7. In general, what is the chief argument presented by the defense in support of a motion to suppress evidence?

8. Explain the significance of the Exclusionary Rule on the admissibility of evidence.
9. List two reasons for granting a trial continuance.
10. List the advantages and disadvantages of granting a motion to separate offenses.
11. What is the primary purpose of a motion to determine the present sanity of an accused?

12. What is the purpose of the pretrial conference?
13. What is a negotiated plea?
14. What are some of the advantages and disadvantages in plea bargaining?

Local Procedure

1. Is the defendant granted the right of discovery in your state?
2. Is the prosecution afforded any right of discovery? If so, to what extent?

3. At what point must the motion to suppress evidence be made during a criminal proceeding?

Endnotes

1. 47 Cal. 2d 566 (1956).
2. 291 F. 646 (1923).
3. 399 U.S. 78 (1970).
4. 367 U.S. 643 (1961).
5. 335 F.2d. 987 (1964).

6. 331 F. 2D. 85 (1964).
7. *Burton* v. *United States,* 391 U.S. 123 (1968).
8. 397 U.S. 742 (1970).
9. 12 Cal. Rptr. 556 (1974).

CHAPTER 10

Courtroom Evidence

*"Give me your evidence," said the King "and don't be nervous, or I'll have you executed
on the spot."*

—LEWIS CARROLL, *ALICE'S ADVENTURES IN WONDERLAND*, 1865

Chapter Outline

Introduction

Hearsay Rule

Rulings on Evidence

Judicial Notice

Relevant Evidence

Rape Shield Laws

Witnesses

Documents

Case Law

Summary

Key Terms

Character evidence

Daubert test

Declarant

Hearsay

Impeachment

Judicial notice

Lay witness

Limited admissibility

Preliminary questions

Rape shield laws

Relevant evidence

Learning Objectives

After completing this chapter, you should be able to:

- Summarize the rules for presenting
  evidence during a trial.

- Explain what constitutes hearsay
  testimony.

- Describe the purposes of the Rules of Evidence.
- Identify and discuss the various rulings on evidence.
- Understand the concept of judicial notice.
- Demonstrate how documents are introduced into evidence.
- Explain what constitutes relevant evidence.
- Discuss the concept of fairness as it relates to the admissibility of evidence.
- Explain the difference between lay and expert witnesses.

INTRODUCTION

The study of evidence is a study of regulation of the process of proving facts. Evidence law was originally almost entirely decisional law. Now it is codified in statutes and court rules. In this chapter, we will examine evidence based on the Federal Rules of Evidence. The Federal Rules did not depart significantly from the common law decisions. Most state rules of evidence are based on the Federal Rules, with only slight differences among the states. Evidence is a very complex and difficult subject for attorneys in law school. In this chapter, we will cover only the highlights to acquaint the readers with the subject.

Evidentiary rules should be construed in a manner to attempt to secure fairness in administration, elimination of unjustifiable expense and delay, and promotion of growth and development of the law of evidence to the end that the truth may be ascertained and proceedings justly determined.

The two basic themes found in the Federal Rules are:

- The Rules favor admissibility of evidence.
- The trial judge has considerable discretion as to the admissibility of evidence.

A trial judge has the authority (discretion) to fashion evidentiary procedures to deal with situations not specifically covered by the rules. In interpreting the Rules, it is important for judges to differentiate when Congress or the legislatures have spoken and finally determined an issue and when they have left room for judicial interpretation. As the Third Circuit Court of Appeals stated in *United States* v. *Pelullo,*[1] while the Rules "are to be liberally construed in favor of admissibility, this does not mean that we may ignore requirements of specific provisions merely because we view the proffered evidence as trustworthy."

Federal Rule 102 establishes a principle of flexibility in the application of the Federal Rules of Evidence. Most states have a similar rule. The U.S. Supreme Court has stated that judicial flexibility has no place when the "plain meaning" of a Federal Rule of Evidence mandates a certain result. However, cases such as *Daubert* v. *Merrell Dow Pharmaceuticals Inc.*[2] and *United States* v. *Mezzanatto*[3] indicate that the Supreme Court is sometimes willing to employ a more flexible approach than a rigid adherence to plain meaning would seem to allow.

HEARSAY RULE

Evidentiary Definitions

STATEMENT A **statement** is (1) an oral or written assertion or (2) nonverbal conduct of a person if it is intended by the person as an assertion.

DECLARANT A **declarant** is a person who makes a statement.

HEARSAY Hearsay is a statement, other than one made by the declarant while testifying at the trial or hearing, offered in evidence to prove the truth of the matter asserted.

A statement is not hearsay if

- The declarant testifies at the trial or hearing and is subject to cross-examination concerning the statement, and the statement is (a) inconsistent with the declarant's testimony and was given under oath subject to the penalty of perjury at a trial, hearing, or other proceeding, or in a deposition, or (b) consistent with the declarant's testimony and is offered to rebut an express or implied charge against the declarant of recent fabrication or improper influence or motive, or (c) one of identification of a person made after perceiving the person; or
- Admission by a party-opponent. The statement is offered against a party and is (a) the party's own statement in either an individual or a representative capacity or (b) a statement of which the party has manifested an adoption or belief in its truth, or (c) a statement by a person authorized by the party to make a statement concerning the subject, or (d) a statement by the party's agent or servant concerning a matter within the scope of the agency or employment, made during the existence of the relationship, or (e) a statement by a coconspirator of a party during the course and in furtherance of the conspiracy. The contents of the statement shall be considered but are not alone sufficient to establish the declarant's authority under subdivision (c), the agency or employment relationship and scope thereof under subdivision (d), or the existence of the conspiracy and the participation therein of the declarant and the party against whom the statement is offered under subdivision (e).

General Rule on Hearsay

Hearsay is inadmissible unless an exception is applicable. Exceptions to the hearsay rule include:

- Affidavits to show grounds for issuing warrants.
- Affidavits to determine issues of fact in connection with motions.
- A statement describing or explaining an event or condition made while the declarant was perceiving the event or condition or immediately thereafter.
- A statement relating to a startling event or condition made while the declarant was under the stress of excitement caused by the event or condition.
- A statement of the declarant's then existing state of mind, emotion, sensation, or physical condition (such as intent, plan, motive, design, mental feeling, pain, and bodily health), but not including a statement of memory or belief to prove the fact remembered or believed unless it relates to the execution, revocation, identification, or terms of the declarant's will.
- Statements made for purposes of medical diagnosis or treatment and describing the medical history, or past or present symptoms, pain, or sensations, or the inception or general character of the cause or external source thereof insofar as is reasonably pertinent to diagnosis or treatment.
- A memorandum or record concerning a matter about which a witness once had knowledge but now has insufficient recollection to enable the witness to testify fully and accurately, shown to have been made or adopted by the witness when the matter was fresh in the witness' memory and to reflect that knowledge correctly. If admitted, the memorandum or record may be read into evidence but may not itself be received as an exhibit unless offered by an adverse party.
- A memorandum, report, record, or data compilation, in any form, of acts, events, conditions, opinions, or diagnoses, made at or near the time by, or from information transmitted by, a person with knowledge, if kept in the course of a regularly conducted business activity, and if it was the regular practice of that business activity to make the memorandum, report, record, or data compilation. The term "business" includes a business, institution, association, profession, occupation, and calling of every kind, whether or not conducted for profit.

- Evidence that a matter is not included in the memoranda reports, records, or data compilations, in any form, to prove the nonoccurrence or nonexistence of the matter, if the matter was of a kind of which a memorandum, report, record, or data compilation was regularly made and preserved, unless the sources of information or other circumstances indicate lack of trustworthiness.

- Records, reports, statements, or data compilations, in any form, of public offices or agencies, setting forth (a) the activities of the office or agency, or (b) matters observed pursuant to duty imposed by law as to which matters there was a duty to report, excluding, however, in criminal cases matters observed by police officers and other law enforcement personnel, or (c) in civil actions and proceedings and against the government in criminal cases, factual findings resulting from an investigation made pursuant to authority granted by law, unless the sources of information or other circumstances indicate lack of trustworthiness.

- Records of vital statistics. Records or data compilations, in any form, of births, fetal deaths, deaths, or marriages, if the report thereof was made to a public office pursuant to requirements of law.

- Absence of a public record or entry. To prove the absence of a record, report, statement, or data compilation, in any form, or the nonoccurrence or nonexistence of a matter of which a record, report, statement, or data compilation, in any form, was regularly made and preserved by a public office or agency, evidence in the form of a certification in accordance with Rule 902, or testimony, that diligent search failed to disclose the record, report, statement, or data compilation, or entry.

- Records of religious organizations. Statements of births, marriages, divorces, deaths, legitimacy, ancestry, relationship by blood or marriage, or other similar facts of personal or family history contained in a regularly kept record of a religious organization. Marriage, baptismal, and similar certificates. Statements of fact contained in a certificate that the maker performed a marriage or other ceremony or administered a sacrament, made by a clergyman, public official, or other person authorized by the rules or practices of a religious organization or by law to perform the act certified, and purporting to have been issued at the time of the act or within a reasonable time thereafter.

- Family records. Statements of fact concerning personal or family history contained in family Bibles, genealogies, charts, engravings on rings, inscriptions on family portraits, engravings on urns, crypts, or tombstones, or the like.

- Statements in ancient documents. Statements in a document in existence twenty years or more, the authenticity of which is established.

- Judgment of previous conviction. Evidence of a final judgment, entered after a trial or upon a plea of guilty (but not upon a plea of nolo contendere), judging a person guilty of a crime punishable by death or imprisonment in excess of one year, to prove any fact essential to sustain the judgment, but not including, when offered by the government in a criminal prosecution for purposes other than impeachment, judgments against persons other than the accused. The pendency of an appeal may be shown but does not affect admissibility.

The following are not excluded by the hearsay rule if the declarant is unavailable as a witness:

1. **Former testimony.** Testimony given as a witness at another hearing of the same or a different proceeding, or in a deposition taken in compliance with law in the course of the same or another proceeding, if the party against whom the testimony is now offered, or, in a civil action or proceeding, a predecessor in interest, had an opportunity and similar motive to develop the testimony by direct, cross, or redirect examination.

Law in Practice

Davis v. *Washington*, 547 U.S. 813 (2006)

Defendant challenged his conviction, arguing that testimony by a 911 operator about a caller identifying him as her assailant was inadmissible hearsay.

How Would You Rule on This Question?

Decision by JUSTICE SCALIA.

The statement identifying defendant during the 911 call was not "testimonial." A 911 call was not designed to establish or prove past facts, but to describe circumstances requiring police assistance. The caller spoke about events as they were actually occurring while facing an ongoing emergency, rather than describing past events. The elicited statements were necessary to resolve the emergency rather than to investigate events.

Miami Herald, March 2, 2007, p. 3B, Col. 1

2. **Statement under belief of impending death.** In a prosecution for homicide or in a civil action or proceeding, a statement made by a declarant while believing that the declarant's death was imminent, concerning the cause or circumstances of what the declarant believed to be impending death.
3. **Statement against interest.** A statement which was at the time of its making so far contrary to the declarant's pecuniary or proprietary interest, or so far tended to subject the declarant to civil or criminal liability, or to render invalid a claim by the declarant against another, that a reasonable person in the declarant's position would not have made the statement unless he or she believed it to be true. A statement tending to expose the declarant to criminal liability and offered to exculpate the accused is not admissible unless corroborating circumstances clearly indicate the trustworthiness of the statement.

RULINGS ON EVIDENCE

Rulings on evidence cannot be assigned as error unless (1) a substantial right is affected and (2) the nature of the error was called to the attention of the judge, to alert him or her to the proper course of action and enable opposing counsel to take proper corrective measures. The objection and the offer of proof are the techniques for accomplishing these objectives. An exception to this requirement is the plain error rule. Under the plain error rule, an appellate court may consider a judicial ruling on the evidence if the ruling was clearly wrong and prejudiced the defendant.

In jury cases, proceedings regarding evidentiary questions are generally conducted, to the extent practicable, outside of the presence of the jury to prevent inadmissible evidence from being suggested to the jury by any means, such as making statements or offers of proof or asking questions in the hearing of the jury.

In some states, each time that the evidence is offered or referred to, the opposing party must renew its objections to the evidence. Most courts take a more flexible approach, holding that the renewal of objections is not required if the issue decided is one that (1) was fairly presented to the trial court for an initial ruling, (2) may be decided as a final matter before the evidence is actually offered, and (3) was ruled on definitively by the trial judge.[4] Other courts distinguished between objections to evidence, which must be renewed when evidence is offered, and offers of proof, which need not be renewed after a definitive determination is made that the evidence is inadmissible.

Preliminary Questions

Preliminary questions concerning the qualification of a person to be a witness, the existence of a privilege, or the admissibility of evidence shall be determined by the court (trial judge). For example, the first question asked a witness, that is, "What is your name?" is considered a preliminary question.

Hearings on the admissibility of confessions shall be conducted outside of the hearing of the jury. Hearings on other preliminary matters shall also be conducted outside of the hearing of the jury when the interests of justice require or when an accused is a witness and so requests. The accused does not, by testifying upon a preliminary matter, become subject to cross-examination on other issues in the case.

Limited Admissibility

When evidence that is admissible as to one defendant or for one purpose, but not admissible as to another defendant or for another purpose is admitted, the court, upon request, will restrict the evidence to its proper scope and instruct the jury accordingly. For example, when evidence that a witness has made a prior inconsistent statement is admitted, the judge will generally instruct the jury that the prior statement was admitted only for the purpose of attacking the creditability of the witness and not for the purpose of showing that the prior statement was true. Federal Rule 195 allows for the **limited admissibility** of evidence for a specified purpose but provides protection by limiting instruction to the nonoffering party who will be prejudiced by the evidence.

Burden on Parties to Object

When evidence is admitted for a limited purpose, or against only one party, the judge should instruct the jury as to the proper scope of the evidence. The burden is on the party who wants the instruction to ask for it.

There is nothing that prohibits a trial judge from providing a limiting instruction sua sponte.[5] There is often good reason for a trial court to avoid giving an instruction that is not requested. The party who is otherwise entitled to an instruction may have made a strategic decision that he or she is better off without one, that is, that an instruction will only serve to emphasize the evidence that the jury has heard, and may suggest a use to which the evidence could be put that the jury might not even have thought about.

The fact that evidence is admissible for a limited purpose does not require that the evidence be admitted. If the prejudicial effect of evidence substantially outweighs its probative value, despite a limiting instruction, then the nonoffering party can argue that the evidence should be completely excluded because any limiting instruction would be inadequate.

A trial judge, in determining the prejudice to be suffered from the offered evidence, must necessarily take into account whether this prejudice can be sufficiently ameliorated by a limiting instruction. A trial judge is required to restrict the evidence to its proper scope and to instruct the jury accordingly if a request is made, but it does not articulate the requirements of a proper request.

Admission of Part of a Document

When a writing or recorded statement or part thereof is introduced by a party, an adverse party may require the introduction at that time of any other part or any other writing or recorded statement which ought in fairness to be considered contemporaneously with it. The rule is an expression of the rule of completeness. The rule is based on two considerations. The first is the misleading impression created by taking matters out of context. The second is the inadequacy of repair work when delayed to a point later in the trial.

The rule of completeness does not prevent the other party from developing the matter on cross-examination or as part of his or her own case. The rule is limited to writings and recorded statements and does not apply to conversations. The rule applies to separate writings and recordings as well as to excised portions of a single writing or recording.

Oral Statements

Where a party introduces a portion of an oral statement, the adversary is entitled to have omitted portions introduced at the same time, insofar as that is necessary to correct any misimpression that the initially proffered portion would create.[6]

Fairness

The fairness rule requires admission of completing evidence only when it ought "in fairness" to be considered with the admitted statement.[7] For example, the rule does not require that "portions of a writing which are neither explanatory of the previously introduced portions nor relevant to the introduced portions be admitted"; the rule does not mean that if any part of a statement is to be admitted, then the entire statement is to be admitted. Sometimes it is difficult to determine whether fairness mandates the admission of allegedly completing evidence.

A good example of the rule's fairness principle arose in *United States* v. *Haddad.*[8] Haddad was a prosecution for a firearms offense. In a postarrest confession, the defendant stated that he knew that marijuana was under his bed, but that he did not know that a gun was under the bed. At trial, the inculpatory statement was admitted as an admission, but the exculpatory statement was excluded as hearsay. The court of appeals found that the confession had been improperly (though harmlessly) redacted to exclude the exculpatory statement about the gun. The court noted that ordinarily, a defendant's self-serving, exculpatory, out-of-court statements would not be admissible. But here the exculpatory remarks were part of the very statement a portion of which the government was properly bringing before the jury, that is, the defendant's admission about the marijuana.

JUDICIAL NOTICE

The concept of **judicial notice** is used when a relevant fact is so well known that to require that it be proved would be a waste of time. For example, a trial judge may take judicial notice that July 4th is a court holiday. A judicially noticed fact must be one not subject to reasonable dispute in that it is either (1) generally known within the territorial jurisdiction of the trial court or (2) capable of accurate and ready determination by resort to sources whose accuracy cannot reasonably be questioned. A party is entitled upon timely request to an opportunity to be heard as to the propriety of taking judicial notice and the tenor of the matter noticed. In the absence of prior notification, the request may be made after judicial notice has been taken. Judicial notice may be taken at any stage of the proceeding.

Law in Practice

Federal Rule of Evidence 201: Judicial Notice of Adjudicative Facts

(a) **Scope of rule.** This rule governs only judicial notice of adjudicative facts.

(b) **Kinds of facts.** A judicially noticed fact must be one not subject to reasonable dispute in that it is either (1) generally known within the territorial jurisdiction of the trial court or (2) capable of accurate and ready determination by resort to sources whose accuracy cannot reasonably be questioned.

(c) **When discretionary.** A court may take judicial notice, whether requested or not.

(d) **When mandatory.** A court shall take judicial notice if requested by a party and supplied with the necessary information.

(e) **Opportunity to be heard.** A party is entitled upon timely request to an opportunity to be heard as to the propriety of taking judicial notice and the tenor of the matter noticed. In the absence of prior notification, the request may be made after judicial notice has been taken.

(f) **Time of taking notice.** Judicial notice may be taken at any stage of the proceeding.

(g) **Instructing jury.** In a civil action or proceeding, the court shall instruct the jury to accept as conclusive any fact judicially noticed. In a criminal case, the court shall instruct the jury that it may, but is not required to, accept as conclusive any fact judicially noticed.

RELEVANT EVIDENCE

Relevant evidence is where it has some tendency as a matter of logic and human experience to make the proposition for which it is advanced more likely than that proposition would appear to be in the absence of that evidence. To identify logically irrelevant evidence, ask, "Does the evidence assist in proving the fact that one party is trying to prove?"[9] Problems of relevancy call for an answer to the question of whether an item of evidence possesses sufficient probative value to justify receiving it in evidence. For example, evidence that a person purchased a revolver shortly prior to a fatal shooting with which he is charged is considered relevant because it may prove that the person was guilty of the fatal shooting if the gun used in the shooting is the same gun that was purchased.

Under the concept of conditional relevancy, probative value depends not only upon satisfying the basic requirement of relevancy, as described above, but also upon the existence of some matter of fact. For example, if evidence of a spoken statement is relied upon to prove notice, probative value is lacking unless the person sought to be charged heard the statement. Does the item of evidence tend to prove the matter sought to be proved?

Exclusion of Relevant Evidence on Grounds of Prejudice, Confusion, or Waste of Time

Although relevant, evidence may be excluded if its probative value is substantially outweighed by the danger of unfair prejudice, confusion of the issues, or misleading the jury, or by considerations of undue delay, waste of time, or needless presentation of cumulative evidence. Case law recognizes that certain circumstances call for the exclusion of evidence which is of unquestioned relevance. These circumstances entail risks that range all the way from inducing decision on a purely emotional basis, at one extreme, to nothing more harmful than merely wasting time, at the other extreme. Situations in this area call for balancing the probative value of and need for the evidence against the harm likely to result from its admission.

Exclusion for risk of unfair prejudice, confusion of issues, misleading the jury, or waste of time all find ample support in the authorities. Unfair prejudice within its context means an undue tendency to suggest decision on an improper basis, commonly, though not necessarily, an emotional one. Surprise is generally not a ground for exclusion under this concept, but unfair surprise may be a ground for exclusion if it is coupled with the danger of prejudice and confusion of issues.

Character Evidence Not Admissible to Prove Conduct, Exceptions, and Other Crimes

Evidence of a person's character or a trait of character is not admissible for the purpose of proving action in conformity therewith on a particular occasion, except:

- Character of the accused. Evidence of a pertinent trait of character offered by an accused, or by the prosecution to rebut the same, or if evidence of a trait of character of the alleged victim of the crime is offered by an accused and admitted, evidence of the same trait of character of the accused offered by the prosecution;

- Evidence of a pertinent trait of character of the alleged victim of the crime offered by an accused, or by the prosecution to rebut the same, or evidence of a character trait of peacefulness of the alleged victim offered by the prosecution in a homicide case to rebut evidence that the alleged victim was the first aggressor;
- Evidence of the character of a witness may be admissible to impeach the witnesses' testimony.
- Evidence of other crimes, wrongs, or acts is not admissible to prove the character of a person in order to show action in conformity therewith. It may, however, be admissible for other purposes, such as proof of motive, opportunity, intent, preparation, plan, knowledge, identity, or absence of mistake or accident, provided that upon request by the accused, the prosecution in a criminal case shall provide reasonable notice in advance of trial, or during trial if the court excuses pretrial notice on good cause shown, of the general nature of any such evidence it intends to introduce at trial.

Character questions arise in two fundamentally different ways: (1) Character may itself be an element of a crime, claim, or defense. A situation of this kind is commonly referred to as character in issue. Illustrations include the competency of the driver in an action for negligently entrusting a motor vehicle to an incompetent driver. No problem of the general relevancy of character evidence is involved, and the present rule therefore has no provision on the subject. (2) **Character evidence** is susceptible of being used for the purpose of suggesting an inference that the person acted on the occasion in question consistently with his character. This use of character is often described as circumstantial. Illustrations are evidence of a violent disposition to prove that the person was the aggressor in an affray or evidence of honesty to disprove a charge of theft. This circumstantial use of character evidence raises questions of relevancy as well as questions of allowable methods of proof.

In most jurisdictions today, the circumstantial use of character is rejected but with important exceptions: (1) an accused may introduce pertinent evidence of good character (often misleadingly described as putting his character in issue), in which event the prosecution may rebut with evidence of bad character; (2) an accused may introduce pertinent evidence of the character of the victim, as in support of a claim of self-defense to a charge of homicide or consent in a case of rape, and the prosecution may introduce similar evidence in rebuttal of the character evidence, or, in a homicide case, to rebut a claim that the deceased was the first aggressor, however proved; and (3) the character of a witness may be gone into as bearing on his credibility.

Character evidence is of slight probative value and may be very prejudicial. It tends to distract the jury from the main question of what actually happened on the particular occasion. It subtly permits the jury to reward the good man or to punish the bad man because of their respective characters despite what the evidence in the case shows actually happened.

RAPE SHIELD LAWS

Pursuant to Federal Rule 412 and similar state rules, the following evidence is not admissible in any civil or criminal proceeding involving alleged sexual misconduct of a victim except as otherwise provided in subdivisions Rule 412 (b) and (c):

1. Evidence offered to prove that any alleged victim engaged in other sexual behavior.
2. Evidence offered to prove any alleged victim's sexual predisposition.

Rule 412(b) Exceptions

In a criminal case, the following evidence is admissible, if otherwise admissible under these rules:

- Evidence of specific instances of sexual behavior by the alleged victim offered to prove that a person other than the accused was the source of semen, injury, or other physical evidence;

- evidence of specific instances of sexual behavior by the alleged victim with respect to the person accused of the sexual misconduct offered by the accused to prove consent or by the prosecution; and
- evidence the exclusion of which would violate the constitutional rights of the defendant.

Procedure to Determine Admissibility

A party intending to offer evidence under Federal Rule 412 (b) must

a. file a written motion at least fourteen days before trial specifically describing the evidence and stating the purpose for which it is offered unless the court, for good cause, requires a different time for filing or permits filing during trial; and

b. serve the motion on all parties and notify the alleged victim or, when appropriate, the alleged victim's guardian or representative.

Before admitting evidence under Rule 412, the **rape shield law**, the court must conduct a hearing in camera and afford the victim and the parties a right to attend and be heard. The motion, related papers, and the record of the hearing must be sealed and remain under seal unless the court orders otherwise.

Federal Rule 412 was amended to also exclude all other evidence relating to an alleged victim of sexual misconduct that is offered to prove a sexual predisposition. This amendment was designed to exclude evidence that does not directly refer to sexual activities or thoughts, but that the proponent believes may have a sexual connotation for the jury. Admission of such evidence would contravene Rule 412's objectives of shielding the alleged victim from potential embarrassment and safeguarding the victim against stereotypical thinking. Consequently, unless the exception is satisfied, evidence such as that relating to the alleged victim's mode of dress, speech, or lifestyle will not be admissible.

The reason for extending the rule to all criminal cases is obvious. The strong social policy of protecting a victim's privacy and encouraging victims to come forward to report criminal acts is not confined to cases that involve a charge of sexual assault. The need to protect the victim is equally great when a defendant is charged with kidnapping, and evidence is offered, either to prove motive or as background, that the defendant sexually assaulted the victim.

Evidence of Similar Crimes in Sexual Assault Cases

In a criminal case in which the defendant is accused of an offense of sexual assault, evidence of the defendant's commission of another offense or offenses of sexual assault is admissible and may be considered for its bearing on any matter to which it is relevant.

In a case in which the prosecution intends to offer evidence under this rule, the prosecutor must disclose the evidence to the defendant, including statements of witnesses or a summary of the substance of any testimony that is expected to be offered, at least fifteen days before the scheduled date of trial or at such later time as the court may allow for good cause.

WITNESSES

Every person is competent to be a witness except as otherwise provided in these rules.

—Federal Rule 601

General Rule of Competency

At common law, only certain individuals were qualified to testify as witnesses. The present rule is that every person is competent to be a witness except as otherwise provided in these rules. This general ground-clearing eliminates all grounds of incompetency not specifically recognized. Disqualifications at common law included religious belief, conviction of crime, and connection with the litigation as a party or interested person or spouse of a party or interested person. American jurisdictions generally have ceased to recognize these grounds. In *United States* v. *Ramirez,*[10] the court of appeals held that the trial court did not abuse its discretion in admitting the testimony of a cocaine addict.

No mental or moral qualifications for testifying as a witness are specified. Standards of mental capacity have proved elusive in actual application. Discretion is regularly exercised in favor of allowing the testimony. The question is one particularly suited to the jury as one of weight and credibility, subject to judicial authority to review the sufficiency of the evidence. Standards of moral qualification in practice consist essentially of evaluating a person's truthfulness in terms of his or her own answers about it.

Competency of Hearsay Declarants

Since a trial judge has the authority in extreme cases to exclude a witness on grounds of incompetency, the question arises of whether the witness' hearsay statements should be excluded as well, even if they would otherwise fit a hearsay exception. This problem occurs fairly frequently in cases raising issues of child abuse, where the victim has made hearsay statements that would be admissible under a hearsay exception—most commonly Federal Rules 803(2), 803(4) or 807—and yet the child is found to be too young to appreciate the consequences of the oath and the responsibilities of being a witness. Most courts have held that a person's incompetency to testify as a witness has no bearing on the admissibility of his or her hearsay statement. The reasoning is that the grounds for admitting the hearsay statement have nothing to do with the witness's ability to appreciate the oath and the consequences of testifying. For example, if the hearsay statement is an excited utterance of a young child, its truthfulness is supported by the fact that the child made the statement while under the influence of a startling event. If this is so, it does not matter that the child has no appreciation of the consequences of the oath; the hearsay statement is reliable anyway.[11]

Nonexpert Witness's Lack of Personal Knowledge

A witness may not testify to a matter unless evidence is introduced sufficient to support a finding that the witness has personal knowledge of the matter. Evidence to prove personal knowledge may, but need not, consist of the witness's own testimony. This rule is subject to the provisions of Federal Rule 703, relating to opinion testimony by expert witnesses.

The rule requiring that a witness who testifies to a fact which can be perceived by the senses must have had an opportunity to observe, and must have actually observed, the fact is a "most pervasive manifestation" of the common law insistence upon "the most reliable sources of information." These foundation requirements may, of course, be furnished by the testimony of the witness himself or herself; hence, personal knowledge is not an absolute, but may consist of what the witness thinks he or she knows from personal perception.

A witness need not be absolutely certain of the event related in order to satisfy the personal knowledge requirement. It is enough that a reasonable juror could find that the witness perceived the event. Moreover, perfect knowledge is not required; the witness can be vague about certain details and still have enough knowledge to testify. A problem in the witness's perception generally goes to weight and not admissibility. For example, the fact that a witness cannot recall specific dates does not require exclusion of that testimony, since inability to recall specific dates does not demonstrate an absence of personal knowledge.[12]

Oath or Affirmation

Before testifying, a witness is required to declare that he or she will testify truthfully, by oath or affirmation administered in a form calculated to awaken the witness's conscience and impress the witness's mind with the duty to do so. Along with cross-examination, the requirement of an oath is designed to ensure that every witness gives accurate and honest testimony. The idea behind the oath requirement is to preserve the integrity of the judicial process by awakening the witness's conscience and making the witness amenable to perjury prosecution if he fibs.[13] Federal Rule 603 states that a witness need not swear an oath, but may merely affirm that he or she will testify truthfully. The affirmation can be given in any form calculated to awaken the conscience of the witness and impress upon the witness the duty to tell the truth. By permitting affirmation as well as oath, many of the difficulties faced by certain members of some religious groups should be alleviated.

In *United States* v. *Ward*,[14] the defendant refused to testify because the trial judge did not permit him to take an altered version of the standard oath. The defendant would have taken an oath that substituted the term "fully integrated honesty" for the word "truth." The court of appeals held that the trial court was in error for refusing to accede to the defendant's demand. It found the defendant's objection to the standard oath to be based on "beliefs that are protected by the First Amendment." The court noted that there is no rigid formula for an acceptable oath. For example, a proffered oath that "I would not tell a lie to stay out of jail" has been properly rejected, since the witness could later say that he or she lied for some purpose other than to stay out of jail, such as to protect a relative.[15]

Impeachment of a Witness

Impeachment is a legal term referring to the process of attacking the credibility of a witness. The rules provide that the credibility of any witness may be attacked by any party, including the party calling the witness. At common law, a party who called a witness could not impeach that witness unless the court declared the witness to be a "hostile witness." This is no longer the rule in most jurisdictions. The rationale for the common-law rule rested on assumptions concerning a party's presumptive support of a witness called by that party and the need to protect the witness from harassment. The Federal Rules recognize that a party does not necessarily vouch for a witness; in fact, a party may have no choice but to call an adverse witness in order to prove a case.

Evidence of Character and Conduct of the Witness

The credibility of a witness may be attacked or supported by evidence in the form of opinion or reputation, but subject to these limitations: (1) the evidence may refer only to character for truthfulness or untruthfulness, and (2) evidence of a truthful character is admissible only after the character of the witness for truthfulness has been attacked by opinion or reputation evidence or otherwise.

Specific instances of the conduct of a witness, for the purpose of attacking or supporting the witness's character for truthfulness, may in the discretion of the court, if probative of truthfulness or untruthfulness, be inquired into on cross-examination of the witness (1) concerning the witness's character for truthfulness or untruthfulness or (2) concerning the character for truthfulness or untruthfulness of another witness as to which character the witness being cross-examined has testified.

Impeachment by Evidence of Conviction of Crime

Evidence that a witness other than an accused has been convicted of a crime is admissible if the crime was punishable by death or imprisonment in excess of one year by the law under which the witness was convicted; and evidence that an accused has been convicted of such a crime shall be admitted if the court determines that the probative value of admitting this evidence outweighs its prejudicial effect to the accused; and evidence that any witness has been convicted of a crime shall be admitted if it involved dishonesty or false statement, regardless of the punishment.

Evidence of a conviction is not admissible if a period of more than ten years has elapsed since the date of the conviction or of the release of the witness from the confinement imposed for that conviction, whichever is the later date, unless the court determines, in the interests of justice, that the probative value of the conviction supported by specific facts and circumstances substantially outweighs its prejudicial effect. However, evidence of a conviction more than ten years old, as calculated herein, is not admissible unless the proponent gives the adverse party sufficient advance written notice of an intent to use such evidence to provide the adverse party with a fair opportunity to contest the use of such evidence.

Evidence of a conviction is not admissible under this rule if the conviction has been the subject of a pardon, annulment, certificate of rehabilitation, or other equivalent procedure based on a finding of the rehabilitation of the person convicted, and that person has not been convicted of a subsequent crime which was punishable by death or imprisonment in excess of one year, or the conviction has been the subject of a pardon, annulment, or other equivalent procedure based on a finding of innocence.

Evidence of juvenile adjudications is generally not admissible. The court may, however, in a criminal case allow evidence of a juvenile adjudication of a witness other than the accused if conviction of the offense would be admissible to attack the credibility of an adult and the court is satisfied that admission in evidence is necessary for a fair determination of the issue of guilt or innocence.

Mode and Order of Interrogation and Presentation

The court exercises reasonable control over the mode and order of interrogating witnesses and presenting evidence so as to (1) make the interrogation and presentation effective for the ascertainment of the truth, (2) avoid needless consumption of time, and (3) protect witnesses from harassment or undue embarrassment.

Cross-examination should be limited to the subject matter of the direct examination and matters affecting the credibility of the witness. A court may, in the exercise of discretion, permit inquiry into additional matters as if on direct examination.

Leading questions should not be used on the direct examination of a witness except as may be necessary to develop the witness's testimony. Ordinarily leading questions should be permitted on cross-examination. When a party calls a hostile witness, an adverse party, or a witness identified with an adverse party, interrogation may be by leading questions.

A witness may be cross-examined on any matter relevant to any issue in the case, including credibility. In the interests of justice, the judge may limit cross-examination with respect to matters not testified to on direct examination.

Prior Statements of Witnesses

In examining a witness concerning a prior statement made by the witness, whether written or not, the statement need not be shown nor its contents disclosed to the witness at that time, but on request the same shall be shown or disclosed to opposing counsel. Evidence of a prior inconsistent statement by a witness is not admissible unless the witness is afforded an opportunity to explain or deny the same and the opposite party is afforded an opportunity to interrogate the witness thereon, or the interests of justice otherwise require.

One of the traditional ways of impeaching a witness is by introducing evidence of a prior inconsistent statement. Under common law, the examining party was required to lay an adequate foundation for the statement at the time the witness testified. This was referred to as "the rule in Queen Caroline's case." That rule required the cross-examining party to confront the witness directly on cross-examination with the inconsistent statement. At that point, the witness would have an opportunity to explain, repudiate, or deny the statement. If the witness denied making the statement, then the trial court could in its discretion permit the cross-examining party to prove that the statement was made.

Federal Rule 613 provides that when a witness is examined concerning a prior statement, this statement need not be shown to the witness at the time of the examination. However, before evidence of the statement can be introduced, the witness must be given some opportunity, at some point in the trial, to explain, repudiate, or deny the statement. On request of opposing counsel, the contents of the statement must be disclosed so that opposing counsel may protect his or her case against unwarranted insinuations that a statement has been made. The time for the showing or disclosure is when the witness is examined about the prior statement, assuming that a proper request is made.

Opportunity for Witness to Explain or Deny the Statement

The basic common-law foundation consists of affording the witness an opportunity for either admitting or denying that a prior inconsistent statement was made and, if he or she admits it, of explaining the circumstances of the statement. The traditional method of confronting a witness with his or her inconsistent statement prior to its introduction is the preferred method of proceeding. In fact, where the proponent of the testimony fails to do so and the witness subsequently becomes unavailable, the proponent runs the risk that the court will properly exercise its discretion to not allow the admission of the prior statement.

Exclusion of Witnesses (Invoking the Rule)

At the request of a party, the court shall order witnesses excluded so that they cannot hear the testimony of other witnesses, and it may make the order of its own motion. This rule does not authorize exclusion of (1) a party who is a natural person, or (2) an officer or employee of a party which is not a natural person designated as its representative by its attorney, or (3) a person whose presence is shown by a party to be essential to the presentation of the party's cause, or (4) a person authorized by statute to be present.

The sequestration of prospective witnesses is a common method of discouraging or preventing collusion and exposing inaccuracies in testimony. Federal Rule 615 provides that at the request of a party, or on its own motion, the court shall order witnesses excluded so that they cannot hear the testimony of other witnesses. Where a victim of a crime is a witness in the criminal case, the sequestration power set forth in Rule 615 has been substantially changed by legislation.

In a criminal case, the Sixth and Fourteenth Amendments entitle a defendant to be present, although the defendant may waive that right in several ways. It is generally held that the police officer in charge of the investigation is within the "officer or employee" exception provided in Rule 615. As noted by the appellate court in *United States* v. *Payan,*[16] a defendant has no right to sequestration of the officer in charge of the investigation.

Opinion Testimony by Lay (Nonexpert) Witnesses

If a witness is not testifying as an expert, the witness's testimony in the form of opinions or inferences is limited to those opinions or inferences which are (1) rationally based on the perception of the witness; (2) helpful to a clear understanding of the witness's testimony or the determination of a fact in issue; and (3) not based on scientific, technical, or other specialized knowledge. **Lay witnesses** often find it difficult to express themselves in language which is not that of an opinion or conclusion. While the courts have made concessions in certain recurring situations, necessity as a standard for permitting opinions and conclusions has proved too elusive and too unadaptable to particular situations for purposes of satisfactory judicial administration. For example, law enforcement agents could testify that the defendant was acting suspiciously without being qualified as experts; however, the rules on experts are applicable where the agents testify on the basis of extensive experience that the defendant was using code words to refer to drug quantities and prices. Courts have permitted lay witnesses to testify that a substance appeared to be a narcotic so long as a foundation of familiarity with the substance has been established. For example, two lay witnesses who were heavy amphetamine users were permitted to testify that a substance was amphetamine; but it was an error to permit another witness to make such an identification where she had no experience with amphetamines.[17] Such testimony is not based on specialized knowledge, but rather is based upon a layperson's personal knowledge. If, however, that witness were to describe how a narcotic was manufactured, or to describe the intricate workings of a narcotic distribution network, then the witness would have to qualify as an expert.[18] In *State* v. *Brown*,[19] the trial court declared that the distinction between lay and expert witness testimony is that lay testimony "results from a process of reasoning familiar in everyday life," while expert testimony "results from a process of reasoning which can be mastered only by specialists in the field." The court in *Brown* noted that a lay witness with experience could testify that a substance appeared to be blood, but that a witness would have to qualify as an expert before he could testify that bruising around the eyes is indicative of skull trauma.

Testimony by Experts

If scientific, technical, or other specialized knowledge will assist the jury to understand the evidence or to determine a fact in issue, a witness qualified as an expert by knowledge, skill, experience, training, or education may testify thereto in the form of an opinion or otherwise if (1) the testimony is based upon sufficient facts or data, (2) the testimony is the product of reliable principles and methods, and (3) the witness has applied the principles and methods reliably to the facts of the case.

The fields of knowledge which may be drawn upon are not limited to the scientific and technical but extend to all specialized knowledge. Similarly, the expert is viewed not in a narrow sense, but as a person qualified by knowledge, skill, experience, training or education. Thus, within the scope of the rule are not only experts in the strictest sense of the word, such as physicians, physicists, and architects, but also the large group sometimes called skilled witnesses, such as bankers or landowners testifying to land values.

The ***Daubert*** **test** set forth a nonexclusive checklist for trial courts to use in assessing the reliability of scientific expert testimony.[20] The specific factors explicated by the *Daubert* court are (1) whether the expert's technique or theory can be or has been tested—that is, whether the expert's theory can be challenged in some objective sense, or whether it is instead simply a subjective, conclusory approach that cannot reasonably be assessed for reliability; (2) whether the technique or theory has been subject to peer review and publication; (3) the known or potential rate of error of the technique or theory when applied; (4) the existence and maintenance of standards and controls; and (5) whether the technique or theory has been generally accepted in the scientific community.

The courts both before and after *Daubert* have found other factors relevant in determining whether expert testimony is sufficiently reliable to be considered by the trier of fact. These factors include:

- Whether experts are proposing to testify about matters growing naturally and directly out of research they have conducted independent of the litigation, or whether they have developed their opinions expressly for purposes of testifying.
- Whether the expert has unjustifiably extrapolated from an accepted premise to an unfounded conclusion.
- Whether the expert has adequately accounted for obvious alternative explanations.
- Whether the expert is being as careful as he would be in his regular professional work outside his paid litigation consulting.
- Whether the field of expertise claimed by the expert is known to reach reliable results for the type of opinion the expert would give.

A review of the case law after *Daubert* shows that the rejection of expert testimony is the exception rather than the rule. The court in *Daubert* stated: "Vigorous cross-examination, presentation of contrary evidence, and careful instruction on the burden of proof are the traditional and appropriate means of attacking shaky but admissible evidence."[21]

When a trial court rules that an expert's testimony is reliable, this does not necessarily mean that contradictory expert testimony is unreliable.

Bases of Opinion Testimony by Experts

The facts or data in the particular case upon which an expert bases an opinion or inference may be those perceived by or made known to the expert at or before the hearing. If they are of a type reasonably relied upon by experts in the particular field in forming opinions or inferences upon the subject, the facts or data need not be admissible in evidence in order for the opinion or inference to be admitted. Facts or data that are otherwise inadmissible shall not be disclosed to the jury by the proponent of the opinion or inference unless the court determines that their probative value in assisting the jury to evaluate the expert's opinion substantially outweighs their prejudicial effect.

Facts or data upon which expert opinions are based may, under the rule, be derived from three possible sources. The first is the firsthand observation of the witness, with opinions based thereon traditionally allowed. A treating physician is an example. The second source, presentation at the trial, also reflects existing practice. The technique may be the familiar hypothetical question or having the expert attend the trial and hear the testimony establishing the facts. The third source consists of presentation of data to the expert outside of court and other than by his or her own perception.

Disclosure of Facts or Data Underlying Expert Opinion

An expert may testify in terms of opinion or inference, and give reasons therefore without first testifying to the underlying facts or data, unless the court requires otherwise. The expert may in any event be required to disclose the underlying facts or data on cross-examination.

Law in Practice

Cuellar v. *United States*, 2008 U.S. LEXIS 4698 (2008)

Humberto Fidel Regalado Cuellar was stopped in southern Texas while driving toward the Mexican border. When asked about a bulge in his pocket, he produced cash that smelled of marijuana. Defendant consented to a search of his vehicle, and officers found $81,000 in cash in a secret compartment. Cuellar was found guilty of attempting to transport the proceeds of unlawful activity to Mexico, knowing that the transportation was designed to conceal or disguise the nature, location, source, ownership, or control of the money.

Was the Evidence Sufficient to Convict Cuellar of Money Laundering?

JUSTICE THOMAS delivered the opinion of Court.

Although the federal money laundering statute, 18 U.S.C.S. § 1956(a)(2)(B)(i), does not require proof that a defendant attempted to "legitimize" tainted funds, the government must demonstrate that the defendant did more than merely hide the money during its transport. Although we agree with the Government that the statute does not require proof that the defendant attempted to "legitimize" tainted funds, we agree with petitioner that the Government must demonstrate that the defendant did more than merely hide the money during its transport. We therefore reverse the conviction since there was not sufficient evidence to support the money laundering charge.

DOCUMENTS

Requirement of Original

To prove the content of a writing, recording, or photograph, the original writing, recording, or photograph is required, except as otherwise provided. Rule 1002 is the best evidence rule that requires the production of an original in order to prove the contents of a writing, recording, or photograph unless an exception is provided in another rule. The traditional rationale of the best evidence rule is that accuracy is promoted by production of the original because the process of copying creates a risk of error.

An exception to the best evidence rule is police testimony as to the contents of a confession. Officers who heard a defendant confess may testify to what they heard even if there is a recording of the confession and a transcript of that recording. A duplicate is admissible to the same extent as an original unless (1) a genuine question is raised as to the authenticity of the original or (2) in the circumstances it would be unfair to admit the duplicate in lieu of the original.

The original document is not required, and other evidence of the contents of a writing, recording, or photograph is admissible, if

1. The original has been lost or destroyed. The original is lost or has been destroyed, unless the proponent lost or destroyed it in bad faith; or
2. The original is not obtainable. No original can be obtained by any available judicial process or procedure; or
3. The original is in the possession of the opponent. At a time when an original was under the control of the party against whom offered, that party was put on notice, by the pleadings or otherwise, that the contents would be a subject of proof at the hearing, and that party did not produce the original at the hearing; or
4. Collateral matters. The writing, recording, or photograph is not closely related to a controlling issue.

Public Records

The contents of an official record, or of a document authorized to be recorded or filed and actually recorded or filed, including data compilations in any form, if otherwise admissible, may be proved by copy, certified as correct, or testified to be correct by a witness who has compared it with the original. If a copy that complies with the foregoing cannot be obtained by the exercise of reasonable diligence, then other evidence of the contents may be given.

Summaries

The contents of voluminous writings, recordings, or photographs which cannot conveniently be examined in court may be presented in the form of a chart, summary, or calculation. The originals, or duplicates, shall be made available for examination or copying, or both, by other parties at a reasonable time and place. The court may order that they be produced in court.

Requirement of Authentication or Identification

One of the general requirements of introducing real evidence, including writings, at trial is that the evidence must be authenticated. This means that someone must lay a sufficient foundation so that the jury is able to determine that the evidence is what it is supposed to be. Similarly, when a witness testifies to statements made by someone else, the witness must be able to identify the person from whom the statements emanated so that the trier of fact is able to properly attribute the statements.

The requirements for authenticating evidence are not burdensome, but they often require that foundational evidence be presented. Courts will not assume that evidence is what the proponent claims simply because on the face of the evidence it is apparent that it might be. In *United States* v. *Skipper,*[22] Skipper was charged with and convicted of possession of crack cocaine with intent to distribute. Police stopped the car that Skipper owned because he was changing lanes erratically. A plastic bag containing crack cocaine was thrown from the driver's side of the car shortly after the lights of the patrol car were activated. Skipper was arrested. At trial, the prosecution introduced criminal evidence of two other convictions for crimes allegedly committed by Skipper. Government Exhibit No. 3 was a certified copy of a judgment against "John Derrick Skipper" indicating that the defendant in that case had pleaded guilty to possession of a controlled substance. An expert testified that the fingerprints on this conviction matched Skipper's fingerprints. Government Exhibit No. 2 was a certified copy of a deferred adjudication order indicating that "John D. Skipper" was placed on ten-year probation for possession of a controlled substance. However, Exhibit No. 2 bore no fingerprints and the government did not otherwise identify Skipper as the person named in the order.

The court of appeals held that the trial judge erred, but the error was harmless in admitting Exhibit No. 2 because the prosecution failed to produce evidence proving that the defendant was the actual John D. Skipper named in the deferred adjudication order. The court held "that the mere similarity in name between a criminal defendant and a person named in a prior conviction alone does not satisfy the identification requirement."

Law in Practice

How Would You Rule in the Following Situation? Did the Accused Receive a Fair Jury Trial?

After a jury convicted Richard Gamache of first-degree murder and sentenced him to death, Gamache's counsel and the trial court learned that during deliberations, court personnel inadvertently gave the jury a videotape that had not been admitted into evidence. During its deliberations, the jury watched the video twice in full and a third time in part before reaching its verdict. The video showed a police interview of Gamache and his codefendants on the day of the murder in which Gamache confessed to the crime in graphic terms. The video showed Gamache explaining, for example, that given the opportunity he would have shot police officers. Quoting Gamache on the video as stating, "If I figured, if I had any idea I was about to be arrested, I'd have started shooting. . . . I figure if I'm going to die, . . . I'm going to take one or two with me").

On appeal, the California Supreme Court held that the jury's access to the tape was indisputably error. The requirement that a jury's verdict "must be based upon the evidence developed at the trial goes to the fundamental integrity of all that is embraced in the constitutional concept of trial by jury. In the constitutional sense, trial by jury in a criminal case necessarily implies at the very least that the evidence developed against a defendant shall come from the witness stand in a public courtroom where there is full judicial protection of the defendant's right of confrontation, of cross-examination, and of counsel. The California Supreme Court found that the error was trial error and not the result of any juror misconduct. Accordingly, it did not apply a presumption of prejudice and proceeded to conduct a harmless-error analysis. The California Supreme Court affirmed the conviction.

The U.S. Supreme Court with four justices dissenting denied the petition for review. See Justice Sotomayor's dissenting opinion at *Gamache* v. *California*, 131 S. Ct. 591, 591-592 (U.S. 2010).

Chain of Custody

In criminal cases, a question of authenticity arises where something is seized from the defendant and then introduced at trial, and the defendant disputes that it is his or hers or argues that the thing has been altered in some way. One way for the prosecution to authenticate the evidence in these circumstances is to establish a chain of custody. Courts have been permissive in determining whether the government has established a sufficient chain of custody. The standard rule is that gaps in the chain of custody go to weight and not admissibility.[23] For example, a one-year gap in the chain of custody for contraband goes to the weight and not the admissibility of the evidence; there is no showing of bad faith on the part of government officials, who are entitled to a presumption that they did not alter the proffered evidence.

The most important chain of custody is the one from the original seizure of the evidence to the analysis of the substance. Given the fungibility of drugs, it is essential to make a connection between the substance seized from the defendant and the substance actually tested. Any substantial gap in this chain of custody or any indication of alteration should be treated as fatal, since otherwise there is an unacceptable risk that the test does not reflect the contents of the substance seized.[24] A gap in the chain occurring after testing can be treated more permissively, given the admissibility of the testing procedure itself and the fact that the only purpose for introducing the substance in court is to illustrate the testimony of government witnesses.

Testimony of a witness who has personal knowledge of a piece of evidence is a classic way of authenticating the evidence. Someone who is an eyewitness to the signing of a document may authenticate the document. A layperson can identify handwriting based upon familiarity with the handwriting. A signature may be the identified by the testimony of a person familiar with the signature. It is not essential for the witness to have been present when the signature was executed.

Handwriting, fingerprints, blood, hair, clothing fibers, and numerous other things can be authenticated by comparison with specimens that have been authenticated. Sometimes the comparison can be done by the jury; at other times, an expert witness will be required, especially when scientific knowledge is needed to make a valid examination of the samples. The trial judge has discretion to exclude specimens when questions as to their authenticity will be confusing and excessively time-consuming.

Sometimes the characteristics of an item will themselves serve to authenticate the item. A letter may be authenticated, for example, by its content and the circumstances indicating that it was a reply to a duly authenticated letter.

One who is familiar with the voice of another may authenticate a conversation or identify the speaker on a tape or other recording. However, if the tape or recording is offered for its truth, hearsay problems still will exist and must be solved following the satisfaction of the authentication requirement.

CASE LAW

Recent Cases

Melendez-Diaz v. *Massachusetts*, 129 S. Ct. 2527 (U.S. 2009)

The defendant Melendez-Diaz appealed his convictions for distributing cocaine and trafficking in cocaine, in violation of Mass. Gen. Laws ch. 94C, §§ 32A and 32E(b)(1). He contended that the Commonwealth of Massachusetts violated his rights under the U.S. Constitution. The Appeals Court of Massachusetts affirmed the conviction and the Supreme Judicial Court of Massachusetts denied review. The U.S. Supreme Court granted certiorari and reversed the conviction based on the violation of the Sixth Amendment right to confront the witnesses against the defendant.

Melendez-Diaz was tried on charges alleging that he distributed cocaine and trafficked in cocaine, in violation of Mass. Gen. Laws ch. 94C, §§ 32A and 32E(b)(1), and the prosecution offered certificates signed by state laboratory analysts, which stated that evidence that was connected to the petitioner was cocaine. The defense objected to admission of the certificates, claiming that their admission violated the defendant's right under the Sixth Amendment to the U.S. Constitution to confront the analysts who signed the certificates, but the trial court overruled the objection and admitted the certificates under Mass. Gen. Laws ch. 111, § 13.

The U.S. Supreme Court held that admission of the certificates violated petitioner's Sixth Amendment right to confront the witnesses against him. The certificates were affidavits, which fell within the core class of testimonial statements covered by the Confrontation Clause, and they were made under circumstances that would have led an objective witness reasonably to believe that they were made for use in a criminal trial. Although the petitioner could have subpoenaed the analysts, that right was not a substitute for his right to confront them.

The Court noted that the Sixth Amendment guarantees a defendant the right to be confronted with the witnesses against him. While the Confrontation Clause guarantees a defendant the right to be confronted with the witnesses "against him," the Compulsory Process Clause guarantees a defendant the right to call witnesses "in his favor" (U.S. Const. amend. 6.). The text of the Amendment contemplates two classes of witnesses—those against the defendant and those in his favor. The prosecution must produce the former; the defendant may call the latter. There is not a third category of witnesses, helpful to the prosecution, but somehow immune from confrontation.

Note: This case was decided on a 5-4 decision and many state prosecutors are unhappy with the results. There will be pressure on the Court to reconsider this rule.

Michigan v. *Bryant*, 131 S. Ct. 1143 (U.S. 2011)

Bryant was convicted of second-degree murder. The Michigan Supreme Court reversed his conviction, holding that the Sixth Amendment's Confrontation Clause rendered a mortally wounded shooting victim's statements inadmissible testimonial hearsay. The State of Michigan's petition for a writ of certiorari was granted to answer the question as to whether the Confrontation Clause of the Sixth Amendment barred admission of the victim's statements.

Police were dispatched to a gas station parking lot and found the victim mortally wounded. Before he died, the victim told the police that he had been shot by Bryant outside defendant's house and had then driven himself to the lot. The officers testified at trial about what the victim had told them. The victim was unavailable at trial because he had died shortly after the shooting. What the victim told the officers was that he fled the shooter's back porch, indicating that he perceived an ongoing threat. The police did not know, and the victim did not tell them, whether the threat was limited to him.

The informality of the exchange suggested that the officers' purpose was to address what they perceived to be an ongoing emergency. The circumstances lacked any formality that would have alerted the victim to or focused him on the possible future prosecutorial use of his statements. Because of these circumstances, the victim's identification and description of the shooter and the location of the shooting were not testimonial hearsay. The Confrontation Clause did not bar their admission at defendant's trial.

The Court reversed the judgment of the Supreme Court of Michigan and the case was remanded for further proceedings not inconsistent with the opinion. It was left to the Michigan courts to decide on remand whether the statements' admission was otherwise permitted by state hearsay rules.

The Court noted that the most important instances in which the Confrontation Clause restricts the introduction of out-of-court statements are those in which state actors are involved in a formal, out-of-court interrogation of a witness to obtain evidence for trial. Even where such an interrogation is conducted with all good faith, introduction of the resulting statements at trial can be unfair to the accused if they are untested by cross-examination.

Whether formal or informal, out-of-court statements can evade the basic objective of the Confrontation Clause, which is to prevent the accused from being deprived of the opportunity to cross-examine the declarant about statements taken for use at trial. When the primary purpose of an interrogation is to respond to an ongoing emergency, its purpose is not to create a record for trial and thus is not within the scope of the Clause. But there may be other circumstances, aside from ongoing emergencies, when a statement is not procured with a primary purpose of creating an out-of-court substitute for trial testimony. In making the primary purpose determination, standard rules of hearsay, designed to identify some statements as reliable, will be relevant. Where no such primary purpose exists, the admissibility of a statement is the concern of state and federal rules of evidence, not the Confrontation Clause.

Summary

- Evidence is a study of the regulations involving the process of proving facts.
- Two themes of the Federal Rules are that (1) the rules favor admissibility of evidence and (2) the trial judge has considerable discretion concerning the admissibility of evidence.
- Hearsay is a statement, other than one made by the declarant while testifying at the trial or hearing, offered in evidence to prove the truth of the matter asserted.
- Hearsay is inadmissible unless an exception is applicable.
- Rulings on evidence cannot be assigned as error on appeal unless a substantial right is affected and the nature of the error was called to the attention of the judge at the time the evidence was offered.

- When evidence is admitted for a limited purpose, the judge should instruct the jury as to the proper scope of the evidence.
- Evidence is relevant where it has some tendency as a matter of logic and human experience to make the proposition for which it is advanced more likely than that proposition would appear to be in the absence of that evidence.
- Admissible relevant evidence may be excluded on the grounds of prejudice, confusion, or waste of time.
- Generally, character evidence is not admissible to prove conduct.
- There are no mental or moral qualifications for testifying as a witness under the Federal Rules.
- A witness should have the opportunity to deny or explain a prior inconsistent statement.
- Expert witnesses include skilled persons.

Review Questions

1. Define hearsay.
2. Under what circumstances is relevant evidence not admissible in court?

3. When may a lay witness state an opinion while testifying in court?
4. Explain the best evidence rule.

Endnotes

1. 964 F.2d 193 (3d Cir. 1992).
2. 509 U.S. 579 (1993).
3. 513 U.S. 196 (1995).
4. *Rosenfeld* v. *Basquiat,* 78 F.3d 84 (2d Cir. 1996).
5. *United States* v. *Mark,* 943 F.2d 444 (4th Cir. 1991).
6. *United States* v. *Haddad,* 10 F.3d 1252, 1259 (7th Cir. 1993).
7. *United States* v. *Wright,* 826 F.2d 938 (10th Cir. 1987).
8. 10 F.3d 1252, 1258 (7th Cir. 1993).
9. D. Paciocco and L. Stuesser, *The Law of Evidence* (Irwin Law, Concord, 1996) at xvii.
10. 871 F.2d 582, 584 (6th Cir. 1989).
11. *United States* v. *Dorian,* 803 F.2d 1439 (8th Cir. 1986).
12. *United States* v. *Powers,* 75 F.3d 335 (7th Cir. 1996).
13. *United States* v. *Zizzo,* 120 F.3d 1338 (7th Cir. 1997).
14. 989 F.2d 1015 (9th Cir. 1993).
15. *United States* v. *Fowler,* 605 F.2d 181 (5th Cir. 1979).
16. 992 F.2d 1387 (5th Cir. 1993).
17. *United States* v. *Westbrook,* 896 F.2d 330 (8th Cir. 1990).
18. *United States* v. *Figueroa-Lopez,* 125 F.2d 1241 (9th Cir. 1997).
19. 836 S.W.2d 530, 549 (1992).
20. *Daubert* v. *Merrell Dow Pharmaceuticals, Inc.,* 509 U.S. 579 (1993).
21. 509 U.S. 579, at 595.
22. 74 F.3d 608 (5th Cir. 1996).
23. *United States* v. *Miller,* 994 F.2d 441 (8th Cir. 1993).
24. *United States* v. *Casamento,* 887 F.2d 1141 (2d Cir. 1989).

CHAPTER 11

Trial: Roles of Major Participants

Injustice anywhere is a threat to justice everywhere.

—MARTIN LUTHER KING JR. [IN A LETTER WRITTEN FROM HIS JAIL CELL IN
BIRMINGHAM, ALABAMA, PUBLISHED IN *ATLANTIC MONTHLY,* AUGUST 1963]

Chapter Outline

Adversary System

Judge

Victim and Defendant

Prosecutor

State Attorney General

Defense Counsel

Clerk of the Court

Bailiff

Court Reporter

Court Commissioner

Case Law

Summary

Key Terms

Adversary system

Bailiff

Contempt

Privileged communication

Learning Objectives

After completing this chapter, you should be able to:

- Describe the roles and responsibilities of the major trial participants.

- Explain the adversarial relationship between the prosecution and defense.

- Discuss the duties and responsibilities of the judge.
- Explain the functions of a state attorney general.
- Discuss the role of the victim in a trial.

- Explain what a bailiff does.
- List the duties of a court reporter.
- Summarize the duties of a court commissioner.

ADVERSARY SYSTEM

Before discussing the actual trial proceedings, the roles of the other major participants in a criminal trial, in addition to the defendant, should be examined. These include the judge, prosecuting attorney, defense counsel, clerk of the court, bailiff, and court reporter. All are considered officers of the court. The function of the jury and the witnesses will be examined later. By the time of the trial, the law enforcement officer will have completed his or her major role in the administration of justice. The investigation will be finished, and the officer's final duty will be serving as a witness and testifying in a truthful, convincing manner.

The Steps in a Jury Trial

Selection of the jury
Prosecutor's opening statement to the jury
Defense's opening statement to the jury. (Defense has the option to delay its opening statement until the presentation of its case.)
Prosecutor's presentation of evidence and direct examination
Defense's cross-examination of prosecutor's witnesses
Prosecution rests
Defense's presentation of evidence and direct examination
Prosecution's cross-examination of defense witnesses
Prosecution's case in rebuttal
Prosecution's closing argument
Defense's closing argument
Prosecution's argument in rebuttal
Judge's instructions to the jury
(*Note:* In some states this comes before arguments.)
Jury deliberations and voting
Pronouncement of the verdict
Hearing on the sentence

The criminal trial procedure varies little—whether the charge is a felony or misdemeanor or whether the trial is a court trial or jury trial. The defendant is entitled to a fair trial before an impartial judge and an honest jury in an atmosphere of judicial calm.

Our justice system is an **adversary system**, meaning that it has two sides. In a criminal trial, these are the prosecution and the defense. Each is permitted to present evidence in its own behalf. Theoretically, both sides come into the trial on an equal basis. But Justice White of the U.S. Supreme Court, in *United States* v. *Wade,* pointed out that our system is not a true adversary system with both sides entering the trial on an equal footing. He stated the following[1]:

Law enforcement officers (and prosecuting attorneys) have the obligation to convict the guilty and to make sure they do not convict the innocent. They must be dedicated to making the criminal trial a procedure for the ascertainment of the true facts surrounding the commission of the crime. To this extent, our so-called adversary system is not adversary at all: nor should it be. But defense counsel has no comparable obligation to ascertain or present the truth. Our system assigns him a different mission. He must be and is interested in not convicting the innocent, but absent a voluntary plea of guilty, we also insist that he defend his client whether he is innocent or guilty. The State has the obligation to present the evidence. Defense counsel need present nothing, even if he knows what the truth is. He need furnish no witnesses to the police, reveal any confidences of his client, nor furnish any other information to help the prosecution's case. If he can confuse a witness, even a truthful one, or make him appear at a disadvantage, unsure or indecisive, that will be his normal course. Our interest in not convicting the innocent permits counsel to put the State to its proof, to put the State's case in the worst possible light, regardless of what he thinks or knows to be the truth. Undoubtedly there are some limits which defense counsel must observe but more often than not, defense counsel will cross-examine a prosecution witness, and impeach him if he can, even if he thinks the witness is telling the truth, just as he will attempt to destroy a witness who he thinks is lying. In this respect, as part of our modified adversary system and as part of the duty imposed on the most honorable defense counsel, we countenance or require conduct which in many instances has little, if any, relation to the search for truth.

JUDGE

Although the terms "judge" and "the court" are used interchangeably, they should be distinguished. The judge presides over the trial proceedings and exercises those duties and power imposed by law. The court is a judicial proceeding presided over by a judge. The judge plays a very important role both before and during the trial. There is a great deal of power and authority, and many decisions are solely at the judge's discretion. Since unscrupulous acts and incorrect legal or procedural rulings could seriously affect the administration of justice, the judge's actions are subject to review by appellate courts. This scrutiny avoids any abuse of power or authority by the judge. Fortunately, most judges are honest individuals who endeavor to do a conscientious job.

Superior or District Court Judges

In most states, the judges of the superior or district court, or its equivalent, are elected by the people of the judicial district where they serve. This district is often the county. These judges are attorneys with past experience in the practice of law. One might wonder why an attorney with a number of years in law practice would wish to become a judge. Probably the most prevalent reason is the prestige that the office holds. Judges are generally held in high esteem within a community. One might be fearful that a judge, being an elected official, would have political obligations that interfere with the ability to carry out his or her functions impartially. As practicing attorneys, most candidates for a judgeship are fairly well known to the people of the community. The campaigning is primarily through personal contacts and the assistance of friends and does not place the victorious judge in a position where he or she is bound to grant political favors. This situation does not mean that members of organized crime have not tried to influence elections, as well as judges, in some areas. However, the great majority of judges have proven to be above this corrupt influence.

Law in Practice

Selection of State Judges

States where the judge is initially selected by a partisan election:

Alabama, Arkansas, Illinois, Indiana, Louisiana, Mississippi, Missouri (in nonmetropolitan areas only), New York, North Carolina, Pennsylvania, Tennessee, Texas, and West Virginia

States where the judge is initially selected by a nonpartisan election:

California, Florida, Georgia, Idaho, Kentucky, Michigan, Montana, Nevada, North Dakota, Ohio, Oklahoma, Oregon, South Dakota, Washington, and Wisconsin

States where the judge is initially selected based on merit:

Alaska, Arizona, Colorado, Connecticut, Delaware, District of Columbia, Hawaii, Iowa, Kansas, Maryland, Massachusetts, Nebraska, New Mexico, Utah, Vermont, and Wyoming

States where the judge is initially appointed by the governor:

Maine, New Hampshire, New Jersey, and Rhode Island

States where the judge is initially appointed by the state legislature:

South Carolina and Virginia

Source: American Judicature Society, *Judicial Selection in the United States: A Compendium of Provisions,* 2nd ed. (Chicago: American Judicature Society, 1993).

Inferior Court Judges

Like superior or district court judges, inferior court judges are elected in most states. They are elected by the people of the judicial district where they serve, but this district is only a portion of a county. The qualifications for this position vary greatly among states. In many outlying rural areas, there is not enough court business to justify a full-time judge, so the judge may be a local practicing attorney elected to act as the judge when court business is required. The judge may also be the operator of a local market or a service station, or may be a retired person who needs a part-time job, as usually there is no requirement that the judge of these courts be trained in law. The fact that these judges are often poorly paid encourages bribery. Some judges work on a commission, receiving a percentage of fines levied, often creating the temptation to fine excessively, particularly in traffic violation cases. The brand of justice meted out in such courts sometimes leaves a great deal to be desired. But again, like superior court judges, most inferior court judges are honest individuals elected because of the community's faith in their honesty and integrity. However, some inferior courts, like municipal courts in some districts, require the judge to be an attorney before acting in the capacity of judge, and the judges of these courts are capable of handling the responsibilities imposed on them.

Function of the Trial Judge

As pointed out in previous chapters, many duties have already been performed by the judge prior to the trial. With the judge sitting as magistrate, arraignments and preliminary hearings will have been held. Further, decisions will have been made on motions presented, appointments of counsel for indigent defendants will be completed, and the right to a speedy and fair trial will have been preserved. Though a fair trial is essential, a perfect trial is not expected.

Law in Practice

A Representative State Code of Conduct for Judges: Oklahoma Code of Judicial Conduct

Chapter 1, App. 4

Canon 3. A Judge Should Perform the Duties of Judicial Office Impartially and Diligently

(A) Judicial Duties in General. The judicial duties of a judge take precedence over all the judge's other activities. The judge's judicial duties include all the duties of the judge's office prescribed by law. In performance of those duties, the following standards apply.

(B) Adjudicative Responsibilities.

(1) A judge should be faithful to the law and maintain professional competence in it. A judge should not be swayed by partisan interests, public clamor or fear of criticism.

(2) A judge should require order and decorum in proceedings before the judge.

(3) A judge should be patient, dignified and courteous to litigants, jurors, witnesses, lawyers and others with whom he the judge deals in official capacity, and should require similar conduct of lawyers, and of his staff, court officials and others subject to the judge's direction and control.

(4) A judge should perform judicial duties without bias or prejudice. A judge should not, in the performance of judicial duties, by words or conduct manifest bias or prejudice, including but not limited to bias or prejudice based upon race, sex, religion, national origin, disability, age, sexual orientation or socioeconomic status, and should not permit staff, court officials and others subject to the judge's direction and control to do so.

(5) A judge should require lawyers in proceedings before the judge to refrain from manifesting, by words or conduct, bias or prejudice based upon race, sex, religion, national origin, disability, age, sexual orientation or socioeconomic status, against parties, witnesses, counsel or others. This Section 3B(5) does not preclude legitimate advocacy when race, sex, religion, national origin, disability, age, sexual orientation or socioeconomic status, or other similar factors, are issues in the proceeding.

(6) A judge should accord to every person who has a legal interest in a proceeding, or that person's lawyer, the right to be heard according to law. A judge should not initiate, nor consider ex parte communications, or consider other communications made to the judge outside the presence of the parties concerning a pending or impending proceeding except that:

(a) Where circumstances require, ex parte communications for scheduling, administrative purposes or emergencies that do not deal with substantive matters or issues on the merits are authorized; provided that the judge reasonably believes that no party will gain a procedural or tactical advantage as a result of the ex parte communication.

(b) A judge may obtain the advice of a disinterested expert on the law applicable to a proceeding before the judge if the judge gives notice to the parties of the person consulted and the substance of the advice, with a record being made, and affords the parties reasonable opportunity to respond.

(c) A judge may consult with court personnel whose function is to aid the judge in carrying out the judge's adjudicative responsibilities or with other judges.

(d) A judge may initiate or consider any ex parte communications when expressly authorized by law to do so.

(7) A judge should dispose of all judicial matters promptly, efficiently and fairly.

(8) A judge should not, while a proceeding is pending or impending in any court, make any public comment that might reasonably be expected to affect the outcome or impair its fairness or make any non-public comment that might substantially interfere with a fair trial or hearing. The judge should require similar abstention on the part of court personnel subject to the judge's direction and control. This Section does not prohibit judges from making public statements in the course of their official duties or from explaining for public information the procedures of the court. This Section does not apply to proceedings in which the judge is a litigant in a personal capacity.

(9) A judge should not, with respect to cases, controversies or issues that are likely to come before the court, make pledges, promises or commitments that are inconsistent with the impartial performance of the adjudicative duties of the office.

During the trial, the judge has the primary responsibility for seeing that justice is carried out. The judge has a duty not only to protect the interests of the defendant but also to protect the interests of the public, ensuring that the guilty are convicted. The judge controls all proceedings during the trial and limits the introduction of evidence and arguments of counsel to relevant and material matters, with a view to the expeditious and effective ascertainment of the truth. The judge must control the conduct of the defendant and the spectators; determine the competency of witnesses and the admissibility of evidence; rule on objections made to questions asked by the attorneys; protect witnesses from harassment during cross-examination; interpret for the jury the laws involved in the particular case; and, in some jurisdictions, comment on the weight of the evidence presented and the credibility of witnesses. In many jurisdictions, the judge sentences the defendant after conviction. If the trial is a court trial, the judge renders a verdict of guilt or innocence. Additional duties during the trial will be enumerated as the discussion of the trial progresses.

CONTEMPT OF COURT A trial is to be conducted in a calm, dignified atmosphere. It is the responsibility of the judge to maintain such an atmosphere. Assisting in this regard is the authority to punish one who interrupts this atmosphere by declaring the offender in contempt of court. **Contempt** is an act that is disrespectful to the court or adversely affects the administration of justice. Any act that embarrasses, hinders, or obstructs the court in the administration of justice may be declared by the judge as contempt of court. Typical acts falling within this category include contemptuous or insulting remarks made to the judge and counsel's persistent arguments with the judge after an admonition to desist has been given. A judge may not go so far as to hold a defense counsel in contempt when counsel is merely defending his client vigorously. Disorderly conduct by a defendant or by the spectators may cause the judge to exercise the right of contempt. A witness who refuses to be sworn in and testify could be held in contempt of court. These acts generally take place within the presence of the judge and are known as direct contempt. The judge may punish the offender summarily—that is, there and then—without a hearing or any other procedure's taking place. The punishment may be imprisonment, a fine, or both.

Not only are insulting remarks made to a judge possible contemptuous acts; may remarks between the prosecuting attorney and the defense counsel may also be considered contemptuous. In *People* v. *Fusaro,* a case in which the two attorneys had exchanged a series of acrimonious remarks, the judge held both in contempt of court. The defense counsel accused the prosecuting attorney of "indulging in crap," to which the prosecuting attorney, according to the judge, "sank to the occasion by voicing an epithet denoting fecal matter of a male bovine."[2] On another occasion, a prosecuting attorney was held in contempt upon using an old southern colloquialism implying that the defendant was the incestuous son of a canine mother.

An interesting development arose out of the *Fusaro* case. The defense counsel was held in contempt and was imprisoned in the middle of the trial. The facts of the case reflect the following: "The record reveals an acrimonious five day trial in which the attorneys mistook bickering and side remarks for vigorous advocacy. The prosecutor . . . was guilty of at least one act of misconduct," and the defense attorney

in his turn cluttered and interrupted the trial with frivolous objections. He aroused the trial judge's ire by permitting a witness to remain in the courtroom despite an exclusion order. He was twice late in returning to the trial after a recess.

On the afternoon of the third day he was 15 minutes late, apologized and explained that the judge of another court had detained him. Outside the jury's presence the trial court held him in contempt for tardiness and imposed a one-day suspended jail sentence.

This exchange of remarks between the prosecuting attorney and defense counsel "indulging in crap" took place thereafter:

> At that point the judge recessed the trial, rebuked the attorneys, indicated that he wanted to consider their behavior and put the matter over to the next morning.
>
> The next morning, outside the jury's presence, the court found both attorneys in contempt.

The prosecuting attorney apologized, and the judge fined him $50. The defense counsel endeavored to justify the language. The judge

> imposed a 24-hour jail sentence on defense counsel, refused to stay the execution and committed him to jail immediately. In view of the jailing, defendant's trial was recessed until the following morning.

The defendant was convicted on four narcotics charges. The conviction was appealed on the grounds that the judge had abused discretion in holding the defense counsel in contempt and immediately imposing a jail sentence. The defendant alleged that the jailing of the counsel prejudiced the defendant in the eyes of the jury and that a speedy trial was denied because of the interruption. Although the appellate court upheld the conviction, the court took a dim view of jailing a defense counsel in the middle of a trial. The court stated the following:

> A trial court has inherent statutory power to exercise reasonable control over the trial in order to insure the orderly administration of justice and to maintain the dignity and authority of the court; it has power to punish summarily for contempts committed in its immediate view and presence. In accordance with the code of the State as punishment for contempt a court may impose a fine not exceeding $500 or up to five days imprisonment or both.

Attorneys as well as others may be held in contempt more than once during a trial and may be punished for each time they are so held. Offenders have been known to receive sentences lasting for years if the sentences are made to run consecutively. The U.S. Supreme Court has held that under these circumstances, the offender is entitled to a trial on the contempt charge. The Court stated that criminal contempt is a crime and that the offender is entitled to the same trial procedure as in any other crime. If the total sentence exceeds six months, the offender is entitled to a trial by jury. If the sentence is not more than six months, the offender may be tried by a judge sitting without a jury, but the Court stated that the trial should be conducted by a judge other than the one holding the offender in contempt because of the possible emotional involvement in the matter.[3] Some states grant a person accused of a crime a jury trial for all violations. The offender would then be entitled to a jury trial even though the sentence would not exceed six months.

The U.S. Supreme Court has considerably restricted the right of a trial judge to take summary contempt action and confused the action that may be taken. But the Court apparently did not eliminate the right entirely. The wording of the Court indicated that if it is necessary to preserve the calm atmosphere and dignity of the court, a judge may exercise the contempt action at the time of the misconduct and may even sentence the person involved. However, if the judge waits until the conclusion of the trial to take the contempt action, the offender is entitled to a trial on the contempt charge.

Defense counsels are held in contempt more frequently than prosecuting attorneys. If a prosecuting attorney indulges in misconduct, the misconduct may be considered prejudicial error, and a conviction may be reversed on appeal.

In addition, acts not performed in the presence of the judge may also be declared as contempt. These acts are known as indirect, or constructive, contempt, and they are usually the result of failure to abide by court orders. For example, jurors may discuss the facts of the case during a recess—in violation of the judge's order not to discuss the case—a juror may refuse to appear in court without sufficient good reason after receiving a summons to appear, or a witness may not appear as directed. Since indirect contempt does not occur in the presence of the judge, a hearing is held to determine whether the alleged offender should be held in contempt. Prior to the hearing, the judge will issue an order requesting the offender to show cause why he or she should not be held in contempt of court. Witnesses both for and against will be questioned at the hearing to assist in determining whether the accused should be held in contempt. If the judge determines that the person should be held in contempt, it would appear that the offender is entitled to a trial on the contempt charge, since the act was not committed in the presence of the judge.

The right of contempt is a powerful weapon, and it is meant to be. It permits a judge to prohibit court proceedings from getting out of hand because of misconduct. It also protects those involved in the court proceedings. If a judge should abuse his or her power of contempt, appeals may be made to a higher court for review and possible remedy.

VICTIM AND DEFENDANT

Victim

The victim of any crime is often the forgotten party in the criminal justice system. For many years, victims were perceived as simply another witness to the crime.[4] The prevailing attitude was that the real victim was the people of the state in which the crime was committed. Families of murder victims could not obtain information regarding the case and were often ignored by overworked and understaffed criminal justice personnel. Within the past twenty years, this attitude has begun to change as we have become more aware of the needs and desires of crime victims.

Law enforcement professionals dealing with crime victims must understand that these victims may be suffering emotional and/or physical trauma as a result of the offense.[5] Care must be taken to ensure that victims understand how the process works and what their rights are. It is also important to realize that there are individuals other than the original victim who have an interest in the process. These parties include the victim's family and friends and, in some situations, the victim's employer. All the appropriate parties should be notified of every significant event within the criminal justice process. Law enforcement professionals must also respect and protect the victim's right to privacy if that is the victim's desire.

Victims of crime will normally have a number of questions and concerns regarding the court system and their involvement in it. One of the most frustrating aspects of this process is the fact that victims often perceive that the defendant has more rights and faster access to the courts than they do.

Defendant

The defendant in a criminal case is guaranteed certain rights within our form of government. Many aspects of the criminal procedure process are controlled by the U.S. Constitution, specifically the Bill of Rights (the original ten amendments to the Constitution). These federal constitutional protections concerning individual rights are, for the most part, binding on state courts.[6]

Law in Practice

Ethical Obligations of a Prosecutor

Under the mandates of the U.S. Constitution, criminal prosecutors engage in a balancing act under conflicting obligations. On the one hand, they must advocate for their clients, the citizenry of the community from which they are appointed or elected; and on the other hand, they must act to protect the criminal defendant's constitutional rights and fairly participate in the search for justice. Because prosecutors have the sole power to initiate judicial action in a criminal case, they are the most powerful players within the criminal justice system. Because there is little independent control over a prosecutor's discretion in charging or not charging a suspect, the prosecutor's ethical and legal commitment to justice is critical. Prosecutors have the ethical and legal obligation to ensure that innocent persons are not unfairly charged and that the evidence against a suspect is, in the judgment of the prosecutor, sufficient to support a specific charge.

[Excerpt from Chris McDonough, Diana Brusca McDonough, and Raymond G. Keenan, "Ethical Obligations of the Criminal Prosecutor" in *Morality and the Law*, pp. 50–64, Roslyn Muraskin and Matthew Muraskin, eds. (Upper Saddle River, NJ: Pearson), 2001.]

These rights attach to the defendant early in the criminal procedure process, and violation of these rights may result in the case's being dismissed. For example, if the defendant confesses to the crime of murder and if that confession is obtained in violation of his or her constitutional rights, it may be suppressed.[7] If the confession is the only link connecting the defendant to the crime, the case may have to be dismissed. When these types of incidents occur, it is very difficult for the victim to understand why the defendant goes free when there has been a confession.

PROSECUTOR

The prosecuting attorney is known by a variety of names. In some places, he or she is known as the district attorney, or the D.A., and in other areas as the county attorney. In the federal system, the title is United States Attorney. The public official role of the prosecuting attorney is comparatively recent. For many years, it was the responsibility of the victim or relatives to prosecute when a crime was committed. Attorneys were employed by these persons to assist in the prosecution. As time passed, it was deemed advisable to have a full-time public prosecutor, since the offense was actually committed against society, and therefore, the office of the prosecuting attorney was established.

In most states, the prosecuting attorney is an elected official of the county. In large urban areas, this is a sought-after position, since it holds prestige, it pays well, and the prosecuting attorney has a number of deputies for assistance. In many places, there may be no staff, and in sparsely settled counties, the position may be only a part-time job. When not engaged in handling official duties, the prosecuting attorney in such counties may have a private law practice. A few states have permitted several counties to form a judicial district and employ a single prosecuting attorney to handle the duties. Many attorneys have no interest in running for the position of prosecuting attorney, since their private practices are more lucrative. Others shun the idea of running as a candidate in an election. As a result, in many counties, the office of the prosecuting attorney is a training ground for younger attorneys willing to run for the office to gain experience and to tide them over financially while building a private practice. In most counties, the prosecuting attorney is a capable and reputable local attorney who has a sincere interest in making certain that justice is done.

Law in Practice

Massachusetts Rules of Professional Conduct Rule 3.8 Special Responsibilities of a Prosecutor

The prosecutor in a criminal case shall:
  (a) refrain from prosecuting a charge that the prosecutor knows is not supported by probable cause;
  (b) make reasonable efforts to assure that the accused has been advised of the right to, and the procedure for obtaining, counsel and has been given reasonable opportunity to obtain counsel;
  (c) not seek to obtain from an unrepresented accused a waiver of important pretrial rights, such as the right to a preliminary hearing, unless a court first has obtained from the accused a knowing and intelligent written waiver of counsel;
  (d) make timely disclosure to the defense of all evidence or information known to the prosecutor that tends to negate the guilt of the accused or mitigates the offense, and, in connection with sentencing, disclose to the defense and to the tribunal all unprivileged mitigating information known to the prosecutor, except when the prosecutor is relieved of this responsibility by a protective order of the tribunal;
  (e) exercise reasonable care to prevent investigators, law enforcement personnel, employees, or other persons assisting or associated with the prosecutor in a criminal case from making an extrajudicial statement that the prosecutor would be prohibited from making under Rule 3.6; . . . (j) not intentionally avoid pursuit of evidence because the prosecutor believes it will damage the prosecution's case or aid the accused.

Law in Practice

Who Prosecutes Felony Cases in the State Courts

Title	States
District Attorney	Alabama, California, Colorado, Georgia, Kansas, Louisiana, Maine, Massachusetts, Mississippi, Nevada, New Mexico, New York, North Carolina, Oklahoma, Oregon, Pennsylvania, Texas, Wisconsin, and Wyoming
County Attorney	Arizona, Iowa, Kansas, Minnesota, Nebraska, New Hampshire, Texas, and Utah
Prosecuting Attorney	Arkansas, Hawaii, Idaho, Indiana, Michigan, Missouri, Ohio, Washington, and West Virginia
Commonwealth Attorney	Kentucky and Virginia
County Prosecutor	New Jersey
District Attorney General	Tennessee
County and Prosecuting Attorney	Wyoming
Solicitor	South Carolina
Circuit Attorney	City of St. Louis
Statewide Prosecution	Alaska, Delaware, and Rhode Island

Note: Some states are listed more than once because different parts of the state use a different system.

Source: Carol DeFrances, Steven Smith, and Louise van der Does, "Prosecutors in State Courts, 1994" (Washington, D.C.: Bureau of Justice Statistics, National Institute of Justice, 1996).

Responsibilities of the Prosecuting Attorney

The prosecuting attorney has a great deal of power, irrespective of personal capabilities or jurisdiction of service. The prosecuting attorney is charged with grave responsibilities to the public that demand integrity, zeal, and conscientious effort in the administration of justice. As stated by the U.S. Supreme Court in the *Gideon* decision, prosecuting attorneys "are everywhere deemed essential to protect the public's interest in an orderly society." The public prosecutor institutes proceedings before magistrates for the arrest of persons charged with or reasonably suspected of committing a public offense. In addition to acting as prosecutor, in most instances he or she represents the county on all civil matters.

The prosecuting attorney enters the justice procedural picture early in the prosecutive process. A great number of arrests are made by law enforcement officers on their own determination that there is reasonable cause to believe that a crime has been committed. Unless the alleged offender is released by the arresting agency without further action being taken, the prosecuting attorney must be consulted to determine whether prosecutive action will be taken against the arrested person. The prosecuting attorney evaluates the weight of evidence against the accused and the nature of the charge in deciding whether to prosecute. If the prosecuting attorney decides against prosecution, the accused will be released. If he or she decides that prosecutive action should be taken, a complaint will be prepared by the prosecuting attorney and filed with the appropriate court. The accused is then taken before a committing magistrate for the initial appearance, or arraignment, as it is referred to in some jurisdictions. Often law enforcement agencies conduct an investigation of alleged violations before making an arrest. In these instances, the prosecuting attorney is usually consulted to determine whether there is sufficient evidence against the accused to justify prosecutive action, whether a complaint should be filed, and whether a warrant of arrest should be obtained. As pointed out in Chapter 5, the prosecuting attorney may prefer to present the charge to the grand jury to determine whether prosecutive action should be taken or whether a secret indictment should be sought. This procedure is followed in felony charges. If the crime for which the arrest was made is a less serious misdemeanor, the prosecutive decision may be left to the discretion of the law enforcement agency involved. Even the preparation of the complaint and the prosecution during the trial may be handled by the officer, and the prosecuting attorney may not appear on the scene unless a special problem arises. In the more serious misdemeanor cases and on felony charges, the prosecuting attorney will be involved from the time of arrest through the appeal.

Law in Practice

Duty of a Prosecutor in a Criminal Case

The National District Attorneys Association states that it is the fundamental duty of prosecutors to seek truth and justice, not merely convictions. If you were the prosecutor, how would you handle the following situations?

You are assigned to prosecute a robbery case. The victim has identified the perpetrator in a photographic lineup and at the beginning of the trial. A detective has testified that the defendant has confessed to the crime. During a break in the trial, the victim tells you that he is not sure whether the defendant was the person who robbed him.

During cross-examination of a rape defendant, you start to doubt the testimony of the victim and begin to believe that the act may have been consensual in nature.

You are in charge of issuing cases, and you are screening one involving a terrorist who was found with explosives and plans to detonate an explosive device on a cruise ship. You discover that the arrest was invalid; therefore, if you do not issue a complaint, he will go free. If you issue the complaint, the investigating officer assures you that he can find other crimes to charge the terrorist with and keep him in confinement.

If the charge is a serious one and the prosecuting attorney decides to prosecute, there are many decisions and duties to perform. The first duty is to determine what charge or charges the evidence will support so that the appropriate accusatory pleading may be filed. The prosecuting attorney must decide whether the charges, when there is more than one, are to be separated into different trials or consolidated into one. In some jurisdictions, if the charge is a felony, it must be decided whether the facts are to be presented in a preliminary hearing or to a grand jury. The information or the indictment must be prepared depending on the type of hearing conducted. Where appropriate, the granting of motions requested by the defense must be disputed.

Law in Practice

Significant Cases Involving the Prosecutor

Berger v. *United States* (1935)	Court notes that the prosecutor's primary interest is in doing justice, not simply winning cases.
Imbler v. *Pachtman* (1976)	Prosecutors enjoy absolute immunity from civil liability when making decisions about initiating and pursuing a criminal prosecution.
Morrison v. *Olson* (1988)	The federal independent counsel law is constitutional.
Burns v. *Reed* (1991)	Prosecutors have only qualified immunity from civil lawsuits concerning advice they give to police officers.
Buckley v. *Fitzsimmons* (1993)	Prosecutors have only qualified immunity from civil lawsuits for statements made during a news conference. They also have only qualified immunity for actions they take during criminal investigations.
Kalina v. *Fletcher* (1997)	A prosecutor may be subject to civil liability for making false statements of fact in an affidavit in support of an arrest warrant.

At the time of the trial, another responsibility is to present enough evidence to prove the defendant guilty beyond a reasonable doubt. The prosecuting attorney must also assist in the selection of the jury, decide what witnesses to call, and determine what physical evidence should be introduced. It is not necessary that every person who has some knowledge of the facts in the case be called, nor is it necessary that all physical evidence collected by the law enforcement officers during an investigation be presented during a trial. The prosecuting attorney must present enough witnesses and physical evidence to ensure the defendant a fair trial, and may not withhold any evidence that would be advantageous to the defendant. If the defense presents witnesses in its behalf, the prosecuting attorney must cross-examine them. The responsibilities of making recommendations to the judge on the severity of the sentence and, in most states, of assisting the state attorney general with appeals also fall to the prosecuting attorney.

Law in Practice

The Elected Prosecutor

The first election of a district attorney in Philadelphia occurred in 1850 [Carole Ramsey, "The Discretionary Power of 'Public Prosecutors in Historical Perspective," 39 *Am. Crim. L. Rev.* 1309 (2002)]. In New York State, private lawyers ceased to represent victims at trial when the district attorney became an elected official in 1846. Private settlements were also eliminated. A complainant might approach the district attorney to urge investigation and prosecution; however, by the second half of the nineteenth century, the district attorney possessed sole discretion over whether to present the victim's charges to the grand jury [N.Y. Const. of 1846, art. X, § 1]. The election of district attorneys represented a move to subject a variety of local officials, including sheriffs and coroners, to the vote. The change ostensibly arose from a desire to increase accountability to the voters. What control should the public have over prosecutors? Consider the two quotes below:

> The . . . main remedy for prosecutorial misconduct [besides administrative supervision, trial court control, and appellate review] is public oversight. State district attorneys typically are elected officials. Misconduct within their offices—even by lawyers whom they have not directly supervised—becomes an issue during elections. Accordingly, media attention and political review by the voters may

provide a deterrent or, at least, a reason for district attorneys to take corrective steps when misconduct is brought to their attention.

[Fred C. Zacharias, "The Professional Discipline of Prosecutors," 79 *N.C.L. Rev.* 721, 765 (2001)]

> I do not suggest that the honorable prosecutor be the slave of his electorate. Indeed, in many matters his duty clearly lies in the defiance of community pressures. But within the confines of the law, I would rather see his discretion guided by an honest effort to discern public needs and community concerns than by personal pique or moralistic impertinence.

[H. Richard Uviller, "The Virtuous Prosecutor in Quest for an Ethical Standard: Guidance from the ABA." 71 *Mich. L. Rev.* 1145, 1153 (1973)]

Law in Practice

Duties of the State of Washington Attorney General's Office

The Attorney General's Office makes a difference every day for the people of Washington—through its work as the state's chief legal officer and through key initiatives such as:

Consumer protection: Fighting ID theft, Internet predators and scams. Find tips to make you a smarter consumer on our All Consuming blog. Attend a free ID theft prevention forum or a shredding event. Learn how to credit issues and better manage your finances.

Government accountability: Promoting open government and protecting private property through the fair use of eminent domain.

Community safety: Protecting children, families, and communities through "Operation: Allied Against Meth." the Youth Internet Safety Task Force, the "Homicide Investigative Tracking System"—or HITS—and the sexually violent predator unit.

As the chief legal office for the State of Washington, AGO attorneys and staff provide legal services to more than 230 state agencies, boards, and commissions, as well as Attorney General's Opinions, antitrust enforcement, and representation for the environment and utility customers.

[Washington State Attorney General Rob McKenna website, www.atg.wa.gov accessed June 9, 2008]

STATE ATTORNEY GENERAL

In most states, the attorney general has broad authority to coordinate local prosecutions. This authority includes the right to prosecute on his or her own and to supervise, assist, and consult local prosecuting attorneys. If a local prosecuting attorney needs assistance or fails to perform his or her duties, the attorney general is free to act. Unless called on by the local prosecutor or unless the local prosecutor fails to prosecute when the facts warrant it, the state attorney general does not ordinarily intervene. There are a few states where the attorney general has no authority over local prosecutions. If there is a malfeasance in office by the local prosecuting attorney in those states, the governor could be called to appoint a special prosecutor to perform the duties of the local prosecutor. When a case is appealed, in most jurisdictions it is the responsibility of the state attorney general to present the case to the appellate court. The attorney general will be assisted by the prosecuting attorney of the county in which the trial took place.

DEFENSE COUNSEL

The defense attorney represents the rights and interests of the defendant. Unlike the prosecutor, who is concerned with justice, truth, and fairness, the defense attorney's obligation as established by the American Bar Association's General Standards of Conduct is to use all of his or her courage, devotion, and skills to protect the rights of the accused. Many defense attorneys interpret this obligation as requiring that they do everything possible to obtain an acquittal even if they know that the defendant in fact committed the offense.

The Sixth Amendment to the U.S. Constitution requires that those who are accused of crimes have a right to be represented by an attorney. The Supreme Court in the landmark case of *Gideon* v. *Wainwright* established the principle that all defendants have a right to counsel in all felony cases even if they cannot afford to hire their own attorney.[8] The Court extended this concept to misdemeanor cases in *Argersinger* v. *Hamilin,* holding that absent a waiver, no person may be imprisoned for any offense, either misdemeanor or felony, unless he or she has been represented by an attorney.[9]

There are basically four types of defense attorneys: public defenders, contract defense services, assigned defense counsel, and private defense counsel. Public defenders are hired and paid for by the government and are appointed to represent those persons charged with crimes who cannot afford to hire an attorney to represent them. Many counties have public defenders' offices that are staffed by very able, aggressive attorneys. However, there are instances when, for a variety of reasons, the public defenders office has a conflict of interest in a case. For example, this conflict might occur if there were two defendants in one case. In this situation, the court might appoint an attorney from the contract defense services to represent one of the two defendants. Contract defense services normally comprise a group of attorneys who have entered into an agreement with the county to represent indigent defendants for a specified amount of money. Assigned defense counsels exist in the majority of the counties in the United States.[10] Many of these counties are small and cannot afford the cost of maintaining a public defenders office. Under the assigned defense counsel format, the court maintains a list of attorneys who are willing to be appointed to represent indigent criminal defendants. When a defendant appears in court, the judge appoints the next attorney on the list to represent this person. The last form of defense attorney is the private defense counsel. These attorneys usually represent those defendants who are capable of paying for their services. Well-known examples of private defense counsel include attorneys such as Johnnie Cochran, F. Lee Bailey, and Alan Dershowitz of the "Dream Team" who represented Hall of Fame football player O.J. Simpson, who was accused of murdering his wife and another person.

Not only do perpetrators have a right to an attorney, the courts have held that the attorney must be competent.[11] Although the Constitution requires competent counsel who will vigorously defend the perpetrator, there is no requirement or right to have an attorney who will knowingly present perjured testimony. In *Nix* v. *Whiteside,* the defense attorney, upon learning that his client was going to take the stand and commit perjury, informed the client that he could not permit such testimony and that if the client insisted upon giving this testimony, the attorney would disclose the perjury and withdraw from the case. The perpetrator testified and did not commit perjury; however, he did file an appeal claiming ineffective counsel. The court disagreed, holding that attorneys who follow their state's rules of professional (ethical) conduct do not violate the Sixth Amendment right to counsel.[12]

Privileged Communication

Defense counsels are often placed in a most awkward position because of the age-old relationship of **privileged communication** between attorney and client. This relationship provides that information furnished to an attorney in confidence by his or her client may not be revealed without the permission of the client. Law enforcement agencies may be unaware of crimes discussed by a client. In one instance, a client told his attorney about two murders that he had committed and where the bodies were buried. The problem created by receiving this information is whether the attorney should furnish it to the appropriate law enforcement agency or keep it in strictest confidence. The answer to this question has been debated by many legal scholars, with no concrete answer forthcoming. It would appear that the better action would be to give the information to the appropriate law enforcement agency so that the bodies could be recovered and relatives notified. Society, as well as the criminal, is entitled to some consideration and justice. In most instances, prosecutive action cannot be taken, since the exclusionary rule would prohibit the use of the information as evidence.

If the facts of a case are such that an attorney cannot accept the responsibility of effectively defending a client, the case should be refused. Once the case is accepted, it is the attorney's duty to remain until it has been brought to a logical conclusion. The defense attorney has many functions to perform, both before and during the trial. A conference with the accused should be held as soon as practically possible. This conference should be private and unobserved even though the accused is in jail at the time. If there are codefendants, the defense counsel must decide whether all of them can be effectively represented without a conflict of interest. If either counsel or one of the defendants feels that being represented by just one counsel would result in prejudice, each defendant is entitled to and must be provided with individual counsel.

Law in Practice

Confidentiality and the Case of Robert Garrow's Lawyers

Robert Garrow was arrested and charged with murder of a young girl. At the time of his arrest, police suspected that Garrow had committed at least two other murders. Garrow admitted these other murders to his defense counsel and told the lawyers where the bodies were. The victims were both teenage girls. Garrow's lawyers, following his directions, found the girls' bodies and photographed them. They did not provide information about their discovery of the bodies to the police. The father of one of the girls thought it might be possible that Garrow was involved in the case of his daughter and approached one of the defense counsel to see if he could obtain information about his daughter. The attorney did not reveal to the father information he had learned from Garrow. After Garrow was convicted of murder, the district attorney brought charges against the defense attorneys. The charges were later dismissed. A state bar committee concluded that the attorneys were bound by the confidentiality of a lawyer-client relationship and that their failure to disclose the information was correct.[13]

The defense counsel will advise the defendant on the plea that should be entered at the arraignment, and counsel will be present for the purpose of cross-examining witnesses at the preliminary hearing. Counsel also has a right to be present during an identification lineup procedure if the defendant has been formally charged; however, the attorney has no right to interfere with the lineup or to prohibit the defendant from participating. The counsel will file those motions that are in the best interest of the defendant. The defendant is entitled to sit with counsel at the counsel table during the trial so that they may confer on the defense. This assistance is another reason why a defendant is entitled to be present during a trial. Defense counsel will cross-examine prosecution witnesses when appropriate and will present such evidence on behalf of the defendant deemed necessary under the circumstances. Further duties of the defense counsel will be pointed out in the discussion of trial procedures.

CLERK OF THE COURT

With the judge, the prosecuting attorney, and the defense counsel all playing dramatic roles during a criminal trial, one could easily overlook the clerk of the court, or county clerk, as the position is also known. This official also has a most important function in the justice system, not only during the trial but before and after it as well. The main function of the court clerk is to maintain all records of a particular case. These records include items such as copies of all the accusatory pleadings and motions that have been filed. The clerk also issues subpoenas and, in many jurisdictions, prepares the jury panel. He or she attends trials to swear in witnesses, marks exhibits, and maintains the evidence that is introduced. The clerk also keeps copies of the court transcripts, judgments rendered, and motions for appeal.

BAILIFF

The court **bailiff** may be a permanent member of the justice system or an individual appointed to assist in a particular trial. In some jurisdictions, the bailiff is a member of the county government and carries the title of marshal. The bailiff assists the judge in maintaining order in the court and calls the witnesses to testify. If the defendant has not been released from custody, it is the duty of the bailiff to guard the defendant in the courtroom. When the jury is sequestered, it is the responsibility of the bailiff to make certain that the jurors are free from all contact with the public; the bailiff will return the jury to the courtroom after they have reached a verdict. In many jurisdictions, the bailiff serves court orders and other court papers.

COURT REPORTER

The responsibility of recording everything said during the trial proceeding belongs to the court reporter. This includes the testimony of all the witnesses, objections made to the attorney's questions, rulings made by the judge, and conferences between the attorneys and the judge. If the case is taken up on appeal, the recorded notes must be transcribed.

The court reporter must be highly skilled to record transactions as they take place, often at a rapid pace. The reporter may record the proceedings in shorthand or with a stenotype machine. When first used in the courtroom, tape recorders were not very reliable. However, today many jurisdictions are using audiotapes to record the trial proceedings. These recorders have increased both their reliability and the quality of recording.

COURT COMMISSIONER

In many judicial districts, court commissioners are appointed to assist trial judges. In most instances, they must possess the same qualifications as the judge, and a commissioner may substitute for a judge in an emergency situation. Otherwise, the commissioners hold hearings on motions filed, set and accept bail, and perform other duties that may be imposed on them by law.

CASE LAW

Recent Cases

Sanchez-Llamas v. *Oregon*, 548 U.S. 331 (U.S. 2006)

Moises Sanchez-Llamas, a Mexican national, argued that his incriminating statements to police in an attempted murder case should have been suppressed because he was not informed of his right under Vienna Convention art. 36 to have the Mexican Consulate notified of his detention.

Sanchez-Llamas, a Mexican national, was convicted of murder, raised a Vienna Convention art. 36 claim for the first time in his habeas petition; the Virginia courts found that the claim was procedurally defaulted.

The Supreme Court held that, assuming that Vienna Convention art. 36 created judicially enforceable rights, suppression of evidence was not an appropriate remedy; the remedial objectives served by the exclusionary rule did not arise in the consular notification context. Also, state rules concerning procedural default were applicable to Vienna Convention art. 36 claims. International Court of Justice decisions precluding application of procedural default rules to Vienna Convention art. 36 claims were not binding. The rule of procedural default applied even to claimed violations of the U.S. Constitution and played an important role in the United States' adversary legal system. The Court affirmed his conviction.

The Court noted that exclusionary rule as it is known is an entirely American legal creation. The exclusionary rule is unique to American jurisprudence. More than forty years after the drafting of the Vienna Convention on Consular Relations, Apr. 24, 1963, 21 U.S.T. 77, 596 U.N.T.S. 261, the automatic exclusionary rule applied in American courts is still universally rejected by other countries. It is implausible that other signatories to the Vienna Convention thought it to require a remedy that nearly all refuse to recognize as a matter of domestic law.

United States v. *Carter*, 2011 U.S. App. LEXIS 5398, 1-3 (4th Cir. N.C. 2011)

Daryl Bernard Carter was found guilty following his jury trial for conspiracy to interfere with commerce by robbery, in violation of 18 U.S.C. § 1951 (2006) (Count 1); interference with commerce by robbery and aiding and abetting (Counts 2, 4); use and carrying of a firearm in relation to a crime of violence and aiding and abetting, in violation of 18 U.S.C.A. § 924(c) (West Supp. 2010) (Counts 3, 5, 7); armed bank robbery and aiding

and abetting (Count 6); and bank robbery (Count 8). He was sentenced to 240 months of imprisonment each for Counts 1, 2, 4, and 8 to be served concurrently; a 292-month term for Count 6 imposed concurrently; a 120-month consecutive term for Count 3; and [*2] 300-month consecutive terms each for Counts 5 and 7, for a total sentence of 1012 months of imprisonment.

On appeal, Carter raises four issues (only one is considered in this note)—whether the district court created the appearance of partiality and prejudice by its extensive questioning of a witness. For the reasons that follow, we affirm.

Carter contended that the district judge's extensive questioning of accomplice Kendrick Tanner created the impression that the judge was partial against him. Carter alleges prejudice from this conduct and argues that he is entitled to a new trial, framing the issue as one of judicial misconduct. As Carter concedes, however, he failed to object to the judge's extensive questioning at trial. Thus, we only review this claim for plain error. See *United States* v. *Godwin*, 272 F.3d 659, 678 (4th Cir. 2001) 679-81 (declining to find plain error despite judge's substantial prejudicial comments, questions, and cross-examination). Although the district court's questioning of Tanner was substantial, we find no prejudice. We find that Carter has failed to meet the demanding burden of showing plain error on appeal. [The U.S. Court of Appeals held that by failing to object at the time the judge was doing the questioning, the defendant waived his right to appeal that issue, and therefore the appellate court could review this issue only if it was "plainly" wrong.]

In re Judicial Misconduct, 630 F.3d 968, 968-970 (9th Cir. 2010)

KOZINSKI, Chief Judge:

Complainant, a pro se litigant, filed a misconduct complaint against a magistrate judge. Instead of filing a statement of facts, complainant attached over a hundred pages of material including what appear to be documents from his underlying civil rights case, various motions purportedly made before the "executive branch, et al," two copies of a letter from a financial specialist, seven photocopies of envelopes, a copy of three receipts, an automated e-mail from PACER and two local court rules. Complainant also attached a filing in which the defendants accused him of "harassment" because he filed "217 pages of attachments" to his motion and filed another motion "consisting of 335 pages."

Under our rules, a judicial misconduct complaint "must contain a concise statement that details the specific facts on which the claim of misconduct or disability is based." Judicial-Conduct Rule 6(b); see also 28 U.S.C. § 351(a). The brief statement of facts required by section 351(a) must be prepared specifically for the misconduct proceeding, although it need not follow a particular form. See Judicial-Conduct Rule 6(a). What matters is that it be concise and set forth the alleged misconduct in a clear and straightforward fashion. The requirement that complainants submit a brief statement of facts is posted on the Ninth Circuit's website and printed on the misconduct complaint form itself. See Ninth Circuit Court of Appeals, Guidelines for Judicial Misconduct or Disability Complaints, http://www.ce9.uscourts.gov/misconduct/judicial_misconduct.html (last visited Dec. 17, 2010).

A complaint of judicial misconduct is a court filing and is therefore subject to the normal constraints on such filings, including the requirement that it conform to procedural rules governing format and content. See In re Complaint of Judicial Misconduct, 527 F.3d 792, 797 (9th Cir. Jud. Council 2008); see also 28 U.S.C. § 358(a). Misconduct complaints that don't comply with section 351(a) or Judicial-Conduct Rule 6(b) are subject to summary dismissal. See 28 U.S.C. § 352(b)(1)(A)(i) (authorizing chief judge to dismiss a complaint that is "not in conformity with section 351(a)"); see also In re Complaint of Judicial Misconduct, 591 F.3d 638, 646 (U.S. Jud. Conference 2009) (dismissing allegations of misconduct "because they do not meet the pleading requirements of Rule 6(b)"); In re Opinion of Judicial Conference Comm. to Review Circuit Council Conduct & Disability Orders, 449 F.3d 106, 111 (U.S. Jud. Conference 2006) (Winter, J., dissenting) (explaining that "complaints . . . may be dismissed summarily" if they "fail to conform with the requirements for submitting a complaint").

Although complainants may attach exhibits to their complaint, the exhibits must directly support the allegations of misconduct or disability in the statement of facts. Cf. Tenth Cir. Misconduct Rule 6.2 ("The complainant should take care to include only documentation that is required to support the specific facts alleged [while excluding e]xcess or irrelevant documentation . . . ."). In a complaint alleging prejudice or bias, for example, excerpts of a trial transcript in which the judge allegedly made racist comments would be appropriate; the entire record would not. See In re Complaint of Judicial Misconduct, 2 Cl. Ct. 255, 261 (1983) (reprimanding attorneys for "filing . . . a torrent of virtually useless paper" in misconduct proceeding).

The Judicial Council receives hundreds of complaints every year, which it must review with limited staff. Rule 6(b)'s requirement that the complaint contain a short and plain statement of the alleged misconduct is designed to focus the review process, conserve resources and ensure that all complaints are reviewed in a timely manner. These goals can't be achieved if the Judicial Council and staff must weed through hundreds of pages of materials looking for something that could possibly amount to misconduct. See In re Complaint of Judicial Misconduct, 591 F.3d at 646 ("Rule 6(b) makes clear that the complaint must be more than a suggestion to a Chief Judge that, if he . . . looks hard enough in a particular direction, he might uncover misconduct."). In conducting an expeditious review pursuant to section 352(a), the chief judge and staff will therefore not examine any documentary materials unless the statement of facts, on its face, presents what appears to be a sufficient allegation of misconduct and specifically points to the pages in the attachment that support the allegations.

As noted, the complaint here contains no statement of facts at all, much less a short and plain one. Without that statement to explain the relevance of the exhibits, the exhibits will be disregarded. Because the complaint makes no allegation of misconduct, it is dismissed.

Briefly Noted

***Reid* v. *Beard*, 2011 U.S. App. LEXIS 6120, 9-11 (3d Cir. Pa., 2011).** Reid's claim on appeal is limited to prosecutorial misconduct. He claimed, among other claims, that the prosecutor had called him a liar in court and had introduced evidence that he was the member of a gang.

The U.S. Supreme Court has held that prosecutorial misconduct is insufficient to overturn a conviction unless it "so infects the trial with unfairness as to make the resulting conviction a denial of due process." *Donnelly* v. *DeChristoforo*, 416 U.S. 637, 643, 94 S. Ct. 1868, 40 L. Ed. 2d 431 (1974). It is not enough to show that a prosecutor's remarks were inappropriate or even deserving of universal condemnation. *Darden* v. *Wainwright,* 477 U.S. 168, 181, 106 S. Ct. 2464, 91 L. Ed. 2d 144 (1986). A reviewing court must "examine the prosecutor's offensive actions in context and in light of the entire trial, assessing the severity of the conduct, the effect of the curative instructions, and the quantum of evidence against the defendant" to determine if prosecutorial conduct rises to a level that infects the trial with such unfairness as to make the resulting conviction a denial of due process. *Moore* v. *Morton*, 255 F.3d 95, 107 (3d Cir. 2001).

The trial court, in its post-verdict opinion, and every other state court that later examined the record, determined that the prosecutorial misconduct in this case—and there was clearly misconduct—did not rise to a level that would require the new trial Reid seeks. The trial court, which was in the best position to consider the effect of any misconduct, carefully considered Reid's allegations, recognized that in some instances the prosecutor went beyond what was permissible, but found that, through curative instructions and other efforts to guarantee a fair trial, the prosecutor's misconduct did not prevent the jury from weighing "the evidence objectively and render[ing] a true verdict." *Commonwealth* v. *Reid*, 25 Phila. 141, 1993 WL 1156018 at *155.

Carter v. *Scribner*, **2011 U.S. App. LEXIS 1592 (9th Cir. Cal. Jan. 24, 2011).** Defendant appealed his conviction for attempted murder based on the fact that his trial defense counsel had previously represented the victim in an unrelated case. The U.S. Court of Appeals noted that "In successive representation, conflicts of interest may arise if the cases are substantially related or if the attorney reveals privileged communications of the former client or otherwise divides his loyalties." *Hovey* v. *Ayers,* 458 F.3d 892, 908 (9th Cir. 2006) (citation omitted). Here, Carter's claim that Clark's previous representation of Lesher resulted in a conflict of interest has no merit. Carter does not produce any evidence to show that Clark's previous representation of Lesher on a charge of auto theft was substantially related to Carter's attempted murder proceeding. Nor does Carter demonstrate how Clark's previous representation of Lesher divides his loyalty to Carter. Carter fails to show how Clark's previous representation of Lesher constituted a conflict, and thus, the court denies the claim.

Summary

- Our system of justice is based on the adversary system.
- The judge presides over the trial proceedings and performs those duties imposed upon him or her by law.
- The trial judge has the primary responsibility during a trial for ensuring that justice is carried out.
- A trial judge has contempt authority. Contempt is an act that is disrespectful to the court or adversely affects the administration of justice.
- The victim is often the forgotten person in the trial.

- The prosecutor's primary duty is to promote justice.
- The prosecutor institutes proceedings before magistrates for the arrest of persons charged with or reasonably suspected of committing a public offense.
- In most states, the state attorney general has broad authority to coordinate local prosecutions.
- The defense counsel has a duty to represent the defendant.
- There are four types of defense attorneys: public defenders, contract defense services, assigned defense counsel, and private retained counsel.

Review Questions

1. What is the primary function of the judge?
2. List four duties of the judge during trial proceedings.
3. What is contempt of court?
4. Name three types of misconduct that might cause one to be held in contempt of court.
5. List five duties and/or responsibilities of the prosecuting attorney.

6. What are some of the problems that a defense attorney encounters with a client?
7. List four duties of a defense counsel.
8. Describe the functions of the following:
   a. the clerk of the court
   b. the bailiff
   c. the court reporter

Local Procedure

1. Does the state attorney general have the authority to assist local prosecuting attorneys in handling prosecutions?

Endnotes

1. 388 U.S. 218 (1967).
2. See *People* v. *Fusaro,* 18 Cal App 3rd 877 (1971).
3. See *Taylor* v. *Hayes,* 418 U.S. 488 (1974) and *Codispoti* v. *Pennsylvania,* 418 U.S. 506 (1974).
4. This section has been adapted from H. Wallace, *Victimology: Legal, Psychological and Social Perspectives* (Boston: Allyn & Bacon), 1996.
5. M. Randell and L. Haskell, "Sexual Violence in Women's Lives," 1/1 *Violence Against Women,* 6 (1995).
6. The Fifth Amendment's right to grand jury indictment and the Eighth Amendment's right regarding excessive bail have not been applied to the states. See *Hurtado* v. *California,* 110 U.S. 516 (1884).
7. If the confession was obtained by coercion, it may not be admitted even for impeachment purposes. See *Mincey* v. *Arizona,* 437 U.S. 385 (1978).
8. 372 U.S. 335 (1963).
9. 407 U.S. 25 (1972). See also *Scott* v. *Illinois,* 440 U.S. 367 (1979), where the U.S. Supreme Court held that the right to counsel only applies where imprisonment is actually imposed rather than merely authorized by statute.
10. Bureau of Justice Statistics Bulletin, *Criminal Defense Systems* (Washington, D.C., U.S. Department of Justice, August 1984), p. 6.
11. *Strickland* v. *Washington,* 466 U.S. 668 (1984).
12. 475 U.S. 157 (1986).
13. See Confidentiality and the Case of Robert Garrow's Lawyers, 25 Buffalo L. Rev. 211, 213–14 (1975).

CHAPTER 12

Jury

*Gentlemen, a court is no better than each man of you sitting before me on this jury. A court is
only as sound as its jury, and a jury is only as sound as the men who make it up.*

—ATTICUS FINCH IN HARPER LEE'S *TO KILL A MOCKINGBIRD*, 1960

Chapter Outline

Key Terms

Challenges for cause
Cross section of community
   standard
Death-qualified jury
Jury list

Jury of one's peers
Jury panel
Peremptory challenge
Sequestered jury

Learning Objectives

After completing this chapter, you should be able to:

- Outline the jury selection process.
- Explain the meaning of "a jury of one's peers."

- Identify the reasons that a
  potential juror may be challenged
  for cause.

265

- Define peremptory challenges and discuss the restrictions on the use of peremptory challenges.
- Explain the rationale behind the sequestering of a jury.

- Discuss the future of the jury system.
- Explain how a jury panel is selected.

INTRODUCTION

Once the trial date has arrived and the prosecution and defense indicate their readiness, the next step is the selection of the jury. However, before entering this phase of the trial proceedings, a few questions need to be answered. First, who are the persons who serve on a jury, and where do they come from? Further, what qualities must they possess to qualify as jurors? A defendant is entitled to be tried in the judicial district in which the crime was committed and to have an impartial jury selected from that district. A criminal would not pick a particular judicial district in which to commit a crime because of greater faith in a jury from that district. This right to be tried within the judicial district in which the crime was committed is included in the Sixth Amendment of the U.S. Constitution. It was included because of the colonists' experience of being hauled away to Great Britain for trials of crimes allegedly committed in the colonies. The jurors were thus picked in Great Britain. Therefore, unless a change of venue is granted because an impartial jury cannot be selected within that district, the fate of one accused of committing a crime rests with those in the judicial district where the crime was committed.

A JURY OF ONE'S PEERS

The only jury qualification set forth in the Sixth Amendment is that it be an impartial jury chosen from the judicial district in which the crime was committed. Similar provisions are included in the constitutions or statutes of the states. Any additional qualifications believed necessary for service as a juror come from suppositions of legislative action. Though not specifically provided for in most state statutes, it is generally conceded that the jury is to comprise the accused's peers. This concept stems from a provision in the Magna Charta that provides that no freeman shall be seized and imprisoned except by judgment of "his peers." This provision did not pertain to a trial jury but to an accusatory jury. The Magna Charta, which was prepared by noblemen for their own benefit, was intended to prohibit the king from seizing and imprisoning a nobleman merely on a whim. Seizure and imprisonment were to occur only after an accusation was determined to be well founded by the judgment of fellow noblemen. Although the Magna Charta was designed primarily for the benefit of noblemen, the lower classes of persons in Great Britain at the time also received benefit from this provision, and it became a part of the due process of law of Great Britain.

Trial by One's Peers

As the trial jury was created, it was assumed that it would comprise one's peers. This concept was brought to America by the colonists. Yet few states have directly indicated that a trial jury must consist of one's peers. More and more often, this concept of trial by peers is directing the selection of juries. In the past, if the jury comprised twelve persons "good and true" picked from the community where the trial was to be held, the nebulous peers qualification had been satisfied. In recent years, a closer look has been taken at the term Jury of **one's peers** and at whether the requirement, though not specifically and formally set forth in the statutes, is met. The dictionary defines peers as one's equals, or those of equal status; one's friends; or associates. To take this definition too literally in composing a jury would imply that a medical doctor could be tried only by a jury comprising other doctors, a farmer by other farmers, a former convict by other convicts, or a sixteen-year-old defendant by other sixteen-year-olds. Such juries would undoubtedly fulfill the peers qualification but would be most difficult to find in some jurisdictions. If such a jury were possible, the chances of jury impartiality would be low. Fortunately, courts have not gone this far in selecting juries. As long as the jury is made up of persons representing a cross section of the community in which the trial takes place, it is regarded as comprising one's peers.

At one time, only white males were qualified to serve as jurors. In fact, most states did not permit women to serve on juries until they were granted the right to vote with the passage of the Nineteenth Amendment to the U.S. Constitution in 1920. Persons of certain races, religions, and national origins were excluded, if not by statutory provision, then by those making the jury panel selection. These exclusions were justified by those responsible for the jury panel, since they were to select only persons who were males, over twenty-one years of age, honest, intelligent, and of good character and sound judgment. It was alleged that members of minority groups did not meet these qualifications. To overcome this practice, the federal government passed legislation stating that no citizen shall be excluded from service on a federal grand jury or a federal petit jury because of race, color, religion, sex, national origin, or economic status and that persons are to be selected at random from a fair cross section of the community.[1]

Cross Section of the Community Standard

Many states have adopted the **cross section of the community standard** to meet the peer group regulation, particularly in view of U.S. Supreme Court decisions. In *Glasser* v. *United States*,[2] the Court stated, "The American tradition of trial by jury, considered in connection with either criminal or civil proceedings, necessarily contemplates an impartial jury drawn from a cross section of the community." The Court has also stated that it is part of the established tradition in the use of juries as instruments of public justice that the jury be a body truly representative of the community. However, what is a truly representative body? Does it pertain only to race, education, age, sex, religion, economic status, or philosophical thinking, or must *all* of these matters be considered when composing a jury panel? These questions were partially answered by the U.S. Supreme Court in *Fay* v. *New York*,[3] where the Court stated the following:

> There is no constitutional right to a jury drawn from a group of uneducated and unintelligent persons. Nor is there any right to a jury chosen solely from those at the lower end of the economic and social scale. But there is a constitutional right to a jury drawn from a group that represents a cross section of the community. And a cross section of the community includes persons with varying degrees of training and intelligence and with varying economic and social positions. Under our Constitution, the jury is not to be made the representative of the most intelligent, the most wealthy or the most successful, nor of the least intelligent, the least wealthy or the least successful. It is a democratic institution, representative of all qualified classes of people.

Only by being able to select a jury from among persons who truly represent a cross section of a community can the accused be assured of an impartial jury.

In order to have a truly representative cross section of a community on a jury panel, more and more jurisdictions are conducting surveys to determine the percentage of persons of minority races and different national origins within the community. In this way, a like percentage can be included on jury panels. Younger people make up a larger percentage of those selected to serve on jury panels. In the past, juries frequently comprised older persons, since they were less likely to suffer financially by serving on juries. As idealistic as it may be to have a truly representative cross section of the community, juries often are not truly representative because many classes of persons suffer financial hardships by serving and are thus excused. However, as long as there is no systematic exclusion of any class of persons, the cross-section requirement is fulfilled. As pointed out by the courts, it is not necessary that a jury include one of each class of persons to be truly representative of a cross section of a community.

When the courts use the term community, they generally mean the judicial district in which the crime was committed. In most instances, the judicial district is the county, but in the case of inferior courts, the judicial district may be only a portion of a county.

When a jury is challenged as not being a true representation of a cross section of a community, the challenge usually is made by a defendant who fails to find one of his or her particular sex, race, or group among those from whom the jury may be chosen. But in *Taylor* v. *Louisiana*,[4] the U.S. Supreme Court held that a defendant may object to the exclusion of a class of persons from the jury panel even though the defendant is not one of the excluded class. In that case, a male defendant objected to the exclusion of women from the jury unless they volunteered for jury duty. The Court pointed out that although 53 percent of persons eligible for jury duty in the judicial district were female, only 10 percent of these had volunteered, and thus there was not a true representation of the cross section of the community. The defendant had a right to object to the exclusion of women from his jury even though he was not a member of the excluded class.

JURY PANEL OR JURY LIST

The procedure of jury selection varies somewhat among states and even among districts within a state. In some larger metropolitan districts, a jury commissioner is often appointed, whose duty it is to select persons within his or her district to be available for jury duty. This group of persons is referred to as a **jury panel** or **jury list**. In other districts, the selection of the panel may fall to the court clerk. In most jurisdictions, the selection of a jury panel is made annually, usually at the beginning of the calendar year. Generally, no guidelines are set forth for selection. As noted, the federal government provided that no person was to be excluded from serving on a jury because of race, religion, and so forth, and that the persons were to be a community cross section picked at random. No procedure was set forth for how those persons were to be randomly selected. This regulation did provide that each federal judicial district must devise and place into operation a written plan for how the jurors were to be selected—whether from voter registration lists or some other source. In this way, the courts would have some record to verify that no class of persons had been systematically excluded.

The official making the selection has almost complete power over the selection of names to be placed on the jury panel, and in most districts, the sources from which he or she obtains the names are solely at his or her discretion. Whatever list is used, the names will be individually placed in a box from which the official will randomly pull those to be placed on the jury panel. For convenience, officials often use the voter registration list, but it is generally not required that a juror be a registered voter. However, this list is often utilized with greater frequency than any other list for two reasons. First, it is more likely to be representative of a cross section of the community than other lists. Second, the qualifications for voting more nearly coincide with those that a juror must possess. However, the supreme courts of some states have held that the use of only voter registration is too restrictive since many members of minority groups do not register to vote. These courts have suggested that other sources in addition to voter registration lists be utilized to get a better cross section of a community. Tax assessors' lists have been used, but this source has been criticized since it has been held that property owners are more likely to be convicting juries than nonproperty owners. Church membership lists have also been used, but with such lists, religious conflicts ensue. Some officials select names randomly from telephone books in the area, or they select every tenth name or some similar numerical sequence. In sparsely settled districts, officials have made selections through personal contact or by selecting names furnished by acquaintances. On one occasion, an official used the membership list of the area League of Women Voters to get a representative number of women on the panel. The use of this list was criticized as being too restrictive in the class of women selected and not a cross section of the women of the community (see *Glasser* v. *United States*). To assure that the jury panel is truly representative of a cross section of a community, some courts require the selection to be made from two lists, such as a voter registration list and a driver's license list.

Juror Qualifications

Although individual juror qualifications may vary somewhat among states, the general qualifications are the same: The person must be a citizen of the United States, eighteen years of age or over, and a resident of the judicial district for a specified time, usually one year. This last qualification has been criticized by some as being too restrictive and not representative of a community, because many residents of a community move more frequently than once a year. In view of this contention, the legislatures of some states have changed the residence requirement from one year to one month. Those upholding the one-year requirement contend that it takes at least a year for a person to learn the thinking and moral standards of a community. For this reason, many states still use the one-year residence requirement.

The person must be in possession of his or her natural faculties, meaning that the person must be able to see, hear, talk, feel, smell, and be comparatively mobile. Some states have passed legislation that a person is not disqualified as a juror because of loss of sight, hearing, or other disabilities that substantially interfere with mobility. This legislation is criticized as being unrealistic by many within the justice system. The belief is that the amount of physical evidence presented during a trial prevents a blind person from adequately functioning as a juror. Similarly, since most evidence presented during a trial is through testimony of witnesses, a person unable to hear the testimony would be unable to perform duties as a juror. A person with limited or impaired mobility may be in a better position to act as a juror unless that impairment prevents the person from sitting where the sights and sounds of the trial are adequate. The proponents of this legislation argue that such persons should not be deprived of the opportunity to perform their civic duty merely because of an impairment. They allege that if there is a reason that the impaired person cannot perform in a particular case, a challenge for cause could be made. This challenge, however, is not without its complications, as we will see later.

Some states hold that a decrepit person may not qualify as a juror. Although the law does not specify the characteristics that make a person decrepit, it appears to be aimed at someone who is of advanced age, cannot move about freely, and may be senile. Determining when one has reached this condition is difficult.

A person must also be of "ordinary" intelligence to qualify as a juror in most states. This is another nebulous term. What might be considered ordinary intelligence by some might not be considered ordinary by others. And by what standards is intelligence to be measured? This qualification has led to the exclusion of competent persons from the jury panel. To establish whether a prospective juror is of ordinary intelligence, many conscientious efforts have been made to devise tests to assist in making the determination. These tests have been challenged by many defendants. They maintain that words unfamiliar to many ethnic groups are included in the tests, thus preventing a jury from being truly representative of the community. Because of these challenges, most such tests have been eliminated. The prospective juror must have sufficient knowledge of the English language to communicate properly and to understand the trial proceedings. Not all persons on voter lists understand English, nor do all have the full use of their natural faculties. Thus, registered voters are not necessarily qualified as jurors. Aliens, those convicted of malfeasance in office, of any felony, or of other high crimes are excluded by most jurisdictions from jury duty. However, even this exclusion has been challenged as excluding a cross section of society.

Some jurisdictions exclude persons who have served as jurors during the preceding year. This is to discourage the professional jurors who continually hang around courthouses attempting to serve on juries because they have little else to do. Whether there is anything wrong with the professional juror is subject to debate.

Obtaining Jurors

Because of the number of persons in a community who do not qualify as jurors, are exempt, or are excused, obtaining a sufficient number of persons who are available for jury duty is not always easy. In one large metropolitan area, the jury commissioner selected 300,000 names in order to maintain a panel of 15,000 persons—the estimated need for the coming year in that district. Generally, it is the responsibility of the official in charge of the jury panel to determine whether the persons selected are qualified to serve or are exempt. To facilitate this determination, many officials will mail a questionnaire to the selected persons, requesting certain information. A sample questionnaire is presented in the accompanying illustration.

The procedure of mailing questionnaires to prospective jurors also has been challenged by defendants. They contend that many members of minority groups do not respond to the questionnaires and thus do not become eligible to be placed on the jury panel. Regardless of these challenges, many jurisdictions still send out questionnaires to assist in obtaining competent persons to act as jurors. The courts recognize that though there is no ideal way to select prospective jurors, the system used is acceptable if no groups of people are eliminated.

When the selection of prospective jurors is completed, those persons found to be competent are placed on the jury panel. As each trial date is set, a number of these persons will be notified to appear in court on that date. The notice is usually by legal document, referred to as a summons, served on the prospective juror by the sheriff, marshal, or other official of the district involved. If the person does not appear as directed after being personally served with the summons, a contempt charge may result unless good cause is shown for not appearing. For example, a prospective juror with a serious illness could not be expected to appear. From the group that appears in court, the trial jury is selected.

The number of persons called to appear in court varies with the type of crime charged and the amount of pretrial publicity that may have been given the case. Usually, no fewer than 25 persons will be summoned to appear in court, and if the charge is murder and the case has received wide publicity, as many as 100 persons may be summoned. There have been times when even with this number, a trial jury could not be picked, and additional persons from the panel had to be called to appear in court. The first twelve names called by the clerk at the time of the trial may not be those of the persons who will serve on the jury.

Typical Jury Questionnaire

Name _____ Address _____

1. Occupation _____ Employed by _____ If
    retired, state former occupation _____
2. Do you own your own business? _____ (Yes or No) Firm name _____
    How many employees? _____
3. Age _____ Condition of hearing _____ Eyesight _____
4. Do you have any physical or mental disability that would interfere with or
    prevent you from serving as a juror? _____ (Yes or No) If so, describe fully.
    Doctor's name _____
5. Can you read and understand English? _____ (Yes or No)
6. Have you ever been convicted of any felony in a state or federal court? _____
    (Yes or No) If your answer is yes, have your civil rights been restored by pardon
    or amnesty? _____ (Yes or No)
7. Have you been a resident of this County and State for one year immediately
    before this date? _____ (Yes or No)
8. Have you served as a juror in this State within the last two years? _____ (Yes
    or No) If yes, when? _____
9. Do you have minor children? _____ Ages: _____
10. Do you have dependents who require your personal constant care? _____ If
    yes, please explain: _____
11. If you are entitled to legal exemption or have legal grounds for excuse from jury
    duty, do you claim it? _____ (Yes or No) If so, explain fully the ground for your
    claim.

I certify (or declare) under penalty of perjury that the answers to the foregoing questions
are true and correct.

Executed in _____ County, State of _____, on the _____ day of
_____, 20____ .

Signature _____

In some districts, the official will not establish a jury panel very far in advance of a trial. As juries are needed, the official will have a number of persons summoned to appear in court on a particular day. At this time, it will be determined whether those summoned are qualified to serve on a jury. The difficulty with this procedure is that many of those summoned may not qualify for jury duty, and more will have to be notified to appear in order that a trial jury may be selected.

When it is established that those persons appearing in court qualify for jury duty, their names will individually be written on slips of paper and placed in a box. When the trial jury is selected, the clerk will pick, at random, twelve individuals (or fewer, depending upon the jurisdiction) who are to act as the trial jurors. They will take seats in an area provided for them, commonly known as the jury box. The prosecuting attorney and the defense counsel very closely scrutinize the jurors to determine whether this is the group with which they wish to rest their case.

EXEMPTION FROM JURY DUTY

Many persons have the qualifications to be a juror but are exempt from jury duty because of their occupations. It is believed that the functions they perform within a community outweigh their responsibility to serve on a jury. Included among those most often exempted from jury duty are members of legislative bodies; members of the armed services on active duty; attorneys and their staffs; ministers and priests; teachers; physicians; correctional officers; law enforcement officers; mail carriers; and most public officers of the county, state, or federal government. (*Note:* In New York City, owners of one-person businesses are not exempt.) However, those persons exempt from jury duty do not have to claim the exemption and are free to serve as jurors if they so choose. Some state statutes do not designate any class of persons who are exempt from jury duty but do include a provision that the court has the authority to excuse a person upon finding that jury service would entail undue hardship on the person or on the public. However, since it is a citizen's civic duty to serve on juries when called, a person may not be excused for a trivial cause or because of mere inconvenience. The courts are considerate of those for whom jury duty would create a real hardship. This group generally includes persons operating one-person businesses requiring individual attention, students in the midst of a school year, mothers with small children, and persons caring for sick dependents. Since jury duty is an inconvenience if not an actual hardship for most persons, many districts will excuse a person from further jury duty during the year if he or she has served for as many as twenty days, or some other predetermined number, as a juror. This does not mean that a juror may be excused in the middle of a trial after serving for twenty days. The juror must continue serving until that particular trial is completed, even if it takes several more weeks.

CHALLENGING JURORS FOR CAUSE

In most instances, by the time the jurors reach the jury box, it will have been determined that each possesses the qualifications necessary to act as a juror. If this has not been determined, the judge or prosecuting attorney will read to the jurors the qualifications necessary, and if anyone seated in the jury box does not possess those qualifications, that juror will be excused and another name will be pulled from the box to replace the excused juror. There have been instances where a person selected to act as a juror did not qualify yet refused to acknowledge the lack of qualification. If either the prosecuting attorney or defense attorney knows that the juror is not qualified, that attorney may challenge the juror's right to serve. For example, it may be known that one of the jurors has been convicted of a felony. That person could be challenged. These challenges are referred to as **challenges for cause**. In other words, there may be some cause why a person should not serve on the jury. There are a number of other reasons why a juror may be challenged for cause besides not being qualified. After viewing the jury, the defense counsel may conclude that it does not represent a cross section of the community because there is no member of the same race, national origin, or age level as the defendant. The defense counsel may then challenge the entire jury panel. If this challenge is made and the judge knows that there was no systematic exclusion of any class of persons, the judge will deny the challenge and the trial activities will proceed. If any other challenges are forthcoming, they will have to be made on other grounds. If the judge questions the possibility of certain classes of persons being excluded, a recess may be declared until doubt is resolved by determining the method used to select the panel.

Preconceived Ideas of Guilt or Innocence

One of the grounds for challenging a juror for cause is preconceived ideas about the guilt or innocence of the defendant. A juror is often asked how much he or she has heard or read about the case through newspapers, radio, and television. In many instances, the juror, or all jurors, may admit hearing or reading about the case. The juror will then be asked if he or she has formed an opinion regarding the guilt or innocence of the defendant. If the juror has, he or she will be challenged for cause, and the judge will undoubtedly excuse that juror unless there is an indication that his or her opinion could be changed as a result of evidence presented during the trial. The problem is whether a juror can in reality throw off an opinion of guilt or innocence already formed irrespective of how strong the evidence may be on either side. The questioning of a prospective juror on a challenge for cause is often referred to as a "voir dire examination."

In almost all instances, the prospective juror who has formed an opinion about the defendant's guilt or innocence prior to a trial has formed that opinion as a result of pretrial publicity given to the case. This circumstance creates a continuing battle between the freedom of the press and the defendant's right to a fair trial by an impartial jury. Publicity is given to many cases, particularly those involving murder charges, and it is almost impossible for prospective jurors not to have learned something about the case. As stated by U.S. Supreme Court Justice Clark in the case of *Irvin* v. *Dowd:*[5]

> It is not required . . . that the jurors be totally ignorant of the facts and issues involved [in a case]. In these days of swift, widespread and diverse methods of communication, an important case can be expected to arouse the interest of the public in the vicinity, and scarcely any of those best qualified to serve as jurors will not have formed some impression or opinion as to the merits of the case. This is particularly true in criminal cases. To hold that the mere existence of any preconceived notion as to the guilt or innocence of an accused, without more, is sufficient to rebut the presumption of a prospective juror's impartiality would establish an impossible standard. It is sufficient if the juror can lay aside his impression or opinion and render a verdict based upon the evidence presented in court.

In the *Irvin* case, pretrial newspaper stories described the defendant as a confessed slayer of six and a parole violator. Because of deep-seated preconceived opinions of the guilt of the defendant by members of the jury, the Court felt that the defendant had been denied a fair trial by an impartial jury.

Returning again to the *Sheppard* v. *Maxwell* case discussed in Chapter 7, the U.S. Supreme Court held that the defendant had been denied a fair trial, as in the *Irvin* case. In the *Sheppard* decision, extensive pretrial publicity accusing the defendant of the crime occurred even though he had not been arrested or charged with the crime. Headlines such as "Why Don't Police Quiz Top Suspect?" appeared, with a demand that Sheppard be taken to police headquarters for questioning. One newspaper described Sheppard in the following language:

> "now proved under oath to be a liar . . . still free to go about his business shielded by his family, . . . protected by a smart lawyer who has made monkeys of the police and authorities, . . . carrying a gun part of the time, . . . left free to do whatever he pleases." After the arrest of the defendant, the publicity intensified and continued throughout the trial. The Court felt that if the prospective jurors did not have a preconceived opinion of the guilt of the defendant, they reached that opinion during the trial primarily from the publicity given the case and not from the evidence presented. [*Sheppard* v. *Maxwell,* 384 U.S. 333 (1966).]

Although the trial judge in the *Sheppard* case endeavored to keep the jurors from being exposed to publicity, the effort was apparently not successful. At the beginning of the trial, the judge stated the following: "I would suggest to you and caution you that you do not read any newspapers during the progress of this trial, that you do not listen to radio comments nor watch or listen to television comments, insofar as this case is concerned. . . . After it is all over, you can read it all to your heart's content." At intervals during the trial, the judge repeated his suggestions. But the "jurors were thrust into the role of celebrities by the judge's failure to insulate them from reporters and photographers. The numerous pictures of the jurors, with their addresses, which appeared in the newspaper before and during the trial itself exposed them to expressions of opinion from both cranks and friends."

As a result of these U.S. Supreme Court decisions, local courts have been encouraged to control information released to the news media. This control does not interfere with the freedom of the press but assists in picking jurors without preconceived opinions on the guilt or innocence of the defendant because of pretrial publicity. The control is designed to prevent the jury from being influenced during the trial by extensive publicity, some of which may be inaccurate. Because of the freedom of the press in this country, much pretrial and during-the-trial publicity is given in many cases, despite gag order controls. Because of pretrial publicity, extensive questioning of prospective jurors takes place to determine whether they have a deep-seated opinion of guilt or innocence that cannot be overcome by the evidence presented during the trial. In some of the more notorious cases, it has taken several weeks just to select a jury.

Challenging the Jurors for Bias

A preconceived opinion on guilt or innocence is not the only grounds for challenging a juror for cause. Another ground is bias, either implied or actual.

Implied bias is set by law and disqualifies a juror from serving. Implied bias may include consanguinity or affinity (that is, kinship or relationship) to within the fourth degree to the victim of the crime or to the defendant. Other examples of implied bias are having a relationship of employer and employee, or landlord and tenant, to either the victim of the crime or the defendant, or having served on a jury that tried another person for the offense charged. Actual bias is prejudice that a juror may admit to having because of a dislike for a particular race, religion, national origin, or class of persons. For example, the juror may admit to a bias against law enforcement officers that would create prejudice against the prosecution.

Since some states do not disqualify prospective jurors because of blindness, an attorney might challenge a blind person for cause if evidence will be presented during the trial requiring visual examination. However, because of the general sympathy for blind people, an attorney should be cautious in excusing a blind person for cause under these circumstances. That same sympathy might be given a prospective deaf juror, causing other jurors to become prejudiced against the attorney. Even though a challenge is made, complications in executing the challenge can occur, as in the following instance. A hearing-impaired person was challenged in a criminal case because of his inability to hear the testimony. He countered the challenge for cause, alleging an inherent right to be a juror. He stated that it was the court's responsibility to supply an interpreter capable of using sign language to translate the testimony for him. The judge concluded that persons could be challenged for cause on other grounds permitted by law and that there was no inherent right to be a juror in all circumstances. The judge further pointed out that even if an interpreter was a practical solution to the challenge, there was always the danger of misinterpretation of the testimony by the interpreter or misconception in the translation by the juror. To further complicate the matter, at the final deliberation, only jurors could be present. The judge's position was further supported by the fact that a person without a sense of smell or feeling could be excused for cause if these faculties were important to the examination of evidence.

Prospective Jurors Opposed to the Death Penalty

Prior to the U.S. Supreme Court decision in *Witherspoon* v. *Illinois,*[6] if a juror was against the death penalty, a challenge for cause could be made in cases carrying a maximum penalty of death. The facts of the *Witherspoon* case show that Witherspoon, the petitioner, was brought to trial in Cook County, Illinois, on a charge of murder. The jury found him guilty and fixed the penalty at death. At the time of trial, an Illinois statute provided the following: "In trials for murder it shall be a cause for challenge of any juror who shall, being examined, state that he has conscientious scruples against capital punishment or that he is opposed to the same."

During the trial, the prosecution eliminated approximately half of the jury panel on a challenge for cause when prospective jurors expressed any qualms about capital punishment. Those persons chosen for the trial jury were ones with no conscientious scruples against the death penalty. Witherspoon took the case to the U.S. Supreme Court on the grounds that a fair trial by an impartial jury representative of the cross section of the community had been denied. Witherspoon maintained that persons who were not against the death penalty were more likely to be convicting jurors. Since many persons were against the death penalty, eliminating those persons from a jury resulted in a jury that was not representative of the community. The Supreme Court agreed with Witherspoon and held that merely having conscientious scruples against capital punishment was not a sufficient cause to disqualify a person from serving on a jury. The Court did state that if a prospective juror advised that under no circumstances could he or she vote to convict a defendant if the death penalty was the sentence, that person could be excused on a challenge for cause. There phrase, "death-qualified jury" is used to indicate a jury in which the members have stated that, if appropriate, they would vote for the death penalty.

In those states in which the death penalty may be imposed upon conviction of certain crimes, the prosecuting attorney may ask whether a prospective juror is opposed to the death penalty. If the juror indicates opposition, the prosecuting attorney may then ask whether the juror could vote for conviction knowing that the death penalty could be imposed. A prospective juror who states that he or she could vote for conviction may not be challenged for cause. The problem created by the *Witherspoon* decision is just what action may be taken against the prospective juror who merely indicates some reservations about being able to vote for conviction. Some appellate courts have held that the prospective juror must state positively that he or she could not consider a guilty verdict, if the penalty is death, in order to have the person challenged for cause. There were three dissenting justices in the *Witherspoon* decision who felt that permissible questioning of prospective jurors on the death penalty would not result in a different kind of jury and that prosecutors would be put to a great deal of trouble for nothing.

The *Witherspoon* decision has caused great complication in the voir dire examination of prospective jurors in capital punishment cases. Some appellate courts have adopted the view that the *Witherspoon* decision holds that to constitutionally excuse a prospective juror for cause due to opposition to the death penalty, the juror must make it unmistakably clear that, first, the juror would automatically vote against the death penalty without regard to evidence presented, or that, second, this attitude toward the death penalty would prevent the prospective juror from making an impartial decision on the defendant's guilt.

Prosecuting attorneys and judges have attempted to abide by the *Witherspoon* decision, but just how strong must the feeling be against the death penalty before a prospective juror is excused? In one case, a prospective juror stated on voir dire examination that she was against the death penalty. The judge asked, "Are you so against the death penalty that you would just automatically vote against the death penalty?" To this the prospective juror stated, "I think there might be a hypothetical case in which so heinous a crime was committed that I would consider the death penalty. But I have not been able to think of a hypothetical case that heinous." With this statement, the judge excused the prospective juror for cause. The defendant in that case was convicted, and the case was automatically appealed to the state supreme court, which reversed the death penalty on the grounds that the prospective juror had been improperly excused as not stating that she would automatically vote against the death penalty. There was a dissenting justice in that case who felt that the juror had been properly excused. The case indicates the difficulty facing the courts in determining when a prospective juror was properly excused for cause in being against the death penalty.[7]

In another state case, a prospective juror was asked whether any personal feelings might prevent his participation in the deliberation of a case carrying a possible death sentence. The prospective juror replied that he was a born-again Christian and did not think that he could have any part of sitting in on a case that would send anyone to the electric chair. With this reply, the judge excused the man. After the defendant was convicted and given the death penalty, the state supreme court in that case reversed the death penalty on the grounds that the prospective juror was improperly excused since it was not made unmistakably clear that the juror's participation in the deliberation of the case was not possible because of the penalty. The dissenting justice in that case felt that the court was only seeking a way to reverse death penalties. Justices who have personal feelings against the death penalty have been able to effectively overrule death penalty sentences by holding that a prospective juror was improperly excused in violation of the *Witherspoon* decision. This treatment has brought about criticism of those justices for not upholding the will of the people.

In the case of *Wainright* v. *Witt,*[8] the U.S. Supreme Court somewhat relaxed the strict rule of the *Witherspoon* decision. In this case, the Court set forth a new standard for determining when a prospective juror may be excused for cause because of his or her views on capital punishment: "That standard is whether the juror's views would prevent or substantially impair the performance of his duties as a juror in accordance with his instructions and his oath. . . . We [the Supreme Court] note that, in addition to dispensing with Witherspoon's reference to 'automatic' decision making, this standard likewise does not require that a juror's bias be proved with 'unmistakable clarity.'" Remember that state appellate courts have the power to make rules for their own trial courts. These rules may be more restrictive than the ones set forth by the U.S. Supreme Court and, as such, may still adhere to the strict rule set forth in the *Witherspoon* decision.

The voir dire examination of prospective jurors can be extensive in any type of case. To limit this examination, some states have passed legislation permitting the trial judge to conduct the voir dire examination. In other states, the trial judge will often call into the courtroom all members of the jury panel selected to appear for the particular trial, and the judge will conduct a portion of the voir dire examination. The panel will be asked whether they have any preconceived opinions on guilt or innocence as a result of pretrial publicity given to the case. The judge may also consider other phases of possible bias. Even though this procedure is followed, the prosecuting attorney and particularly the defense counsel are permitted a reasonable voir dire examination opportunity. Some judges conduct no voir dire examinations, since they believe that selecting the jury is the prerogative of the attorneys involved and that any interference with it is a denial of their rights. Most attorneys enjoy the privilege of conducting voir dire examinations in challenging for cause, since it gives them an opportunity to become better acquainted with the jurors who are finally selected. Some courts frown on this reason for voir dire examinations as having no place in the justice system. These courts hold that voir dire examinations by the attorneys are for determining whether a juror should be disqualified by a challenge for cause. In these courts, the attorneys are limited to questions pertinent to the cause for which they may be attempting to disqualify the juror. Other courts permit a certain amount of freedom when questioning a prospective juror. This aids the attorneys in determining whether a peremptory challenge should be exercised when an undesired juror cannot be disqualified for cause. As long as the attorneys' questions relate to a challenge for cause, the questioning can be almost limitless, particularly when the cause is for bias. For this reason, some judges try to limit the questioning to matters directly relating to the particular case involved. If a judge is too restrictive in permitting the questioning by the defense counsel, a conviction could be reversed on appeal through the allegation that the jury was not impartial.

PEREMPTORY CHALLENGE

After the prosecution and defense have exhausted their challenges for cause, there is one more opportunity to remove an undesired juror or jurors. Each attorney is given the right to excuse a juror whom he or she may not want on the jury. The right to excuse a juror under these circumstances is known as a **peremptory challenge**. Both the prosecution and the defense have a certain number of peremptory challenges that permit either attorney to excuse a juror without stating a reason. The challenges are granted based upon the theory that they assist the attorneys in more nearly selecting an impartial jury. A prosecuting attorney, for example, may exercise the right of peremptory challenge to excuse a juror who, during challenge for cause, indicated reservations against the death penalty but could vote for a conviction if the evidence against the defendant was strong enough. Even though this is the real reason the juror was excused, the attorney does not have to give the reason. A defense attorney may excuse a juror who stated during challenge for cause that he or she believed that the defendant was guilty but that this feeling could be controlled and the juror guided by the evidence of the case.

Prohibiting the Peremptory Challenge

Generally, the trial judge has no authority to prohibit a juror from being excused on a peremptory challenge. However, the U.S. Supreme Court in *Batson* v. *Kentucky*[9] held that an attorney may not use peremptory challenges to exclude persons from a jury solely on the basis of race. Batson was of the black race, and during the jury selection, the prosecuting attorney excluded all persons of this race from the jury by the use of his peremptory challenges. The Supreme Court stated the following:

> Although a prosecutor ordinarily is entitled to exercise permitted peremptory challenges for any reason at all as long as that reason is related to the outcome of the case to be tried . . . the Equal Protection Clause [of the Fourteenth Amendment] forbids the prosecutor to challenge potential jurors solely on account of their race or on the presumption that black jurors as a group will be unable impartially to consider the State's case against a black defendant.

The Supreme Court of one state held that "peremptory challenges may not be used to remove prospective jurors solely on the basis of presumed group bias. We define group bias as a presumption that certain jurors are biased merely because they are members of an identifiable group distinguished on racial, religious, ethnic, or similar grounds."[10] The Court in the *Batson* case based its decision primarily on the violation of the Equal Protection clause of the U.S. Constitution. But some state courts have limited the use of peremptory challenges to exclude members of a certain group on the theory that a defendant is entitled to be tried by an impartial jury representative of a cross section of the community. The exclusion of members of a defined group by the use of peremptory challenges denies the defendant that right. The prosecution has the same right to question the use of peremptory challenges by the defense in the exclusion of certain classes of persons. The prosecution is also entitled to have the case tried by a jury representative of a cross section of the community.

The *Batson* decision did not eliminate all use of peremptory challenges to exclude from a jury persons of a defined group. But when it becomes apparent that such an attempted exclusion is taking place, the opposing side may question the procedure. The trial judge has the responsibility to determine whether there is a justification for the exclusions. If the offending attorney can establish a bona fide justification for the exclusions, the peremptory challenges will stand. The justification is generally based on some attitude displayed by the excluded juror, such as being unduly friendly toward the defendant or his attorney or displaying an unwholesome attitude toward law enforcement.

As in the challenge for cause, when a juror is excused by the peremptory challenge, the court clerk will pick another name from the jury panel box, and that prospective juror will take the seat of the excused juror in the jury box. That juror and any others who may replace excused jurors may be questioned to determine whether they should be challenged for cause.

Thus, another time-consuming procedure occurs in the selection of the jury. The number of peremptory challenges for the prosecution and the defense varies among states. Some states grant the prosecution and defense an equal number of peremptory challenges, usually ten each. Other states grant the defense ten challenges and the prosecution only five. Some jurisdictions grant more peremptory challenges for felony trials than for misdemeanor trials. Where the maximum penalty is death, most jurisdictions permit twice as many peremptory challenges as in noncapital cases.

Holding Challenges in Reserve

Both the prosecuting attorney and the defense attorney will usually hold one or two of their peremptory challenges in reserve. The reason is that a person who is most unsatisfactory to one side or the other may have his or her name drawn from the panel, leaving no way to disqualify this person for cause. If all the peremptory challenges have been exhausted, there is no way of preventing that person from being a juror. The person may have a history of never having voted for conviction or having a known dislike for a particular race or religion, yet this dislike cannot be established in questioning for cause. Defense attorneys generally do not like to have law enforcement officers, either active or retired, on a jury, since such persons tend to assume guilt from the mere arrest and formal charging of the defendant. This tendency may be impossible to establish in order to excuse the officer on cause, but no cause is needed in the peremptory challenge.

Law in Practice

Snyder v. Louisiana, 128 S. Ct. 1203 (2007)

Defendant Snyder was convicted of first-degree murder in a Louisiana state court and was sentenced to death. He petitioned for a writ of certiorari to the Supreme Court of Louisiana which had rejected his claim that the prosecution exercised some of its peremptory jury challenges based on race, in violation of *Batson* v. *Kentucky*. The U.S. Supreme Court granted certiorari (agreed to review his claim). Eighty-five prospective jurors were questioned as members of the jury panel (individuals called for jury duty). After the challenges for cause, there were thirty-six potential jurors left on the jury panel; five of the thirty-six were black; and all five of the prospective black jurors were eliminated by the prosecution through the use of peremptory strikes. When defense counsel made a *Batson* objection concerning the strike of one black juror, a college senior who was attempting to fulfill his student-teaching obligation, the prosecution offered two race-neutral reasons for the strike: (1) the juror looked very nervous throughout the questioning; and (2) he was going to miss his student-teaching class. The Court held that it could not presume that the trial judge credited the prosecutor's assertion that the juror was nervous. The student-teaching obligation reason failed, however, because a university dean had told the court that the juror's missing up to a week would not cause a problem and the juror did not express any concern about serving on the jury.

How Would You Rule?

JUSTUCE ALITO delivered the opinion of the Court:

The Constitution forbids striking even a single prospective juror for a discriminatory purpose. On appeal, a trial court's ruling on the issue of discriminatory intent must be sustained unless it is clearly erroneous. The trial court has a pivotal role in evaluating *Batson* claims. With respect to the first reason, the Louisiana Supreme Court was correct that nervousness cannot be shown from a cold transcript, which is why the trial judge's evaluation must be given much deference. The second reason proffered for the strike of the juror—his student-teaching obligation—fails even under the highly deferential standard of review that is applicable here.

The Court reversed the judgment and remanded the case for further proceedings. [Trial judge was directed to determine whether he credited the prosecutor's assertion that the juror was nervous. If the trial judge does not credit the assertion, then the trial judge would be required to order a new trial.]

Both prosecuting attorneys and defense attorneys will question prospective jurors for cause as extensively as the court will permit. This questioning enables them to get a better idea of how a particular prospective juror may think or react in reaching a verdict. The attorneys may then utilize their peremptory challenges more effectively.

Accepting Jurors

All attorneys engaged in the trial of cases, whether civil or criminal, constantly try to analyze persons in an effort to determine who make the best jurors. There is no way to predict how a person will react in each instance, but attorneys feel that certain groups or classes of persons tend to react in more definite patterns than others. For example, defense attorneys feel that minority groups who have encountered hardships and discrimination tend to be more tolerant of defendants than members of white Anglo groups of medium or higher income. Younger persons are alleged to be more permissive and forgiving in their attitudes toward a defendant, particularly if the defendant is also a younger person. For that reason, defense attorneys try to have more persons between the ages of eighteen and twenty-one on jury panels as well as more members of minority groups. But obtaining these classes of people for jury duty is not easy. Many younger persons attending school are excused so that their school year will not be interrupted. If not in school, many are married and are in a lower-income bracket, as are many in minority groups who are excused from jury duty because of the extreme financial hardship that might be suffered. In most jurisdictions, the compensation for jury duty is meager, since it is considered to be a civic duty to serve on a criminal trial jury. Jurors in some areas receive only $5 a day plus a small mileage fee. It has been recommended that the compensation be increased in order that younger persons and members of minority groups in lower-income brackets can afford to serve on the jury. But court costs are already extremely high, and each increase in jury fees makes them that much greater, another burden on the taxpayer. A few jurisdictions have increased jurors' compensation to ease the financial hardship suffered by those who serve, as well as to obtain a wider selection of persons.

U.S. Supreme Court Decisions Regarding the Peremptory Challenge

Case	Key Ruling
Batson v. *Kentucky* (1986)	The Court ruled that under the Fourteenth Amendment, prosecutors are barred from using peremptory challenges to remove black jurors because of their race.
Powers v. *Ohio* (1991)	The Court concluded that a defendant has the standing to object to race-based exclusion of jurors by the use of peremptory challenges on the grounds of equal protection, even if the defendant is not of the same race as the challenged jurors.
Edmonson v. *Leesville Concrete Co.* (1991)	The Court held that the Batson ruling applies to attorneys in civil lawsuits. A private party in a civil action may not use peremptory challenges to exclude jurors on the basis of race.
Georgia v. *McCollum* (1992)	On the basis of Batson, the Court prohibited the exercise of race-based peremptory challenges by defense attorneys in criminal cases.
J.E.B. v. *Alabama* (1994)	The Court held that the Equal Protection Clause of the Fourteenth Amendment bars discrimination in jury selection on the basis of gender. Discrimination in jury selection, whether based on race or gender, causes harm to the litigants, the community, and the individual jurors who are wrongfully excluded from participation in the judicial process.
Snyder v. *Louisiana* (2007)	A juror's student-teaching obligation, given as a race-neutral reason for a peremptory strike, failed even under a highly deferential standard of review because a university dean had told the court that the juror's missing up to a week would not cause a problem and the juror did not express any further concern about serving on the jury.

Many attorneys feel that the most satisfactory juror is one who takes pride in serving on a jury, takes the duty seriously, endeavors to conscientiously evaluate the evidence presented during the trial, and attempts to arrive at a just verdict. The financial burden upon the juror should not be great, and he or she should not have to worry about children or day-care issues.

After the prosecution and defense have exhausted their challenges for cause, have no desire to further exercise their right of peremptory challenges, and indicate to the judge that they are satisfied with the jury selected, the jury will be sworn to perform their duty. The oath administered to the jurors will in substance be that each of them will endeavor to reach a true and just verdict based on the evidence of the case. After the jurors have been sworn in, the trial begins. Some jurisdictions still swear jurors individually, but most jurisdictions administer the oath to the jury as a group once they have been selected and accepted by both sides and by the judge.

Law in Practice

Gonzalez v. *United States*, 76 U.S.L.W. 4261 (2008)

Defendant was charged with five felony drug offense counts. After his counsel consented, a magistrate rather than the trial judge presided at voir dire. After the guilty verdict, petitioner argued on appeal that it was error not to obtain his own consent to the magistrate presiding at voir dire.

How Would You Rule?
JUSTICE KENNEDY delivered the opinion of the Court.

Because the acceptance of a magistrate at the jury selection phase was a tactical decision. Constitutional concerns did not require a different interpretation as defendant had conceded that a magistrate was capable of competent and impartial performance of the judicial tasks involved in jury examination and selection. Although a criminal defendant could demand that a U.S. Const. art. III judge preside over the selection of a jury, the choice to do so reflected considerations more significant to the realm of the attorney than to the accused. [Conviction affirmed.]

ALTERNATE JURORS

Records reveal that often during a lengthy trial, one or more jurors become incapacitated and cannot continue. If this happens and the defendant does not agree to continue the trial with those jurors who remain, the judge must declare a mistrial and the trial must be restarted. If several weeks have elapsed before the juror becomes incapacitated, having to start the trial again is frustrating as well as expensive. To avoid the possibility of having to start a new trial, most states have statutes providing that alternate jurors may be selected at the discretion of the trial judge. Determining the approximate time that the prosecution and defense plan to take in presenting their sides of the case enables the judge to decide whether and how many alternate jurors should be selected.

Alternate jurors are selected in the same manner as regular jurors. The alternates may be challenged for cause, and usually one additional peremptory challenge is granted for each alternate selected. The judge may decide that only one alternate will be necessary, or he or she may decide on more if the trial is to be extremely lengthy. Usually not more than four alternates are selected. If there is more than one alternate and one of the regular jurors becomes incapacitated, the clerk will draw the name of the alternate who will be substituted for the incapacitated juror. Some states permit an alternate to be substituted for the incapacitated juror up to the time that the case is given to the jury for deliberation. Other states permit an alternate to be substituted anytime before the verdict is reached. The alternate jurors must be situated in the courtroom where they can observe all the proceedings and can hear all that takes place. Usually, an area next to the jury box is reserved for alternate jurors to facilitate their ability to see and hear. After selection, the alternate jurors are given the same oath as the regular jury.

The use of the alternate juror system has been criticized by some legal scholars. They allege that the alternate juror creates a jury of thirteen instead of twelve, particularly if the alternate is substituted during the deliberation. It has been alleged that permitting a substitution during the deliberation handicaps the alternate juror, since he or she has not had the benefit of the group dynamics during the preceding deliberation. Because of these criticisms, some states do not permit substitution after the deliberation begins, and once the case is given to the jury for a verdict, the alternate juror or jurors are discharged. The problem created by discharging alternate jurors at the time of deliberation is that, after a lengthy trial, the deliberation could take several days and a juror could possibly become incapacitated during that time. If this happens, the jury would have to be dismissed and the trial started over, thus defeating the purpose of the alternate juror system. Those jurisdictions permitting the substitution of an alternate juror during deliberation either allow the deliberation to start anew or require that the alternate be thoroughly briefed on the deliberation up to the time of the substitution.

The alternate juror system has also been criticized as unfair to the defendant, because the alternate juror, knowing that chances of substitution are slight, may not take much interest in the case and be unable to properly evaluate the evidence during deliberation if substituted. To eliminate this possibility, it has been proposed that, if alternate jurors are to be selected, the entire jury—including alternates—should be selected at one time. At the time the case is given to the jury for deliberation, the court clerk would draw twelve names from the jury selection box. In this way, none of the jurors would know who were regulars or alternates until all the evidence of the case had been presented, and all would have an equal interest in the presentation.

Although the alternate juror system has been criticized by some as being unfair to the defendant, these criticisms seem shallow compared with the benefits gained by having a juror who can replace one who may become incapacitated. It must be remembered that the alternate juror system was established because, in most instances, a defendant will not agree to continue a trial with less than a full jury should one of the jurors become incapacitated. The refusal to continue with the trial is usually based on the belief that delays in a trial work to the defendant's advantage. In addition, it is impossible to make every situation arising in the justice system ideal for the defendant. In fact, many in the justice system feel that the system is already tilted heavily in favor of the defendant.

SEQUESTERING THE JURY

Once the jury has been selected and sworn in, the judge must decide whether it is to be sequestered, or locked up. When a jury is sequestered, it is segregated from all outside contact. The primary reason for a **sequestered jury** is to protect its members from possible outside influence in arriving at their verdict. When not in the courtroom, the jurors are kept together as a body at all times under the guard of a bailiff or some other court officer. They eat together and are housed in a hotel, motel, or some other convenient place until the trial is concluded. Even the newspapers that they may be permitted to read or the news broadcasts that they may listen to must be monitored to ensure that nothing that might affect their verdict is brought to their attention. As was pointed out in the *Sheppard* case, the jury was aware of the extensive news media publicity throughout the trial. According to the U.S. Supreme Court, the publicity influenced the jury in their opinion on guilt, and the Court reversed the conviction. The Court suggested that the judge should have had greater control over the news releases or should have sequestered the jury during the trial to prevent undue influence. Generally, it is held that when a jury is not sequestered, the judge has the authority to forbid the jurors from reading any newspapers or listening to any broadcasts about the case, and if they should inadvertently read about or listen to something about the case, they are to disregard it.

In a few states, the jury must be sequestered during a trial on certain charges; otherwise, sequestering is at the discretion of the judge. The jury may be sequestered at any time during the trial proceedings. It may be sequestered on the judge's own decision or at the request of either the prosecution or the defense. If the jury is not sequestered during the presentation of the evidence, it will usually be sequestered during the deliberation when the trial pertains to a serious charge. In a few jurisdictions, the jury must be sequestered during the deliberation. If the jury is sequestered, the alternate jurors are sequestered as well, but are generally sequestered separately from the regular jury. In those jurisdictions where the jury is sequestered at the judge's discretion prior to the time of deliberation, most judges hesitate to sequester the jury because of the hardship imposed. The jurors lose all contact with their families and friends during the period of sequestration. Most of the jurors are unacquainted with one another before the trial begins, yet they must be housed together. Often personality clashes occur, affecting their judgment during the deliberation. From the standpoint of the taxpayer, sequestering a jury is expensive because taxes pay for housing and feeding the jury during this period. Most jurors dislike being sequestered, and when that possibility is apparent, prospective jurors will do everything possible to be excused from that particular trial. Thus, in addition to the hardships experienced by the jurors themselves, selecting a jury becomes even more difficult than usual. When a jury is sequestered during a trial at the request of the prosecution or defense, it is the policy of the judge not to inform the jury which side made the request in order to avoid any prejudice by the jurors toward that side. Whether the jury is sequestered or not, each time the court is adjourned, the judge must advise the jurors against discussing the facts of the case among themselves or with others and against forming any opinions about the case until the time of deliberation.

Law in Practice

Dixon v. *United States*, 548 U.S. 1 (2006)

Defendant admitted that, while purchasing firearms, she provided an incorrect address and falsely stated that she was not under indictment for a felony. Defendant alleged that she acted under duress because her boyfriend threatened to kill her or hurt her daughters if she did not buy the guns for him. Defendant contended that the district court's instructions to the jury erroneously required her to prove duress by a preponderance of the evidence instead of requiring the Government to prove beyond a reasonable doubt that she did not act under duress.

How Would You Rule on Her Appeal?

JUSTICE STEVENS delivered the opinion of the Court.

The duress defense, like the defense of necessity, may excuse conduct that would otherwise be punishable, but the existence of duress normally does not controvert any of the elements of the offense itself. Criminal liability is normally based upon the concurrence of two factors, an evil-meaning mind and an evil-doing hand. Like the defense of necessity, the defense of duress does not negate a defendant's criminal state of mind when the applicable offense requires a defendant to have acted knowingly or willfully; instead, it allows the defendant to avoid liability because coercive conditions or necessity negates a conclusion of guilt even though the necessary mens rea was present. At common law, the burden of proving affirmative defenses—indeed, all circumstances of justification, excuse or alleviation—rest on the defendant. [The Court affirmed the judgment.

FUTURE OF THE JURY SYSTEM

Interviews with persons who have accepted their duty to serve on criminal juries reveal that many become disenchanted with the jury system. The most common complaint concerns the time spent by prospective jurors waiting to be called for duty on a particular case. Many wait for hours in the uncomfortable surroundings of the courthouse halls. Some even wait all day without being called, only to be ordered to return the next day to suffer a similar experience. This waiting usually stems from last-minute requests for continuances, hearings on other motions presented, or plea bargaining.

Many persons believe that average jurors are neither able to cope with the facts of the more complex trials nor able to understand and abide by the instructions given them by the judge. Some feel that too many jurors permit emotions and personality conflicts to interfere with judgment in arriving at a verdict. In those states where a unanimous verdict must be returned, one juror may prevent such a verdict from being rendered just because of an emotional or personality conflict, thereby hampering the justice system. Many persons believe that our justice system would not come to a sudden halt if the jury system were abolished and verdicts were decided by a body of three or more judges. Irrespective of what persons may think or believe, as long as the Sixth Amendment guarantee to a trial by jury is in effect, the jury system will not be eliminated.

Law in Practice

Rules for the Jurors in the O.J. Simpson Trial

The rules below were provided to the jury in the murder trial of the former football star O.J. Simpson. Realizing that the O.J. Simpson case was provoking unusual interest, Judge Lance Ito, with suggestion from the attorneys on both sides, drew up the following document:

> Date: 23 September 1994
> Department 103
> HON. LANCE A. ITO, Judge
> D. ROBERTSON, Deputy Clerk

Superior Court of the State of California in and for the County of Los Angeles

People vs. Orenthal James Simpson

Case #BA097211

Court Order

Each juror and alternate juror selected to serve in this matter is ordered and directed to:

1. Not to read or listen to or watch any accounts or discussions of this case reported by newspapers, television, radio, or any other news media.
2. Not to visit or view the premises or place where the offense or offenses charged were allegedly committed or any premises or place involved in this case unless directed by the court to do so.
3. Not to converse with other jurors or with anyone else upon any subject connected with the trial unless and until permitted to do so by the court.
4. Not to request, accept, agree to accept, or discuss with any person receiving or accepting, any payment or benefit in consideration for supplying any information concerning this trial for a period of 180 days from the return of a verdict or the termination of the case, whichever is earlier.
5. Promptly to report to the court any incident within their knowledge involving an attempt by any person improperly to influence any member of the jury.

Dated: _____, 19_____

_____
Hon. Lance A. Ito
I agree to the above order and understand that if I violate the provisions of this order that I can be ordered to pay a sanction to the court of up to $1,500 for each violation pursuant to Code of Civil Procedure Section 177.5, to reimburse or make payment to the County of Los Angeles for costs caused by a violation pursuant to California Rules of Court, Rule 227, or punished by a fine or imprisonment for contempt pursuant to Code of Civil Procedure Section 1218.

Dated: _____, 19_____

_____
Juror
Additional Instructions

(continued)

After about six weeks the attorneys and the judge decided that the first set of rules were not strong enough, so the following regulations were devised:

Date: 12 December 1994
Department 103
HON. LANCE A. ITO, Judge
D. ROBERTSON, Deputy Clerk

Superior Court of the State of California in and for the County of Los Angeles

People vs. Orenthal James Simpson

Case #BA097211

Court Order

During the course of this trial, and until further order of this court, the trial jurors and alternates in this case shall NOT read any newspaper article or other written account including magazines or books or watch any television programs dealing with this case, the defendant or his family, the victims or their families, the attorneys or any other matter concerning this case. The court will distribute to the jurors and alternates the local daily newspaper of their choice, edited to remove any coverage of this case. Jurors and alternates shall NOT listen to any radio programming. Each juror and alternate may listen to audio tapes and compact disks, including books on tape that do not concern this case. Jurors and alternates who need current weather and traffic information may get this information by dialing (213) 962-3279.

Jurors and alternates shall NOT watch:

1. ANY television news program or news break.
2. ANY television "*tabloid*" program such as Hard Copy, A Current Affair, Inside Edition, American Journal, or Premiere Story.
3. ANY television talk show such as Marilu, Leeza, Jenny Jones, Sally Jessy Raphael, Oprah, Donahue, Good Morning America, Today, CBS This Morning, The Montel Williams Show, The Maury Povich Show, Ricki Lake, Rolonda, Rush Limbaugh and Geraldo.
4. ANY television news magazine program such as 60 Minutes, 20/20, Dateline, Eye to Eye, 48 Hours, or Primetime Live.
5. ANY entertainment news magazine such as Entertainment Tonight and EXTRA.
6. CNN, CNN Headline News, CNBC, The E! Channel, Sports Center on ESPN, Press Box on Prime Ticket, The News on MTV, any news or talk show on BET and Dennis Miller Live on HBO.
7. The Tonight Show (Jay Leno) and The Late Show with David Letterman.

Jurors and alternates MAY watch:

1. Normal television entertainment programming, including sports and home shopping channels, not excluding above, however. Jurors are strongly cautioned to avoid watching advertisements for upcoming news broadcasts known as "teasers."
2. Cable or satellite television channels: American Movie Classics, Showtime, Cinemax, The Disney Channel, The Movie Channel, The Shopping Channel, The Family Channel, The Cartoon Channel, Turner Classic Movies, MTV, Discovery Channel, Arts and Entertainment (A&E), Bravo, Lifetime, Nashville, Nickelodeon and Home Box Office.
3. Movies and other programming on video tape that do not involve this case, the defendant or his family, the victims or their families, or the attorneys and their families.

Any questions regarding this order shall be directed to the Clerk of the Court.

IT IS SO ORDERED.

CASE LAW

Recent Cases

Gonzalez v. *United States*, 553 U.S. 242 (U.S. 2008)

Homero Gonzales was charged with five felony drug offense counts. After his counsel consented, a magistrate judge presided at voir dire of perspective jurors. After the guilty verdict, Gonzalez argued on appeal that it was error not to obtain his own consent to the magistrate presiding at voir dire. The United States Court of Appeals for the Fifth Circuit affirmed the judgment of conviction.

The Court noted that the question was whether it sufficed for counsel alone to consent to the magistrate's role in presiding over voir dire and jury selection or whether a defendant had to give his or her own consent. Case law established that the additional duties 28 U.S.C.S. § 636(b)(3) permitted the magistrate to undertake included presiding at voir dire and jury selection, provided there was consent and no objection. In this case, express consent by counsel sufficed to permit a magistrate to preside over jury selection in a felony trial, pursuant to the authorization in § 636(b)(3), because the acceptance of a magistrate at the jury selection phase was a tactical decision. Constitutional concerns did not require a different interpretation as petitioner had conceded that a magistrate was capable of competent and impartial performance of the judicial tasks involved in jury examination and selection. Although a criminal defendant could demand that a U.S. Const. art. III judge preside over the selection of a jury, the choice to do so reflected considerations more significant to the realm of the attorney than to the accused.

Petitioner criminal defendant was convicted of first-degree murder in a Louisiana court and was sentenced to death. He petitioned for a writ of certiorari to the Supreme Court of Louisiana, which had rejected his claim that the prosecution exercised some of its peremptory jury challenges based on race, in violation of *Batson* v. *Kentucky*. Certiorari was granted.

Snyder v. *Louisiana,* 552 U.S. 472 (U.S. 2008)

Eighty-five prospective jurors were questioned as members of a jury panel. Thirty-six of these survived challenges for cause; 5 of the 36 were black; and all five of the prospective black jurors were eliminated by the prosecution through the use of peremptory strikes.

When defense counsel made a Batson objection concerning the strike of one black juror, a college senior who was attempting to fulfill his student-teaching obligation, the prosecution offered two race-neutral reasons for the strike: (1) the juror looked very nervous throughout the questioning; and (2) he was going to miss his student teaching class.

The Court in reversing the conviction stated that it could not presume that the trial judge credited the prosecutor's assertion that the juror was nervous. The student-teaching obligation reason failed even under a highly deferential standard of review because a university dean had told the court that the juror's missing up

to a week would not cause a problem and the juror did not express any further concern about serving on the jury. The implausibility of the explanation was reinforced by the prosecutor's acceptance of white jurors who disclosed conflicting obligations that appeared to have been at least as serious. [The judgment of the Louisiana Supreme Court was reversed and the case was remanded for further proceedings.]

The Court noted that *Batson* v. *Kentucky* provides a three-step process for a trial court to use in adjudicating a claim that a peremptory challenge was based on race. First, a defendant must make a prima facie showing that a peremptory challenge has been exercised on the basis of race; second, if that showing has been made, the prosecution must offer a race-neutral basis for striking the juror in question; and third, in light of the parties' submissions, the trial court must determine whether the defendant has shown purposeful discrimination. . . . In considering a Batson objection, or in reviewing a ruling claimed to be Batson error, all of the circumstances that bear upon the issue of racial animosity must be consulted.

Briefly Noted

Batson v. *Kentucky* 476 U.S. 79, 106 S.Ct. 1712, 90 L.Ed.2d 69 (1986). The State's privilege to strike individual jurors through peremptory challenges, is subject to the commands of the "Equal Protection Clause." Although a prosecutor ordinarily is entitled to exercise permitted peremptory challenges "for any reason at all, as long as that reason is related to his view concerning the outcome" of the case to be tried, the Equal Protection Clause forbids the prosecutor to challenge potential jurors solely on account of their race or on the assumption that black jurors as a group will be unable impartially to consider the State's case against a black defendant.

Summary

- The only qualification set forth in the Sixth Amendment is that a jury be an impartial jury.
- The concept of a jury of one's peers actually refers to a jury that is selected fairly and impartially from a cross section of the community.
- The procedures for selecting a jury vary from state to state.

- Jurors must be U.S. citizens, eighteen years of age or older, and residents of the judicial district for a specified period of time.
- Certain individuals are exempt from mandatory jury duty but may volunteer to serve on a jury.
- Potential jurors may be challenged for cause based on the concept that they will not be fair and impartial.

- Peremptory challenges may not be used to exclude a certain gender or racial group from a jury.
- A death-qualified jury is one in which the members have stated that, if appropriate, they would vote for the death penalty.

- The primary reason for sequestering a jury is to eliminate possible outside influence.

Review Questions

1. Who are one's peers as the term relates to a jury?
2. In what amendment is found the right to trial by an impartial jury?
3. What is a jury panel or jury list?
4. List four qualifications for being a juror.
5. What persons may be exempt from jury duty, and why is the exemption granted?

6. What is meant by challenging a juror for cause?
7. List three possible challenges for cause.
8. What is the purpose of permitting a challenge for cause?
9. What is a peremptory challenge?
10. Who are alternate jurors, and why are they selected?
11. What is meant by sequestering the jury?
12. Explain the purpose of sequestering a jury.

Local Procedure

1. What are the qualifications for a juror?
2. If a juror becomes incapacitated, may he or she be replaced by an alternate during the deliberation?

3. Must the jury be sequestered? If so, at what point during the trial?
4. How many peremptory challenges are permitted to the prosecution and the defense?

Endnotes

1. See 18 U.S. Code, section 1861.
2. 328 U.S. 128 (1942).
3. 332 U.S. 261 (1947).
4. 419 U.S. 522 (1975).
5. 366 U.S. 717 (1961).

6. 391 U.S. 510 (1968).
7. *People* v. *Velasquez,* 26 Cal.3d 425 (1980).
8. 83 L.Ed. 2d 841 (1985).
9. 476 U.S. 79 (1986).
10. *People* v. *Johnson,* 47 Cal.3rd 1194 (1989).

CHAPTER 13

Trial Procedure

Whatever disagreement there may be as to the scope of the phrase "due process of law" there can be no doubt that it embraces the fundamental conception of a fair trial, with the opportunity to be heard.

—OLIVER WENDELL HOLMES, IN *FRANK* V. *MANGUM,* 237 U.S. 309 (1915)

Chapter Outline

Key Terms

Cross-examination

Deposition

Direct examination

Directed verdict

Preponderance of evidence

Reasonable doubt

Rebuttal evidence

Redirect examination

Subpoena duces tecum

Syndromes

Learning Objectives

After completing this chapter, you should be able to:

- Explain the purposes of opening statements.

- Discuss the concept of reasonable doubt and the burden of proof.

- Describe the presentation of testimony and the examination of witnesses.
- Explain the consequences of a finding of not guilty by reason of insanity.
- List the purposes of subpoenas.

- Explain the functions of closing arguments.
- Identify the grounds upon which a judge may issue a directed verdict.
- Discuss the issues concerning syndromes.

OPENING STATEMENTS

In order that the jury may be informed of both the charge against the defendant and the plea entered, it is the policy of most courts to have the accusatory pleading read to the jury. If the charge is a felony, the accusatory pleading will be an information or an indictment, depending on the circumstances. If the charge is a misdemeanor, the accusatory pleading is usually a complaint that may or may not be read, depending upon the custom of the jurisdiction.

Prosecuting Attorney Opening Statement

After the jury has been sworn in and the charge read to them, the prosecution is the first to present its evidence. The prosecution goes first because they have the burden of proof. Prior to calling the first witness, the judge will ask the prosecuting attorney whether he or she wishes to make an opening statement. An opening statement will be made in most instances, since it provides an opportunity to explain further the charge against the defendant. By making an opening statement, the prosecuting attorney is able to outline the evidence planned for the trial, thereby allowing the jury to more intelligently follow the presentation of the prosecution's side of the case. The opening statement is probably more important in jury trials than in court trials because it orients the jury to what is to follow and prepares them for the evidence.

The prosecuting attorney has considerable latitude in referring to the evidence that he or she plans to introduce during the trial, but the statements are not considered facts of the case. If for some reason the evidence is not admitted, the jury may not consider the attorney's statements as evidence of the case. It has been held to be prejudicial error for a prosecuting attorney to mention evidence known to be inadmissible. Prejudicial error may result from a statement or an act of misconduct by a prosecuting attorney or a witness that will prevent the defendant from getting a fair trial or that is so prejudicial that either a mistrial will be declared or a conviction will be reversed on appeal. It is also prejudicial error for a prosecuting attorney to refer to the defendant as an ex-convict or to imply that he or she has committed prior crimes. A defendant is entitled to be tried on the facts stated in the accusatory pleading; any reference to other crimes or prior convictions is considered to be so prejudicial against the defendant that the judge may declare a mistrial at that time. If the judge does not declare a mistrial and the defendant is convicted, the conviction may be reversed on appeal.

Defense Counsel Opening Statement

After the prosecuting attorney has completed the opening statement, the judge will often ask whether the defense attorney wishes to make an opening statement. In some jurisdictions, the judge may delay the defense attorney's opening statement until after the prosecution has presented its side of the case. Many defense attorneys believe that it is a mistake to make an opening statement before the prosecution has completed its side of the presentation of the evidence, since the defense strategy may change. If an opening statement is made before the prosecution presents its side of the evidence, statements may be made that will not conform with the defense strategy, and the jury may be confused about what happened or may question the innocence of the defendant. In making an opening statement immediately after the prosecuting attorney has made his or her opening statement, the defense attorney may alert the prosecution to an anticipated defense; most defense attorneys try to avoid this. Many defense attorneys waive the right of making an opening statement at any time, since they feel that the disadvantages outweigh the advantages. Often defense witnesses do not measure up to expectation or do not appear at all. If their testimony has been previously outlined, the jury may question the validity of the defense.

On the other hand, some defense attorneys believe that it is a mistake not to make an opening statement immediately following the opening statement of the prosecuting attorney. They theorize that the prosecuting attorney will have made a favorable impression on the jury and that it is dangerous not to challenge that statement immediately. These defense attorneys state that it is not necessary to go into any detail of the defense at that time. They can merely inform the jury that the defense plans to present evidence to prove that the facts of the case are not as alleged by the prosecuting attorney. These defense attorneys will request the jury to keep an open mind until the defense has the opportunity to present contrary evidence.

REASONABLE DOUBT

In our system of justice, the defendant in a criminal case is presumed to be innocent until proved otherwise. The U.S. Supreme Court has held in a number of cases proving a criminal charge *beyond a* **reasonable doubt** is constitutionally required though not included in the Bill of Rights. This Court stated the following in the case of *In re Winship:*

> . . . it is the duty of the Government to establish guilt beyond a reasonable doubt. This notion—basic in our law and rightly one of the boasts of a free society—is a requirement and safeguard of due process of law in the historic, procedural content of due process . . . that guilt in a criminal case must be proved beyond a reasonable doubt and by evidence confined to that which long experience in the common law tradition, to some extent embodied in the Constitution, has crystallized into rules of evidence consistent with that standard. These rules are historically grounded rights of our system, developed to safeguard men from dubious and unjust convictions, with resulting forfeitures of life, liberty and property. . . .
>
> The requirement of proof beyond a reasonable doubt has this vital role in our criminal procedure for cogent reasons. The accused during a criminal prosecution has at stake interests of immense importance, both because of the possibility that he may lose his liberty upon conviction and because of the certainty that he would be stigmatized by the conviction. Accordingly, a society that values the good name and freedom of every individual should not condemn a man for commission of a crime when there is reasonable doubt about his guilt. . . .
>
> Moreover, use of the reasonable doubt standard is indispensable to command the respect and confidence of the community in application of the criminal law. It is critical that the moral force of the criminal law not be diluted by a standard of proof which leaves people in doubt whether innocent men are being condemned. It is also important in our free society that every individual going about his ordinary affairs have confidence that his government cannot adjudge him guilty of a criminal offense without convincing a proper factfinder of his guilt with utmost certainty.[1]

The term reasonable doubt is familiar to all. Yet many jurors are confused about the real meaning of the term and when reasonable doubt has been proved. They desire some explanation, but the more one tries to interpret the meaning of reasonable doubt, the more confusing it becomes. To further confuse the issue, some courts and statutes state that the defendant must be proved guilty beyond a reasonable doubt and to a moral certainty. A statute of one state defines reasonable doubt as follows:

> It is not a mere possible doubt, because everything relating to human affairs, and depending upon moral evidence, is open to some possible or imaginary doubt. It is that state of the case, which, after the entire comparison and consideration of all the evidence, leaves the minds of jurors in that condition that they cannot say they feel an abiding conviction . . . of the truth of the charge.

After reading this definition, there is some question whether the jury would have any better understanding of the meaning of reasonable doubt than before. To state it in a simpler form, it is that doubt that a juror may have after weighing all the evidence of the case and is still not satisfied that the defendant is guilty of the crime charged.

WITNESSES

The defendant is entitled to be confronted by the witnesses against him or her. As stated by the U.S. Supreme Court in *California* v. *Green,* this confrontation

> (1) insures that the witness will give his statements under oath thus impressing him with the seriousness of the matter and guarding against the lie by the possibility of a penalty for perjury; (2) forces the witness to submit to cross examination, the "greatest legal engine ever invented for the discovery of the truth"; (3) permits the jury that is to decide the defendant's fate to observe the demeanor of the witness in making his statement, thus aiding the jury in assessing his credibility.[2]

Since the defendant has the right to be confronted by opposing witnesses, most of the prosecution's evidence attempting to prove guilt beyond a reasonable doubt will be presented through the testimony of witnesses. As indicated earlier, the U.S. Constitution has been interpreted to require that a defendant has a right to confront and cross-examine all witnesses against him or her. However, this right is not absolute.[3] For example, hearsay statements of another person may be admitted against the defendant even though he or she does not have the opportunity to cross-examine the person making those statements. The U.S. Supreme Court also examined another aspect of this constitutional right when it addressed the issue of the use of closed-circuit television in child abuse cases in *Maryland* v. *Craig.*[4]

In October 1986, a Howard County grand jury charged Sandra Ann Craig with a number of child abuse offenses. The victim, Brooke, was a six-year-old girl who from August 1984 to June 1986 attended a prekindergarten and kindergarten center owned and operated by Craig. In March 1987, before the case went to trial, the state sought to invoke a Maryland statute that allowed the judge and jury to view the victim via closed-circuit television. The victim was to be located in a separate room outside the presence of the defendant. Although the defendant and her attorney could view the television and ask questions, they would not be allowed to physically confront the victim.

In support of its motion, the state presented expert testimony that Brooke, as well as a number of other children who were alleged to have been abused, would suffer serious emotional distress that they could not reasonably communicate if required to testify in the courtroom and face the defendant. Another expert testified that Brooke would probably stop talking and would withdraw and curl up into a ball if she were in the same room as the defendant. The trial court ruled that because of the possible distress that the victims would suffer in seeing the defendant, the closed-circuit television would be authorized.

In upholding such a procedure, the U.S. Supreme Court held that a strict reading of the Confrontation Clause would do away with every hearsay exception and that this was too extreme a result. Therefore, the Court held that the Confrontation Clause reflects a preference for face-to-face confrontations at trial, but that this preference must occasionally give way to considerations of public policy and the necessities of the case. Thus, the holding in *Maryland* v. *Craig* allows the use of closed-circuit television under certain circumstances in child-abuse cases. Specifically, there must be a state statute that authorizes such a procedure, and the state must establish that the child is unable to face his or her accused molester in person.

There are two kinds of witnesses: the lay, or ordinary, witness and the expert witness. The lay witness is an individual who has some personal knowledge of the facts of the case derived from personal perceptions, that is, from what was seen, heard, or felt. An expert witness is an individual who has knowledge and skill in a particular field that is beyond the knowledge of the average person. The expert witness gives the judge and the jury the benefit of acquired knowledge, often in the form of an opinion, to assist them in arriving at the truth of a matter. The jury may either accept the opinion of the expert or reject it, as they see fit. Before an expert witness may testify, the side calling this witness must qualify him or her as an expert. By training, experience, or education, the expert witness must prove knowledge or skill in a particular field above that of the average person. This expertise is established by questioning the witness about his or her ability in a particular field. The judge must then declare the witness to be qualified as an expert before testimony or an opinion on the facts of the case can be given. Establishing the qualifications of the expert witness is referred to as a voir dire examination.

It is not necessary for the prosecution to call every person who has some knowledge about the facts of the case to be a witness. The prosecuting attorney must call enough witnesses to prove the defendant guilty beyond a reasonable doubt. It is difficult to determine how many witnesses this step will take in any given case. At first glance, it may appear that the prosecuting attorney should not gamble on how many witnesses should be called, but should call all who may know something about the case. However, to accept testimony from every person who may have some personal knowledge about the case could be time-consuming and could cause the jury to become weary and lose interest in the prosecution's presentation. But the prosecution will call all the witnesses necessary to completely relate the story of what happened in the case. In addition, a few witnesses will probably be called to corroborate the testimony of other witnesses. The prosecution will have to present those witnesses necessary to establish that a crime was committed—that is, it will have to prove the elements of the crime. This process of proving that a crime was committed is known as establishing the corpus delicti.

The sequence in which the witnesses are called to testify may not result in the presentation of the events in the same sequence in which they occurred. The prosecuting attorney will decide the sequence in accordance with how the facts can best be presented in a logical, understandable manner.

SUBPOENA

Persons are officially notified to appear in court as witnesses by a legal document known as a subpoena. Subpoenas will be issued for the attendance of both prosecution and defense witnesses. Depending upon the jurisdiction, a subpoena may be issued by a judge, prosecuting attorney, clerk of the court, or public defender.

Occasionally, a witness will be commanded to bring books, papers, documents, or other physical evidence to court. If so, a "**subpoena duces tecum**" will be issued to the witness. The subpoena duces tecum follows the same general form as the subpoena, but it includes a description of the material that the witness is to produce in court and a statement of the relevance of the requested evidence to the trial.

Generally, a subpoena or subpoena duces tecum may be served by anyone, but most frequently it will be served by an officer of the court. Service is made by personally delivering a copy of the subpoena to the witness. After the service is made, the person serving the subpoena will make a written return on a copy of the subpoena stating the date, time, and place that the service was made.

It has been held that a person owes a duty to society to appear and testify as a witness in criminal cases when subpoenaed to do so. Because of this duty, witnesses generally are not compensated when appearing to testify. Yet it is recognized that a witness should not suffer undue financial hardship in performing duty as a witness. Since a subpoena is valid anyplace within the state in which it is issued, most jurisdictions provide for the payment of reasonable travel expenses to a witness who must travel a great distance to testify.

In some jurisdictions, before a witness can be compensated, the judge involved in the trial must endorse the subpoena with a statement that the witness is a material witness and that this attendance is absolutely necessary. Once a witness has appeared in court, it is common practice to have the judge order the witness back instead of issuing a new subpoena for a new date.

Witnesses Failing to Appear

The failure of a witness to appear as commanded in a subpoena can bring about contempt of court charges unless good cause for not appearing can be shown. In addition to being held in contempt, the witness, if subpoenaed by the defense, can in some states be civilly sued by the defendant for failure to appear. It is not necessary for a person to be served with a subpoena to be a witness. The witness may orally agree to appear but cannot be held in contempt for failing to be present at the trial.

In the past, since a subpoena was good only within the state in which it was issued, there was no way to command the appearance of a witness who was out of the state. Today, most states have adopted the Uniform Act to Secure the Attendance of Witnesses from without the State in Criminal Cases. This act enables a court to command the appearance of a material witness beyond the jurisdiction of the court because the witness resides in another state. The court in which the witness is needed to appear will issue a certificate naming this person as a material witness, the date and place at which he or she is to appear, and the approximate number of days that the person will be needed as a witness. This certificate is transmitted to the appropriate court in the state where the needed witness resides. The court in that state will order the witness to come before it for a hearing to determine whether the person is a necessary and material witness and whether any undue hardship will be caused by the person's appearing in the other state as a witness. If the judge concludes that the person is a necessary and material witness and that no hardship will be suffered, the person will be tendered expense money and ordered to appear in the demanding court as a witness. Should the person fail to appear as commanded, contempt of court charges may be filed in the state where the material witness resides. The witness is immune from arrest on any prior crimes committed in the demanding state while in the state to testify.

Excluding Witnesses

Prior to the time that any of the witnesses testify, the judge must decide whether the witnesses may remain in the courtroom or should be excluded until after they have testified. This decision may be made on the judge's own motion or on the request of either the prosecution or the defense. The primary purpose for excluding witnesses from the courtroom is to prevent them from trying to corroborate the testimony of other witnesses. The effort to corroborate another witness's testimony is not always done with an intent to falsify. It may be done because one witness may be uncertain of some of the facts. Although witnesses are excluded from the courtroom, it is almost impossible to keep them from conversing about their testimony even though the judge admonishes them against such action.

EXAMINATION OF WITNESSES

The Oath

Before being permitted to testify, an oath must be administered in which the witness promises to tell the truth. Throughout the history of trial by jury, witnesses have given an oath that their allegations are true. In the past, these oaths have involved a call to the deity to assist the oath giver in substantiating the truthfulness of the statements made, as well as a call for assistance in telling the truth. It was the general belief that, after giving such an oath, should one falsely testify, divine punishment would result. So strong was the belief in divine punishment at common law that if one did not believe in God, one was considered incompetent to testify.

Although most jurisdictions presently do not prescribe wording for the oath administered to a witness, generally a call to the deity to assist the witness in telling the truth is still included. Oaths that are administered to witnesses today are substantially as follows: "Do you hereby solemnly swear to tell the truth, and nothing but the truth, in the matter now pending before this court, so help you God?" At one time, while this oath was being administered, the witness was required to raise the right hand and lay the left hand on a Bible. Most jurisdictions have dispensed with the use of the Bible in administering the oath, but the witness is still required to raise his or her right hand during its administration.

AFFIRMATION Although there is no requirement that the word God be mentioned in the oath, it usually is included. Some persons consider it objectionable to "swear to God" to tell the truth. They feel this way either because they believe that the use of the word God under the circumstances is sacrilegious or because they do not believe in a God and object to swearing to something in which they have no belief. To accommodate these individuals, courts permit them to affirm to tell the truth. When either the court clerk or another court officer administers the oath or affirmation, or swears in the witness, as the procedure is known, the witness is asked to stand and be sworn. If the oath is found objectionable, the witness will advise the officer that the truth will be affirmed. The officer will then require the witness to raise the right hand, and the officer will state words to this effect: "Do you hereby solemnly affirm to tell the truth and nothing but the truth in the matter now pending before this court?" This procedure has been referred to as an affirmation. Whether a witness swears to tell the truth or affirms to tell the truth, both procedures are technically known as the "oath."

A few legal scholars argue that administering the oath is a useless procedure and a waste of time, since it does not guarantee that the witness will testify truthfully. But the great majority of persons engaged in the trial of cases believe that administering the oath to the witness gives a certain legal solemnity to the occasion and may cause the witness to reflect upon the necessity to tell the truth. As is stated in the Federal Rules of Criminal Procedure, the wording of the oath may be of any nature that will awaken the witness to the necessity of telling the truth.

Even though the oath may not guarantee that the truth will be told, the witness may be prosecuted for perjury if testimony is intentionally falsified after the oath is administered. This threat may be enough to encourage some witnesses to testify truthfully, when they might not otherwise do so.

REFUSAL TO BE SWORN If a witness refuses to be sworn, a contempt of court charge can be filed against the witness. The only exception to the administration of the oath to a witness is in the case of a small child or a mentally retarded person who may not understand the meaning of the oath. Under these circumstances, before the child or mentally retarded person is allowed to testify, the judge will conduct a voir dire examination to determine whether the prospective witness knows that it is wrong to tell a falsehood and that it is necessary to tell the truth. If this can be established by the judge through questioning the prospective witness, the oath will be eliminated.

Direct Examination

After the oath has been administered to the witness, the witness will begin his or her testimony; that is, facts will be related within the witness's knowledge of the case. Prior to making any statements about the case, the witness will be required to state his or her name and correct spelling of the name for identification purposes. Because of threats that have been made to law enforcement officers and their families, some jurisdictions permit the officers to give their headquarters address instead of their home address. After the identification data are furnished by the prosecution witness, the prosecuting attorney will start the examination. The questioning of the witness by the side that calls him or her is known as **direct examination**. Unless restricted by the trial judge, the prosecuting attorney may approach the direct examination in one of two ways or in a combination of both. The prosecuting attorney may request the witness to relate in his or her own words the facts about the case. This procedure is sometimes referred to as the narrative approach. The prosecuting attorney may also use the short-question-and-answer approach. Both procedures have their advantages and disadvantages. The narrative approach permits the witness to tell the story in a more logical form so that the jury may be better able to follow the testimony. But unless the witness is familiar with the rules of evidence, irrelevant material and hearsay evidence may be included, or facts may be related that the prosecuting attorney wishes to avoid. By asking the witness short, direct questions, the prosecuting attorney has greater control over the facts to be related and can limit the testimony to relevant facts. The short-question-and-answer form of examination is frequently time-consuming, and sometimes this type of testimony becomes boring to the jury. If a witness is shy or perhaps somewhat reluctant to testify, it may be necessary to revert to the short-question-and-answer procedure.

During the direct examination, the attorney may not ask the witness leading questions. A leading question is one that indicates the desired answer to the witness. For example, the attorney may ask the witness, "You did see the defendant threaten the victim with a knife, didn't you?" Clearly, the attorney wants a yes answer. But by rephrasing the question, the witness may be asked, "Did you see the defendant threaten the victim with a knife?" Although the attorney may still desire a yes answer, that wish has not been indicated to the witness, and the witness is free to give either a yes or no answer. The mere fact that a question calls for a yes or no answer does not make it a leading one, but if phrased to indicate the answer desired, it is a leading question. The reason these questions are not generally permitted during direct examination is that the witness is usually favorable to the side that calls the witness, and thus there may be a tendency to assist that side irrespective of the truth if a desired answer is indicated.

Occasionally, a witness called by the prosecution will display hostility toward the prosecution, making the expected testimony difficult to obtain. Under these circumstances, the prosecuting attorney may request the judge to declare for the record that the witness is a hostile witness. If the witness is declared to be hostile, the prosecuting attorney may then ask leading questions. This type of questioning is permitted because it is assumed that the witness will answer truthfully, because of the displayed hostility, even though a desired answer is indicated. Although a hostile witness may be asked leading questions during direct examination, using that method does not mean that obtaining the desired testimony from the witness will become any less difficult. To be declared a hostile witness, a person must display hostility and uncooperativeness. The mere fact that a witness does not meet expectations or is reluctant to furnish information will not be sufficient grounds for the judge to declare the witness hostile.

A limited use of leading questions is permitted in the examination of children, senior citizens, and mentally retarded persons in order to assist them in telling their stories. Leading questions may also be asked concerning identifying matters, such as name, address, and place of employment of the witness, since these matters are usually not in controversy. Occasionally, a leading question may be permitted to assist in refreshing the memory of a witness.

Objections to Questions

During the direct examination by the prosecuting attorney, the defense attorney may object to some of the questions asked. If so, the objection will be indicated to the judge, who must rule upon the objection. After an objection is made, the witness should not answer the question until the judge has ruled on it. If the judge believes that the objection is well founded, he or she will sustain the objection, meaning that the witness may not answer the question. If the judge does not agree with the objection, he or she will overrule the objection, whereupon the witness must answer. There are many reasons the defense attorney may object to a question. The question may call for an answer that would be hearsay information; it may be leading; or it may require the witness to state an opinion about some matter. If the prosecution asks an improper question or one that calls for information that is not admissible, unless the defense attorney objects the answer is permitted to go into the record of the case and generally is not grounds for appeal should the defendant be convicted. For this reason, defense attorneys make frequent objections during the trial. From a psychological standpoint, defense attorneys may also inject objections from time to time in an effort to lessen the impact of the testimony of the prosecution's witnesses.

Occasionally, a witness will become overzealous in answering the prosecuting attorney's questions and will answer a question to which an objection is made before the judge is able to rule on it. If the objection is overruled, no serious consequences result, other than the judge's becoming irritated because the witness did not wait for the ruling. However, if the objection is sustained, the answer has been improperly given, and therefore it must be stricken from the record and the jury advised to disregard the answer. But the problem is, can a jury completely forget such a statement? Knowing the difficulty of disregarding some statements, especially if the answer is highly prejudicial against the defendant, the judge may declare a mistrial, and the case will have to be restarted with a different jury. In addition, the witness could be held in contempt of court, particularly if previously admonished against answering before the judge can rule on an objection.

Cross-Examination

After the prosecuting attorney has concluded questioning the witness on direct examination, the defense attorney is permitted to cross-examine the witness. The primary purpose of **cross-examination** is to assist in arriving at the truth. Cross-examination enables the opposition or adversary to challenge the witness's veracity, accuracy, and prejudices. One of the basic reasons that the accused is entitled to confront adverse witnesses is to enable cross-examination. This right was made mandatory on the states by the case of *Pointer* v. *Texas*.[5] The U.S. Supreme Court stated the following in the *Pointer* decision:

> . . . We hold today that the Sixth Amendment's right of an accused to confront the witnesses against him is likewise a fundamental right and is made obligatory on the States by the Fourteenth Amendment.
>
> It cannot seriously be doubted at this late date that the right of cross-examination is included in the right of an accused in a criminal case to confront the witnesses against him. And probably no one, certainly no one experienced in the trial of lawsuits, would deny the value of cross-examination in exposing falsehood and bringing out the truth in a trial of a criminal case . . . the right of cross-examination is one of the safeguards essential to a fair trial.

If the defense attorney believes that the witness told the truth during the direct examination and nothing is to be gained by cross-examining the witness, the right to cross-examine that particular witness may be waived. Cross-examination is at best a dangerous procedure for a defense attorney. Before deciding whether to cross-examine a witness, the defense counsel must carefully weigh whether there is more to be lost than gained by the cross-examination. If a witness was telling the truth during direct examination, the cross-examination may merely result in the witness's being able to reemphasize the story to the jury. There is also the possibility that the witness may become emotionally upset by vigorous cross-examination, thus often receiving the sympathy of the jury.

IMPEACHMENT On the other hand, if a witness testified falsely during direct examination, has made prior inconsistent statements, or has colored the testimony because of some prejudice, these facts may be disclosed to the jury only through cross-examination. Cross-examination under these circumstances is necessary in order that the jury may disregard the testimony or give it the proper weight. This devaluation of the testimony by cross-examination is referred to as impeachment in the field of evidence.

Generally, cross-examination is an unpleasant experience for both the witness and the attorney. As we pointed out, if the witness told the truth during direct examination and cannot be upset by cross-examination, the defense attorney may suffer the unpleasantness of the witness's retelling the story to the jury. Many times a defense attorney does not receive the answer anticipated during cross-examination, but the attorney is usually bound by the answer and thus often is powerless to overcome the damage the answer may cause. If a witness testifies truthfully during direct examination, there is usually little to fear from cross-examination. However, a few attorneys feel that the only way to properly represent the defendant in a criminal case is to vigorously cross-examine all witnesses. If the witness has given testimony particularly damaging to the defense, the defense attorney may endeavor to devalue the testimony by belittling or embarrassing the witness during cross-examination. Although having the responsibility of protecting a witness from overzealous cross-examination, the judge may not unduly restrict the defense attorney from vigorous cross-examination. Occasionally, a witness may have been indiscreet in some action or statement made that may be brought out during cross-examination, and the judge will be powerless to prevent this embarrassment. If the witness, and particularly the law enforcement officer, has testified discreetly in conduct and content, any attempt at embarrassment by the defense attorney may result in enhancing the officer's testimony. Juries often react unfavorably to this cross-examination tactic.

Although leading questions may not generally be asked during direct examination, they are permitted on cross-examination if the attorney feels that utilizing them is an advantage. Leading questions are frequently asked during vigorous cross-examination. The reason these questions are permitted during cross-examination is that usually the witness who is being cross-examined is not favorable to the side doing the cross-examining, and the witness will not give a desired answer, even though it is indicated, unless it is the truth.

LIMITED CROSS-EXAMINATION States differ in the extent of the cross-examination. A majority of the states limit the cross-examination to the facts brought out during direct examination. This procedure is referred to as limited or restricted cross-examination. Other states permit the witness to be cross-examined about any pertinent facts in the case that may be within the knowledge of the witness. This procedure is known as unlimited or unrestricted cross-examination. Those favoring restricted cross-examination allege that attorneys are able to control the material that is presented by a witness and may prepare the presentation in a more logical manner. This method enables the jury to follow the facts more closely as they unfold. Those who advocate unrestricted cross-examination allege that the unrestricted procedure saves time, in that a witness may be examined extensively while on the stand rather than being recalled at a later time. Also, the procedure eliminates objections by the opposing side that the questions asked during cross-examination did not pertain to matters brought out during direct examination. In those states following the restricted cross-examination procedure, witnesses are usually cautioned to confine their answers to questions asked during direct examination and not to volunteer additional information, since they may subject themselves to unnecessary and extensive cross-examination. This outcome is one of the dangers of permitting the story to be told in the witness's own words, since facts may be included that could be used to devalue the testimony during cross-examination. Whether the restricted or unrestricted procedure is followed, witnesses are seldom permitted to give the facts in their own way during cross-examination. The cross-examiner desires to control the testimony and can better do so by confining the questions to ones that require short answers, often only a yes or no.

REDIRECT EXAMINATION AND RECROSS-EXAMINATION After the defense attorney has completed his or her cross-examination, the judge will permit the prosecuting attorney to further question the witness. This questioning is known as **redirect examination**. The questioning must be confined to clarifying facts brought out during cross-examination. Sometimes the defense attorney will require that the witness answer a question with only a yes or no, but the answer does not reflect the true situation without further explanation. When the prosecuting attorney further questions the witness after cross-examination, the answers can be explained more fully by the witness. Seldom will a judge permit any new material to be brought forth during the redirect examination. To do so would start the entire questioning process again and could encourage sloppy practice by attorneys by not properly preparing the direct examination. Unless the prosecuting attorney believes that redirect examination will be beneficial, it may be waived.

If the prosecuting attorney further questions the witness on redirect examination, at the conclusion of this questioning the defense attorney is entitled to re-cross-examine the witness on facts stated on redirect examination. After this series takes place, the witness is excused and the next witness is called. The same sequence of examinations may take place with each prosecution and defense witness who is called, or the sequence could stop after the direct examination. When the entire series is repeated with each witness, criminal trials can become very lengthy.

Refusal to Answer Questions

The witness must answer all questions asked throughout the entire examination. The only exception is that if the answer to a question will incriminate the witness, the witness may refuse to answer. An incriminating answer is one that would subject the witness to prosecution. The Fifth Amendment to the U.S. Constitution provides that one may not be compelled to witness against oneself. But all other questions must be answered even though the answer may be embarrassing or life-endangering to the witness or his or her family. The degrading or endangering questions must be pertinent to the case, however, and not asked merely to embarrass the witness. Otherwise, the judge may not permit the question to be answered. Refusal to answer questions occurs more frequently during cross-examination than during direct examination. It is during cross-examination that the witness is questioned by the adversary, and it is then that questions may be asked that the witness would be hesitant to answer. If a witness persists in refusing to answer a question that is not incriminating, the entire testimony may be stricken from the record and the jury advised to disregard it. It is held that a witness may not testify to those facts that may be favorable and refuse to testify to matters that may be unfavorable. In addition to having the testimony stricken from the record, the witness could be held in contempt of court until the questions are answered.

There are times during a trial when arriving at the truth of what happened is more important than the prosecution of a witness incriminated by answering a question. Under these circumstances, the witness may be granted immunity from prosecution by the judge. If immunity is granted, the witness must answer all questions.

Examination by the Judge and Jury

Although it is the primary responsibility of the prosecution and defense to call and examine the witnesses whom they believe are necessary, witnesses may also be called by the trial judge if deemed necessary in the interest of justice. Most jurisdictions permit the judge to question prosecution and defense witnesses if such questioning may furnish information not brought forth by the prosecutor or defense counsel. Occasionally, a juror may wish to question a witness in order to clarify some point. Most judges will permit a limited amount of questioning by a juror if it is felt that the questioning is in good faith, but such questioning could very easily get out of hand, since some jurors may desire to get into the act and become counsels. The questioning of witnesses by jurors is generally not encouraged. When a juror wishes to ask a witness a question, the judge usually will require the juror to write the question on a slip of paper and have it handed to the judge, who will ask the question for the juror. This precaution keeps a juror from trying to become one of the questioning attorneys.

Introduction of Physical Evidence

During the investigation of a crime, officers will usually discover physical evidence, or material objects, that are pertinent to the crime. These objects, such as a latent fingerprint developed at a crime scene and identified as that of the defendant, often assist in connecting the defendant to the crime. Physical evidence may include objects taken during a robbery or burglary that were found in the possession of the defendant. These objects may be described by the officer who found them, and it is not necessary that they be presented in court. But in almost all instances, the prosecuting attorney will introduce these objects as evidence in order to substantiate the officer's testimony and to emphasize the facts of the case. These physical objects must be introduced by witnesses who can connect the objects with the crime charged. The witness will have to describe where the object was found, when, and under what circumstances. Who can forget the controversy surrounding the bloody glove in the O.J. Simpson murder trial? Once the object is introduced into evidence, the jury may examine it and consider it part of the facts of the case.

Viewing the Crime Scene

There are times when a judge may feel that a jury can better follow the testimony of the witnesses if they view the area in which the crime was committed. Under these circumstances, the judge will order the jury, as a body, to be taken to the crime scene by an officer of the court. Since viewing the crime scene is, in a sense, receiving facts of the case, the viewing in some jurisdictions is considered as evidence of the case. For that reason, the prosecuting attorney, defense attorney, defendant, and judge must accompany the jury. It has been established as improper for a jury, either as individuals or as a group, to view the crime scene without authorization from the judge.

In making the decision, the judge must consider several factors. If photographs of the crime scene are displayed to the jury, will that display accomplish as much as the actual viewing? Have material changes taken place in the crime scene that may cause more confusion than clarification?

Prosecution Rests

After presentation of all the prosecution witnesses and physical evidence that the prosecuting attorney believes is necessary, the prosecuting attorney will usually state, "The prosecution rests, your honor. . . ." This statement is an indication to all those involved in the trial that the prosecution has presented the evidence that it believes is sufficient to convince the jury that the defendant is guilty beyond a reasonable doubt. In other words, the prosecution rests its side of the case in the hands of the jury with the hope of getting a favorable verdict.

Judgment of Acquittal

After the prosecution rests, the defense may present evidence in its own behalf. Before doing so, however, the usual procedure is for the defense counsel to request permission from the judge to approach the bench—that is, permission to speak to the judge. Permission is usually granted, and the defense attorney then will request that the jury be excused so that a motion can be made for a judgment of acquittal.

If the judge permits the motion to be argued, the defense attorney will endeavor to convince the judge that the prosecution failed to establish that a crime was committed or that the defendant committed it. Or the defense attorney may contend that the prosecution failed to present enough evidence to substantiate, or uphold, a conviction on appeal. If the judge agrees with the defense attorney, the judge has the authority to take the case out of the hands of the jury and enter a judgment of acquittal, which is a bar to any further action against the defendant on the crime charged. This procedure is also referred to as a motion for a **directed verdict**. However, the directed verdict has another meaning in some states. In such states, if a motion for a directed verdict is granted, the judge instructs the jury to return a verdict of not guilty. The jury is not bound by this direction in some states. The jury may disregard the motion and return a verdict of guilty. A few states contend that a judge does not have the right to enter either a motion of acquittal or a directed verdict, since the procedure takes the case out of the hands of the jury, who are the exclusive judge of the facts of the case.

The reason that a defense attorney will request the jury to be excused during the time the motion is made for a judgment of acquittal is that if the motion is not granted, the jury may be convinced that the judge believes the defendant guilty. This belief could affect their verdict. The motion for a judgment of acquittal or a directed verdict does not always have to be argued. The judge may be convinced that the evidence presented by the prosecution does not support a conviction. The judge may then make a motion to enter a judgment of an acquittal or may direct a verdict of acquittal.

However, even though convinced at the time the prosecution rests that the defendant is guilty beyond a reasonable doubt, the judge may neither enter a judgment of conviction nor direct a verdict of conviction. Such action would be denying the defendant the right to a trial by jury.

DEFENSE PRESENTATION

If the judge does not agree to enter a judgment of acquittal or to direct a verdict of acquittal, the defense attorney must make a decision. He or she must decide whether to allow the case to go to the jury at that time with the hope that they have some doubt about the guilt of the defendant or whether evidence should be presented in behalf of the defendant in an effort to create such a doubt. Generally, if there is any defense that can be presented, the defendant's attorney will present evidence rather than take a chance on the jury's returning a guilty verdict. If the defendant has admitted guilt to counsel but refuses to enter a plea of guilty, presenting a defense may be a difficult task for the defense attorney.

Defense Approaches

If the charge is homicide or aggravated assault, the defense may attempt to prove that the defendant committed the act in self-defense. In the case of a forceful rape, the defense may allege that the victim consented to the act of intercourse with the defendant. One of the more prevalent defenses is the alibi defense. Also, a defense attorney will occasionally endeavor to prove that the defendant is of such good character that a crime as charged in the accusatory pleading could not have been committed. This is not always an easy defense to present, particularly if the defendant has a criminal record. The moment that the defendant endeavors to prove reputable character through witnesses, the prosecution can discredit the testimony by showing the defendant's criminal record. This is one of the few times that the past record of a defendant may be introduced in evidence.

Should the Defendant Testify

While planning the defense, an attorney must decide whether the defendant should be permitted to testify. Often it is not an easy decision to make, since many factors must be considered. The attorney must consider the impression that the defendant may make on the jury while testifying. If the defendant has a criminal record, and particularly a conviction on a felony, this may be brought out during cross-examination. On the stand, the defendant is treated the same way as any other witness in most jurisdictions, and witnesses may be impeached by revealing certain past convictions. Being aware of the defendant's past record of convictions could affect the jury's verdict. If the defendant does take the stand, what will be the jury's reaction to this failure to testify and to explain personal knowledge of the facts?

In the distant past, if the defendant did not take the stand in his or her own defense, the failure to do so could be commented on by the prosecuting attorney and the judge as the case was being summarized to the jury. But in the case of *Griffin* v. *California,* the U.S. Supreme Court held that such comments are improper, since they tend to force the defendant to be a witness against himself or herself in violation of the Fifth Amendment of the U.S. Constitution.[6] The facts of the *Griffin* case reflect that the defendant was convicted of murder in a jury trial. The defendant did not testify at the trial on the issue of guilt, and the trial judge instructed the jury that a defendant has a constitutional right not to testify. But the judge told the jury the following: "As to any evidence or facts within his knowledge, if he does not testify or if, though he does testify, he fails to deny or explain such evidence, the jury may take that failure into consideration as tending to indicate the truth of such evidence and as indicating that among the inferences that may be reasonably drawn therefrom those unfavorable to the defendant are the most probable."

The petitioner (the defendant) had been seen with the deceased on the evening of her death, the evidence placing him with her in the alley where her body was found. The prosecutor made much of the failure of the petitioner to testify (and made the following statements to the jury):

> The defendant certainly knows whether Essie Mae (the deceased) had this beat up appearance at the time he left her apartment and went down the alley with her.
>
> What kind of a man is it that would want to have sex with a woman that he beat up if she was beat up at the time he left?
>
> He would know that. He would know how she got down the alley. He would know how the blood got on the bottom concrete steps. . . .
>
> These things he has not seen fit to take the stand and deny or explain. And in the whole world, if anybody would know, this defendant would know. Essie Mae is dead, she can't tell you her side of the story. The defendant won't.

The case was taken to the U.S. Supreme Court on a writ of certiorari to consider whether comment on the defendant's failure to testify violated the self-incrimination clause of the Fifth Amendment made applicable to the states by the Fourteenth Amendment. The Supreme Court pointed out that a defendant has a constitutional right to remain silent and not testify, and permitting the prosecuting attorney and judge to comment on the defendant's failure to testify was

> a penalty imposed by the courts for exercising a constitutional privilege. It cut down on the privilege by making its assertion costly. It is said, however, that the inference of guilt for failure to testify as to facts peculiarly within the accused's knowledge is in any event natural and irresistible, and that comment on the failure

does not magnify that inference into a penalty for asserting a constitutional privilege. What the jury may infer, given no help from the court, is one thing. What it may infer when the court solemnizes the silence of the accused into evidence against him is quite another.

The defendant's Fifth Amendment right against self-incrimination and the fact that the exercise of that right may not be called to the attention of the jury were both clearly illustrated by the *Griffin* case. However, in most jurisdictions, if the defendant does take the stand and fails to explain certain facts that logically should have been explained, that failure may be commented on by the judge and the prosecuting attorney. The theory behind this permitted comment is that it is held that a defendant should not be able to testify on only those matters that are beneficial but fail to explain other facts that may be unfavorable. Another problem created for a defense attorney arises when the client insists on taking the stand and the attorney does not believe such action to be wise. Does a defendant have a right to testify in his or her own behalf over the objections of counsel? This question has not been answered in all jurisdictions, but a few have held that a defendant does have a right to present evidence in his or her own behalf, even to testifying over the objections of counsel. The court of one state made this comment concerning the right of a defendant to testify:

> We are satisfied that the right to testify in one's own behalf is of such fundamental importance that a defendant whose timely demands to take the stand contrary to the advice given by his counsel has the right to give an exposition of his defense before a jury. The defendant's insistence upon testifying may in the final analysis be harmful to his case, but the right is of such importance that every defendant should have it in a criminal case. Although normally the decision whether a defendant should testify is within the competence of the trial attorney where, as here, a defendant insists that he wants to testify, he cannot be deprived of that opportunity.[7]

However, the defendant does not have a right to have his or her attorney present perjured testimony. The courts have stated that there is no Sixth Amendment right to an attorney's knowingly presenting perjured testimony. In one case, the defendant told his attorney that although he never saw a gun in the victim's hand, he was going to take the stand and raise the issue of self-defense. His attorney told him that such conduct would be perjury, and if the defendant attempted to testify in that manner, the attorney would disclose the perjury and withdraw from the case. The defendant testified but did not raise the self-defense issue. He was convicted and appealed, claiming he was denied effective counsel since the attorney's refusal to allow him to testify in the way he wanted violated his right to counsel. The U.S. Supreme Court held that it was not a violation of the defendant's Sixth Amendment right for his counsel to act in accordance with state laws governing professional conduct.[8]

REBUTTAL BY THE PROSECUTION

After the defense has presented its side of the case and rests, the prosecution may present additional evidence to meet or rebut that presented by the defense. The presentation of **rebuttal evidence** is permitted because, in most instances, the prosecution will have no advance knowledge of the approach that the defense may take in an effort to prove the defendant not guilty. Although after resting the prosecuting attorney may have felt that the defendant was proved guilty beyond a reasonable doubt, the defense may have created some new doubt by presenting its evidence. The evidence presented by the defense may not have been based upon actual facts. For example, the defense may have tried to prove that the defendant was at some place other than that where the crime was committed, creating a doubt in the minds of the jury about the guilt of the defendant. This alibi evidence may have been attempted through perjured testimony. To allow this testimony to stand unchallenged by the prosecution would be an injustice to society. The only way that this testimony can be effectively challenged, except through cross-examination, is for the prosecution to present further testimony to prove that the defendant was at the scene of the crime.

Generally, no new evidence pertaining to the guilt of the defendant may be presented during the rebuttal. This is the case because permitting new evidence would cause the entire sequence of the trial examination procedure to take place again. The only time that additional evidence may be introduced is when new material evidence has been discovered. The prosecution must be in a position to convince the judge that the newly discovered evidence was not available when the prosecution first presented its side of the case and that its discovery was not because of carelessness, inadequate investigation, or poor preparation. In the interest of justice, the judge may permit the newly discovered evidence to be introduced, but the defense may again present evidence in an effort to overcome that presented by the prosecution. This presentation is sometimes referred to as the rejoinder in some jurisdictions and as the defense rebuttal in others.

After the prosecution has finished the rebuttal, the defense may again make a motion for a judgment of acquittal to be entered. If this motion is denied by the judge, the next procedure, depending upon the procedure of the jurisdiction, is either presentation of closing arguments by the prosecution and the defense or instruction to the jury on the law of the case.

Depositions

Sometimes during a trial, a witness for one side or the other is unable to attend court to testify, yet the testimony of that witness is material to the case. Rather than continuing the trial until the witness is able to appear in court, an out-of-court written statement, or **deposition**, given under oath, will be taken from the witness. Before a deposition may be taken, the opposing side must be notified that a deposition is to be taken at a particular time, date, and place. This notice is necessary so that the opposing side may be present to cross-examine the witness. The deposition is usually in a question-and-answer form much as the testimony would be given in court. The deposition will be read to the jury at the appropriate time during the trial, and the information will become part of the facts of the case. Because of the right of the defendant to be presented with the witnesses against him or her, some states do not permit the prosecution to introduce depositions in evidence.

NOT GUILTY BY REASON OF INSANITY

Because the procedure on the defense of not guilty by reason of insanity differs among states, a discussion of that defense is in order at this time. Not all states permit a separate plea of not guilty by reason of insanity. In those states where this plea is not permitted, the insanity defense is alleged by the defense after the prosecution rests in the same manner as other defenses that the defendant may use, such as the alibi of self-defense. Under these circumstances, the prosecution will present its evidence to prove the defendant guilty beyond a reasonable doubt.

After the presentation of this evidence, the defendant alleges that he or she cannot be held criminally liable for the crime since he or she was insane at the time of committing the act. The defendant then presents evidence in his or her behalf in an endeavor to prove that he or she was insane at the time. This type of defense can catch the prosecution by surprise, and obtaining rebuttal evidence may be difficult. Further, with this type of defense being alleged, the prosecution has a double burden. Not knowing of the insanity defense in advance, the prosecution usually must present much evidence to prove that the defendant committed the crime, but by claiming the insanity defense, the defendant is in a sense admitting the act but alleging that there is no criminal liability. To rebut this allegation, the prosecution must prove that the defendant was sane at the time the crime was committed. Because of the element of surprise to the prosecution by the insanity defense and the double burden imposed upon the prosecutor, efforts have been made to have this defense included in the right of discovery by the prosecution. In those jurisdictions permitting a separate plea of not guilty by reason of insanity, the prosecuting attorney is not surprised and usually has ample opportunity to prepare the case to meet the allegation.

In those states where a separate plea of not guilty by reason of insanity is permitted, unless the defendant enters that plea, sanity is presumed at the time that the crime was committed, and no defense of insanity may be entered. A few states permit the defendant to enter dual pleas. The defendant may enter a plea of not guilty and at the same time enter a plea of not guilty by reason of insanity. When the dual pleas are entered, the trial on the not guilty plea will be tried first. If the defendant is found not guilty, no further action may take place. But if the defendant is found guilty, a second trial takes place to determine the sanity of the defendant at the time the crime was committed. These trials may be heard by the same jury or different juries, depending on the wishes of the defendant or the procedure of the jurisdiction involved. In some states, the two trials are consolidated into one.

Burden of Proof

States differ in their approach regarding the burden of proof on the insanity issue. Some states contend that, by entering the plea of not guilty by reason of insanity, the defendant has admitted the conduct. Having admitted guilt, the defendant is not entitled to the presumption of innocence, and the prosecution has no burden of proof on the guilt issue. Since it is presumed that all persons are sane unless, and until, proved otherwise, in some states the defendant has the burden of proving insanity at the time the crime was committed. Having this burden, the defense will open the trial proceedings by presenting the defendant's evidence first, followed by the prosecution. In the effort to prove insanity, the defendant may produce expert witnesses in the field of psychology, who, after examining the defendant, may express their opinions on the defendant's mental state at the time the crime occurred. The defense counsel may call witnesses acquainted with the defendant to express their opinions on the defendant's sanity for corroboration with the opinions of the experts. The amount of proof that the defendant must present differs among states. Some states require the defendant to prove insanity by a **preponderance of evidence**; other states require that insanity be proved to the satisfaction of the jury. The line of demarcation between these proofs is very fine, but it is conceded that the defendant does not have to prove beyond a reasonable doubt that the crime was committed while he or she was insane.

After the defendant has presented evidence to prove insanity, the prosecution has the responsibility of going forward with the evidence and proving that the defendant was sane at the time of the act. How much evidence must the prosecution present to prove sanity? Merely going forward with the evidence generally implies meeting the evidence of the opposition. The consensus is that the prosecution must do more than meet the evidence. There must be more than a doubt about the sanity of the defendant before the jury can conclude that the defendant was sane at the time the crime occurred. Most jurisdictions contend that the prosecution still has the burden of proving the defendant sane beyond a reasonable doubt. In fact, in some jurisdictions, if the defendant enters the plea of guilty by reason of insanity, the prosecution opens the trial and presents evidence to prove the defendant sane beyond a reasonable doubt, and the defense may meet that evidence by merely creating a doubt about sanity at the time the act was committed.

Test for Sanity

Determining sanity is not easy. Whatever procedure is followed, the ultimate determination to be made is whether the defendant was in such a state of mind at the time the crime was committed that he or she cannot be held legally responsible. Some acceptable test must be applied. The problem becomes more complicated because it is not the defendant's present state of mind that is at issue. As has been previously pointed out, unless a defendant is mentally capable of defending himself or herself, the trial cannot take place. Since the case is going to trial, it has been adjudged that the defendant is presently sane. It is necessary then to go back in time in attempting to establish the sanity of the defendant. Even the most knowledgeable experts in the field of psychology can give only an opinion of the mental condition at the time of the crime unless the defendant was under a doctor's treatment.

Devising a test that will accurately establish a defendant's mental condition months before has been very difficult. For many years in England, the "wild beast test" was used. This test has also been referred to as the good and evil test. It was held that if an accused did not know any more than a wild beast would when the crime was committed, then no criminal responsibility could result from the act. In other words, if the accused had no more conception of good and evil than a wild beast while committing the crime, he could not be held responsible. The good and evil test was used until it was replaced by the right and wrong test in 1843.[9] In that case, Daniel M'Naughten was indicted for the murder of Edward Drummond, private secretary to Sir Robert Peel, the prime minister of Great Britain. M'Naughten mistook Drummond for Peel, whom M'Naughten felt was persecuting him. M'Naughten was found not guilty by reason of insanity. The acquittal generated so much public indignation in London, including that of the Queen, that the judges were called before the House of Lords and asked to explain the test that was used to determine the sanity of M'Naughten. The judges answered the inquiry with the following test, which the jury was to consider in determining the sanity of one accused of crime. The judges stated that

> the jurors ought to be told in all cases that every man is to be presumed to be sane, and possess a sufficient degree of reason to be responsible for his crimes, until the contrary be proved to their satisfaction; and that to establish a defense on the ground of insanity, it must be clearly proved that, at the time of the committing of the act, the party accused was laboring under such a defect of reason, from disease of mind, as not to know the nature of the act he was doing; or, if he did know it, that he did not know he was doing what was wrong. The mode of putting the latter part of the question to the jury on these occasions has generally been whether the accused at the time of doing the act knew the difference between right and wrong.

Various Insanity Defense Standards

Test	Legal Standard of Mental Illness	Final Burden of Proof
M'Naughten	"Didn't know what he was doing or didn't know it was wrong."	Balance of probabilities
Irresistible Impulse	"Could not control his conduct."	Beyond a reasonable doubt
Durham	"The criminal act was caused by his mental illness."	Beyond a reasonable doubt
Substantial capacity	"Lacks substantial capacity to appreciate the wrongfulness of his conduct or to control it."	Beyond a reasonable doubt
Present federal law	"Lacks capacity to appreciate the wrongfulness of his conduct."	Clear and convincing evidence

The test has been referred to as the M'Naughten test. It has since been followed in England and has been adopted by many states in this country. Although the test has been criticized by some legal scholars and psychologists, it has been replaced in only a few states.

The M'Naughten test continues to have acceptance because it is generally felt that no better test has been devised and that the jury is better able to understand it than other tests that have been suggested.

Because of the confusion surrounding the M'Naughten test, in 1887 some jurisdictions adopted the Irresistible Impulse test. The landmark case in this area was *Parsons* v. *State,* where an Alabama court set forth the modern version of the Irresistible Impulse test.[10] This test holds that a person will be considered insane if, as a result of a disease of the mind, he or she was unable to control his or her behavior. Just as the name of this test implies, if the defendant could prove that he or she was suffering from a disease of the mind so that there was an impulse to commit criminal acts that he or she could not control, then the defendant would be considered insane. The current trend is to revert to only the M'Naughten test.

This test also was controversial, and in 1954 the U.S. Court of Appeals in Washington, D.C., decided the case of *Durham* v. *United States.*[11] Although this decision was also controversial, some jurisdictions adopted its rationale as their test for insanity. The court stated that the "rule" to be followed in determining criminal responsibility is as follows:

> It is simply that an accused is not criminally responsible if his unlawful act was the product of mental disease or mental defect. . . .
>
> Whenever there is some evidence that the accused suffered from a diseased or defective mental condition at the time the unlawful act was committed, the trial court must provide the jury with guides for determining whether the accused can be held criminally responsible. We do not, and indeed could not, formulate an instruction which would be either appropriate or binding in all cases. But under the rule now announced, any instruction should in some way convey to the jury the sense and substance of the following: If you the jury believe beyond a reasonable doubt that the accused was not suffering from a diseased or defective mental condition at the time he committed the criminal act charged, you may find him guilty.

The same problems inherent in the M'Naughten test regarding mental disease or defect were present in the *Durham* case. The Durham test has been severely criticized in the case of *United States* v. *Currens,* where the court said it is too vague and indefinite to be workable in the determination of criminal responsibility.[12] The Durham test does not give the jury any real guidelines to determine whether an unlawful act was the product of a mental disease or mental defect.

The other major test used is the American Law Institute's substantial capacity test (also known as the ALI test). The Model Penal Code uses the ALI test. It is also being used in a growing number of states. The test is found in Section 4.01 of the Model Penal Code and is as follows:

1. A person is not responsible for criminal conduct if at the time of such conduct as a result of mental disease or defect he lacks substantial capacity either to appreciate the criminality (wrongfulness) of his conduct or to conform his conduct to the requirements of the law.
2. As used in the Article, the terms mental disease or defect do not include abnormally manifested only by repeated criminal or otherwise antisocial conduct.

The primary difference between the M'Naughten and ALI tests is that the M'Naughten test requires the defendant to show total mental impairment, whereas the ALI test requires the defendant to show only that he lacked the "substantial capacity" to conform his or her conduct to the requirements of law, that is, lack of self-control.

A number of states now use the "guilty, but mentally ill" procedure for handling the insanity issue. Under this procedure, when an insanity defense is raised, the court, if the evidence permits, may find the defendant guilty but mentally ill. In most states, when the defense is raised, the case is tried without regard to the insanity defense. If a finding of guilty results, the jury is asked to determine whether the defendant is insane.

Syndromes

Starting in the 1980s, a range of **syndromes** that affect the mental state of the defendant have been presented to excuse or justify the conduct of the defendant. One of the most famous is the Twinkie defense. When considering nutrition and criminal behavior, consider that Americans buy 700 million Twinkies a year—80 percent of them on impulse. Over 50 billion Twinkies have been sold in the past sixty years.

On May 22, 1979, Dan White, a former San Francisco, California, county supervisor, was convicted of voluntary manslaughter for the November 1978 killing of San Francisco Mayor George Moscone and Supervisor Harvey Milk. White was originally charged with first-degree murder (a capital offense). The prosecutor argued to the jury that White was guilty of cold-blooded murder. It was established that White had gone to city hall to talk to the mayor. He had entered through a window to avoid the metal detector at the main entrance. At the time, he was carrying a snub-nosed revolver. He shot Mayor Moscone and Supervisor Milk nine times with the weapon, killing both of them. White readily admitted killing both the mayor and the supervisor, the latter being his most vocal opponent on the San Francisco Board of Supervisors.

White's defense attorney, Douglas Schmidt, presented evidence to establish that White had suffered from "diminished capacity" caused by a "biochemical change" in his brain. According to the defense's theory of the case, White was incapable of the premeditation, deliberation, and malice required to obtain a murder conviction. Evidence at the trial indicated that White was a manic depressive with a high degree of stress caused by financial and other personal problems. A defense medical expert testified that White suffered from a "genetically caused melancholia," and at the time, he was "discombobulated." Defense witnesses, who comprised family members, friends and experts, testified about White's moods and his diet. One defense psychiatrist testified that White's compulsive diet of candy bars, Twinkies, and Cokes was evidence of a deep depression and resulted in excessive sugar intake, which either caused or aggravated a chemical imbalance in his brain. The Twinkie defense or syndrome apparently has not been successfully used since the Dan White trial. California has since abolished this defense.

XYY SYNDROME Some efforts have been made by defense attorneys to use the alleged effects of the XYY syndrome as an insanity defense. This defense is based upon the theory that individuals with an abnormal complement of chromosomes are legally insane and as such cannot be held criminally responsible for their acts. Generally, courts have been rejecting this defense, primarily because geneticists, in studying the extra Y chromosomes, differ in their opinions concerning the effects. It is generally conceded that not all individuals with an abnormal complement of chromosomes are, by nature, involuntarily aggressive. Also, these experts hold that it cannot be stated with certainty that a criminal act is the result of an abnormal complement of chromosomes.

PMS SYNDROME Another widely discussed defense is the premenstrual stress syndrome (PMS). The problems with the PMS defense are, first, that the defense must establish that PMS is a disease; second, that the defendant suffers from PMS; and third, that the PMS must cause the mental impairment that excuses the conduct. Premenstrual syndrome, or premenstrual tension (PMT), is believed to affect approximately 40 percent of American women between the ages of twenty and forty.[13] Normally, the symptoms begin ten to fourteen days prior to the onset of the menstrual period and become progressively worse until the onset of menstruation. In some women, PMS continues for several days after the onset. Common symptoms include irritability, anxiety, mood swings, depression, migraine headaches, fainting, dizziness, and allergies.

As one woman stated, "There is a pervasive sense of things always falling apart." Susan Lark, in her book *Premenstrual Syndrome Self-Help Book,* states that severely afflicted women are most vulnerable to extreme behavior during this time.[14] Katherine Dalton, an English physician, reports an increase in the likelihood of accidents, alcohol abuse, suicide attempts, and crimes committed by some women suffering from premenstrual tension. In "Menstruation and Crime," she states that in many cases, the affected women have Dr. Jekyll and Mr. Hyde personality splits; that is, they are "mean," "witchy," and "irritable" during the PMT period. They often yell at their children, pick fights with their husbands, and snap at friends and coworkers. After the symptoms end, they often spend the rest of the month trying to repair the damage done to these relationships.[15] There is a lot of skepticism regarding the PMS/PMT defense, which has generally not been successful.

BATTERED SPOUSE SYNDROME In recent years, wives who have killed their abusing spouses have attempted to use the battered spouse defense. In the 1980s, *The Burning Bed,* a popular film that was based on a real-life case, depicted a woman who killed her husband while he slept. The husband had apparently abused and threatened her. When he went to sleep, she set fire to the bed, killing him. Traditionally, self-defense is not available in these cases because at the time of the killings, the spouses were not in imminent danger. As one court stated, a battered woman cannot reasonably fear imminent life-threatening danger from her sleeping spouse. For the most part, courts have rejected the battered spouse syndrome as a defense for spousal killings. A growing minority of courts have, however, held that the fact that the other spouse was sleeping does not preclude self-defense. When courts allow persons who have been abused to use self-defense as a shield to liability, this practice is known as the imperfect self-defense plea.

The use of the imperfect self-defense plea received national attention when two sons claimed they had been sexually abused since childhood and therefore found it necessary to kill their mother and father. Eric and Lyle Menendez, along with a series of family violence experts, testified that, as a result of the continued sexual abuse, they believed that they were in imminent danger of death or great bodily injury.

An increasing number of courts are accepting the use of the imperfect self-defense plea in battered women cases. There is a gradual acceptance that some women can be trapped emotionally in an abusive relationship and honestly believe that they must kill their abusers to survive.[16] However, a number of courts still do not recognize this syndrome. In *State* v. *Stewart,* evidence at trial indicated that Mike Stewart had abused Peggy Stewart during their marriage and had sexually abused her two daughters by an earlier marriage. On one occasion, he shot one of Peggy's cats and then held the gun to Peggy's head and threatened to pull the trigger.

Peggy left Mike and moved to Oklahoma. Because Peggy was suicidal, she was committed to a hospital. Mike came to the hospital, checked her out, and took her back home. As they drove back home to Kansas, Mike told Peggy that it was all in her head, and that from now on, he would decide what was right for her. When they arrived home, Mike forced her to have oral sex, and then he went to bed. Later that day, as Mike slept, Peggy heard voices in her head repeating over and over, "kill or be killed." She then took a gun that she had hidden in the house and killed him with it. The court ruled that the facts do not constitute self-defense and that the state does not recognize the battered spouse syndrome. To excuse a killing under these circumstances would be the same as permitting capital punishment to be used for spousal abuse.[17]

Law in Practice

Clark v. *Arizona*, 548 U.S. 735 (2007)

Eric Clark shot and killed a police officer conducting a traffic stop. The defendant was found incompetent to stand trial and was committed to a state hospital for treatment. Two years later, the same trial court found his competence was restored and ordered him to be tried for murder. At trial, defendant did not contest the shooting or the death, but relied on his undisputed paranoid schizophrenia at the time of the incident in denying that he had the specific intent to shoot a law enforcement officer or knowledge that he was doing so, as required by Ariz. Rev. Stat. § 13-1105(A)(3). Clark challenged the 1993 amendment to Arizona's insanity rule which modified Arizona's insanity test to read: A defendant will not be adjudged insane unless he demonstrates that at the time of the commission of the criminal act he was afflicted with a mental disease or defect of such severity that he did not know the criminal act was wrong. The change eliminated the defense of diminished capacity. Was the revised statute constitutional?

How Would You Rule?

JUSTICE SOUTER delivered the opinion of the Court.

Due process does not prohibit Arizona's use of an insanity test stated solely in terms of the capacity to tell whether an act charged as a crime was right or wrong. Arizona has declined to adopt a defense of diminished capacity (allowing a jury to decide when to excuse a defendant because of greater than normal difficulty in conforming to the law). The State's choice would be undercut if evidence of incapacity could be considered for whatever a jury might think sufficient to raise a reasonable doubt about mens rea, even if it did not show insanity. In other words, if a jury were free to decide how much evidence of mental disease and incapacity was enough to counter evidence of mens rea to the point of creating a reasonable doubt, that would in functional terms be analogous to allowing jurors to decide upon some degree of diminished capacity to obey the law, a degree set by them, that would prevail as a stand-alone defense.

Irrespective of the sanity test or defense that is applied, if the jury finds the defendant to have been sane at the time the crime occurred, the only procedure left is sentencing. On the other hand, if the jury finds that the defendant was insane when the crime was committed, the accused is, in theory, entitled to be released. If the defendant was found to have been insane when committing the crime, in most jurisdictions confinement will be in a mental hospital under a civil commitment to make certain that there is no threat to society. One court went so far as to hold that "an accused person who is acquitted by reason of insanity is presumed to be insane and may be committed for an indefinite period to a hospital for the insane."[18] In another decision, it was stated that "even where there has been a specific finding that the accused was competent to stand trial and assist in his own defense, the court would be well advised to invoke the code provision so that the accused may be confined as long as the public safety and his welfare require."[19]

CLOSING ARGUMENTS

After both sides have presented their evidence, the next procedure in most jurisdictions is the closing arguments by the prosecuting attorney and the defense attorney. Closing arguments are merely a summarization of the evidence presented during the trial. Attorneys have mixed emotions regarding the value of closing arguments. Some attorneys allege that they have no effect on the jury and are a waste of time. Other attorneys feel that a closing argument may be the difference between losing a case and winning it. Irrespective of the viewpoints, in most criminal trials, both the prosecution and the defense will give closing arguments. There is no limit on the length of a closing argument. The attorneys may take only a few minutes or they may take several days, depending on the length of the trial. The judge does have the right to limit the time involved, but he or she cannot be too restrictive. With the possible exception of an insanity trial, the usual procedure is for the prosecuting attorney to give the closing argument first, followed by the defense. After the defense has completed its closing argument, the prosecuting attorney may give a rebuttal argument. Some jurisdictions reverse this procedure and permit the defense attorney to present the closing argument first, followed by the prosecution.

It is considered improper for the attorneys to appeal to the sympathy or emotions of the jurors, but frequently the closing arguments are a dramatic performance that results in an emotional appeal. In fact, during the questioning of the jurors for cause, attorneys may inject questions designed to later enable them to weave the personal lives of some of the jurors into the closing arguments. At this point in the trial, each side is endeavoring to sell the jury on the fact that its side is entitled to the verdict.

Closing Argument by the Prosecution

During the closing argument, the prosecuting attorney will summarize the evidence presented, emphasizing the strong points that indicate guilt. To substantiate the closing statements, the physical evidence already introduced may be displayed again. The prosecuting attorney may state that the evidence clearly proves that the defendant is guilty of the crime charged. It is held to be prejudicial error, however, for the prosecuting attorney to state that from personal knowledge, the defendant is known to be guilty, implying that information not brought forth during the trial is in his or her possession. The courts have stated that the right to discuss the merits of a case, regarding both the law and the facts, is very wide, and that the prosecuting attorney has the right to state what the evidence shows and what conclusions are to be drawn. The adverse party cannot complain if the reasoning is faulty and the deductions are illogical, since such matters are ultimately for the consideration of the jury. It has been held that the prosecuting attorney should be circumspect in remarks concerning the defendant and his or her counsel, but the use of derogatory epithets does not necessarily represent misconduct.

In the case of *People* v. *Jones*,[20] the prosecuting attorney referred to the defendant's behavior as consistent with animalistic and felonious tendencies, and also implied that there was a strange, twisted reason for the actions of the accused. The U.S. Supreme Court in that case stated the following:

> We recognize that prosecutors, like all others who have responsible roles in the trial of a criminal case, are human; as humans they may be affected by the tensions of a trial to the point of error and, on occasion, even to misconduct. We recognize, too, that the great increase in crime and the corresponding increase in the number of prosecutions in recent years has placed a heavy burden on district attorneys, who frequently must rely on inexperienced deputies to try cases. Be that as it may, prosecutors should be ever aware that in all they do and say they are representatives of the government of whom the public, including those who are prosecuted, are entitled to expect a high degree of ethical conduct.
>
> . . . while some of the references to the appellant (defendant), more particularly, "animalistic tendencies" and "felonious tendencies" were quite strong, we hold that, under the facts of this case, they were within the bounds of legitimate argument and did not constitute misconduct.

Following such arguments by the prosecuting attorney, the judge will often instruct the jury that the closing arguments are not to be considered as evidence in the case and that the jury is to disregard any statements not based on the evidence. If a prosecuting attorney does indulge in misconduct during the closing argument, the misconduct could lead to a mistrial being declared at the time or to a reversal of a conviction on appeal.

Closing Argument by the Defense

Technically, the same rules of conduct that apply to the prosecuting attorney also apply to the defense attorney. In many cases, the defense counsel emphasizes the presumption of innocence and the high burden of proof borne by the prosecutor.

Since defense counsel misconduct is not appealable if the defendant is acquitted, the defense attorney often has considerable freedom in arguing the case to the jury. An appeal will often be made to the sympathy of the jury. It may be pointed out that in rendering a guilty verdict, the jury will deprive the defendant of freedom and companionship with his or her family. In one case, the defendant appeared in court wearing long hair and a shaggy beard. In the argument to the jury, the defense counsel stated that in looking over the jury, no member representative of the defendant's peer group could be seen. The defense attorney recalled a trial some 2,000 years before at which the defendant also was wearing a beard, had long hair, and was tried without peer group representation. Keeping that fact in mind, the defense attorney felt that the appearance of the defendant would not deter the jury from rendering a verdict in favor of acquittal. Although the defense attorney may be dramatic in appealing to a jury, there are times when the jury may resent what they feel to be an insult to their intelligence in defense counsel arguments.

Even though represented by an attorney, occasionally a defendant will insist upon making a closing argument in addition to the one given by the attorney. Whether this will be permitted is at the judge's discretion. If the defendant is self-represented, a closing argument is always permitted.

Rebuttal Closing Argument

After the defense attorney has concluded the closing argument for the accused, the prosecuting attorney is entitled to make a rebuttal closing argument. Statements and challenges presented during the defense attorney's closing argument can be met.

CASE LAW

Recent Cases

Carey v. *Musladin*, 549 U.S. 70 (U.S. 2006)

Mathew Musladin, a prison inmate, was convicted in state court of murder but asserted that his right to a fair trial was prejudiced because the victim's family wore buttons depicting the victim during the inmate's trial. Upon the grant of a writ of certiorari, petitioner prison warden appealed the judgment of the U.S. Court of Appeals for the Ninth Circuit that held that the inmate was entitled to a writ of habeas corpus.

Members of the victim's family sat in the front row of the spectators' gallery wearing buttons displaying the victim's image. The trial court denied Musladin's motion to order the family members not to wear the buttons. The California Court of Appeal upheld Musladin's conviction, stating that he had to show actual or inherent prejudice to succeed on the buttons claim; as providing the test for inherent prejudice; and ruling that he had not satisfied that test. The Federal District Court denied Musladin's habeas petition, but the Ninth Circuit reversed and remanded, finding that the state court's decision "was contrary to, or involved an unreasonable application of, clearly established Federal law. The Supreme Court reversed the decision of the court of appeals.

The Supreme Court noted that the lower court had concluded that the state court failed to consider whether the wearing of the buttons during the inmate's trial created an unacceptable risk of impermissible factors coming into play in the trial.

The U.S. Supreme Court stated that since it had not previously consider whether spectator conduct at trial was inherently prejudicial, there was no clearly established federal law for the state court to apply. The Court's previous considerations of prejudicial courtroom conduct involved only state action, and the Court had never held that the test for prejudice from state conduct was equally applicable to spectator conduct. Therefore, the state's denial of relief to the inmate could not be in conflict with clearly established federal law.

Briefly Noted

Smith v. ***Spisak,*** **130 S. Ct. 676 (2010).** Defense counsel's inadequate closing argument did not violate Sixth Amendment because there was no reasonable probability that a better closing argument without the defects would have changed the result because, inter alia, the jurors had fresh in their minds the State's evidence regarding the killings and the inmate's boastful and unrepentant confessions.

Michigan v. ***Bryant,*** **131 S. Ct. 1143 (2011).** Where the primary purpose of an interaction between a mortally wounded shooting victim and the police was to enable the police to meet an ongoing emergency, his identification and description of the shooter and the location of the shooting were not testimonial statements. Their admission at trial did not violate the Confrontation Clause.

United States v. ***Comstock,*** **130 S. Ct. 1949 (U.S. 2010).** Neither Congress' power to criminalize conduct, nor its power to imprison individuals who engage in that conduct, nor its power to enact laws governing prisons and prisoners, is explicitly mentioned in the United States Constitution. But Congress nonetheless possesses broad authority to do each of those things in the course of carrying into execution the enumerated powers vested by the Constitution in the Government of the United States, U.S. Const. art. I, § 8, cl. 18—authority granted by the Necessary and Proper Clause.

McDaniel v. ***Brown,*** **130 S. Ct. 665 (U.S. 2010).** The appellate court's reversal for insufficiency of the evidence is in effect a determination that the government's case against a defendant was so lacking that the trial court should have entered a judgment of acquittal. Because reversal for insufficiency of the evidence is equivalent to a judgment of acquittal, such a reversal bars a retrial. To make the analogy complete between a reversal for insufficiency of the evidence and the trial court's granting a judgment of acquittal, a reviewing court must consider all of the evidence admitted by the trial court, regardless of whether that evidence was admitted erroneously.

Summary

- One purpose of an opening statement is to orient the jury to evidence that will follow.
- Because the prosecution has the burden of proof, it presents its case first.
- The defense may present an opening statement immediately after the prosecutor's or may delay it until the defense presents its case.
- The defendant is presumed innocent until his or her guilt is established beyond a reasonable doubt.
- The term "beyond a reasonable doubt" is difficult to define and does not mean proof beyond a moral certainty.
- The defendant is entitled to confront the witnesses against him or her. The right of confrontation includes the right to cross-examine the witness.
- Witnesses are officially notified to appear as witnesses by the use of subpoenas.
- If a witness voluntarily appears, there is no requirement to have a subpoena issued.
- Witnesses who fail to appear as ordered by a subpoena are subject to sanctions for contempt of court.
- Prior to questioning a witness, an oath must be given. If the witness objects to being sworn in, the witness may affirm that his or her testimony will be truthful.
- There is no requirement that the word God be included in an oath.
- The order of examination of a witness is direct examination, cross-examination, redirect, and recross.
- Most states put the burden of establishing an insanity issue upon the defense.
- The purpose of closing arguments is to summarize the evidence.

Review Questions

1. What is the purpose of the opening statement?
2. Define reasonable doubt.
3. What amendment guarantees a defendant the right to be confronted with the witnesses against him or her?

4. What is the purpose of a subpoena?
5. In what way does the oath differ from the affirmation?
6. Why was the affirmation adopted?
7. What is direct examination?
8. Define a leading question.
9. What is the primary purpose of cross-examination?

10. Must the defendant present evidence in his or her own behalf?
11. What is the purpose of rebuttal by the prosecution?
12. State the purpose of the M'Naughten test.
13. What purpose do closing arguments serve?

Local Procedure

1. In your home state, may a defendant enter a plea of not guilty by reason of insanity, or is insanity raised only as a defense?

2. Is the M'Naughten test or some other test for insanity followed in your home state?

Endnotes

1. 397 U.S. 358 (1970).
2. 399 U.S. 149 (1970).
3. Portions of this section dealing with the use of closed-circuit television have been adapted from H. Wallace, *Family Violence: Legal, Medical, and Social Perspectives* (Boston: Allyn & Bacon), 1996.
4. 110 S.Ct. 3157 (1990).
5. 380 U.S. 400 (1965).
6. 380 U.S. 609 (1965).
7. See *People* v. *Robles,* 85 Cal.Rptr. 166 (1970).
8. *Nix* v. *Whiteside,* 475 U.S. 157 (1986).
9. 8 Eng. Reprint 718 (1843).
10. 81 Ala. 577, 2 So. 854 (1887). It should be noted that the Irresistible Impulse test actually predated the M'Naughten test. For an excellent historical discussion of the evolution of these early insanity rules, see Paul Keedy, "Irresistible Impulse as a Defense in Criminal Law," 100 *Univ. of Penn. Law Review* 956–961 (1952).
11. 214 F.2d 862 (D.C. Cir. 1954).
12. 290 E. 2d 751 (1961).
13. Susan Lark, *Premenstrual Syndrome Self-Help Book* (Los Angeles: Forman), 1984, p. 19.
14. Katherine Dalton, "Menstruation and Crime," *British Medical Journal* No. 3, 1961, p. 1752.
15. J. H. Morton et al., "A Clinical Study of Premenstrual Tension," *American Journal of Obstetrics and Gynecology,* No. 65, 1953, pp. 1182–1191.
16. H. Wallace, "Battered Women Syndrome: Self-Defense and Duress as Mandatory Defenses? The History and Acceptance of the Battered Women Syndrome in American Courts," *The Police Journal,* London, 1994, pp. 231–238.
17. *State* v. *Stewart,* 763 P.2d 572 (Kansas, 1988).
18. See *Orencia* v. *Overholser,* 82 U.S. App. D.C. 285 (1947).
19. See *Barry* v. *White,* 62 U.S. App. D.C. 69 (1933).
20. 86 Cal.Rptr 516 (1970).

CHAPTER 14

Instructions and Deliberation of the Jury

A jury verdict is a quotient of the prejudices of twelve people. . . .

—KENNETH GRUB, ATTORNEY

Chapter Outline

Instructions to the Jury

Deliberations

Case Law

Summary

Key Terms

Allen charge

Charging the jury

Consciousness of guilt

Deliberations

Foreperson

Hung jury

Learning Objectives

After completing this chapter, you should be able to:

- Summarize instructions to and deliberations of a jury.
- Explain the judge's requirement to instruct the jury on various issues.
- Discuss the deliberation process.
- List the duties of the prosecutor and defense counsel in preparing jury instructions.
- Explain the restrictions on a judge's ability to comment on the evidence.
- List the materials that may be taken into the jury's deliberation room.
- Discuss the Allen instructions and why a judge would give an Allen charge.
- Explain the problems involved in less than unanimous verdicts.

INSTRUCTIONS TO THE JURY

On completion of the closing arguments, in most jurisdictions, the judge instructs the jury on the law applicable to the case. Instructing the jury is also known as **charging the jury** or as the charge to the jury. In a few states, the judge may instruct the jury prior to the closing arguments in order that the attorneys involved may include comments on the instructions during their closing arguments. During the charge to the jury, the judge will summarize the points of law explained to them during the trial and instruct them on their function as jurors. Also, the judge will instruct the jury on any additional laws applicable that were not explained as the trial progressed.

Defense and Prosecution Recommendations

As a general rule, the prosecuting attorney and defense attorney prepare written instructions that they desire to be given to the jury. These instructions are furnished to the judge prior to the closing arguments. After reviewing these instructions, the judge selects those that appear to be applicable. Other instructions not suggested by the attorneys may also be given. The judge has the responsibility of instructing the jury on the laws applicable whether requested to do so or not.

The defendant is entitled to instructions being given on all pertinent evidence, regardless of its importance. The failure to give an instruction concerning pertinent evidence, whether requested or not by the defense, could be grounds for the reversal of a conviction on appeal. However, a judge does not have to give instructions that are repetitive or that include some statement of fact in the form of evidence in the case.

The judge also has the responsibility of instructing the jury in clear and understandable language. Too often the instructions are lengthy, complicated, and difficult for the jury to understand. For example, an instruction on the meaning of reasonable doubt may be confusing to the jury, but the defendant is entitled to an instruction on the presumption of innocence. The judge will read to the jury the definition of reasonable doubt as set forth in Chapter 13. The jury will be informed that a defendant in a criminal action is presumed innocent until the contrary is proved and that if there is a reasonable doubt of guilt, the defendant is entitled to an acquittal. The effect of this presumption places on the state the burden of proving guilt beyond a reasonable doubt.

The following are samples of additional instructions generally given to a jury. The jury will be informed that it is the function of the judge to interpret the law but that the jury is the exclusive judge of the facts. The jury must determine those facts only from the evidence presented in court, and it must conscientiously consider and weigh the evidence during the trial. It must also carefully determine the credibility of each witness. In measuring the credibility of a witness, the jury may consider the demeanor of the witness as he or she testifies; the opportunity of the witness to have gained the facts about which he or she testifies; and the witness's ability to observe, retain, and communicate the matters. The jury will be informed that it must not consider as evidence any statement made by the attorneys involved, nor is the jury to speculate on what an answer to a question may have been when an objection to the question was sustained. Nor may the jury consider in its deliberation on the verdict any statement that was stricken from the record. The jurors will be advised that they must not be governed by mere sentiment, sympathy, passion, or prejudice in arriving at a verdict and that they must reach a just verdict regardless of the consequences of that verdict. The jurors will also be informed that it is their duty to consult one another and to deliberate on a just verdict but that the verdict is to express the individual opinion of each juror. The jury will then be advised of the previously mentioned presumption of innocence and reasonable doubt instructions.

The foregoing instructions are applicable in all criminal trials but are not all-inclusive of those that may be given in a trial proceeding. In addition to these general instructions, more specific instructions applicable to the particular case will be included. Instructions may be given on the meaning of direct and circumstantial evidence. The jury will be informed that direct evidence directly proves the fact in issue, whereas circumstantial evidence proves a fact by an inference drawn from another set of facts having been proved. At this point in the instructions, the jury is often again hopelessly lost in the explanation. The right of an expert witness to give an opinion on controversial questions is explained. It is explained that the jury may consider the qualifications of the expert and must give the testimony the proper weight. The meaning of intent and motive may be explained. If an alibi defense was alleged, the judge will inform the jury that if they have reasonable doubt about the defendant's being present at the scene of the crime, an acquittal should result. The meaning of **consciousness of guilt** will be explained, as well as those acts that may fall within that category, such as a suspect's running from a crime scene.

The jury will be informed that the defendant has a right not to testify and that no inference of guilt is to be drawn from the failure to testify. Since most jurisdictions permit a jury to return a verdict to a lesser degree of crime than that charged in the accusatory pleading, the jury will be given an instruction to this effect. Most jurisdictions permit the jury to take the written instructions given by the judge with them during deliberations.

Comments by the Judge

States differ materially in permitting a judge to comment on the evidence of a case and the credibility of witnesses. About half of the states prohibit comments by the judge on the evidence and credibility of the witnesses, since it is believed that such comments are an invasion of the function of the jury. A few states and federal courts grant considerable freedom to a judge to comment on the evidence and the credibility of the witnesses. It has been stated that the judge should be a real factor in the administration of justice and not a mere referee of the adversary system. The judge must summarize the evidence in an impartial and instructive manner, but he or she may point out weaknesses in the evidence of the prosecution and defense or may question the credibility of witnesses. However, the judge's right to comment on the evidence and witnesses is not unlimited. Courts have stated that the judge must be fair, objective and impartial, and must not ignore evidence favorable to the defendant. It has been held improper for the judge to directly state the belief that the defendant is guilty. Comments in one case were considered improper when the judge indicated to the jury that in viewing the evidence in its most favorable light to the defendant, one was still left with the conclusion that the defendant was guilty. The judge further stated that if he were deciding the case, the accused would be found guilty.

Law in Practice

Abdul-Kabir v. *Quarterman*, 127 S. Ct. 1654 (2007)

Ted Calvin Cole, his stepbrother Michael Hickey, and Michael's wife, Kelly, decided to rob and kill Kelly's grandfather, Raymond Richardson, to obtain some cash. Two days later they did so. Cole strangled Richardson with a dog leash; the group then searched the house and found $20 that they used to purchase beer and food. The next day, Michael and Kelly surrendered to the police and confessed.

The police then arrested Cole who also confessed. Cole was tried by a jury and convicted of capital murder. After a sentencing hearing, the jury was asked to answer two special issues:

"Was the conduct of the defendant, TED CALVIN COLE, that caused the death of the deceased, RAYMOND C. RICHARDSON, committed deliberately and with the

(continued)

reasonable expectation that the death of the deceased or another would result?

"Is there a probability that the defendant, TED CALVIN COLE, would commit criminal acts of violence that would constitute a continuing threat to society?"

Cole presented two categories of mitigating evidence. The first consisted of testimony from his mother and his aunt, who described his unhappy childhood. Cole's aunt testified that Cole seemed incapable of expressing any emotion. The second category of mitigating evidence came from two expert witnesses—a psychologist and the former chief mental health officer for the Texas Department of Corrections—who discussed the consequences of Cole's childhood neglect and abandonment. Dr. Jarvis Wright, the psychologist, spent 8 to 10 hours interviewing Cole and administering an "extensive battery of psychological tests." He testified that Cole had "real problems with impulse control" apparently resulting from "central nervous damage" combined with "all the other factors of his background." He also testified that Cole had likely been depressed for much of his life, that he had a "painful" background, and that he had "never felt loved and worthwhile in his life." Providing an analogy for Cole's early development, Dr. Wright stated that "the manufacturing process had botched the raw material horribly."

The trial judge instructed the jury to take into consideration evidence presented at the guilt phase as well as the sentencing phase of the trial but made no reference to mitigating evidence. Under the provisions of the Texas criminal code, the jury's affirmative answers to these two special issues required the judge to impose a death sentence.

Petitioner Jalil Abdul-Kabir, formerly known as Ted Calvin Cole, contends that there is a reasonable likelihood that the trial judge's instructions to the Texas jury that sentenced him to death prevented jurors from giving meaningful consideration to constitutionally relevant mitigating evidence.

JUSTICE SCALIA wrote the Court's opinion.

Our line of cases in this area has long recognized that before a jury can undertake the grave task of imposing a death sentence, it must be allowed to consider a defendant's moral culpability and decide whether death is an appropriate punishment for that individual in light of his personal history and characteristics and the circumstances of the offense. There is no perfect procedure for deciding in which cases governmental authority should be used to impose death. But a statute that prevents the jury in all capital cases from giving independent mitigating weight to aspects of the defendant's character and record and to circumstances of the offense proffered in mitigation creates the risk that the death penalty will be imposed in spite of factors which may call for a less severe penalty. When the choice is between life and death, that risk is unacceptable and incompatible with the commands of the Eighth and Fourteenth Amendments. For that reason, the judgment of the Court of Appeals in this case must be reversed. The case is remanded for further proceedings consistent with this opinion.

Comments to the jury may be made before or after the instructions, at the judge's discretion. Except in states where the judge gives the instructions to the jury prior to the closing arguments, the jury begins its deliberations once the instructions are given.

DELIBERATIONS

If the jury has not been sequestered prior to being given the case, the judge must decide whether or not to do so during **deliberations**. As we pointed out earlier, in some states the jury must be sequestered during the deliberations. In other states, it is at the discretion of the judge. The jury may decide on the verdict in the courtroom, but in most instances they will retire to some private and convenient place for deliberations. This place is generally referred to as the jury room.

Inside the Jury Room

While deliberating, the jurors will be under the guard of an officer of the court. The court officer will have been sworn to keep the jurors together, not permit any person to speak to them, and not speak to them himself or herself except on orders of the court. During the deliberation, no one—not even the officer in charge of the jury—may be present in the jury room except the jurors. On one occasion, an alternate juror was inadvertently given permission by the officer in charge of the jury to sit in the jury room merely to observe during the deliberation. On learning of this, the judge declared a mistrial although the alternate juror did not in any way engage in the deliberation. The courts of a few states, however, have permitted an alternate juror to be sequestered with the other jurors during the deliberation, but only after the judge has instructed the alternate juror not to participate in the deliberation.

In one case, the officer in charge of the jury was also a material witness for the prosecution. He and other officers transported the jury back and forth to their hotel while the jury was being sequestered, and these officers also ate at the same table with the jurors and conversed with them. Although it was alleged that there was no conversation about the facts of the case during these associations, the U.S. Supreme Court held that the presence of the officer interfered with the defendant's right to be tried by an impartial jury. The presence of the officer, according to the Court, may have established rapport with the jury that may have affected their verdict of guilty.[1]

In reference to only jurors being present during the deliberation, we return to the problem encountered by the hearing-impaired person who becomes a juror. By necessity, this juror's interpreter must be present during the deliberation to interpret the communication that takes place among the jurors as they attempt to arrive at a verdict. How may it be determined that the deliberation was accurately interpreted, or was that juror somehow influenced by the interpretation? Would it be held that the interpreter was an extra juror present during the deliberation? If the defendant was convicted, could the defense challenge on appeal the presence of the interpreter during the deliberation, or would this challenge have been waived by the lack of challenge for cause during jury selection? Only future cases will decide the answers to these questions.

Prior to beginning the deliberation, the jury will select one of their members to act as the **foreperson**—their leader and spokesperson. If, during the deliberation, the jury desires further instructions on the law or information concerning the case, the foreperson will advise the officer in charge, who in turn will notify the judge of the request. The judge, in most instances, will require that the jury be returned to the courtroom for the requested information. It is considered improper for the officer in charge to act as a messenger carrying information from the judge to the jury.

Materials Inside the Jury Room

On beginning the deliberation, the jury may take with them any and all documents introduced during the trial. However, in many jurisdictions, the jury may not take any depositions with them. The reason for this prohibition is that to permit the jury to take the depositions would possibly allow them to give greater weight to the testimony of a witness not present over one who was present. The rules of evidence in most states provide that the jury may take any document introduced and also permit the jury to take any exhibits or physical evidence, such as a gun, plaster of paris cast, or fingerprint, that may have been introduced. Courts in some jurisdictions have held that the jury should be permitted to take with them all evidence introduced, including depositions, any prepared transcript or recorded testimony, and personal notes as long as the defendant is not unduly prejudiced and the jury is not likely to use the evidence improperly.

A great majority of the states permit jurors to take notes at the discretion of the judge. Judges differ in their attitudes toward note-taking. Some judges argue that most jurors are not trained in the art of taking notes. Not being trained, they may take down trivial matters and overlook important facts, or they may try to take down everything and get hopelessly lost in the process, missing material testimony as it is presented. It is argued also that the better note-takers will tend to dominate the deliberation or that jurors will quarrel over whose notes are a correct record of the testimony. Those arguing in favor of note-taking by jurors allege that it is asking too much of a juror to remember all the testimony during a lengthy trial and that permitting notes to be taken enables the jurors to refresh their memory during the deliberation. Usually, the reporter's transcript is not available at the time of the deliberation, and unless the jurors have their notes, the only way that testimony may be recalled in some instances is to have the jury returned to the courtroom and the reporter's notes read to the jury. This procedure is time-consuming, and judges often frown on this activity when engaged in too frequently by a jury. It is argued that the benefits derived from a juror's taking notes during a trial far exceed any detriment that may be suffered.

Law in Practice

The Judge's Instructions to the Jury in a Criminal Case

No. B-96-MO19-O-PR-B

The State of Texas	§	In the 156th District
v.	§	Court of
Michael Runnels	§	Bee County, Texas

Charge of the Court

LADIES AND GENTLEMEN OF THE JURY:

The Defendant, MICHAEL RUNNELS, stands charged by indictment with the offense of Assault on a Public Servant, alleged to have been made on a correctional officer on or about the 1st day of April A.D., 2006, in Bee County, Texas. The Defendant has plead[ed] not guilty.

1.

Our law provides that a person commits the offense of assault if he intentionally and knowingly causes bodily injury to another.

Such assault is aggravated assault when committed upon a guard employed by the Texas Department of Criminal Justice–Institutional Division in the lawful discharge of his official duty when the person committing the assault knows or has been informed that the person assaulted is such a guard.

2.

By the term "bodily injury" is meant physical pain, illness or any impairment of physical condition.

3.

A person acts intentionally, or with intent, with respect to a result of his conduct when it is his conscious objective or desire to cause the result.

A person acts knowingly, or with knowledge, with respect to a result of his conduct when he is aware that his conduct is reasonably certain to cause the result.

4.

Now, if you find, from the evidence, beyond a reasonable doubt that on or about the 1st day of April, 2006, in Bee County, Texas, MICHAEL RUNNELS TDCJ #698369, did then and there knowingly or intentionally cause bodily injury

to Robert D. Hill, a public servant, to-wit: a Correctional officer with the Texas Department of Criminal Justice–Institutional Division, Garza East Unit, in Beeville, Bee County, Texas, by striking Robert D. Hill in the head and face with a closed fist, while Robert D. Hill was lawfully discharging an official duty and the defendant knew that Robert D. Hill was a public servant, then you will find the Defendant guilty of Aggravated Assault on a Correctional Officer.

Unless you so find beyond a reasonable doubt, or if you have a reasonable doubt thereof, you will find the defendant not guilty.

5.

A guard or Correctional Officer employed by the Texas Department of Correction is justified in using force against a person in custody when and to the degree the guard or Correctional Officer reasonably believes the force is necessary to maintain the security of the penal institution, the safety or security of other persons in custody or employed by the penal institution, or his own safety or security.

Therefore, if you find that Robert D. Hill used force against MICHAEL RUNNELS and that while doing so he did not reasonably believe that the use of force was necessary to maintain the security of the Penal Institution, the safety or security of other persons in custody or employed by the Penal Institution, or his own safety or security, you will next consider the defense of self-defense.

6.

"Reasonable belief" as used herein means a belief that would be held by an ordinary and prudent person in the same circumstances as Robert D. Hill.

Upon the law of self-defense, a person is justified in using force against another when and to the degree he reasonably believes the force is immediately necessary to protect himself against the other's use or attempted use of unlawful force. A person is under no obligation to retreat to avoid the necessity of repelling or defending with force less than deadly force, against an attack or threatened attack. The use of force against another is not justified if the actor provoked the other's use or attempted use of unlawful force, unless the actor abandons the encounter, or clearly communicates to the other his intent to do so reasonably believing he cannot safely abandon the encounter and the other nevertheless continues or attempts to use unlawful force against the actor.

"Reasonable belief" as used herein means a belief that would be held by an ordinary and prudent person in the same circumstances as defendant.

You are instructed that it is your duty to consider all the relevant facts and circumstances surrounding the alleged assault, including the previous relationship, if any, existing between the accused and Robert D. Hill, together with all relevant facts and circumstance going to show the condition of the mind of the defendant at the time of the alleged offense. In considering all the foregoing, you should place yourself in the defendant's position and view the circumstances from his standpoint alone, at the time in question.

Now if you find and believe from the evidence beyond a reasonable doubt that on the occasion in question the defendant, MICHAEL RUNNELS, intentionally and knowingly caused bodily injury to Robert D. Hill by striking him in the head and face with his (the defendant's) closed fist and that Robert D. Hill used force against Michael Runnels without reasonably believing that the use of force was necessary to maintain the security of the Penal Institution, the safety or security of other persons in custody or employed by the Penal Institution, or his own safety or security, but you further find from the evidence, or you have a reasonable doubt thereof, that from the words or conduct, or both, of Robert D. Hill, viewed from the standpoint of the defendant at the time, it reasonably appeared to the defendant that his person was in danger of bodily injury and there was created in his mind a reasonable expectation or fear of bodily injury from the use of unlawful force at the hands of Robert D. Hill, and that acting under such apprehension and reasonably believing that the use of force on his part was immediately necessary to protect himself against such use or attempted use of unlawful force against him, the defendant struck Robert D. Hill with his fist to defend himself, then you will acquit the defendant.

7.

You are instructed that certain evidence was admitted in evidence before you in regard to the defendant's having been charged and convicted or reprimanded of offenses other than the one for which he is now on trial. Such evidence cannot be considered by you against the defendant as any evidence of guilt in this case. Said evidence was admitted before you for the purpose of aiding you, if it does aid you, in passing upon the weight you will give his testimony, and you will not consider the same for any other purposes.

8.

A grand jury indictment is the means whereby a Defendant is brought to trial in a felony case. It is not evidence of guilt nor can it be considered by you in passing upon the question of guilt of the Defendant. The burden of proof in all criminal cases rests upon the State throughout the trial, and never shifts to the Defendant.

All persons are presumed to be innocent and no person may be convicted of an offense unless each element of the offense is proved beyond a reasonable doubt. The fact that a person has been arrested, confined, or indicted for, or otherwise charged with, the offense gives rise to no inference of guilt at his trial. The law does not require a defendant to prove his innocence or produce any evidence at all. The presumption of innocence alone is sufficient to acquit the defendant unless the jurors are satisfied beyond a reasonable doubt of the defendant's guilt after careful and impartial consideration of all evidence in the case.

The prosecution has the burden of proving the defendant guilty and it must do so by proving each and every element of the offense charged beyond a reasonable doubt and if it fails to do so, you must acquit the defendant.

It is not required that the prosecution prove guilt beyond all possible doubt; it is required that the prosecution's proof excludes all "reasonable doubt" concerning the defendant's guilt.

A "reasonable doubt" is a doubt based on reason and common sense after a careful and impartial consideration of all the evidence in the case. It is the kind of doubt that would make a reasonable person hesitate to act in the most important of his own affairs.

Proof beyond a reasonable doubt, therefore, must be proof of such a convincing character that you would be willing to rely and act upon it without hesitation in the most important of your own affairs.

In the event you have a reasonable doubt as to the defendant's guilt after considering all the evidence before you, and these instructions, you will acquit him and say by your verdict, "Not guilty."

You are the exclusive judges of the facts proved, the credibility of the witnesses and the weight to be given their testimony, but the law you shall receive in these written instructions, and you must be governed thereby.

After you retire to the jury room, you should select one of your members as your presiding juror. It is his/her duty to preside at your deliberations, vote with you, and when you have unanimously agreed upon a verdict, to certify to your verdict by using the appropriate form attached hereto, and signing the same as Presiding Juror.

No one has any authority to communicate with you except the officer who has you in charge. During your deliberations in this case, you must not consider, discuss, nor relate

(continued)

any matters not in evidence before you. You should not consider nor mention any personal knowledge or information you may have about any fact or person connected with this case which is not shown by the evidence.

After you have retired, you may communicate with this Court in writing through the Officer who has you in charge. Do not attempt to talk to the officer, the attorneys, or the Court concerning any question you may have. After you have reached a unanimous verdict, the presiding juror will certify thereto by using the appropriate form attached to this charge and signing his/her name as Presiding Juror. You may now retire to consider your verdict after argument of counsel.

_____
Judge Presiding

No. B-96-MO19-PR-B

The State of Texas	§	In the 156th District
v.	§	Court of
Michael Runnels	§	Bee County, Texas

Verdict Sheet

I.

We, the Jury, find the Defendant, MICHAEL RUNNELS, guilty of the offense of Assault on a Public Servant as charged in indictment.

_____
Presiding Juror

OR

II.

We, the Jury, find the Defendant, MICHAEL RUNNELS, not guilty.

_____
Presiding Juror

Length of Deliberation

How long the jury may deliberate on a case before reaching a verdict will depend largely on the length of the trial and on how convincing the evidence may have been. The jury may decide on a verdict after conferring for a few minutes or they may take days. In many instances, they cannot agree at all. The jury that cannot agree on a verdict is referred to as a **hung jury**. When this situation occurs, the jury is discharged, and a mistrial may be declared by the judge. The trial will have to be restarted with a new jury. It is not unusual for a trial to end with a hung jury. As we previously pointed out, most juries in a criminal case consist of twelve persons. In a great majority of the states, the verdict must be unanimous: that is, all the jurors must agree on either guilt or innocence. To get twelve people to agree on the guilt or innocence of an accused is often difficult.

Judges would rather permit a reasonable amount of time for deliberation than have to start the case over with a new jury, since this step is both time-consuming and expensive. Most judges will do their utmost to encourage a jury to reach a verdict. A judge may call the jury back into the courtroom from time to time to determine whether the foreperson believes that a verdict can be reached. The judge may even inquire about how the jury is numerically split in reaching a verdict, but it is considered improper for the judge to ask how they are split on guilt or innocence. If the foreperson inadvertently states how the jury is split on guilt or innocence, it is not generally considered to be a reversible error. The judge must be circumspect in urging the jury to reach a verdict. He or she must not do or say anything that may be interpreted as a threat to the jury or as forcing a verdict on the jury. Any statement or instruction to the jury at this point that could be interpreted as coercive is considered improper and could result in the reversal of a conviction on appeal. An instruction has been held to be coercive when a judge emphasizes that a verdict must be reached because of the simplicity of the evidence or when a judge threatens to lock up the jury until the verdict is agreed on. In one case, a jury had been deliberating from Monday until Wednesday afternoon before Thanksgiving. Late Wednesday afternoon, the judge called the jurors in and indicated that it would be wise for them to agree on a verdict soon so that it would not be necessary to sequester them over the Thanksgiving holiday. After deliberating for a few more hours, the jury returned a guilty verdict. The conviction was reversed on appeal because of the threat by the judge to the jury.

After a judge has made an inquiry about the possibility of the jurors' reaching a verdict, the judge will discharge the jury if the foreperson feels that the jury is hopelessly deadlocked and cannot agree on a verdict. If possible, the judge will avoid this action. The jury may be asked to further consider the matter, particularly if the majority is for a verdict, with only one or two persons disagreeing. In some states, the judge may read to the jury what is referred to as the **Allen charge** or Allen instruction. This instruction has been called the "dynamite charge," since its purpose is to blast the jury into action so that they will arrive at a verdict. This charge was originally approved by the U.S. Supreme Court in the case of *Allen* v. *United States*.[2] The Allen instruction is substantially as follows:

> Ladies and gentlemen of the jury, in a large proportion of cases and perhaps strictly speaking, in all cases, absolute certainty cannot be attained or expected. Although the verdict to which a juror agrees must, of course, be his own verdict, the result of his own convictions and not a mere acquiescence in the conclusion of his or her fellows, yet in order to bring twelve minds to a unanimous result, you must examine the questions submitted to you with candor and with a proper regard and deference to the opinions of each other. You should consider that the case must at some time be decided, that you are selected in the same manner and from the same source from which any future jury must be selected, and there is no reason to suppose the case will ever be submitted to twelve men or women more intelligent, more impartial or more competent to decide it, or that more or clearer evidence will be produced on the one side or the other. And with this view, it is your duty to decide the case, if you can conscientiously do so.
>
> In order to make a decision more practicable, the law imposes the burden of proof on one party or the other in all cases. In the present case, the burden of proof is on the prosecution to establish every part of it beyond a reasonable doubt. And if in any part of it you are left in doubt, the defendant is entitled to the benefit of the doubt and must be acquitted. But in conferring together, you ought to pay proper respect to each other's opinions and listen with a disposition to be convinced to each other's arguments.
>
> And on the other hand, if much the larger of your panel are for a conviction, a dissenting juror should consider whether a doubt in his or her own mind is a reasonable one, which makes no impression upon the minds of so many men or women equally honest, equally intelligent with himself or herself and to have heard the same evidence with the same attention and with an equal desire to arrive at the truth and under the sanction of the same oath.
>
> And on the other hand, if a majority are for acquittal, the minority ought seriously to ask themselves whether they may not reasonably and ought not to doubt the correctness of a judgment, which is not concurred in by most of those with whom they are associated, and distrust the weight or sufficiency of that evidence which fails to carry conviction to the minds of their fellows.
>
> That is given to you as a suggestion of the theory and rationale behind jurors coming to a decision one way or the other. So the Court is going to ask you to retire and continue in your deliberations.

The courts in some states are opposed to the reading of the Allen instruction to a jury. These courts are of the opinion that the jury may interpret the instruction as commanding them to reach a verdict. Yet many courts consider the Allen instruction to be a proper reminder to the jurors of their obligation to attempt to arrive at a just verdict and not allow personal pride, prejudice, or personalities to interfere with their judgment. As was stated by Justice Burger in the case of *Fulwood* v. *United States*[3]:

> The Allen charge is a carefully balanced method of reminding jurors of their elementary obligations, which they lose sight of during protracted deliberations. It is perfectly valid to remind them that they should give some thought to the views of others and should reconsider their position in light of those views. The charge as given here did not require the jury to reach a verdict but only reminded them of their duty to attempt an accommodation. While it suggests to the minority that they reconsider their position in light of a majority having a different view, it reminds them that they should not acquiesce in a verdict which does not represent their own convictions.

Instead of using the Allen instruction to encourage jurors to arrive at a verdict, the courts of some states have adopted the instruction recommended by the American Bar Association, which is in substance the following:

> It is your duty, as jurors, to consult with one another and to deliberate with a view to reaching an agreement, if you can do so without violence to individual judgment. Each of you must decide the case for yourself, but do so only after an impartial consideration of the evidence with your fellow jurors. In the course of your deliberations, do not hesitate to reexamine your own views and change your opinion if convinced it is erroneous. But do not surrender your honest conviction as to the weight or effect of evidence solely because of the opinion of your fellow jurors, or for the mere purpose of returning a verdict.

Even if the Allen instruction or a similar instruction is read to the jury, they still may be unable to reach a verdict. Some persons may have sincere doubts about the guilt or innocence of a defendant and so will not retract that doubt, regardless of the urging of the majority of the jurors. Unfortunately, there are also persons who, for reasons of their own, delight in opposing the majority on any issue. When these individuals are on juries, reaching a verdict is almost impossible. As the old story goes, when the judge inquired of a jury foreperson regarding the possibility of reaching a verdict, the foreperson replied that the jury was still attempting to arrive at an agreement but that doing so would take time. The foreperson then suggested that the judge order eleven dinners and one bale of hay in order that they might eat before further deliberations.

Less-Than-Unanimous Verdicts

To avoid hung juries caused by one or two jury members, some states have broken with the traditional unanimous verdict rule in criminal trials. Legislation has been passed in these states permitting less-than-unanimous verdicts to be reached in certain criminal cases. All states require that the verdict be unanimous in cases in which the maximum penalty may be death but vary somewhat in the number required to arrive at a verdict. Some states require an eleven-to-one verdict and some a nine-to-three verdict. The less-than-unanimous verdict has received the sanction of the U.S. Supreme Court in two companion cases decided in 1972.[4] In the *Johnson* case, the defendant was convicted of robbery by a nine-to-three verdict in the Criminal District Court of the Parish of Orleans. In the *Apodaca* case, the facts reveal that Robert Apodaca, Henry Morgan Cooper, Jr., and James Arnold Madden were convicted, respectively, of assault with a deadly weapon, burglary in a dwelling, and grand larceny, before separate Oregon juries, all of which returned less-than-unanimous verdicts. The vote in the case of Cooper was ten to two, the minimum requisite vote under Oregon law for sustaining a conviction. Johnson as well as the defendants in the *Apodaca* case took their convictions to the U.S. Supreme Court on the ground that they had been denied their guarantee of a trial by jury as provided by the Sixth Amendment and made applicable to the states by the Fourteenth Amendment. These defendants contended that permitting the conviction of a less-than-unanimous verdict did not constitute a trial by jury.

Johnson alleged that when a jury rendered such a verdict, the prosecution had failed to prove the defendant guilty beyond a reasonable doubt, thus violating the right to due process of law. The Court did not agree with this contention and stated the following:

> We conclude that as to the nine jurors who voted to convict, the State satisfied its burden of proving guilt beyond a reasonable doubt. The remaining question under the Due Process Clause is whether the vote of three jurors for acquittal can be said to impeach the verdict of the other nine and to demonstrate that guilt was not in fact proved beyond such doubt. We hold that it cannot.
>
> Of course, the State's proof could be regarded as more certain if it had convinced all 12 jurors instead of only nine; it would have been even more compelling if it had been required to convince and had, in fact, convinced 24 or 36 jurors. But the fact remains that nine jurors—a substantial majority of the jury—were convinced by the evidence. In our view disagreement of three jurors does not alone establish reasonable doubt, particularly when such a heavy majority of the jury, after having considered the dissenters' views, remains convinced of guilt. That rational men disagree is not in itself equivalent to a failure of proof by the State, nor does it indicate infidelity to the reasonable doubt standard. Jury verdicts finding guilt beyond a reasonable doubt are regularly sustained even though the evidence was such that the jury would have been justified in having a reasonable doubt; even though the trial judge might not have reached the same conclusion as the jury; and even though appellate judges are closely divided on the issue [of] whether there was sufficient evidence to support a conviction.

In the *Apodaca* decision, the Supreme Court further discusses the reasonable doubt argument as well as upholding the right of the states to permit a less-than-unanimous verdict and still uphold the Due Process Clause. In the *Apodaca* decision, the Court stated the following:

> In *Williams* v. *Florida,* we had occasion to consider a related issue: whether the Sixth Amendment's right to trial by jury requires that all juries consist of 12 men. After considering the history of the 12-man requirement and the functions it performs in contemporary society, we concluded that it was not of constitutional stature. We reach the same conclusion today with regard to the requirement of unanimity.
>
> Like the requirement that juries consist of 12 men, the requirement of unanimity rose during the Middle Ages and had become an accepted feature of the common-law jury by the 18th century.
>
> Our inquiry must focus upon the function served by the jury in contemporary society. As we said in *Duncan,* the purpose of trial by jury is to prevent oppression by the Government by providing a safeguard against the corrupt or overzealous prosecutor and against the compliant, biased, or eccentric judge. Given this purpose, the essential feature of a jury obviously lies in the interposition between the accused and his accuser of the common sense judgment of a group of laymen. A requirement of unanimity, however, does not materially contribute to the exercise of this common sense judgment. As we said in *Williams,* a jury will come to such a judgment as long as it consists of a group of laymen

representative of a cross section of the community who have the duty and the opportunity to deliberate, free from outside attempts at intimidation, on the question of a defendant's guilt. In terms of this function we perceive no difference between juries required to act unanimously and those permitted to convict or acquit by votes of 10 to two or 11 to one. Requiring unanimity would obviously produce hung juries in some situations where nonunanimous juries will convict or acquit. But in either case, the interest of the defendant in having the judgment of his peers interposed between himself and the officers of the State who prosecute and judge him is equally well served.

The defendants in the *Apodaca* case contended, as did Johnson, that a unanimous verdict was necessary in order to comply with the beyond-a-reasonable-doubt requirement for guilt, but the Court stated as follows:

We are quite sure that the Sixth Amendment itself has never been held to require proof beyond a reasonable doubt in criminal cases. The reasonable doubt standard developed separately from both the jury trial and the unanimous verdict. As the Court noted in the *Winship* case, the rule requiring proof of crime beyond a reasonable doubt did not crystallize in this country until after the Constitution was adopted. And in that case, which held such a burden of proof to be constitutionally required, the Court purported to draw no support from the Sixth Amendment.

Defendant's argument that the Sixth Amendment requires jury unanimity in order to give effect to the reasonable doubt standard thus founders on the fact that the Sixth Amendment does not require proof beyond a reasonable doubt at all. The reasonable doubt argument is rooted, in effect, in due process and has been rejected in *Johnson* v. *Louisiana.*

Mr. Justice Powell in his concurring opinion made some comments worthy of noting in upholding the less-than-unanimous verdict. Among other comments, he stated:

. . . There is no reason to believe, on the basis of experience in Oregon or elsewhere, that a unanimous decision of 12 jurors is more likely to serve the high purpose of jury trial, or is entitled to greater respect in the community, than the same decision joined in the 10 members of a jury of 12. The standard of due process assured by the Oregon Constitution provides a sufficient guarantee that the government will not be permitted to impose its judgment on an accused without first meeting the full burden of its prosecutorial duty. . . .

Removal of the unanimity requirement could well minimize the potential for hung juries occasioned either by bribery or juror irrationality. Furthermore, the rule that juries must speak with a single voice often leads, not to full agreement among the 12 but to agreement by none and compromise by all, despite the frequent absence of a rational basis for such compromise. . . .

The petitioners (defendants) contended that their right to a jury comprising a cross section of a community was interfered with by the less-than-unanimous verdict. Their petitions alleged that unless unanimity is required, the viewpoint of a minority of the jurors representing minority groups is excluded from discussion during the deliberation. They also alleged that whether the verdict is conviction or acquittal, it may be the unjust product of racism, bigotry, or an emotionally inflamed trial. To this contention, Mr. Justice Powell stated the following:

Such fears materialize only when the jury's majority, responding to these extraneous pressures, ignores the evidence and the instructions of the court as well as the rational arguments of the minority. The risk, however, that a jury in a particular case will fail to meet its high responsibility is inherent in any system which commits decisions of guilt or innocence to untrained laymen drawn at random from the community. In part, at least, the majority-verdict rule must rely on the same principle which underlies our historic dedication to jury trial; both systems are premised on the conviction that each juror will faithfully perform his assigned duty. . . . Even before the jury is sworn substantial protection against the selection of a representative but willfully irresponsible jury is assured by the wide availability of peremptory challenges and challenges for cause. The likelihood of miscarriage of justice is further diminished by the judges' use of full jury instructions, detailing the applicable burdens of proof, informing the jurors of their duty to weigh the views of fellow jurors, and reminding them of the solemn responsibility imposed by their oaths. Trial judges also retain the power to direct acquittals in cases in which the evidence of guilt is lacking, or to set aside verdicts once rendered when the evidence is insufficient to support a conviction. Furthermore, in cases in which public emotion runs high or pretrial publicity threatens a fair trial, judges possess broad power to grant changes of venue, and to impose restrictions on the extent of press coverage.

   In light of such protections it is unlikely that the Oregon "ten-of-twelve" rule will account for an increase in the number of cases in which injustice will be occasioned by a biased or prejudiced jury. It may be wise to recall Mr. Justice White's admonition in *Murphy* v. *Waterfront Comm'n,* that the Constitution "protects against real dangers, not remote and speculative possibilities."

Since the U.S. Supreme Court has given sanction to less-than-unanimous verdicts, it is highly possible that other states in the future will adopt this verdict requirement.

   It has been argued that there is no sound reason, other than tradition, for the requirement of the unanimous verdict. The origin of the unanimous verdict is unclear. By the latter part of the fourteenth century, the unanimous verdict was required, but it was not the jury verdict as we know it today. As pointed out in the history of the jury trial, in the fourteenth century, convicted persons were often subject to cruel and unusual punishment. It has been alleged that one of the reasons for the unanimous verdict at that time was to avoid such punishment as often as possible. Those who are for the less-than-unanimous verdict allege that since the convicted person is not subjected to cruel and unusual punishment today, there is no need for the unanimous verdict. The less-than-unanimous verdict would also eliminate many hung juries, resulting in fewer retrials and saving court costs.

   The arguments of those who oppose the less-than-unanimous verdict are just as strong. It is stated that abolishing the unanimous verdict in order to prevent hung juries is a shallow argument and not sufficient reason for such an action. Some argue, as did Mr. Justice Douglas in his dissent in the *Johnson* case, that the less-than-unanimous verdict prohibits the minority members of the jury from presenting their arguments, which might prevent a conviction when the minority have a real doubt of guilt. It is also argued that if this verdict is permitted, the next step may be eliminating the presumption of innocence or proving the defendant guilty beyond a reasonable doubt. It should be pointed out that the Bill of Rights says nothing about twelve persons specifically being required to compose a jury, a verdict's being unanimous, proving the defendant guilty beyond a reasonable doubt, or presuming innocence. These rights of the accused have been established by tradition but allegedly have a constitutional standard, and any break with this standard will weaken our justice system.

   The U.S. Supreme Court, however, in *Burch* v. *Louisiana,*[5] held that the verdict of a jury comprising only six persons must be unanimous for "nonpetty offenses." The Court stated that "to hold anything less than a unanimous verdict by a jury of only six persons would be a threat to the constitutional guarantee of a trial by an impartial jury."

CASE LAW

Recent Cases

Williams v. *Florida* 399 U.S. 78 (1970)

JUSTICE WHITE delivered the opinion of the Court.

Prior to his trial for robbery in the State of Florida, petitioner filed a "Motion for a Protective Order," seeking to be excused from the requirements of Rule 1.200 of the Florida Rules of Criminal Procedure. That rule requires a defendant, on written demand of the prosecuting attorney, to give notice in advance of trial if the defendant intends to claim an alibi, and to furnish the prosecuting attorney with information as to the place where he claims to have been and with the names and addresses of the alibi witnesses he intends to use. In his motion petitioner openly declared his intent to claim an alibi, but objected to the further disclosure requirements on the ground that the rule "compels the Defendant in a criminal case to be a witness against himself" in violation of his Fifth and Fourteenth Amendment rights.

The motion was denied. Petitioner also filed a pretrial motion to impanel a 12-man jury instead of the six-man jury provided by Florida law in all but capital cases. That motion too was denied. Petitioner was convicted as charged and was sentenced to life imprisonment. The District Court of Appeal affirmed, rejecting petitioner's claims that his Fifth and Sixth Amendment rights had been violated. We granted certiorari.

I.

Florida's notice-of-alibi rule is in essence a requirement that a defendant submit to a limited form of pretrial discovery by the State whenever he intends to rely at trial on the defense of alibi. In exchange for the defendant's disclosure of the witnesses he proposes to use to establish that defense, the State in turn is required to notify the defendant of any witnesses it proposes to offer in rebuttal to that defense. Both sides are under a continuing duty promptly to disclose the names and addresses of additional witnesses bearing on the alibi as they become available. The threatened sanction for failure to comply is the exclusion at trial of the defendant's alibi evidence—except for his own testimony—or, in the case of the State, the exclusion of the State's evidence offered in rebuttal of the alibi.

We need not linger over the suggestion that the discovery permitted the State against petitioner in this case deprived him of "due process" or a "fair trial." Florida law provides for liberal discovery by the defendant against the State, and the notice-of-alibi rule is itself carefully hedged with reciprocal duties requiring state

disclosure to the defendant. Given the ease with which an alibi can be fabricated, the State's interest in protecting itself against an eleventh-hour defense is both obvious and legitimate. Reflecting this interest, notice-of-alibi provisions, dating at least from 1927, are now in existence in a substantial number of States. The adversary system of trial is hardly an end in itself; it is not yet a poker game in which players enjoy an absolute right always to conceal their cards until played. We find ample room in that system, at least as far as "due process" is concerned, for the instant Florida rule, which is designed to enhance the search for truth in the criminal trial by insuring both the defendant and the State ample opportunity to investigate certain facts crucial to the determination of guilt or innocence.

Petitioner's major contention is that he was "compelled . . . to be a witness against himself" contrary to the commands of the Fifth and Fourteenth Amendments because the notice-of-alibi rule required him to give the State the name and address of Mrs. Scotty in advance of trial and thus to furnish the State with information useful in convicting him. No pretrial statement of petitioner was introduced at trial; but armed with Mrs. Scotty's name and address and the knowledge that she was to be petitioner's alibi witness, the State was able to take her deposition in advance of trial and to find rebuttal testimony. Also, requiring him to reveal the elements of his defense is claimed to have interfered with his right to wait until after the State had presented its case to decide how to defend against it. We conclude, however, as has apparently every other court that has considered the issue, that the privilege against self-incrimination is not violated by a requirement that the defendant give notice of an alibi defense and disclose his alibi witnesses.

The defendant in a criminal trial is frequently forced to testify and to call other witnesses in an effort to reduce the risk of conviction. When he presents his witnesses, he must reveal their identity and submit them to cross-examination, which in itself may prove incriminating or which may furnish the State with leads to incriminating rebuttal evidence. That the defendant faces such a dilemma demanding a choice between complete silence and presenting a defense has never been thought an invasion of the privilege against compelled self-incrimination. The pressures generated by the State's evidence may be severe but they do not vitiate the defendant's choice to present an alibi defense and witnesses to prove it, even though the attempted defense ends in catastrophe for the defendant. However "testimonial" or "incriminating" the alibi defense proves to be, it cannot be considered "compelled" within the meaning of the Fifth and Fourteenth Amendments.

Very similar constraints operate on the defendant when the State requires pretrial notice of alibi and the naming of alibi witnesses. Nothing in such a rule requires the defendant to rely on an alibi or prevents him from abandoning the defense; these matters are left to his unfettered choice. That choice must be made, but the pressures that bear on his pretrial decision are of the same nature as those that would induce him to call alibi witnesses at the trial: the force of historical fact beyond both his and the State's control and the strength of the State's case built on these facts. Response to that kind of pressure by offering evidence or testimony is not compelled self-incrimination transgressing the Fifth and Fourteenth Amendments.

In the case before us, the notice-of-alibi rule by itself in no way affected petitioner's crucial decision to call alibi witnesses or added to the legitimate pressures leading to that course of action. At most, the rule only compelled petitioner to accelerate the timing of his disclosure, forcing him to divulge at an earlier date information that the petitioner from the beginning planned to divulge at trial. Nothing in the Fifth Amendment privilege entitles a defendant as a matter of constitutional right to await the end of the State's case before announcing the nature of his defense, any more than it entitles him to await the jury's verdict on the State's case-in-chief before deciding whether or not to take the stand himself.

Petitioner concedes that absent the notice-of-alibi rule the Constitution would raise no bar to the court's granting the State a continuance at trial on the ground of surprise as soon as the alibi witness is called. Nor would there be self-incrimination problems if, during that continuance, the State was permitted to do precisely what it did here prior to trial: take the deposition of the witness and find rebuttal evidence. But if so utilizing a continuance is permissible under the Fifth and Fourteenth Amendments, then surely the same result may be accomplished through pretrial discovery, as it was here, avoiding the necessity of a disrupted trial. We decline to hold that the privilege against compulsory self-incrimination guarantees the defendant the right to surprise the State with an alibi defense.

II.

In *Duncan* v. *Louisiana,* 391 U.S. 145 (1968), we held that the Fourteenth Amendment guarantees a right to trial by jury in all criminal cases that—were they to be tried in a federal court—would come within the Sixth Amendment's guarantee. Petitioner's trial for robbery on July 3, 1968, clearly falls within the scope of that holding. See *Baldwin* v. *New York,* ante, p. 66; *DeStefano* v. *Woods,* 392 U.S. 631 (1968). The question in this case then is whether the constitutional guarantee of a trial by "jury" necessarily requires trial by exactly 12 persons, rather than some lesser number—in this case, six. We hold that the 12-man panel is not a necessary ingredient of "trial by jury," and that respondent's refusal to impanel more than the six members provided for by Florida law did not violate petitioner's Sixth Amendment rights as applied to the States through the Fourteenth.

We had occasion in *Duncan* v. *Louisiana,* supra, to review briefly the oft-told history of the development of trial by jury in criminal cases. That history revealed a long tradition attaching great importance to the concept of relying on a body of one's peers to determine guilt or innocence as a safeguard against arbitrary law enforcement. That same history, however, affords little insight into the considerations that gradually led the size of that body to be generally fixed at 12. Some have suggested that the number 12 was fixed upon simply because that was the number of the presentment jury from the hundred, from which the petit jury developed. [399 U.S. 78, 88] Other, less circular but more fanciful reasons for the number 12 have been given, "but they were all brought forward after the number was fixed," and rest on little more than mystical or superstitious insights into the significance of "12." Lord Coke's explanation that the "number of twelve is much respected in holy writ, as 12 apostles, 12 stones, 12 tribes, etc.," is typical. [399 U.S. 78, 89] In short, while sometime in the 14th century the size of the jury at common law came to be fixed generally at 12, that particular feature of the jury system appears to have been a historical accident, unrelated to the great purposes which gave rise to the jury in the first place. The question before us is whether this accidental feature of the jury has been immutably codified into our Constitution.

This Court's earlier decisions have assumed an affirmative answer to this question. The leading case so construing the Sixth Amendment is *Thompson* v. *Utah,* 170 U.S. 343 (1898). There the defendant had been tried and convicted by a 12-man jury for a crime committed in the Territory of Utah. A new trial was granted, but by that time Utah had been admitted as a State. The defendant's new trial proceeded under Utah's Constitution, providing for a jury of only eight members. This Court reversed the resulting conviction, holding that Utah's constitutional provision was an ex post facto law as applied to the defendant. In reaching its conclusion, the Court announced that the Sixth Amendment was applicable to the defendant's trial when Utah was a Territory, and that the jury referred to in the Amendment was a jury "constituted, as it was at common law, of twelve persons, neither more nor less." 170 U.S., at 349. Arguably unnecessary for the result, this announcement was supported simply by referring to the Magna Carta, and by quoting passages from treatises which noted—what has already been seen—that at common law the jury did indeed consist of 12. Noticeably absent was any discussion of the essential step in the argument: namely, that every feature of the jury as it existed at common law—whether incidental or essential to that institution—was necessarily included in the Constitution wherever that document referred to a "jury." Subsequent decisions have reaffirmed the announcement in Thompson, often in dictum and usually by relying—where there was any discussion of the issue at all—solely on the fact that the common-law jury consisted of 12. . . .

Briefly Noted

Renico v. *Lett*, **130 S. Ct. 1855 (U.S. 2010).** When a judge discharges a jury on the grounds that the jury cannot reach a verdict, the Double Jeopardy Clause does not bar a new trial for the defendant before a new jury. Trial judges may declare a mistrial whenever, in their opinion, taking all the circumstances into consideration, there is a manifest necessity for doing so. The decision to declare a mistrial is left to the sound discretion of the judge, but the power ought to be used with the greatest caution, under urgent circumstances, and for very plain and obvious causes. The "manifest necessity" standard for declaring a mistrial cannot be interpreted literally, and a mistrial is appropriate when there is a "high degree" of necessity. The decision whether to grant a mistrial is reserved to the broad discretion of the trial judge.

Summary

- On completion of the closing arguments, the judge charges (instructs) the jury on the law of the case.
- Counsel for both sides submits requests for instructions to the judge in a hearing outside of the presence of the jury. Any objections to the proposed instructions must be made during the hearing.
- States differ on what comments a judge may make to the jury regarding the state of the evidence.

- During deliberations, only jury members may be present.
- Any evidence admitted in the trial may be taken into the jury room for consideration during deliberations.
- Some states permit jury findings based on less-than-unanimous verdicts.
- When the jury comprises only six members, the verdict must be unanimous.

Review Questions

1. What is the purpose of the charge to the jury?
2. List five points of law that a judge may explain to the jury before it goes into deliberation.
3. What is the purpose of the deliberation?
4. What may the jury take with it during the deliberation?
5. Define a hung jury.
6. What is the purpose of the Allen instruction?

Local Procedure

1. In your home state, may the judge comment on the weight of the evidence and the credibility of the witnesses?
2. May the Allen instruction be read to the jury?
3. Must the jury reach a unanimous verdict?
4. May an alternate juror be sequestered with the jury during deliberations?

Endnotes

1. *Turner* v. *Louisiana,* 379 U.S. 466 (1965).
2. 164 U.S. 492 (1896).
3. 369 F2nd 960 (1967).
4. *Johnson* v. *Louisiana* 406 U.S. 356 (1972); *Apodaca* v. *Oregon,* 406 U.S. 404 (1972).
5. 60 L.Ed.2d 96 (1979).

CHAPTER 15

The Verdict and Appeals

In this court dissents have gradually become majority opinions.

—SUPREME COURT JUSTICE FELIX FRANKFURTER IN
GRAVES V. *NEW YORK*, 360 U.S. 466, 1939

A murder trial is the most solemn proceeding known to the law. . . . Such trials are invariably dignified and deliberate so far as the conduct of the legal side of the case is concerned. No judge, however unqualified for the bench; no prosecutor, however light-minded; no lawyer, however callous, fails to feel the serious nature of the transaction or to be affected strongly by the fact that he is dealing with life and death. A prosecutor who openly laughed or sneered at a prisoner charged with murder would severely injure his case. The Jury, naturally, is overwhelmed with the gravity of the occasion and the responsibility resting upon them.

—NEW YORK PROSECUTOR ARTHUR TRAIN, 1909

Chapter Outline

Verdict	Case Law
Appeals	Summary
Appellate Court Citations	

Key Terms

Boykin advisement	Mistrial
Impaneled jury	New trial
Manifest necessity	Verdict

Learning Objectives

After completing this chapter, you should be able to:

- Describe the various types of appeals.
- Outline the appeal process.
- Describe various trial outcomes including verdicts, new trials, and mistrials.

- Explain the meaning of a verdict.
- Discuss when a defendant is entitled to a mistrial.
- Identify when a defendant after a mistrial may be subjected to a new trial.
- List the grounds that a defendant can use on appeal to obtain a new trial.

- Explain the process for the pronouncement of judgment and the arrest of judgment.
- Discuss the issues regarding the release of a defendant during an appeal.
- List those situations in which the prosecution may appeal.

VERDICT

Derived from the Latin word *verdictum*, the word **verdict** means "a true declaration." In a court trial, the verdict is the decision of the judge. In a criminal trial, the verdict is the decision of the jury. Once the verdict in a criminal trial has been agreed on, the foreperson will so advise the bailiff, the officer who is in charge of the jury. The bailiff will then inform the judge, who will reconvene court in order that the verdict may be received. Since the deliberation often takes considerable time, the judge usually will adjourn court on the case while the jury is deliberating. This action permits the judge to perform other duties while being available at all times to furnish further instructions or information that the jury may request while deliberating. After the court is reconvened, the judge will instruct the bailiff to return the jury to the courtroom. On their arrival, the judge may request that their names be called to make certain that all the jurors are present. If a juror is missing, the judge may have to declare a mistrial unless the juror's whereabouts can be determined and his or her presence can be immediately obtained. After all the jurors are accounted for, the judge will ask the foreperson whether the jury has agreed on a verdict. If the foreperson answers in the affirmative, the judge may ask him or her to announce the verdict; if the verdict is in writing, the judge may request that it be given to the clerk of the court to read. Not all jurisdictions require that the verdict be in writing and signed by the foreperson. Whether it is required to be in writing or not, most jurisdictions furnish forms to the jury on which they may record their verdict. The defendant must be present at the time the verdict is announced in open court unless his or her whereabouts cannot be determined. In that case, the verdict may be announced in the absence of the accused.

After the verdict is announced, the prosecution or the defense may request that the jurors be polled individually to determine how each voted on the verdict. When the verdict must be unanimous, if one or more jurors allege that the verdict does not express all the jurors' opinions, the judge may instruct the jury to return to the jury room for further deliberation. If the facts warrant such action, the judge may discharge the jury and declare a mistrial.

If the jury finds the verdict to be not guilty, the defendant is entitled to immediate release if in custody. If the defendant is out on bail, the security will be returned to the person who posted it, since it will have served its purpose. In either event, the defendant is free from further prosecution on the crime charged.

If the defendant is found guilty, the next procedural step is sentencing. A few other matters should be considered before the discussion of the sentencing. The jury may have found the defendant guilty as charged in the accusatory pleading, or the jury may have found the defendant guilty of a lesser degree. It is possible that the jury found the defendant guilty on some of the charges stated in the accusatory pleading and not guilty on others. In addition to finding the defendant guilty, the jury may be called upon to determine whether the defendant was armed at the time that a crime was committed. All these matters may affect the sentence imposed. Once the verdict is announced in open court, it will be recorded in the record of the case. At this point, the jury is entitled to be discharged unless it is involved in the sentencing procedure. If it is a court trial, the judge has the responsibility of rendering the verdict.

Even though the jury returns a verdict of guilty, most jurisdictions permit the judge to modify the verdict. If the judge believes that the evidence shows the defendant was not guilty to the degree that the jury found him or her guilty, the judge may modify the verdict by finding the defendant guilty of a lesser degree or lesser crime included in the criminal act. A few states permit the judge to go one step further. The guilty verdict of a jury may be set aside and a judgment of acquittal entered, or the judge may set aside the verdict and dismiss the charge. In either event, the judge's action in this regard is usually a bar to any further prosecutive action against the defendant. The right of a judge to set aside the entire verdict is very powerful. But such action is permitted on the grounds that if the evidence is insufficient to establish the defendant guilty beyond a reasonable doubt, the judge must set aside the verdict in the interest of justice. However, a judge may not set aside a verdict of not guilty, since this action would deny the defendant the right of a trial by jury.

New Trial and Mistrial

If a judge believes that the prosecution has failed to prove the defendant guilty beyond a reasonable doubt, the judge may enter a judgment of acquittal in some jurisdictions. This action occurs before the case is turned over to the jury for deliberation and takes the case out of their hands. But if the judge is permitted to set aside the jury's guilty verdict, the case is taken from the jury after it has fulfilled its function. This action often draws criticism from jurors, since it voids their function. To avoid this criticism, judges will grant a motion for a **new trial** rather than enter the judgment of acquittal or set aside the verdict.

Law in Practice

Watson v. *United States*, 128 S. Ct. 579 (2007)

Michael Watson pleaded guilty in federal court to a drug trafficking offense but asserted that an additional mandatory minimum sentence was improperly imposed for using a firearm during and in relation to the offense.

JUSTICE SOUTER delivered the Court's opinion.

The question is whether a person who trades his drugs for a gun "uses" a firearm during and in relation to a drug trafficking crime within the meaning of 18 U.S.C. § 924(c)(1)(A). We hold that he does not.

Watson gave prescription narcotics to a government informant or an undercover officer in exchange for the firearm. Defendant's trade of the narcotics for the firearm did not constitute use of the firearm during and in relation to the drug transaction within the ordinary or natural meaning of the term "use" in § 924(c)(1)(A). While a trade of a firearm for drugs would constitute use of the firearm by the recipient of the drugs to accomplish the trade, the converse was not true since defendant merely received the firearm and did not in any manner use the firearm. The judgment affirming defendant's sentence was reversed, and the case was remanded for further proceedings.

After a jury has returned a verdict of guilty, the defense may request that a new trial be granted. Generally, a new trial may be granted only on the motion, or request, of the defendant, and not on the judge's own motion. If a new trial is granted, the case will therefore be heard again from the beginning, usually before the same judge, but with a new jury. The grounds for granting a new trial are specifically set forth in the codes of most states. These grounds usually include such matters as the jury's receiving evidence of the case out of court; the jurors separating without permission of the court after being sequestered; the verdict's being decided on by lot or by means other than a fair expression of opinion; misconduct of the jurors, preventing the defendant from receiving a fair trial; or a guilty verdict's being returned that was not supported by the evidence. Although it has been stated that a new trial may be granted only on statutory grounds, courts have held that new trials should be granted on nonstatutory grounds when a failure to do so would result in a denial of a fair trial to the defendant. In one case, the judge stated in comments to the jury that, in all his experience as a lawyer and judge, he had never seen so many defense witnesses, including the defendant himself, whose truthfulness was in doubt. Even though the judge informed the jurors that it was their duty to weigh the credibility of the witnesses, he felt that, after a guilty verdict was returned by the jury, a new trial should be granted in the interest of justice. In this way, the judge was correcting his own remarks that bordered on directing the jury to return a verdict of guilty.

One of the more frequent grounds used for granting a new trial is newly discovered evidence by the defense. In order for a defendant to take advantage of this ground, the defense must be in a position to prove to the satisfaction of the judge that the newly discovered evidence is material and that the evidence could not with due diligent search have been discovered by the time of the first trial. It has been held by some courts that the newly discovered evidence must be of sufficient importance to indicate a probable acquittal in a new trial. This evidence must be more than just a repetition of the evidence presented by the defense during the first trial unless the repetitive evidence would materially strengthen previously presented evidence.

The prosecution has the right to argue against the granting of a new trial. It may endeavor to prove that there was not due diligent search before the first trial to justify a new trial, or it may argue against other grounds presented by the defense. It is not always necessary for the prosecution to argue against the motion for a new trial. The judge may deny the motion without any argument's being presented.

Granting a new trial is not to be confused with declaring a **mistrial**. The motion for a new trial may not be made until a verdict of guilty has been rendered. A mistrial may be declared anytime during the trial proceedings, on the judge's own motion or at the request of the defense. The right of the prosecution to request a mistrial is somewhat restricted and not permitted in all jurisdictions. A mistrial may be declared any time that there is misconduct that is so prejudicial that the defense would be denied a fair trial. The misconduct may occur early in the trial proceedings. For example, if, during the opening statement by the prosecuting attorney, he or she refers to the defendant as an ex-con or otherwise imply a past criminal record, the judge may decide that the remarks were so prejudicial that the defendant could not get a fair trial. The judge may at that time declare a mistrial. If the mistrial is declared at that point in the proceedings, not too much trial time is lost; but if the misconduct comes late in the trial, such as just before deliberation, much time, energy, and money will have been wasted.

Sometimes, rather than declare a mistrial, the judge will instruct the jury to disregard the misconduct and inform them that it is not to affect them in rendering a verdict. This admonition is not always effective, since jurors cannot always erase something that they have heard. If the defendant is convicted, the failure to declare a mistrial may be grounds for reversal on appeal. As stated, a judge may declare a mistrial when the jury cannot agree on a verdict. Defendants have argued that the inability of a jury to agree on a verdict indicates both that the prosecution has not proved the defendant guilty beyond a reasonable doubt and that the defendant is entitled to a judgment of acquittal. This argument has been rejected by the U.S. Supreme Court. The Court held that the defendant may be retried under these circumstances. The Court stated that it recognizes "society's interest in giving the prosecution one complete opportunity to convict those who have violated its laws."[1] However, before a mistrial may be declared when a jury cannot agree on a verdict, the judge must weigh the situation carefully. Courts have held that if a judge declares a mistrial too quickly when further deliberation would have resulted in a verdict, the defendant has been deprived of the "valued right to have his trial completed by a particular tribunal." But if the judge fails to declare a mistrial when the jury cannot agree on a verdict after lengthy deliberation, there is a risk that a verdict may result from pressure by some jurors on others that would deny the jurors an opportunity for individual expression.

If a mistrial is declared at the request of the defense, generally, the case can be tried again at the discretion of the prosecuting attorney. The retrial is not considered a violation of the double jeopardy guarantee, since the defendant, in requesting a mistrial, waives the guarantee against double jeopardy. However, some jurisdictions hold that unless there is sufficient cause to declare a mistrial or unless the defendant agrees to the mistrial, jeopardy may have set in, and the defendant cannot be retried. If the misconduct prejudicial to the prosecution was committed by defense counsel or by the accused, the prosecution may have little or no remedy.

However, in *Arizona* v. *Washington*, the U.S. Supreme Court did uphold the action of the trial judge in declaring a mistrial at the request of the prosecution when a defense attorney made improper statements to the jury during the opening argument. The trial judge concluded that the remarks were so prejudicial that the prosecution would be denied the right to have the case tried before an impartial jury. The Supreme Court stated that before a trial judge could declare a mistrial over the objections of the defense, it must be established that there was a **"manifest necessity"** for such action. In other words, there must be sufficient evidence to prove that such action should be taken. The Court stated the following:

> Because of the variety of circumstances that may make it necessary to discharge a jury before a trial is concluded, and because those circumstances do not invariably create unfairness to the accused, his valued right to have the trial concluded by a particular tribunal is sometimes subordinate to the public interest in affording the prosecutor one full and fair opportunity to present his evidence to an impartial jury. Yet in view of the importance of the right, and the fact that it is frustrated by any mistrial, the prosecutor must shoulder the burden of justifying the mistrial if he is to avoid the double jeopardy bar. His burden is a heavy one. The prosecutor must demonstrate "manifest necessity" for any mistrial over the objections of the defendant.

Yet in *Carsey* v. *United States*,[2] the U.S. Court of Appeals held that the improper remarks made by the defense attorney to the jury during the closing argument could have been corrected if the judge had instructed the jury to disregard the improper remarks of the defense attorney. The court held that declaring a mistrial was improper and that the defendant had been placed in jeopardy and could not be retried.

In a dissenting opinion in the *Carsey* case, Justice Tamm took the opposite view from that of the majority, stating as follows:

> When appellant's (defendant's) trial counsel, in his closing plea to the jury, advised the jury of two prior mistrials he did it deliberately for the purpose of creating doubt of the defendant's guilt in the minds of the jurors who, understandably, would ask themselves whether a reasonable doubt of guilt had not been established when two prior juries, upon the same evidence, had been unable to reach a verdict. If the prosecutor had made the same statement to the jury for the purpose of injecting into their thinking a fact completely outside of the evidence before them, we would label it as both a "foul blow" and an "improper method calculated to produce a wrongful conviction." I am unwilling and unable to agree that the questioned statement herein was proper when made by defense counsel when it so obviously would have been improper if made by Government counsel. The statement would have been [an] adequate and proper basis for the granting of a mistrial if the prosecutor had made it, and I must conclude that it was proper and adequate for the trial judge's action when it was made by defense counsel. Defense counsel's initial statement created and triggered the factual situation resulting in the mistrial, despite the majority's feeble attempt to transfer the responsibility to the prosecuting attorney.
>
> The majority opinion places a premium on chicanery and invites the defense counsel to engage in it by its "you cannot lose" result. If this opinion is to prevail, defense counsel may resort to trickery in the court room secure in the knowledge that if he gets by with it he will have the benefit of his misconduct, and if he does not a mistrial will be declared and thereby he reaps an even greater reward for his unethical behavior.

The facts of another case indicate that during the trial recess, the defendant, who was out on bail, approached a drinking fountain in the courthouse hall, drew a cup of water, and handed it to one of the women jurors, at the same time carrying on a conversation with her. Thereafter, the defendant proceeded to give other members of the jury drinks of water. This conduct was observed by an officer, who informed the judge. After court reconvened, the judge questioned the officer on the stand about the incident and declared a mistrial. The defense attorney endeavored to place the defendant on the stand to prove that no conversation pertaining to the facts of the case took place. The defense attorney also tried to accept the blame for the misconduct of the defendant by stating that he had failed to admonish the defendant against having any contact with the jury. The judge's opinion was that the defendant was endeavoring to make a favorable impression on the jury, and a mistrial was declared. In addition, the defendant was held in contempt of court. On retrial, the defendant entered a plea of once in jeopardy that the judge refused to accept, and the defendant was found guilty on the original charge of attempted robbery. The defendant appealed the conviction on the grounds that the guarantee against double jeopardy had been violated by the retrial. The appellate court agreed with the defendant. The court stated the following:

> An impaneled jury refers to a jury that the trial judge has accepted and has constituted as the jury to hear a case. Once a jury has been **impaneled** and sworn to try a defendant, jeopardy attaches, and its subsequent discharge when not authorized by law or by defendant's consent, is equivalent to an acquittal and constitutes former jeopardy barring retrial.
>
> As to what constitutes sufficient cause to authorize the discharge of a jury, the courts have required a showing that there exists some legal necessity resulting from physical causes beyond the control of the court.
>
> The determination as to whether the required legal necessity exists is a matter left to the discretion of the trial court. However, "the power of the Court to discharge a jury without the consent of the prisoner is not an absolute, uncontrolled discretionary power. It must be exercised in accordance with established legal rules and a sound legal discretion in the application of such rules to the facts and circumstances of each particular case, and in this State is subject to review by an appellate court."
>
> The trial court's action in summarily declaring a mistrial solely on the basis of the officer's testimony that he had observed defendant talking with two of the jurors during the recess on their way back to the court room from the water cooler was unjustified and constituted an abuse of discretion. Before the matter was ruled on defendant should have been given a reasonable opportunity to present his version of the incident and with proper participation by his counsel.[3]

This decision has been criticized by many legal scholars on the basis that the judge did have sufficient cause to declare a mistrial. It is alleged that the misconduct by the defendant in contacts with the jury could not help creating some favorable impression to the detriment of the prosecution. It is further alleged that if a material witness for the prosecution had made this contact with the jury, the judge undoubtedly would have declared a mistrial, since the defendant could not have received a fair trial from an impartial jury.

Arrest of Judgment and Pronouncement of Judgment

If a new trial is not granted after the verdict is rendered, the next procedure is the pronouncement of judgment by the judge. Pronouncement of judgment is usually thought of as the oral sentencing of the defendant by the judge. But technically, it entails more than the oral statement of what the sentence will be. The pronouncement of judgment is reduced to a written document generally known as the judgment. This judgment will set forth the plea entered, the verdict, and, if guilty, will reflect the sentence or other disposition of the case—all of which are entered in the case record. Technically, the pronouncement of judgment is made whether there is an acquittal or a conviction, but in many jurisdictions, it is synonymous with the pronouncement of the sentence. In misdemeanor cases, most jurisdictions permit the pronouncement of judgment in the absence of the defendant. In a felony conviction, the presence of the defendant is required unless he or she cannot be located after due diligent search; in this case, pronouncement of judgment may be made in his or her absence.

Jurisdictions vary somewhat in the time within which the pronouncement of judgment must take place after a guilty plea is entered or a guilty verdict is returned. In misdemeanor convictions in some jurisdictions, the pronouncement may be made immediately; if not, it must take place within a few days. Other jurisdictions provide that the pronouncement of judgment may not occur in fewer than six hours and not more than five days. The six-hour limit allows time for the convicted defendant to arrange personal affairs before serving time. In felony convictions, a considerable delay is usually permitted in the pronouncement of judgment. The delay permits time for a presentence investigation, conducted in order that a more equitable sentence may be imposed. The delay is usually not longer than one month. It is to the advantage of both society and the convicted defendant to have sentence pronounced without unnecessary delay. The defendant is entitled to know the sentence as soon as possible in order that the term may begin. As for society's interest, there is little comfort in having a felon free on bail who may be in a position to commit other crimes while awaiting the pronouncement of sentence.

Prior to the pronouncement of judgment, the defendant may file a motion in the arrest of judgment or, in most jurisdictions, the judge may enter the motion. In many jurisdictions, the law provides that at the time the convicted defendant is brought before the judge for pronouncement of judgment, the judge must inquire of the defendant, "Is there any legal reason why judgment should not be pronounced?" It is at this time that the defendant will show legal cause for the arrest of judgment. Some jurisdictions hold that making the inquiry of the defendant is a useless procedure, and the defendant is entitled to make a motion at any time after the verdict is rendered.

The motion for the arrest of judgment is made on statutory grounds. These grounds include such matters as present insanity of the defendant. If it is determined that the defendant is insane at the time of the pronouncement of judgment, it must be postponed until sanity has been restored, since a defendant may not be sentenced while insane. The motion may be on the grounds that there was some defect in the accusatory pleading that had not been successfully challenged previously, such as the failure to state that a crime had been committed. If the motion for arrest of judgment is denied or none is entered, the next procedure is the pronouncement of the sentence. In most jurisdictions, before the sentence is pronounced, the defendant is entitled to make a statement in his or her own behalf. This statement is generally a plea for leniency or consideration in the sentencing. If a judge fails to grant the defendant an opportunity to make a statement, the sentence may be set aside on appeal. The case does not have to be retried under the circumstances, but the sentence will be set aside and the case will be sent back to the trial court for resentencing after the defendant has been given an opportunity to speak. After the defendant has made a plea, if any, to the judge or jury, he or she will be sentenced. Before entering into the sentencing procedure, the appeals that may be taken by the defendant or the prosecution should be discussed. The outcome of the appeal could determine whether a defendant serves a sentence.

APPEALS

Appeal by the Defendant

If convicted, a defendant will usually appeal the conviction to the appropriate appellate court if there is any basis at all for the appeal. The defendant's appeal may be well founded, since some error may have been committed during the trial that was prejudicial. Or the defendant may attempt to appeal the case merely to delay serving the imposed sentence.

FREEDOM PENDING APPEAL Generally, the defendant must file a notice of appeal within a few days after the pronouncement of judgment. Whether the defendant remains free on bail pending the outcome of appeal is largely within the discretion of the judge. The defendant has no inherent right to remain free from custody once convicted, since the presumption of innocence is lost. In determining whether a defendant should be free pending the appeal, the judge may consider whether the efforts to appeal were based on frivolous grounds; whether the appeal was merely a delaying tactic to avoid serving the sentence; whether there may be a temptation to flee the jurisdiction of the court pending the appeal; or whether the defendant may be a threat to the community if free on bail.

Whether the defendant remains free on bail or is incarcerated, the judge in most instances will have sentenced the defendant. If the defendant remains free on bail, no time will be served until the outcome of the appeal is determined. If the conviction is reversed, the defendant will not have served any time. But if the defendant is incarcerated pending the appeal, the sentence will have begun to be served. If the conviction is reversed and the defendant is not retried or cannot be retried, little can be done to compensate for the time spent in prison other than to clear the name of the accused. But if the conviction is affirmed or if the defendant is retried after a reversal, credit will be given for the time spent in incarceration pending the appeal. Not all appeals are made immediately after a conviction. An appeal may not be taken until several years of a sentence have been served. These appeals are usually based on the result of some U.S. Supreme Court decision that changes the justice procedure in some manner and is made retroactive; that is, the decision is applicable to all convictions irrespective of when the case was tried. If the decision is not made retroactive, it is applicable only to those defendants whose cases have not been decided previous to the U.S. Supreme Court's decision.

Law in Practice

Appellate Court Structure of Various States

States with only a court of last resort

Delaware, Maine, Montana, New Hampshire, Nevada, Rhode Island, South Dakota, Vermont, West Virginia, and Wyoming

States with a court of last resort and one intermediate-level court of appeals

Alaska, Arizona, Arkansas, California, Colorado, Connecticut, Florida, Georgia, Hawaii, Idaho, Illinois, Iowa, Kansas, Kentucky, Louisiana, Maryland, Massachusetts, Michigan, Minnesota, Missouri, Nebraska, New Jersey, New Mexico, North Carolina, Ohio, Oregon, South Carolina, Utah, Virginia, Washington, and Wisconsin

States with a court of last resort and two intermediate-level courts of appeals

Alabama, New York, Pennsylvania, and Tennessee

States with a state supreme court and a court of criminal appeal (both courts of last resort) and one intermediate-level court of appeals

Oklahoma and Texas

Note: In Oklahoma and Texas, the state supreme court is the court of last resort for civil matters, and the court of criminal appeals is the court of last resort for criminal cases.

Not all efforts by a defendant to appeal a conviction to an appellate court are successful. Sufficient grounds must be alleged in order for the appellate court to hear the appeal. The grounds on which a defendant may appeal a case are numerous. Whatever grounds are alleged, it must be shown that the error committed during the trial was sufficiently prejudicial that the defendant was denied a fair trial or that there was a miscarriage of justice. Some of the grounds most frequently alleged on appeal are as follows: There was insufficient probable cause to make a lawful arrest; a confession that was improperly obtained was admitted as evidence; physical evidence was introduced that was unlawfully seized; a failure was made to grant a change of venue; there was insufficient representation of competent counsel; a failure to give pertinent instructions to the jury existed; a denial of a new trial was made; or there was a failure to declare a mistrial when there was prejudicial misconduct.

METHOD OF APPEAL Upon appealing the case, the defendant, through counsel or on his or her own, will submit to the appropriate appellate court a brief that sets forth the alleged error committed during the trial with citations of appellate court decisions upholding the contended error. A transcript of the trial proceedings will accompany the brief. The prosecution will submit a brief in an effort to show why the conviction should be affirmed and not reversed. The appellate court will review the briefs and the transcript. After doing so, it may conclude that there is no ground for appeal, and the court will deny a hearing on the matter. A hearing date will be set if the appellate court feels that the appeal is worthy of a hearing. At the hearing, the defense attorney and the prosecution's representative, usually the state attorney general, assisted by the prosecuting attorney who was responsible for the conviction, will be present to argue their sides of the case. The defendant is usually not present, since he or she has no inherent right to be present at an appeal hearing. After the hearing, the appellate court justices will consider the matter and conclude whether the conviction should be affirmed or reversed. In making its determination, the appellate court will consider whether there was error or conduct that was so prejudicial that the defendant was denied a fair trial. Sometimes the appellate court will hold that there was error or misconduct during the trial but that this was not serious enough to deny the defendant a fair trial. Under these circumstances, the error is referred to as harmless error.

If the appellate court denies the defendant a hearing on the appeal, there is little the defendant can do about the decision. The appellate court may be called the court of last resort; its decision is usually final unless the defendant can prove that one of the constitutional guarantees was violated, and then the defendant may eventually appeal to the U.S. Supreme Court. The Supreme Court may or may not grant a hearing, depending upon the validity of the alleged violation. It may grant a hearing in an effort to determine whether there was a violation; if there was, the Supreme Court will reverse the conviction. If the Supreme Court denies the hearing or affirms the conviction, no further appeal can be taken by the defendant.

RETRIAL AFTER REVERSAL If a conviction is reversed by either the state appellate court or the U.S. Supreme Court, the states differ on whether the defendant may be retried. If the reversal is based on the fact that a law is unconstitutional, that jeopardy had attached, or that a law is too vague in wording to indicate the violation, there cannot be a retrial. But if the reversal is based on the introduction of illegally seized evidence or an improperly obtained confession, in many states the defendant may be retried, and the improperly introduced evidence will not be admissible during the retrial. The prosecuting attorney has to determine whether the other evidence was sufficient in obtaining a conviction. If not, the charge will undoubtedly be dismissed. A few states do not permit a retrial on reversal of a conviction, since it would be a violation of the guarantee against double jeopardy. Other states hold that on appealing a conviction, the defendant waives the double jeopardy guarantee. If a defendant is successful in getting a conviction reversed on appeal and is retried and convicted, may the judge impose an increased sentence after the new trial? This question was answered by the U.S. Supreme Court in the case of *North Carolina* v. *Pearce*.[4] The Court in that decision held that if identifiable misconduct by the defendant took place after the first trial, the judge might impose an increased sentence, but the increase should not be based on the fact that the defendant has appealed his or her case. The Court stated the following:

> Due process of law requires that vindictiveness against a defendant for having successfully attacked his first conviction must play no part in the sentence he receives

after a new trial. And since the fear of such vindictiveness may unconstitutionally deter a defendant's exercise of the right to appeal or collaterally attack his first conviction, due process also requires that a defendant be freed of apprehension of such a retaliatory motivation on the part of the sentencing judge.

In order to assure the absence of such a motivation, we have concluded that whenever a judge imposes a more severe sentence upon a defendant after a new trial, the reasons for his doing so must affirmatively appear. Those reasons must be based upon objective information concerning identifiable conduct on the part of the defendant occurring after the time of the original sentencing proceedings. And the factual data upon which the increased sentence is based must be made part of the record, so that the constitutional legitimacy of the increased sentence may be fully reviewed on appeal.

Justice White, who concurred in part with the majority opinion, stated that in his opinion, he would "authorize an increased sentence on retrial based on any objective, identifiable factual data not known to the trial judge at the time of the original sentencing proceeding." Only future decisions will tell whether the Court would sanction this reason for an increased sentence, rather than the majority's limited reason of "identifiable conduct" by the defendant after the original sentence. The Court did conclude that on an increased sentence after a new trial, the defendant must be given credit for the time served on the original sentence.

Law in Practice

Steps in a Criminal Appeal

Appeal	A challenge to a decision or ruling by a lower court.
Mandatory Appeals	An appeal the appellate court is required to hear. Generally, the intermediate court of appeals is required to accept an appeal of a decision by a general trial court.
Discretionary Appeal	Appellate court may accept or reject the appeal.
Notice of Appeal	The party filing an appeal must submit a written notice of appeal to the court to which the party plans to appeal. Generally, the period of time in which a notice of appeal must be filed is short. Many states have a ten-day period after judgment is announced.
Trial Record	The party filing the appeal must make arrangements with the court reporter to prepare a transcript of the trial and the exhibits to be filed with the appellate court.
Appellate Brief	The party filing an appeal must submit a brief which consists of the written assignments of error, written arguments as to why the decision was wrong, and citations of authority relied on in the brief.
Rebuttal Brief	The opposing party submits a rebuttal brief stating why the decision should not be reversed.
Oral Arguments	The appellate court may or may not order the parties to present oral arguments on the case.
Written Decision	The appellate court will issue a written decision containing its decision and the reasons for it.
Disposition	The appellate court orders the case affirmed, remanded, and reversed and remanded.
Affirmed	The decision is upheld. The appellate court found no reversible error. *Note:* About 85 percent of criminal convictions are upheld.
Remanded	The appellate court returns the case to the lower court and orders the lower court to hold a hearing on a specific issue or make a determination on a specific issue.
Reversed and Remanded	The decision is set aside, and the case is returned to the trial court for either a new trial or a dismissal of the charges.

Appeal by Prosecution

States vary considerably concerning the prosecution's right of appeal. A few states deny the prosecution any right to appeal, since it would result in a violation of the guarantee against double jeopardy. Some permit a limited right of appeal by the prosecution when the appeal does not involve the double jeopardy guarantee. Generally, an appeal may be taken by the prosecution on a judge's order setting aside or dismissing an accusatory pleading. But the appeal may be taken only when the setting aside or dismissal was before the trial began; otherwise, jeopardy will have set in. An appeal may also be taken on a grant of a new trial, an arrest of judgment, or a modification of a verdict or punishment imposed. In most states, the prosecution has no right to appeal a case when an acquittal verdict has been rendered. As stated in *Washington* v. *Arizona*, a judgment of acquittal is final regardless of how errone-ously it may have been arrived at. However, a few states do allow an appeal by the prosecu-tion after a verdict of acquittal has been returned. The appeal is followed when the prosecution alleges that a serious error was made by the judge on a ruling of law or proce-dure. The appeal is permitted so that guidelines may be established for future cases, but the appellate court has no authority to reverse the acquittal.

An increasing number of states allow the prosecution to appeal a judge's order suppress-ing evidence. It is generally held that where such an appeal is permissible, the appeal may be taken only on an order suppressing evidence that was made before the trial began and may not be taken during the trial. Some states do not permit an appeal of an order suppressing evidence that was made even before the trial. The courts of these states hold that the prosecution is no more disadvantaged by an erroneous ruling before the trial than one during the trial when such ruling leads to an acquittal.

Appeal Involving a Guilty Plea

As we previously discussed, since a plea of guilty is equal to a conviction, this fact must be ex-plained to the defendant before the plea may be accepted. Therefore, it is paradoxical to permit a defendant to appeal a conviction resulting from a voluntary plea of guilty, but some states do permit a defendant to appeal a guilty plea. The grounds for the appeal are based upon some alleged constitutional, jurisdictional, or other grounds concerning the legality of the proceed-ings. For example, the defendant may allege that the judge failed to explain the significance of the guilty plea as required by *Boykin* v. *Alabama*, that the judge denied the defendant the right to withdraw the guilty plea, or that there was a violation of the agreement pertaining to the plea bargain. When the trial judge advises a defendant as to his or her rights before the judge accepts a guilty plea, the advisement is considered as the "**Boykin advisement**." There have been times when a defendant was denied a request for suppression of evidence and thereafter entered a plea of guilty, knowing that the trial would result in conviction. Under these circumstances, the defendant may appeal the guilty plea in an effort to determine whether the evidence should have been suppressed.

APPELLATE COURT CITATIONS

Judges of the appellate courts are generally referred to as justices. The number of justices composing an appellate court varies from one state to another as well as from one appellate court to another. Many states have only a single appellate court, which is generally referred to as the supreme court. Other states have a bilateral appellate court system in which there is an appellate court and a supreme court. Usually only three justices will compose an appel-late court, whereas the supreme court varies, usually from five to nine justices. Not all justices must agree on the decision, only a majority. Once the decision is made, one of the justices agreeing with the majority will put the decision in writing, stating whether the conviction was upheld or reversed, and the reasoning behind the decision. A dissenting justice, if any, may or may not decide to write a dissenting opinion, setting forth the reasons for disagreement with the majority.

Recording Court Decisions

The decisions handed down by the appellate courts are recorded in official publications so that they may act as guidelines for future cases. Each decision is given a citation number in order that the decision may be filed, indexed, and located by attorneys, judges, and others having occasion to refer to a particular decision. The citation will include the name, or title, of the case; the name of the official record book; the volume and page number; and the year in which the decision was handed down by the appellate court.

The following is a typical example of an appellate court citation: *State* v. *Tison*, 142 Ariz. 446 (1999). *State* v. *Tison* is the title of the decision; 142 refers to the volume number of the official record; Ariz. is an abbreviation for the state of Arizona, indicating that the decision is that of the Arizona Supreme Court; 446 is the page number where the decision begins; 1999 is the date or year in which the decision was handed down by the Arizona Supreme Court. Sometimes the date will precede the volume and page number. The way that the titles of the decisions refer to the persons involved varies among the states. Instead of the title being *State* v. *Tison*, the title may be *Tison* v. *State*, depending on the manner in which the appeal was taken. In some states, the word *People* or *Commonwealth* is substituted for *State*.

In addition to the appellate decision's being published in official publications, the decisions, particularly those of the U.S. Supreme Court, are included in the publications of private companies. A different citation is reflected for these publications. In order that a particular decision may be more readily located by a judge or an attorney, both the official citation and the citation of private companies are included when a case decision is referred to. For example, the West Publishing Company in St. Paul, Minnesota, publishes the decisions of the supreme courts of the various states. These decisions are reported by geographic areas. This reporting system is known as the National Reporter System. The supreme court decisions of the states of Iowa, Michigan, Minnesota, Nebraska, North Dakota, South Dakota, and Wisconsin are published in the *North Western Reporter*, and the citation carries the abbreviation of NW. Returning to the case of *State* v. *Tison*, 142 Ariz. 446, there may be the additional citation of 690 P.2d 747 (1999). The P. indicates that the decision can be located in the *Pacific Reporter* of the National Reporter System. The 2d indicates the second series of the *Pacific Reporter* volumes. The supreme court decisions of the states of Connecticut, Delaware, Maine, Maryland, New Hampshire, New Jersey, Pennsylvania, Rhode Island, and Vermont are published in the *Atlantic Reporter*, abbreviated as A. The supreme court decisions of the states of Illinois, Indiana, Massachusetts, New York, and Ohio are published in the *North Eastern Reporter*. The decisions of the supreme courts of the states of Alaska, Arizona, California, Colorado, Hawaii, Idaho, Kansas, Montana, Nevada, New Mexico, Oklahoma, Oregon, Utah, Washington, and Wyoming are published in the *Pacific Reporter*. The *South Eastern Reporter* includes the supreme court decisions of the states of Georgia, South Carolina, Virginia, and West Virginia. The *Southern Reporter* publishes the decisions of the supreme courts of the states of Alabama, Florida, Louisiana, and Mississippi. The *South Western Reporter* publishes the decisions of the supreme courts of the states of Arkansas, Missouri, Kentucky, Tennessee, and Texas. If a decision is handed down by the U.S. Supreme Court on an alleged violation of a constitutional guarantee, the following is an example of the official citation that would be used: *Batson* v. *Kentucky*, 476 U.S. 79 (1986). The U.S. Supreme Court decisions are also published by the West Publishing Company in a publication known as the *Supreme Court Reporter*, abbreviated as S.Ct. The *Batson* decision would be cited as 106 S.Ct. 1712. The Lawyers Cooperative Publishing Company also publishes the U.S. Supreme Court decisions in a publication known as the *Supreme Court Reporter* Lawyer's Edition, abbreviated as L.Ed. Thus the *Batson* decision may be cited as 90 L.Ed.2d 69. Or a decision may carry all three citations as follows: *Batson* v. *Kentucky*, 476 U.S. 79, 106 S.Ct. 1712, 90 L.Ed.2d 69 (1986).

In those states in which there is an appellate court below the supreme court, the decisions of these appellate courts are also published in an official publication. These decisions can usually be distinguished from the decisions of the supreme court by the abbreviation App. appearing after the abbreviation of the state.

CASE LAW

Recent Cases

Puckett v. *United States*, 129 S. Ct. 1423 (U.S. 2009)

James Puckett sought certiorari review of a judgment from the United States Court of Appeals for the Fifth Circuit, which affirmed his conviction and sentence after concluding that Puckett failed to meet his burden of showing plain error under Fed. R. Crim. P. 52(b) on his claim that the government failed to meet its obligations under a plea agreement.

The Court noted that the government conceded that it violated the plea agreement when it objected to a reduction for acceptance of responsibility after petitioner assisted in another crime while awaiting sentencing. The Court of Appeals found that petitioner forfeited the breach of plea agreement claim by failing to raise it in the district court. The Court found that contrary to petitioner's claim, the government's breach did not retroactively cause his guilty plea to have been unknowing or involuntary.

The Court noted that if a litigant believes that an error has occurred (to his detriment) during a federal judicial proceeding, he must object in order to preserve the issue. If he fails to do so in a timely manner, his claim for relief from the error is forfeited. No procedural principle is more familiar to the United States Supreme Court than that a right may be forfeited in criminal as well as civil cases by the failure to make timely assertion of the right before a tribunal having jurisdiction to determine it.

The Court stated that plea bargains are essentially contracts. When the consideration for a contract fails–that is, when one of the exchanged promises is not kept—the court does not say that the voluntary bilateral consent to the contract never existed, so that it is automatically and utterly void; the court says that the contract was broken. The party injured by the breach will generally be entitled to some remedy, which might include the right to rescind the contract entirely; but that is not the same thing as saying the contract was never validly concluded. When a

defendant agrees to a plea bargain, the government takes on certain obligations. If those obligations are not met, the defendant is entitled to seek a remedy, which might in some cases be rescission of the agreement, allowing him to take back the consideration he has furnished, that is, to withdraw his plea. But rescission is not the only possible remedy; in Santobello, the United States Supreme Court allowed for a resentencing at which the government would fully comply with the agreement—in effect, specific performance of the contract. In any case, it is entirely clear that a breach does not cause the guilty plea, when entered, to have been unknowing or involuntary. It is precisely because the plea was knowing and voluntary (and hence valid) that the government is obligated to uphold its side of the bargain.

Yeager v. *United States*, 129 S. Ct. 2360 (U.S. 2009)

Following an acquittal on fraud and securities fraud charges and a mistrial on insider trading and money laundering charges under 15 U.S.C.S. §§ 78j(b) and 78ff, 17 C.F.R. § 240.10b5-1, and 18 U.S.C.S. § 1957, defendant Yeager was retried on the mistried counts. He moved to dismiss. The district court denied the motion, and the United States Court of Appeals for the Fifth Circuit affirmed. The Supreme Court granted certiorari. The Supreme Court reversed and remanded the case to the U.S. Court of Appeals.

The Court noted that Yeager was accused of making false and misleading statements about a corporation's product development. He allegedly sold more than 700,000 shares of the corporation's stock at prices inflated by the alleged deception. The jury could not reach a verdict on the insider trading and money laundering counts. Defendant argued that his acquittals on the fraud and securities fraud charges precluded his retrial on the insider trading and money laundering charges under the issue-preclusion component of the Double Jeopardy Clause of the Fifth Amendment.

The Fifth Circuit determined that the jury must have found that defendant did not have any insider information and that a conflict between the acquittals and the hung counts barred the application of issue preclusion. The Supreme Court held that the hung counts should not have been considered in the issue-preclusion analysis. If possession of insider information was a critical issue of ultimate fact in all of the charges against defendant, a jury verdict that necessarily decided that issue in his favor would protect him from further prosecution. On remand, the Fifth Circuit could reconsider whether the acquittals necessarily decided that issue.

The Court noted that when an issue of ultimate fact has once been determined by a valid and final judgment of acquittal, it cannot again be litigated in a second trial for a separate offense. To decipher what a jury has necessarily decided, courts should examine the record of a prior proceeding, taking into account the pleadings, evidence, charge, and other relevant matter, and conclude whether a rational jury could have grounded its verdict upon an issue other than that which the defendant seeks to foreclose from consideration. The inquiry must be set in a practical frame and viewed with an eye to all the circumstances of the proceedings.

The Court also noted that a hung count is not a "relevant" part of the record of the prior proceeding for double jeopardy purposes. Because a jury speaks only through its verdict, its failure to reach a verdict cannot—by negative implication—yield a piece of information that helps put together the trial puzzle. "Record" is defined as the official report of the proceedings in a case, including the filed papers, verbatim transcript of the trial or hearing (if any), and tangible exhibits.

Summary

- The term "verdict" means a true declaration.
- In a bench trial, the judge decides the verdict.
- In a jury trial, the jury decides the verdict.
- If the judge believes that the prosecution has failed to establish the guilt of the defendant, the judge should enter a directed verdict of acquittal.
- A mistrial occurs when, because of an event, the judge concludes that a fair trial is impossible.

- The pronouncement of judgment is normally considered the oral sentencing of the defendant by the judge in open court, but technically it also includes the written judgment of the judge.
- The defendant may appeal his or her conviction or sentence or both.
- The prosecution has only limited rights of appeal.

Review Questions

1. What is a verdict?
2. Where is the verdict announced?
3. Must the defendant be present when the verdict is announced?
4. In what way are a mistrial and a new trial alike? In what way do they differ?
5. What is meant by an arrest of judgment?
6. What does the term "pronouncement of judgment" mean?
7. List three grounds on which the defendant may appeal a conviction.
8. Why is the prosecution limited in its right to appeal a verdict of acquittal in most jurisdictions?
9. What is the purpose of an appellate citation?
10. Explain the meaning of the following citation: *Batson* v. *Kentucky,* 476 U.S. 79 (1986).

Local Procedure

1. In your home state, may the prosecution appeal a verdict of acquittal?
2. If an appellate court reverses a conviction, may the defendant be retried?

Endnotes

1. *Arizona* v. *Washington,* 54 L.Ed. 2d 717 (1978).
2. 392 F. 2d (1967).
3. *People* v. *Huff,* 63 Cal.Rptr. 317 (1967).
4. 397 U.S. 711 (1969).

CHAPTER 16

Sentencing

You have so many options when you sentence. You can put a defendant on probation, order him to be put on work-release and go to a half-way house, or send him to an institution. But what it comes right down to is that there is no alternative that's any good. I guess you could call it a judge's dilemma.

—CHARLES HALLECK, JUDGE, SUPERIOR COURT OF THE DISTRICT OF COLUMBIA, 1976

Chapter Outline

History of Punishment

Types of Sentencing and Sentences

Death Penalty

Fines

Case Law

Summary

Key Terms

Definite sentence

Deterrence

Indefinite sentence

Indeterminate sentence

Probation

Rehabilitated

Suspended sentence

Learning Objectives

After completing this chapter, you should be able to:

- Describe various sentencing goals.
- Summarize the history of punishment and various types of punishment.
- Describe various types of sentences.
- Explain how an appropriate sentence is determined.
- Summarize the offender's rights during sentencing.

- Outline facts about and the arguments for and against the death penalty.
- Define terms related to sentencing.
- Explain the prohibitions against cruel and unusual punishment.

HISTORY OF PUNISHMENT

Imprisonment as Punishment

Under Roman law, imprisonment as punishment was illegal. In early English history, imprisonment was a means of holding the offender for trial and sentencing but not for punishment. The imprisonment of convicted offenders was, and still is, a troublesome and an expensive form of punishment.

Thus, we find that in earlier times, swifter and less expensive forms of punishment were inflicted. Some imprisonment as a form of punishment was used at common law in England for a few minor offenses, such as vagrancy. The ecclesiastical courts also imposed imprisonment on convicted clergymen in some instances. But death penalty, mutilation, and banishment were still the most frequently imposed forms of punishment. When a convicted person was banished from England, not only was the offender required to leave home, family, and friends, but his property was also confiscated by the king or the church. Banishment became another source of revenue for both king and church. It is alleged that as many as 100,000 persons were banished to the American colonies from England before the colonies received independence. As late as the early 1800s, England had more than 200 violations carrying a possible death penalty. But shortly thereafter, imprisonment and banishment to Australia were substituted for the death penalty as a form of punishment.

Present Sentencing Procedure

Each rule of conduct written throughout history has required that a punishment be established for convicted violators. Usually, the more serious the crime, the more severe the punishment. But which punishments should be inflicted for each particular crime has plagued society for centuries. Even today, the sentencing of a convicted offender may be the most complex part of the judicial process. Convicting the offender may be easier than deciding what should be done after the conviction. In primitive times, retaliation was the philosophy behind punishment, and the victim inflicted any punishment he or she desired. As more organized societies were developed, those in the judicial process began to make an effort to fit the penalty to the crime committed. Nevertheless, vengeance or retaliation against the offender was still prevalent in the thoughts of those trying to establish appropriate punishments. The problem became what penalty the offender should be subjected to in order to satisfy society's desire for vengeance and still have the penalty fit the crime. Thus, in the early sentencing process, a thief might have a hand cut off, a perjurer might have the tongue cut out, and a male adulterer might be castrated. The punishment continued to be cruel and severe.

Law in Practice

Sentencing Philosophies

Retribution	A person has infringed upon the rights of others and therefore deserves to be penalized to a degree commensurate with his or her criminal activity.
Incapacitation	To prevent crime, it is necessary to deprive the individual of the opportunity to commit crime (e.g., by confinement).
Deterrence	Punishing criminals to prevent future crimes. Punishment should focus on the crime committed, not on the defendant.
Specific Deterrence	Punishment designed to prevent a specific person from committing a future crime.
General Deterrence	Punishment designed to prevent others from committing future crime.
Rehabilitation	The concept that the criminal needs to be treated rather than punished. Punishment should be based on the needs of the defendant rather than the severity of the crime.

Law in Practice

What Should a Judge Consider Before Deciding on the Sentence? 18 U.S. Code § 3553

Imposition of a sentence

(a) Factors to be considered in imposing a sentence. The court shall impose a sentence sufficient, but not greater than necessary, to comply with the purposes set forth in paragraph (2) of this subsection. The court, in determining the particular sentence to be imposed, shall consider—

(1) the nature and circumstances of the offense and the history and characteristics of the defendant;

(2) the need for the sentence imposed—

(A) to reflect the seriousness of the offense, to promote respect for the law, and to provide just punishment for the offense;

(B) to afford adequate deterrence to criminal conduct;

(C) to protect the public from further crimes of the defendant; and

(D) to provide the defendant with needed educational or vocational training, medical care, or other correctional treatment in the most effective manner;

(3) the kinds of sentences available

[*Note:* The above federal statute applies only to federal judges.]

As time passed, imprisonment became the generally accepted way of punishing an offender, and society turned from the retaliatory approach to the isolation philosophy of punishment. Instead of trying to get even with the offender, society attempted to protect itself by imprisonment. As long as the offender was confined, society would be free of recurrent harm. As a result, when penitentiaries were first built in the United States, they were built with the idea of confining the offenders in maximum security to isolate them from society for the prescribed length of the sentence. The offenders became known as inmates. These penitentiaries were fortresslike structures. There were high walls with gun towers surrounding the buildings and cell blocks. Inmates spent much time locked in their cells. They were required to wear a distinctive uniform; for a long time, the uniform was made of black and white striped material. Many of the penitentiaries built in the late 1800s and early 1900s are still in use.

Isolation as Punishment

With punishment based on the isolation theory, the problem was how long an offender should be isolated for society's protection. Early in our history, the sentencing of an offender to imprisonment was solely the responsibility of the trial judge. In most instances, there were no guidelines to assist in determining how long an offender should be confined. As a result, there was a great discrepancy among judges in the sentence imposed for the same offense. Much depended on the judge's attitude and personal philosophy. When legislators began to establish appropriate penalties for each crime, they concentrated on the felony. There is considerable difference among states on the sentences that may be imposed. In some states, legislation has been passed providing a minimum and maximum number of years that an offender must serve for the conviction of a particular crime. For example, an offender convicted of burglary may receive a sentence of not less than one year in prison and not more than ten years. In other states, the law sets forth the maximum length of imprisonment that may be imposed. The law may provide that an offender may not be sentenced for a term longer than ten years. Under this system, an offender could be sentenced to a single hour in confinement, and this outcome has occurred in a few instances. As will be seen, under both systems, the trial judge has great leeway in deciding the sentence to be imposed. As legislators considered the penalties for felonies, misdemeanors were also considered. As with felonies, the length of the sentence to be imposed was usually left to the trial judge, with the maximum set forth in the state statutes.

Other Possible Penalties

Although imprisonment became one form of punishment, it is not the only penalty that may be imposed on a convicted offender. The types of sentences possible for criminal offenders are set forth in the codes of the various states. Penalty is still referred to as punishment in most codes. A penalty may be one or a combination of the following: imprisonment; fine; probation; suspended sentence; and in some states, the death penalty. Removal from public office and the disqualification to hold public office are also listed as forms of punishment in some states.

In a few jurisdictions, the terms "punishment" and "sentence" imply imprisonment. Therefore, probation is not considered to be a sentence but rather a disposition of the case. However, in most jurisdictions, the term sentence is the judgment of the court after conviction. The sentence is the final disposition of the trial, whether by imprisonment, suspended sentence, probation, or fine. But punishment is sometimes more closely associated with imprisonment than are other forms of sentence. Technically, punishment means any unpleasantness that the convicted offender may suffer. Any restrictions placed upon the offender, whether by imprisonment, suspended sentence, or probation, are forms of unpleasantness, as is the financial hardship imposed by a fine.

Deterrence

As reformists in the justice system continued to study punishment, its purpose shifted from isolation theory to **deterrence**. The movement to rehabilitate the offender followed. As our study will emphasize, the isolation approach has not been entirely abandoned, since there are inmates from whom society is safe only during their confinement. Neither deterrence nor rehabilitation is applicable to some hardened criminals.

Law in Practice

Identity Theft: A Top Concern

Determinate Sentencing	Until the 1970s in most jurisdictions, the judge imposed a specific number of years of imprisonment.
Indeterminate Sentencing	In the 1970s, many jurisdictions adopted indeterminate sentencing, which was based on the rehabilitation model and allowed judges to impose a sentencing range. Corrections officials and parole boards decided the actual length of time served.
Mandatory Minimums	In the 1960s, most jurisdictions required that a defendant serve a minimum prison sentence for selected offenses.
Return to Determinate Sentencing	1976: Maine became the first state in the modern era to return to determinate sentencing. 1977: California, Illinois, and Indiana enacted determinate sentencing laws.
Sentencing Guidelines	1980: Minnesota was the first state to create a sentencing commission and adopt sentencing guidelines.
Sentencing Reform Act	1984: Federal sentencing guidelines were adopted and parole was abolished in federal courts effective 1987.
Truth in Sentencing Laws	1984: These laws require offenders to serve a substantial portion of their prison sentence. They are most often used for violent offenses.
Statistical Evidence	1987: In *McCleskey* v. *Kemp,* the U.S. Supreme Court rejected the use of statistical information to prove racial discrimination in the use of the death penalty.
Federal Sentencing Guidelines	1989: In *Mistretta* v. *United States,* the U.S. Supreme Court held that the federal sentencing guidelines and Sentencing Commission do not violate the constitutional separation of powers.

Megan's Law	1994: New Jersey adopted a law requiring convicted sex offenders to register with local police departments following the rape and murder of seven-year-old Megan Kanka. Other states quickly enacted similar laws.
Polly's Law	1994: California passed a three-strikes law named after murder victim Polly Klaas. By 1995, twenty-four states and the federal government had passed three-strikes laws.
San Diego County v. *Romero*	1996: The California Supreme Court held that judges have discretion in counting prior convictions for purposes of applying the three-strikes law.
Edwards v. *United States*	1997: The U.S. Supreme Court refused to hear a challenge that federal sentencing laws dealing with crack cocaine are racially discriminatory.
United States v. *Booker* and *United States* v. *Fanfan*	2005: The U.S. Supreme Court held that the federal sentencing guidelines established under the Federal Sentencing Reform Act were unconstitutional. The Court held that the guidelines were not binding on judges and that compliance by judges was discretionary.
Roper v. *Simmons*	2005: The U.S. Supreme Court held that it was unconstitutional to impose the death penalty for a crime committed by an offender prior to his or her eighteenth birthday.
Baze v. *Rees*	2008: The constitutionality of a lethal injection protocol was affirmed because inmates had not carried their burden of showing that the risk of pain from maladministration of a concededly humane lethal injection protocol, and the failure to adopt untried and untested alternatives constituted cruel and unusual punishment under the Eighth Amendment.

Whatever sentence is imposed, its primary purpose is for the protection of society. The protection may be a result of isolating the offender from society or deterring the offender from committing future crimes, thus serving as an example to others inclined to commit crimes. The protection may also be through rehabilitation so that the offender will refrain from committing future crimes.

TYPES OF SENTENCING AND SENTENCES

To better understand the deterrence and rehabilitation theories of sentencing, we should discuss the type of sentence to be imposed. Perhaps in no other area of the justice system is there greater variance among states than in the sentencing phase of the justice proceedings.

Misdemeanor Sentencing

Upon conviction of a misdemeanor charge, the statutes of most states provide that the penalty imposed shall not exceed one year of imprisonment and/or a $1,000 fine. As stated, in most jurisdictions, the sentence is imposed by the trial judge, and if imprisonment is imposed, the time is generally served in a county or city jail. Most jurisdictions permit the judge to suspend the sentence and place the offender on probation; to grant probation with the provision that a certain amount of time must be spent in imprisonment; or merely to impose a fine.

Although the laws of most states provide that an offender convicted on a misdemeanor charge may not be sentenced for a period of more than one year, it is possible for him or her to serve more than a single year. This occurs when the offender is convicted on more than one misdemeanor charge. The judge may impose a sentence for one year on each charge and have the sentences run consecutively. A consecutive sentence is one that must be served before the next begins. A consecutive sentence for minor convictions is the exception; in most instances, if the offender is convicted on more than one charge, the judge will provide that the sentences are to be served concurrently, that is, at the same time.

Felony Sentencing

In a majority of the states, it is still the prerogative of the trial judge to impose the sentence. But in some states, the jury will impose the sentence, and in a few states, a jury must be impaneled to impose the sentence even though a jury trial has been waived. If the convicted offender is imprisoned, in some states the length of the sentence that must be served is determined by a board or committee appointed for that purpose. Generally, depending upon the jurisdiction, the types of imprisonment or sentence that may be imposed are the **definite sentence**, the **indefinite sentence**, or the **indeterminate sentence**. Although the sentences are classified as such, confusion has arisen because a definite sentence in one state may be known as an indefinite sentence in another state. Irrespective of their names, we will discuss each classification so that the reader will have some insight into the sentencing procedures followed in the various states.

DEFINITE SENTENCE As imprisonment began to be substituted for other forms of punishment, there were few guidelines to assist judges in deciding on the number of years to be imposed. Since retribution, or social retaliation, was still the primary purpose behind punishment, lengthy sentences were often imposed. Some judges became arbitrary and discriminatory in imposing sentences. To overcome this practice, legislation was passed in most states setting forth a pre-scribed sentence, or a definite mandatory sentence, to be required of one convicted of a particular offense. The theory behind the definite sentence was that it would be applied equally to all, irre-spective of race, religion, or social or economic status. The judges no longer had any control over the length of time to be served. On conviction, the mandatory sentence was imposed, and the offender was required to serve that period of time. After serving the prescribed period of time, the offender was released back into society, but never was the offender released prior to that time. The first major change in the definite sentencing procedure came with the introduction of the conditional release. A few states passed legislation permitting the governing board of the penal system to grant time off from the definite sentence for good behavior. If, as an inmate, the convicted offender's behavior was proper, the sentence was reduced by a few days each month. Good behavior principally consisted of complying with prison rules.

The definite sentence was severely criticized by reformists as being inflexible. The definite sentence did not permit any aggravating or mitigating factors, such as age of the offender, prior criminal record, or other circumstances surrounding the commission of the crime to be considered. Since the definite, or mandatory, sentencing procedure was inflexible, judges often dismissed a charge against an offender rather than impose a severe definite sentence when there were mitigating circumstances. An offender was then permitted to go unpunished. Because of the inflexibility of the definite sentence, it has all but disappeared from the justice system.

Indefinite Sentence

As the definite sentence lost favor, it was replaced by the indefinite sentence. In some states, the indefinite sentence is referred to as the indeterminate sentence or as the non-determinate sen-tence. Technically, there is a difference in the application of the indefinite, or non-determinate sentence and the indeterminate sentence. With the appearance of the indefinite sentence, legis-lative bodies passed statutes prescribing the maximum penalty that could be imposed on the convicted offender. For example, if an offender were convicted of armed robbery, the statute might state that the offender "shall not be imprisoned for a period of more than thirty-five years." Under the indefinite sentencing procedure, the imposition of the sentence was returned to the judge in most states. A few states provided for the jury to impose the sentence.

The theory behind the indefinite sentence was that it enabled the sentence to fit the offender and not the crime. The sentencing body would weigh the situation and impose the number of years deemed to be just under the circumstances. Since sentencing is far from an exact science, determining the number of years to be served was, and still is, a difficult prob-lem. The problem is magnified because an individual's future conduct is difficult, if not impossible, to predict. Society's reaction to imposed sentences is also unpredictable. There are persons who would lead us to believe that vengeance plays no part in the sentencing procedure of our civilized society. However, realistically, society's vengeance may still be felt in a community when an atrocious crime is committed. Thus, in imposing a sentence, it must be of sufficient length to satisfy the desire for social retaliation but not so long as to discourage the offender from wanting to reform. In most instances, when legislation was passed prescribing the maximum sentence to be imposed, that time was long enough that the most vengeful individual could not take exception. It was the duty of the sentencing body to impose the exact length of a sentence. Since there were no guidelines on the length of an equitable sentence, it often reflected the judge's or the jury's feelings and philosophy. There were wide discrepancies between judges and juries in the sentences imposed for the same offenses. Also, some judges became very lenient in the sentences they imposed.

To overcome this leniency and to assist in establishing some sentencing guidelines, the legislatures of several states passed statutes that prescribed both a minimum and a maximum sentence. For example, on a conviction of armed robbery, the penalty prescribed may state that the offender "shall not serve less than five years' and not more than thirty-five years' imprisonment." It became the responsibility of the judge or jury to decide on an appropriate number of years between the minimum and the maximum allowed.

PRESENTENCE INVESTIGATIONS To assist judges in attempting to arrive at an equitable sentence and to more nearly make the sentence fit the offender, many judges require a presentence investigation. The presentence investigation is usually conducted by a staff member of the probation department. It generally includes such matters as the offender's family status, educational background, work experience, and prior criminal record. It also includes circumstances surrounding the commission of the crime. Whether it was a crime of passion, a thrill, or an emotional involvement may have an impact on the sentence to be prescribed. The offender's attitude toward the crime will be reported. The investigation will also show whether the offender is remorseful over having committed the crime or is only unhappy about being caught. Even with the assistance of the information contained in a presentence report, the sentence to be imposed still involves a difficult decision for the judge. Not all judges have staffs available to them to make presentence investigations, so in most instances, they must rely solely on their contact with the offender during the trial and their own insight regarding what sentence should be imposed. The judge may consider the mental state of the offender at the time the crime was committed. Was the offender in a state of diminished capacity? Was his or her mental condition so diminished by intoxication or drugs that the offender could not have formulated an intent, created a motive, or entertained malice toward the victim? If so, the judge may impose a lesser penalty. Some states have permitted diminished capacity to be pleaded as a defense to a criminal charge, but currently this use has been abolished in most states and may be considered only by the judge at the time of sentencing.

JURIES IMPOSING SENTENCES Juries generally do not have access to any presentence investigative material. When the jury imposes the sentence, it is too often nothing more than a calculated guess on what is appropriate. Often juries will be either extremely harsh or very lenient in sentencing, because of deep emotional involvement with a crime committed in their community. The sentence of the jury is often the result of a compromise brought about by bargaining over the verdict. Attempting to get a jury to arrive at what may be an equitable sentence is often more difficult than reaching a unanimous verdict. One may wonder why juries are permitted to impose the sentence in some states in view of the problems involved. This practice is a carryover from colonial days. The colonists frequently had unpleasant experiences with the royal judges, as well as some postindependence judges, who were too arbitrary and discriminatory in the imposition of sentences. To overcome these problems, a few state legislatures provided that the imposition of the sentence was to be the prerogative of the jury.

Whether a sentence is imposed by a judge or a jury, it will stipulate the exact number of years to be served. At first glance, it would appear that this sentencing procedure is of the definite type. Definite and indefinite sentences differ in that with the definite sentence, the law prescribes a definite mandatory number of years that must be served by all offenders on conviction of a particular crime. With the indefinite sentence, the law prescribes either a maximum amount of time that may be imposed or a minimum and a maximum, and from this indefinite period of time, the judge or jury will decide upon a definite amount of time for the sentence.

With the passing of time and the growing interest in rehabilitation, the indefinite sentence has become even more indefinite because, after serving a portion of the sentence, the inmate may become eligible for parole, thereby shortening the time to be served. Parole will be discussed more fully later in the chapter. Because the exact number of years that must be served is indefinite, or indeterminate, and because of the possibility of parole, this sentencing procedure is referred to as the indeterminate sentence in some states.

Indeterminate Sentence

The true indeterminate sentence removes the sentencing of a prescribed number of years from the hands of a judge or a jury. The length of the sentence is determined by a board or committee appointed for that purpose sometime after the imprisonment has been pronounced. The primary purpose of the indeterminate sentence is to permit the sentence to more nearly fit the offender and to assist in the rehabilitation process. But this was not the original purpose of the indeterminate sentence. On the continent of Europe during the seventeenth and eighteenth centuries, the indeterminate sentence was used to lengthen the sentences of dangerous criminals for protective detention after they had served their original sentences. This procedure eventually died out in Europe. The indeterminate sentence was adopted in this country, but for a different reason. This sentence permitted a mitigation of the sentence that might otherwise have been imposed with the view that the indeterminate sentence would assist the offender in reforming. When this sentence was first adopted in this country, the offender was imprisoned for an indeterminate time in order to accomplish physical, emotional, and mental rehabilitation so that his or her renewed freedom would no longer endanger the welfare of society. Once the offender arrived at this status, as decided by a board of managers of the penal system, he or she was entitled to be released. Thus, the inmate could be held for an indeterminate period, even for an entire lifetime—until reaching that point of physical, emotional, and mental rehabilitation where there was no threat to society on his or her release.

Law in Practice

Ayers v. *Belmontes,* 549 U.S. 7 (2006)

Fernando Belmontes, the respondent, was tried in 1982 in the Superior Court of the State of California in and for the County of San Joaquin. A jury returned a verdict of murder in the first degree and then determined he should be sentenced to death. The issue before the U.S. Supreme Court concerns a jury instruction in the sentencing phase. In the sentencing phase of his trial, the defendant offered mitigating evidence, including evidence of a pre-crime religious conversion, to show that he would make positive contributions to society if he were incarcerated instead of executed. The trial court instructed the jury under Cal. Penal Code § 190.3(k) (1988) to consider any other circumstance which extenuated the gravity of the crime even though it was not a legal excuse for the crime. The inmate argued that this instruction by the trial judge violated his Eighth Amendment right to present all mitigating evidence in a capital sentencing proceeding because it did not fully consider his precrime evidence.

How Would You Rule?

JUSTICE KENNEDY delivered the Court's opinion.

The Supreme Court found that there was not a reasonable likelihood that the jury applied the instruction in a way that prevented the consideration of constitutionally relevant evidence. As the inmate sought to extrapolate future behavior from precrime conduct, his mitigation theory was analogous to good-character evidence, which fell within factor (k)'s purview.

The instructions as a whole made it clear that the jury was to take a broad view of mitigating evidence; nothing barred the jury from viewing the inmate's future prospects as extenuating the gravity of the crime. Where a defendant in a death penalty cases seeks to extrapolate future behavior from precrime conduct, his mitigation theory is analogous to good-character evidence and held to fall within the purview of Cal. Penal Code § 190.3(k) (1988). Both types of evidence suggest the crime stemmed more from adverse circumstances than from an irredeemable character. A "forward-looking" future-dangerousness inquiry is not independent of an assessment of personal culpability.

Very few states have adopted the true indeterminate sentencing procedure. Under this procedure, the legislature prescribes both the minimum and the maximum terms for each offense punishable by imprisonment in the state prison. Upon conviction of such an offense, and if neither a new trial nor probation is granted, the trial judge does not specify the length of imprisonment but merely sentences the defendant as prescribed by law. A board appointed by the governor then determines, within statutory limits, the length of time that the offender will actually be required to serve. This board is frequently referred to as the parole board.

The indeterminate sentence has been interpreted to mean that on being sentenced as prescribed by law, the offender has been sentenced to the maximum time prescribed by the statutes for the particular offense. But the indeterminate sentence process permits the shortening of the offender's sentence on a showing of rehabilitation. The theory behind the indeterminate sentence is to give the inmate a great incentive to reform so that the sentence will be reduced in length from the maximum prescribed.

When Is an Offender Rehabilitated?

Determining when an offender has been **rehabilitated** to a point where there is no longer a threat to society on release is an almost impossible task. Some never reach that point and have to serve the maximum time. However, each inmate is entitled eventually to have the length of his or her sentence determined by the board. In making the determination, the board will take many things into consideration. Each penal institution maintains a file or cumulative folder on each inmate. The board will study the file and hold a hearing at which the inmate may appear to plead the case. Generally, the hearing will not be held until the inmate has served six months to one year of the maximum time prescribed. By holding the hearing after the inmate has started serving a portion of the sentence, the board has an opportunity to study the inmate's reaction to incarceration, since these data, as well as much other information, will be included in the cumulative file. The file will contain the name and age of the inmate, the place and time of conviction, the charge for which the inmate was convicted, and the minimum and maximum sentence prescribed by the statutes. The presentence investigative report will be included to provide the board with background knowledge on the inmate. Also included may be the results of tests given to the inmate upon incarceration, as well as a record of the inmate's efforts to improve academically by attempting to learn some salable work skill. The board will consider the general attitude of the inmate toward society, law, and authority as expressed by the inmate in the appearance before the board.

After a review of the entire matter, the board will endeavor to arrive at some equitable length of time to be served. The board may conclude that the inmate should serve six years on a sentence prescribed by law to be not less than one year and not more than ten years. The board may conclude further that the inmate should serve four of those years in actual confinement and the other two years on parole. After the time has been set, if the inmate demonstrates an inability to conform to prison regulations or no attempt to reform has been made, the board has the authority to reset the length of the sentence, even requiring the inmate to serve the maximum time. For this reason, it has been interpreted that an offender sentenced under the indeterminate sentence procedure is sentenced to the maximum prescribed, and any time less than the maximum is based on the rehabilitation of the inmate. It has been held that the indeterminate sentence grants the inmate no vested right to a permanently fixed length of sentence at any time.

Advantages and Disadvantages of the Indeterminate Sentence

The indeterminate sentence has been attacked by inmates on the allegation that it violates the due process of law because of its uncertainty, and, as such, is cruel and unusual punishment. However, to date, these attacks have been unsuccessful, since the courts have found that the sentence is fixed at the maximum and that it is the inmate's reformation that permits the maximum to be reduced. The courts have held that as long as a minimum and a maximum sentence prescribed by the legislature are not disproportionate to the offense committed, the sentence is not cruel and unusual. It has been stated that whether a particular punishment is disproportionate to the offense is a question of degree. Courts have described a disproportionate punishment as one in which the length of the sentence is so disproportionate as to shock the moral sense of all reasonable people or the community.

The proponents of the true indeterminate sentencing procedure allege that a board is in a better position than a judge to determine the sentence that should be imposed. The board comes in contact with all convicted offenders who are imprisoned, whereas judges are in contact with only those convicted in their particular court. The board therefore is able to view the inmates' progress in an overview as one large unit and can follow this progress during confinement as well as parole. As such, the board can weigh what sentence is more likely to be equitable. The board also has personal contact with the inmate during confinement and, before determining the sentence, can study his or her responses to treatment over a period of months. The judge must make a sentence determination at the end of a trial—without any guidelines on a defendant's reaction to the rehabilitation processes. As previously stated, judges under both the indeterminate and the indefinite sentencing procedures are able to retain jurisdiction over a defendant by granting probation in lieu of imposing a sentence of imprisonment.

Suspended Sentence and Probation

The right of benefit of clergy was carried a step further in England during the thirteenth and fourteenth centuries. This right may be called the forerunner of the **suspended sentence**. Under certain circumstances, an accused was permitted to have a trial transferred from the king's court to the ecclesiastical court. By so doing, the offender was able to avoid the death penalty but still might be imprisoned for life. However, in most instances, the offender was only mutilated in some minor way and released back into society. The philosophy of the right of benefit of clergy was brought to America by the colonists. Instead of the possibility of a transfer of courts, either some other punishment was substituted for the death penalty or the judge might suspend carrying out the death penalty for the lifetime of the offender, depending on good behavior.

The suspended sentence is recognized in our system of justice today, but in most instances it is coupled with a period of probation. In many jurisdictions, there cannot be a suspended sentence without probation being imposed for a prescribed period. In those jurisdictions where the suspended sentence is permitted without probation, the judge merely suspends imposing a sentence. The offender is free to return to society. Generally, no restrictions are placed on the offender other than good behavior during the period of the suspended sentence. If the offender breaks the law again, the judge may impose a sentence on the original charge as well as the new charge if the offender is convicted.

Probation, like the suspended sentence, permits the convicted offender to remain free from custody, but by being placed on probation, the offender is under the supervision of some person who assists him or her in leading a law-abiding life. The person is usually a public officer known as a probation officer. The primary purpose of the suspended sentence and probation is to rehabilitate the offender. When the convicted offender is granted a suspended sentence or probation, it is assumed that there is no threat to society by the offender's remaining free from custody.

ORIGINS OF PROBATION Probation, primarily of American origin, is an outgrowth of the suspended sentence and is the newest form of correctional treatment for the offender. Probation is believed to have begun in America when a cobbler, John Augustus, attended a police court in Boston, Massachusetts, in August 1841. He decided to post bail for a man charged with being a common drunkard. The judge permitted Augustus to post the bail and ordered the defendant to return in three weeks for sentencing. When the man returned, the judge noted an improvement in his attitude. Instead of sentencing the defendant to imprisonment, the judge fined him one cent and court costs. Encouraged by his first experience, Augustus posted bail for other first offenders who seemed worthy of consideration. In each case, Augustus agreed to supervise the activities of the offenders and to report to the judge on their progress. Augustus continued this work until his death in 1859. It was continued by Rufus R. Cook, a chaplain of a county jail. In 1878, Massachusetts passed a law providing for the appointment of a paid probation officer for the courts in Boston. At the same time, experiments were being made in the use of probation in England. Although probation made its appearance in America in the mid-1800s, it was not until well into the twentieth century that probation as a form of sentencing came into extensive use.

Probation is a form of clemency, and an offender has no inherent right to demand to be placed on probation. In most states, there are certain violations for which probation may not be granted. Otherwise, in most jurisdictions, the judge has wide discretionary power to grant probation. In most instances, the judge's decision is final. Prior to granting probation, the judge may, or in some cases must, have a probation or presentence investigation conducted to determine whether the offender could benefit from probation. This investigation is generally conducted by a probation officer, who may or may not give a recommendation on whether probation should be granted. In most states, the recommendation is not binding upon the judge, and probation may be granted even though not recommended by the probation officers, or vice versa. Probation is often granted as a result of plea bargaining. But the mere fact that an offender enters a guilty plea is no assurance that there will be benefits from probation or that society is better protected by the granting of probation.

One of two procedures is usually followed in granting probation. On conviction, the judge merely suspends pronouncing any sentence and places the offender on probation for a prescribed time. Or the judge may impose a sentence such as a prescribed period of imprisonment, but the execution of the sentence will be suspended, and the offender will be placed on probation for a prescribed time. The time that the offender may be placed on probation is generally at the discretion of the judge, but in most instances it is not for a period longer than the maximum time of imprisonment for the particular crime.

CONDITIONS OF PROBATION The general condition imposed on the offender, when placed on probation, is that he or she be a law-abiding individual during the period of probation. Many other restrictions may also be imposed at this time. For example, the judge may restrict the offender's area of travel and associates, or the offender may be prohibited from patronizing bars. Restitution for damages or injuries caused while violating the law may be required. In some instances, as a condition of probation, the offender must agree to having his or her person or home searched without a warrant at any time by either a probation officer or a law enforcement officer. When these conditions are imposed, however, it is generally held that the search may not be a harassment procedure but that it is to be made only when there is probable cause to believe that the offender has violated probation. Whenever restrictions are placed on an offender, it has been stated that the restrictions should have some connection with the crime committed. For example, in one case, the defendant was convicted of grand theft. Prior to the conviction, the defendant had given birth to three illegitimate children fathered by different men. As a condition of probation, the judge advised the defendant that she was not to become pregnant out of wedlock again during the probation period. She did become pregnant out of wedlock, and the judge then revoked her probation and sentenced her to prison. She appealed the sentence as constituting cruel and unusual punishment. The appellate court agreed with her and reversed the case, sending it back to the judge for further consideration. The appellate court stated that the trial judge might be commended for the attempt to prevent illegitimacy but that the attempt should have been made in a different manner, since the restriction on pregnancy had no connection with the crime committed. However, judges frequently require a person placed on probation to do work for charity organizations, a requirement that appears to have no connection with the crime committed. There are times when a judge may grant probation with the stipulation that a short time be spent in imprisonment. Some reformists have criticized the use of imprisonment for one placed on probation as being a handicap to the rehabilitation process. Others justify the imprisonment as being a means of awakening the offender to the realization of what could happen if probation is violated.

There is a difference among states on the question of whether a convicted offender may refuse probation. In some states, it is held that the offender does not have to give consent to being placed on probation; therefore, there is no right to refuse to accept probation. In other states, it is held that the convicted offender must give consent to be placed on probation. Although probation is generally preferable to imprisonment, a judge, in granting probation, may impose certain restrictions that the offender may feel are intolerable. In this case, the offender may prefer a limited time of imprisonment. Since probation is not considered a form of punishment but a rehabilitation process, it is believed that the convicted offender should be willing to be placed on probation. Otherwise, the rehabilitative effect of probation is lost. There are a few states in which an offender may be placed on probation prior to conviction. On a complaint being filed, an offender can be placed on probation, thereby avoiding a conviction. It is felt that the consent of the offender is necessary under these circumstances. In some states, this procedure is known as diversion.

REVOCATION OF PROBATION If, during the period of probation, the offender, known as a probationer, violates the law or fails to abide by other restrictions that may have been imposed, the probation may be revoked and the probationer sentenced to imprisonment. Whether or not probation is revoked is at the discretion of the trial judge. In *Gagnon* v. *Scarpelli,* the U.S. Supreme Court held that before probation may be revoked, the probationer is entitled to a hearing, stating the following:

> Probation revocation, like parole revocation, is not a stage of a criminal prosecution, but does result in a loss of liberty. Accordingly, we hold that a probationer, like a parolee, is entitled to a preliminary and final revocation hearing, under the conditions specified in *Morrissey* v. *Brewer.* . . .

CRITICISM OF PROBATION Generally, one would not quarrel with the primary purpose of probation, which is rehabilitating the offender. But many persons both in and out of the justice system believe that judges grant probation too often. Probation has been granted to prevent overcrowding of prisons. It has also been granted to offenders who have no incentive to mend their ways. In one case, for example, an offender was convicted of burglary and placed on three years' probation. While on probation, the offender was convicted on another burglary charge, and the same judge again placed the offender on probation, to run concurrently with the probationary period of the prior conviction. For this reason, some states have passed legislation that prohibits an offender from being placed on probation after conviction for certain crimes or for using a gun while committing crimes. In spite of the efforts to curb the use of probation, it is still used extensively. At any given time, more than two million persons are on probation in the United States.

Law in Practice

Punishment for Sex Offenders

"Once a sex offender, always a sex offender?"

Anonymous

Jill Levenson in a recent survey found that 75 percent of the general public believes that sex offenders will reoffend. Sex crime researchers Hanson and Morton-Bourgon conducted a large-scale analysis of recidivism rates among adult sex offenders and concluded that the recidivism rate was 24 percent within fifteen years, which is considerably less than the rate for many other crimes. The researchers noted that it was 35 percent for child molesters of boy victims.

Levenson also found in her study that 50 percent of the general public believes that treatment for sex offenders is not effective. Hanson and Morton-Bourgon concluded that treatment, especially counseling, does make a difference. They also concluded that the more recent studies indicate significantly larger treatment benefits than do the older studies. The researchers also found that the majority of treatment programs include two components: cognitive-behavior, which aims to change sexual deviant thoughts, and relapse prevention, which aims to teach sex offenders how to anticipate and cope with problems.[1]

DEATH PENALTY

The toughest part of this job is sentencing. I've lost all kinds of sleep over sentences. I find it dreadful.

—MALCOLM MUIR, JUDGE, U.S. DISTRICT COURT, 1982

I think a judge's education is very imperfect when it comes to the sentencing process especially in death penalty cases.

—EDWARD DAVIS, FORMER CHIEF OF POLICE, LOS ANGELES, 1973

Heated arguments have taken place over the years concerning the merits of the death penalty. Those who oppose the death penalty do so principally on the grounds that it has no place in a civilized society. They hold that the death penalty is a form of cruel and unusual punishment, and further allege that it does not act as a deterrent. An equal number contend that the death penalty is a deterrent and as such should be retained. But they concede that the deterrent effect does not function effectively, because, as previously pointed out, for any deterrent to be effective, the punishment must be swift and sure. In fact, the time interval between the imposition of the death penalty and the execution makes the death penalty anything but swift in coming and sure in being carried out.

Cruel and Unusual Punishment

The question of whether or not the death penalty is cruel and unusual punishment in violation of the Eighth Amendment was placed before the U.S. Supreme Court in the case of *Furman* v. *Georgia.*[2] The Court held in that case that the death penalty as such was not cruel and unusual punishment but that the indiscriminate manner in which it was applied made the death penalty cruel and unusual punishment in violation of the Eighth Amendment.

The Court in the *Furman* decision indicated that perhaps, if the death sentence was to be made mandatory for all of equal guilt, the sentence would not be discriminatory and thus would not violate the cruel and unusual punishment provision of the Eighth Amendment. As a result, many state legislatures passed statutes making the death penalty mandatory on conviction for certain crimes. This mandatory sentence took from the jury or judge the right to determine the sentence to be imposed on conviction for crimes previously carrying the alternate sentence of life imprisonment or death.

However, the U.S. Supreme Court, in *Woodson* v. *North Carolina,*[3] overruled as cruel and unusual punishment a North Carolina statute making the death penalty mandatory. The Court held that such a statute did not allow any consideration to be given to the character and record of the offender. The Court stated, "Consideration of both the offender and the offense in order to arrive at a just and appropriate sentence has been viewed as a progressive and humanizing development."

Consequently, those state statutes making the death penalty mandatory had to be revised to conform with the *Woodson* decision. Statutes were then passed allowing the jury or judge to take into consideration aggravating or mitigating circumstances in imposing the alternate sentence of life imprisonment or death. A Georgia statute of this nature was upheld by the U.S. Supreme Court in *Gregg* v. *Georgia.*[4] In reaffirming that the death penalty was not in violation of the Eighth Amendment guarantee against cruel and unusual punishment, the Court stated the following:

> The imposition of the death penalty for the Crime of murder has a long history of acceptance both in the United States and in England. The common-law rule imposed a mandatory death sentence on all convicted murderers. And the penalty continued to be used into the 20th century by most American States, although the breadth of the common-law rule was diminished, initially by narrowing the class of murders to be punished by death and subsequently by widespread adoption of laws expressly granting juries the discretion to recommend mercy.
>
> It is apparent from the text of the Constitution itself that the existence of capital punishment was accepted by the Framers. At the time the Eighth Amendment was ratified, capital punishment was a common sanction in every State. Indeed, the First Congress of the United States enacted legislation providing death as the penalty for specified crimes. The Fifth Amendment, adopted at the same time as the Eighth, contemplated the continued existence of the capital sanction by imposing certain limits on the prosecution of capital cases: "No person shall be held to answer for a capital, or otherwise infamous, crime unless on a presentment or indictment of a Grand Jury . . . ; nor shall any person be subject for the same offense to be twice put in jeopardy of life or limb; . . . nor be deprived of life, liberty, or property, without due process of law. . . ." And the Fourteenth Amendment, adopted over three-quarters of a century later, similarly contemplates the existence of the capital sanction in providing that no State shall deprive any person of "life, liberty, or property" without due process of law.
>
> For nearly two centuries, this Court, repeatedly and often expressly, has recognized that capital punishment is not invalid per se.

In holding that the death penalty is not a violation of the guarantee against cruel and unusual punishment, the dissenting justices in the *Furman* case stated as follows:

> Punishments are cruel when they involve torture or a lingering death; but the punishment of death is not cruel, within the meaning of that word as used in the Constitution. It implies there something inhuman and barbarous, something more than the mere extinguishment of life. . . .
>
> The traditional humanity of modem Anglo-American law forbids the infliction of unnecessary pain in the execution of the death sentence. . . . The cruelty against which the Constitution protects a convicted man is cruelty in the method of

punishment, not the necessary suffering involved in any method employed to extinguish life humanely.

The gas chamber, electric chair, hanging, lethal injection, and firing squad have all been sanctioned by the Court as humane means of carrying out the death penalty.

In the *Gregg* decision, the Court made some interesting comments on the death penalty as a deterrent as well as a necessary form of punishment to satisfy society's demand for justice. The Court stated the following:

> The death penalty is said to serve two principal social purposes: retribution and deterrence of capital crimes by prospective offenders.
>
> In part, capital punishment is an expression of society's moral outrage at particularly offensive conduct. This function may be unappealing to many, but it is essential in an ordered society that asks its citizens to rely on legal processes rather than self-help to vindicate their wrongs. "The instinct for retribution is part of the nature of man and channeling that instinct in the administration of criminal justice serves an important purpose in promoting the stability of a society governed by law. When people begin to believe that organized society is unwilling or unable to impose upon criminal offenders the punishment they deserve, then there are sown the seeds of anarchy—of self-help, vigilante justice, and lynch law." Retribution is no longer the dominant objective of the criminal law, but neither is it a forbidden objective nor one inconsistent with our respect for the dignity of men. Indeed, the decision that capital punishment may be the appropriate sanction in extreme cases is an expression of the community's belief that certain crimes are themselves so grievous an affront to humanity that the only adequate response may be the penalty of death.
>
> Statistical attempts to evaluate the worth of the death penalty as a deterrent to crimes by potential offenders have occasioned a great deal of debate. The results simply have been inconclusive. Although some of the studies suggest that the death penalty may not function as a significantly greater deterrent than lesser penalties, there is no convincing empirical evidence either supporting or refuting this view. We may nevertheless assume safely that there are murderers, such as those who act in passion, for whom the threat of death has little or no deterrent effect. But for many others the death penalty undoubtedly is a significant deterrent.

Alternate Sentencing Procedure

Since the *Woodson* decision held that the alternate sentencing procedure must be followed, it is important to discuss the procedure's development. For many years, the death penalty was made mandatory upon the conviction of certain specified crimes in most states. Jurors aware of this situation knew that on voting for a guilty verdict, they were voting for the execution of a human being. Many jurors had reservations about the death penalty. When it came time to vote on the verdict, they could not bring themselves to vote guilty irrespective of the strength of the evidence of guilt. This inability to vote for a guilty verdict caused many trials to end with hung juries. In an effort to overcome this problem, the legislatures of many states enacted statutes setting forth alternate sentences of life imprisonment or death on conviction of certain crimes. The statutes further provided that the jury in the jury trial was to make the decision about which penalty was to be imposed. Under these circumstances, the juror with reservations about the death penalty could still vote for a guilty verdict but be in a position to vote for life imprisonment after the conviction. In 2002, the U.S. Supreme Court held that the factual determination about the existence of "aggravating factors" that make a convicted murder eligible for the death penalty must be made by the jury and not the judge.

When the alternate sentence was made possible, one of two procedures was generally followed. In some states, a trial was first held to determine the guilt or innocence of the accused. If the accused was found guilty, a second trial was held to determine whether the death penalty was to be imposed or whether the sentence was to be life imprisonment. In other states, only one trial was held. The jury would deliberate first on the guilt or innocence of the accused, and, if the jury voted a guilty verdict, then they would then deliberate on the penalty to be imposed. Both procedures have received the sanction of the U.S. Supreme Court. Under both procedures, the juror with reservations about imposition of the death penalty could still vote for a guilty verdict without voting for the death of the defendant.

During the trial or sentence determination hearing, the jury must consider both aggravating and mitigating circumstances, and weigh them against each other. The *Gregg* decision listed such aggravating circumstances as a murder committed by a convict under a sentence of imprisonment; a murder committed by one previously convicted of murder or a felony involving violence; a murder committed at the time the defendant committed another murder; a murder committed while committing or attempting to commit robbery, rape, arson, burglary, or kidnapping; a murder committed for the purpose of avoiding arrest; and a murder committed in an especially cruel or atrocious manner. As to mitigating circumstances, the Court suggested that it be taken into consideration whether the defendant had no significant prior criminal record; whether the murder was committed while the defendant was under some emotional stress; whether the defendant was an accomplice of another person who actually did the murder and whether the defendant's participation in the homicidal act was relatively minor; whether at the time of the murder the defendant was acting under a diminished capacity; and whether the defendant was of youthful age.

In most jurisdictions, when the death penalty is imposed, the case is automatically appealed to the highest appellate court within the jurisdiction. The court will review the facts of the case to determine whether the conviction should be affirmed and whether the death penalty is justified from the evidence presented. The appellate court may affirm both the conviction and the death penalty, or it may affirm the conviction but hold that the death penalty is not justified under the circumstances. In this instance, either the case will be returned to the trial court for revision of the sentence or, depending on the court, the life sentence may be imposed automatically. If the appellate court reverses the conviction, the penalty phase will not be considered.

The death penalty may be imposed in approximately two-thirds of the states and within the federal system, yet opponents undoubtedly will continue to attempt to have it abolished as being cruel and unusual punishment. In fact, in their dissenting opinions in the *Gregg* decision, Justices Marshall and Brennan were adamant in their contention that the death penalty is cruel and unusual punishment and thus a violation of the Eighth Amendment guarantee.

Death Penalty as Excessive Punishment for the Crime of Rape

Appellate courts have from time to time held that a particular sentence is excessive and disproportionate to the crime committed, and thus the sentence is cruel and unusual punishment. In such an instance, the sentence will be set aside and the case referred to the trial court for resentencing. What is considered excessive punishment is not easily determined and often rests largely upon the personal viewpoints of the justices involved. In *Coker* v. *Georgia*,[5] the U.S. Supreme Court held that the death penalty for the rape of an adult woman was excessive and disproportionate to the crime.

Law in Practice

Kennedy v. *Louisiana*, 554 U.S. 407 (U.S. 2008)

Patrick Kennedy, a Louisiana prisoner, was sentenced to death and sought certiorari review of a judgment from the Supreme Court of Louisiana, which upheld his capital sentence following his conviction under La. Rev. Stat. Ann. § 14:42 (1997 and Supp. 1998) for the aggravated rape of an eight-year-old child. The Supreme Court reversed the judgment and remanded the case for further proceedings.

The Court noted that the Supreme Court of Louisiana rejected Kennedy's argument that the death penalty for the rape of a child under the age of twelve was disproportionate, and it upheld the constitutionality of La. Rev. Stat. Ann. § 14:42 under the Eighth Amendment.

The Court, however, held that the Eighth Amendment barred the State of Louisiana from imposing the death penalty on Kennedy. Based both on consensus and its own independent judgment, the Court held that a death sentence for one who raped but did not kill a child, and who did not intend to assist another in killing the child, was unconstitutional under the Eighth and Ninth Amendments. After reviewing the history of the death penalty for the crime of child rape, current state statutes and new enactments, and the number of executions since 1964, the Court concluded that there was a national consensus against capital punishment for the crime of child rape. The Court also concluded in

its independent judgment that the death penalty was not a proportional punishment for the crime of child rape.

The Court noted that the Eighth Amendment, applicable to the States through the Fourteenth Amendment, provides that excessive bail shall not be required, nor excessive fines imposed, nor cruel and unusual punishments inflicted. The Eighth Amendment proscribes all excessive punishments, as well as cruel and unusual punishments that may or may not be excessive. The United States Supreme Court explained in *Atkins* and *Roper* that the Eighth Amendment's protection against excessive or cruel and unusual punishments flows from the basic precept of justice that punishment for a crime should be graduated and proportioned to the offense. Whether this requirement has been fulfilled is determined not by the standards that prevailed when the Eighth Amendment was adopted in 1791 but by the norms that currently prevail. The Eighth Amendment draws its meaning from the evolving standards of decency that mark the progress of a maturing society. This is because the standard of extreme cruelty is not merely descriptive, but necessarily embodies a moral judgment. The standard itself remains the same, but its applicability must change as the basic mores of society.

Subsequent Death Penalty Legislation

Since the *Coker* decision was handed down, the U.S. Supreme Court has invalidated the death penalty in two other landmark cases, establishing new approaches to death penalty limitations. In the case of *Godfrey* v. *Georgia*,[6] the Court held that the sentence of death amounted to cruel and unusual punishment when pronounced on the defendant Godfrey, even though two murders had been committed. The Court quoted the Georgia statute providing that the death penalty could be invoked when the offense of murder was "outrageously or wantonly vile, horrible or inhuman." The Court held that to fall within that category, the evidence must demonstrate that the offender committed the murder through torture, depravity of mind or an aggravated battery before killing the victim. In the Godfrey case, the facts indicate that the defendant shot both victims in the head with a shotgun and that they died instantly. There was no evidence of serious suffering by the victims that would justify the death penalty under the Georgia statute. There were dissenting justices in that case who felt that the killings by the defendant did fall within the statute as being outrageously or wantonly vile, horrible, and inhuman. In the case of *Enmund* v. *Florida*,[7] the facts reveal that Enmund and two other defendants entered into a conspiracy to rob a victim of money. The three went to the home of the victim, Kersey, and two of the robbers approached Kersey to commit the crime. Kersey resisted and called for help. His wife came to the rescue and wounded one of the robbers. In retaliation, the robbers killed both Kersey and his wife. During this time, Enmund was sitting in the getaway car. After the killing, the three left the scene of the crime but were later identified, arrested, and tried on a charge of first-degree murder. In accordance with the Florida statute providing that "the killing of a human being while engaged in the perpetration of or in the attempt to perpetrate the offense of robbery is murder in the first degree even though there is no intent to kill, and for which upon conviction the death penalty may be imposed," all three defendants were convicted of first-degree murder and sentenced to death.

Enmund appealed the death sentence on the grounds that the death penalty under the circumstances was in violation of the cruel and unusual punishment clause of the Eighth Amendment of the U.S. Constitution. Enmund alleged that he did not participate in the actual killing and had no intent to kill during the robbery, and as such, the death penalty as applied was disproportionate to the crime he committed. The U.S. Supreme Court agreed with Enmund that the death penalty in his instance was cruel and unusual punishment. The Court stated the following:

> We have no doubt that robbery is a serious crime deserving serious punishment. It is not, however, a crime so grievous an affront to humanity that the only adequate response may be the penalty of death. It does not compare with murder, which does involve the unjustified taking of human life. Although it may be accompanied by another crime, robbery by definition does not include the death of another person. The murderer kills; the robber if no more than that, does not. Life is over for the victim of the murderer; for the robbery victim, life is not beyond repair. As we said of the crime of rape in the *Coker* case, we have the abiding conviction that the death penalty, which is unique in its severity and irrevocability, is an excessive penalty for the robber who, as such, does not take human life.

The dissenting justices in the *Enmund* case felt that the death penalty was not disproportionate to the crime of felony murder even though Enmund did not actually kill or intend to kill the victims. They pointed out that Enmund planned the robbery and assisted in carrying it out by going with the other two defendants to the victim's home and sat in the getaway car to aid in the escape after the robbery. As such, he was as guilty of murder as the other two defendants.

The majority of the justices in the *Enmund* case did not rule out all death penalty sentences in which a coconspirator did not actually do the killing, but as stated by one of the dissenting justices, to invoke the death penalty in such instances there must be proving of intent at the time that the robbery was planned. This requirement could be most difficult, since intent is a state of mind, and proving the state of mind when a robbery was planned is troublesome. Imposing the intent phase in such cases does preclude the death penalty's being imposed in most instances.

The U.S. Supreme Court in *Tison* v. *Arizona*[8] modified the intent ruling set forth in the *Enmund* decision. The Court in the *Tison* case stated that although the defendants had no specific intent to kill the victims of their crime, their mental state was one of such "reckless disregard for human life" that the death penalty was not cruel and unusual punishment under the circumstances.

The facts of the *Tison* case indicate that Gary Tison was serving a life sentence for the murder of a guard in an attempted escape. After serving a number of years in prison, Gary Tison's wife and his three sons, Raymond, Donald, and Ricky, conspired to assist him in escaping. In furtherance of the conspiracy, they assembled an arsenal of weapons, which the Tison brothers smuggled into the Arizona State Prison, where Gary Tison was serving time. The brothers armed Gary Tison and his cellmate, Randy Greenwalt, who also was serving a life sentence for murder. The five were able to overpower the guards and forced them and the visitors who were present at the time into a closet. The five fled the prison grounds in the Tisons' Ford and proceeded to a house nearby where the brothers had secreted a Lincoln automobile.

The five abandoned the Ford and proceeded in the Lincoln toward Flagstaff, going by way of back desert roads. On the way, a tire blew out on the Lincoln, so they decided to flag down a motorist and steal his car. Raymond stood in front of the Lincoln to flag a car while the others hid beside the road.

One car passed; then a Mazda automobile containing John Lyons, his wife, his two-year-old son, and John's fifteen-year-old niece stopped to render aid. As Raymond showed John Lyons the flat tire, the others emerged and, at gunpoint, forced the Lyons family into the back seat of the Lincoln. Raymond and Donald Tison drove the Lincoln down a dirt road further into the desert, followed by Gary, Ricky Tison, and Greenwalt in the Mazda. After traveling a short distance, both cars stopped, and Gary Tison blasted the radiator of the Lincoln with a shotgun, presumedly to further disable it. The Lyons family were made to stand in front of the Lincoln, where John Lyons pleaded with the group to spare his family's life and requested that they be given water so that they could survive in the desert. He asked as well for the five to take the Mazda and go on their way. Gary Tison ordered his sons to get some water from the Mazda. The sons did not know why their father gave them that order except that he seemed to be confused about what to do because of the baby. As the boys were returning with the water, they saw Gary Tison and Randy Greenwalt brutally murder the entire Lyons family, including the baby, with blasts from shotguns. The five men then got into the Mazda and drove away. Several days later, the group encountered a police roadblock. During a shootout, Donald Tison was killed. Gary Tison escaped but died of exposure from the desert heat. Greenwalt, Ricky Tison, and Raymond Tison were captured, tried, convicted of murder, and given the death penalty.

Ricky and Raymond Tison appealed their death penalty sentence to the U.S. Supreme Court on the grounds set forth in the *Enmund* decision, alleging that their death penalty was cruel and unusual punishment, since they had no intent to murder the victims of the crime. The Court rejected their contention. The Court pointed out that the Tison brothers were major participants in a long series of events leading up to the murder of the four victims and that, after the killing, the brothers further assisted in the escape. The Court maintained that they should have anticipated that serious injury or death would occur as a result of their activities. The Court also held that the whole mental attitude of the Tison brothers was one of "reckless indifference to the value of human life" and that this reckless disregard of human life was every bit as shocking to the moral sense as an intent to kill. As such, it was sufficient to justify the death penalty and was not in violation of the Eighth Amendment guarantee against cruel and unusual punishment.

Attention is called to the fact that even though an appellate court reverses the death penalty, the offender is not necessarily set free. In most instances, the sentence will be reduced from the death penalty to life imprisonment without the possibility of parole or to life imprisonment only, depending on the statutes of the particular state. A life sentence without the possibility of parole may also be changed to life imprisonment by a governor at any time. Under a life sentence, most offenders are eligible for parole after serving a term of approximately twelve years. That possibility does not mean that the offender will be paroled after that period, but an offender sentenced for life usually does not serve until his or her death.

Retarded Defendants

In 2002, the U.S. Supreme Court held, by a 6-3 decision, that the Constitution's ban on cruel and unusual punishment bars the execution of mentally retarded people. The decision was a turnaround for the Court that thirteen years earlier had found no reason to bar the execution of the mentally retarded. The *Atkins* v. *Virginia* case involved Daryl Atkins, who had an I.Q. of 59. He had been sentenced to death for a murder and a robbery committed when he was eighteen years old. The majority decision of the Court noted that the tide of public opinion had turned and that now most states either prohibit capital punishment altogether or ban its use against the mentally retarded. Also, they noted that public opinion polls have demonstrated a steadily dwindling public enthusiasm for capital punishment in general. At the time of the decision, about twenty states allowed the execution of retarded persons. The decision failed to provide guidance to the states on what constitutes mental retardation for the purposes of the capital punishment prohibition.

FINES

The origin of the fine as a form of punishment is lost in history. Its early use as a form of punishment served a dual purpose. Money or property was taken from the wrongdoer and paid to the victim of the crime or to his or her relatives. The fine was also a source of revenue for the king or church, depending on the law that was broken. As other means of reimbursing the victim of a crime became available, such as civil suits, the fine was no longer used for that purpose, but fines were levied as a source of revenue for the government. The fine is still employed as a form of punishment for minor crimes.

The use of the fine as punishment in serious cases has dwindled considerably since the decision of *Williams* v. *Illinois* was handed down by the U.S. Supreme Court.[9] The statutes of most states provide for a penalty of imprisonment plus a specific amount of money that can be imposed in the form of a fine. This provision is applicable to most felonies as well as misdemeanors. As a result, judges in the past were able to impose a maximum time of imprisonment plus a fine. If unable to pay the fine, the convicted offender was imprisoned and "worked out" the fine by being given credit in a prescribed daily amount. In the *Williams* case, the U.S. Supreme Court held that imprisoning one who was indigent and unable to pay the fine beyond the maximum amount of imprisonment prescribed by law was in violation of the Equal Protection Clause of the Fourteenth Amendment. The facts of the *Williams* case show that Williams was convicted of petty theft and received the maximum sentence provided by law, which was one year imprisonment and a $500 fine. Williams was also taxed $5 court costs. "The judgment directed, as permitted by statute, that if Williams was in default of payment of the fine and court costs at the expiration of the one-year sentence, he should remain in jail pursuant to the Illinois Criminal Code to work off the monetary obligations at the rate of $5 per day." The Court in that case stated the following:

> . . . Thus, whereas the maximum term of imprisonment for petty theft was one year, the effect of the sentence imposed here required appellant (Williams) to be confined for 101 days beyond the maximum period of confinement fixed by the statute since he could not pay the fine and costs of $505. . . .
>
> We conclude that when the aggregate imprisonment exceeds the maximum period fixed by the statute and results directly from an involuntary nonpayment of a fine or court costs we are confronted with an impermissible discrimination which rests on ability to pay, and accordingly, we reverse.
>
> Nothing in today's decision curtails the sentencing prerogative of a judge because, as noted previously, the sovereign's purpose in confining an indigent beyond the statutory maximum is to provide a coercive means of collecting or "working out" a fine. After having taken into consideration the wide range of factors underlying the exercise of his sentencing function, nothing we now hold precludes a judge from imposing on an indigent, as on any defendant, the maximum penalty prescribed by law.
>
> It bears emphasis that our holding does not deal with a judgment of confinement for nonpayment of a fine in the familiar pattern of alternative sentence of "$30 or 30 days." We hold only that a state may not constitutionally imprison beyond the maximum duration fixed by statute a defendant who is financially unable to pay a fine. A statute permitting a sentence of both imprisonment and fine cannot be parlayed into a longer term of imprisonment than is fixed by the statute since to do so would be to accomplish indirectly as to an indigent that which cannot be done directly. We have no occasion to reach the question whether a State is precluded in any other circumstances from holding an indigent accountable for a fine by use of penal sanction. We hold only that the Equal Protection Clause of the Fourteenth Amendment requires that the statutory ceiling placed on imprisonment

for any substantive offense be the same for all defendants irrespective of their economic status.

Although the U.S. Supreme Court did not rule out the alternative penalties, such as thirty days in jail or a $30 fine, some appellate courts contend that application of such alternative penalties necessarily results in different treatment for the rich offender and the poor one. The nature of the penalty actually inflicted by the thirty days in jail or $30 fine depends on the offender's financial ability and personal choice. If the offender chooses and is able to pay the fine, imprisonment may be avoided. If he or she chooses imprisonment, the fine may be avoided. If the offender is unable to pay the fine, imprisonment cannot be avoided. Thus, the indigent offender has no choice, and the alternative penalties work as a violation of the Equal Protection Clause. However, to date, the alternative penalty procedure has not disappeared from the justice system, and fines will continue to be imposed as a form of penalty for some time to come.

CASE LAW

Recent Cases

Abbott v. *United States*, 131 S. Ct. 18 (U.S. 2010)

Defendants Kevin Abbott and Carlos Gould in unrelated cases were convicted of drug and firearm offenses, including 18 U.S.C.S. § 924(c) which provided a minimum mandatory sentence for using, carrying, or possessing a weapon in connection with a crime of violence or drug trafficking crime. Upon grants of writs of certiorari, the defendants appealed their sentences under § 924(c), which were affirmed in the U.S. Courts of Appeals for the Third and Fifth Circuits.

The Supreme Court noted that Section 924(c) imposed a five-year minimum sentence, in addition to any other term of imprisonment, for possessing a weapon while committing a predicate offense, except to the extent a greater minimum sentence is provided by § 924(c) or any other provision of law. The defendants contended that, since their predicate offenses provided minimum sentences greater than five years, these other provisions of law precluded the imposition of the additional five-year sentences.

The U.S. Supreme Court unanimously held that the defendants' sentences were proper since § 924(c) required the highest mandatory minimum specified for the defendants' conduct in § 924(c), unless another provision of law, specifically directed to conduct proscribed by § 924(c), imposed an even greater mandatory minimum. In determining whether a greater minimum sentence was otherwise provided by any other provision of law, the key question was whether other law provided for the conduct § 924(c) proscribed, that is, possessing a firearm in connection with a predicate crime. Rather than implausibly limiting sentences, the

"except" clause was intended to ensure that violators of § 924(c) served at least five years.

The Court noted that a defendant is subject to a mandatory, consecutive sentence for a conviction under 18 U.S.C.S. § 924(c), and is not spared from that sentence by virtue of receiving a higher mandatory minimum on a different count of conviction. A § 924(c) offender is not subject to stacked sentences for violating § 924(c). If he possessed, brandished, and discharged a gun, the mandatory penalty would be ten years, not 22. He is, however, subject to the highest mandatory minimum specified for his conduct in § 924(c), unless another provision of law directed to conduct proscribed by § 924(c) imposes an even greater mandatory minimum.

Graham v. *Florida*, 130 S. Ct. 2011 (U.S. 2010)

Terrance Graham, a juvenile, was charged as an adult. The defendant pleaded guilty to armed burglary with assault and attempted robbery, was adjudicated guilty after violating conditions of probation, and received the maximum sentence of life imprisonment without parole. Upon the grant of a writ of certiorari, the defendant appealed the judgment of the First District Court of Appeal of Florida which affirmed the defendant's sentence.

The defendant contended that, as a juvenile who did not commit or intend to commit homicide, the sentence of life imprisonment without parole constituted cruel and unusual punishment.

The U.S. Supreme Court held that the Eighth Amendment prohibited the imposition of a life-without-parole sentence on the juvenile offender who committed a nonhomicide crime and, while the defendant need not be guaranteed eventual release from the life sentence, he must have some realistic opportunity to obtain release before the end of the life term. The practice of sentencing a juvenile who did not commit a homicide offense to life without parole was exceedingly rare and a national community consensus developed against it, and none of the recognized goals of penal sanctions, in other words, retribution, deterrence, incapacitation, and rehabilitation, provided an adequate justification for the sentence. Further, it could not be conclusively determined at the time of sentencing that the juvenile defendant would be a danger to society for the rest of his life, and a sentence of life without parole improperly denied the juvenile offender a chance to demonstrate growth, maturity, and rehabilitation.

Roper v. *Simmons* 125 S. Ct. 1183; 2005 U.S. LEXIS 2200 (2005)

[Christopher Simmons, a juvenile, committed murder at the age of seventeen. He was tried and sentenced to death.]

JUSTICE KENNEDY delivered the opinion of the Court.

This case requires us to address, for the second time in a decade and a half, whether it is permissible under the Eighth and Fourteenth Amendments to the Constitution of the United States to execute a juvenile offender who was older than 15 but younger than 18 when he committed a capital crime. In *Stanford* v. *Kentucky,* 492 U.S. 361, 106 L. Ed. 2d 306, 109 S. Ct. 2969 (1989), a divided Court rejected the proposition that the Constitution bars capital punishment for juvenile offenders in this age group. We reconsider the question.

At the age of 17, when he was still a junior in high school, Christopher Simmons, the respondent here, committed murder. About nine months later, after he had turned 18, he was tried and sentenced to death. There is little doubt that Simmons was the instigator of the crime. Before its commission Simmons said he wanted to murder someone. In chilling, callous terms he talked about his plan, discussing it for the most part with two friends. Simmons proposed to commit burglary and murder by breaking and entering, tying up a victim, and throwing the victim off a bridge. Simmons assured his friends [that] they could "get away with it" because they were minors.

The State sought the death penalty. As aggravating factors, the State submitted that the murder was committed for the purpose of receiving money; was committed for the purpose of avoiding, interfering with, or preventing lawful arrest of the defendant; and

involved depravity of mind and was outrageously and wantonly vile, horrible, and inhuman.

The jury recommended the death penalty after finding [that] the State had proved each of the three aggravating factors submitted to it. Accepting the jury's recommendation, the trial judge imposed the death penalty.

Simmons obtained new counsel, who moved in the trial court to set aside the conviction and sentence. After these proceedings in Simmons' case had run their course, this Court held that the Eighth and Fourteenth Amendments prohibit the execution of a mentally retarded person. *Atkins* v. *Virginia,* 536 U.S. 304, 153 L. Ed. 2d 335, 122 S. Ct. 2242 (2002). Simmons filed a new petition for state postconviction relief, arguing that the reasoning of *Atkins* established that the Constitution prohibits the execution of a juvenile who was under 18 when the crime was committed.

> The Missouri Supreme Court agreed. It held that since Stanford, a national consensus has developed against the execution of juvenile offenders, as demonstrated by the fact that eighteen states now bar such executions for juveniles, that twelve other states bar executions altogether, that no state has lowered its age of execution below 18 since Stanford, that five states have legislatively or by case law raised or established the minimum age at 18, and that the imposition of the juvenile death penalty has become truly unusual over the last decade.

We granted certiorari and now affirm.

The Eighth Amendment provides: "Excessive bail shall not be required, nor excessive fines imposed, nor cruel and unusual punishments inflicted." The provision is applicable to the States through the Fourteenth Amendment. As the Court explained in *Atkins,* the Eighth Amendment guarantees individuals the right not to be subjected to excessive sanctions. The right flows from the basic "precept of justice that punishment for crime should be graduated and proportioned to the offense." By protecting even those convicted of heinous crimes, the Eighth Amendment reaffirms the duty of the government to respect the dignity of all persons.

The prohibition against "cruel and unusual punishments," like other expansive language in the Constitution, must be interpreted according to its text, by considering history, tradition, and precedent, and with due regard for its purpose and function in the constitutional design. To implement this framework, we have established the propriety and affirmed the necessity of referring to "the evolving standards of decency that mark the progress of a maturing society" to determine which punishments are so disproportionate as to be cruel and unusual.

In *Thompson* v. *Oklahoma,* 487 U.S. 815, (1988), a plurality of the Court determined that our standards of decency do not permit the execution of any offender under the age of 16 at the time of the crime. The plurality opinion explained that no death penalty State that had given express consideration to a minimum age for the death penalty had set the age lower than 16. The plurality also observed that "[t]he conclusion that it would offend civilized standards of decency to execute a person who was less than 16 years old at the time of his or her offense is consistent with the views that have been expressed by respected professional organizations, by other nations that share our Anglo-American heritage, and by the leading members of the Western European community." The opinion further noted that juries imposed the death penalty on offenders under sixteen with exceeding rarity; the last execution of an offender for a crime committed under the age of sixteen had been carried out in 1948, forty years prior.

Bringing its independent judgment to bear on the permissibility of the death penalty for a fifteen-year-old offender, the Thompson plurality stressed that "[t]he reasons why juveniles are not trusted with the privileges and responsibilities of an adult also explain why their irresponsible conduct is not as morally reprehensible as that of an adult." According to the plurality, the lesser culpability of offenders under 16 made the death penalty inappropriate as a form of retribution, while the low likelihood that offenders under 16 engaged in "the kind of cost-benefit analysis that attaches any weight to the possibility of execution" made the death penalty ineffective as a means of deterrence. With Justice O'Connor concurring in the judgment on narrower grounds, the Court set aside the death sentence that had been imposed on the fifteen-year-old offender.

The next year, in *Stanford* v. *Kentucky,* 492 U.S. 361 (1989), the Court, over a dissenting opinion joined by four Justices, referred to contemporary standards of decency in this country and concluded [that] the Eighth and Fourteenth Amendments did not proscribe the execution of juvenile offenders over 15 but under 18. The Court noted that 22 of the 37 death penalty States permitted the death penalty for 16-year-old offenders, and, among these 37 States, 25 permitted it for 17-year-old offenders. These numbers, in the Court's view, indicated there was no national consensus "sufficient to label a particular punishment cruel and unusual." A plurality of the Court also "emphatically reject[ed]" the suggestion that the Court should bring its own judgment to bear on the acceptability of the juvenile death penalty.

The same day the Court decided Stanford, it held that the Eighth Amendment did not mandate a categorical exemption from the death penalty for the mentally retarded. *Penry* v. *Lynaugh,* 492 U.S. 302, (1989). In reaching this conclusion it stressed that only two States had enacted laws banning the imposition of the death penalty on a mentally retarded person convicted of a capital offense. According to the Court, "the two state statutes prohibiting execution of the mentally retarded, even when added to the 14 States that have rejected capital punishment completely, [did] not provide sufficient evidence at present of a national consensus."

Three Terms ago the subject was reconsidered in *Atkins.* We held that standards of decency have evolved since *Penry* and now demonstrate that the execution of the mentally retarded is cruel and unusual punishment. The Court noted objective indicia of society's standards, as expressed in legislative enactments and state practice with respect to executions of the mentally retarded. When *Atkins* was decided only a minority of States permitted the practice, and even in those States it was rare. On the basis of these indicia, the Court determined that executing mentally retarded offenders "has become truly unusual, and it is fair to say that a national consensus has developed against it."

The inquiry into our society's evolving standards of decency did not end there. The *Atkins* Court neither repeated nor relied upon the statement in Stanford that the Court's independent judgment has no bearing on the acceptability of a particular punishment under the Eighth Amendment. Instead we returned to the rule, established in decisions predating Stanford, that "the Constitution contemplates that in the end our own judgment will be brought to bear on the question of the acceptability of the death penalty under the Eighth Amendment." Mental retardation, the Court said, diminishes personal culpability even if the offender can distinguish right from wrong. The impairments of mentally retarded offenders make it less defensible to impose the death penalty as retribution for past crimes and less likely that the death penalty will have a real deterrent effect. Based on these considerations and on the finding of national consensus against executing the mentally retarded, the Court ruled that the death penalty constitutes an excessive sanction for the entire category of mentally retarded offenders, and that the Eighth Amendment "places a substantive restriction on the State's power to take the life of a mentally retarded offender."

Just as the *Atkins* Court reconsidered the issue decided in *Penry*, we now reconsider the issue decided in Stanford. The beginning point is a review of objective indicia of consensus, as expressed in particular by the enactments of legislatures that have addressed the question. This data gives us essential instruction. We then must determine, in the exercise of our own independent judgment, whether the death penalty is a disproportionate punishment for juveniles.

As in *Atkins*, the objective indicia of consensus in this case—the rejection of the juvenile death penalty in the majority of States; the infrequency of its use even where it remains on the books; and the consistency in the trend toward abolition of the practice—provide sufficient evidence that today our society views juveniles, in the words *Atkins* used respecting the mentally retarded, as "categorically less culpable than the average criminal."

A majority of States have rejected the imposition of the death penalty on juvenile offenders under 18, and we now hold this is required by the Eighth Amendment.

JUSTICE STEVENS, with whom JUSTICE GINSBURG joined, concurred. [Omitted.]

Summary

- Imprisonment as punishment was not used in early English history.
- Banishment was one of the first forms of punishments.
- Today, imprisonment is one of the most common forms of punishment.
- In most states, the judge determines the sentence. In a few states, like Texas, the defendant may choose to be sentenced by a jury.
- Most states require a presentence investigation prior to the imposition of a sentence for a felony conviction.
- Probation is one of the most popular forms of punishment today.
- The U.S. Constitution prohibits cruel and unusual punishments.
- The death penalty is considered excessive punishment for the crime of rape.
- The use of fines as punishment has dwindled since the *Williams* v. *Illinois* case.

Review Questions

1. What amendment includes the guarantee against cruel and unusual punishment?
2. Why was imprisonment not used as a form of punishment in early criminal procedures?
3. What contribution did William Penn make to the sentencing procedure?
4. What is the primary purpose behind sentencing an offender?
5. List the different forms of punishment that may presently be imposed upon a convicted offender.
6. Explain the significance of each of the following types of sentences:
   a. The definite sentence
   b. The indefinite sentence
   c. The indeterminate sentence
7. What is the primary purpose of granting probation?
8. Why has the alternative sentence of a fine of $30 or thirty days in jail been criticized?

Local Procedure

1. Which type of sentence is imposed—indefinite or indeterminate—in your home state?
2. Who sentences the defendant—the judge, the jury, or some other body?

Endnotes

1. Hal Arkowitz and Scott Lilienfeld (2008, May) "Misunderstood crimes" *Scientific American,* pp. 78–80.
2. 408 U.S. 238 (1972).
3. 428 U.S. 280 (1976).
4. 428 U.S. 153 (1976).
5. 433 U.S. 584 (1977).
6. 446 U.S. 420 (1980).
7. 458 U.S. 782 (1982).
8. 95 L.Ed. 2d 127 (1987).
9. 339 U.S. 235 (1970).

CHAPTER 17

Collateral Proceedings and Writs

What we seek is the reign of law, based upon the consent of the governed and sustained by the organized opinion of mankind.

—WOODROW WILSON, ON THE LEAGUE OF NATIONS,
IN A SPEECH AT MOUNT VERNON, JULY 4, 1918

Chapter Outline

Extradition

Writs

Case Law

Summary

Key Terms

Certiorari

Extradition

Habeas corpus

International extradition

Rendition

Unlawful Flight Statute

Writ

Learning Objectives

After completing this chapter, you should be able to:

- Summarize the right to and restrictions on habeas corpus.

- Outline the procedures involved in extradition.

- Explain the use of the writ of certiorari.

- Explain the importance of habeas corpus.

- Discuss the Uniform Criminal Extradition Act.

INTRODUCTION

In this chapter, we will examine the two collateral proceedings that are essential to the judicial process. Collateral proceedings refer to those proceedings that are not part of the normal judicial process involved in the conviction and sentencing or the acquittal of a defendant but that are a necessary part of the criminal justice system. The collateral proceedings discussed in this chapter are extradition and writs.

EXTRADITION

From a sequential standpoint, **extradition** should have been included in the discussion on arrest, but in view of the technicalities involved in this subject, we believe that its discussion will be more understandable if delayed until this point. Extradition is the procedure followed in returning an accused from one state or foreign country to the state where the crime was committed for the purpose of prosecution. The extradition proceedings may be international or interstate. Interstate extradition is referred to by some legal writers as **rendition**.

Interstate Extradition

Interstate extradition is based upon Article IV, Section 2, of the U.S. Constitution. This section provides that "A person charged in any state with treason, felony, or other crime, who shall flee from justice, and be found in another state, shall on demand of the executive authority of the state from which he fled, be delivered up, to be removed to the state having jurisdiction over the crime." Because of certain deficiencies of this provision in covering all phases of extradition, most states have adopted the Uniform Criminal Extradition Act. Prior to the act's adoption, it was necessary to prove that an accused had actually fled from the state in which the crime was committed to avoid prosecution. The act makes it unnecessary to prove that the accused fled from justice. The mere presence of the accused in another state is all that is necessary. Prior to the adoption of the act, an accused who was found in another state to which he or she had not voluntarily gone could not be extradited. For example, in one case, a fugitive was wanted for robbery in Utah but fled to Oklahoma. While in Oklahoma, the offender committed a bank robbery and was sentenced to serve a federal sentence in the penitentiary in Leavenworth, Kansas. Utah attempted to extradite the fugitive from Kansas after the completion of the bank robbery sentence. It was held that since the fugitive did not voluntarily flee to Kansas, he could not be extradited. The adoption of the act permits extradition from any state even though the accused did not voluntarily go to that state. An accused may be extradited on either a misdemeanor or a felony charge. However, because of the expense and procedure involved, fugitives are seldom extradited on a misdemeanor charge.

REQUIREMENTS FOR EXTRADITION In order to extradite an accused, there must be a warrant of arrest outstanding against that individual based on an accusatory pleading filed in the county in which the crime took place. After determining that the accused is in another state, the prosecuting attorney of the county in which the crime was committed will make an application to the governor of his or her state. The application is a request for the governor to make a demand on the governor of the state where the accused is presently located for the return of the fugitive to the demanding state for prosecution. The application must show the name of the fugitive, the crime charged, the approximate time and date of the offense, the circumstances surrounding the commission of the crime, and the state and location where it is believed that the fugitive is located. It must also be alleged that the fugitive was in the demanding state at the time that the crime was committed. The application, along with copies of the accusatory pleading and a warrant, will be submitted to the governor of the demanding state. On approval of the application for extradition, the governor of the demanding state will appoint an officer to deliver the extradition papers to the governor of the state in which the fugitive is located, with a demand that the fugitive be returned to the demanding state for prosecution. The state in which the fugitive is located is generally referred to as the asylum state.

ACTING ON THE EXTRADITION REQUEST On receipt of the papers, the governor will review them in an effort to determine whether the fugitive should be surrendered to the demanding state. The governor may request the attorney general, or any prosecuting attorney of his or her state, to conduct an investigation to assist in making the determination. The investigation may include an inquiry to determine that the person sought is actually the one charged in the demanding state, and the offender's identity must be established with certainty. An inquiry may be made by the asylum state to make certain that the accused has been substantially charged in the demanding state. This is a determination of whether or not a complaint has been filed or an indictment returned and a warrant of arrest issued. The governor of the asylum state may wish to be satisfied that the accused sought was in the demanding state at the time the crime was committed and that he or she then left the demanding state. If the investigation concludes that the fugitive should be surrendered, the governor will issue a governor's warrant of arrest directing some officer to place the fugitive under arrest. After the arrest is made, the fugitive will be taken before a local magistrate, who will set a date for an extradition hearing. If the offense for which the fugitive is being extradited is a bailable offense in the demanding state, the local magistrate may set bail in order that the fugitive may post bail and be free from custody pending the extradition hearing. The hearing is usually set within a few days after the arrest. During the hearing, two major facts will be considered. First, is the fugitive in custody the person named in the accusatory pleading of the demanding state? Second, was the fugitive in the demanding state at the time the crime was committed? If the magistrate has any reservations about either of these issues, a request may be made that the demanding state present further evidence to prove the identity and whereabouts of the fugitive. The fugitive is entitled to the assistance of counsel at the hearing and to present evidence in his or her own behalf. If the magistrate is satisfied that the fugitive at the hearing is the one named in the accusatory pleading and was in the demanding state at the time that the crime was committed, the fugitive will be turned over to the custody of an officer of the demanding state for return to that state. Evidence of the fugitive's guilt or innocence is not pertinent at the hearing and will not be presented. After returning to the demanding state, the fugitive may be prosecuted on any charge, not just the one named in the extradition proceedings. In fact, the fugitive does not even have to be prosecuted on that charge if the prosecuting attorney wishes to substitute a different charge.

THE FUGITIVE ALREADY ARRESTED Not all fugitives wanted in another state are first arrested on a governor's warrant. Frequently, an individual is arrested on a minor local charge, after which it is determined that there is an outstanding warrant of arrest for that individual in another state. The laws of most states permit a temporary detention of the arrested person until extradition proceedings can be instituted. Many times, extradition proceedings are waived under these circumstances. If the person in custody waives the right to extradition proceedings, the waiver will eliminate the application to the governor of the demanding state and the other extradition formalities previously described. Upon agreeing to waive extradition, the arrested person is taken before a local magistrate, from whom consent to be returned to the demanding state will be given. Usually, the consent is given in writing. The magistrate will then order the arrested person's return to the demanding state.

REFUSAL TO EXTRADITE Although the U.S. Constitution provides that a person charged with a crime who has fled a state shall, upon demand, be "delivered up" to the demanding state, there have been times when a governor of an asylum state has refused to honor this constitutional provision. Both the U.S. Supreme Court and many state courts have held that the governor of an asylum state has the duty to abide by the demand, but there is no authority that can compel the governor to extradite a person wanted for prosecution. It has been held, however, that the governor of the asylum state must, within a reasonable time, either abide by the demand or refuse to extradite. The action cannot just be postponed indefinitely. The demanding state is entitled to know whether the fugitive is to be returned or not.[1] It has also been held that the asylum state has no right to question the merits or motives of the demanding state. The guilt or innocence of the offender is the sole responsibility of the demanding state.

In one case, the supreme court of an asylum state ordered a local court to investigate the conditions of the prison in the demanding state from which the offender escaped before the asylum state would authorize the extradition of the offender. However, the U.S. Supreme Court held in the case of *Pacileo* v. *Walker*[2] that the state supreme court had exceeded its authority. The facts of the *Pacileo* case indicate that Walker, the defendant, escaped from an Arkansas prison and was later apprehended in California. The governor of Arkansas requested that Walker be extradited to Arkansas to serve the remainder of his sentence. The governor of California signed the extradition papers, but the California Supreme Court ordered a local court to investigate the conditions of the Arkansas prison system to determine whether they violated the Cruel and Unusual Punishment Clause of the Eighth Amendment to the U.S. Constitution. The local sheriff who was charged with the responsibility of making the investigation contended that the courts of the asylum state did not have the authority to investigate the prison conditions of the demanding state. The sheriff's contention was appealed to the U.S. Supreme Court, which held that once the governor of the asylum state signs the extradition papers, the courts of that state may consider only whether or not the extradition documents of the demanding state and asylum state are in order. Any further inquiry is beyond the local court's authority. The Court held that this issue had been previously decided in other cases.

Federal Law Against Unlawful Flight

Interstate extradition proceedings are not to be confused with the procedure followed under the federal Unlawful Flight to Avoid Prosecution Statute. In the 1930s, gangsters began to plague local law enforcement officers by going into a community and committing a series of serious crimes and then immediately fleeing to parts unknown. These officers were often handicapped in their efforts to locate the gangsters, because many times they fled to another state. Because of the seriousness of the situation, Congress passed the Unlawful Flight to Avoid Prosecution Statute. This statute permits the federal government, through the Federal Bureau of Investigation (FBI), to assist in locating and arresting badly wanted fugitives. When a fugitive is identified as having left the state where a crime was committed, the local prosecuting attorney can have a local warrant of arrest issued. The U.S. Attorney for that district is then requested to file a complaint charging the fugitive with the violation of the **Unlawful Flight Statute**. A warrant is issued on the federal complaint giving the FBI the authority to locate and arrest the fugitive. In most instances, the local prosecuting attorney must agree to handle extradition proceedings, since the statute was passed to assist in locating and arresting the fugitive and not for return to the demanding state. Originally, the statute permitted assistance in only a few major crimes; however, it now permits assistance to be given for any felony violation.

International Extradition

International extradition is based entirely on treaties with certain countries; these treaties specify the crimes for which an accused may be extradited. In most instances, political crimes are excluded. If a fugitive is extradited from a foreign country, he or she may be prosecuted only on the extradition charge. This safeguard prevents countries from extraditing a political fugitive under the pretext of a specified crime and then instigating prosecution for an alleged attempt to overthrow a government or for another political or unspecified crime. International extradition is handled in the United States through the Department of State. Instead of the governor of the demanding state directly contacting the officials in the asylum country, the governor will forward the demand for extradition to the secretary of state. The secretary of state will submit the demand to the officials of the asylum country, requesting that the fugitive be surrendered to officials of the United States in order that he or she be returned to this country for prosecution. If those officials decide that extradition is in order, the fugitive will be surrendered to this country. As in the case of the governor who does not honor the constitutional provision on interstate extradition, little can be done to compel a foreign country to extradite a person wanted in this country, with the exceptions of registering a protest or breaking a treaty. In most instances, however, the asylum country honors the demand. Treaties differ somewhat among countries. Some treaties provide that any person may be extradited for the specified crimes; other treaties exempt citizens of that particular country. This provision could hamper extradition, since many countries recognize dual citizenship. The lack of a treaty between two countries does not prevent one of them from surrendering a wanted fugitive to the other. Under these circumstances, the fugitive may be prosecuted for any crime unless the two countries agree otherwise.

WRITS

A **writ** defies simple definition. Legally, a writ is defined as a mandatory precept, under seal, issued by a court, and commanding the person to whom it is addressed to do or not to do some act. One might think of a writ as a written order issued by a court directing some other court officer to do or not to do a particular act. A number of writs may be issued by a court, but only the more frequently encountered ones will be discussed here.

Writ of Habeas Corpus

The writ of **habeas corpus** has been termed the great writ because its purpose is to obtain the prompt release of one who is being unlawfully detained. The right to this writ is embodied in the U.S. Constitution and in the laws of all the states. The statutes of the states read similarly to the following: Every person unlawfully imprisoned or restrained of liberty, under any pretense whatever, may request a writ of habeas corpus to inquire into the cause of the imprisonment or restraint. The person who believes that he or she is being unlawfully imprisoned, or someone in that person's behalf, may petition the appropriate court to have a writ of habeas corpus issued. Generally, a writ of habeas corpus may be issued by a judge of the superior court or its equivalent, or by a justice of an appellate court. In most states, the judge of the inferior court has no authority to issue a writ of habeas corpus.

The petition must state the place of confinement, the officer or person doing the confining, and the facts explaining why the petitioner feels unlawfully imprisoned. If the reason is valid, the writ will be issued and served on the person holding the prisoner, commanding that the prisoner be brought before the issuing court for a hearing to determine whether there is sufficient cause to confine the prisoner. A copy of the writ is furnished to the local prosecuting attorney in order that evidence may be presented endeavoring to prove the legality of the imprisonment. But the burden of proof is on the imprisoned person to prove by a preponderance of evidence that the imprisonment is unlawful. If the offense for which the person is imprisoned is a bailable one, the person is entitled to post bail pending the habeas corpus hearing.

If, after hearing the evidence presented by the prisoner and the prosecuting attorney, the judge concludes that the prisoner is being unlawfully detained, an order for the prisoner to be set free will be issued. The prisoner may not be charged further on that offense unless additional evidence is developed showing reasonable cause for an arrest and commitment by a legal process. If the judge concludes that the imprisonment was lawful, the prisoner will remain in custody to await the appropriate judicial processes.

The early use of the writ of habeas corpus was limited to obtaining the immediate release of one unlawfully restrained. But in recent years, the use of this writ has been broadened materially to make it applicable in a number of situations. For example, if an offender believes that the bail set for release is excessive, a writ of habeas corpus may be filed in an effort to get a reduction in bail. Further, if a convicted person believes that the sentence is excessive, the writ may be filed to have a determination made on this issue. This writ has also been used to determine the effectiveness of counsel. One of the more extensive uses made of the writ in recent years has resulted from some appellate court decisions, particularly those of the U.S. Supreme Court, that affect the rights of one convicted. For example, the *Witherspoon* decision held that a prospective juror could not be challenged for cause just because the juror had reservations against the death penalty. This decision caused writs of habeas corpus to be filed by all those convicted and given the death penalty in trials in which prospective jurors had been excused for cause as being against the death penalty. These writs requested that the sentence of death be reduced to life imprisonment. This action was possible, since the U.S. Supreme Court made the *Witherspoon* decision retroactive. When a decision is made retroactive, it is effective even though a trial is completed and the appeal period has passed. If a decision is not made retroactive, only those offenders whose trial or appeal has not been completed may take advantage of it.

The writ is also the way that the death penalty in state criminal trials is traditionally attacked in federal court. In the past, convictions were voided years after the defendants were found guilty. The process has also been used to delay the imposition of the death penalty. To eliminate this possibility, in 1996 the U.S. Congress passed the Antiterrorism and Effective Death Penalty Act. This act establishes limitation periods for the bringing of habeas actions and requires that federal courts generally defer to state courts' determinations. Under the act, a habeas corpus petitioner will normally have one year in which to seek relief. If the claim has been adjudicated in state court, relief will not be available unless the state court's adjudication resulted in a decision that is either contrary to or involved an unreasonable application of clearly established federal law as determined by the U.S. Supreme Court, or was based on an unreasonable determination of the facts in light of the evidence presented in the state court proceedings. The presumption of correctness accorded state courts' factual findings was also strengthened. Second or successive habeas corpus actions presenting new claims must be dismissed unless the claim is shown to rely on a new, previously unavailable rule of constitutional law or unless the factual predicate for the claim could not have been discovered previously through due diligence and the new facts would be sufficient to establish by clear and convincing evidence that, except for the error, no reasonable fact finder would have convicted.[3]

Law in Practice

House v. *Bell*, 547 U.S. 518 (2006)

In 1985, a Tennessee jury convicted petitioner Paul House of Carolyn Muncey's murder and sentenced him to death. The State's case included evidence that FBI testing showing semen consistent (or so it seemed) with House's on Mrs. Muncey's clothing and small bloodstains consistent with her blood, but not House's on his jeans. In the sentencing phase, the jury found the aggravating factor that the murder was performed while House was committing, attempting to commit, or fleeing from the commission of rape or kidnapping. House's appealed his conviction and the conviction was affirmed.

Twenty years later, House, by a writ of habeas corpus, asserted that new evidence conclusively established that semen on the victim's clothes was that of the victim's husband and indicated that bloodstains on his clothes resulted from spillage from samples of the victim's blood and that the victim's husband was the likely murderer.

As a federal judge, should you allow the defendant to contest his conviction, almost twenty years after it was affirmed?

JUSTICE KENNEDY delivered the opinion of the Court.

Out of respect for the finality of state-court judgments federal habeas courts, as a general rule, are closed to claims that state courts would consider defaulted. In certain exceptional cases involving a compelling claim of actual innocence the federal courts will make an exception.

As a general rule, claims forfeited under state law may support federal habeas relief only if the prisoner demonstrates cause for the default and prejudice from the asserted error. While there was no showing of conclusive exoneration, consideration of House's claims was warranted despite procedural default since it was more likely than not that no reasonable juror viewing the record as a whole would lack reasonable doubt. Although sexual assault was not an element of the offense, the semen evidence was used to infer the inmate's motive and to support the death penalty, and the only other forensic evidence, the bloodstains, was shown to be of questionable origin. Further, testimony that the husband confessed and evidence that the alcoholic husband regularly abused the victim potentially indicated the husband as the murderer. The case was remanded for a new hearing on the evidence. [On May 28, 2008, a federal judge in Nashville, Tennessee ordered the prosecutor to either start a new trial by June 17, 2008, or release Paul House from prison. The prosecutor stated to the press that he had new evidence that Paul House had committed the murder, but failed to describe the new evidence. (*Source:* Associated press news release, May 29, 2008)]

Writ of Certiorari

This writ is issued by an appellate court to permit the review of a decision or judgment by a lower court. It is often issued when other means of appeal are not possible. The writ of **certiorari** is granted by a state supreme court to review a lower court's decision in order to establish guidelines to be followed in future cases by either trial judges or lower appellate courts. This is particularly the case if there is some doubt concerning a law or procedure. This writ is automatically issued in most jurisdictions to review a case when the death penalty is imposed to determine whether the facts warrant a conviction and the imposition of the death penalty. The U.S. Supreme Court issues this writ to review the decision of a state appellate court when there may be a possible denial of a U.S. constitutional guarantee. Generally, the U.S. Supreme Court accepts only about 2 percent of the writs that are filed with the Court. The *Coker* decision is a good example. Coker was convicted of forceful rape and sentenced to death in a trial court in Georgia. The Georgia Supreme Court affirmed both the conviction and the death penalty. The U.S. Supreme Court granted Coker a writ of certiorari in order to determine whether the death penalty was excessive for the conviction of rape and, thus, a violation of the Eighth Amendment.

Law in Practice

Certiorari

Certiorari is a Latin word meaning to be informed of, or to be made certain in regard to. It is also a term used for certain appellate proceedings for re-examination of actions of a trial court, or inferior appeals court. The U.S. Supreme Court uses the term certiorari in the context of appeals.

Petition for Writ of Certiorari (Cert Petition). A document which a losing party files with the Supreme Court asking the Supreme Court to review the decision of a lower court. It includes a list of the parties, a statement of the facts of the case, the legal questions presented for review, and arguments as to why the Court should grant the writ.

Writ of Certiorari. A decision by the Supreme Court to hear an appeal from a lower court.

Cert. Denied. The abbreviation used in legal citations to indicate that the Supreme Court denied a Petition for Writ of Certiorari in the case being cited.

CASE LAW

Recent Cases

Munaf v. *Geren*, 553 U.S. 674 (U.S. 2008)

The detainees were American citizens who voluntarily traveled to Iraq. Each was detained by the Multinational Force-Iraq (MNF–I). The first detainee allegedly took part in insurgency activities. An injunction was issued barring his removal from U.S. or MNF–I custody. The second detainee had been found guilty by an Iraqi criminal court of kidnapping, although that conviction had been vacated and remanded. The court of appeals found that the second detainee's conviction precluded habeas jurisdiction. The Supreme Court held that habeas jurisdiction existed under § 2241(c)(1) in both cases because the detainees were American citizens held by American forces who answered only to an American chain of command. However, the detainees were not entitled to habeas relief. Iraq had a sovereign right to prosecute the detainees for crimes allegedly committed in Iraq. Habeas could not be used to defeat the criminal jurisdiction of a foreign sovereign, even if application of that sovereign's laws would allegedly violate the U.S. Constitution. The detainees' claims that their transfer to Iraqi custody would likely result in torture presented a matter for the political branches, not the judiciary.

Excerpts from the Court's decision

The federal habeas statute provides that a federal district court may entertain a habeas application by a person held in custody under or by color of the authority of the United States, or in custody in violation of the Constitution or laws or treaties of the United States. 28 U.S.C.S. § 2241(c)(1), The statute applies to persons held in custody under or by color of the authority of the United States.

An individual is held "in custody" by the United States when the United States official charged with his detention has the power to produce him. The disjunctive "or" in § 2241(c)(1) makes clear that actual custody by the United States suffices for jurisdiction, even if that custody could be viewed as "under color of" another authority.

The jurisdiction of a nation within its own territory is necessarily exclusive and absolute. A sovereign nation has exclusive jurisdiction to punish offenses against its laws committed within its borders, unless it expressly or impliedly consents to surrender its jurisdiction. A foreign nation has plenary criminal jurisdiction over all Americans who commit offenses against its laws within its territory. This is true with respect to American citizens who travel abroad and commit crimes in another nation whether or not the pertinent criminal process comes with all the rights guaranteed by the United States Constitution. When an American citizen commits a crime in a foreign country, he cannot complain if required to submit to such modes of trial and to such punishment as the laws of that country may prescribe for its own people.

Beard v. *Kindler*, 130 S. Ct. 612 (U.S. 2009)

Joseph Kindler and another individual burglarized a store and were arrested. Kindler killed the other person before he could testify against the inmate. Kindler was convicted of capital murder, and the jury recommended a death sentence. Before the trial court could consider the Kindler's postverdict motions or the jury's death recommendation, he escaped twice. Pursuant to Pennsylvania's fugitive forfeiture rule, the trial court denied the motion to reinstate his challenges to his conviction and sentence. The trial court formally imposed the death sentence. The federal appellate court found that the fugitive forfeiture rule was not "firmly established" and therefore was not an independent and adequate procedural rule sufficient to bar review of the merits of a habeas petition in federal court.

The Supreme Court determined that remand was warranted because a discretionary state procedural rule could serve as an adequate ground to bar federal habeas review. Nothing inherent in such a rule rendered it inadequate for purposes of the adequate state ground doctrine. A discretionary rule could be "firmly established" and "regularly followed."

The Court stated that a federal habeas court will not review a claim rejected by a state court if the decision of the state court rests on a state law ground that is independent of the federal question and adequate to support the judgment.

Comment by author: Jeffery A. Beard, who is named in the case, was the secretary of the Pennsylvania Department of Corrections. The Supreme Court recognizes in this case that if the decision is based on a state law and not a federal issue that the state court has final authority. It is unclear from reading the decision as to why Kindler did not allege that the Pennsylvania fugitive statute violated the U.S. Constitution and was therefore a federal issue.

Summary

- Interstate extradition is often referred to as rendition.
- International extradition is regulated by treaties between the countries involved.
- Interstate extradition involves the governor (or a representative of the governor) of the requesting state sending a request for extradition to the governor of the receiving state (where the accused is located).
- A person being extradited has a right to a judicial hearing in the receiving state before he or she is extradited.
- The receiving state has no obligation to honor a request for extradition.
- It is a violation of federal law to cross state boundaries in order to avoid prosecution in another state.
- The writ of habeas corpus is termed "the great writ."
- The writ is used to test the legality of confinement.

Review Questions

1. What is extradition?
2. Upon what is international extradition based?
3. Upon what is interstate extradition based?
4. In relation to prosecution, how do international and interstate extradition differ?
5. In what way did the Uniform Criminal Extradition Act correct certain weaknesses in the extradition procedure?
6. Briefly outline the procedure that must be followed in extraditing an offender.
7. What is the purpose of each of the following writs:
   a. Habeas corpus?
   b. Certiorari?

Local Procedure

1. Has your state adopted the Uniform Criminal Extradition Act?
2. Does your state have statutory procedures for handling writs?

Endnotes

1. *State of South Dakota* v. *Brown*, 144 Cal.Rptr. 758 (1978).
2. 449 U.S 86 (1981).
3. 18 U.S. Code 3663A.

CHAPTER 18

Victims' Rights

*Rape is the only crime in which the victim becomes the accused and, in reality,
it is she who must prove her good reputation, her mental soundness, and
her impeccable propriety.*

—FREDA ADLER, 1975

Chapter Outline

Historical Perspective
Restitution
Compensation

Victim Impact Statements
Summary

Key Terms

Restitution
Symbolic restitution
Victim compensation

Victim impact statement
Victim service provider
Victims' Bill of Rights

Learning Objectives

After completing this chapter, you should be able to:

- Discuss restitution in historical perspective.
- Explain how a typical victim's compensation program works.

- List the various benefits that victims of crime may receive from state compensation programs.
- Explain the various types of restitution available.

- Explain the purpose of victim impact statements and the issues involved in their use by the courts.

- Define and explain the various victims' service providers available.

HISTORICAL PERSPECTIVE

The majority of this book has focused on the criminal justice system and the offender. Understanding how we respond to offenders is an important part of the criminal justice process; however, we must also understand how the victim of a crime fits within this system. This chapter will examine a newly emerging trend in the United States, that of victim interaction in the criminal justice system.[1] During the late 1960s, victims of crime began volunteering to serve within various victim assistance programs. As these crime victims continued to speak out about their treatment in the criminal justice system, the states and the federal government reacted by establishing commissions to study crime and its consequences.

The federal government responded by establishing the Law Enforcement Assistance Administration (LEAA). This agency provides funds to law enforcement agencies for a variety of purposes, including the establishment of victim and witness programs.[2] In 1975, the LEAA called a meeting in Washington, D.C., of various victim advocates to discuss methods of increasing victims' rights. One of the consequences of this meeting was the formation of the National Organization for Victim Assistance (NOVA). Today, NOVA is considered by many to be one of the leading victim rights organizations in the world.

Gains and Losses

During the late 1970s and early 1980s, the movement foundered. Lack of funding by the federal government caused many community-based victim organizations and service providers to cease operations. Additionally, within the movement, issues such as professionalism and training caused increasing divisiveness. The movement began to splinter into specialized groups that focused on specific issues. Several sexual assault and domestic violence organizations, such as the National Coalition Against Sexual Assault, were established to address the specific needs of those victims.[3] Although there was tension among various service providers because of diminishing funding and disagreement regarding specific goals, there was also progress in other areas of the victims' movement during this period. Parents of Murdered Children (POMC) was founded by Robert and Charlotte Hullinger in 1978, and Mothers Against Drunk Driving (MADD) was founded by Candy Lighter in 1980. Both of these organizations continue to have an impact on victims' rights and the victims' movement.

Increased Public Awareness

From 1982 to 1986, victims' organizations began to use the media to increase public awareness of crime victim issues. President Ronald Reagan and Congress responded to this heightened awareness with actions that would eventually have long-term consequences for the victims' movement. In 1982, President Reagan appointed a Task Force on Victims of Crime. This task force published a report that has since become a platform for victims' rights.[4]

In 1984, another key event took place when Congress passed the Victims of Crime Act (VOCA).[5] The Office for Victims of Crime (OVC) was created in the Department of Justice to implement the task force's recommendations. OVC provides grants to states for programs with direct services for victims of all crimes. VOCA also established the Crime Victims Fund to provide money to local victim assistance programs and state victim compensation programs. The fund receives money from federal criminal fines, penalties, and bond forfeitures.

Question: "How important do you think it is for the judicial system to provide victims and their families with each of the following?"

	Very Important	Somewhat Important	Not Too Important	Not at All Important	Not Sure
Right to be notified about and places of trials and related hearings	84%	13%	1%	1%	1%
Right to be physically present at trials and related hearings	82	15	1	0	1
Opportunity to discuss case with prosecutor during plea bargaining	72	18	3	3	4
Opportunity to discuss case with prosecutor during trial	57	28	6	4	4
Opportunity to make statement prior to sentencing about how crime affected them	72	20	5	2	2
Right to be paid for stolen or damaged property or injuries received in crime	81	15	2	1	1

*Percentages may not add to 100 because of rounding.

Source: Kathleen Maguire and Ann L. Pastore (eds.), *Sourcebook of Criminal Justice Statistics 1992*. U.S. Department of Justice Statistics (Washington, D.C.: Government Printing Office, 1993). p. 199, Table 2.49.

Increased Professionalism

From 1984 to the present, the victims' movement has been characterized by an increase in the professionalism of its advocates and providers. In earlier years, the victims' movement was marked by strong, dynamic leaders with vision and determination. At present, it has expanded beyond the ability of any one person's ability to influence its direction. It is now a national movement with a tremendous influence on local, state, and national politics.

Universities are expanding their victim-related courses. Organizations such as NOVA are offering increased training opportunities, and in 1995 the U.S. Department of Justice sponsored the first National Victim Assistance Academy in Washington, D.C. This academy was repeated in 1996 using distance-learning technology to link three universities in a joint academic effort. It continues to be offered on various college campuses across the nation.

The public awareness of victim issues continues to grow, and victim advocates have become an acknowledged force in modern politics. **Victim service providers** are realizing that their profession requires multidisciplinary training. There is a growing awareness that to be accepted by other professionals requires continuing education, certification, or other acknowledged credentials. This increased professionalism should translate into more sophisticated interventions and a faster rate of progress within the victims' movement.

Additional Laws

Increased professionalism also means increased knowledge and insight into the problems of victims. Congress has acknowledged the plight of victims by passing a **Victims' Bill of Rights**. By 1990, two-thirds of the states had enacted similar types of laws protecting victims. In 1994, Congress enacted the Violent Crime Control and Law Enforcement Act. Title IV of that law is the Violence Against Women Act (VAWA). Congress mandated that various professions form partnerships and work together to respond to all forms of violence against women.

The U.S. Attorney General is required to report to Congress annually on the grants that are awarded under the act and to ensure that research examining violence against women is encouraged. The report must include the number of grants, funds distributed, and other statistical information. Additionally, the report must assess the effectiveness of any programs that are funded under VAWA.

VAWA provides funding for a variety of research-based studies. It also requires that federal agencies engage in research regarding violence against women. For example, the National Institute of Justice is mandated to conduct four important projects: (1) the development of a research agenda that will address violence with particular emphasis on underserved populations; (2) the assessment of establishing state databases to record the number of sexual and domestic violence incidents; (3) a study to determine how abusive partners obtain addresses of their victims; and (4) an examination with other agencies of the battered woman syndrome.[6]

In 2000, Congress passed the Victims of Trafficking and Violence Prevention Act. Division A of the act addresses the issue of trafficking of persons into the sex trade, slavery, and slavery-like conditions through prosecution of traffickers and assistance for victims of trafficking. This act increases penalties for slavery and trafficking crimes and provides for restitution for trafficking victims. Division B of the act expands VAWA and also expands the definition of a victim of terrorism to include a person who is a national of the United States or an officer or employer of the U.S. government who is injured or killed as a result of a terrorist act or mass violence outside the United States.

The Concept of a "Victim" Under Alaska Law

Alaska Statutes

Section 12.55.185. Definitions. In this chapter, unless the context requires otherwise, "victim" means:

A. a person against whom an offense has been perpetrated;

B. one of the following, not the perpetrator, if the person specified in (A) of this paragraph is a minor, incompetent, or incapacitated:
   i.   an individual living in a spousal relationship with the person specified in (A) of this paragraph; or
   ii. a parent, adult child, guardian, or custodian of the person;

C. one of the following, not the perpetrator, if the person specified in (A) of this paragraph is dead:
   i.   a person living in a spousal relationship with the deceased before the deceased died;
   ii. an adult child, parent, brother, sister, grandparent, or grandchild of the deceased; or
   iii. any other interested person, as may be designated by a person having authority in law to do so.

Source: Alaska state legislature.

Several laws were added to aid victims of the September 11, 2001, terrorist attacks. Title IV of the Air Transportation Safety and System Stabilization Act of 2001 established the September 11th Victim Compensation Fund of 2001 to address the economic and noneconomic losses of victims of this specific act of terrorism. (The final rules regarding this act were published March 6, 2002.) The USA Patriot Act of 2001 addresses the needs and concerns of victims of terrorist acts, including immigrant victims of the attacks on September 11, 2001. The Victims of Terrorism Tax Relief Act of 2001 exempts from income taxes any individual who dies as a result of wounds or injury incurred from the terrorist attacks.

In what may become one of the most critical dates in the history of victims' rights, on June 25, 1996, President Bill Clinton proposed a Victims' Rights Constitutional Amendment to the U.S. Constitution. In a speech made in the Rose Garden of the White House announcing this amendment, President Clinton stated that after studying all the alternatives, he was convinced that the only way to fully safeguard the rights of victims was to amend the Constitution to guarantee victims certain rights.[7]

The Victims' Rights Constitutional Amendment faces a long and complex process before it becomes law. It must be approved by Congress and then adopted by three-quarters of the states to become part of the Constitution. It is not something that will happen in a few weeks or months, and there are those who already claim that the proposed amendment is too detailed and should be made broader. No matter what the outcome, the simple fact that such an amendment has actually been proposed is a significant acknowledgment of the plight of victims of crimes.

Law in Practice

Need Information on Victims' Rights and Protections?

The National Center for Victims of Crime (NCVC) has established an extensive web site on victims' rights and protections. Visit the Web site at www.victimlaw.info.

The site is a unique resource to exercise, implement, and enforce victims' rights and protections. It was developed by NCVC and contains more than 15,000 user-friendly database features, including:

- Victims' rights statutes
- Tribal laws
- Constitutional amendments
- Court rules
- Administrative code provisions
- Attorney general opinions
- Case summaries of related court decisions.

The site provides four ways to search for content:

- Topical—by selecting one or more topics within a right
- Term—search by entering one or more search terms
- Contents—by a list of all laws within the data base
- Citation—find a specific document by entering a citation.

Selected Landmarks in Victims' Rights and Services

1965[8]

- The first crime victim compensation program is established in California.
- By 1970, five additional compensation programs are created in New York, Hawaii, Massachusetts, Maryland, and the Virgin Islands.

1972

- The first three victim assistance programs are established:
  - Aid for Victims of Crime in St. Louis, Missouri
  - Bay Area Women Against Rape in San Francisco, California
  - Rape Crisis Center in Washington, DC

1973

- The results of the first National Crime Victimization Survey are released. The survey, commissioned by the President's Commission on Law Enforcement and the Administration of Justice, asks U.S. household members about their exposure to crime. It is intended to complement what is known about crime from the FBI's annual compilation of crimes reported to law enforcement agencies.

1974

- The Law Enforcement Assistance Administration (LEAA) funds the first victim/witness programs in Brooklyn and Milwaukee
- District attorneys' offices, plus seven others through a grant to the National District Attorneys Association, to establish model assistance programs for victims, encourage victim cooperation, and improve prosecution.
- The first law enforcement-based victim assistance programs are established in Fort Lauderdale, Florida, and Indianapolis, Indiana.
- Congress passes the Child Abuse Prevention and Treatment Act, which establishes the National Center on Child Abuse and Neglect. The new center establishes an information clearinghouse and provides technical assistance and model programs.

1975

- The first "Victims' Rights Week" is organized by the Philadelphia District Attorney.
- Citizen activists from across the country unite to expand victim services and increase recognition of victims' rights through the formation of the National Organization for Victim Assistance (NOVA).

1976

- The National Organization for Women (NOW) forms a task force to examine the problem of battering. It calls for research into the problem, along with money for battered women's shelters.

- The first national conference on battered women is sponsored by the Milwaukee Task Force on Women in Milwaukee, Wisconsin.
- In Fresno County, California, Chief Probation Officer James Rowland creates the first victim impact statement to provide the judiciary with an objective inventory of victim injuries and losses at sentencing.
- The first hotline for battered women is started by Women's Advocates in St. Paul, Minnesota.
- Women's Advocates and Haven House in Pasadena, California, establish the first shelters for battered women.
- Nebraska and Wisconsin become the first states to abolish the marital rape exemption.

1977

- The National Association of Crime Victim Compensation Boards is established by the existing twenty-two state victim compensation programs to promote the creation of a nationwide network of compensation programs.
- Oregon becomes the first state to enact mandatory arrest in domestic violence cases.

1978

- The National Coalition Against Sexual Assault is formed to combat sexual violence and promote services for rape victims.
- The National Coalition Against Domestic Violence (NCADV) is organized as a voice for the battered women's movement on a national level.
- Parents of Murdered Children (POMC), a self-help support group, is founded in Cincinnati, Ohio.
- Minnesota becomes the first state to allow probable cause (warrantless) arrests in cases of domestic assault, regardless of whether a protection order has been issued.

1979

- Frank G. Carrington, considered by many to be "the father of the victims' rights movement," founds the Crime Victims' Legal Advocacy Institute, Inc., to promote the rights of crime victims in the civil and criminal justice systems. The nonprofit organization is renamed VALOR, the Victims' Assistance Legal Organization, in 1981.
- The Office on Domestic Violence is established in the U.S. Department of Health and Human Services but is later closed in 1981.
- The World Society of Victimology is formed to promote research relating to crime victims and victim assistance, advocate for victims' interests, and advance cooperation of international, regional, and local agencies concerned with crime victims' issues.

1980

- Mothers Against Drunk Driving (MADD) is founded after the death of 13-year-old Cari Lightner, who was killed by a repeat drunk-driving offender. The first two MADD chapters are established in Sacramento, California, and Annapolis, Maryland.
- Congress passes the Parental Kidnapping Prevention Act of 1980.
- Wisconsin passes the first "Crime Victims' Bill of Rights."
- The First National Day of Unity is established in October by NCADV to mourn battered women who have died, celebrate women who have survived the violence, and honor all who have worked to defeat domestic violence.
- The first Victim Impact Panel is sponsored by Remove Intoxicated Drivers (RID) in Oswego County, New York.

1981

- President Ronald Reagan proclaims the first "National Victims' Rights Week" in April.
- The abduction and murder of six-year-old Adam Walsh prompt a national campaign to raise public awareness about missing children and enact laws to better protect children.
- The Attorney General's Task Force on Violent Crime recommends that a separate national task force be created to examine victims' issues.

1982

- In a Rose Garden ceremony, President Reagan appoints members of the Task Force on Victims of Crime, which holds public hearings in six cities across the nation to focus attention on the needs of crime victims. The Task Force's Final Report offers sixty-eight recommendations that become the framework for the advancement of new programs and policies. Its final recommendation, to amend the Sixth Amendment of the U.S. Constitution to guarantee that ". . . the victim, in every criminal prosecution, shall have the right to be present and to be heard at all critical stages of judicial proceedings . . ." becomes a vital source of new energy to secure state victims' rights constitutional amendments.
- The Victim and Witness Protection Act of 1982 bring "fair treatment standards" to victims and witnesses in the federal criminal justice system.
- California becomes the first state to amend its constitution to address the interests of crime victims by establishing a constitutional right to victim restitution.

(continued)

- The passage of the Missing Children's Act of 1982 helps guarantee that identifying information about missing children is promptly entered into the FBI National Crime Information Center (NCIC) computer system.
- Congress abolishes, through failure of appropriations, the Law Enforcement Assistance Administration; many grassroots and system-based victim assistance programs close.

1983

- The Office for Victims of Crime (OVC) is established by the U.S. Department of Justice within the Office of Justice Programs to implement recommendations from the President's Task Force on Victims of Crime. OVC establishes a national resource center, trains professionals, and develops model legislation to protect victims' rights.
- U.S. Attorney General William French Smith establishes a Task Force on Family Violence, which holds six public hearings across the United States.
- U.S. Attorney General Smith issues the first Attorney General Guidelines for Victim and Witness Assistance, which outlines standards for federal victim and witness assistance and implementation of victims' rights contained in the federal Victim and Witness Protection Act of 1982.
- In April, President Reagan honors crime victims in a White House Rose Garden ceremony.
- The First National Conference of the Judiciary on Victims of Crime is held at the National Judicial College in Reno, Nevada, with support from the National Institute of Justice. Conferees develop recommendations for the judiciary on victims' rights and services.
- President Reagan proclaims the first National Missing Children's Day in observance of the fourth anniversary of the disappearance of six-year-old Etan Patz.
- Wisconsin passes the first Child Victim and Witness Bill of Rights.
- The International Association of Chiefs of Police Board of Governors adopts a Crime Victims' Bill of Rights and establishes a Victims' Rights Committee to focus attention on the needs of crime victims by law enforcement officials nationwide.

1984

- The passage of the Victims of Crime Act (VOCA) establishes the Crime Victims Fund, made up of federal criminal fines, penalties, and bond forfeitures, to support state victim compensation and local victim service programs.
- President Reagan signs the Justice Assistance Act, which establishes a financial assistance program for state and local government and funds 200 new victim service programs.

- The National Center for Missing and Exploited Children is established as the national resource agency for missing children. The Center was mandated as part of the Missing Children's Assistance Act of 1982.
- The Task Force on Family Violence presents its report to the U.S. Attorney General with recommendations for action, including improving the criminal justice system's response to battered women and establishing prevention and awareness activities, education and training, and data collection and reporting.
- The National Minimum Drinking Age Act of 1984 is enacted, providing strong incentives to states to raise the minimum age for drinking to twenty-one, saving thousands of young lives in years to come.
- The Spiritual Dimension in Victim Services is founded to involve the faith community in violence prevention and victim assistance.
- Congress passes the Family Violence Prevention and Services Act, which earmarks federal funding for programs serving victims of domestic violence.
- Concerns of Police Survivors (COPS) is organized at the first police survivors' seminar held in Washington, DC, by 110 relatives of officers killed in the line of duty.
- A victim/witness notification system is established within the Federal Bureau of Prisons.
- Victim/witness coordinator positions are established in the U.S. Attorneys' Offices within the U.S. Department of Justice.
- California State University, Fresno, initiates the first Victim Services Certificate Program offered for academic credit by a university.
- OVC establishes the National Victims Resource Center, now named the Office for Victims of Crime Resource Center (OVCRC), to serve as a clearinghouse for OVC publications and other resource information.

1985

- The National Victim Center (renamed the National Center for Victims of Crime in 1998) is founded in honor of attempted-murder victim Sunny von Bulow to promote the rights and needs of crime victims and to educate Americans about the devastating effect of crime on our society.
- The United Nations General Assembly adopts the Declaration of Basic Principles of Justice for Victims of Crime and Abuse of Power that serves as the basis for victim service reform at national and local levels throughout the world.

1986

- OVC awards the first grants to support state victim assistance and compensation programs.

- Two years after its passage, the Victims of Crime Act is amended by the Children's Justice Act to provide funds specifically for the investigation and prosecution of child abuse.
- Rhode Island passes a victims' rights constitutional amendment granting victims the rights to restitution, to submit victim impact statements, and to be treated with dignity and respect.
- MADD's "Red Ribbon Campaign" enlists motorists to display a red ribbon on their automobiles, signaling a pledge to drive safely and soberly during the holidays. This national public awareness effort has since become an annual campaign.
- By year's end, thirty-five states have established victim compensation programs.

1987

- The American Correctional Association establishes a Task Force on Victims of Crime.
- NCADV establishes the first national toll-free domestic violence hotline.
- October is officially designated as National Domestic Violence Awareness Month to honor battered women and those who serve them.
- In a 5-4 decision, the U.S. Supreme Court rules in *Booth* v. *Maryland* (482 U.S. 496) that victim impact statements are unconstitutional (in violation of the Eighth Amendment) when applied to the penalty phase of a capital trial because "only the defendant's personal responsibility and moral guilt" may be considered in capital sentencing. Significant dissenting opinions are offered.

1988

- The National Aging Resource Center on Elder Abuse is established by a cooperative agreement among the American Public Welfare Association, the National Association of State Units on Aging, and the University of Delaware. Renamed the National Center on Elder Abuse, it continues to provide information and statistics.
- *State* v. *Ciskie* is the first case to allow the use of expert testimony to explain the behavior and mental state of an adult rape victim. The testimony is used to show why a victim of repeated physical and sexual assaults by her intimate partner would not immediately call the police or take action. The jury convicts the defendant on four counts of rape.
- The Drunk Driving Prevention Act is passed, and all states raise the minimum drinking age to 21.
- Amendments to the Victims of Crime Act legislatively establish the Office for Victims of Crime, elevate the position of Director by making Senate confirmation

necessary for appointment, and encourage state compensation programs to cover victims of domestic violence, homicide, and drunk driving. In addition, VOCA amendments, at the behest of MADD and POMC, add a new "priority" category for funding victim assistance programs for "previously underserved victims of violent crime."
- OVC establishes a Federal Emergency Fund for victims in the federal criminal justice system.

1989

- In a 5-4 decision, the U.S. Supreme Court reaffirms in *South Carolina* v. *Gathers* its 1987 decision in *Booth* v. *Maryland* that victim impact evidence and arguments are unconstitutional when applied to the penalty phase of a capital trial. Again, significant dissenting opinions are offered.
- The legislatures in Texas and Washington pass victims' rights constitutional amendments. Both are ratified by voters.

1990

- Congress passes the Hate Crime Statistics Act, requiring the U.S. Attorney General to collect data on the incidence of certain crimes motivated by prejudice based on race, religion, sexual orientation, or ethnicity.
- The Student Right to Know and Campus Security Act, requiring institutions of higher education to disclose murder, rape, robbery, and other crimes on campus, is signed into law by President George H.W. Bush.
- Congress passes the Victims of Child Abuse Act, which features reforms to make the federal criminal justice system less traumatic for child victims and witnesses.
- The Victims' Rights and Restitution Act of 1990 incorporates a Bill of Rights for federal crime victims and codifies services that should be available to victims of crime.
- Congress passes legislation proposed by MADD to prevent drunk drivers and other offenders from filing bankruptcy to avoid paying criminal restitution or civil fines.
- The Arizona petition drive to place the victims' rights constitutional amendment on the ballot succeeds, and the amendment is ratified by voters.
- The first National Incidence Study on Missing, Abducted, Runaway and Thrownaway Children in America shows that more than one million children are abducted annually.
- The National Child Search Assistance Act requires law enforcement to enter reports of missing children and unidentified persons into the FBI's NCIC computer system.

(continued)

1991

- California State University, Fresno, approves the first bachelor's degree program in victimology in the nation.
- The National. Center for Victims of Crime releases America Speaks Out, the results of the first national public opinion poll to examine citizens' attitudes about violence and victimization.
- In a 7-2 decision in *Payne* v. *Tennessee* (501 U.S. 808), the U.S. Supreme Court reverses its earlier decisions in *Booth* v. *Maryland* (1987) and *South Carolina* v. *Gathers* (1989) and rules that testimony and prosecutorial arguments commenting on the murder victim's good character, as well as how the victim's death affected his or her survivors, do not violate the defendant's constitutional rights in a capital case.
- The New Jersey legislature passes a victims' rights constitutional amendment, which is ratified by voters in November.
- In an 8-0 decision, the U.S. Supreme Court rules in *Simon & Schuster* v. *New York Crime Victims Board* that New York's notoriety-for-profit statute was overly broad and unconstitutional. Notoriety-for-profit statutes had been passed by many states by this time to prevent convicted criminals from profiting from the proceeds of depictions of their crimes in the media or publications.
- The Washington Secretary of State implements the nation's first Address Confidentiality Program, which provides victims of domestic violence, stalking, and sexual assault an alternative, confidential mailing address and secures the confidentiality of two normally public records—voter registration and motor vehicle records.
- By the end of 1991, seven states have incorporated victims' rights into their state constitutions.

1992

- In a unanimous decision, the U.S. Supreme Court—in *R.A.V.* v. *City of St. Paul*—strikes down a local hate crimes ordinance in Minnesota. The ordinance had prohibited the display of a symbol which one knew or had reason to know "arouses anger, alarm, or resentment in others on the basis of race, color, creed, religion or gender," and was found to violate the First Amendment.
- Five states—Colorado, Kansas, Illinois, Missouri, and New Mexico—ratify victims' rights constitutional amendments.
- Twenty-eight states pass antistalking laws.
- Massachusetts passes a landmark bill creating a statewide computerized domestic violence registry and requires judges to check the registry when handling such cases.

1993

- Congress passes the International Parental Child Kidnapping Act, which makes unlawful removal of a child from outside the United States with the intent to obstruct the lawful exercise of parental rights a federal felony.
- President William J. Clinton signs the "Brady Bill," requiring a waiting period for the purchase of handguns.
- Congress passes the Child Sexual Abuse Registry Act, establishing a national repository for information about child sex offenders.
- Twenty-two states pass antistalking statutes, bringing the total number of states with antistalking laws to 50, plus the District of Columbia.

1994

- President Clinton signs a comprehensive package of federal victims' rights legislation as part of the Violent Crime Control and Law Enforcement Act. The Act includes:
  - The Violence Against Women Act (VAWA), which authorizes more than $1 billion in funding for programs to combat violence against women.
  - Enhanced VOCA funding provisions.
  - Establishment of a National Child Sex Offender Registry.
  - Enhanced sentences for drunk drivers with child passengers.
- Kentucky becomes the first state to institute automated telephone notification to crime victims of their offender's status, location, and release date.
- OVC establishes the Community Crisis Response program, using the NOVA model, to improve services to victims in communities that have experienced a crime resulting in multiple violent victimizations.

1996

- The Community Notification Act, known as "Megan's Law," amends the Child Sexual. Abuse Registry law to provide for notifying communities of the location of convicted sex offenders.
- President Clinton signs the Antiterrorism and Effective Death Penalty Act, providing $1 million to strengthen antiterrorism efforts, make restitution mandatory in violent crime cases, and expand compensation and assistance for victims of terrorism both at home and abroad, including victims in the military.
- The Mandatory Victims' Restitution Act, enacted as Title II of the Antiterrorism and Effective Death Penalty Act, allows federal courts to award "public harm" restitution directly to state VOCA victim assistance programs. The act makes restitution in federal cases mandatory, regardless of the defendant's ability to pay. It also requires federal courts to order restitution to victims of fraud.

- The VOCA definition of "crime victim" is expanded to include victims of financial crime, allowing this group to receive counseling, advocacy, and support services.
- The National Domestic Violence Hotline is established by Congress to provide crisis intervention information and referrals to victims of domestic violence and their friends and family.
- The Church Arson Prevention Act is signed in response to an increasing number of acts of arson against religious institutions around the country.
- The Drug-induced Rape Prevention Act is enacted to address the emerging issue of drug-facilitated rape and sexual assault.
- The Office of Juvenile Justice and Delinquency Prevention, within the U.S. Department of Justice, issues the Juvenile Justice Action Plan, which includes recommendations for victims' rights and services within the juvenile justice system for victims of juvenile offenders.

1997

- Congress enacts a federal anti-stalking law as part of the National Defense Authorization Act for Fiscal Year 1997.

1998

- Congress enacts the Child Protection and Sexual Predator Punishment Act of 1998, providing for numerous sentencing enhancements and other initiatives addressing sex crimes against children, including crimes facilitated by the use of interstate facilities and the Internet.
- Congress passes the Crime Victims with Disabilities Awareness Act, representing the first effort to systematically gather information about the extent of victimization of individuals with disabilities. This legislation directs the attorney general to conduct a study on crimes against individuals with developmental disabilities. In addition, the Bureau of Justice Statistics must include statistics on the nature of crimes against individuals with developmental disabilities and victim characteristics in its annual National Crime Victimization Survey by 2000.
- The Identity Theft and Deterrence Act of 1998 is signed into law. This landmark federal legislation outlaws identity theft and directs the U.S. Sentencing Commission to consider various factors in determining penalties, including the number of victims and the value of losses to any individual victim. The act further authorizes the Federal Trade Commission to log and acknowledge reports of identity theft, provide information to victims, and refer complaints to appropriate consumer reporting and law enforcement agencies.

2000

- Congress passes a new national drunk driving limit of 0.08 blood alcohol concentration (BAC) with the strong support of MADD and other victim advocacy organizations, as well as leading highway safety, health, medical, law enforcement, and insurance groups. The new law, passed with strong bipartisan support, requires states to pass 0.08 "per se intoxication" laws or lose a portion of their annual federal highway funding.
- Congress reauthorizes the Violence Against Women Act of 2000, extending VAWA through 2005 and authorizing funding at $3.3 billion over the five-year period. In addition to expanding federal stalking statutes to include stalking on the Internet, the act authorizes:
- The Internet Crime Complaint Center web site, www.ic3.gov, is created by the U.S. Department of Justice, Federal Bureau of Investigation, and the National White Collar Crime Center to combat Internet fraud by giving consumers a convenient way to report violations and by centralizing information about fraud crimes for law enforcement.
- Congress passes and the president signs the Trafficking Victims Protection Act of 2000. This new law significantly strengthens criminal enforcement, prosecution, and penalties against traffickers; provides new protections to victims; and enables victims of severe forms of trafficking to seek benefits and services available to other crime victims.

2001

- Congress passes and President Bush signs the USA PATRIOT Act of 2001, a package of antiterrorism legislation that includes changes to the Victims of Crime Act (VOCA), including increasing the percentage of state compensation payments reimbursable by the federal government and allowing OVC to fund compliance and evaluation projects.
- The Child Abuse Prevention and Enforcement Act and Jennifer's Law increase the annual Crime Victims Fund set-aside for child abuse victims from $10 million to a maximum of $20 million, and allow the use of Byrne grant funds for the prevention of child abuse and neglect. Jennifer's Law authorizes $2 million per year through Fiscal Year 2002 for states to apply for grants to cover costs associated with entering complete files of unidentified crime victims into the FBI's NCIC database.

2002

- By the end of 2002, all 50 states, the District of Columbia, the U.S. Virgin Islands, Puerto Rico, and Guam have established crime victim compensation programs.

(continued)

2003

- Congress makes the Office on Violence Against Women (formerly the Violence Against Women Office within the Office of Justice Programs) a permanent, independent office within the U.S. Department of Justice.
- Congress passes and President Bush signs the PROTECT Act of 2003—also known as the "Amber Alert" law—which creates a national AMBER network to facilitate rapid law enforcement and community response to kidnapped or abducted children.
- The American Society of Victimology (ASV) is established at the first American Symposium on Victimology held in Kansas City, Kansas. The ASV serves as a forum for academicians and practitioners on all topics related to victimology in partnership with the World Society of Victimology.
- The Prison Rape Elimination Act of 2003 is enacted to track and address the issue of rape in correctional institutions and develop national standards aimed at reducing prison rape.
- Congress establishes January as National Stalking Awareness Month.
- The Fair and Accurate Credit Transactions Act of 2003 is enacted to provide new protections against identity theft and help victims of identity theft recover their financial losses.
- Congress passes and President Bush signs the Trafficking Victims Protection Reauthorization Act. Along with reauthorizing programs created under the first TVPA, this legislation strengthens prevention efforts, supports prosecution of offenders, simplifies the process by which victims are certified eligible for benefits, and allows benefits and services to be available for victims' family members who are legally allowed to come to the United States. The legislation also creates a civil cause of action for victims of forced labor or forced prostitution.

2004

- The Identity Theft Penalty Enhancement Act is enacted, defining aggravated identity theft as stealing another person's identity in connection with the commission of other specified felonies. The legislation also prohibits the court from ordering an offender's sentence for identity theft to run concurrently with a sentence imposed on the same offender for any other crime.
- Congress passes and President Bush signs the Justice for All Act of 2004, which includes the Scott Campbell, Stephanie Roper, Wendy Preston, Louarna Gillis, and Nila Lynn Crime Victims' Rights Act, providing substantive rights for crime victims. For the first time, the law provides mechanisms at the federal level to enforce the rights of crime victims, giving victims

and prosecutors legal standing to assert victims' rights, authorizing the filing of writs of mandamus to assert a victim's right, and requiring the attorney general to establish a victims' rights compliance program within the Department of Justice. The legislation authorizes $155 million in funding over the next five years for victim assistance programs at the federal and state level. This omnibus crime legislation also provides funding for DNA testing, crime labs, sexual assault forensic examiners, and programs for post-conviction DNA testing.

2005

- The U.S. Department of Justice establishes an online national sex offender registry that provides real-time access to public sex offender data nationwide with a single Internet search.
- OVC and the Bureau of Justice Assistance initiate a landmark program to establish teams of law enforcement task forces and victim services to respond to human trafficking. The primary goals of this program are to develop sustainable programs to combat human trafficking through proactive law enforcement and prosecution at all levels of government, to coordinate U.S. Attorneys' Offices' efforts, to collaborate with victim service providers, and to increase the identification and rescue of trafficking victims.

2006

- Congress passes and President Bush signs the Violence Against Women and Department of Justice Reauthorization Act of 2005. This extension of the Violence Against Women Act includes provisions for early intervention, prevention, and health care, and promotes a national commitment to keep women and children safe from fear and abuse.
- Congress passes and President Bush signs the Trafficking Victims Protection Reauthorization Act of 2005. This law expands the Trafficking Victims Protection Act of 2000 by enhancing efforts to fight domestic trafficking in persons.
- The United States Court of Appeals for the Ninth Circuit decides *Kenna* v. *U.S. District Court for the Central District of California*, in which the court considered whether the Crime Victims' Rights Act portion of the Justice for All Act gave victims the right to speak at sentencing hearings. The case involved a father and son who swindled dozens of victims. The defendants pled guilty to wire fraud and money laundering. More than sixty victims submitted victim impact statements. At the father's sentencing hearing, several victims spoke about the effects of the crimes, but at the son's sentencing the judge refused to allow the victims to speak. The court held that the district judge had

made a mistake, and made three important points: (1) in passing the Crime Victims' Rights Act, it was the intent of Congress to allow victims to speak at sentencing hearings, not just to submit victim impact statements; (2) victims have a right to speak even if there is more than one criminal sentencing; and (3) the remedy for a crime victim denied the right to speak at a sentencing hearing is to have the sentence vacated and a new sentencing hearing held in which the victims are allowed to speak.

2007

- For the first time ever, the Crime Victims Fund deposits surpass a billion dollars, totaling $1.02 billion.

Information and Referrals about Victims' Rights, Services, and Criminal and Juvenile Justice Resources:

Battered Women's Justice Project 800-903-0111

Bureau of Indian Affairs, Indian Country Child Abuse Hotline 800-633-5155

Childhelp USA National Hotline 800-4-A-CHILD

Child Welfare Information Gateway 800-394-3366

Federal Trade Commission Identity Theft Hotline 877-ID-THEFT

Mothers Against Drunk Driving 800-GET-MADD

National Center for Missing and Exploited Children 800-843-5678 TDD 800-826-7653

National Center for Victims of Crime, National Crime Victim Helpline 800-FYI-CALL TTY 800-211-7996

National Children's Alliance 800-239-9950

National Clearinghouse for Alcohol and Drug Information 800-729-6686 Español 877-767-8432 TDD 800-487-4889

National Crime Prevention Council 800-NCPC-911

National Criminal Justice Reference Service/800-851-3420 Office for Victims of Crime Resource Center

National Domestic Violence Hotline 800-799-SAFE TTY 800-787-3224

National Fraud Information Hotline 800-876-7060

National Organization for Victim Assistance 800-TRY-NOVA

National Organization of Parents Of Murdered Children, Inc. 888-818-POMC

National Resource Center on Domestic Violence 800-537-2238 TTY 800-553-2508

National Sexual Violence Resource Center 877-739-3895 TTY 717-909-0715

Office for Victims of Crime Training and Technical Assistance Center 866-OVC-TTAC TTY 866-682-8880

Rape, Abuse, & Incest National Network 800-656-HOPE

Resource Center on Domestic Violence, Child Protection and Custody 800-527-3223

RESTITUTION

Introduction

The 1982 *Final Report of the President's Task Force on Victims of Crime* included several key points regarding restitution.[9] The report recommended that legislation be enacted requiring judges to order restitution for property loss and personal injury in all cases unless the judge explicitly finds that restitution is not appropriate. However, it went on to point out that although restitution is a proper goal to be pursued, it has limitations. The report noted that restitution cannot be ordered unless the perpetrator is caught and convicted. Even if it is ordered, the offender often has no resources with which to make any payments. Finally, those perpetrators who can make payments may take many years to finally pay off the balance. In the interim, the victim is left to bear the cost of the crime.[10]

As a result of this report and other factors influencing the victim's movement over the past two decades, a number of laws have been enacted addressing the issue of restitution. Hillenbrand reports that one of the reasons these laws have been enacted may be the change in perception regarding restitution. She states that society began to view restitution not as a way to punish or rehabilitate the offender, but as a method of bringing justice to victims.[11] Other authorities argue that laws mandating restitution have been passed as politically correct, with little or no thought given to their effect. This situation has resulted in a system that does not deliver on its promise of making victims whole. Consequently, victims become more disillusioned with the criminal justice system when they learn that the court order mandating the offender to pay restitution carries no weight or authority.[12]

Even the definition of **restitution** causes conflict. It represents many things to many people. The victim may view restitution as a way to regain financial loss and punish the offender, whereas the court may see it as a method of instilling responsibility in the offender. The agency charged with collecting restitution may view it as simply one more task for an already overburdened department. Traditionally, restitution is a court-ordered sanction that involves payment of compensation by the defendant to the victim for injuries suffered as a result of the defendant's criminal act.

Restitution as we know it today can be traced to the criminal laws that authorized suspended sentences and the use of probation. By the late 1930s, several states had passed laws that allowed judges to order restitution as a condition of granting probation.[13] This process viewed restitution as part of the correctional process. In the late 1970s and 1980s, the victims' movement began to argue that restitution should be viewed as protecting victims from suffering financial hardship rather than as punishing or rehabilitating the offender.

The modern concept of restitution in the criminal justice system serves a variety of purposes in the administration of justice. Restitution attempts to establish a relationship between the perpetrator and the victim in an effort to make the offender aware of the financial consequences suffered by the victim as a result of the offender's acts. Another purpose of restitution is to advance the concepts of personal responsibility and accountability to the victim. A third idea regarding restitution holds that though it cannot undo the wrong, it can assist the victim financially and emotionally and at the same time educate the offender. Finally, restitution serves to punish the offender. The funds used to pay restitution must come from the offender and thus have a continuing impact on him or her.[14]

Law in Practice

Status of Crime Victim Compensation Programs in the United States

Each state in the United States, as well as the District of Columbia, the U.S. Virgin Islands, Guam, and Puerto Rico, operates a crime victim compensation program to provide financial assistance for victims of violent or personal crime. Each state administers its own program in accordance with its state statute. The U.S. Department of Justice provides supplemental Victims of Crime Act (VOCA) funding and technical support to the states. The following information is generally applicable to all state compensation programs. For information regarding specific programs, contact the programs directly.

Eligibility Requirements

Report to police Usually within 72 hours; exceptions are made for good cause.

Filing period One year is typical; exceptions are made for good cause.

Victims of terrorist acts Compensation is payable through the federal Antiterrorism Emergency Reserve for residents and nonresidents who are injured or killed in acts of terrorism within the United States or for U.S. nationals, officers, and/or employees of the U.S. government who are injured or killed in acts of terrorism outside the United States. In addition, some state compensation programs provide benefits to victims of terrorism.

Claimants The following parties are eligible for compensation in most states:

- Victims of crime
- Dependents of homicide victims
- Relatives of victims of crime
- Citizens of foreign countries

Procedures

The claimant must file an application with the compensation agency in the state where the crime occurred. Based on information submitted by the victim, the agency determines if the claimant is eligible and has suffered a financial loss. In most states, the victim can appeal the agency's decision to deny or reduce the amount of compensation.

Benefits and Award Limits

Maximum benefits available to victims from the state programs average about $25,000, though a number of states have higher or lower maximums.

Compensable costs All states will cover the following:

- Medical expenses
- Mental health counseling
- Lost wages for disabled victims

- Lost support for dependents of homicide victims
- Funeral and burial expenses

In addition, many states cover the following:

- Travel for medical treatment
- Services to replace work previously performed by the victim
- Crime scene cleanup
- Moving expenses
- Essential medical personal property (such as prosthetic devices and glasses)

- Rehabilitation
- Attorneys' fees

Emergency awards Some states provide emergency awards or expedite processing for victims faced with extraordinary financial needs.

Funding sources Most states obtain their funding from fees or charges assessed against offenders. Some states receive appropriations from general revenue. OVC provides supplemental funds from federal criminal fines and penalties.

Source: Information taken from the Office for Victims of Crime, *U.S. Department of Justice's Directory of International Crime Victim Compensation Programs, 2004–2005* (Washington, D.C.: Government Printing Office, 2005, pp. 81–82.)

Types of Restitution

Restitution can now be ordered for a wide variety of criminal acts, including sex crimes, child sexual abuse, telemarketing fraud, and domestic violence.[15] Restitution can also be ordered to pay for lost wages, child care, and other expenses involved in attending court hearings.[16] Additionally, there are many different types of restitution.[17]

The most common form of restitution is financial, which requires the offender to make payments directly to the victim of the crime. Financial community restitution requires the offender to make payments to a community agency such as a restitution center, which then pays the victim. Individual service restitution requires the offender to perform a service for the victim. For example, the offender might be required to repair or replace property he or she damaged during the commission of the crime. Community service restitution requires the offender to perform some beneficial service to the community. In this type of restitution, which is sometimes referred to as **symbolic restitution**, society serves as the symbolic victim. Finally, some states authorize restitution fines. Restitution fines differ from actual restitution in that they are collected and deposited in the state's crime victim compensation fund. These monies then become part of the fund's operating expenses.

Restitution may be tied to different aspects of a defendant's sentence and is frequently imposed at the earliest possible time in the criminal process. Additionally, many plea agreements call for restitution. Imposing payment as a condition of probation is the most commonly used method of collecting restitution. A court order may also follow the defendant to the correctional institution. Many states now require inmates to work while incarcerated; while working in prison, they normally receive only a minimal amount of money (usually far less than the minimum wage). Several states have passed laws requiring that a portion of that amount, no matter how small, be set aside for payment as restitution to the victim. An increasing number of states are implementing policies that require restitution to be established as a condition of parole. States are also passing laws that provide that any restitution order in a criminal case will also be considered a civil order for remuneration from the defendant to the victim and may be processed in civil courts.

Problems with Restitution

Restitution is a complex process that involves a number of different professionals working in the criminal justice system. Unfortunately, these professionals are usually overworked and under-budgeted. Many of them claim that collecting and disbursing restitution is someone else's job.[18] This perception leads to poor communications and diminished accountability among agencies within the criminal justice system and, in turn, causes poor consultation and communication with victims. Since there may not be one agency controlling or coordinating restitution, judges may impose insufficient or excessive restitution orders.

Many victims feel dissatisfied with the restitution process. Some believe that the amount imposed in the court order was insufficient. Others feel powerless as they search for answers to their questions, only to be directed from one agency to another.[19]

Occasionally, multiple perpetrators are involved in one crime against a single victim. If the prosecution grants one of the perpetrators immunity to testify against the others, the victim will not be able to receive a court order of restitution against that defendant. By the same token, there are crimes involving single perpetrators and multiple victims. Deciding which victim should receive the perpetrator's limited funds can create great difficulties.

Another obvious problem with restitution is the socioeconomic status of the perpetrator. In a majority of cases, he or she is poor and unlikely to earn the money necessary to make full restitution. Additionally, juvenile offenders are often incapable of obtaining or holding on to jobs that might provide them with the funds necessary to pay the court-ordered restitution.

COMPENSATION[20]

Introduction

Victims often suffer physical injury, emotional and mental trauma, and financial loss as a result of a crime. The financial loss to crime victims can cause additional stress as they worry about paying hospital and doctor bills, physical recovery from their injuries, and their ability to return to work. Crime victim compensation programs exist to provide financial assistance to victims and to reduce some of these stressors. These programs exist in all fifty states, as well as the District of Columbia, and many will pay for medical care, mental health counseling, lost wages, and, in the case of homicides, funeral costs and loss of support.[21] Although no amount of money can replace the use of an arm or the loss of a loved one, it can help victims preserve their financial stability and dignity and thereby assist in the recovery process.

As we discussed, in 1984 Congress enacted VOCA, which established a Crime Victims Fund, supported by revenues from federal offenders. This revenue was based upon fines, penalty assessments, and forfeited appearance bonds. When VOCA was enacted, the fund ceiling, or amount that could be allocated to the fund, was $100 million. Amendments to VOCA occurred in 1986, 1988, 1990, and 1992, when Congress removed the ceiling. Although deposits fluctuate from year to year, the total amount deposited in the fund from its inception to 2004 was more than $3.1 billion.[22] Some of this money is available to the Administrative Office of the U.S. Courts, which established and administers a centralized National Fine Center. This center receives all the fines, assessments, and penalties and collects money from those who failed to pay on time. Other monies are used to improve the investigation and prosecution of child abuse cases, including those child abuse acts committed against Native Americans. However, most of the money in the fund is used to support state victim compensation and victim assistance service programs. **Victim compensation** is a direct payment to, or on behalf of, a crime victim for crime-related expenses such as unpaid medical bills, mental health counseling, funeral costs, and lost wages.[23] Victim assistance includes services such as crisis intervention, counseling, emergency transportation to court, temporary housing, advocacy, and criminal justice support.[24]

VOCA also established special assessments for individual crimes that are levied on every conviction. Additionally, VOCA has a "Son of Sam" provision that requires royalties from the sale of literary rights or any other profits derived from a crime to be deposited in the Crime Victims Fund and held for five years to satisfy any civil judgment that a victim may obtain. If no judgments are filed, these funds become part of the general Crime Victims Fund.[25]

Victim assistance programs include organizations that provide a wide variety of services to victims of state and federal crimes. More than 8,000 agencies or organizations provide services to victims, and nearly 3,000 of those organizations received some VOCA funding.[26]

Program Operation

California established the first compensation program in 1965, and within three years, five other states created similar programs. California's is still the largest program in the nation; it pays out about a third of the total benefits paid by all programs combined.[27] The median annual payout per state is approximately $2 million.

Every state administers a crime victim compensation program through a central agency.[28] These agencies are organized and funded statewide, with administration, claims investigation, and decision making handled by each state's headquarters. There is an ongoing debate among those in the field regarding centralization versus decentralization of compensation services.[29] Most victim compensation programs are small agencies employing only a handful of staff. The lack of personnel creates delays in processing claims, prevents the training of groups regarding their right to compensation, and does not allow for specialized services such as bilingual staff. Some agencies are using student interns or volunteers to carry out staff functions. These programs provide assistance to victims of both federal and state crimes. Although each state compensation program is independently run, most programs have similar eligibility requirements and offer the same types of benefits. The maximum state award generally ranges between $10,000 and $25,000.[30] Victims applying for compensation must comply with certain requirements, including reporting the crime and filing claims by certain deadlines. In most states, the victim initiates the process by calling the compensation agency. Program staff then mails an application to the victim, who fills it out and returns it to the compensation agency. Once the claim form is received, it is processed by an investigator or a claims specialist. These employees do not go out into the field to obtain their information; rather, they collect data using letters, telephone calls, and other techniques. These investigators must verify a wide variety of information, including the fact that the crime was reported to the proper law enforcement agency and the existence of appropriate documentation of medical expenses. They must also obtain data regarding funds paid by insurance companies and determine the amount, if any, of lost wages.

Once all pertinent information is gathered, the victim compensation agency will decide whether or not to make an award and, if so, how much it should be. In most states, victims may appeal a denial of benefits. These appeals are heard by a different panel from the one that made the original determination. Some states require that the appeal be heard by a judge.

Eligibility

Not all victims of every crime are eligible for state compensation. In general, the majority of states limit compensation to victims who suffered injuries as a result of the criminal conduct of another and to survivors of homicides (i.e., relatives and friends). Additionally, there is some disparity among eligibility requirements in these programs, with some states mandating that the victim suffer some sort of physical injury and others allowing for physical or mental injures. Most of the states allow the parents of deceased victims to collect compensation.

A majority of states disallow some classes of persons from eligibility. Most states preclude firefighters and police officers from receiving victim compensation awards. The rationale for this exclusion is that if their injuries are job related, they are eligible for other state programs, such as worker's compensation. Some states exclude convicted prisoners from filing claims while they are in jail or prison, or are serving probation or parole. VOCA requires states to provide compensation to nonresidents victimized within a state as well as to persons who are subject to federal jurisdiction, such as Native Americans. Additionally, residents of one state who are victimized in another state are eligible in their home state if the state where the crime occurred does not allow those victims compensation.

In the past, domestic violence victims were summarily denied compensation. Many states denied these claims because of the belief that the victim contributed to his or her own injuries by staying in the relationship or that any award would benefit the wrongdoer if he or she was still living with the victim. In a way similar to the change in attitudes toward victims of drunk driving, our altered perception of domestic violence victims has resulted in a change in policy in most states. The great majority of all states now include domestic violence as a compensable crime.

Law in Practice

McEvoy v. *Feigenbaum*, 2007 Conn. Super. LEXIS 1456 (2007)

On October 14, 2003, Victorya McEvoy received a phone call indicating that the former wife of a man she was dating was coming to her house armed with weapons intending to kill her and her friend. After calling the police, she and her friend fled and called the police, who intercepted the former wife with her weapons, without any contact ever taking place with McEvoy. On December 15, 2005, McEvoy applied to Connecticut's Judicial Department Office of Victim Service, claiming to have suffered from anxiety, fear, and difficulty in sleeping. That office denied her claim on January 29, 2004, and on February 16, 2004, she requested a review of that decision by a victim compensation commissioner. After a series of telephone conferences in May and June 2004, she filed a brief on August 13, 2004, and additional medical documentation demonstrating that she had incurred the following costs; two separate bills for dental treatments in the amounts of $220 and $500. Conn. Gen. Stat. § 54-201 permitted payment of victim compensation for expenses actually and reasonably incurred as a result of the personal injury or death of the victim and any other loss resulting from the personal injury or death of the victim. The statute defined "personal injury" to mean actual bodily harm and mental anguish that is the direct result of bodily injury. She produced letters from a dentist opining that her nervous condition as a result

of the threatening incident caused her to grate her teeth at night resulting in damage to a crown, which necessitated the dental work.

Should She Collect Victim's Compensation for Mental Anguish Suffered Although There Was No Personal Injury?

Superior Court of Connecticut, Judicial District of Hartford held:

The Victims' Compensation Act, Section 54-201, defines "personal injury" to mean (A) actual bodily harm and mental anguish which is the direct result of bodily injury . . ." This is a much more restrictive definition than that in the Workmen's Compensation Act because it requires a specific bodily injury as a threshold in qualifying for compensation under the Victim's Compensation Act. It appears that such a requirement is intended to eliminate vague claims of emotional distress, difficult to validate and having an unlimited claim exposure. The claimed physical and emotional injuries claimed by McEvoy in this case are not sufficient to elicit compensation under the act because they did not result from an initial bodily injury as required by the plain language of the statute, even if actual body injuries subsequently occurred.

Some state compensation programs have very few domestic violence claims. The staff of these programs believes that is the case because victims underreport this form of violence. Additionally, certain minority groups may not report because exposing male offenders to public attention violates cultural norms. Finally, many program staff believes that police add information to their reports that serves to disqualify victims of domestic violence. For instance, police officers may include details to indicate that a domestic violence victim may have contributed to his or her injuries. However, the officers might not include that same information in a barroom altercation between strangers where misconduct is far more common and likely.[31]

Kelly v. *California*, 129 S. Ct. 564, 564-568 (U.S. 2008): Excerpts from the Justices' Comments Denying the Writ of Certiorari

JUDGES: Statement of JUSTICE STEVENS respecting the denial of the petitions for writs of certiorari. JUSTICE BREYER, dissenting from the denial of the petitions for writs of certiorari.

The petitions for writs of certiorari are denied. JUSTICE SOUTER would grant the petition for a writ of certiorari in No. 07-11073.

Statement of JUSTICE STEVENS respecting the denial of the petitions for writs of certiorari.

These two capital cases raise questions concerning the admissibility of so-called "victim impact evidence" during the penalty phase of a capital trial. The term is a misnomer in capital cases because the evidence does not describe the impact of the crime on the victim—his or her death is always an element of the offense itself. Rather, it describes the impact of the victim's death on third parties, usually members of the victim's family.

In the first of these cases, petitioner Douglas Kelly was convicted of murdering 19-year-old Sara Weir. 42 Cal. 4th 763, 68 Cal. Rptr. 3d 531, 171 P.3d 548 (2007). The prosecution played a twenty-minute video consisting of a montage of still photographs and video footage documenting Weir's life from her infancy until shortly before she was killed. The video was narrated by the victim's mother with soft music playing in the background, and it showed scenes of her swimming, horseback riding, and attending school and social functions with her family and friends. The video ended with a view of her grave marker and footage of people riding horseback in Alberta, Canada—the "'kind of heaven'" in which her mother said she belonged. [The full video is available online at http://www.supremecourtus.gov/opinions/video/kelly_v_california.html case file.]

In the second case, petitioner Samuel Zamudio was convicted of robbing and murdering Elmer and Gladys Benson. 43 Cal. 4th 327, 75 Cal. Rptr. 3d 289, 181 P.3d 105 (2008). Two of the victims' daughters and two of their grandchildren testified about the effects of the murders on themselves and their families. During one daughter's testimony the prosecution played a video containing 118 photographs of the victims at various stages of their lives, including their childhood and early years of marriage. The photographs showed the couple raising their children, serving in the military, hunting, fishing, vacationing, bowling, celebrating holidays and family events, and attending recognition dinners for Gladys's community service. "The last three photographs in the montage showed, in order, Gladys's grave marker with the inscription readable, Elmer's grave marker with the inscription readable, and both grave markers from a distance,

each accompanied by a vase of flowers." Id., at 363, 181 P. 3d, at 134.

In both cases the California Supreme Court upheld the admissibility of the videos. The court explained that the video admitted during Kelly's sentencing "expressed no outrage" and contained no "clarion call for vengeance," but "just implied sadness." 42 Cal. 4th, at 797, 171 P. 3d, at 558. Similarly, the court held that the video shown during Zamudio's penalty phase proceedings was "not unduly emotional." 43 Cal. 4th, at 367, 181 P. 3d, at 137. Only one dissenting justice expressed any concern that the evidence had the potential to "imbue the proceedings with 'a legally impermissible level of emotion.'" 42 Cal. 4th, at 803, 171 P. 3d, at 575 (Moreno, J., concurring and dissenting). No member of the court suggested that the evidence shed any light on the character of the offense, the character of the offender, or the defendant's moral culpability.

I

Victim impact evidence made its first appearance in this Court's jurisprudence in 1987. *Booth* v. *Maryland*, 482 U.S. 496, 107 S. Ct. 2529, 96 L. Ed. 2d 440 (1987). In earlier landmark cases, such as *Williams* v. *New York*, 337 U.S. 241, 69 S. Ct. 1079, 93 L. Ed. 1337 (1949), and *Lockett* v. *Ohio*, 438 U.S. 586, 98 S. Ct. 2954, 57 L. Ed. 2d 973 (1978), evidence probative of the culpability and character of the offender and the circumstances of the offense had marked the outer limits of the kind of evidence admissible in capital sentencing. Consistent with that precedent, in our first encounter with victim impact evidence, the Court announced a rule that categorically "prohibit[ed] a capital jury from considering victim impact evidence" that "described the personal characteristics of the victims and the emotional impact of the crimes on the family." Booth, 482 U.S., at 501-502, 107 S. Ct. 2529, 96 L. Ed. 2d 440. It was the unique character of the death penalty that justified Booth's per se rule: The opinion relied on the fact that death is a "punishment different from all other sanctions," id., at 509, n. 12, 107 S. Ct. 2529, 96 L. Ed. 2d 440, and on our earlier admonition that any decision to impose the death sentence must "be, and appear to be, based on reason rather than caprice or emotion," id., at 508, 107 S. Ct. 2529, 96 L. Ed. 2d 440 (quoting *Gardner* v. *Florida*, 430 U.S. 349, 358, 97 S. Ct. 1197, 51 L. Ed. 2d 393 (1977) (opinion of STEVENS, J.)).

Throughout the late 1970s and for much of the following decade, the fact that "death is a different kind of punishment from any other that may be imposed in this country," id., at 357 , 97 S. Ct. 1197, 51 L. Ed. 2d 393, had justified

(continued)

placing limits on its permissible applications, see, for example, *Godfrey* v. *Georgia*, 446 U.S. 420, 433, 100 S. Ct. 1759, 64 L. Ed. 2d 398 (1980) (plurality opinion), and requiring special procedural protections for the defendant, see *Lockett*, 438 U.S., at 604, 98 S. Ct. 2954, 57 L. Ed. 2d 973 (plurality opinion). Our decision in Booth flowed naturally from the same principle.

Beginning in the late 1980s, however, changes in the Court's capital jurisprudence began to weaken the procedural and substantive safeguards on which we had earlier insisted. In *Tison* v. *Arizona*, 481 U.S. 137, 107 S. Ct. 1676, 95 L. Ed. 2d 127 (1987), rather than adhere to the rule announced in *Enmund* v. *Florida*, 458 U.S. 782, 102 S. Ct. 3368, 73 L. Ed. 2d 1140 (1982), which prohibited death sentences for defendants who neither killed nor intended to kill a victim, a majority of the Court held that felony murder could qualify as a capital offense. Soon thereafter, the Court rejected a challenge to a death sentence based on evidence that a victim's race enhanced the likelihood that a Georgia jury would impose the death penalty. *McCleskey* v. *Kemp*, 481 U.S. 279, 107 S. Ct. 1756, 95 L. Ed. 2d 262 (1987). As Justice Blackmun presciently observed, the fact that "death is different" was fast becoming a justification for applying "a lesser standard of scrutiny" in capital cases. See id., at 347, 348, 107 S. Ct. 1756, 95 L. Ed. 2d 262 (dissenting opinion).

Confirming that observation, the Court's 1991 opinion in *Payne* v. *Tennessee*, 501 U.S. 808, 111 S. Ct. 2597, 115 L. Ed. 2d 720, overruled Booth in short order, giving prosecutors a powerful new weapon in capital cases. At issue in Payne was the admission of penalty phase testimony by the mother of a deceased victim. The woman testified about the effect of the crime on her surviving grandson, who had witnessed the murder of his mother and baby sister and had himself nearly been killed by the same attack. Her testimony powerfully conveyed her grandson's suffering, but "she[d] no light on the defendant's guilt or moral culpability." Id., at 856, 111 S. Ct. 2597, 115 L. Ed. 2d 720 (STEVENS, J., dissenting). By its very poignancy, the testimony "encourage[d] jurors to decide in favor of death rather than life on the basis of their emotions rather than their reason." Ibid. Yet, despite the inherent danger posed by such testimony, the Court rejected Booth's per se rule barring the admissibility of victim impact evidence in capital proceedings. Declaring such evidence to be "simply another form or method of informing the sentencing authority about the specific harm caused by the crime in question," 501 U.S., at 825, 111 S. Ct. 2597, 115 L. Ed. 2d 720, the Court held that prosecutors should be permitted to present evidence "offering a quick glimpse of the life which [the] defendant chose to extinguish" and "demonstrating the loss to the victim's family and to society . . . result[ing] from the defendant's homicide," id., at 822, 111 S. Ct. 2597, 115 L. Ed. 2d 720 (internal quotation marks omitted).

Given Payne's sharp retreat from prior precedent, it is surprising that neither the opinion of the Court nor any of the concurring opinions made a serious attempt to define or otherwise constrain the category of admissible victim impact evidence. Instead, the Court merely gestured toward a standard, noting that, "[i]n the event that evidence is introduced that is so unduly prejudicial that it renders the trial fundamentally unfair, the Due Process Clause of the Fourteenth Amendment provides a mechanism for relief." Id., at 825, 111 S. Ct. 2597, 115 L. Ed. 2d 720. That statement represents the beginning and end of the guidance we have given to lower courts considering the admissibility of victim impact evidence in the first instance.

II

In the years since *Payne* was decided, this Court has left state and federal courts unguided in their efforts to police the hazy boundaries between permissible victim impact evidence and its impermissible, "unduly prejudicial" forms. Following *Payne*'s model, lower courts throughout the country have largely failed to place clear limits on the scope, quantity, or kind of victim impact evidence capital juries are permitted to consider. See generally, Logan, "Through the Past Darkly: A Survey of the Uses and Abuses of Victim Impact Evidence in Capital Trials," 41 Ariz. L. Rev. 143 (1999). Not only have courts allowed capital sentencing juries to hear brief oral or written testimony from close family members regarding victims and the direct impact of their deaths; they have also allowed testimony from friends, neighbors, and coworkers in the form of poems, photographs, hand-crafted items, and—as occurred in these cases—multimedia video presentations. See Blume, "Ten Years of Payne: Victim Impact Evidence in Capital Cases," 88 Cornell L. Rev. 257, 271-272 (2003) (collecting cases).

Victim impact evidence is powerful in any form. But in each of these cases, the evidence was especially prejudicial. Although the video shown to each jury was emotionally evocative, it was not probative of the culpability or character of the offender or the circumstances of the offense. Nor was the evidence particularly probative of the impact of the crimes on the victims' family members: The pictures and video footage shown to the juries portrayed events that occurred long before the respective crimes were committed and that bore no direct relation to the effect of crime on the victims' family members.

Equally troubling is the form in which the evidence was presented. As these cases demonstrate, when victim impact evidence is enhanced with music, photographs, or video footage, the risk of unfair prejudice quickly becomes overwhelming. While the video tributes at issue in these cases contained moving portrayals of the lives of the victims, their primary, if not sole, effect was to rouse jurors' sympathy for the victims and increase jurors' antipathy for the capital defendants. The videos added nothing relevant to the jury's deliberations and invited a verdict based on sentiment, rather than reasoned judgment.

I remain convinced that the views expressed in my dissent in *Payne* are sound, and that the per se rule announced in Booth is both wiser and more faithful to the rule of law than the untethered jurisprudence that has emerged over the past two decades. Yet even under the rule announced in *Payne*, the prosecution's ability to admit such powerful and prejudicial evidence is not boundless.

These videos are a far cry from the written victim impact evidence at issue in *Booth* and the brief oral testimony condoned in *Payne*. In their form, length, and scope, they vastly exceed the "quick glimpse" the Court's majority contemplated when it overruled *Booth* in 1991. At the very least, the petitions now before us invite the Court to apply the standard announced in *Payne*, and to provide the lower courts with long-overdue guidance on the scope of admissible victim impact evidence. Having decided to tolerate the introduction of evidence that puts a heavy thumb on the prosecutor's side of the scale in death cases, the Court has a duty to consider what reasonable limits should be placed on its use.

VICTIM IMPACT STATEMENTS

History of Victim Impact Statements[32]

A new series of rights is emerging in our judicial system. These rights confer upon the victim or upon the relatives of deceased victims the opportunity to speak out or be heard during various phases of the criminal justice process. As with many rights that converge on a single point, there is an actual or a potential conflict. How we handle this conflict is a reflection of the morals and ethics of our society. This section reviews the history of these various rights and examines the rationale behind the current status of the law as it relates to victim impact statements.

One of the most controversial "rights" bestowed upon victims is the victim impact statement. In essence, the **victim impact statement** presents the victim's point of view to the sentencing authority. Providing the sentencing authority with all relevant information is not a new phenomenon in the criminal justice system. For many years, courts have accepted information regarding the defendant prior to the imposition of a sentence. Traditionally, presentence reports have been used by judges to determine the proper punishment for criminal defendants. The report, which is normally prepared by a probation officer, details the defendant's background, education, and criminal record. Many of these reports also include information concerning the victim of the crime.[33]

Victim impact evidence is now admitted in sentencing for a wide variety of criminal acts, including those that fall within the realm of family violence. However, the law on admissibility and use of victim impact statements is based upon use of this evidence during death penalty cases. To understand the nature of victim impact statements, it is necessary to review how this evidence is used in the most serious types of criminal cases—those involving capital punishment.

The use of victim impact evidence during the sentencing phase of a criminal raises serious constitutional issues. The right to confront witnesses comes head-to-head with the right to have all relevant evidence placed before the sentencing authority. Intense feelings were aroused in the U.S. Supreme Court when it addressed this issue.

Constitutional Issues

In *Booth* v. *Maryland,* the U.S. Supreme Court initially addressed the use of victim impact statements in a sentencing jury's determination.[34] In 1983, John Booth and Willie Reed bound and gagged an elderly couple. Believing that the couple might be able to identify them, Booth stabbed them numerous times with a kitchen knife. The trial judge in *Booth* allowed the jury to consider a victim impact statement that detailed the family's and the community's respect and admiration for the victims as well as the impact of the murder on the victims' family.[35]

The Supreme Court, in reversing the death sentence, held that it was impermissible to allow the jury access to such evidence in the sentencing phase of a death penalty proceeding.[36] The Court listed three factors that precluded the prosecution from introducing evidence of the homicide's impact on the victim's family.

First, in holding that the victim impact statement (VIS) impermissibly allows the jury to focus on the victim rather than the defendant, the Court stated the following:

> When the full range of foreseeable consequences of a defendant's actions may be relevant in other criminal and civil contexts, we cannot agree that it is relevant in the unique circumstances of a capital sentencing hearing. In such a case, it is the function of the sentencing jury to "express the conscience of the community on the ultimate question of life or death." When carrying out this task the jury is required to focus on the defendant as a "uniquely individual being." The focus of a VIS, however, is not on the defendant, but on the character and reputation of the victim and the effect on his family. These factors may be wholly unrelated to the blame-worthiness of a particular defendant.[37]

The Court was particularly moved by the fact that the capital defendant does not typically choose his or her victim and, in fixing the punishment, there should be no correlation between the murder and the grief experienced by the victim's family.

Second, the Court held that the sentence of death should not turn on the characteristics of the victim and the victim's family. Specifically, the Court recognized that the imposition of the death penalty should not be determined on the basis of the ability of the victim's family to articulate their anguish and bereavement, whether the victim did or did not leave behind a family, or on the fact that the victim was a stellar member of the community.[38] These factors focus attention on the victim and away from the central inquiry of whether the defendant's characteristics and background are such that the death sentence is warranted.[39]

Finally, the Court stated that because a VIS contains the subjective perceptions and feelings of family members, the defendant has limited rebuttal opportunity.[40] Further, to the extent that the defendant is given an opportunity to rebut such information, "[t]he prospect of a 'mini-trial' on the victim's character is more than simply unappealing, it could well direct the sentencing jury from its constitutionally required task—determining whether the death penalty is appropriate in light of . . . the crime."[41]

In summing up the Court's holding that introduction of the VIS violates the Eighth Amendment's prohibition against cruel and unusual punishment, Justice Powell stated that such evidence would serve no other purpose than to inflame the jury and divert it from its obligation to be fair and impartial.[42] It should be apparent that at the time of the decision in *Booth* v. *Maryland,* the relevant considerations at the sentencing phase of a murder trial were those aspects of the defendant's background or character, or those circumstances that extenuated or mitigated the defendant's culpability.

South Carolina v. *Gathers* followed the rationale of *Booth* and held unconstitutional the imposition of a death penalty based upon prosecutorial remarks that were considered inflammatory.[43] Demetrius Gathers and three companions sexually assaulted and killed Richard Haynes, a man they encountered in a park. During the incident, the perpetrators ransacked a bag the victim was carrying. The bag contained several articles pertaining to religion, including a religious tract entitled "Game Guy's Prayer." During the sentencing phase of the trial, the prosecutor's argument included references to Haynes's personal qualities and included a reading of the "Game Guy's Prayer." The Supreme Court reversed the sentence, stating that such references to the qualities of the victim were similar to the *Booth* holding prohibiting victim impact statements. The Court determined that such evidence was likely to inflame the jury and thus violated the defendant's Eighth Amendment rights. In a well-reasoned and logical dissent, Justice O'Connor stated, "Nothing in the Eighth Amendment precludes the community from considering its loss in assessing punishment nor requires that the victim remain a faceless stranger at the penalty phase of a capital case." The dissent by Justice O'Connor was a signal that the winds of judicial temperament might be changing.

In *Payne* v. *Tennessee,* the court completely reversed itself and allowed to stand the imposition of a death sentence that was based in part on evidence contained in a victim impact statement. In 1987, Pervis Tyrone Payne entered the apartment of Charisse Christopher and her two children. Payne stabbed Charisse and the children numerous times with a butcher knife. Charisse and her daughter, Lacie Jo, died; however, three-year-old Nicholas survived.

Payne was caught and convicted for the murders. During the penalty phase, four witnesses testified regarding the defendant's background, reputation, and mental state. All these witnesses urged the jury not to impose the death penalty. In rebuttal, the prosecution called the maternal grandmother, who was caring for Nicholas. She was allowed to testify, over the defendant's objection, that Nicholas continued to cry out, calling for his dead mother and sister. The witness was also allowed to testify regarding her personal grief over the loss of her loved ones.

During closing arguments, the prosecutor hammered on the pain and suffering that Nicholas and his deceased family had endured, stating the following:

> But we do know that Nicholas was alive. And Nicholas was in the same room. Nicholas was still conscious. His eyes were open. He responded to the paramedics. He was able to follow their directions. He was able to hold his intestines in as he was carried to the ambulance. So he knew what happened to his mother and baby sister.
>
> There is nothing you can do to ease the pain of any of the families involved in this case. There is nothing you can do to ease the pain of Bernice or Carl Payne, and that's a tragedy. There is nothing you can do basically to ease the pain of Mr. and Mrs. Zvolanek, and that's a tragedy. They will have to live with it for the rest of their lives. There is obviously nothing you can do for Charisse and Lacie Jo. But there is something you can do for Nicholas.
>
> Somewhere down the road Nicholas is going to grow up, hopefully. He's going to want to know what happened. And he is going to know what happened to his baby sister and his mother. He is going to want to know what kind of justice was done. He is going to want to know what happened. With your verdict, you will provide the answer.[44]

The jury sentenced Payne to death, and the case was then appealed to the U.S. Supreme Court. Payne contended that the trial court erred when it allowed the maternal grandmother to testify. Relying on *Booth* and *Gathers,* Payne argued that such evidence was a violation of his Eighth Amendment rights. After reviewing the principles that have guided criminal sentencing over the ages, the Court stated that the consideration of the harm caused by the crime has been an important factor in the exercise of judicial discretion. The majority opinion went on to state that neither *Booth* nor *Gathers* even suggested that a defendant, entitled as he or she is to individualized consideration, is to receive that consideration wholly apart from the crime committed. The Court stated that victim impact evidence is simply another form or method of informing the sentencing authority about the specific harm caused by the crime in question.[45]

Thus the U.S. Supreme Court overruled *Booth* and *Gathers* to the extent that they prohibited introduction of evidence or argument regarding the impact of the crime on the victim, families, and community. In addition, the Court's decision clearly stated that the decision regarding the admission of such evidence was the prerogative of the individual states. The Court ruled that it would not intervene unless the evidence introduced was so unduly prejudicial that it rendered the trial fundamentally unfair.[46] If this possibility occurred, the Court reasoned, the Due Process Clause of the Fourteenth Amendment provides a mechanism for relief.

The decision was not without heated dissent. In a dissenting opinion, Justices Marshall and Blackmun uttered words that will ring in the halls of justice and law school classrooms forevermore: "Power, not reason, is the new currency of this Court's decision making."[47] The justices went on to point out that the Court was disregarding the accepted judicial principle of stare decisis.[48]

The decision also generated controversy in the academic world when a series of articles appeared condemning the Court for both allowing victim impact evidence and appearing to repudiate its acceptance of stare decisis.[49] Although the dissent and certain individuals within the academic community may condemn the majority's opinion, it is now clearly the law of the land. In addition, the Supreme Court's decision enhances the victims' rights movement in the United States. It allows individual states to determine what is relevant evidence in the death penalty phase of a capital crime. Some would argue that the decision in *Payne* leaves prosecutors and defense attorneys scrambling to determine what type of evidence is admissible under the guise of victim impact statements. The answer is simply this: Evidence that does not result in rendering a trial fundamentally unfair is proper. This concept of fundamental fairness is not a new, untested, or ill-defined doctrine.

There is a long history defining acts by the state that are classified as fundamentally unfair. The doctrine of fundamental fairness has its roots in two early cases. In *Powell* v. *Alabama,* several black youths were accused of repeatedly raping two young white girls. They were caught, tried, and convicted. Their conviction was overturned on the ground that the failure of the trial court to appoint counsel until the day of the trial was a violation of the defendants' due process.[50] In *Brown* v. *Mississippi,* a sheriff hung the defendant from a tree and whipped him until he confessed to the murder of a white man. The Supreme Court held that such actions are revolting to the sense of justice, and the confession was suppressed.[51]

Law in Practice

Kenna v. *United States* Dist. Court, 435 F.3d 1011, 2006 U.S. App. LEXIS 1369 (9th Cir. Cal. 2006)

Moshe and Zvi Leichner, father and son, swindled scores of victims out of almost $100 million. While purporting to make investments in foreign currency, they spent or concealed the funds entrusted to them. Each defendant pleaded guilty to two counts of wire fraud and one count of money laundering. More than sixty of the Leichners' victims submitted written victim impact statements. At Moshe's (the father's) sentencing, several, including petitioner W. Patrick Kenna, spoke about the effects of the Leichners' crimes—retirement savings lost, businesses bankrupted and lives ruined. The district court sentenced Moshe to 240 months in prison.

Three months later, at Zvi's sentencing, the district court heard from the prosecutor and the defendant, as required by Federal Rule of Criminal Procedure 32(i)(4). But the court denied the victims the opportunity to speak. It explained:

> I listened to the victims the last time. I can say for the record I've rereviewed all the investor victim statements. I have listened at Mr. Leichner's father's sentencing to the victims and, quite frankly, I don't think there's anything that any victim could say that would have any impact whatsoever. I—what can you say when people have lost their life savings and what can you say when the individual who testified last time put his client's [sic] into this investment and millions and millions of dollars and ended up losing his business? There just isn't anything else that could possibly be said.

The district judge refused to let the victims speak. Zvi (the son) was sentenced to 135 months in prison. Kenna, one of the victims, filed a timely petition for writ of mandamus pursuant to the Crime Victims' Right Act (CVRA), 18 U.S.C. § 3771(d)(3). He sought an order vacating Zvi's sentence, and commanding the district court to allow the victims to speak at the resentencing.

How Would You Rule as an Appellate Judge?

Decision by the U.S. Court of Appeals for the Ninth Circuit:

The criminal justice system has long functioned on the assumption that crime victims should behave like good Victorian children—seen but not heard. The Crime Victims' Rights Act sought to change this by making victims independent participants in the criminal justice process. The CVRA guarantees crime victims eight different rights, and unlike the prior crime victims' rights statute, allows both the government and the victims to enforce them.

Kenna and the district court disagree over the scope of one of the rights guaranteed by the CVRA: "The right to be reasonably heard at any public proceeding in the district court involving release, plea, sentencing, or any parole proceeding." 18 U.S.C. § 3771(a)(4). Kenna contends that his right to be "reasonably heard" means that he is entitled to speak in open court at Zvi's sentencing, if that is how he chooses to express himself. The district court argues that the words "reasonably heard" vest the judge with discretion about how to receive the views of the victims, and that the judge is entitled to limit Kenna to written victim statements or his prior statements at Moshe's sentencing. No court of appeals has considered the scope of this CVRA right, and the two district courts that have closely considered it have reached opposite conclusions.

The district court committed an error of law by refusing to allow petitioner to allocute at Zvi's sentencing and we must therefore issue the writ. We turn now to the scope of the remedy. Kenna asks us to vacate Zvi's sentence, and order the district court to resentence him after allowing the victims to speak. The problem is that the CVRA gives district courts, not courts of appeals, the authority to decide a motion to reopen in the first instance. See 18 U.S.C. §3771(d)(5). Moreover, defendant Zvi Leichner is not a party to this mandamus action, and reopening

his sentence in a proceeding where he did not participate may well violate his right to due process. It would therefore be imprudent and perhaps unconstitutional for us to vacate Zvi's sentence without giving him an opportunity to respond.

We think it advisable to let the district court consider the motion to reopen in the first instance. In ruling on the motion, the district court must avoid upsetting constitutionally protected rights, but it must also be cognizant that the only way to give effect to Kenna's right to speak as guaranteed to him by the CVRA is to vacate the sentence and hold a new sentencing hearing. We note that if the district court chooses not to reopen the sentence, Kenna will have another opportunity to petition this court for mandamus pursuant to the CVRA. Likewise, defendant will be able to contest any change in his sentence through the normal avenue for appeal (assuming he has not waived such rights as part of the plea bargain).

Law in Practice

Victims' Rights Constitutional Amendment

Section 1. To ensure that the victim is treated with fairness, dignity, and respect, from the occurrence of a crime of violence and other crimes as may be defined by law pursuant to section two of this article, and throughout the criminal, military, and juvenile justice process, as a matter of fundamental rights to liberty, justice and due process, the victim shall have the following rights: to be informed of and given the opportunity to be present at every proceeding in which those rights are extended to the accused or convicted offender; to be heard at any proceeding involving sentencing, including the right to object to a previously negotiated plea, or to a release from custody; to be informed of any release or escape; and to a speedy trial, a final conclusion free from unreasonable delay, full restitution from the convicted offender, reasonable measures to protect the victim from violence or intimidation by the accused or convicted offender, and notice of the victim's rights.

Section 2. The several States, with respect to a proceeding in a State forum, and the Congress with respect to a proceeding in a United States forum, shall have the power to implement further the rights established in this article by appropriate legislation.

Source: Office for Victims of Crime (Washington, D.C.), 1996.

The doctrine of fundamental fairness accepts the concept that due process is a general command that requires states to provide the defendant with a fair trial. If the admission of the victim impact evidence "revolts the sense of justice" or "shocks the conscience" of the court, such admission would be error under the Due Process Clause.

Victim impact evidence is now an accepted part of the judicial process. The ability of a victim of family violence to inform the court of the impact of the offender's acts on his or her life can only benefit the victim and continue to educate the public regarding the dynamics of violence.

Summary

- Historically, the victim has been a forgotten part of the criminal justice process.
- The victims' rights movement in the United States began in the late 1970s.
- In 1982, President Ronald Reagan appointed a Task Force on Victims of Crime.
- In 1984, the VOCA was enacted.

- The Final Report of the Task Force recommended that an order of restitution be required in sentencing an individual convicted of a crime against an individual.
- Today, restitution can now be ordered for a wide variety of criminal acts.

- Most states have some form of victim compensation program to reduce the trauma of victimization.
- Victims have the right to present a victim's impact statement in a criminal trial during the sentencing procedures.

Review Questions

1. Explain why the historical perspective of restitution is important in understanding today's models.
2. List reasons why an incarcerated prisoner should not have to make restitution to a victim. Assume that you are the prisoner's advocate and must convince a judge of your position.
3. Explain how a typical compensation program is funded and operates.
4. Describe the various eligibility requirements for receiving compensation.
5. List the various benefits that victims of crime may receive under a state compensation program.

6. Explain and give concrete examples of fundamental fairness. Can you list ways in which a victim impact statement would violate this constitutional standard?
7. Should law enforcement officers inform the victim of a crime about victim impact statements? Prepare a form that should be given to victims outlining their rights.
8. How can we ever determine whether victim impact statements serve a valid purpose in the criminal justice system? How would you structure such a study? What are the pitfalls inherent in these types of studies?

Local Procedure

1. Who handles compensation claims in your county? Contact them and determine whether they have handouts that explain their duties.
2. Who coordinates restitution in your court system?
3. Are different types of restitution available in your jurisdiction? List the types.

4. Attend a sentencing hearing at your local courthouse. Was the victim present? Did he or she make a victim impact statement? Do you think it had any effect on the sentencing of the offender? Explain your reasoning.

Endnotes

1. Portions of this chapter have been adapted from Harvey Wallace, *Victimology: Legal, Psychological and Social Perspectives* (Boston: Allyn & Bacon), 1997.
2. Emilio C. Viano, *Victim/Witness Services: A Review of the Model* (Washington, D.C.: Government Printing Office), 1979.
3. M. Largen, "Grassroots Centers and National Task Forces: A History of the Anti-Rape Movement," 32 *Aegis,* pp. 46–52 (Autumn 1981).
4. Final Report of the President's Task Force on Victims of Crime (Washington, D.C.: Government Printing Office), December 1982.
5. Victims of Crime Act of 1984, 42 U.S. Code, section 10601 (1984).
6. Jeremy Travis, "Violence Against Women: Reflections on NIJ's Research Agenda," *National Institute of Justice Journal* vol. 34, pp. 34–42, (February 1996).
7. "Remarks by the President at Announcement of Victims' Constitutional Amendment," Press Release, The White House, Office of the Press Secretary, Washington, D.C., June 25, 1996, p. 2.
8. The material for this section is based on the information and data published by the Office of Crime Victims, NCJRS (2008) pamphlet "Landmarks in Victims' Rights and Services".
9. Final Report of the President's Task Force on Victims of Crime.
10. Ibid. at 38.
11. Susan Hillenbrand, "Restitution and Victim Rights in the 1980s." In A. J. Lurigio, W. G. Skogan, and R. C. Davis (eds.), *Victims of Crime: Problems, Policies, and Programs* (Newbury Park, CA: Sage), 1990.
12. Carol Shapiro, "Is Restitution Legislation the Chameleon of the Victims' Movement?" In B. Gateway and J. Hudson (eds.), *Criminal Justice, Restitution, and Reconciliation* (Monsey, NY: Willow Tree Press), 1990.
13. L. F. Frank, "The Collection of Restitution: An Overlooked Service to Crime Victims," vol. 8, *St. John's Journal of Legal Commentary* 107 (1992).

14. National Victim Assistance Academy Text (unpublished 1998), pp. 21–105.

15. Attorney General Guidelines for Victim and Witness Assistance, 1995 (U.S. Department of Justice, Washington, D.C.), 1995.

16. 18 U.S. Code, section 3663(b), as amended by section 40504 of P.L. 103–322 (1994).

17. National Victim Assistance Academy Text, pp. 21–10–8, 21–10–11.

18. Michael D. Harris, "No One Wants Responsibility for Restitution," *Los Angeles Daily Transcript,* January 6, 1995, p. A-1.

19. National Victim Assistance Academy Text, p. 21–10–7.

20. Much of the material that appears in this section has been adapted from various federally funded projects, including NACVCB's *Crime Victim Compensation: A Fact Sheet and Crime Victim Compensation: An Overview* (National Association of Crime Victim Compensation Boards, Alexandria, Va.), July 1, 1994; *Crime Victim Compensation,* Dale G. Parent, Barbara Auerbach, and Kenneth E. Carlson, *Compensating Crime Victims: A Summary of Policies and Practices*, Office of Justice Programs (Washington, D.C.: U.S. Department of Justice), January 1992; *Compensating Crime Victims and Focus on the Future: A Systems Approach to Prosecution and Victim Assistance,* National Victim Center, MADD, and American Prosecutors Research Institute (U.S. Department of Justice, Washington, D.C.), no date; hereinafter, *Focus on the Future.*

21. *Crime Victim Compensation*, p. 112.

22. "Victims of Crime Act Crime Victims Fund," *OVC Fact Sheet* (Office for Victims of Crime, Washington, D.C.), 2005.

23. Ibid.

24. Ibid.

25. *Compensating Crime Victims*, p. 2.

26. Ibid.

27. *Compensating Crime Victims*, p. 2.

28. Ibid.

29. *Compensating Crime Victims,* p. 7.

30. "Victims of Crime Act Crime Victims Fund," *OVC Fact Sheet* (Washington, D.C.: Office for Victims of Crime), 1996.

31. *Compensating Crime Victims*, p. 21.

32. The information for this section was based on Harvey Wallace, *Family Violence; Legal, Medical and Social Perspectives* (Boston: Allyn & Bacon), 2008.

33. See Phillip A. Talbert, The Relevance of Victim Impact Statements to the Criminal Sentencing Decision, 36 UCLA L Rev 199, 202–11 (1988), and Maureen McLeod, Victim Participation Criminal Law Bull at Sentencing, 22, 501, 505–11 (1986).

34. *Booth* v. *Maryland,* 482 U.S. 496 (1987).

35. Ibid. at 500–01.

36. Ibid. at 509. The Court did, however, carefully note that information typically contained in a victim's statement is generally admissible in noncapital cases and may be considered in capital cases if directly related to the circumstances of the crime. Id. at 508 n. 10. For example, the Court noted that the prosecution may produce evidence regarding the characteristics of the victim to rebut an argument made by the defendant (e.g., the victim's peaceable nature to rebut the claim of self-defense). Ibid.

37. Ibid. at 507–07 (citations omitted).

38. Ibid. at 505–07.

39. Ibid. at 507–08.

40. Ibid.

41. Ibid.

42. Ibid.

43. 490 U.S. 805 (1989).

44. 115 L.Ed.2d 728–729.

45. 115 L.Ed.2d 734–735.

46. 115 L.Ed.2d 735.

47. 115 L.Ed.2d 748.

48. 115 L.Ed.2d 756.

49. See Jimmie O. Clements, Jr., Case Note, Criminal Law—Victim Impact Evidence: The Scope of the Eighth Amendment Does Not Include a Per Se Bar to the Use of Victim Impact Evidence in the Sentencing Phase of a Capital Trial, Payne v. Tennessee. 23 St. Mary's L.J. 517(1991); Aida Alaka, Note, Victim Impact Evidence, Arbitrariness and the Death Penalty: The Supreme Court Flipflops in *Payne* v. *Tennessee*, 23 Loy. U. Chi. L.J. 581(1992); K. Elizabeth Whitehead, Case Note, Mourning Becomes Electric: Payne v. Tennessee's Allowance of Victim Impact Statements During Capital Proceedings, 45 Ark. L. Rev. 531(1992).

50. *Powell* v. *Alabama,* 287 U.S. 45, 53 S.C. 55, 77 L.Ed. 158 (1932).

51. U.S. 278, 56 S.Ct. 461, 80 L.Ed. 682 (1936).

Outline of Trial Procedure

In order that the reader may better understand the trial procedures, an outline of the general procedure in a criminal trial is included here. Depending upon the jurisdiction, there may be some slight deviation from the procedures set forth.

1. Selection of jury
2. Swearing in of jury (trial technically begins at this time)
3. Reading of charge and plea
4. Opening statement by prosecuting attorney
5. Opening statement by defense (this may be waived entirely or until prosecution rests)
6. Calling of first prosecution witness and administration of the oath
7. Direct examination
8. Cross-examination (may be waived)
9. Redirect examination (may be waived)
10. Re-cross-examination (may be waived)
11. Calling of additional prosecution witnesses, administration of oath, direct examination, and other procedure as in case of first witness
12. Prosecution rests
13. Motion for judgment of acquittal by defense (if denied, then the following procedure)
14. Opening statement by defense (if not previously given)
15. Calling of first defense witness and procedure followed as in case of first prosecution witness
16. Defense rests
17. Rebuttal presentation by prosecution
18. Closing arguments by prosecution and then by defense
19. Rebuttal closing argument by prosecution
20. Instructing the jury
21. Deliberation
22. Return of verdict (if guilty verdict returned, then the following procedure)
23. Request for new trial by defense (if denied, then the following procedure)
24. Sentencing the defendant

Motion for the Production and Inspection of Evidence and Information That May Lead to Evidence

PEOPLE V. *ROBERT LEE GRANT*

Case No. 98-02145

Re: *Brady* v. *Maryland,* 373 U.S. 83, 10 L.Ed.2d 215, 83 S.Ct. 1194

Comes now, Robert Lee Grant, defendant in the above styled and numbered cause by and through his attorney of record, and respectfully requests the Court to order the prosecution to produce for inspection all evidence and information which may lead to favorable evidence as to the issue of the Defendant's guilt or innocence and punishment, including, but not limited to the following exculpatory evidence:

I.

Any major use of force paperwork, Internal Affairs Investigation paperwork, or other employer disciplinary reports involving acts of the complaining witness or any witnesses testifying on behalf of the State since their employment by the institution. Such evidence is material and exculpatory as bearing upon the witnesses' motive for testifying, their bias and prejudice against the Defendant, their credibility and is necessary in order for the Defendant to properly exercise his Sixth Amendment right to confront the witnesses against him.

II.

Any and all evidence that a witness called by the State during this trial has committed perjury or has previously made any statement or given any testimony which conflicts with or contradicts the testimony given by said witness during the trial of this cause.

III.

All statements of all persons, whether they have testified or not, who have been interviewed by the prosecution or any agent thereof and who have personal knowledge of facts of this cause which could be deemed favorable to the Defendant, as to the issues of guilt, innocence or punishment.

IV.

All exculpatory evidence and facts which are known or by the exercise of due diligence should be known by the prosecution, including facts known to investigators of the District Attorney's office, investigators or other institution employees which are relevant to have a hearing upon the guilt or innocence of the Defendant, the credibility to the State's witnesses or mitigation of punishment.

V.

The Defendant submits to the Court that the failure or refusal to produce any or all of the foregoing evidence or information by the prosecution constitutes a suppression of evidence and a violation of the Fifth, Sixth, and Fourteenth Amendments of the United States Constitution and substantially fair trial. *Brady* v. *Maryland,* 373 U.S. 83 (1963); *United States* v. *Agurs,* 427 U.S. 97 (1976); *Ashe* v. *Texas,* 319 E2d 80 (5th Cir. 1963); *Moore* v. *Illinois,* 408 U.S. 786 (1972); *United States* v. *Bagley,* 473 U.S. 677, 105 S.Ct. 3375, 87 L.Ed.2d 481 (1985); *United States* v. *McKellar,* 798 F.2d 151 (5th Cir. 1986); *Woods* v. *State,* 713 S.W.2d 276 (Tex.Cr.App. 1974).

WHEREFORE, PREMISES CONSIDERED, the Defendant prays that this Honorable Court will grant this motion in all things.

Respectfully submitted

Attorney for Defendant

GLOSSARY

Abandonment: The concept that once property has been abandoned, its former owner has no reasonable right of privacy in it.

Abstract goals: The underlying principles upon which our justice system is based.

Adversary system: Our concept of justice, in which one side represents the plaintiff or state and the other side represents the defendant, while the judge acts as the independent referee.

Aggravation or circumstances in aggravation: Facts which tend to justify the imposition of a more severe punishment.

Allen charge: An instruction given a deadlocked jury in attempt to get the jury to reach a verdict.

Alternate juror: A person who sits with the jury during the trial and is prepared to serve as a jury member if one of the regular jurors is excused or disqualified.

Appointed counsel: A counsel that has been appointed by the judge to represent the defendant.

Arraignment: A hearing before a court having jurisdiction in which the identity of the defendant is established, the defendant is informed of the charges and of his or her rights, and in some states the defendant is required to enter a plea.

Arrest: The seizure of a person to answer for a criminal charge.

Atonement: A designated price to be paid or duty to be performed by an offender to the victim or victim's family when a certain crime was committed.

Bail: A form of pretrial release in which the defendant is required to post money or property to ensure his or her presence at trial.

Bailiff: An individual assigned to assist the judge and the jury and to perform other duties assigned by the judge.

Bench trial: A trial by a judge without a jury.

Bench warrant: A warrant issued by the judge during a trial. It is issued from the judge's bench.

Booking: The process that officially records an entry into detention after an arrest.

Boykin advisement: The required advice that a judge must give a defendant in open court before the judge can accept a guilty plea. Based on the Supreme Court case of *Boykin* v. *Alabama.*

Brady material: Material that tends to be beneficial to the defendant's case must be provided to defense prior to trial. Based on the Supreme Court decision in *Brady* v. *Maryland.*

Certiorari: A petition to an appeals court to invoke its jurisdiction.

Challenges for cause: A challenge to a potential juror based on the juror's qualifications or lack of impartiality.

Change of venue: Moving of the trial to a different geographical location.

Character evidence: Evidence of a person's character that tends to prove that the individual did or did not commit a certain act.

Charging the jury: The act of a judge in instructing the jury.

Civil contempt: The willful continuing failure or refusal of any person to comply with a court's lawful writ, subpoena, process, order, rule, or command that by its nature is still capable of being complied with.

Code of Hammurabi: One of the first-known attempts to establish a written code of conduct.

Competency: Refers to the mental state of the defendant at the time of trial. A defendant must be able to assist his or her counsel in defending of the case.

Complaint: A written statement made upon oath before a judge, magistrate, or official authorized by law to issue warrants of arrest, setting forth essential facts constituting an offense and alleging that the defendant committed the offense.

Consciousness of guilt: The concept that reflects on the defendant's knowledge of his or her level of guilt.

Constitutional right to speedy trial: The defendant's right to a speedy trial guaranteed by the Sixth Amendment. Speedy trial time starts when prosecution is commenced.

Constructive contempt: Any criminal or civil contempt other than a direct contempt. [See Direct contempt.]

Consular immunity: The limited immunity granted to consuls and their deputies as representatives of a foreign government.

Contempt: The violation of court order or disruption of court proceedings.

Continuance: The delay of a trial at the request of one of the parties.

Conviction in absentia: Conviction of a defendant in which the defendant is not present in court.

Court rules: Rules issued by the courts to regulate the process in the courts in the areas not regulated by statutes, regulations, and other rules.

Court trial: A trial by a judge without a jury.

Criminal contempt: Either misconduct of any person that obstructs the administration of justice and that is committed either in the court's presence or so near thereto as to interrupt, disturb, or hinder its proceedings; or willful disobedience or resistance of any person to a court's lawful writ, subpoena, process, order, rule, or command, where the dominant purpose of the contempt proceeding is to punish the contemptor.

Cross-examination: The examination of a witness by the party that did not call the witness; used to weaken the witness's testimony.

Cross section of community standard: The requirement that the jury panel or list be representative of a cross section of the community.

Curtilage of a dwelling house: A space, necessary and convenient and habitually used for family purposes and the carrying on of domestic employments. It includes the garden, if there is one, and it need not be separated from other lands by a fence.

Daubert test: A test used by the courts to determine if certain scientific evidence should be admitted into evidence.

Death-qualified jury: A jury in which the members have indicated that under appropriate circumstances they would vote for the death penalty.

Declarant: An individual making a formal statement.

Definite sentence: A sentence that has a specified period of confinement or definite terms.

Deliberations: The closed sessions of a jury in which the jury attempts to reach a verdict.

Demur: The formal mode of disputing the sufficiency in law of the pleadings contained in the complaint.

Deposition: A form of pretrial discovery in which a witness is questioned under oath and the other parties are given an opportunity to be present and ask questions. Used more in civil than in criminal cases.

Determination of guilt: A verdict of guilty by a jury, a finding of guilty by a court following a nonjury trial, or acceptance by the court of a plea of guilty.

Deterrence: Punishment based on the goal of deterring future criminal activity.

Diplomatic immunity: The immunity granted to diplomatic officers, their staffs, and their families by which they are free from local jurisdiction and as such cannot be arrested or detained for any offense unless they are permanent residents or citizens of the United States.

Direct contempt: The disorderly or insolent behavior or other misconduct committed in open court, in the presence of the judge, that disturbs the court's business, where all the essential elements of the misconduct occur in the presence of the court and are observed by the court, and where immediate action is essential to prevent diminution of the court's dignity and authority before the public.

Direct examination: The initial questioning of a witness by the party that originally called the witness.

Directed verdict: A verdict by the judge when the judge concludes that the evidence is such that a jury could not legally find the defendant guilty.

Due process: Those procedures that effectively guarantee individual rights in the face of criminal prosecution and those procedures that are fundamental rules for fair and orderly legal proceedings.

Duplicate: A counterpart produced by the same impression as the original, or from the same matrix, or by means of photography, including enlargements and miniatures, or by mechanical or electronic re-recording, or by chemical reproduction, or by other equivalent techniques which accurately reproduce the original.

Effective counsel: An attorney who exercises the normal standards of effectiveness in representing his or her client.

Evidence relating to past sexual behavior: Such a term includes, but is not limited to, evidence of the complaining witness's marital history, mode of dress, and general reputation for promiscuity, nonchastity, or sexual mores contrary to the community standards and opinion of character for those traits.

Evidentiary hearing: A hearing held by the trial court to resolve contested factual issues.

Exclusionary Rule: The rule used to exclude evidence that was obtained by the violation of a constitutional right such as an illegal search.

Exoneration of bail: The court's act in dissolving bail after the defendant has appeared in court as required.

Expectation of privacy zone: The living area immediately surrounding a home where the residents have an expectation of privacy.

Extradition: The surrender by one state or nation to another state or nation of a person who is charged with a crime in the requesting state.

Farce or sham test: A test formerly used to determine if the defense counsel adequately represented the defendant. The defense must be more than a sham or farce.

Foreperson: The individual jury member who has been selected by the other jurors as their spokesperson.

Former acquittal: A defense based on double jeopardy in which defendant claims that he or she has been acquitted of the charged offense.

Fruit of the Poisonous Tree: Additional evidence discovered from information obtained as the result of a constitutional violation such as an illegal search.

Gag order: An order by the judge to the parties to a lawsuit to refrain from discussing the case with the press.

Grand jury: An investigative body that meets to determine whether there is sufficient evidence to support an indictment against a defendant. The grand jury may also investigate the conduct of public officials and agencies.

Habeas corpus: A writ that orders the custodian of a prisoner to appear in court and explain why the individual is being held in confinement.

Harmless error: Any error, defect, irregularity, or variance which does not affect substantial rights and shall be disregarded.

Hearsay: A statement, other than one made by the declarant while testifying at the trial or hearing, offered in evidence to prove the truth of the matter asserted.

Hung jury: A jury that cannot agree on a verdict.

Impaneled jury: A jury that has been selected and sworn in by the judge.

Impartial trial by jury: A jury that starts the case without any preconceived opinions regarding the guilty or innocence of the defendant.

Impeachment: The attempt to limit or discredit evidence that has been admitted.

Indefinite sentence: A sentence that has no fixed term and may be adjusted to fit the offender.

Independent state grounds: A decision based on a state constitution or statute that does not involve an interpretation of federal law.

Indeterminate sentence: A sentence in which the period of confinement or other punishment is to be determined based on the need of the offender.

Indictment: A written statement charging the defendant or defendants named therein with the commission of an indictable offense, presented to the court by a grand jury, endorsed "A True Bill," and signed by the foreperson. The term indictment includes presentment.

Indigent defendant: A defendant who lacks the resources to afford to hire his or her attorney.

Information: A written statement charging the defendant or defendants named therein with the commission of an indictable offense, made on oath, signed, and presented to the court by the district attorney without action by a grand jury.

Initial appearance: The first appearance by the defendant in a criminal case before a judge. Generally, at the initial appearance, the defendant is informed of the charges against him or her and advised of his or her rights. In some states it is the same as an arraignment.

Insanity: The abnormal mental state of the defendant at the time that the crime was committed.

International extradition: Extradition of a fugitive from another country subject to the extradition treaties between the two countries.

Joiner: The consolidated trial of a case by joining charges or defendants.

Judgment: The adjudication of the court based upon a plea of guilty by the defendant, upon the verdict of the jury, or upon the court's own finding following a nonjury trial that the defendant is guilty or not guilty.

Judicial notice: The act of a court in accepting certain facts without the necessity to present evidence to prove them, such as the fact that New York is a state, a fact that a court can take judicial notice of.

Jurisdiction: The power of a court to act in regard to the individual or subject matter.

Jury list: A jury panel. The list of potential jurors that have been summoned from which a jury may be selected.

Jury of one's peers: A jury composed of a cross section of the community that was selected in a fair and impartial manner.

Jury panel: The list of potential jurors that have been summoned from which a jury may be selected.

Law enforcement officer and officer: Any person vested by law with a duty to maintain public order or to make arrests for offenses.

Lay witness: A nonexpert witness.

Legislative immunity: Statutory provisions that grant limited immunity to legislative members while attending or going to legislative sessions.

Limited admissibility: Evidence that is admitted for a limited purpose only.

Locked-down jury: A jury that has been sent to the deliberations room to start deliberations on the findings.

Magistrate: A judicial officer with the power to issue a warrant, including magistrates, district judges, superior court judges, and any other judicial officer authorized by law to conduct a preliminary examination of a person accused of a crime or issue a warrant.

Manifest necessity: In reference to a mistrial, a condition in which the judge concludes that it is necessary to declare a mistrial.

Material witness: A witness whose presence is deemed necessary for the trial of the case. A person designated as a material witness may be required to post security to ensure his or her presence at trial.

Mentally incompetent: Refers to an accused who lacks sufficient present ability to assist in his or her defense by consulting with counsel with a reasonable degree of rational understanding of the facts and the legal proceedings against the defendant.

Miranda **warning:**   Warnings required before officers can interrogate a suspect who is in detention.

Mistrial: The act of a judge in terminating a trial before it is concluded because of errors or issues that call into question the fairness of the trial.

Mitigation or circumstances in mitigation: Facts that tend to justify the imposition of a lesser punishment.

Motion to suppress evidence: A motion presented prior to trial to determine the admissibility of certain items of evidence.

Negotiated plea: A plea that has been agreed upon by the defendant and the state; a plea bargain.

New trial: A retrial of a defendant with a new jury.

Nolo contendere: A plea of no contest that supports a conviction if accepted by the judge.

Notice-of-alibi defense: A requirement that the defendant provide the prosecution with advance notice that an alibi defense will be used.

Open fields: The concept that the Fourth Amendment's restrictions on unreasonable searches and seizures do not apply to items in open fields.

Opening statements: Statements made by counsel prior to the presentation of evidence. The statements are not considered evidence and should not contain arguments on behalf of a party.

Order to show cause: An order in response to a habeas corpus petition directing the respondent (warden) to file a return. The order to show cause is issued if the petitioner (prisoner) has made a prima facie showing that he or she is entitled to relief; it does not grant the relief requested. An order to show cause may also be referred to as granting the writ.

Orientation goals: Those goals of the justice system that are oriented in one of two opposite directions—law and order or individual rights.

Original: Concerning a writing or recording, the writing or recording itself or any counterpart intended to produce the same effect by a person executing or issuing it. An original of a photograph includes the negative or any print therefrom. If data are stored in a computer or similar device, any printout or other output readable by sight, shown to reflect the data accurately, is an original.

Peremptory challenge: A challenge that a party has to eliminate a potential juror. Each side has a limited number of peremptory challenges. While the party peremptorily challenging a potential juror normally is not required to provide a reason for the challenge, the challenge may not be used to exclude one gender or race from the jury.

Petty offenses: Offenses which have a maximum jail time of six months and a fine of not more than $500.

Plain errors: Errors or defects affecting substantial rights that may be noticed, although they were not brought to the attention of the court.

Plain View Doctrine: The concept that looking at items in plain view is not a search because there is no reasonable expectation of privacy concerning items in plain view.

Pragmatic goals: Criminal justice goals related to preventing crime and developing better environmental conditions in the neighborhoods that foster law-abiding behavior.

Precept: A warrant or legal document issued by a court directing a person to comply with the terms of the precept.

Preliminary hearing: A proceeding before a judicial officer to determine if a crime has been committed, whether the crime occurred within the jurisdiction of the court, and whether there are reasonable grounds to believe that the defendant committed the crime.

Preliminary questions: Basic questions like name and address asked of a witness when the witness is first called to testify.

Preponderance of evidence: The normal burden of proof required in civil cases where the moving party is required to establish that it was more likely than not that a certain event occurred or a fact exists.

Pretrial discovery: The right of parties to obtain evidence from the other parties prior to the commencement of the trial.

Pretrial diversion: An agreement between the parties to a criminal case that the charges will be dropped if the defendant successfully meets the conditions for diversion.

Private person arrest: An arrest by a person who does not have a peace officer status.

Privileged communications: Communications between individuals that are protected from discovery or use in a trial. Generally, communications between a party and his or her attorney are privileged.

Probable cause: Exists when the facts and circumstances within the officer's knowledge, and of which he or she has reasonably trustworthy information, are sufficient to cause a reasonably cautious person to believe that an offense has been or is being committed.

Probation: Placing a defendant on conditioned release subject to revocation if the defendant violates the terms of the release.

Public defender: An attorney who works for the state and has the duty of defending indigent defendants.

Public trial: A trial that the public has a right to attend.

Rape shield laws: Laws designed to protect a rape victim and limit the admission of the victim's prior sexual history.

Reasonable cause to believe: A basis for belief in the existence of facts which, in view of the circumstances under and purposes for which the standard is applied, is substantial, objective, and sufficient to satisfy applicable constitutional requirements.

Reasonable doubt: The burden of proof that is required before a defendant may be convicted of a crime. The burden is on the prosecution to prove a fact with a high degree of certainty.

Reasonable suspicion: A suspicion based on facts or circumstances which by themselves do not give rise to the probable cause requisite to justify a lawful arrest, but which give rise to more than a bare suspicion, that is, a suspicion that is reasonable as opposed to imaginary or purely conjectural. A suspicion based on facts that would cause a reasonable person to conclude that criminal activity is ongoing or has occurred.

Rebuttal evidence: Evidence to rebut or negate evidence presented by the other party.

Redirect examination: The examination by the party who called the witness to cover matters that were covered in the cross-examination.

Rehabilitated: The conclusion that a defendant has reformed.

Release on own recognizance: Release of a defendant without bail upon his or her promise to appear at all appropriate times, sometimes referred to as "personal recognizance."

Relevant evidence: Evidence having any tendency to make the existence of any fact that is of consequence to the determination of the action more probable or less probable than it would be without the evidence.

Rendition: Another term for interstate extradition.

Resisting arrest: The act of resisting a lawful arrest; a crime.

Restitution: Court-ordered sanction that involves payment of compensation by the defendant to the victim for injuries suffered as a result of the defendant's criminal activity.

Retained counsel: Counsel that has been selected and employed by the defendant.

Return: The law enforcement officer executing an arrest warrant shall endorse thereon the manner and date of execution, shall subscribe his or her name, and shall return the arrest warrant to the clerk of the court specified in the arrest warrant.

Right of confrontation: The constitutional right of a defendant to confront the witnesses against him or her. It includes the right to cross-examine the witness.

Right of discovery: The right of either a prosecutor or a defendant to discover certain evidence in possession of the other party.

Right of the press and the public to access to criminal trials: The constitutional right of the public and the press to attend a criminal trial granted by the First Amendment.

Right to trial by jury: Right of a defendant to have his or her case decided by a fair and impartial jury.

Search: A governmental intrusion into an area where a person has a reasonable expectation of privacy.

Search warrant: A written order, in the name of the state or municipality, signed by a judge or magistrate authorized by law to issue search warrants, directed to any law enforcement officer, commanding him or her to search for personal property and, if found, to bring it before the issuing judge or magistrate.

Seizure: Taking any person or thing or obtaining information by an officer pursuant to a search or under other color of authority.

Self-representation: A defendant's acting as his or her own attorney.

Sequestered jury: A jury that has been secluded from the public and the press. Generally, a jury is sequestered during the deliberation phase of the trial.

Severance: The act of dividing multiple charges or defendants into separate trials.

Spousal privilege: A communication is confidential if it is made privately by any person to his or her spouse and is not intended for disclosure to any other person. An accused in a criminal proceeding has a privilege to prevent his or her spouse from testifying as to any confidential communication between the accused and the spouse. The privilege may be claimed by the accused or by the spouse on behalf of the accused. The authority of the spouse to do so is presumed. There is no privilege under this rule in a proceeding in which one spouse is charged with a crime against the other person or property of (1) the other, (2) a child of either, (3) a person residing in the household of either, or (4) a third person committed in the course of committing a crime against any of them.

Standards: Detail goals to improve the justice system.

Standby counsel: An attorney appointed by a judge to be available to consult with the defendant in cases where the defendant represents himself or herself.

Statute of limitations: The time within which criminal proceedings must commence after the commission of the crime. Some crimes, such as murder, have no statute of limitations.

Statutory right to a speedy trial: Defendant's right to a speedy trial, which is guaranteed by a statute.

Stop and frisk: The act of stopping a person for investigative purposes and frisking him or her for the presence of a weapon.

Subpoena duces tecum: A subpoena of a witness that also orders the witness to bring certain documents to court.

Subpoenas: Orders issued by the clerk of the court in which a criminal proceeding is pending at any time for witnesses required by any party for attendance at trial and at hearings, for taking depositions, or for any other lawful purpose.

Summons: An order issued by a judicial officer or, pursuant to the authorization of a judicial officer, by the clerk of a court, requiring a person against whom a criminal charge has been filed to appear in a designated court at a specified date and time.

Suspended sentence: An adjudged sentence whose imposition is suspended under certain conditions, and upon compliance with the conditions the sentence is vacated. If the conditions are not complied with, the suspension is vacated and the sentence is imposed.

Symbolic restitution: A beneficial service to the community that the defendant is ordered to perform because of his or her criminal misconduct.

Syndromes: Mental conditions that are often presented to excuse or justify the conduct of the defendant.

Temporary detention: A brief investigative detention.

***Terry* stop:** An investigative stop by an officer to determine if criminal activity is ongoing.

***Terry*-type stop:** A detention that will ordinarily be for a fairly short duration and that will be no longer than necessary to effectuate the purpose of the detention.

Torts: A private or civil wrong or injury that is addressed in civil court.

Trial by ordeal: An ordeal in which the accused was required to perform some physical task to prove his or her innocence.

Unlawful flight: Fleeing the jurisdiction of a court to avoid criminal proceedings. Addressed by the Unlawful Flight Statue.

Venue: The geographic location of the court.

Verdict: A judgment by the court. In a criminal court, it refers to the finding of guilty or not guilty.

Victim: A person against whom a criminal offense has allegedly been committed, or the spouse, parent, lawful representative, or child of someone killed or incapacitated by the alleged criminal offense, except where the spouse, parent, lawful representative, or child is also the accused.

Victim impact statements: Statements which victims or victim representatives are permitted to submit for court consideration at sentencing time.

Victim service providers: Organizations that provide services to victims of crime.

Victims' Bill of Rights: Statutory legislation that provides certain basic rights to a victim during the trial of a criminal case.

Victim compensation: Payments made to victims in an attempt to lessen the impact of the crime upon them.

Voir dire: The preliminary examination of a potential juror to determine qualifications to serve as a juror; preliminary examination of a witness to determine his or her competency to speak the truth.

Waiver of error: No party may assign as error on appeal the court's giving or failing to give any instruction or portion thereof, or to the submission or the failure to submit a form of verdict, unless the party objects thereto before the jury retires to consider its verdict, stating distinctly the matter in which the party objects and the grounds of his or her objection.

Work product: Discovery cannot be required of legal research or of records, correspondence, reports, or memoranda to the extent that they contain the opinions, theories, or conclusions of the prosecutor, members of the prosecutor's legal or investigative staff or law enforcement officers, or of defense counsel or defense counsel's legal or investigative staff.

Writ: A mandatory precept (warrant), under seal, issued by a court and commanding a person to whom it is addressed to do or not to do some act.

INDEX